PRAISE FOR *TITHING*

Doug LeBlanc's collection of profiles of tithers will open your eyes to how giving can be a practice that shapes rather than an obligation that weighs. Along the way, it also breaks down stereotypes of what kind of person tithes. Rather than teaching or preaching stewardship, this book lets givers from across a wide theological spectrum tell their own stories. Their motivations turn out to be as diverse as their backgrounds, and equally varied are the fruits the discipline bears in their lives. If you have not yet "tested God in this," you may find yourself intrigued enough by their stories to try.

Rev. Beth Maynard
Editor, *Get Up Off Your Knees: Preaching the U2 Catalog*

Which of the following best describes a person who tithes: a conservative evangelical, an Episcopal priest, a progressive activist, a pacifist, a Roman Catholic monsignor, a black church pastor, an Eastern Orthodox author, or a Seventh-day Adventist convert from Judaism? Answer: all of the above, of course! Douglas LeBlanc's book explodes stereotypes and demonstrates that tithing has a way of reordering our priorities so that our focus is not on the issues that perpetually divide us but on giving back to the God who gave everything to us in Jesus. These are inspiring, often surprising stories of God's grace at work in unlikely people, unexpected places, and extraordinary ways. At the same time, they prove that the discipline of tithing isn't just for the super-spiritual: it's something we are *all* called to do.

Fr. Nathan J.A. Humphrey
Editor, *Gathering the Next Generation: Essays on
the Formation and Ministry of GenX Priests*

TITHING

Test Me in This

Douglas LeBlanc

THOMAS NELSON
Since 1798

NASHVILLE   DALLAS   MEXICO CITY   RIO DE JANEIRO

Published in Nashville, Tennessee, by Thomas Nelson. Thomas Nelson is a trademark of Thomas Nelson, Inc.

Thomas Nelson, Inc., titles may be purchased in bulk for educational, business, fund-raising, or sales promotional use. For information, please e-mail SpecialMarkets@ThomasNelson.com.

All Scripture quotations, unless otherwise indicated, are taken from the HOLY BIBLE: NEW INTERNATIONAL VERSION®. © 1973, 1978, 1984 by International Bible Society. Used by permission of Zondervan Publishing House. All rights reserved.

Scripture quotations marked KJV are taken from The King James Version of the Bible. Public domain.

Scripture quotations marked NRSV are taken from the NEW REVISED STANDARD VERSION of the Bible. © 1989 by the Division of Christian Education of the National Council of the Churches of Christ in the U.S.A. All rights reserved.

Scripture quotations marked NASB are taken from the NEW AMERICAN STANDARD BIBLE®, © The Lockman Foundation 1960, 1962, 1963, 1968, 1971, 1972, 1973, 1975, 1977, 1995. Used by permission.

ISBN 978-0-8499-4608-0 (trade paper)

Library of Congress Cataloging-in-Publication Data

Tithing : test me in this / [compiled by] Douglas LeBlanc.
    p. cm.
    Includes bibliographical references.
    ISBN 978-0-8499-0095-2 (hardcover)
    1. Christian giving. 2. Tithes. 3. United States—Religious life and customs. I. LeBlanc, Douglas.
    BV772.T58 2009
    248'.6—dc22

                              2009031702

Printed in the United States of America
10 11 12 13 14 RRD 9 8 7 6 5 4 3 2 1

In honor of my father

CONTENTS

ACKNOWLEDGMENTS

I THANK MY FRIENDS DAVID HANDY, TREVA HOUSER, Michael Noyes, Phoebe Pettingell, Vernon Plack, Tim Ridolfi, and David Virtue for their regular questions and encouraging words about my progress toward a complete manuscript.

The warmth of a dinner conversation with Jon Sweeney helped me form a vision for in-person interviews with the tithing believers I write about in this book.

Steve Levin of the *Pittsburgh Press-Gazette* helped me find Rabbi Yisroel Miller. Lee Penn helped me find John Schwiebert and, like other friends, asked about the book regularly.

Maren Tompkins of All Saints Episcopal Church, Pasadena, and Kathy Norquist of Eternal Perspective Ministries coordinated busy calendars and never lost patience with my requests for help.

My parish priest, Charles Alley of St. Matthew's Episcopal Church, Richmond, offered gentle accountability, empowering prayer, and helpful responses to my draft chapters.

My wife, Monica, blessed my decision to set aside other freelance writing and concentrate on this book for a season. At too many points in our marriage, Monica graciously has allowed my editorial passions to diminish our financial security. She also found important relevant passages for the introduction. I am humbled by her generous love.

FOREWORD

The seven ancient practices of the faith were once called the seven ancient disciplines; but times change, and words change with them. The notion of *discipline* fell out of favor over the years, *practices* seeming more voluntary and therefore less foreboding. By any name, however, the seven come into the life of faith as means of monitoring or directing both the workings of the physical body and the passage of time. Three of the seven—fasting, the sacred meal, and tithing—govern the body, its product and its appetite. The other four—the keeping of the hours, the hallowing of the Sabbath, the observance of the liturgical year, and the making of pilgrimage—govern or give contour to the passage of time.

Of the seven, only two seem to most of us to be awkward or, perhaps, even a bit beyond the pale. That is, fasting and tithing seem somehow more private than do the other five—less subject to conversation and easily more subject to omission, even by the devout. Of that pair, tithing is most assuredly the more difficult to discuss; yet ironically, it and the sacred meal were the first of the seven given us to observe. Like the sacred meal, tithing was established so early in our story that Abram, from whom the first tithe was taken by the Melchizedek, was still Abram and not yet renamed as Abraham. Centuries later,

Christian theology was destined to make much of that fact, St. Paul arguing that Levi and all the priestly line had themselves paid tithes when they were "still in the loins of their father, Abraham."

Regardless of how old or how embroidered its history among us is, however, we Christians tend to bristle or resist or retreat when we are instructed by our clergy or our theo-logians in the requirement laid upon us to tithe. The instinctive reaction is that the organization, whatever "the organization" is in our particular case, only wants our money, and that any concern for the spiritual benefits of the tithe is purely secondary, if not tertiary. Beyond that, and assuming that some of us do surmount that line of instinctive resistance, there is the nagging sense that tithing is legalistic—far more legalistic, in fact, than are any of the other six. It seems, in our post-Reformation minds, to be part of an old order, something that should have passed on with the coming of New Testament grace.

Tithing is, in sum, then, a truly difficult topic to broach and an almost impossible one to treat sympathetically, much less persuasively. I knew that completely and unequivocally when I approached Doug LeBlanc about writing this volume as part of the Ancient Practices Series. He and I have been colleagues and associates for years; and for all those years, I have admired the clarity of his thought, the steady, unobtrusive consistency of his

Christian devotion, and his quite remarkable skill in making complicated things clear to the rest of us. He seemed to me, therefore, to be the logical choice for writing about this, the most difficult of the ancient seven.

To say that Doug was enthusiastic in his response and filled with eagerness for the project would be about as far from the truth as one could get. It was more a matter of considerable silence, then a question or two, and then the only possible comment, "I'll have to pray about it." He did, and the result is in your hands now as you read this.

In true LeBlanc fashion, he has chosen not to address tithing in long essays about its history among us or with critiques and tedious theological arguments. Instead, in what I think was a stroke of genius or the angels or both, he has chosen to discover men and women who do tithe and are willing to say, publicly and on the record, why they do so. It is their stories in their words that Doug has collected here.

Will this book turn its readers into tithers? Who knows? And perhaps that is not even the point. Perhaps the point is that reading this book will convince us, first, that tithing is possible and, second, that it is one the seven practices for very good and formative reasons. After that, whether we choose to assume the discipline or choose to not assume it is a matter for each of us to decide in prayer. The difference for all of us, though, will be that none of us will ever again be able to occupy a default position of taking no position. In reading, we will have discovered that each of us must decide, just as we will have seen for ourselves what it is we are deciding.

Phyllis Tickle
General Editor
Ancient Practices Series

INTRODUCTION

IN THE EARLY 1990S, I WAS PART OF A HOME BIBLE STUDY connected to a small church in Colorado Springs. It was the first time I had lived in any city other than my birthplace of Baton Rouge, Louisiana. This home group, and others that preceded it, gave me a sense of belonging—not merely in a city and state that were entirely new to me, but also with brothers and sisters in a Christian church. My memories of these home groups are mostly warm ones.

One memory, while not distinctly unpleasant, still leaves me perplexed nearly twenty years later. I remember more than one meeting in which one of our members inveighed against tithing as a mere legalism, a way for modern Christians to escape the much costlier demands of authentic discipleship. This brother was especially keen on arguing that God wants everything we call our own, not merely 10 percent of it.

All of this was fine as theological fodder and as something to meditate on between meetings, but our meetings were taking place in modern suburbia. Members of our group were not known for giving away vast quantities of money, serving in soup kitchens together, or doing much of anything more than meeting together in perfect comfort, drinking coffee or soda, and discussing our faith as something that made our already pleasant lives more pleasant still.

Since then, something in me has felt skeptical when I encounter prosperous American Christians who speak of tithing in tones that sound almost contemptuous, who write joyless books about the very notion of tithing as pastorally insensitive, or who dismiss Christian leaders as opportunists who ought to find honest work in some other form of sales.

I grew up in a home in which tithing was not the norm until I was a teenager. My brother became a Christian through the Jesus Movement. My bewildered father, a gentle soul and World War II veteran, became convinced that my brother had gone off the deep end and began reading the Bible—in search, I think, of a passage in which Jesus urged people to follow him, but not to be excessive about it. Within a year, both my parents came to faith through a renewal movement called Faith Alive.

My father soon announced that our family would transfer from the pious but excessively formal parish in which I grew up to another Episcopal parish, which hosted the Faith Alive weekend that changed our family's life. Also within a year, or at least so it seemed, my father announced that he and Mom would begin tithing. Mom loudly resisted, for a time, but soon enough she realized that Dad was committed, and when the newly converted Lester Louis LeBlanc was committed to something he believed God was calling him to do, resistance was futile.

From that day on, the lesson was lived out before my eyes: my parents tithed off their gross income, and it went to our newfound spiritual home. Dad believed the matter was clear enough in Malachi 3:10: "'Bring the whole tithe into the storehouse, that there may be food in my house. Test me in this,' says the LORD Almighty, 'and see if I will not throw open the floodgates of heaven and pour out so much blessing that you will not have room enough for it.'"

Dad read Scripture faithfully, and he had an almost intuitive sense for cutting to the spiritual heart of a question. I loved to talk about theology with Dad, who had to drop out after elementary school, because what he lacked in education he overcame with wisdom and humility. My theological conversations with Dad never encompassed the Fathers of the church. I was too young to give much thought to the Fathers, and if Dad read them, he did not try to counter my callow opinions by rubbing my face in his deeper learning.

My father died in 1992, after heart surgery that was a technical success but led to a month in intensive care and an attack of pneumonia. I know that Dad would be pleased to recognize, in the Fathers, an affirmation of the principles he lived by when he decided that the LeBlancs would be a tithing household.

The Didache ("The Teaching"), more fully known as
The Teaching of the Lord to the Gentiles by the Twelve Apostles,
stresses the importance of Christians giving generously:

Give to everyone who asks you, and do not demand it back,
for the Father wants something from his own gifts to be
given to everyone. Blessed is the one who gives according
to the command, for he is innocent. . . . Do not be one who
stretches out the hands to receive but withdraws them when
it comes to giving. If you earn something by working with
your hands, you shall give a ransom for your sins. You shall
not hesitate to give, nor shall you grumble when giving, for
you will know who is the good paymaster of the reward. . . .
But every genuine prophet who wishes to settle among you
is worthy of his food. Likewise, every genuine teacher is,
like the worker, worthy of his food. Take, therefore, all the
first fruits of the produce of the wine press and threshing
floor, and of the cattle and sheep, and give these first fruits
to the prophets, for they are your high priests. But if you
have no prophet, give them to the poor. If you make bread,
take the first fruit and give in accordance with the commandment. Similarly, when you open a jar of wine or oil,
take the first fruit and give it to the prophets. As for money
and clothes and any other possessions, take the first fruit
that seems right to you and give in accordance with the
commandment.[1]

A passage from *The Conferences* of John Cassian speaks more explicitly of tithing as the starting point of Christian giving:

> And so if even those who, faithfully offering tithes of their fruits, are obedient to the more ancient precepts of the Lord, cannot yet climb the heights of the gospel, you can see very clearly how far short of it those fall who do not even do this.[2]

In the Fathers, we see not only an assumption that Christians ought to continue the Jewish custom of tithing, but also some attention to how Christian leaders ought to distribute these gifts:

> Let [the bishop] use those tenths and first-fruits, which are given according to the command of God, as a man of God; as also let him dispense in a right manner the free-will offerings which are brought in on account of the poor, to the orphans, the widows, the afflicted, and strangers in distress, as having that God for the examiner of his accounts who has committed the disposition to him. Distribute to all those in want with righteousness, and yourselves use the things which belong to the Lord, but do not abuse them; eating of them, but not eating them all up by yourselves: communicate with those that are in want, and thereby show yourselves unblameable before God.[3]

One of the Christians I write about in these pages, Frederica Mathewes-Green, cited three of the saints of the early church, and in turn she was drawing from research by the work of Randy Alcorn, who had already talked with me about his life in giving:

- "'The Jews were constrained to a regular payment of tithes; Christians, who have liberty, assign all their possessions to the Lord, bestowing freely not the lesser portions of their property, since they have the hope of greater things." (Irenaeus)

- "'Tithes are required as a matter of debt, and he who has been unwilling to give them has been guilty of robbery. Whoever, therefore, desires to secure a reward for himself . . . let him render tithes, and out of the nine parts let him seek to give alms." (Augustine)

- "'If anyone shall not do this he is convicted of defrauding and supplanting God." (Jerome)[4]

I have a lively theological curiosity and have worked as a religion writer for most of my career, but I am no theologian or exegetical writer. To the extent that I am capable of exhortation or teaching, it is mostly through telling the stories of other people's lives. I am prone to a near fundamentalism that is common among old-school journalists:

it's not about you, and keep the first person singular out of your narrative as much as possible. In these pages, I try to limit the first person singular to what background is important to my earlier experiences, in several cases, with the people I am writing about.

In writing these stories, I traveled to seven states and a dozen cities within those states. I make no pretense of this brief book being an exhaustive treatment of tithing or the theology related to it. It is more of a journalist's pilgrimage, one in which my subjects discuss how tithing—or a still larger vision of God's abundant generosity—has affected other aspects of their spiritual lives. Of necessity, some chapters spend more time on the broader spiritual story of these lives than on the details of their tithing.

> *Tithing tends not to be accompanied by daily or even weekly reflection. Often it is more of a background habit, a reminder that our lives are not our own.*

Unlike daily, structured prayer or time spent reading Scripture, tithing tends not to be accompanied by daily or even weekly reflection. Often it is more of a background habit, a reminder that our lives are not our own. Tithing is like prayer in the sense that God is working out his purpose and generously offers us a voluntary place in his purpose. God no more needs the money that flows through our bank accounts than he needs to be informed, through prayer, about the ways in which we hope he will intervene in our lives.

Instead, God is at all times bringing healing and redemption into our world and, to the extent we are ready to cooperate in those goals, God will use us. As we open our otherwise tight grip on what we think of as our money, we begin to realize it has come our way only by the grace of God. As we draw closer to people who need the compassion of Christ, we end up—perhaps even unwittingly—drawing closer to God. It is all God's idea and work, ultimately, but we may choose to become his instruments.

1

CONTINUITY IN THE TRADITION

Gregory and Frederica Mathewes-Green

In the summer of 1991, Frederica Mathewes-Green attended the Episcopal Church's 69th General Convention, which met that year in Phoenix. I had admired Frederica's witty articles in the national newsletter of Feminists for Life, which she edited for a few years, and this convention was my first opportunity to meet a woman who was quickly becoming one of my favorite writers. From a distance, I saw Frederica handing out free copies of a document printed on a modern imitation of parchment. The document was the Baltimore Declaration, an effort by six Episcopal priests—including Frederica's husband, Father Gregory—to identify ten points of theological struggle for the church. The closest the declaration came to causing any change in the Episcopal Church was the publication of a thoughtful and largely ignored book,

Reclaiming Faith: Essays on Orthodoxy in the Episcopal Church and the Baltimore Declaration.[1]

I interviewed Frederica during that convention, and I have forgotten most of what we talked about. What I remember, though, is her crying. That year's convention featured a daily morning Bible study combined with the Holy Eucharist. Deputies, bishops, journalists, and visitors gathered together at round tables in a vast and gloomy exhibit hall to read Scripture together and discuss what they thought God might be saying to the convention on any given day.

One morning the text told the wonderful story of John the Baptist leaping for joy, in utero, merely upon hearing the voice of the pregnant Blessed Virgin Mary as she greeted her cousin Elizabeth. Frederica, who was attending this convention not only to help promote the Baltimore Declaration but also to volunteer with NOEL (the National Organization of Episcopalians for Life), pointed out the clear pro-life lessons to be drawn from this passage. Frederica's tablemates disagreed with this plain-sense reading of the text. As Frederica told me about this encounter, she cried, explaining that she was not crying because her feelings were hurt but because she was so heartbroken for the church. Frederica and I have been friends ever since.

The General Convention of 1991 was the final national convention that Frederica attended as an Episcopalian.

The convention's anemic response to the Baltimore Declaration, and its refusal to affirm that Episcopal clergy ought to limit their sexual activity to the covenant of marriage, convinced the Mathewes-Greens that they should think about serving in another Christian church. They considered the Roman Catholic Church and what are called continuing Anglican churches—bodies that broke away from the Episcopal Church after it decided to ordain women to the priesthood and adopted a modern version of the Book of Common Prayer (1979). Frederica had attended Virginia Theological Seminary at the same time as her husband, as they both explored whether to become Episcopal priests. When the Mathewes-Greens decided to leave the Episcopal Church, they ultimately joined the Self-Ruled Antiochian Orthodox Christian Archdiocese of North America, a branch of Orthodoxy that has been most pastoral toward Protestants—evangelical Protestants in particular—whose search for a deeper spiritual life has led them toward the East. Frederica told her family's story in her book *Facing East: A Pilgrim's Journey into the Mysteries of Orthodoxy*.[2]

During their childhoods, Gregory was Episcopalian and Frederica was Catholic. They made no pretense of Christian faith when they met each other, and Frederica read a Hindu prayer during their wedding. They were hippies, Frederica was a self-described hairy-legged feminist,

"I'm not sure what it was that inspired us to begin tithing. I remember that we were doing it right from the beginning."

"We were both new Christians, new to seminary, and, for me, new to the Episcopal Church," Frederica said. "I'm not sure what it was that inspired us to begin tithing. I remember that we were doing it right from the beginning, during our seminary years. We were janitors at Church of the Resurrection; we each got twenty dollars a week, and that was our only income, apart from our being on work-study scholarship. We might have gotten a little bit of income from the work we did at the seminary. So for each twenty dollars, we put two dollars in the basket."

IMPOVERISHED SEMINARIANS

and their spirituality was syncretic. On their honeymoon, however, Frederica found herself kneeling before a statue of Jesus and hearing the unmistakable yelps of the Hound of Heaven. When they attended seminary together in 1974 and 1975, they were still zealously renewed Christians— and they began tithing. It was not an easy commitment to make, but it would shape the rest of their life together as Christian disciples.

Gregory said, "We knew it was one of those things that committed Christians, biblical Christians, did, and obviously it said something about our commitment of our material things to God."

Frederica recalled their financial struggles during their time in seminary: "Our rent was one hundred dollars a month, and our weekly food budget was ten dollars. I remember it was a splurge to get a container of yogurt. We were vegetarians that year. That helped us save a little bit of money, that first year in seminary. We were extremely poor, poorer than most people would admit. I remember they had just invented ziplock bags, and I was at a school picnic or something, and I was saving the bags and washing them out and putting them out to dry. One of the other students teased me about exaggeratedly acting like I was poor, but I *was* poor. We hadn't bought a box of ziplock bags. My dad had sent us something in several bags, so we saved those bags and kept rewashing them. I didn't buy a mop, because it was eight dollars, and I could mop the floor with a sponge. It was a real sacrifice—to give 10 percent of twenty dollars is a large sacrifice—but we felt very determined about it from the beginning. In thirty-four years of marriage, we have never *not* tithed. Every month we've given 10 percent or more."

"I think we were aware that being truly committed Christians was going to be a life-changing thing, and there wasn't going to be any part of our lives that wasn't touched by that, so it had to mean something for our pocketbooks," Gregory said. "We certainly were biblically literate enough to know what the tithe was."

"I remember a little controversy we were in at the time," Frederica said of her senior year, when she was a part-time student. "We were on campus a couple of days a week, and I didn't want to pay two dollars for the campus lunch. In the cafeteria it was family style; everybody put in two dollars and they put the dishes on the table, but I wanted to bring food from home. The fear was that I hadn't paid and that I might eat some of the food out of the bowls as I sat there eating my sandwich. The administration was very insistent that I put in my two dollars. 'It's just two dollars, that's all you've got to pay.' But I was the one paying the bills, and I knew that we just didn't have an extra two dollars, so I wanted to bring my peanut-butter sandwich. The decision, I guess to force my hand, was that I was not allowed to come into the dining room unless I paid two dollars. So I'd go to classes, talk to my classmates, say good-bye, and then sit in the lobby and eat my sandwich. I think eventually they decided it was safe to let me back in. I think I was allowed to have some of the coffee, but none of the food."

Frederica laughs heartily as she recalls the resolution of this standoff. Gregory describes her as "holding court" while eating in the spacious lobby of the refectory, as her fellow students often gathered around to commiserate with her.

A SECOND POVERTY

Gregory and Frederica speak fondly of this time, as they believe it established patterns of generosity and trust in God that served them well, especially when Gregory made the financially costly decision to leave a well-paying career as an Episcopal priest and to plant Holy Cross, a new Antiochian Orthodox mission in metropolitan Baltimore. Gregory refers to that period as "our second poverty."

Frederica landed a full-time job in 1992 in which she helped work on a pro-life referendum for Maryland. Knowing the financial sacrifices that lay ahead, Gregory and Frederica saved all the income from Frederica's job so they could use it as a cushion in the future. "As we were looking toward becoming Orthodox, we were quite nervous about it, because we had three children, and we'd have to find health insurance somehow, and we'd have to move out of the rectory," Frederica said. "I kept saying, 'Lord, if you give us ten tithers, we will have our church.' We were surprised, as we kind of canvassed the Episcopal parish, that not very many people wanted to join us. We thought that in a high Episcopal church, you just jump off that onto the escalator and go to the slightly higher Orthodox Church. We were surprised that we didn't get very many takers—more arrived as the year went by, but not right away. I kept saying, 'Ten tithers make one income.' I kept praying, 'Give us ten tithers,' and we got five.

"It was very threadbare there for a while. Right from the start, the church decided what Gregory's income was going to be, and it was $1,500 a month or something. It was quite low. They determined that this was our income from February 14, 1993, the first day we had worship, but they couldn't pay it, so month after month went by and we would draw on our savings to pay him the salary, and the church would still owe us. But we kept tabs of how much was owed, and within those first three years it was all paid off. They got to where they could pay a salary and then pay a little bit more to make up the prior shortfall. It's another example of how God brings things together. If it hadn't been for that job with the referendum, I don't know what we would have done. But everything was arriving at the time it was needed, not before, and we were able to make it work."

Gregory wondered during some weeks and months whether he should drive a truck for United Parcel Service. "Looking back, you can see it so much clearer. But as we all know, sometimes being in the midst of creative activity, you don't always know that it's increasingly getting better," he said.

"We insisted that the church tithe to the diocese, and the diocese at that point was providing very little financial support for mission priests," Frederica said. "They sent us $200 a month, and our mission's income was about $2,000 a month, so we sent them $200 a month back. These identical checks would cross in the mail as they supported us and we paid our tithe to the diocese."

For the first several years of its life, Holy Cross met in a community center near Catonsville. In 1997 it bought a church building in Linthicum, near Baltimore-Washington International Airport. The Mathewes-Greens live just around the corner from the church. The building they bought was constructed for a Methodist congregation and had become Full Gospel Mission Church, a Korean congregation, by the time Holy Cross purchased it. The members of Holy Cross poured hundreds of hours into transforming it from a Pentecostal worship space into the icon-rich and incense-friendly church it is today.

As Holy Cross has grown, Gregory has worked his way back toward a reliable income and Frederica has developed a vocation as a prolific author (nine books) and speaker (pro-life groups, churches, college lectures). "As things have gotten better, as Holy Cross Church has put down roots and thrived, I decided (I think it was a year and a half ago) to actually break through the wall to 20 percent," she said. "We gave 20 percent for a year, kind of nervous, but turned out great. It's so true that you can't outgive God."

AN ANCIENT TRADITION

In Eastern Orthodox theology, the Mathewes-Greens have found an anchor for a spiritual discipline they had begun in the mid-1970s, and a deeper explanation for what that spiritual discipline is meant to achieve. "When we became Orthodox, it didn't feel like a radical departure from our sense of what tithing was about and stewardship questions," Gregory said. "It felt like a deepening of it, and we could see much more continuity in the tradition. We could see almost immediately the connection with the whole idea of spiritual disciplines, of the Orthodox emphasis on *theosis*—being like God, growing into the image of God.

"Since clearly one of God's characteristics is generosity—the overflowing of his compassion, his love, and his self-giving—there are different ways the church gifts us in exercising that in ourselves. When we give, the muscle grows, the God-likeness. In the Sermon on the Mount, where Jesus talks about prayer and fasting and almsgiving, those three seem to have a special connection—not just because Jesus talked about them in the same sermon, but also because they're three facets of the Christian life that demonstrate our commitment to the dominion of God over everything and also give us ways to internalize that work.

"By all that, I mean that the dominion of God is over the whole material world. We're given some control over it, but we demonstrate that we know he has the lordship and the dominion, because we tithe. It's even kind of a sacramental illustration, I think."

"The Orthodox continuity with the ancient practices was something we frankly didn't believe until we had been in the church for a while, and we saw that they really fasted on Wednesday and Friday, and maintained other practices from the first century onward. You can just drop into the devotional literature or the records at any point in history, in all of these different ethnic backgrounds, out of touch with each other for centuries, and find that the practices are still the same," Frederica said.

"All these practices are training wheels toward learning how to live fully in the kingdom."

Gregory cites author Randy Alcorn's image of tithing as a set of training wheels for Christians who want to become serious about their giving. He believes the same is true of fasting. "All these practices are training wheels for learning how to live fully in the kingdom," he said. "At this point in our lives, we need the training wheels, for the most part. Tithing is a really good example, because it may feel like a constriction at first, like training wheels, but after a while grace does move a person to a place where, in a sense, you can take those wheels off and feel truly more generous in your heart, not having to worry so much at the end of the month, 'Did we give the 10 percent?' It's less about the mechanics of it than the growth that really does happen into grace.

"I would say it's really the same dynamic in most of the spiritual disciplines. We come into a fallen world as fallen people, and our relationship to the fallen world is just not as it was meant to be by God. I don't get it right in relation to money; I don't get it right in relation to my stomach; I don't get it right in relation to the use of time or any of these things. In the tradition, there are these great mechanisms and disciplines that help me get it right."

Looking back on their decades of tithing, Gregory and Frederica see consistent evidence of God's faithfulness and his call on them to grow in generosity. "Things have been tougher sometimes, financially, but there's never really been a strong temptation to stop tithing," Gregory said. "What there has been is a realization that we really can give more. God has given us so much, not just financially but in so many different ways, that one of the ways we can clearly give back is by supporting various ministries and outreach and so forth beyond the tithe, which we always give to 'the storehouse,'[3] which we understand as being the church."

"Even at the beginning, we could see that tithing did not make us impoverished," Frederica said. "In fact, somehow we ended up having more money. There were a couple of times, that first year in seminary, we went and looked in the savings account and mysteriously found an extra fifty dollars there that we hadn't put in. That happened at least twice, and we were never able to discover where it came from. (That was in the day when you actually would give them the bank book, and they would stamp it and give it back.) We would get unexpected refunds, bonuses, or things we were never looking for.

"When we tithe, the blessings keep flowing in faster than we can bail them out again."

"That has continued to happen—over and over, things we had expected to pay for would somehow be free, or money that we weren't looking for would just land in the mailbox. It feels like bailing out a leaking boat. When we tithe, the blessings keep flowing in faster than we can bail them out again."

2

SO THAT OTHERS MAY SIMPLY LIVE

Ron and Arbutus Sider

IF YOU'RE TRAVELING ONLY A FEW HUNDRED MILES TO interview the author of *Rich Christians in an Age of Hunger*,[1] somehow it feels more fitting to ride a train than to book a flight. I didn't know the address for Ron and Arbutus Sider's home as I set out on a chilly March morning to talk with them. I rode Amtrak's Silver Meteor from Richmond to the Thirtieth Street station in downtown Philadelphia and then hopped on a commuter train for a brief ride to the Queen Lane station. I called Ron Sider's cell phone number, and within minutes he picked me up in the family car. It's a short drive from the station to the Siders' home, and when I noticed some of the street names in this neighborhood just off Germantown Avenue, my little gray cells came alive. Could it be? Was this the neighborhood of the late and mourned magazine *The Other Side* and its sister ministry, Jubilee Fellowship?

This was the place, and the Siders lived in this same home when the magazine and Jubilee were in their prime. It would be difficult to overstate the importance of *The Other Side* in developing many evangelicals' social consciences from the mid-1960s onward. By the time *The Other Side* closed in late 2004, it had become mostly a voice of liberal Protestantism, although it belonged to the Evangelical Press Association until the end. In its best days, *The Other Side* was the magazine most likely to make evangelicals struggle with the gospel's implications for racial justice, capital punishment, or the relation between sugar and global poverty.

The Siders bought this home in 1975 for $15,000, as part of a multihouse community that at its peak attracted thirty-five adults living in a six-block area. The late John Alexander, son of *The Other Side*'s founding editor and a respected author in his own right, lived across the street. Richard K. Taylor, coauthor with Ron of *Nuclear Holocaust and Christian Hope*,[2] also belonged to Jubilee.

Members of Jubilee shared cars and tools and encouraged one another to live simply. Within small groups, members of the community disclosed their tax returns to each other and discussed how they spent their incomes. Speaking of taxes: the Siders have never had a full audit by the IRS, although the service did challenge the Siders' charitable giving a few years ago. "I didn't even have to supply them with all the cancelled checks," Ron said. "They were satisfied with a copy of the check ledger."

Jubilee thrived for about five years, but the Siders broke from it in 1980. Within about eighteen months, Jubilee disintegrated. "I thought that what we were trying to do was right," Ron said. "If you really work hard at Christian community and share deeply, you inevitably hurt each other. You can't live that close together and not have real fights and disagreements." The hope, the Siders said, was that continued conversation, prayer, and openness to change would lead to reconciliation and unity. That unity did not come about. The Siders, among others, withdrew from Jubilee but remained in their home in Germantown. Ron said that the failure of Jubilee was one of the great disappointments of his life.

FROM ONTARIO TO NEW HAVEN

What has drawn me to talk with the Siders is an idea that ultimately grew into the book *Rich Christians:* the proposal of a graduated tithe. The idea is fairly simple: Family members agree to a base amount of what they need to live on for a year. They tithe on that base amount. For every additional $1,000 of income they receive, they increase their giving by 5 percent. In *The Graduated Tithe*—an InterVarsity Press booklet published in 1978, one year after *Rich Christians*—Ron mentioned that his family had agreed to a base amount of $8,000 (for Ron, Arbutus, and their three children).[3]

Talking to the Siders in their comfortable and aging home, I soon realized that the graduated tithe is not the central focus of their financial discipleship as Christians. Instead, the theme that the Siders return to again and again is simple living. It's right there on the opening page of *The Graduated Tithe*: *"The rich must live simply that the poor may simply live.*—Dr. Charles Burke (1975)"[4]

> *The graduated tithe is not the central focus of their financial discipleship as Christians. Instead, the theme that the Siders return to again and again is simple living.*

Both Ron and Arbutus grew up immersed in such teachings—she as the fourth child of a family living in an Amish and Mennonite community, and he as a son of the Brethren in Christ. Both communities stressed simplicity, economic sharing, the need to resist a proud and materialistic culture, not using extravagant display, and striving for peace. They were both born in 1939 and both grew up in Southern Ontario, Canada.

They moved to the United States for Ron to pursue graduate studies at Yale, where he earned both a master's degree and a PhD. He took a leave of absence from his doctoral studies to earn a bachelor of divinity from the Yale Divinity School. While attending the divinity school, Ron did interim ministry at a local church.

One weekend, Ron was preparing a sermon on world hunger. His usual approach to a sermon was to describe a problem, draw lessons from relevant Scripture verses, and suggest actions that believers may take to address the problem. The idea of the graduated tithe came to him as he worked on the sermon. By 1972, he had developed an article on the graduated tithe for *HIS*, a collegiate magazine published by InterVarsity Press.[5] He later proposed a booklet for IVP on the graduated tithe and on world hunger. As he wrote that book in 1975 and early 1976, "it grew like Topsy and became *Rich Christians in an Age of Hunger*."

During the Siders' years in New Haven, they became aware of a clash between simple living and the styles of dress and home furnishings that were common among Ron's classmates and professors. They noticed, for instance, that other people did not have plastic curtains in their homes. Arbutus cut her long hair and bought a coordinated outfit, including a hat and gloves, to wear at church. "We put much more of an emphasis on the outward appearance than we had ever done before," she said. "We were putting pressures on ourselves because we were adapting to a new culture."

The Siders emphasize that the pressures were self-imposed rather than based on anything said to them. Even so, they were uneasy about being shaped by those self-imposed pressures. "I grew up in a home that was very modest and simple," Arbutus said. "The ability to go to high school was a really big thing for me. [Simple living] was always, for me, part of my faith commitment. I was a good little girl who wanted to follow Jesus."

Fitting in was a concern for several years, and the pressures eased in the fall of 1968, when Ron took a job at an inner-city campus of Messiah College. Ron taught at Messiah for ten years, and they lived at Messiah College's Temple University Campus in North Philadelphia for seven of those years. Arbutus recalls an international student telling her, "Stop putting yourself down. I love your home. I feel very much at home here." Arbutus chokes up as she remembers the moment.

"I can remember the point at which I let go of the burden of having to be like everyone else and reclaimed being who I was," she said. "I reclaimed the freedom of simplicity. The freedom to live simply so others can simply live has been a joy to reclaim. That's what makes the graduated tithe not a burden or an oppressive thing but a guide on this freedom journey."

While living in New Haven, the Siders did not lose touch with the social consciences of the churches that formed them. Arbutus, who taught in a one-room school-house in Ontario, found work as a teacher in North Haven's public schools. She used a Laundromat in an African-American neighborhood, and her friends worried about her safety. "I was doing just fine until some of our friends learned I was using *that* Laundromat." She never felt imperiled and kept doing her laundry there.

Ron and Arbutus had an education in black-white relations by getting to know their landlord. He was a custodian at Yale who had to work two full-time jobs—plus his income from renting out two apartments above his home—to provide a good income for his family. "We were in their living room, watching on their television set, during the aftermath of Martin Luther King's death," Arbutus said. They also got to share the experience when their landlord's son made return visits from college and asked why progress on civil rights was so slow.

"By the time we moved to North Philadelphia, I was becoming a full-time mom," she said. "After a year or two, it became clear I wanted to be involved in the neighborhood." She became involved in citywide advocacy for students and their parents, and her advocacy included speaking before the city council and school board. "That felt comfortable. I believed in what I was doing."

Arbutus believes she earned a figurative master's degree in systems thinking through those years of activism: "Ron was writing about systemic evil, and I was seeing it on an urban level." She advocated for public schools, but as she listened to inner-city mothers' hopes for their children, she became convinced that private Christian schools also are important. She helped found Philadelphia Mennonite High School, which opened in 1998. The Siders attend Oxford Circle Mennonite Church, which they appreciate for its economic, racial, and educational diversity.

For twenty years, Arbutus had a private practice as a marriage and family therapist. She stepped away from that practice in 2007. She's drawn to work with people in recovery and with couples, helping them to stay together or to get married. "It's a challenge and a real satisfaction to be walking alongside couples like that." For Arbutus, an important concern is consistently spending real time with people in need. She believes that such commitments of time help Christians realize the world of hurt that surrounds them and give them the chance to embody God's compassionate response to suffering. She considers this a crucial question for a comfortable Christian's discipleship: "This year, with whom am I rubbing shoulders who reminds me that the rest of the world does not have what we have?"

"This year, with whom am I rubbing shoulders who reminds me that the rest of the world does not have what we have?"

MAKING ROOM FOR BRAND-NAME SHOES

In the pages of *Rich Christians* and other books, Ron is a fairly strict critic of consumerism. Among his recommendations for resisting consumerism are "laughing regularly at TV commercials" and "developing family slogans like, 'Who are you kidding?' and 'You can't take it with you!'" During our visit he told a story related to this paragraph in

Rich Christians:

For a decade, my own savings bank used a particularly enticing ad: "Put a little love away. Everybody needs a penny for a rainy day. Put a little love away." Responsible saving is good stewardship. But promising that a bank account guarantees love is unbiblical, heretical, and demonic. This ad teaches the big lie of our secular, materialistic society. But the words and music were so seductive that they danced through my head hundreds of times.[6]

The bank that Ron mentioned in this paragraph was the Philadelphia Savings Fund Society (PSFS), which sponsored a math contest that the Siders' oldest son,

Ted, won as an elementary-school student. The Siders attended an awards ceremony at the top of the high-rise PSFS Building in Philadelphia's central city. Ron ended up sitting at the same table with an executive who was in charge of the ad campaign. He told her about his critique of the ad. She said it was the most successful campaign PSFS had run. She also agreed that its message was immoral.

The relentless message of *Rich Christians*—that more than a billion people live in grinding poverty and that affluent Christians ought to change their own lives to help relieve that suffering—has led some of Sider's critics to accuse him of being a socialist or an ascetic killjoy. As Ron and Arbutus describe it, they strived to apply the principles of simple living in ways that were not burdensome as their children grew up. "It's one thing to apply it when your kids are one and three and quite another when they're in high school and then on to college," Ron said. When the Siders' two sons mentioned the importance of name-brand shoes among their peers, the parents did occasionally relent and agree to buy such shoes. Ron said that keeping cars until they were no longer reasonably functional, staying in their small modest house in an interracial neighborhood, and buying their clothes mostly at thrift stores were the primary ways they resisted the consumerist tide.

Their commitment to simple living affected their approach to vacations, which they usually linked to Ron's speaking engagements. Three times during the 1980s, the formative years for their two sons and one daughter, the family took cross-country camping trips to reach speaking engagements in the West. Those vacations celebrated the freedom of simplicity without losing any important sense of having fun together, Arbutus said.

More recently, Ron and Arbutus thought carefully before they agreed to join another couple in sharing the use of a modest cabin in northern Maine. Each summer they now spend three to five weeks at the cabin. The cabin relies on gas lighting and gas appliances, and the toilet is outside. The location gives Ron ready access to fishing, a hobby he has long enjoyed. "In some ways it's like being in Ontario, where we grew up," Arbutus said. "We don't live in poverty, and we certainly don't live without the very nice benefits of middle-class life," Ron said.

Ron seems mostly amused by charges of asceticism. He speaks warmly of his long friendship with the Christian apologist John Warwick Montgomery, who worried that Ron was an ascetic and invited him to come along to a meeting of a group dedicated to gourmet dining. Ron told his friend that he would gladly tag along, so long as Montgomery paid for the meal. Ron also recalls talking, during a conference where he gave a speech, with a missionary at Columbia Bible College who felt guilty about enjoying large, fluffy towels when she returned to the United States. "Please don't feel guilty," he remembers saying to her. "I want you to delight in that. The material world is good. It's not that God doesn't want you to have any of these goods of the earth. It's a question of balance."

Ron said, "I've never thought that the reason for living more simply was that somehow living more simply was itself a virtue. Asceticism has never been one of my temptations. We really want people to know about Jesus, so we want the missionary task to flourish, and we think God wants people to have economic justice and not live in poverty. It takes resources to do both of those things."

For that matter, the father of the graduated tithe has held that idea with an open hand over the years, and he sounds untroubled that it has not become a widespread practice among his fellow evangelical Christians. "I very seldom meet people who say they've been applying it," he said. "I've never felt that the graduated tithe is a biblical demand that everyone must follow." He estimates that only five to ten times since the publication of *Rich Christians* in 1977 have people mentioned the importance of the graduated tithe in their lives. In contrast, nearly every time he travels, he meets people who thank him for publishing *Rich Christians* and say the book has affected how they live.

Arbutus said the graduated tithe is not an end in itself but a structure for achieving the higher purposes of simple living and supporting the work of God's kingdom. She compared it to the structure provided by a married couple's pledge of lifelong commitment. Despite their longstanding commitment to the graduated tithe, the Siders warn against treating even basic tithing in a legalistic manner.

The graduated tithe is not an end in itself but a structure for achieving the higher purposes of simple living and supporting the work of God's kingdom.

Tithing is not a biblical demand like sexual fidelity or honesty, Ron said. "It's an Old Testament principle that makes enormous sense, and it's a great starting point. I wouldn't say to a desperately poor single mom, 'You've got to tithe or you're disobeying God.'" Indeed, Arbutus has discouraged impoverished people from tithing when it's clear that their income does not allow paying their bills and tithing. "It's fine for impoverished people to give 2 or 3 or 5 percent," she said.

"We are entirely Christ's," Ron said. "Every part of our being is committed to Christ, which means all of our money is his, all of our resources and property and time are his. We need to be asking, 'How does God want me to use my time and my skills and my money?' For most

American Christians, the tithe as the maximum is just absurd—not because it's a legalistic norm, but that, given what the Bible says, and the needs of the world, and our incredible wealth, we ought to be giving a lot more. I think most American Christians are living in sin by the way they spend their money."

3

MISSIONAL LIVING AFTER KATRINA

Jerry and Stacy Kramer

WHEN I VISITED FATHER JERRY KRAMER AND HIS WIFE, Stacy, at the Free Church of the Annunciation, two trailer homes no longer dominated the small parking lot on the west side of the church. This normally would be cause for rejoicing, especially on aesthetic grounds, but these were not normal times. Like most of New Orleans, the neighborhood known as Broadmoor was devastated in late August 2005 when the western edge of Hurricane Katrina lashed the city. Katrina came close to fulfilling decades-long predictions of a hurricane leaving greater metropolitan New Orleans entombed in water. The two trailers in Annunciation's parking lot represented the heart of this small Episcopal congregation's post-Katrina existence—not only its survival but also its freshly renewed ministry in Broadmoor.

Jerry negotiated with a dealer in Texas to buy the trailers because he knew the church could not afford to wait for help from the Federal Emergency Management Agency. One trailer served as the church's worship space and emergency housing for a flooded-out parishioner. Another trailer provided office space for Jerry and for the Broadmoor Improvement Association. The association was the rallying point for Broadmoor residents as they fought the city's initial redevelopment plans, which would have rezoned this mixed-income neighborhood—from the poor to the middle class to Walter Isaacson's childhood home—out of existence. From both of the trailers, Jerry and other leaders of Annunciation oversaw the parish's ministry of distributing cleaning supplies, food, clothes, and truckloads of other donated items from across the nation. Because of the trailers' role in the resurrection of Annunciation, the parking lot seemed almost diminished without them.

Walking around the block that houses Annunciation, I missed the trailers less. At Jena Street and South Claiborne Avenue stands the church's restored nave. Creating a small new narthex on the west side has decreased noise from the four-lane, hectic Claiborne Avenue. Before Katrina, an entrance at the back of the church offered no buffer between the street and the worship space. The narthex also gives new prominence to a stained-glass window that depicts Jesus standing on the

Sea of Galilee and reaching for a panicked Saint Peter, after the impulsive Peter tried to join Jesus in walking on water. Before Katrina, that window was above the back door and difficult to notice. Now the window is hard to miss as you walk in from the new side entrance, or if you're walking by on Claiborne after dark. In the months after Hurricane Katrina, Annunciation's nave was so damaged by putrid floodwaters that Jerry urged his people not to expect that they would worship within it again. Bishop Charles Jenkins of the Episcopal Diocese of Louisiana presided over a tearful deconsecration of the nave, which stood on this corner for nearly a century.

Next door to the nave, in the former rectory, Jerry hopes to fulfill a post-Katrina vision for a neighborhood coffee-house with free Wi-Fi. On the corner of Jena and South Derbigny streets is a neighborhood playground built by volunteers and filled with brightly colored equipment donated by a nonprofit organization called KaBOOM. On Derbigny Street is a former two-story home that's been remodeled to house the church's youth ministry. Between the Youth House and the playground is Gabriel House, another remodeled two-story residence that is now home to the Broadmoor Improvement Association and Annunciation's church offices. Here, in a sunlit office decorated with icons and burning candles, Jerry and Stacy Kramer sat to discuss their life as a tithing couple.

MAKING A COVENANT

Jerry is a perpetual-motion entrepreneur, but Stacy is the reason the Kramers began tithing. When Stacy was twenty-seven, her mother encouraged her to read a book about tithing. The book was by a member of the Unity School of Christianity, and although Stacy does not believe Unity's underlying theology, she found the author's case on tithing both convincing and well grounded in Scripture. Stacy was so persuaded that she wrote an individual covenant with God, modeled after the covenant between Jacob and God as described in Genesis 28:20–22:

> Then Jacob made a vow, saying, "If God will be with me and will watch over me on this journey I am taking and will give me food to eat and clothes to wear so that I return safely to my father's house, then the LORD will be my God and this stone that I have set up as a pillar will be God's house, and of all that you give me I will give you a tenth."

Stacy also was struck by God's call to tithing in Malachi 3:6–12: "It's the only place in Scripture where God says, 'Test me in this,'" Stacy said, contrasting the passage with the repeated warning throughout Scripture against putting the Lord to the test.

In her covenant, Stacy pledged to tithe off her net income for six months. As Stacy honored her promise, her income increased unexpectedly. She worked at a hospital that was imposing a salary freeze, but she received a $7,000 salary adjustment. "To a tither and to God, there is no such thing as a fixed income or a salary freeze," she said. In contrast, she said her life suddenly turned hellish after she decided to skip tithing when money seemed tighter. She worried about money more, and a bill for emergency surgery amounted to roughly the same amount she would have tithed. From this experience, she concluded that God puts his followers' money to use one way or another: "Don't you want to cooperate and experience God's blessings?"

"If you call yourself a Christian, the starting point is the tithe. . . . God likes for you to give sacrificially, to give and not know how you're going to eat."

Stacy grew up poor, and she said that made her focus on material comfort as a young adult. "I'm a born-again cheapskate. I was a taker and not a giver," she said. For Stacy, tithing was the beginning of learning how to give. "If you call yourself a Christian, the *starting point* is the tithe," she said. "God likes for you to give sacrificially, to give and not know how you're going to eat."

TITHING FOR LOVE

Stacy became such an ardent proponent of tithing that she did not want to marry any man who failed to appreciate the importance of the discipline. Tithing was a new concept to Jerry when he met Stacy. Jerry was a stewardship consultant to Catholic dioceses, mostly in Texas, and thought he was doing well to give twenty dollars during the weekly offering. Jerry said that most of the parishioners he worked with as a stewardship consultant were giving one-half of 1 percent of their income.

Jerry remembers with amusement that his life goal was to be a partner in a Catholic stewardship-consulting firm. He attributes this very precise goal, and his aptitude for the work, to his childhood. Young Jerry had to ask for his allowance each week, making the case for why he deserved it and explaining how he intended to spend it. By his early thirties, Jerry had achieved his life goal. Being a stewardship consultant was lucrative enough for Jerry to earn a six-figure income and for the Kramers, who were married in 1996, to enjoy an upper-middle-class life in a gated community in Houston. They both laugh about their perception during those years that they were struggling to make ends meet. "Your money is where your faith hits the road," Jerry said. "Look at your check register, and you'll know what you're worshipping.

For many years we were worshipping Blockbuster Video and Domino's Pizza."

"Your money is where your faith hits the road. . . . Look at your check register, and you'll know what you're worshipping."

A crucial shift occurred when Jerry decided to become an Episcopal priest. Becoming close with two priests at St. Christopher's Episcopal Church in League City, Texas—Walter Ellis and later Jim Smalley—deepened his sense of calling. Jerry sensed that God wanted more of him than just raising money. "Giving is essentially a fruit of faith and not the end in itself," Jerry said. "I knew the bigger issue was calling and challenging people to deeper faith. It wasn't a crisis of stewardship; it was a crisis of discipleship. If you disciple people effectively and lead them to real, transformative faith, the money takes care of itself."

Jerry had explored a possible call to the priesthood much earlier in life while he was still a Catholic. Now Jerry felt further called to serve as a missionary in Africa. His seminary experience had prepared him for missionary service, and Africa now seemed to beckon. Jerry wanted to experience the flourishing church there and participate in what God was doing in East Africa. First, though, the Kramers had a financial hurdle they wanted to clear. Even with Jerry's six-figure income, the Kramers had accumulated $30,000 in credit-card debt.

In the early years of their marriage the Kramers tithed on their net income, and Jerry thought that tithing meant giving 5 percent to your church and 5 percent to a charity. Stacy pressed for giving the first 10 percent to the church where they worshipped—she calls it giving "10 percent to your house." The Kramers resolved together that they would begin tithing on their gross and asked God to guide them in clearing their credit-card debt. Both God and the Kramers honored their ends of that covenant, and the Kramers have tithed off their gross income ever since.

KATRINA CHANGES EVERYTHING

After several years of back-and-forth travel, the Kramers and their three children served as missionaries in Tanzania for fourteen months before returning to the United States. In late January 2005, Jerry interviewed with Annunciation's search committee. Within a week, the committee invited him to become the church's next rector.[7] Only a few months into Jerry's time as rector of Annunciation, Hurricane Katrina slammed into the Gulf coasts of Louisiana and Mississippi. Six feet of water flooded the church and its parish hall for about three weeks. Gangsters broke into the parish hall and made the upstairs room their hangout. Jerry said that nurses at Baptist Memorial Medical Center, located across Claiborne from the church, told him they saw the gangsters come and go by boat, trading drugs and exchanging gunfire by day, eating and drinking in the parish hall by night.

The Kramers had evacuated safely to Baton Rouge when Katrina approached the coast. A week after Katrina struck, Jerry returned to survey the damage at Annunciation. After stumbling along Napoleon Avenue and finally borrowing a fishing boat from neighboring merchants, a bewildered Jerry found his way to the church. Upstairs in the parish hall, he found junk food, switchblades, and a battery-powered boom box still playing music—all left behind by the looters who had rifled through the building in search of any valuables they could steal.

In the nave, Jerry found the sort of catastrophe caused by floodwaters. Pews had moved throughout the room and were still floating in the hazardous water, which had become, across greater New Orleans, a toxic and revolting mix of fuel, garbage, feces, and decaying bodies. Jerry said that as he stood in the nave, both looking upon the damage and being filmed for a televised news report, he could not imagine where to begin putting the pieces back together.

Annunciation began putting the pieces back together by

trying to help relieve the suffering of its neighbors. It not only distributed relief supplies from its parking lot, but with the help of St. Luke's Episcopal Church in Baton Rouge, it offered similar help several miles east to the Lower Ninth Ward, where devastation was even worse than in Broadmoor. Jerry recruited Robert Perry, a bus driver for the city of New Orleans and a member of Annunciation, to drive an RV on weekdays and help distribute the supplies from the parking lot of an abandoned Walgreens. Robert had evacuated to Atlanta and was planning a return to Delaware, where he grew up, but this new mission convinced Robert to return to New Orleans and to stay.

Annunciation helped launch a new Episcopal mission in the Lower Ninth Ward, which met in one of the few scattered homes there that was not totally destroyed by Katrina. The Diocese of Louisiana asked the Walgreen Company if it would donate the abandoned store for continuing relief and development work in the Lower Ninth Ward. The company agreed, and All Souls Church found a larger space in which to worship. When the archbishop of Canterbury met with the Episcopal Church's bishops in New Orleans in late September 2007, he visited the building and blessed the congregation with holy water. Neighborhood children watched as Rowan Williams, the archbishop of Canterbury, with his shock of wiry hair and a full beard, blessed the church amid billowing incense.

BECOMING A MISSIONAL CHURCH

Two and a half years after Hurricane Katrina struck, as I listened to Jerry and Stacy Kramer describe how the storm transformed their struggling little parish, I cautiously asked whether they felt the church was somehow stronger—better, even—because of going through the ordeal together. Jerry sensed my hesitation. "There's no need to dance around the issue," he said. "Stacy and I have discussed this many times, and the answer is yes. Even today, knowing all that it would entail, we would choose to go through it again. Our marriage was pushed to the brink, but we have a tighter bond than ever because of what we went through together."

"God is always up to something good. Our purpose as a church is to find out what God wants to do through us and be available to him."

As Jerry sees it, Hurricane Katrina helped Annunciation move from being a mostly unnoticed neighborhood church, struggling just to survive, to a missional church that the residents of Broadmoor now know with affection because of its role in preserving the neighborhood and helping people in their moments of greatest need. "God is a missional God," Jerry said. "God is always up to something good. Our purpose as a church is to find out what God wants to do through us and be available to him."

Katrina sharpened Annunciation's focus because it clarified which members were ready to be missional. In the wreckage after Katrina, Jerry told his congregation that Annunciation "would not be a mere chaplaincy, worshipping a stained-glass window and a prayer book." To those members who wanted to return to what Annunciation was before Katrina, Jerry suggested that several Episcopal parishes along the posh and elegant St. Charles Avenue might be more appropriate places to worship. "I know that many of the old guard didn't sign up for this kind of church. But we had to become something different in the wake of Katrina. A sleepy, inward-looking chaplaincy wasn't going to cut it. I have no problem with people going elsewhere if our church isn't their cup of tea. We know our mandate, and we're unapologetic about it. Go where you're going to be fed. We now seem to feed people who want to make a real difference for our community and for the world."

In the weeks after Katrina, a neighbor who was contemplating suicide stopped by Annunciation's relief center instead. That day, a member of Annunciation listened sympathetically, hugged her, and gave her a Bible. The neighbor became a steady volunteer and a member of Annunciation. Robin Yeager, a kitchen worker at Annunciation, prayed with a parishoner for the first time in her years of working there, and she became a Christian. Before then, Jerry said, she was just treated as hired help.

The parish hall, which had been thoroughly flooded and trashed after Katrina, is now restored. It served as the relief supply warehouse for nearly two years. Rooms on the second floor have been transformed into dormitory-style bedrooms that house volunteers for the long term. Barring another hurricane strike, rebuilding New Orleans could take another decade.

Jerry said that Annunciation has been the site of remarkable cooperation between conservative and liberal Episcopalians. Indeed, Annunciation has hosted volunteer teams from liberal parishes, such as St. Columba's in Washington, D.C., and from conservative ex-Episcopal churches, such as Truro in Fairfax, Virginia, sometimes with overlapping time together. For suburban conservatives, Jerry said, Annunciation provides a chance to encounter the urban poor as more than an abstraction. For wealthy liberal parishes, Annunciation provides hands-on work rather than just a place to send a check. For parishes across the spectrum, New Orleans is a good practice ground for the culture shock of serving somewhere in the developing world. "We're just dangerous and Third World enough to provide that kind of training," Jerry said.

The Kramers do not credit tithing for everything in their spiritual pilgrimage from a gated community in Houston to missionary work in Tanzania and building a missional church in post-Katrina New Orleans. They do say, however, that tithing was an important part of learning to keep material things in perspective, setting aside idols, and trusting entirely in God.

Members of Annunciation gained a deeper appreciation of the generosity inspired by tithing. Despite losing so much and living so precariously, the parish has increased its local giving 60 percent. One day a new member grew cautious about giving away too many emergency supplies and wanted to cut back. A member with more experience stressed Annunciation's teachings about giving freely and trusting God to provide. The next day another truckload of much-needed supplies arrived.

"The focus of biblical tithing is on what you can do, out of a grateful heart, to serve God, not on what you can get out of God."

The Kramers faced a test of their commitment in Christmas 2005, when they were down to a household balance of fifteen dollars and no money to buy gifts for their children. They had already pledged several thousand in support to an orphanage in Tanzania, and they honored the pledge. Then Stacy received a check from a friend in Texas who insisted that she use it exclusively for buying the children's Christmas gifts.

"The focus of biblical tithing is on what you can do, out of a grateful heart, to serve God, not on what you can get out of God," Stacy said. "I don't want a Mercedes-Benz. If someone gave me one, I would give it to another person. I think that as Christians, we are called to be down-wardly mobile."

4

EARNEST MONEY

John Schwiebert

PRESIDENT GEORGE H. BUSH IS CREDITED WITH CALLING Portland, Oregon, "Little Beirut" because of violent protests that broke out there as he visited the city in 1990. Metanoia Peace Community United Methodist Church is resolutely nonviolent, but the posters dotting its sloping yard make clear that this spacious corner of Northeast Eighteenth and Tillamook streets is not Bush County. Elsewhere in the yard stands a peace pole, a gift from a Portland city commissioner, which expresses the wish MAY PEACE PREVAIL ON EARTH. "Ten Reasons Why the U.S. Must Leave Iraq" appear at the front door of the building Metanoia calls the Eighteenth Avenue Peace House.

The Rev. John Schwiebert met me at the door of Peace House, and we settled into a quiet room to discuss Metanoia Peace Church's history and its commitment to tithing. John

is a tall and slender man who speaks quietly and deliber-
ately, offers steady and friendly eye contact, and laughs
when remembering some of the stranger moments of being
a peace activist. Once, when spending the weekend in jail,
he and other protesters learned of their impending release
as they watched a televised news broadcast. This was news
not only to the protesters but also to the jail's guards.

John grew up in Caldwell, Idaho, attended the College
of Idaho, and then spent three years at Drew Theological
Seminary in New Jersey. He settled in Oregon in 1972.
"I've lived more than half my life right here in Portland," he
said. John is countercultural but pragmatic—a few times he
expressed astonishment at how so many people do not
understand the basics of handling money. He's idealistic
but candid about times when the community's ideals have
not worked out very well. Metanoia, which welcomes
people "regardless of age, race, nationality, gender, sexual
orientation, economic status, or experience with Christianity
or a faith community," hired Joyce McManus, a lesbian, as
copastor in 1993. Within two years, 80 percent of the church
decided it could not afford to keep her on staff. Metanoia
lost some of its members as a result and ultimately paid
$60,000 to buy out the interests of McManus and her part-
ner in a nearby home the church had purchased.

Metanoia is a small, intentional community that began
forming in mid-1985. In the New Testament, the Greek

word *metanoia* refers to changing one's mind, or repenting. The core founders of Metanoia—John and his wife, Pat, and Bruce and Ann Huntwork—knew each other through their longtime involvement in peace protests and nonviolent direct action. Metanoia defines the latter as "active confrontation of specific instances of violence and injustice, sometimes using illegal means (civil disobedience), but only in a manner which is faithful to the principles of nonviolence in word and deed, as practiced by Jesus, Gandhi, the Berrigan brothers and others."[1] Indeed, John recalls that part of his courtship with Pat involved their attending rallies against the Vietnam War.

"We had a sense that the call to Christian discipleship was much more radical than most churches conceived of it."

Metanoia felt like a natural name for the community because of the founders' shared experiences. "Because we were doing nonviolent, Gandhi-style civil disobedience, we were organized into affinity groups. There was a group of us who were Christian, and self-consciously so, and we were part of this other movement that had all kinds of people in it. We needed a name for our affinity group, so we called it Metanoia. That was before we created Metanoia Peace Community. When we later began meeting and talking about a new congregation, Metanoia was a name we were already using," John said. "We had been a part of churches before, and we had a sense that the call to Christian discipleship was much more radical than most churches conceived of it. We talked about things like turning away from rugged individualism, which was rampant in our society, to actually embracing community—not separating ourselves from, but marching to a different drum than the dominant culture. There was certainly a countercultural aspect of it, and we understood Metanoia to imply that. You change direction."

Unlike some other intentional Christian communities in the United States, such as Jesus People USA in Chicago, or The Word of God in Ann Arbor, Metanoia never grew into a membership of several hundred. A history on Metanoia's Web site (www.metanoia.org) tells of thirty adults enrolling in a School of Christian Living "designed to build community and prepare individuals for membership and leadership."[2] Nineteen people completed the course and became Metanoia charter members.

Membership at Metanoia is not simply a matter of placing your name in the church records and showing up for worship at your leisure. A covenant commits full members of the church to these disciplines:

- Participate weekly in the Sunday gatherings of the community.

- Regard all of our personal income and possessions as a resource to be shared, beginning with the tithe (10%).
- Meet regularly with other members in a small Covenant Member Group, where we allow others to hold us accountable for living out this covenant.
- Meet monthly with other members in a gathering of the full membership.
- Devote time daily to meditation, prayer, silence and other acts of devotion, both alone and with others (the journey inward).
- Be in mission to the world, as evidenced in specific acts of compassion and justice (the journey outward).
- Live our lives in response to God's call, seeking guidance from other members in an ongoing process of discernment of that call.
- Support and uphold one another, as together we participate in building up the body of Christ.
- Continue in membership until, in conversation with our fellow members, we have together come to discernment that we are being called to some other place or relationship.[3]

Today, John said, there are sixteen committed members of Metanoia, half of whom live together at Peace House. There are another thirty-five "sojourning members," people who identify with Metanoia's mission but have not signed on to the membership covenant. Worship services at Metanoia normally attract about twenty-five people. Only John and one sojourning member of Metanoia, a civil-rights activist named Lisa Clay, chose to discuss their experiences with tithing.

If a member of Metanoia lives at Peace House, it could seem that asking for a tithe is a bit redundant, like expecting cloistered nuns to wear a veil during their waking hours. Instead, though, the tithe is the starting place for all covenant-committed members of Metanoia to begin a journey into the generosity of God.

"If you become a member of Metanoia, you agree that tithing is the platform in which you enter into membership. You start there," John said. "One metaphor that I like to use, and we talked about it a lot in the early part of Metanoia, was the tithe as earnest money. As with most real-estate transactions, and certainly this house, the process starts with your saying, 'I want to buy this house, and as an indication of my seriousness about this, I'm putting down $10,000 of earnest money, which tells you that I intend to follow through on it.' If the seller follows through and I don't, then the seller gets to keep the money."

"If you become a member of Metanoia, you agree that tithing is the platform in which you enter into membership. You start there."

"We said, okay, what we're aiming for in our community life is to share all things in common, so that nothing you ever receive in any kind of income is a resource that you're not willing to share," he said. "Some of the money you have to keep for yourself, in order to keep yourself from falling into poverty. Some of the money you need to give away to other people. But the tithe, the 10 percent, is your earnest money that you give every month or every week, which is your way of saying I am fully committed to this. 'Seek first the kin-dom of God[4] and all these other things will be added unto you' has been a powerful conviction for us, I think. The more we saw ourselves investing in the kin-dom of God, the less we had to worry about where resources were going to come from. They just seemed to come. That's been powerfully true for us."

CREATING A COMMUNITY

Two things have helped Metanoia's finances: the clean purchase of Peace House, and Pat Schwiebert's career in helping grief-stricken families who lose unborn children or newborns to an early death (www.griefwatch.com).

Pat learned many skills working with dying patients, John said. "At the same time, she had also been doing childbirth education, and when she encountered people whose children died before, during, or after childbirth, she was a real help to them. They told their stories about how sometimes insensitive the hospital staff was, not knowing what to do. Of course staff members felt bad, but they tended to isolate emotionally from the parents. She started teaching and writing about how medical professionals can understand grief and help people. She wrote a book called *When Hello Means Goodbye*,[5] which was addressed to parents, and told them how to help get what they need when they confront that kind of situation, how to deal with their own grief, and how to help others help them with their grief.

"She was working for the Oregon Health & Science University at the time, and Oregon Health & Science University published the book. The foundation was a nonprofit organization, and at a certain point they said, 'We've got too many of these small enterprises, and we ought to spin some of them off.' What we realized was that we were a nonprofit. By that time, we had formed Metanoia Peace Community United Methodist Church. There wasn't enough space up at the Oregon Health & Science University anyway, because the program was growing, so we moved it in here. So now it's a part of Metanoia Peace Community. Since we ship books and other supplies from here, and even do some of the printing here in the basement area, the proceeds from the sale of those materials helps pay the bills. It helps pay property tax and helps pay the costs of maintaining the building. Of course we live here, too, and don't have to pay rent or house payment somewhere else. The amount of money we're able to leverage because of those economies is substantial. We're able to contribute to other groups and to do a significant amount of ministry for our size."

Metanoia purchased Peace House after the Schwieberts saw, during a morning jog, that the building was available. A bank in St. Louis had seized it in a foreclosure. "The price for it was $120,000 in 1986. We didn't have cash. We had a house, and Bruce and Anne had another house. We had already been talking to them about forming this new community and about forming a new church. They said, 'We're in on it if you want to do it.' We knew we would have to come up with the cash, because there was another buyer standing in line who had cash. We went to twenty-six different friends and borrowed money on simple promissory notes, unsecured loans, and we did it in, like, two and a half weeks. We put it all together, handed them the cash, took the title to the house, and then as soon as we got Metanoia formed and incorporated, we deeded the house over to the church.

"We knew there couldn't be any appearance of laundering money or pretending that it belonged to the church when it really belonged to us," John said. "Part of creating the community was that we had essentially renounced private property, and the rest of our lives we expect to live in community with other people and not go out of this life owning anything. It just became a part of our conviction.

"The title has in it that if Metanoia Peace Community should ever cease to exist, the ownership of the property would automatically transfer to the [Portland-based] Oregon-Idaho Conference of the United Methodist Church. I don't know what they'll do with it, but it's very clear that we reserve no rights to it. On the other hand, we had a document written out between the residents of the house and Metanoia Peace Community United Methodist Church Incorporated that said we could live in the house if we paid all the costs for operating it. We do that. Part of the cost comes out of the Grief Watch program. Since I've retired, and the church doesn't have to pay any salary, the church budget agrees to pay half of the utilities."

RESCUED BY A TITHE

Lisa Clay has been a sojourning member of Metanoia since the early 1990s. Lisa said she learned about the importance of tithing from attending small and struggling but Spirit-filled churches in her earlier years. She tells two dramatic stories of her experiences with tithing during her years with Metanoia.

One story involves fellow members of Metanoia coming to her sudden rescue. "One day I was walking down the street and I needed $400. Some terrible thing had happened and I was on a very, very low income, and raising my children pretty much by myself," she said. "I needed $400, and it was really urgent, and I was so down. I heard this horn, and I looked up and there was this family. They were probably having as bad a struggle as I was. She and her kids had gotten some kind of blessing. She and all of her kids gave me their tithes, and it came to $400. It created love, through tithing, just letting the Holy Spirit lead. The exact amount! That kind of thing sticks in your head."

Lisa's other story involves a dilemma she faced after receiving an $80,000 settlement from a civil-rights lawsuit against a store. She hesitated about tithing and was ill at ease until she decided that tithing needed to be her top priority. "I was swimming around, so confused. In my heart I knew something was wrong, and that's what was wrong: I hadn't put God first," she said. "The next day, everything fell into place. It was almost instantaneous." She gave the tithe to Metanoia, which placed the entire $8,000 into the pastor's discretionary fund. John Schwiebert assured Lisa that if more needy families came to her attention, he stood ready to help them through the tithe she had surrendered to God.

5

TREASURES IN HEAVEN

Randy Alcorn

RANDY ALCORN'S COMMITMENT TO THE PRO-LIFE cause cost him his thirteen-year vocation as pastor of Good Shepherd Community Church, located about five miles southeast of his home in the Portland suburb of Gresham. In God's economy, however, Randy developed a much wider pastorate through his popular books, including novels and nonfiction. His books have created a few million dollars in royalties and he has given away all of the royalties to Christian ministries. A few themes thread their way through most of Randy's books: Jesus has redeemed us by his death on the cross, heaven and hell are real, and God calls his people to lives of sacrifice for the sake of his eternal kingdom.

Randy welcomed me to his office behind his home. The office was lined with framed book covers and sports memorabilia. It's definitely guy space, but much tidier than a bachelor's apartment. Randy mentioned that he would need to check his blood sugar periodically. He was diagnosed as an insulin-dependent diabetic in 1985. We both set up recording devices, chose soft drinks from a small refrigerator, and sat to talk about how God is using the son of a tough-minded tavern owner to spread some lessons about the costs of discipleship.

Randy grew up in Portland in a non-Christian household. He began attending Powell Valley Community Church to be around a young woman named Nanci. He became a Christian through that church, and Nanci eventually became his wife. Randy said he was drawn early in his Christian life toward people who made heroic sacrifices for their faith—people like the late Richard Wurmbrand, who was tortured by communists in Romania and later led a ministry called Voice of the Martyrs; and Brother Andrew, who repeatedly risked arrest by smuggling Bibles behind the Iron Curtain. "For several years I didn't give much to the church. Instead I gave a whole lot to parachurch Christian ministries, especially those working with persecuted Christians," he said.

Randy became aware of tithing when his pastor preached on the importance of supporting the local congregation. He remembers that the sermon drew on

Galatians 6:6: "Anyone who receives instruction in the word must share all good things with his instructor."

Randy said he was already giving "significantly beyond 10 percent" outside the congregation. "However, what I determined to do at that point was to give 10 percent to the church. When I gave 10 percent to the church, I sensed the vested interest that I then had. By that time I understood what Jesus was saying in Matthew 6:20–21, in terms of storing up for ourselves treasures in heaven, and when you give to something, where your treasure is, there will your heart be also."

Randy said he was persuaded that tithing was the least he could do for his congregation, and that he never looked on it legalistically. "I was prone even back then to do my homework and research. It just became clear that, as a New Testament follower of Christ, in the most affluent society in human history, there's no way I could ever justify giving less than 10 percent when God had required that, really, of the poorest Israelite. Here I know the grace of Jesus. Why would I not give more? It seemed like a good starting place. I wouldn't have articulated it that way, but looking back, I think that really was what I was experiencing."

"As a New Testament follower of Christ, in the most affluent society in human history, there's no way I could ever justify giving less than 10 percent when God had required that, really, of the poorest Israelite."

Randy earned a bachelor's degree in theology from Multnomah Bible College and a master's degree from Western Seminary, both in Portland. While studying at Multnomah, he became a part-time youth pastor at Powell Valley Community Church. Shortly after completing his master's degree in 1977, he became one of two original pastors at Good Shepherd Community Church, where he remained as a pastor until 1990. He had neither grown bored with his responsibilities nor fallen into moral failure. Instead, he joined a group trying to protect the lives of the unborn at Lovejoy Surgicenter—so named because it is on the corner of Northwest Twenty-fifth Avenue and Northwest Lovejoy Street in Portland. The *Los Angeles Times* reported in 1998 that the facility "performs nearly half of all abortions in Oregon, as well as offering podiatry, vasectomies, tubal ligations and plastic surgery."[1]

GAINING STRENGTH THROUGH BROKENNESS

Randy was among the Christians who participated in pro-life rescues beginning in the 1980s. In fact, one of his books—*Is Rescuing Right?*—made the case for nonviolent civil disobedience at abortion clinics.[2] For Randy and thirty-three other protesters, it proved a costly decision. Allene Klass, owner of Lovejoy Surgicenter, took the protesters to court on charges of trespass and nuisance. She won the case, and the jury imposed a judgment of $8.2 million on the protesters.

Randy already was a published author by then, but royalties were not his primary income when the judgment came down. "Once we gave the books and the royalties completely over to the Lord, book sales dramatically increased, which I think itself was interesting, kind of God's way of saying, 'Put them in my hands, and the causes go to things I'm concerned about, that I have a vested interest in.' I knew I needed to provide for my family. My wife didn't work outside the home, and we didn't want her to. There was any number of things I could do, but the problem was, I couldn't make over minimum wage. Whatever job I was going to do, 25 percent of what was above minimum wage could be garnished. I did not want a dime to go to an abortion clinic. I could work hard, but at the end of the day, if a large chunk of this money was going to an abortion clinic, that was just unthinkable."

Randy resigned as pastor of Good Shepherd, and he founded Eternal Perspective Ministries. "The ministry pays me minimum wage plus benefits so that I can write books, which—by God's grace—are earning millions of dollars," Randy said. "It's crazy, humanly speaking, but it works great."

Randy was not alone in his response: the *Times* also

reported that Lovejoy Surgicenter had collected only about $250,000 of the $8.2 million judgment. The judgment stood for ten years and then was renewed for another ten years. Randy expects the judgment will expire on its twentieth anniversary, but he is not likely to change his financial choices. When the first ten-year judgment period was about to expire, the board of Eternal Perspective Ministries—having no idea that the judgment would be extended—offered to give the Alcorns access to the book royalties. After discussing the offer and praying about it, the Alcorns declined—and soon learned that the judgment had been extended.

Being part of that $8.2 million judgment and being diagnosed as a diabetic have been two of the most powerful experiences in Randy's spiritual life. They have "ultimately been a cause of not only growth but also rejoicing about that growth," Randy said. "My point, of course, is not that those were easy or that they remain easy. They haven't been, and they aren't. But I see such great ways that God has used those things in my life. I was very independent. My health had been good. My father owned a number of taverns and was the most independent human being you have ever known, and he was extremely healthy and strong. Even though I came to Christ when I was in high school, in pastoral ministry I discovered—and the people who worked with me, I'm sure, discovered—that I was self-reliant. Now, I was a Jesus-loving Christian who was seeking to draw upon God's empowerment in what I did. But pretty much I got up, got out of bed, worked long hours, did what I did, and didn't really need to rely on any-one that much.

"When I became an insulin-dependent diabetic, all of a sudden I had to take blood tests throughout the day. I had to take insulin. Sometimes I have low blood sugar where my body isn't working right and my mind isn't working right. So the strong body and strong mind that I had, now, peri-odically, are not strong. A few times a week, I experience what I think an Alzheimer's patient experiences. The only difference is I can drink some orange juice and in fifteen or twenty minutes I'm fine. I can vividly remember what it was like to be in a thick fog and not accurately perceive what's happening around me."

Randy cites the apostle Paul's passage from 2 Corinthians 12:7–9: "'To keep me from becoming conceited because of these surpassingly great revelations, there was given me a thorn in my flesh, a messenger of Satan, to torment me. Three times I pleaded with the Lord to take it away from me. But he said to me, 'My grace is sufficient for you, for my power is made perfect in weakness.' Therefore I will boast all the more gladly about my weaknesses, so that Christ's power may rest on me."

"I resigned from pastoral ministry, which I loved.

Looking back at it, what God wanted me to do with the rest of my life—I'm convinced that is what I'm doing now," Randy said. "I believe he used the years of pastoral ministry to prepare me for writing, mentoring, and speaking. Because I loved pastoral ministry, I don't think I ever would have stepped away from it. He yanked me away from it.

"Here is an abortion clinic—people whose lives are dedicated to the killing of children, who bring these lawsuits, who bring these writs of garnishment from courts against me, that end up making it necessary that I no longer be a pastor. God used them as God used Joseph's brothers, as Joseph says in Genesis 50:20: 'You meant evil against me, but God meant it for good.'[3] That's exactly what has happened in our lives. I'm so grateful. I would not have it any other way, as hard as those years were."

> *"God used them as God used Joseph's brothers, as Joseph says in Genesis 50:20: 'You meant evil against me, but God meant it for good.' That's exactly what has happened in our lives."*

Randy saw, for instance, that his daughters Karina, then twelve, and Angela, ten, showed courage of their own. Just before the lawsuit went to trial, Lovejoy Surgicenter offered to drop charges against him. He was the only defendant to receive such an offer. The Alcorns held a family meeting to discuss the offer. Randy remembers Karina saying that if Lovejoy Surgicenter wanted him out of the case, God probably wanted him to remain part of the lawsuit. "She said what I believed in my heart, but I just couldn't say those words to my family. I would have if I'd had to," Randy said. "God graciously allowed my twelve-year-old to say that, and my ten-year-old said, 'Yeah!' She was right there with her sister. Nanci agreed too, as much as she wanted the situation to go away." Randy reminded his daughters that they could lose their house and might have to leave their school. Were they still willing? They nodded. "I get tears in my eyes when I think about it, even now."

"Our daughters, to this day, speak of those days with a sense that they grew," Randy said. "They prayed, and they saw God answer prayers. I think it's very likely, had they not gone through that, they would not be the young women they are, in terms of being sold out to Christ."

TITHING AND TRAINING WHEELS

Being among those penalized for their pro-life protests enabled Randy to do more of what he already wanted to do: scale down his living expenses and give far more money to the kingdom of God. Through Eternal Perspective Ministries, the Alcorns have given away more than $4 million to ministries that engage in evangelism, pro-life and pro-family activism, famine relief, child sponsorship and orphan aid, and activism against human trafficking.

Randy defends tithing against charges of legalism, though he also expresses sadness that some Christians see tithing as the summum bonum of stewardship, rather than the starting place.

Randy defends tithing against charges of legalism, though he also expresses sadness that some Christians see tithing as the summum bonum of stewardship, rather than the starting place. "You'd think it was this extraordinary act of sacrifice and devotion that only great saints would actually give 10 percent. People talk about Old Testament giving and New Testament giving, and one of the greatest misconceptions is that the Old Testament was the tithe, required giving, and New Testament is freewill giving, freewill offering. The Old Testament is *full* of freewill offerings," he said.

"A remarkable number of people, and I've had long conversations with many of them, give absolutely nothing and view the tithe as a legalistic Old Testament thing. To give a tithe would be, to them, like offering an animal sacrifice. It would be ungodly to do it. And of course, they look around and say there are these people who are into tithing as legalism. And there *are* people, absolutely, into tithing as legalism. And I'm completely against that."

Randy explained why God wants more. "What I always say to people is that if you take the standard of 10 percent and say God required it of the poorest people in Old Testament Israel, and now that we're under the grace of Jesus and we have the indwelling Holy Spirit and we live in this incredibly affluent culture, do you think he would expect less of us? Does God still have expectations of New Testament people? Clearly he does. In fact, Jesus' message is, 'You have heard that it was said, but I say to you.' And then what does he do each time? He raises the bar.

"New Testament giving—Acts 2 and Acts 4 are very explicit on this—is this contagious liquidating of assets and giving to those in need. How far beyond 10 percent was that? That was taking an already existing asset, liqui-dating it, and giving the entire thing away. That's giving away 100 percent of that asset, not 100 percent of your income. They gave away what many Christians today, in equivalent terms, might give away over a lifetime, and many would not even give that much."

"New Testament giving—Acts 2 and Acts 4 are very explicit on this—is this contagious liquidating of assets and giving to those in need."

Randy likes to call tithing the training wheels of Christian giving. "The point of putting on training wheels is actually to get you up and get you going to learn how to ride a bike. I think for many Christians tithing can be a very good thing, in that it gets them going on the path of giving in a disciplined way that has some objectivity to it that is measurable," he said. "God's goal is that your life would be lived by the grace of Jesus. Look at 2 Corinthians 8 and 9, the longest New Testament passage on giving, and just study that passage and meditate on it. That's separate from the tithing issue. If you actually capture the spirit of 2 Corinthians 8 and 9 and it becomes a reality in your life, you can forget about tithing."

Not long before I left Randy's home office, our conversation turned to Malachi 3, and especially to God's challenge in verse 10 that the Israelites test him by daring to tithe from their produce. "It's as if God is saying there is something very special about giving. He doesn't say, 'Don't commit adultery. Test me in this. Give *not committing adultery* a try and see if I don't bless you.' God doesn't take his commands and reduce them to the level of 'Oh, give it a try and see if it works.' It's as if he's making a special case out of giving, and he's saying, 'Yes. Test me in this and see if I don't bless you.'

"There's a New Testament equivalent to that. Luke 6:38 is a close parallel to Malachi 3:10, where Jesus says, 'Give, and it will be given to you. A good measure, pressed down, shaken together and running over, will be poured into your lap." Anyone who says, 'Oh, Malachi 3, that's Old Covenant, and it's restricted to that'—no. Luke 6 is very close. 'Watch me abundantly provide for you.' And this is Jesus; this is not King David or Solomon, who are living in splendor. This is Jesus, who doesn't have a rock to lay his head on. He's got the clothes on his back, and not much more. And Jesus is saying, 'Just watch what happens when you give. My heavenly Father is going to overflow.'

"Jesus is saying, 'Just watch what happens when you give. My heavenly Father is going to overflow.' "

"In Malachi, why is that promise there? I think it's because God longs for his people to live the life of grace, to live the life of freewill offering, and see how much fun it is and how God abundantly provides and blesses it."

6

"NEVER TELL ME
WHAT YOU WON'T DO"

Jerald January

As I drove from Chicago's Loop to Vernon Park Church of God on the city's South Side, I knew Jerald January only through the memorable title of his memoir, *A Messed-Up Ride or a Dressed-Up Walk,*[1] and through what I could gather on his church's Web site (www.vpcog.org). In talking with Jerald, I heard heartbreaking stories of casual racism, broken business agreements, and Jerald's sometimes vanquished dreams of promoting a Christian healing that crosses racial barriers. I also heard of perseverance and God's faithfulness, and of how a commitment to tithing has his church on the verge of constructing a spacious new multipurpose campus about sixteen miles south of its current location.

Tragedy struck early in Jerald's life when he saw his

mother fatally shot during a domestic dispute. He remembers hearing the shot and seeing his mother's blood on the kitchen floor. "No one knew I saw her murdered until I was about fourteen years old," he said. "My brothers and I were told that she died in a car accident, but I was there when he shot her. I was a kid, so no one thought that I remembered anything."

Jerald's paternal grandparents took over as his surrogate parents, raising him in inner-city Detroit. The title of his memoir comes from his grandfather's saying that "a messed-up ride is better than a dressed-up walk." He wrote:

I understood what my grandfather was saying: Let your pride do what it wants to do. You can look great and "dressed-up" and walk to where you need to be, and never get there on time or at all. Or, you can realize that sometimes you're forced to be in circumstances that don't look good to you, but they will get you where you need to be. The ride is "messed up," but at least you're getting there.

Occasionally, though, it is better to have a dressed-up walk. I can't forget what Rosa Parks showed us all. Blacks in Montgomery could have ridden the bus and supported a system that counted them less than human. Instead, they chose to walk to and from church for a full year dressed as domestics, blue-collar workers, and professionals. That dressed-up walk brought a lot of good to the country?

Jerald's book tells of his growing up in Detroit; attending Ferris State College in Big Rapids, Michigan; starting a family in Chicago in the late 1970s and seeing that marriage fail; remarrying in 1985; and working with needy youth in Denver in the early 1990s.

"We lived in a very, very modest house in Detroit. My grandparents and my father raised us. We didn't have a whole lot. My granddad and my grandma believed if you pray and you trust God, he'll let you do anything in the world you want to do," Jerald said. "My grandfather was not allowed to go past sixth grade. He grew up in a town where some of the boys weren't allowed to go past sixth grade because they were black. He said, 'When I was a little boy they told me, "Nigger, you don't need no more education."' He'd always say, 'If I had a high-school diploma, I would have been president of the United States,' because he was such a wise man. To the day he died, he talked about the fact that they never let him go to high school."

Jerald did not face the same severity of obstacles, but he has compiled some broken dreams along the way. A publisher declined to print his next manuscript, *A Second Time*, so he founded his own company, CoolSprings Publishing, Inc.[3] In *A Second Time*, Jerald suggests that the Old Testament prophet Jonah was, to put it plainly, a bigot. "It wasn't a book on reconciliation," he said. "It was a book from a sermon I had preached at Focus on the

Family, which I did only one time. It was something James Dobson was having for denominational leaders. I wanted to talk about the real divisions between blacks and whites in church. That was it. In my study I found that, pretty much, Jonah was a bigot. That's all. He had seen what had happened to his forefathers, and he'd rather die in the ocean than for God to save those people."

A *Second Time* led to another dashed dream. Jerald appeared on *The 700 Club* to promote the book, and Christian Broadcasting Network subsequently tried to sponsor a conference featuring both Jerald and Jim Cymbala of the Brooklyn Tabernacle. "They based a conference around my book and Jim Cymbala's book on bringing people together from different cultures," he said. "Even though they showed our commercial for thirty days straight, twice on every show, we got a call back saying, 'For the first time in the history of *The 700 Club*, we cannot sell this conference. Our people will not come to hear about blacks and whites loving each other.' They had some great posters. Boy, the artwork was awesome. I was looking forward to doing it, but they said, 'We can't sell it; the people don't want it.'"

Still, one of the most crippling setbacks Jerald experienced was for a touring event he envisioned called the Urban Block Party. "It was a concept God gave me—when the prodigal comes home, kill the fatted calf, and have a big party. We used to have block parties where I grew up—twice a year they block off the neighborhood. But this was like a super show, free of charge to the public. Anybody could come," he said.

Urban Block Party would unite famous athletes from professional football and basketball with actors and singers in a scripted show. Jerald and a partner had lined up corporate sponsorships to cover roughly $93,000 in tour expenses. Then disaster struck. "In a matter of four weeks, my entire life fell apart," Jerald said. "Everything that we had worked for, it just seemed like it had crumbled to dust." One of the tour's major sponsors suddenly backed out of the tour, claiming it had not realized that the majority of its participants were—well, that they were black.

"What? What are you talking about?" Jerald said, looking back at that time. "Eighty-three percent of the NFL is black. We're giving them entrée with the best athletes in the world, and you guys say you love the Lord. It was so close to the event that I didn't have time to get $93,000 together. Everything was booked; it was over the Christmas holidays. I ended up cancelling it. We ate a lot of debt. Some people let us off the hook; some didn't."

Taking the advice of his wife, Jerra, Jerald drove to a secluded retreat center for concentrated prayer. "God didn't say anything to me. I read the Scriptures, and I prayed," Jerald said. "I was saying, 'Just give me a hint. What did I do wrong? Why did this happen like this?' Nothing. On my way home I was stopping to get some gas for my truck, and heard the Holy Spirit whisper, 'Do you love me?' It had to be God, because I wasn't even thinking about God. I was just thinking of how I was going to get out of this debt. I was just pumping gas and said, 'Yeah, Lord, I love you.' Nothing else. About fifteen miles from my exit to go home, I heard the Lord say to me, 'Never tell me what you won't do.' I had told him, 'I will never pastor. Never.'"

"I heard the Lord say to me, 'Never tell me what you won't do.'
I had told him, 'I will never pastor. Never.'"

"I'M THE JOSHUA"

Jerald began preaching at age twenty, but he said that seeing too many wrecked lives of senior pastors had left him resisting the idea of being a senior pastor himself. Ultimately God used the financial collapse of the Urban Block Party to move Jerald toward becoming pastor of Vernon Park Church of God.

"'This church had contacted me three times in a year and a half, and I said there was no way in God's green earth that I would pastor a church,'" he said. "'The last thing I wanted to do was pastor a church on the South Side of Chicago. 'Lord, let's not go that way. I live in

Colorado Springs.' Even if I was going to move, I had an offer to go to work for a large Christian businessmen organization, to be a mentor to CFOs and CEOs.

"As much as I didn't want to pastor, I knew God wanted me here. I didn't tell them that, though. They asked me to come here and speak at a meeting for young people. It was in the spring of 1999, in the week after the Lord had spoken to me. I wasn't going to pastor, but I thought, *Lord, if I at least go and preach, maybe you'll ease up off me a little bit.* I came and spoke on a Sunday morning. They only had one service then, with about two hundred members. It was just a common service, to me. I wasn't particularly good, and it wasn't a particularly good service. But from Monday to Thursday, every night I spoke, more and more people came. By Thursday it was standing room only, and people were standing in the hallways. One trustee said, 'We haven't had this in years.' My wife leaned over to me and said, 'I think God's setting us up.'"

Soon afterward Jerald accepted the church's offer, but only as an interim pastor. "After about a year, I thought, *Okay, maybe I'm supposed to be here.* I never let them install me as the pastor, though. I was the pastor, but we never had any installation services. I signed a one-year contract. I figured they may not like me, and I might not like them. I love God, but I know enough guys fail at this thing. I was coming into a church that, even though it's prestigious, it was not very healthy financially. It was a nice building, but it had problems."

Jerald said he made a deal with God: if, within a year, the church grew from 200 people to about 350, and if tithes and offerings increased, he would stay. He was not, he stressed, paid on commission. By the next February, the church had grown from 230 to about 300. "The church was getting healthier; the offerings went up $2,000 or $3,000 a Sunday. We were able to pay off some bills," he said. "Someone asked me, 'Why did you do it that way?' There are about six million people in Cook County. If I can't attract 350 of them, I'm not the guy for the job. I have other skills. I can go do something else."

Jerald is the second pastor of Vernon Park Church of God, which Claude and Addie Wyatt founded in a garage in 1955. "I'm the Joshua," Jerald said.

A TURNING POINT IN TITHING

A turning point in the congregation's life came when Jerald began teaching a class called "Right Relationship to Wealth" on Wednesday nights. "I wanted people to understand what the Bible really says about money. People told me, 'We have never heard this like this before. You made it so plain.'"

Trustees told Jerald that offerings shot up from $7,500 a week to $11,000 a week. "Some people put little notes in [the collection basket] saying they had never understood what tithing was. Some people even went back as far as a year and made up every tithe they had missed. I had never told anyone to do anything like that. I really never believed that the offering should be a big part of the service." The offering now lasts only a few minutes, and Jerald jokes that it occurs just before the benediction, so people can withhold their offerings if the sermon annoyed them.

Membership in the church has continued growing. Vernon Park now has about eleven hundred members. For a time, the church expanded its schedule to three services on Sunday. Jerald said he found that schedule too exhausting, and he scaled back to two services. With that growth has come a sense of outgrowing Vernon Park's current facility. Jerald believes he heard the Lord say to him, "Build me a house."

"I thought, *Okay, Lord, we'll build another church.* As my studies went on, I sensed he wasn't just talking about building a church. As I was reading the words of Jesus, 'In my Father's house are many mansions,'[4] I had this concept about a campus, a holistic campus where we not only have a church but also have a place for a seniors building, an athletic building, maybe twelve or thirteen acres."

Eventually a member of Jerald's church spotted land

in Lynwood, Illinois, owned by the survivors of an immigrant farmer. The member knocked on the farmhouse door, introduced himself, and explained that his pastor had a vision for a multipurpose campus. Jerald was hoping to find land at about $135,000 an acre, compared to prices ranging between $190,000 and $500,000 elsewhere in Cook County. He heard from the family's attorney that the survivors were willing to sell all the property to Vernon Park—if the church was willing to buy all forty-three acres of the farm.

"It was a whole-faith thing," Jerald said. "I told God, 'Okay, God, we're a tithing church; we give. We even tithe off of what people give us to other ministries around the country and around the world. But we're not a big church. We're what we call a tweener church—we're too big to be small, too small to be big.'"

When trustees from the church met with family members, at first Jerald could not believe the price was as low as it was: $18,000 an acre. "They said, 'Pastor, this makes absolutely no sense. We got there, and there was no negotiation. The owner just said, 'If the church shows up, offer them the land for this amount of money.' I said, 'Guys, this is $18,000 an acre. The houses across the street—four houses per acre—start at $400,000.' It just didn't make any sense to me. I said, 'This is great: $637,000 for forty-three acres of prime land on a main street half a block from the expressway. Something's wrong—Jimmy Hoffa's buried on it—*something*.' My faith should have been better than that, but it wasn't."

At the closing, the youngest of the farmer's three daughters began crying.

Asking her sisters' permission, she told the story of their parents, who came to this country as immigrant sharecroppers. The farmer asked God for his own land, praying that if God would grant that dream, "he would use it to God's glory and be a secret tither to ministries all over the world," Jerald said. "No one would ever know, but he would make God proud that he gave him that land. In Lynwood this old man was famous, because his rows were so straight. He didn't have the best equipment, but everybody knew how much he loved God. She said, 'Papa taught us how to pray, walking through the corn out there on that land.'"

Jerald sees further significance in the purchase. In the early years of the farm's life, blacks weren't allowed to live in that southern part of Cook County. It was Ku Klux Klan territory.

In time the church acquired still another thirty-five acres, at the same price per acre, from a neighbor who was the farmer's best friend for many years. Ultimately, the church bought just over seventy-five acres of land for a bit more than $1 million.

Jerald's plan for the property, which will be called Vernon Park Village, comprises twenty-two acres for the church and offices; forty-four acres for housing, especially retirement condos; and on the front end, mostly retail and commercial, with one corner of luxury rentals for retired people.

Jerald is confident the church will retain a ministry to needy people in its new location. "Less than a mile from us is the poorest neighborhood in the state of Illinois, Ford Heights. Our missions ministry for the church is already putting together programs—not just food programs, but education programs for the children. We're already meeting with four different school boards in that area. We're looking forward to it. There's a trailer park less than a quarter of a mile from where we are."

Jerald said that tithing has been a guiding principle throughout his Christian life, and he has suffered when he strayed from it. He credits his grandparents with teaching him about tithing. "They always went to church. My grandmother was a Baptist, and my grandfather was a Methodist. No matter whose church we went to, the offering plate never went by unless they put money in it. They made us put money in. They gave us money, and that quarter could buy a lot of penny candy. That wasn't odd to us. They were always blessed. They weren't well-educated people, but they were always blessed," he said.

Jerald said that tithing has been a guiding principle throughout his Christian life, and he has suffered when he strayed from it.

"I have seen what happens when you don't tithe, in my own life, twice. I had become, for some reason, a tither of convenience. If things were going okay, I convinced myself that I could skip it this time. I remember having a house foreclosed. I had to apologize to my wife, because I knew it was my fault. I don't know where I picked up that habit, but somewhere in my late twenties and early thirties I was doing that, and I filed for bankruptcy and everything. From that day to this day, we have not ceased to tithe, plus give 5 percent in offerings, on everything that we own. Everything. It's been twenty-one years. I don't care if I was unemployed or not. I don't care what it was from. We always do that. We've never needed anything. We've never gone hungry. We tell people that we believe that same mantle has fallen on our church."

7

DEEP GLADNESS MEETS DEEP HUNGER

Kevin Jones

In October 2002, reporter Kevin Jones wrote about "Confessing the Faith," a national conference of conservative activists within mainline Protestant churches. Kevin's report left no doubt about which side he was on. He opposed these conservatives, but he also expressed a grudging respect for their perseverance. "From what I've seen, they are playing a deeply sophisticated and subtle game and playing it in a relentless and patient style, determined to take the time it takes to win," he wrote in an online article. "Are progressives playing at that level? Are we willing to?"[1]

Kevin and his wife, the Reverend Rosa Lee Harden, immersed themselves for a time in the culture wars of the Episcopal Church. They launched a popular Web site,

Every Voice Network, which offered original reporting and frequent commentary. By 2004 they developed a multimedia curriculum, Via Media, which used many of the techniques (video content followed by small-group discussions over dinner) of the Alpha course, a popular introduction to the Christian faith. Via Media's theology was considerably different, though: while Alpha flows from the charismatic and evangelical stream of Anglicanism, Via Media flows from the liberal stream.

Kevin was a force to be reckoned with, and a somewhat intimidating one at that. Drawing on his years of experience as a reporter of both religion and business news, Kevin delved into public records that established connections between conservative activist groups and wealthy benefactors. A few of the headlines from Kevin's stories during the Episcopal Church's General Convention of 2003 convey what a happy warrior he was: "Anglican Imperialism: How the AAC [American Anglican Council] Funds International Allies," "[Gene] Robinson Controversy: Allegations Weak, Timing Suspicious," "Conservatives Plot Next Steps."[2]

Still, one of the things I most remember from that General Convention was when reporters stood in line for more than an hour, waiting for the seats allotted to us when the House of Bishops would debate whether to approve of Gene Robinson as the first Episcopal Church bishop who spoke openly of his gay partner before his election was approved. As reporters stood by, fighting away boredom with occasional small talk, Kevin walked along the line, offering free bottles of water. "I'll take one," I said, marking the first time I spoke with him. This was an almost inconsequential moment, but it also was a glimpse of Kevin as something more than a happy warrior.

I saw more of this side of both Kevin and Rosa Lee in May 2004, when I traveled to Jackson, Mississippi, to learn more about their Via Media curriculum. I attended as a reporter rather than a subscriber of the curriculum, and I wanted to interview the publishers about their vision and their goals. After a daylong training session, Kevin and I chatted by a hotel pool while Rosa Lee worked in some therapeutic swimming. Kevin and Rosa Lee invited me to join them and several other friends for a meal at a Red Hot & Blue restaurant, a barbecue chain in which the late conservative firebrand Lee Atwater made an early investment. Among those who have lived in the South, eating barbecue together covers a multi-tude of conflicts. What I remember most about that evening was riding back to the hotel with Kevin and Rosa Lee after dinner. We took a few detours so they could drive past homes they had helped build as part of Habitat for Humanity in Jackson.

They spoke fondly of their involvement with Habitat, a time they used not only to build houses but also to

broaden the Jackson chapter's vision of long-term community transformation.

"Maybe we should do a better job of quantifying the
economic costs of poverty to get folks in," Kevin said.
"That's a lot of what Rosa Lee did with Habitat in Jackson,
to get people involved. It wasn't that you wanted to just
care about housing for poor folks, but she could talk about
lower policing costs, lower social-service costs, higher
property taxes, higher economic-development quotients—
oh, and poor folks get houses, and the percentage of them
that finish high school is so much greater. You have to find
a way to sell good to people with small hearts. It's a continual challenge."

"You have to find a way to sell good to people with
small hearts. It's a continual challenge."

As I think back on those years of Every Voice Network
and Via Media, it becomes clear that even then Kevin
wanted to do more than take sides in the Episcopal
Church's vigorous but often circular debates. Even in 2002,
when he took on the Association for Church Renewal, his
online biography included this paragraph: "He is currently
working toward building a community that will re-vision
the roles of business and capitalism. Read more about that
budding work at collectiveintelligence.net."[3]

Kevin and Rosa Lee tithe, but Kevin thinks of tithing as too modest a goal for stewardship. "I think we have a responsibility with our resources. It's more like the talents parable: what did we do with what came our way?" he

HOLISTIC GENEROSITY

so is Rosa Lee's church, Holy Innocents, which has about two hundred members.

I asked Kevin to tell me more about Good Capital, and we agreed that an in-person interview in San Francisco was a good idea. Kevin and Rosa Lee live in a modest-sized and eco-friendly apartment in the Noe Valley neighborhood. Good Capital's office is within walking distance, and

I visited the Collective Intelligence Web site on occasion, but I found it a bit heavy on Web jargon and contemporary economic theory. I noticed that Kevin had become involved in the Anglican Malaria Project, and I wrote him once to say I missed his voice in our shared church's debates—mostly because of his willingness to step back from the battle on occasion and comment on the power struggles on both sides. Kevin wrote back to say he was feeling too fulfilled in his work with Good Capital, LLC (www.goodcapital.net), to be very tempted by church politics.

said. "Tithing seems like an obligation, whereas the parable of the talents seems like a relationship, a transaction, a gift, and return of that gift. That makes more sense to me."

"I think we have a responsibility with our resources. It's more like the talents parable: what did we do with what came our way?"

As a Silicon Valley entrepreneur, Kevin built one company, Net Market Makers, to $18 million in revenues, and sold it for $30 million in early 2000. Kevin demurs about how much of his wealth he will invest in Good Capital as one of its three principals, but the company intends to invest $1 million to $3 million per deal in ten to twelve enterprises. Good Capital says the company also will seek investments from "high-net-worth individuals, religious capital, and foundations."[4]

Kevin said Good Capital wants to challenge the traditional approach to philanthropy, which he sees as an inadequate and miserly response to a world in need. Kevin believes that Andrew Carnegie's two "Gospel of Wealth" essays, first published by *North American Review* in 1889, sold Americans on a philosophy that treated the market as a force of nature best left unregulated. "Philanthropy is so completely emasculated that 95 percent of a foundation is built on a capital-management vehicle and it has a 5 percent donation arm out the back," he said. "That's really

TITHING

what foundations are. They only have to distribute 5 percent of their corpus every year toward their product or their service. That's being dethroned in a radical and big and good way by something called mission-related investing. There are some big foundations driving it but also some smaller, catalytic foundations driving it—the F. B. Heron Foundation, the Meyer Memorial Trust, and the Annie E. Casey Foundation, where they want at least 2 percent of that 95 percent to be invested in line with the mission."

When a philanthropic foundation gives away only 5 percent of its corpus in a year, "philanthropy is in this little encapsulated bubble. The way we think about our money, we have two pockets. We have the investment pocket and a little bitty giving pocket. That's allowed by a thing called externalities," he said. "There are two areas of externalities: environmental and social. Global warming has put the environment on the balance sheet, so it's no longer an externality. It's a cost that's being factored in by every business. The reinsurance companies are asking insurance companies, 'What's the exposure of this business to global warming or other climate change?' Poverty, unfortunately, is not on the balance sheet, so it's still an externality. When Wal-Mart externalizes the cost of health care to the state by not paying benefits, it can maximize profits, but it doesn't mean that there's not a social cost. We're bearing that cost, but we allow corporations to do that."

Good Capital also works against an assumption that foundations need to think about the social good only when making grants. He cites a series of articles by the *Los Angeles Times* that said the Bill and Melinda Gates Foundation, in the *Times*'s words, "reaps vast financial gains every year from investments that contravene its good works."[5]

"There's a complete dichotomy from the investment side of the house, where they say they have a fiduciary responsibility, a legal responsibility, to grow the corpus and so they can't think about mission. Mission is just out the back. It's kind of the wrong end of the horse, as my friend Jed Emerson [a lecturer at the Stanford School of Business] says. That series of articles is causing a huge move, basically, to say, 'Do we have a Gates Foundation exposure in our portfolio?'" Kevin said.

> *"It's a deeper level of stewardship. It means asking,*
> *'What is my money doing to the planet and to the people?'"*

"I don't walk to talk about philanthropy. I want to talk about you and your assets and what you want to do with them in the world. We're raising a fund where it's on the line between giving and investing. You don't just look at risk and return, but you look at risk and return and your impact. It's a deeper level of stewardship. It means asking, 'What is my money doing to the planet and to the people?' I think that's what we're responsible for. If we use philanthropy, we're using old, outdated cultural frames that lock us into the doctrine that was laid down by Andrew Carnegie. We want to dethrone the current myths of capital. We think it's a devil's bargain, and the times are such that we have to do it. The planet demands it, and the people demand it."

Good Capital does not want to limit its definition of responsible investment to as narrow a category as fair trade. Kevin said that concept has become so broad as to be almost meaningless. "We're looking to invest in fair-trade companies that offer a living wage all the way down but are organic all the way down. It's really interesting: You can't get a premium for fair trade, because if you say *fair trade* you just reach the Birkenstock kind of hippie crowd, the pity crowd—you can be in your caftans and buy your fair trade caftans. Some of these folks aren't using the words *fair trade* anymore. They want to get beyond that. They're calling it *sustainable sourcing*. It's environmentally sound and socially sound. There's an old formulation of things like fair trade that people are starting to get beyond, in terms of crafts and artisanal things. In coffee, fair trade is asking, 'Is it organic? Is it shade-grown? Is it fair trade?' Well, Sam's Club can do that, so they're moving in there."

Kevin mentions two examples of the kinds of business in which Good Capital plans to invest: Evergreen Lodge and Better World Books. Kevin personally invested in

Evergreen Lodge as a startup, and Good Capital announced in April 2008 that it would provide Better World Books with up to $2.5 million in growth capital.

Evergreen Lodge (www.evergreenlodge.com) is a bed-and-breakfast on the west side of Yosemite National Park that also trains at-risk young people as season interns. "A third of their population consists of people from halfway houses, young men and women," Kevin said. "There's a cost to the intake of those folks. You have to find the right ones who can learn a career in a hotel or restaurant. There are social workers on staff, as well as kids from the ghetto who have never been to the Sierras. It has a huge impact. They're working around college kids, who have always had a different set of options and hopes than kids from the ghettos, so that causes a change. And then there's outplacement to hotels that have learned to work with them. There's a hard cost to that. It's about $300,000 to $400,000 a year in hard costs, and there are some soft costs. 'At-risk' means there's some risk with these kids. They don't have work habits. They haven't been in a supervised situation with positive goals before, a lot of them. But it still makes 12 percent. There's a subsidization of a social mission inside a for-profit business."

Better World Books sells both new and used books, and many of its used books come from both college campuses and libraries. At the top of its online store (www.betterworldbooks.com), Better World keeps tallies of how many used books it has kept out of landfills and how much money it has contributed to help spread literacy across the world. Better World offers the customary shipping options, from standard to urgent, but it uses Carbonfund.org to make its shipments carbon-neutral.

"The reason we got to them, and not another fund, is that they wanted to give away more than any other investor would deal with," Kevin said of Better World Books. "They wanted to give away 10 percent top line. We said that's not going to work. You can give away 5 percent top line and give 5 percent of your stock to your nonprofit literacy partners—Room to Read, Books for Africa, based on their performance. Our investors will give up 5 percent of that return that we could have gotten, and you give up 5 percent of your company, and we can strike a deal. That's the thing we did, and we will report every year on the pounds of books that didn't go to the landfill because they were sold online, the tons of carbon offset because they ship carbon-neutral, and then the number of books that go to the literacy groups."

A LONG SEARCH FOR JUSTICE

In describing the spiritual aspect of his work with Good Capital, Kevin reached for an observation by essayist and novelist Frederick Buechner. Rosa Lee helped him recall how Buechner defines *vocation* in his book *Wishful Thinking: A Seeker's ABC*: "The place God calls you to is the place where your deep gladness and the world's deep hunger meet."[6]

"I am finding more meaning in my everyday tasks, which has a spiritual dimension. There's the impact I know we're having on people's lives with the companies we're investing in, and yet we're doing it with a level of professional skill that took me thirty-five years of my life to acquire," he said. "I'm bringing more of myself to it, as opposed to just my professional self. I can talk about what things really mean and why we're doing it and why we should bear the cost of doing good. This is a load our capital should carry.

> *"I am finding more meaning in my everyday tasks, which has a spiritual dimension. There's the impact I know we're having on people's lives with the companies we're investing in."*

"I can talk to my kids in a different way. My kids are pretty much fringe left, permaculture farmers in intentional communities. I can talk about the impact I'm trying to have on the world in a way that makes sense to them. That's really important. I couldn't do that while I was in business. I get no satisfaction out of traditional business anymore. I know how to do it, but it's a game that is empty to me. I can bring my whole self to this in a way that I've never brought my whole self to business before. We've had things where I did good *over here* and I did business *over there*. This is a unifying thing that breaks down the compartmentalization that I had to live within when I was in traditional business."

Kevin has explored ways to help the poor for much of his life. "I became a Christian in 1970 via the Jesus Movement. They asked me to open my heart, and that scared me to death. I thought I was with some bloodletting cult," he said. "I lived in a house with other converts through college and went to Southern Baptist seminary to work with poor folks. I discovered I did not have the temperament to be a community activist."

He worked with the Anglican Malaria Project, but that, too, became a lesson in what sort of work he's equipped to do. "We discovered that well-meaning entrepreneurial white folks coming in with a great solution in Mozambique had so much to learn," he said. "It was a great learning enterprise. I learned that I am much better at being an advocate than I am in on-the-ground direct service with the level of incremental change that happens with really poor folks in Africa. A fast-moving entrepreneur is not the same profile as a community organizer. I worked on it for two years. We set up a great system, and then I realized I wasn't the person to push it forward."

Kevin traces his passion for helping the poor to his growing up in a working-class home. "We were the single blue-collar, financially challenged family within a larger, white-collar, affluent family. My father repaired washing machines. The uncles who were doctors and lawyers cut the turkey at Thanksgiving. We got the meat they didn't want, down at the end of the table. That got pointed out to them at one dinner. They informed my father and mother that all was right with the world and we'd continue to be down at the foot of the table. That made me aware that simply speaking about injustice to those in power or those with money did not cause them to change.

"Even asking did not change the basic power structures. My first tactic, which I employed half a dozen times, was to become one of the guys at the head of the table," he said. "But after doing that several times, I realized my heart was with the people down at the foot of the table. I was over fifty before I realized that becoming rich and powerful was not really much of an answer, that working to restructure the capital markets, and business, and the way people think about power and money, was at the heart of what I want my life to be about."

8

A SENSE OF COMMUNITY

Mark Kellner

WHEN MY FELLOW JOURNALIST MARK KELLNER AGREED to discuss tithing with me, we met at an open-air mall in downtown Silver Spring, Maryland, and then made our way to a Thai restaurant. It was a slightly chilly Saturday night in mid-September. When I first met Mark in early 2000, we got together at a P. F. Chang's at Fashion Island, another open-air mall, in Newport Beach, California. I suppose that if Mark and I have a serendipitous final meeting just before we die, or before the Second Coming of Christ, it will be at a Mongolian barbecue in a city yet to be determined. Mark and I came to know each other because we're both journalists with a particular fond-ness for writing about religion. From the moment I first spoke to Mark regarding this book, he emphasized that he would speak only for himself and not for any past or current church or employer. I agreed to make that clear.

His pilgrimage through the American religious land-scape is offbeat, if not even exotic. First, the bird's-eye view: Jewish childhood, teenage years with the Worldwide Church of God, seventeen years as a member of the Salvation Army, and now more than ten years as a member of the Seventh-day Adventist Church. His interest in American religions is not merely journalistic. In most of the changes in his chosen places of worship—except for a three-year respite at Marble Collegiate Church, the home of Norman Vincent Peale's gospel of positive thinking—Mark has committed himself to churches that make no small demands of their members.

"I find it interesting to see people who make a commit-ment and who stick to it—especially when that commitment is sort of countercultural and when it can involve real sac-rifice," Mark said. To complement this thought, Mark tells the joke about the respective sacrifices that a hen and a pig make so a farmer may have a breakfast of eggs and bacon. You probably know the punch line: the pig turns to the hen and says, "You're making a commitment. I'm making a sacrifice."

"I find it interesting to see people who make a commitment and who stick to it—especially when that commitment is sort of countercultural and when it can involve real sacrifice."

A CONVERSION INTERRUPTED

If Mark were handling this transition sentence, he might frame it as a joke: "How did a nice Jewish boy from Queens wind up in a church like this?" It's a long story, but this narrative will hit the highlights.

"I figured out at a very early age who the Messiah was," Mark said. "I was playing hooky one day from school, and Billy Graham was on the television. Now, there was no warning, there was no crawl along the bottom of the screen that said, 'Warning! Jewish people do not need to watch this!' And so I watched, and what Billy Graham said made sense. It made a lot of sense. This was shortly before my thirteenth birthday. My folks came home and I said, 'Guess what? I'm a Christian.' And they said, 'Guess what? You're not.' At the age of thirteen, in the Jewish tradition, one is confirmed in a bar mitzvah as an adult member of the faith. My parents were in the process of spending what was, for those days, a very handsome sum of money—thousands of dollars. They essentially suppressed my Christianity then. I went along, I was a little changeable then, although obviously something stuck in the back of my mind."

By 1975, Mark joined Herbert W. Armstrong's Worldwide Church of God.[1] At the time the Worldwide Church of God—Mark calls it simply the Worldwide Church—practiced a multilayered approach to tithing that made a mandatory 10 percent look like child's play. "In the Worldwide Church, tithing was mandated very strongly," Mark said. "You had your first tithe, which was 10 percent off the top, sent in to the headquarters in Pasadena. There was a second tithe, which was to be retained by the member, and—every three years after baptism—a third tithe, which also went to headquarters. Ostensibly that third tithe was for the care of widows and orphans in the church. In actuality, those who were critical of Herbert Armstrong suggested that among the widows and orphans was a Grumman Gulfstream II jet, and that some of the widows may have been young lady friends of Garner Ted Armstrong, who was ousted during my association with the Worldwide Church."

Mark expressed a fondness for how the Worldwide Church advised its members to spend their second tithe: "The second tithe, that was kind of a brilliant thing. This was all from Leviticus, of course. The second tithe was meant to defray your expenses at the church's annual camp meeting called the Feast of Tabernacles—ten days, usually in a resort area of some stripe or another. You went away from home, you saved up your money, and you went to town—not riotously, not in debauchery, per se. You basically went out and you had a good time. It was supposed to be a foretaste of heaven. You know, I like that."

Other than the second tithe, however, most of what

Worldwide Church members gave supported the work of their headquarters—and a widely reported lavish lifestyle favored by its founder. "Of course, there were suggestions," Mark said. "For example, as you were planning for the festival, the suggestion was to send in a *tithe of the tithe* to maintain the assembly halls and campgrounds and meeting places that the church did own. They didn't own local build-ings, but they would have these regional places to gather. There was pressure, shall we say, to contribute festival offer-ings, and reasonably healthy ones at that. Armstrong's view was that we were in the gun lap toward the end of every-thing, so why get your teeth fixed? Give money to the work."

Looking back, Mark does not resent the Worldwide Church's higher-than-average sense of tithing. "I was a kid; I was a teenager. Herbert Armstrong spent $10 mil-lion building one of the finest auditoriums on the West Coast, the Ambassador Auditorium in Pasadena. There's $20 of mine somewhere in there, but in the perspective of history it's not a whole lot," Mark said. Instead, Mark left the Worldwide Church less because of its rigorous demands on tithing but because he was disenchanted by how poorly he believed Herbert Armstrong treated his family mem-bers and subordinates. "What did trouble me toward the end, and what has always troubled me in observing tithing situations or situations involving church finance, is when you treat the people below you worse than you take care of yourself. Herbert did that with just about everyone he came into contact with, including his children."

Mark said little about his time with Marble Collegiate Church, except to offer this compliment for how that church handled its stewardship messages: "Every fall they did something that made an impression on me and that I wish more churches would do.

"On a series of Sunday mornings, people would come up and give a testimony about their commitment to tithe and what that did for them."

"Every fall, [Marble Collegiate Church] did something that made an impression on me and that I wish more churches would do. On a series of Sunday mornings, people would come up and give a testimony about their commitment to tithe and what that did for them."

Mark does not say a great deal more about the Salvation Army, but its hymnody and theology left a lasting impression. "The battle within the Salvation Army, very briefly, is whether they're going to end up as primarily or largely a social services agency or whether they're going to remain true to their evangelical roots. William Booth was very concerned about evangelism, and social service evolved as a way to get the gospel to people. The idea was not just to go around and do good works and set up canteens at house fires. The idea was to win people for Christ."

Mark said his tithing was less consistent during his years with Marble Collegiate Church and the Salvation Army. "We have all sorts of wonderful choruses in the Salvation Army. One is 'I am not under law but under grace / It was grace that rescued me / It was grace that set me free / I have sought, I have found the hiding place / I am not under law but under grace.' When the budget was tight, I would sort of turn to that, and to a companion chorus from the Salvation Army: 'Grace there is my every debt to pay / Blood to wash my every sin away / Power to keep me spotless day by day / For me, for me.'"

BECOMING ADVENTISTS

Mark said his attraction to Adventism occurred when he and his wife had hit a plateau in their experience with the Salvation Army. "One day, I was listening to the radio and I heard a commercial for a fellow who was giving a series of public lectures. I happened to know that the fellow was a Seventh-day Adventist. I also knew that my wife was not overly favorable toward Seventh-day Adventism. In order to get her to go to these lectures, I did what any self-respecting husband would do in a similar situation: I told her only half the truth. I said, 'Listen, here's a guy who's going to give these lectures on Bible archaeology, on the pyramids, on the pharaohs.' And he *was* doing this. She agreed to go, and we kept going. We accepted the Seventh-day Adventist message. I was baptized as a Seventh-day Adventist in April 1999. My wife was baptized a couple of weeks later."

Beneath the frequent asides and a delivery akin to Jackie Mason's, Mark is serious about his faith. He commits himself to a church that celebrates its Christian Sabbath on Saturday, urges its members to abide by a vegetarian diet, and teaches this on tithing: "God's plan for the support of His work on this earth is through the tithe and freewill offerings of His people. The tithe is the main source of funding for the total proclamation of the gospel to all the world by the Seventh-day Adventist Church."[2]

The Seventh-day Adventist Church says much more than this about tithing, of course. Its "Guidelines on the Use of Tithe" run just over sixteen hundred words, laying down strict rules for how Adventist leaders are to distribute the tithes they collect and where they collect them (within their own geographical conferences or divisions).[3]

"We talk in the church about people 'returning tithes' because we believe, as the Bible says, that 'the earth is the LORD's, and the fullness thereof.'"

Mark questions whether the tithe is a biblical requirement, but he trusts his church's teaching about its importance in supporting the church. Mark uses an

Adventist phrase—to *return tithe*—when referring to his giving. "'We talk in the church about people' returning tithes'
because we believe, as the Bible says, that 'the earth is the
LORD's, and the fullness thereof,'"[4] he said. "If everything
belongs to him, if he owns the cattle on a thousand hills, I
don't own the cattle but I get to use them. I'm returning to
God what he has given me."

So, then, Mark returns tithes. "I have no problem with
adhering to and supporting the church's position. I do find
things in Scripture and in history that raise questions.
Tithing was to be done on agricultural goods. As far as I
know, there's no mention in Scripture of tithing on money.
There are scriptures where it is sort of implied or where
you can *infer* something—such as when Paul talks about
setting aside on the first day of the week an offering.[5] But
Paul, who would certainly have known the custom of tithing from his Pharisaical training, did not say, 'On the first
day of the week, get your tithe ready.' Was it a special
offering? Was it something else? Were offerings meant to
be something one gives from money, and the tithe was
from agricultural produce? Let's face it: one of the things
people in my denomination are accused of is legalism. I
don't really think that those who are truly Christian at
heart within our denomination are legalists. I do not
observe the Sabbath to get to heaven, however imperfectly
I may or may not observe it. I do it out of love. And I do

it because I read the fourth commandment fairly literally, I guess."

BELONGING TO THE BODY OF CHRIST

Mark also affirms tithing because it gives a sense of belonging to some larger body of Christians, some larger purpose other than personal fulfillment.

"Community is important, and I believe going to church is important. Now, how do I apply this to tithing? I have experienced this very keenly, both in Seventh-day Adventism and in the Salvation Army. When you join a church of that nature—in one sense, particularly with the Salvation Army, you are part of an international community. I have been in Japan. I was in Kobe after the Hengchun earthquake, and we were in a tiny little Salvation Army building. There were some Japanese Salvation Army officers, myself, and other people from the United States. We all sat around the same table. We had the same hymns. They were singing in Japanese; we were singing in English. There's a sense of community there.

"As a Seventh-day Adventist, I have been in Nairobi, Kenya, where I have been the only Caucasian person in a congregation of one thousand people renting an auditorium at the University of Nairobi. They were singing mostly in Swahili. I was trying to sing in Swahili because they had the hymnal in front of me. When I was in the city of Kaunas in Lithuania, and we were all together singing Jack Hayford's song 'Majesty,' they were singing in Lithuanian, and I was singing in English. You feel a part of a larger fellowship than you do otherwise," he said.

"Tithing is a similar thing. By contributing and being a part financially of the church at the local level, the district level, the regional level, the national level, and the world level—because the tithe money in our denomination flows upward—it's a great linking thing."

Creating a sense of connection is important in helping church members know they belong in a community and in encouraging them to stay in that community. "We've got tons of people coming into the church through the front door of the church, and we're grateful for it. Sometimes we will lose some of them through the back door because they haven't been nurtured properly or they don't feel connected for some other reason. That's why I believe connection is important," Mark said.

"When you decide to become a Seventh-day Adventist, you have to be pretty hard-core. If you're going to rearrange your life in that fashion, I would like to see someone stay committed to it. Now if they elect to leave, I wish them Godspeed and pray they'd return and reconsider, but I'm not trying to imprison people. I want people to be happy doing what they're doing, and I want them to be happy being a part of the fellowship. That's where the connection comes in. I think there's value in going to a church every week, going to a building that is not your home, that is not your familiar surroundings, and coming together with other people. The Scripture says do not forsake the assembling of yourselves together.[6] I don't know of too many people who leave a church or a community or a faith group where they're happy."

Mark sees tithing as both expressing and creating a deeper sense of connection with each other and with God. "It is a way of establishing a bond that you wouldn't have otherwise. By being in that channel, if you will, being in that mind-set, I certainly think that God is more able to show favor in a way that we recognize it. Strictly speaking, if you really want to get Talmudic about it, every moment in our lives is an incredible gift from God. I know from my own circumstances that there has been more than one occasion where I should have been dead, a long time ago. God has elected to keep me alive, to a certain point. I've heard it said that we are immortal until we have completed the mission that God has given us," he said.

"I wouldn't want to deny it to the people who well and truly need this for whatever reason, but you can essentially turn on your television any Sunday morning and go to church, and have almost every element of a church service except maybe the guy snoring next to you. And you send in your offering to the television preacher, and all is well. But that kind of sterility and that kind of being in a silo, if you will, I find very troubling. It's better when you smash the silo and you become a part of a community. I'm borrowing a metaphor from the IT industry, where data has been kept in all these compartments, silos, and the whole idea now is to smash everything and let all the information mix. When you get people out of their shells and into the community, that's where the miracles happen."

"When you get people out of their shells and into the community, that's where the miracles happen."

9

"THE ESSENCE OF GOD IS ALWAYS TO BE GIVING"

Ed Bacon

IN THE MID-1990S, AS PART OF MY WORK FOR A CONSER-
vative activist group within the Episcopal Church, I began
reporting on the annual conference of the Association of
Diocesan Liturgy and Music Commissions (ADLMC).
One thing stands out from ADLMC's annual meetings:
hearing a message by the Reverend J. Edwin Bacon Jr. for
the first time. Ed was fairly new as rector of All Saints in
Pasadena, one of the best-known liberal congregations in
the Episcopal Church.

What was most memorable about Ed's talk had little to
do with liturgy or music. Rather, he described a congregation that calls its members to give. Ed told how he would
host new parishioners at his home and urge them to become
involved in one of the parish's plethora of service-oriented

groups—including COLORS (Christians Offering Love to Overcome Racism in Society), GAIA (the Global AIDS Interfaith Alliance), and Night Basketball and Books, which helps low-income children and adolescents.

Almost as an aside, he mentioned that All Saints encourages its members to tithe. Ed's talk caught me by surprise. Given my assumptions about this congregation, and given the standard topics of ADLMC addresses, I had expected little more than political bromides and perhaps a peacock-like display of liturgical novelties. Ed's talk brought me up short. I thought, *Here is a liberal congregation spreading a gospel that makes some demands on your soul and on your time. Here is a place where you will not be praised effusively just for showing up on Sunday morning.*

When Ed concluded his remarks at ADLMC, I walked forward to thank him. In the ten-plus years since then, I've always enjoyed seeing Ed. We are usually on opposite sides of our shared denomination's political and theological divides. What we share is a sense that those questions matter. If you're an activist within the church long enough, you befriend people on the other side of your favorite questions—or you avoid becoming friends with them. Life is richer when Ed Bacon is your friend.

Knowing of Ed's emphasis on tithing added a sense of poignancy to news reports involving the congregation's conflict with the Internal Revenue Service. All Saints caught the unblinking eye of the IRS after its previous rector, the Reverend George F. Regas, preached a sermon two days before the presidential election of 2004. George did not endorse either major candidate, but he did imagine Jesus saying to George W. Bush, "Mr. President, your doctrine of preemptive war is a failed doctrine. Forcibly changing the regime of an enemy that posed no imminent threat has led to disaster."

In June 2005, All Saints received an IRS letter saying that its tax-exempt status could be revoked because of that sermon's political content. One thing was clear, even from a distance: the IRS chose its target poorly. All Saints retained a Washington law firm to fight the investigation until the agency backed down. The IRS backed down in September 2007, saying it had concluded that the church had "intervened in the 2004 Presidential election campaign" but adding, "We note that this was a one-time occurrence and that you have policies in place to ensure that the Church complies with the prohibition against intervention in campaigns for public office."

"There was never any doubt about the course that we were going to take," Ed said over breakfast in a hotel restaurant adjacent to All Saints. "We always knew that we were going to fight this. We knew it was unjust, in the first place. If we had to fight to the Supreme Court, we would do that. If the Supreme Court ruled against us, we would continue on with our identity. Nobody ever blinked an eye about that."

For his part, George also was clear that no IRS investigation—or even a revocation of tax-exempt status—would affect the parish clergy's collective will to address political questions from the pulpit. "That congregation is so profoundly committed to being a prophetic church, to trying speak truth to power and all that means, and they have become such significant leaders in that world, that the IRS could not ever change that. They could make it more difficult, but it wouldn't change anything. People would dig deeper," George said in his office at the nonprofit Regas Institute in downtown Pasadena. "The whole business of the freedom of the pulpit is so central—not only for the progressive pulpit, but also for the conservative pulpit. The freedom to speak truth as you have come to understand it is very important. Anything that mitigates that is a huge impoverishment to being true to the message, true to what God's calling us to be."

All Saints believes it stands in the line of a prophetic tradition, "particularly of Isaiah, Hosea, Amos, and Jesus," Ed said. "Isaiah and Amos are very clear that God finds beautiful worship repugnant if it doesn't lead you to go into the world and change the world for the widows and the orphans and everybody who is disenfranchised and marginalized. All Saints is not about just showing up. All Saints is about showing up for beautiful, transformative, moving corporate worship, but it is always, always in the interest of taking the transformation you have experienced in worship to the world, to transform the world, so that it can be what God's dream always was when God created the world.

"The essence of my stewardship theology is the belief that we are God's colleagues. In order for us to be energetic, inspired, empowered colleagues of God, we have to put our money where our mouth is. When you give, you release so much more energy for God, because it's so energizing and inspiring to be a giver."

"The essence of my stewardship theology is the belief that we are God's colleagues. In order for us to be energetic, inspired, empowered colleagues of God, we have to put our money where our mouth is."

TWO INFLUENTIAL RECTORS

All Saints Episcopal Church celebrated its 125th anniversary in 2008, and the celebration included a $45 million capital campaign to expand space for worship, Christian education, and community activism. All Saints sits on prime real estate in Pasadena. City Hall is just across Euclid Street, and Fuller Theological Seminary is one block east. With its gothic architecture and well-tended courtyard, All

Saints is a picturesque campus that sometimes appears in films and television shows.

It would be tempting to think that All Saints is rolling in money. When people mention their assumptions about All Saints, "I tell them that we don't have deep pockets. We don't have an endowment of much more than $1 mil-lion, which is really just unheard of," Ed said. "We're not a member of the Consortium of Endowed Episcopal Parishes, and our $5 million budget comes from the giving of the people. We have a very small endowment, we get 5 percent from that, and we've got some revenue that comes in from our parking lot, but that's it. All the other stuff comes from pledges, some special gifts that we go out and get from time to time, and the offering plate. We have a lot of people who have modest incomes. In this economic downturn, we've had three people who suddenly were homeless because they lost their jobs." Parishioner Peggy Phelps, who has given the church $50,000 annually for the past decade, agrees that the endowment is comparatively small, and she bemoans it: "We have a smaller endowment here than the SPCA does. That's shocking."

All Saints has a long tradition of political engagement, but its emphasis on tithing appears more directly tied to the arrival of George Regas as its rector in 1967, and Ed Bacon's continuing emphasis on tithing since becoming rector in 1995. Both men say they had come to appreciate tithing before they arrived at All Saints. George learned of tithing's importance while serving as a vicar, fresh out of seminary, at a tiny mission in Pulaski, Tennessee. Two parishioners told him that if the mission hoped to ever have any money, he needed to talk about tithing. "My systematic entry into the tithing world was one of self-interest," he said.

A native of Tennessee, he had studied at the famously progressive Episcopal Theological School (now Episcopal Divinity School) in Cambridge, Massachusetts, and returned to his home state during the early stirrings of the civil-rights movement to lead a mission in what was then Ku Klux Klan country. "It was a hard three years, but they were an important three years and they were three years of growth."

From Tennessee he became rector of Grace Church in Nyack, New York, which had seven hundred communicants. After George served there for two years, his bishop, Horace Donnegan, appointed him chairman of the diocesan stewardship committee. George sought advice from one of his parishioners, Wheeler Conkling, who stressed that leaders teach tithing most effectively by relying on public testimonies given by tithers. "He was the most affluent person in Nyack who was in the heart of my ministry," George said. "He was a successful businessperson who was deeply committed to the ministry of the church and to tithing. When I could get Wheeler Conkling in Nyack to witness to his Christian discipleship and to what tithing had meant to him, you'd better believe people listened. Not only was he a successful businessperson, but he was the very heart of the ministry of the church."

"It was just a given in [my father's] life that he wanted to give back because this country had given him so much. Generosity meant that he gave back. That planted itself deeply in me."

George also credits his father for teaching him about generosity. His father came to the United States as a penniless immigrant from Greece and eventually became a moderately successful restaurateur. Because his father started his life in America in such need," "He was a very generous human being, and so generosity was just part of my growing up. He didn't know anything about tithing."

His father often said that your checkbook tells the story of your priorities." "That was real for him. When we were talking about what we could do or not do, he would say, 'Look at the checkbook, son. Look where we're spending the money.' I can remember, as a young boy, being surprised at the amount of money he gave to Saint James Episcopal Church. I never asked him about it. I was too young. He died when I was twenty-one. I never talked to him about what motivated that. It was just a given in his life that he wanted to give back because this country had given him so much. Generosity meant that he gave back. That planted itself deeply in me."

Ed also credits his father, and the first priest he worked for in Atlanta, with teaching him about tithing. "My father was a Baptist minister and also an educator. He and mother always tithed. He preached tithing," he said. "When I began my career or vocation as an Episcopal priest, my boss, Dan Matthews, said, 'It's time for you to be tithing, and I know you know the importance of tithing. And you and Hope are not tithing. I want you to know that if you want to be a fruitful priest in the Episcopal Church, and you're going to be a rector of a church, it's important that you tithe, because of all the benefits.' I didn't have to ask him, 'What are the benefits?' I didn't resist that at all. I just said, 'You're absolutely right,' and so we immediately began tithing, and have ever since."

> *"If you want to be a fruitful priest in the Episcopal Church, and you're going to be a rector of a church, it's important that you tithe, because of all the benefits."*

WHY PEOPLE GIVE

Some of Ed's parishioners smile as they describe his challenging parishioners to give and then adds, "I hope I'm not asking too little of you." All Saints conveys its emphasis on tithing primarily through people giving their testimonies—speaking during church about how they have grown into more generous givers—and in related articles through the parish newsletter, *Saints Alive*.

"I think people intrinsically know that when they give, that's when they're happy, that's when they're joyful," Ed said. "I think that underneath that is something that they might never say: when you give of yourself, to a faith community and to others, that's one of the places where you get to discover the image of God that is within you. The essence of God is always to be giving. God is a giver. God is a giver of life; God is a giver of health; God is a giver of forgiveness; God is a giver of mercy and compassion; God is a giver of energy to transform the world to be a just and peaceful place. I think that there is a spiritual phenomenon that goes on when you give generously. The by-product is joy and happiness, but the deepest thing that is going on is that you're expressing the image of God within you. I think that people feel connected with God in a way that's as powerful as having a mystical experience during prayer or while gazing at the sunset."

Several members of All Saints reinforced Ed's perspective as they discussed their giving to the church. Vestry member Gloria Pitzer said that she and her husband were already increasing their giving when their life together took a challenging turn. "My husband lost his job, and all of a sudden we were tithing. I like to call it the case of the inadvertent tither," she said. "Living generously is learned. It's learned from hearing how other people are freed by doing it. I don't think you're born as a giver. It's freed me from the guilt of holding on to my money and worrying about what I'm going to part with. It's freed me to be generous in other giving as well."

> *"Living generously is learned. It's learned from hearing how other people are freed by doing it."*

Cooper Thornton moved to Los Angeles from Nashville to pursue acting. Cooper and his wife, Laura, an ordained minister, felt at home in the atmosphere of All Saints. "It's exciting for something so uncomfortable to be out on the table. You've named the elephant in the room," Cooper said of the church's emphasis on tithing. Cooper appreciates tithing as one of the several spiritual disciplines—such as prayer and serving the needy—that sometimes are easier to see in a liturgical church. "The disciplines just give much more of a shape to my life. It gives me a connection to a global faith community that shares a lot of the same disciplines."

Kate Gasparrelli-Byrne credits her parents' emphasis on generosity with helping her be open to tithing. "I don't like the word *tithing.* It sounds like a tax we pay to God," she said. Nevertheless, she tithes and considers generosity a crucial aspect of living as a Christian. "You can't make life like this," she said, clinching a fist. "You have to make life like this," she said, opening her hand again. "You can stretch and give at a level that's uncomfortable for you and trust that the universe will be there to support you. This is the heart of tithing; we are in this together. Tithing becomes a natural extension of how you aggregate what you care about. If you're not tithing, you're preventing the Holy Spirit from working in your life in a major way."

"*This is the heart of tithing: we are in this together. Tithing becomes a natural extension of how you aggregate what you care about. If you're not tithing, you're preventing the Holy Spirit from working in your life in a major way.*"

Dottie Simmons, director of strategic planning and operations for Home Box Office, grew up in the African Methodist Episcopal Church. "I eventually got to a place where giving to God *first* meant I truly believed that my needs will be met regardless of my apparent circumstances in this material world," she said. "When I first began tithing, I made significantly less than I do now, so of course that 10 percent had more of an impact on my finances, but my thinking really changed. Within months I had enough money for all of my *needs* and I found myself *wanting* less."

Richard Beatty, who works at Jet Propulsion Laboratories, has taken his engineering skills on short-term visits to Armenia and Malawi through an All Saints program called Transformation Journeys. "I've never heard it as required or that you're a bad person if you don't tithe," he said. "Rather, it's been an invitation. It makes me feel a lot more of a bond with the place, more informed, and much happier to be a part of it."

When many of these All Saints parishioners discussed their lives of giving, they also mentioned Warrington "Warry" MacElroy, a longtime member of All Saints. "Have you talked to Warry?" they said. "You have to talk to Warry."

Warry, who is retired, made himself available on short notice during my final day of meeting with members of All Saints. He was dressed in casual but elegant clothes, but the more striking thing about him was a ready smile and eyes that radiated peace. "Up until 1973, I was a respectable Christian, I was a good boy. I did what I was supposed to do," he said.

Then he attended Cursillo[1] and became a born-again and charismatic Christian. Through a friend at work, he saw a pro-tithing pamphlet published by Seventh-day Adventists. He read the pamphlet, was impressed by its message, and felt that God said to him, "Warry, after all

I've done for you, do you think I would ask you to tithe and not make it possible for you to do that?"

He had to triple his donations to reach 10 percent.

"Now I'm scared to stop," he said. "I have no desire to stop. It's what we're supposed to be doing. It is one of the most simple and direct ways of discovering an up close and personal God." Like Stacy Kramer of New Orleans, Warry cites God's words in Malachi 3:10: "'Test me in this,' says the LORD Almighty, 'and see if I will not throw open the floodgates of heaven and pour out so much blessing that you will not have room enough for it.'"

LIVING WATER

When Ed Bacon talks with new members of All Saints—or with members who otherwise need help in learning some principles of generosity—he compares the two very different bodies of water that he saw during a tour of Israel. First, he describes the vibrancy surrounding the Sea of Galilee, which he witnessed from the deck of a restaurant at the seashore. "There were people in rowboats and speedboats, folks way out in fishing boats, people on Jet skis, people picnicking along the banks. For centuries people have made their business a fishing business because the place is so full of fish," he said.

"Next, I talk about going to the Dead Sea on the same tour, and there's no life there. The only thing that's going on is in one or two spots you go and get this mud on your face and it's supposed to be good for your skin. You can go out and float because of all the salt. But there is no boating, no picnicking, no foliage, no greenery. It's desolate.

"That is the essence of life, and that is the essence of what makes you alive, when you not only receive the graces of God but you also give the graces of God away very liberally, very generously."

"The difference between those two bodies of water is that the Sea of Galilee not only receives the Jordan River, but it releases the Jordan River; it gives. The Dead Sea only has water coming in. Nothing is flowing out, except through evaporation. That is the essence of life, and that is the essence of what makes you alive, when you not only receive the graces of God but you also give the graces of God away very liberally, very generously."

10

"DO THEY TELL SUCH STORIES ABOUT ME AND YOU?"

Yisroel Miller

ABOUT TWENTY-FIVE THOUSAND JEWS LIVE IN GREATER Pittsburgh, and the largest concentration of Jewish families is in the neighborhood known as Squirrel Hill. Visit Squirrel Hill on a Friday evening or a Saturday, and you will see steady streams of people walking, sometimes in the middle of side streets, to the neighborhood's eight prominent synagogues, including Congregation Poale Zedeck, at the corner of Shady and Phillips avenues. This Orthodox synagogue, where Austro-Hungarian immigrants worshipped beginning in the late nineteenth century, is rich in stained glass. The Pittsburgh History and Landmarks Foundation helps support and protect this gem of a sacred space.

I arrived early for an afternoon interview with Yisroel Miller, who became the rabbi of Poale Zedeck in 1984.[1]

I walked around the block and then sat on the front steps of the building, enjoying the whimsical manner in which Shady Avenue branches off and forms a triangular corner with Tillbury Avenue. A man opened the door from behind me. "Are you the rabbi?" I asked. He was instead the building's caretaker, he told me good-naturedly. After I explained I was there to interview Rabbi Miller, he wished me a pleasant visit to "Congregation PZ," as he called it.

The office entrance for Congregation PZ is protected by an intercom system, but I arrived at the door at an opportune moment and walked in behind an older member of the congregation. A staff member seemed nervous about my unexplained presence until I mentioned that I was there to see Rabbi Miller.

The rabbi greeted me warmly, and we stepped into a study lined with hundreds of books, most of them in Hebrew. As an air conditioner hummed in one corner, we sat, and the rabbi was soon walking me through Orthodox Jewish thinking on tithing in a patient voice of instruction. Our conversation was not strictly catechetical, but Rabbi Miller is a man who loves to teach—not merely because it is his role in this congregation, but also because he loves and reveres the law that he's explaining.

"My father was a rabbi. Growing up in a rabbinic home, the one thing that was clear to me was that I did not want to become a rabbi," he said. "I'm sure that's true of many clergy children. But I had an interest in the study of Jewish learning, which we call Torah. In Judaism, the study of your religion is a sacrament, one of the outstanding religious deeds one does, and as a teenager I met some charismatic people who gave me an insight into the fire of Jewish learning. I spent several years doing that, and I found I wanted to share it with other people.

"I eventually came to Pittsburgh on a fellowship program, after ordination, which allowed me to continue some of my studies and reach out to laypeople who wanted to study and learn more about Judaism, both those who are already committed and those who are searching. One of the places I did my teaching was in this synagogue. When the rabbi moved on, the congregation turned to me and asked, 'Would you be our spiritual leader?' That had not been my career plan, but I had a mentor—it's very important in our tradition to have a living mentor—and he said, 'If they ask you, you don't say no.' I took the position, and now I've been here twenty-four years."

INTERPRETING TORAH

On that warm summer day, Rabbi Miller's instruction was methodical. He defined the law that God gave through Moses, he explained today's prevailing consensus interpretations of that law, and he provided examples of righteous Jews who have lived in accord with the law.

"Among the commandments in the five books of Moses is that of tithing. Tithing is from agricultural produce, and the staples in ancient Israel were grain [wheat and barley], wine, and olive oil," he said. "Our tradition is that Jewish farmers in the land of Israel are to tithe those, which are given to those in need. When we change from an agricultural society to an urban one, and money becomes the medium of exchange, the question is, is there an obligation to take tithes from other forms of income? The consensus opinion is that there is an obligation.

"The general consensus is that giving tithes is a commandment, a fulfillment of God's will."

"But it's a question again: is that the original obligation of the Bible, or is it something the rabbis added? If it's something the rabbis added, it's still seen as something God wanted to be in agricultural society. Since now we are making money other ways, God would certainly want the idea of charity to continue. There are those of the opinion that, although tithing is a commandment, you find in Judaism a distinction between an obligation that has virtually no exceptions or a righteous deed that may not be a binding obligation. The general consensus is that giving tithes is a fulfillment of God's will. To give a tithe to a charity is an obligation. To give a tithe of one's income may be very difficult for some people, and it's generally not seen as a binding obligation that everyone must do. It is something to be encouraged, though.

"'We are a religion of law, and I should explain that. Many people think that once you put things into law codes, you drain the life out of them. There's always that danger, but we feel that as long as it's amorphous, it's not coded that this is what you need to do, human beings will stretch any obligation infinitely. By codifying it into law, we say, 'This is what you do.' We're not trying to take the spirit out of it.

"'We have books on virtually every commandment to fulfill. 'Honor thy father and mother.' All right—Jews, Christians, people around the world, are in favor of that, but Jews have books on the subject. What does that mean? 'Do not go about as a tale-bearer.' Most people consider that proper conduct. We consider it a biblical command-ment. As such, there are laws on it, and people study books of law on what it means to gossip. What may one say, what may one not say, when may one make exceptions? The effect of the study is not to take the spirit out of the law. On the contrary, it sensitizes you to it. On a day when I'm studying the laws about 'thou shalt not gossip'—which of course are always the writer's exhortations, essentially, and stories—when I'm studying one of those books, on that day I tend to gossip less than I would otherwise. It makes me a more spiritual being. The same thing is true with the laws of charity in general and tithing in particular."

The third chapter of Malachi is a central focus of rabbis' teachings on tithing. Rabbi Miller said, "The rabbis say, based on a verse in one of the prophets where God says, 'Test me in this. Bring the tithe to the storehouse and see if I do not give you blessings without end.'² The Talmud says on this that in general it's wrong to test God. You can't say, 'Well, God, I'm going to pray really hard today, and I better win the lottery tonight or else. That's the test if you're really here.' As Woody Allen said, 'Send me a sign, like a deposit in a Swiss bank.' The Talmud says do not test God. Don't expect a payoff. An exception when you may test God: start giving a tithe, and see if you don't get paid back. I'm not sure there's a guarantee, or perhaps the payment will be in other forms, besides monetary. But in general, devout Jews like to say, nothing bad will happen if you're giving charity. Don't worry about becoming impoverished, but we're not talking about giving away all your income. But giving a tithe—our tradition is, it's good for you."

> *"An exception when you may test God: start giving a tithe, and see if you don't get paid back . . . In general, devout Jews like to say, nothing bad will happen if you're giving charity."*

LEARNING GENEROSITY BY STORIES

Rabbi Miller tells the story of how one act of non-osten-tatious kindness created a cross-generational blessing between two families. "There was a rabbi, and someone in a neighboring community passed away, leaving behind a widow and an orphaned child. They were destitute. This was a couple of generations ago. The rabbi helped raise money for the widow and the orphan. The orphan went on to become the dean of a major rabbinical school. Of course, the orphan knew nothing about the rabbi who had helped his family when he was a child. The rabbi's grandson wanted to become a rabbi, and he went to a certain school and didn't do well. He was a round peg in a square hole. So he tried another school. It was like a prep school. When you're going for the rabbinate, there are prep schools. He went to a couple of schools and was unsuccessful.

"So someone said to him, 'Why don't you go visit the dean of this very prestigious rabbinical school? It's like a grad school. He's a very wise man.' So this kid went to the dean, the rabbi, and the dean said, 'Why don't you enroll here?'"

The student was doubtful that he could do any better at this prestigious school, but the dean persuaded him to audit classes and to live with the dean as he made the tran-sition back into academic studies.

"So the young man ended up living in the rabbi's house. The dean got him into the school against five thousand normal regulations. The young man ended up in the school. Today's he a very successful rabbi in New Jersey," Rabbi Miller said. "I know the young man, and I know the great rabbi, the dean. And if you'll tell me it's a coincidence that the young man's grandfather helped the orphan, who does not know this, and that this dean of students felt the need to help this young man, I just see it as one simple example of payback. There are many such stories."

Rabbi Miller cites two works in English, written primarily for contemporary Jews who do not know Hebrew or whose knowledge of the language is very limited. One book is *Guide to Halachos* [laws]: *A Quick Reference Manual of What You Can Do in Common Occurring Situations.*[3] Another provides an English translation of teachings on tithing by Rabbi Israel Meir Kagan (1840–1883), who began writing anonymously as a Polish grocer but eventually achieved a sustained influence on Orthodox Jews across the world.[4] Both books provide clear explanations of how to calculate what one should give in a year, and describe options on how to distribute that money. The emphasis is more on charitably meeting other people's needs than on supporting the synagogue as an institution.

Rabbi Kagan is better known as Chafetz Chaim, after his first book, and many stories tell of his godly life. "His wife wanted him to study." Rabbi Miller said. "She ran the store most of the day, and he studied, and when he was forty years old, he saw that there were many Jews who are not aware that gossip is sinful. It's not a nice thing to do, but you wouldn't think of it like someone who embezzles from the bank. He said, 'Thou shalt not steal. It's a sin. Thou shalt not bear tales. It's a sin.' There are books about honesty in business. There were no books written about tale-bearing. It's mentioned, but a whole book? He wrote a whole book on the subject, followed by another book. He published it anonymously. He wasn't looking for honor. The book is called *Who Wants to Live?* or *Who Wants Life?* In Hebrew, it's *Chafetz Chaim.*[5] Since people did not know his name, it was anonymous, they referred to the author of this book as Chafetz Chaim, and that's the way he's known till this day. He went on to write many other books, including a book on general obligations toward others, in which he includes the obligation, the commandment, the mitzvah, of tithing."

Rabbi Miller continued: "They tell stories about him that I would not believe, except that I have met his students. He had a student from Germany. Russia was fighting Germany, and he was arrested as a spy. So Chafetz Chaim, Rabbi Kagan, was called to the stand as a character witness. The attorney wanted to explain to the judge, 'Who is this man?' So the attorney said, 'Your honor, I'll tell you a story about this man. He was one day walking on the street and someone stopped him and asked if he could change a ten-dollar bill. So Chafetz Chaim pulled out his wallet and started to make the change, and that person grabbed the wallet and started running down the street. Chafetz Chaim, an elderly man already, started running after him, saying, "I forgive you! I forgive you!"' So the judge said to the attorney, 'You believe that story is true?' The attorney said, 'I don't know, Your Honor, but do they tell such stories about me and you?'"

One reason for Chafetz Chaim's widespread respect, Rabbi Miller believes, was that he *lived* the tradition. "If you talk about the outstanding rabbis, to be on the very top rung of those who are respected, you need a combination of outstanding scholarship and outstanding character. If you are a professor of Talmudic studies and you know a lot but the character doesn't seem to match, even if you're a decent fellow, you'll never make the top rung—partly because it's not an official position. It's accepted, and people tend to accept those they feel are living the tradition. The person who follows the rituals but does not have love for his neighbor is not following the tradition."

Modern secular culture is making it more difficult for people to appreciate generous giving as an individual and personal action.

Rabbi Miller is concerned that modern secular culture is making it more difficult for people to appreciate
generous giving as an individual and personal action. He
mentions going on a tour to Israel in a group of one hundred and fifty people, and giving each person one dollar
to share with a needy person. Some members of the tour
were so stumped by that simple opportunity that they
asked if they could give their money back to the rabbi
and let him distribute the money.

"It's hard to give away your money, but if as soon as
you get your paycheck you put 10 percent into your charity
checking account, then it's not yours anymore," Rabbi
Miller said. In the Jewish tradition, "You're not allowed to
give all your tithe in one place. You have to be available if
people need you for something. If a poor person, someone
in need, comes knocking at your door, you can't say, 'Well,
I gave all my money to some other cause.' One has to reach
out to a variety of causes. For instance, an Orthodox Jew
will make sure to give a certain amount of charity to people
in need and give another certain amount of charity to the
meaning and maintenance of Judaism—the synagogue,
schools. In our faith, study is so important, to support a
Jewish school that teaches Judaism is vital. Generally, we
tell people that if the community has a choice of one building, either a synagogue or a school for children, make it the
school. If you have the school, you'll end up with a

synagogue. If you have a synagogue and no school, you'll end up with neither.

In the Jewish tradition, "You're not allowed to give all your tithe in one place. You have to be available if people need you for something."

"There are many people who ask me if they're allowed to use their tithe in other ways." The rabbi mentions the giving of some members of his congregation. "I know there is someone who has a charity account. He said to me, 'Rabbi, if you ever know of anybody in need, let me know.' I'll tell him about a case now and then, usually without the name, and he'll send me a check. There are good people everywhere, and it is so inspiring to see people who are charitable and it gives them joy. Occasionally rabbis will come to town for various causes, like a major rabbinical school in Israel, or a major rabbinical school in New York City, and I'll write a letter of recommendation, give their contacts. There was a gentleman—he has passed on since—he was not a learned Jew, but he had done well in business, and he said to me, 'Rabbi, if you ever have anybody visiting who's collecting for something you think is worthy, please bring him around.' I would bring someone to him. It's not just that he would welcome people with a smile. Afterward he would call me and say, 'Thank you so much for bringing that person to me, that I could help him out.' There are a number of souls like that.

"There are others who use their tithing to give support to families in need without knowing where the support comes from. Or even better, sometimes, do it in a way that they don't even know that they're getting a gift. For instance, to hire someone to do a service and to pay them extra—and they don't realize that the extra is a way of helping them."

Rabbi Miller said that one of his mentors empha-sized the principle of tithing one's time and treasures just as much as tithing one's income. Such service takes a variety of forms. "There are Jewish funeral homes, but we have volunteers who do special bathing and clothing of the dead, and the honors to be done to them. People give of their time to do that. It's a tithe of one's time, to help prepare dead bodies for burial. There are people in New York City who started an ambulance service. Because of the nature of New York, if someone needs an ambulance, one can wait quite a while. Some orthodox Jews, a few decades ago, made a private ambulance ser-vice, and it's staffed totally by volunteers. You don't have to be Jewish to use it, and they don't put it in the Yellow Pages, because if everyone would use it, they would not have enough people to staff it. But it's there, and there are volunteers who go out, and virtually every large syna-gogue in New York has people who belong to that organization, who are trained to give CPR, first aid, whatever it takes.

"There are imaginative ways of giving of one's time, beyond giving of one's financial resources."

"I know other people who volunteer, who give of their time. If you don't have AAA and your car breaks down, people are available twenty-four hours a day in shifts. There are imaginative ways of giving of one's time, beyond giving of one's financial resources."

11

RIGHTEOUS NUMBERS CRUNCHING

John and Sylvia Ronsvalle

THE MINISTRY KNOWN AS EMPTY TOMB, INC., IS BASED in a modestly sized office building within walking distance of the University of Illinois at Urbana-Champaign. In the weeks before I met with its founders, John and Sylvia Ronsvalle, I suggested a discussion of about an hour. Sylvia responded with a more generous and open-ended schedule that included lunch followed by a lengthy interview. The Ronsvalles met me at the Champaign train station, graciously helped me arrange for an earlier return to Chicago that evening, and gave me a driving tour of the university campus. As we drove past Memorial Stadium, the imposing brick structure where the Fighting Illini play football, the Ronsvalles talked about how many people collectively spend hundreds of thousands of dollars annually to secure coveted skyboxes there.

Sylvia describes empty tomb, which the Ronsvalles founded in the early 1970s, as a Christian research and service organization. That's an understatement on the order of saying the Salvation Army occasionally helps a homeless person. Sylvia says, "When we chose the name in the early 1970s, the lower case was an attempt on our part to state, in a non-triumphalistic way, that Jesus did, indeed, rise from the dead, and to state that truth in a casual and accessible fashion." For reporters writing stories about the state of giving in churches, empty tomb is the go-to think tank. The Ronsvalles crunch statistics so vigorously that in 2010 they plan to publish the twentieth edition of *The State of Church Giving*, a challenging report of nearly two hundred pages.[1] They praise whatever progress they find, such as the decision of Cornerstone Church in Simi Valley, California, to devote half its budget to missions. Still, they also catalog just how little priority most churches give to worldwide evangelism or to fighting preventable childhood deaths in developing nations.

Recent subtitles of *The State of Church Giving* offer some hint of what the Ronsvalles think as they survey the landscape each year: "Abolition of the Institutional Enslavement of Overseas Missions" (2007), "Global Triage, MDG 4 [Millennium Development Goals], and Unreached People Groups" (2008). On the back cover of the 2008 edition, they add a trio of Bible verses, all of which include the numbers 3:16 and convey God's concern for transforming the world:

John 3:16: "'For God so loved the world, that he gave his only begotten Son, that whosoever believeth in him should not perish, but have everlasting life.'" (KJV)

1 John 3:16–17: "'This is how we know what love is: Jesus Christ laid down his life for us. And we ought to lay down our lives for our brothers. If anyone has material possessions and sees his brother in need but has no pity on him, how can the love of God be in him?'" (NIV)

The Revelation to John 3:16: "'So, because you are luke-warm, and neither cold nor hot, I am about to spit you out of my mouth.'" (NRSV) [2]

But empty tomb is not just a research organization. The *service* part of its mission statement includes helping the poor of Champaign with food, clothes, furniture, bills, home repair, prescription costs, layettes for newborns, and Christmas gifts. Much of empty tomb's building is devoted to storing supplies that local Christians donate and help distribute to the needy.

One interior wall, which bears the weight of the struc-ture, honors the members of many churches that donated money and labor during construction. Church members signed the two-by-fours behind the wall.

Sylvia recalls that when she and John began their work among the poor, some black children in Champaign had red hair because of malnutrition. "'There was dire poverty, and many churches were not involved," she said. "We just started saying, 'Jesus cares,' and people in need would start showing up on our doorstep." The Ronsvalles began helping people in immediate need of clothing, food, or furniture. "The local work started because we saw need. We met people. They needed food. From there we started asking, 'What more can we do?'"

The Ronsvalles began with a larger vision than merely helping the poor on behalf of people who did not want to get involved with the poor. Sylvia quotes what John emphasized from the beginning of empty tomb: "We're not going to take care of the poor. We are going to provide discipleship opportunities." When a woman from one church began delivering food, she told other church members about her experiences. Another hundred people from that church signed up to join their sister in similar ministry. "It's important for people to meet people—and then, suddenly, you can love them," Sylvia said. "The bigger ideas make sense because they grow out of this care."

"SHE JUST WANTS TO SAVE THE WORLD"

Concern for the poor and for evangelizing the world weaves through the Ronsvalles' years together. Except for a year of teaching English in China, they've spent their married life together in this small university town. John and Sylvia had met on campus, but John really caught Sylvia's attention in December 1969, when they saw each other in a pub near the university campus. The pub meeting occurred just after Sylvia had accompanied her sister Mary to watch a documentary about Vietnam. "I was in a power struggle with God during my junior year in college on who would be in charge of my life," Sylvia said. "It all came to a head one night. My sister, who was into bands and traveling, came down, and we were going out to the bars. She, of all things, said, 'Let's go and watch some television.' There was a show on the Vietnam War.

"As I was watching, as they were talking to this general about how they were going to now put the Vietnamese in charge as the Americans pulled out, I saw big white letters across the TV screen that said *death*. It was clear to me, and it said everything apart from Jesus Christ leads to death. I was Miss Let's Make Everything Fine. I ran out of the viewing room in tears and ran into the bathroom. I decided that I had to quit school the next day and be a missionary, because that's one of the things I felt God wanted."

From there, Sylvia and Mary went to the pub. John, who was general chairman of the Graduate Student Association, walked in and sat at the table with Sylvia and Mary. He asked, "What's wrong with Sylvia?"

"Nothing. She just wants to save the world," Mary said.

"That was like red meat to John," Sylvia told me. "My sister left the table, he sat down, and he started this two-hour sentence about how you get students on the faculty senate at the University of Illinois and you eventually evangelize the world for Jesus Christ. It all connected, through many rivulets. As he was talking, just as I had heard that everything apart from Jesus Christ leads to death, the same Voice said, 'I want you to help this man. You've been so busy telling me what you wouldn't do, you couldn't hear what I wanted you *to do*. I want you to help this man.'"

Sylvia agreed to help John. "That's when I signed up, and he started taking me out for dinner. We were working on getting students on the faculty senate every night. And I thought, *Thank you, God; at least you've given me a rich man*. It turned out he was spending all his savings in a very irresponsible fashion," she said.

John laughed quietly.

"When we got married, we were poor-poor," Sylvia said. "I'm talking *food stamps* poor-poor. We lived in an unoccupied house and eventually moved into public housing." During their last six years in public housing, the Ronsvalles did not take a rent subsidy from the government, and they ended up paying more for their public housing than some friends paid on mortgages.

The Ronsvalles lived in a public housing project known as Bradley Park. "We moved in there, and it was pretty scary. We found water all over the floor, and it turned out that it was raw sewage that had backed up in these apartments since they were built," Sylvia said.

The Ronsalles began a years-long campaign that involved bucking officials with the Department of Housing and Urban Development, who insisted that residents of the public-housing complex were causing the sewer problems. Eventually the Ronsalles helped convince the city council to authorize a study of the sewer problem. The study proved that the sewer lines had been installed incorrectly, and the majority of apartments were repaired.

"We can't just live someplace. It has to make a difference in the kingdom," Sylvia said, laughing lightly.

MOVING AT SCALE

Listening to John Ronsvalle gives some idea of the intensity behind empty tomb's name for itself. "If Jesus Christ really, really got up from the dead, and was really, really, really God, that's pretty big news; that's very, very important," he said. "It's hard to convey now the sense I had in high school that, 'If this is true, wow!' Everything else falls by the wayside in terms of importance. But it didn't seem like people were taking it that seriously."

If Christians truly believe that Jesus Christ conquered

death with his physical resurrection, and that he will return to earth someday as both triumphant king and the righteous judge of humanity, they ought to behave accordingly, John reasons. They ought to make financial choices that give top priority to God and his purposes. The church, to use one of John's favorite themes during our interview, ought to "move at scale."

If Christians truly believe that Jesus Christ conquered death with his physical resurrection, and that he will return to earth someday as both triumphant king and the righteous judge of humanity, they ought to behave accordingly.

"We are not moving at scale. We are playing at Christianity," John said. To drive his point home, John relies on an observation from the Southern Baptist Convention that 2,800 missionaries could complete the job of reaching all remaining people groups that have never heard the gospel of Jesus. Assuming a cost of $65,000 for each missionary, the total cost of world evangelism would be $182 million.[3]

That sounds like a lot, but John tosses other numbers in for context: About 1.14 million American households have a net worth of $5 million or more. Using a very strict doctrinal definition of the word *evangelical*, roughly 7 percent (or nearly 80,000 households) of evangelicals have a net worth of $5 million or more, with an annual income of about $400,000. Now consider: Americans spend $70 billion per year on soft drinks. A mere $5 billion a year would stop child deaths from preventable diseases around the world.

Repeatedly during our interview, John returned to the figure of $182 million, and of how easy it would be to achieve: a mere 2 cents per day in evangelical churches. He refers to the failure to meet this need as outrageous and scandalous. "During the last thirty-five years that we've been active, two major things have happened. One, Franky Schaeffer called for getting arrested for protesting abortion. And, more recently, the Micah Challenge; they're really gearing up on the Millennium Development Goals."

John is frustrated that both those cases of social involvement primarily amount to asking that *governments* help relieve suffering. "In all of this, there's no mobilization to get this job done," he said, whacking his papers of statistics that show an achievable goal of world evangelism.

"I think it's poor political science to ask people to vote to do something they won't do voluntarily," Sylvia said. "What we saw in a lot of the major social movements was generally an overflow out of the church of personal conviction, and those people convinced people. Abolition, the women's movement, the prison reform movement, child labor laws—all of these grew out of actively concerned church people who were there out of faith, and then it became more efficient to do it governmentally."

"We hear about winning the world for Christ, and I don't think we're very seriously working at that in any intelligent way," John said. "It seems like the Great Commandment is a major directive that Jesus gave us, and it seems like the Great Commission is easily seen as flowing from the Great Commandment. Why do we want to see somebody become saved? It's out of love for them. If we love them, word and deed come together."

"The Great Commission is easily seen as flowing from the Great Commandment. Why do we want to see somebody become saved? It's out of love for them. If we love them, word and deed come together."

"OUR MONEY *IS* US"

The Ronsvalles decided early on that they would tithe. "I did not come from a tithing household, and as far as I know, John didn't," Sylvia said. "We had two rooms to live in and seventy-five dollars a month plus food stamps and empty tomb's vehicle and phone line. We would occasionally get a doughnut at Eisner's. I remember the exact moment we decided to tithe. We were in the parking lot; we were driving a '56 Ford pickup. We were in our jeans—I had two pairs of jeans and five tops—and I said to John, 'John, we don't tithe.' He looked at me and we both said, 'Yeah, but we're so poor.' We looked at each other, and we agreed we had to tithe. That was the end of the discussion."

The Ronsvalles tithe on their donation-based income and on the value of their medical coverage. They donate a lot back into empty tomb. John understands Matthew 23:23 as Jesus' implicit affirmation of the tithe as the starting point for a person concerned with righteousness ("'Woe to you, teachers of the law and Pharisees, you hypocrites! You give a tenth of your spices—mint, dill and cumin. But you have neglected the more important matters of the law—justice, mercy and faithfulness. You should have practiced the latter, without neglecting the former").

They set aside 10 percent with each new pay period, usually distributing it to a church and causes as they see needs arise. "Actually it's kind of fun to have that money set aside," Sylvia said. "You have it, it's there, and you see the need. It's not like 'Oh, I wish I could help,' but 'How much do we want to give here?' It becomes, 'What does God want to do?'"

For the Ronsvalles, tithing is not only a matter of obeying God. It is also a conscious way to resist the self-worship that accompanies greed and stinginess.

For the Ronsvalles, tithing is not only a matter of obey-ing God. It is also a conscious way to resist the self-worship that accompanies greed and stinginess. "One of the things we've concluded is that our money is us," Sylvia said. "It's a direct function of who we are. It's two concepts. One is of our current time and talent—our work, our energy, our volunteering. But money is really our *stored* time and talent. It's what we have invested and built up. Our parents, when you have an inheritance, that's them.

"The fact is, our money is just another form of us. Ephesians 5:5 and Colossians 3:5 both point out that greed is idolatry. Idolatry is worship, essentially, of self rather than God, which is why we cannot have any other gods. All other gods, besides Jehovah Yahweh, really come back to us. If we are not coming to terms with our money, there is a part of ourselves that we are worshipping, reserving from God, keeping from God. That's why tithing is a spiritual discipline, in the sense that it's really one of the most basic ways of coming to terms with idolatry. If you don't have your money in order, then you don't have yourself, in a very real sense."

In one essay they've published online, the Ronsvalles quote a fellow Christian as asking them, "If I'm not trusting God with my money, am I really trusting him with my eternal salvation?" Sylvia adds: "If we see money as a way to pay the bills, then whether I tithe is a consumer decision: 'Can I afford to live in a bigger house? Can I afford to tithe? Can I afford to take a vacation?' But if, in fact, I understand that money is nothing more than my efforts in a different form, then what I do with it directly has to do with my heart. It reflects who I am, where I'm investing myself."

After so many years of studying the world's needs and the church's poor giving patterns, the Ronsvalles struggle to reconcile the two. John said they sometimes think of Christians in comparison to two figures from J.R.R. Tolkien's Lord of the Rings trilogy: the Ents (slow-moving trees) and Théoden, the king who spends much of the narrative in an enchanted stupor.

"It's greed-induced apathy. It's like people in this country are under the influence of drugs, and it is the drug of affluence," Sylvia said. She cites Jacques Ellul's observation, in *Money and Power*,[4] that Jesus speaks of Mammon as a personal being in Matthew 6, and she elaborates on it. "Mammon is competing for your soul with God. The church in the United States, with all the blessings we've had, has had two choices: You can take those resources and lay them at God's feet, or you can be consumed by them and become like Théoden, become like the Ents, become drugged. It would take visionary moral leadership to wake people up, and you're not seeing it."

Still, the Ronsvalles have not reached a point of despair, and they are amused at the thought of retirement. "How do you ever stop speaking the truth? This isn't a career. This, is like, what we're stuck with. You just have to do this, like breathing," Sylvia said. "It's an issue of faith. We don't get to sign up for results. We sign up to speak the truth."

Epilogue

STEWARDSHIP IS A THANKSGIVING TO GOD

Thomas McGread

IN MID-SEPTEMBER 2008, I FLEW TO WICHITA, KANSAS, to talk with Monsignor Thomas McGread, a pioneer of stewardship in Catholic circles. Because of his vision for stewardship, members of parishes in the Diocese of Wichita may send their children to diocesan schools without having to pay tuition. Monsignor Thomas spent thirty-one years of his vocation, until his retirement in 1997, as the pastor of St. Francis of Assisi Catholic Church in downtown Wichita. He later also worked as stewardship director for the diocese. He brought to the parish and the diocese an approach to stewardship that challenged its members to ask how much of their time and talents they were returning to God in thanksgiving for his grace.

"Christ died for us, and that's why we go to Mass: to thank him. Stewardship is really a thanksgiving to God," he said while sitting in his small apartment. "We have all kinds of time for entertainment and for sports, yet we have no time for God. And yet we expect to end up in heaven. We want to *prepare* for that life. We called it a way of life rather than just a program. You want to live this way, living with Christ."

"Christ died for us, and that's why we go to Mass: to thank him. Stewardship is really a thanksgiving to God."

This way of life included round-the-clock Adoration of the Blessed Sacrament, which Monsignor Thomas credits with drawing people closer to the heart of Jesus and—by natural extension—toward showing more of God's generosity.

Monsignor Thomas, who came to the Diocese of Wichita in the 1960s as one of eight immigrant priests from Ireland, still speaks with a moderate Irish accent. He is the kind of gentle old priest who, closing in on eighty when I interviewed him, will call a longtime parishioner "Child" as she calls him with a prayer concern. The monsignor is a man of no long speeches. He answers questions with more than yes or no, but he limits himself to simple statements of fact.

Though he helped the U.S. Conference of Catholic Bishops prepare a pastoral letter, "Stewardship: A

Disciple's Response,"[1] he is concerned that bishops sometimes hinder progress on stewardship.

"The biggest drawback is that some of the bishops are kind of scared of stewardship, like they don't quite understand it," he said. "A lot of them think it's about money. Even when the bishops wrote the pastoral, they were worried about calling it stewardship. They wanted to call it 'Disciple's Response.' But we convinced them that *stewardship* was a biblical word. Christ talked about being a good steward quite a lot, so let's explain what it means. There's a whole lot more than money in the whole thing. The main thing was time."

"Every Scripture passage, practically, has something about stewardship in it."

In about 1983, Monsignor Thomas began presenting workshops for Catholic Stewardship Consultants of Augusta, Georgia. His health struggles—he's had six heart bypass surgeries, and his legs have failed him—prevent him from giving live presentations any longer, and the consultancy relies on video recordings from the monsignor's healthier years.

In presenting a theology of stewardship to his people, the monsignor said, he relied on no curriculum: "Just the Bible. There's enough in the Bible for that. Every Scripture passage, practically, has something about stewardship in it."

What I find especially striking about the monsignor is

that he said so little about the legacy of his work that surrounds us. When I called ahead to arrange our interview, I
had the impression that he might live in a suburban condo-
minium or house. Instead, he lives in an assisted-care
facility that is adjacent to the diocese's Spiritual Life Center,
a sprawling conference center. The same campus includes
a home for retired priests.

All of these buildings were constructed during Monsignor
Thomas's years as the diocese's stewardship director. He did
not volunteer this information, but he acknowledged it
when I asked. Just to the east of the Spiritual Life Center is
Ascension Cemetery, developed at the same time. Here lie
some of the Irish priests who came to America at the same
time as the monsignor. Here he will rest as well.

Though he is not as infirm as Pope John Paul II was in
his final years of life, the monsignor reminds me of that
pontiff. This is how saints grow old and prepare to meet
God. After we talked, I walked through Ascension Cemetery,
where I marveled at a towering golden sculpture of the
risen Christ, which stares out across the flat Kansas plains.
I found a section devoted to children's graves, and one was
decorated with a small knickknack bearing the image of
SpongeBob SquarePants.

All this redemptive use of land is possible because one
priest challenged his small and mostly poor congregation to
begin spending more time with God. Suddenly I was crying.

Study Guide

TITHING: TEST ME IN THIS

Douglas LeBlanc

> *"Stand at the crossroads and look; ask for the ancient paths, ask where the good way is, and walk in it, and you will find rest for your souls."*
>
> —Jeremiah 6:16

INTRODUCTION

Do you believe that every part of our lives comes from God and belongs to him? If so, how does tithing fit into his work in our lives? In what ways does it express our thankfulness to him in the same way that regular prayer or partaking in communion does?

How is tithing a reflection of the compassion that God shows us?

CHAPTER 1: CONTINUITY IN THE TRADITION: GREGORY AND FREDERICA MATHEWES-GREEN

The life-long commitment of the Mathewes-Greens to tithing continued even when they were impoverished students. In what ways does this reflect their idea that regular practices—such as tithing—are like training wheels on our faith?

If tithing became as second-nature to us as prayer, how could this affect our relationship with God and our compassion to those around us?

CHAPTER 2: SO THAT OTHERS MAY SIMPLY LIVE: RON AND ARBUTUS SIDER

The Siders practice a simple way of life in order to give more to the church and their community. In what ways could living simply change your view of the world and those around you? What benefits could a simpler life have other than the ability to give more?

Ron Sider points out that the focus of a simple life is not deprivation and hardship but balance in a world out of control with consumerism. In what areas of your life could simpler choices mean less stress and more openness with your family and faith?

CHAPTER 3: MISSIONAL LIVING AFTER KATRINA: JERRY AND STACY KRAMER

The Kramers had already committed to tithing prior to Katrina, pointing out that they had once "worshiped" Blockbuster and Domino's Pizza. If you broke down your budget, where would your biggest expenditures fall? Are there focus points in your life that distract you from your faith journey?

After Katrina, survival meant sacrifice, dedication, and renewed commitments. In what ways do smaller crises in our lives reorder our thinking about what's important? How does tithing remind us that the point of our faith is to serve God, not persuade him to give to us?

CHAPTER 4: EARNEST MONEY: JOHN SCHWIEBERT

For John Schwiebert and the members of the Metanoia congregation, tithing is akin to putting earnest money down on a house—a recognizable commitment to follow through with your promised purchase . . . or commitment to the faith.

In what ways is this belief reflected in the stories they share of financial rescues and blessings?

How does tithing fit in with other disciplines—fasting, prayer, etc.—taken on as a commitment to serving God?

CHAPTER 5: TREASURES IN HEAVEN: RANDY ALCORN

How is committing to a tithe, or only 10 percent of our income, a reflection of "where our treasures are"? Do other "treasures" overshadow the investment or focus of that 10 percent?

What do the financial choices Randy Alcorn has made tell us about his commitment to God and his pro-life work? Could you make a similar commitment to a cause you believe in?

CHAPTER 6: "NEVER TELL ME WHAT YOU WON'T DO": JERALD JANUARY

In the early part of his life, despite his commitment to God, Jerald January stood in God's way. What lessons can each of us take from the message: never tell God what you won't do? In what ways have you seen these lessons play out in your own life?

How do you think a commitment to tithing would reflect a renewed commitment to God?

CHAPTER 7: DEEP GLADNESS MEETS DEEP HUNGER: KEVIN JONES

Kevin Jones developed his attitudes toward money and social activism during his childhood, as part of the only blue-collar home in a large but otherwise white-collar family. In what ways has your upbringing affected your attitudes toward money and tithing?

Kevin also sees the use of money and other resources as a relationship issue, a way of stewarding the gifts God has bestowed on us. When you consider tithing or other gifts, where do you place the priorities?

CHAPTER 8: A SENSE OF COMMUNITY: MARK KELLNER

Mark Kellner believes that tithing is a commitment to community as well as to God. In what ways can you see the tithes of your faith community working to spread the word and work of God?

How does dedicating yourself to the practice of tithing help bond you with the church and the work they do in the world?

CHAPTER 9: "THE ESSENCE OF GOD IS ALWAYS TO BE GIVING": ED BACON

Ed Bacon believes that professing believers are colleagues of God—we are in this with him, and showing up is not enough. We should desire to give to others as he does, with our time, talent, and resources.

Tithing isn't always about finances. In what ways do you

give back to the church, to God, with the other gifts in your life?

How do you think that making a choice for constant and committed giving change your relationship with those around you?

CHAPTER 10: "DO THEY TELL SUCH STORIES ABOUT ME AND YOU?":YISRAEL MILLER

How do the stories about the charity of others encourage us to follow the practice of tithing? Why do we admire those who sacrifice for others when we are reluctant to make the same choices? In what way does fear prevent us from giving of our own resources?

CHAPTER 11: RIGHTEOUS NUMBERS CRUNCHING: JOHN AND SYLVIA RONSVALLE

John and Sylvia Ronsvalle present some amazing figures in their reports, including how little each believer would have to give to evangelize the world. When you tithe, do you equate the money with service to God or just to your local church?

Are you aware of how your local church uses funds in the local community or for global missions?

EPILOGUE: STEWARDSHIP IS A THANKSGIVING TO GOD: THOMAS MCGREAD

How do best express your thanks to God for all he has given you?

NOTES

Introduction

1. Michael W. Holmes, ed. and trans., *The Apostolic Fathers in English*, 3rd. ed. (Grand Rapids: Baker, 2006), 163–64, 165, 170.
2. Philip Schaff, *Sulpitius Severus, Vincent of Lerins, John Cassian,* "How Those Who Live Under the Grace of the Gospel Ought to Go Beyond the Requirement of the Law." Accessed June 10, 2009, through the Christian Classics Ethereal Library: http://www. ccel.org/ccel/schaff/npnf211.iv.vi.v.v.html.
3. Philip Schaff, *Fathers of the Third and Fourth Centuries: Lactantius, Venantius, Asterius, Victorinus, Dionysius, Apostolic Teaching and Constitutions, Homily,* "Of First-Fruits and Tithes, and After What Manner the Bishop is Himself to Partake of Them, or to Distribute Them to Others." Accessed June 10, 2009, through the Christian Classics Ethereal Library: http://www.ccel.org/ ccel/schaff/anf07.ix.iii.iv.html.
4. Randy Alcorn, *Money, Possessions and Eternity* (Carol Stream, IL: Tyndale, 2003), 185.

Chapter 1: Continuity in the Tradition

1. Ephraim Radner and George R. Sumner, *Reclaiming Faith: Essays on Orthodoxy in the Episcopal Church and the Baltimore Declaration* (Grand Rapids: Eerdmans, 1993).
2. Frederica Mathewes-Green, *Facing East: A Pilgrim's Journey into the Mysteries of Orthodoxy* (New York: HarperSanFrancisco, 1996).
3. See Malachi 3:10.

Chapter 2: So That Others May Simply Live

1. Ronald J. Sider, *Rich Christians in an Age of Hunger: Moving from Affluence to Generosity* (Downers Grove, IL: InterVarsity, 1977).
2. Ronald J. Sider and Richard K. Taylor, *Nuclear Holocaust and Christian Hope: A Book for Christian Peacemakers* (Downers Grove, IL: InterVarsity, 1983).
3. Ronald J. Sider, *The Graduated Tithe* (Downers Grove, IL: InterVarsity, 1978).

4. Ibid., 3.

5. Ron Sider, "The Ministry of Affluence: A Graduated Tithe," *HIS* 33, No. 3 (December 1972), 6–8.

6. Sider, *Rich Christians in an Age of Hunger*, 44.

7. Jerry Kramer announced in September 2009 that he was leaving Annunciation and preparing to return to missionary work in Tanzania.

Chapter 4: Earnest Money

1. Metanoia Peace Community, "Glossary of Terms," s.v. "Non-Violent Direct Action," available at http://www.metanoiaumc.org/glossary2.htm.

2. Ibid., "A Brief History," available at http://www.metanoiaumc.org/briefhistory.htm.

3. Ibid., "Membership Covenant," available at http://www.metanoiaumc.org/membercovenant.htm.

4. Like some other progressive Christians, when John refers to the kingdom of God, he tends to the drop the letter *g*, as he believes that *kin-dom* sounds less patriarchal.

5. Paul Kirk and Pat Schwiebert, *When Hello Means Goodbye* (Portland: Oregon Health & Science University/Perinatal Loss, 1985).

Chapter 5: Treasures in Heaven

1. Amy Cornel1ussen, "Abortion Foes Face Resolute Opponent," *Los Angeles Times*, January 25, 1998. Available at http://articles.latimes.com/1998/jan/25/local/me-11913.

2. Randy Alcorn, *Is Rescuing Right?* (Downers Grove, IL: InterVarsity, 1990).

3. Genesis 50:20 NASB.

Chapter 6: "Never Tell Me What You Won't Do"

1. Jerald January and Steve Wamberg, *A Messed-Up Ride or a Dressed-Up Walk: A Stirring Autobiography of Hope for the City, Love for God, and a Faith That Stays the Course* (Grand Rapids: Zondervan, 1994).

2. Ibid., 12–13.

3. Jerald January, *A Second Time* (Hazel Crest, IL: CoolSprings Publishing, 1996).

4. John 14:2 KJV.

Chapter 7: Deep Gladness Meets Deep Hunger

1. Kevin Jones, "The Rise of the Right in the Republican Party," report from Indianapolis, November 2, 2002. Available at http://www.theocracywatch.org/Report_From_Indianapolis. html.

2. These and other articles are available at www.everyvoice.net/ archive.

3. Every Voice Network: Anglican Voices United for Justice, "About Our Team," Kevin Jones. Available at http://www. everyvoice.net/archive/modules.php?op=modload&name=Stat ic&mod=About2&file=index.

4. Good Capital, "FAQs," available at http://www.goodcap.net/ faqs.php.

5. Edmund Sanders and Robyn Dixon, "Dark Cloud over Good Works of Gates Foundation," *Los Angeles Times*, January 7, 2007. Available at http://www.latimes.com/news/la-na-gatesx07jan07,0,290910,full.story.

6. Frederick Buechner, *Wishful Thinking: A Seeker's ABC* (New York: Harper One, 1993, rev. ed.), s.v. "vocation."

Chapter 8: A Sense of Community

1. Theologians have written at length about the problems of the Worldwide Church of God's theology during its first sixty years of existence. By the mid-1990s, leaders of the church rethought the theology of founder Herbert W. Armstrong and ultimately repudiated it. In April 2009, the church changed its name to Grace Communion International.

2. Seventh-day Adventist Church, "Guidelines on the Use of Tithe," available at http://www.adventist.org/beliefs/ guidelines/main_guide4.html.

3. Ibid.

4. 1 Corinthians 10:26 KJV.

5. See 1 Corinthians 16:2.
6. See Hebrews 10:25

Chapter 9: "The Essence of God Is Always to Be Giving"

1. For more information on the Cursillo movement, see http://www.natl-cursillo.org/whatis.html.

Chapter 10: "Do They Tell Such Stories About Me and You?"

1. Yisroel Miller has since become the rabbi of the House of Jacob Congregation in Calgary, Alberta, Canada.
2. See Malachi 3:10.
3. Nachman Schachter and Moshe Heinemann, *Guide to Halachos: A Quick Reference Manual of What You Can Do in Common Occurring Situations* (New York: Feldheim, 2003).
4. *Ahavath Chesed: The Love of Kindness as Required by God* (New York: Feldheim, 1976).
5. *Chafetz Chaim: A Lesson a Day* (New York: Artscroll/Mesorah, 1995).

Chapter 11: Righteous Numbers Crunching

1. *The State of Church Giving Through 2006: Global Triage, MDG 4, and Unreached People Groups*, 18th ed. (Champaign, IL: Empty Tomb, Inc., 2008). Available at http://www.emptytomb.org/pubs.html.
2. Ibid., back cover.
3. Ibid., 65–67, 118.
4. Jacques Ellul, *Money and Power*, 2nd ed. (Downers Grove, IL: InterVarsity, 1985).

Epilogue: Stewardship Is Thanksgiving to God

1. "Stewardship: A Disciple's Response" (Washington, D.C.: United States Conference of Catholic Bishops, 2002), available at http://www.usccb.org/stewardship/disciplesresponse.pdf.

ABOUT THE AUTHOR

Douglas Leblanc is Editor at large for *The Living Church* and has also written for *Christian Research Journal, Christianity Today,* Compassion International, and Anglicans United. He and his wife live near Richmond, Virginia, where they attend Saint Matthew's Episcopal Church.

THE ANCIENT PRACTICES SERIES

PHYLLIS TICKLE, GENERAL EDITOR

Finding Our Way Again by Brian McLaren

In Constant Prayer by Robert Benson

Sabbath by Dan B. Allender

Fasting by Scot McKnight

Tithing by Douglas LeBlanc

The Sacred Meal by Nora Gallagher

The Liturgical Year by Joan Chittister

The Sacred Journey by Charles Foster

*Stand at the crossroads and look; ask for the ancient paths,
ask where the good way is, and walk in it,
and you will find rest for your souls.*

—JEREMIAH 6:16 NIV

THOMAS NELSON

Since 1798

Lindsey Barem... years of revie... ...est and ma... ...e worst restaurants
exhaustive... ...finity... ...ground for ...ry writing. She is
prestigious André Simo... ...tat... cookbook, In... ...e of the Potato; an
cooking with members ...elebration of Sou... ...hortlisted for the
helped Simon Hopkinso... 1993); and th... ...ed book on
to write *Roast Chicken* and *Other Stories* (winner ...oth the 1995 André
Simon Award and the Glenfiddich Cookery Book of the Year Award),
and this was followed by *The Prawn Cocktail Years* and *The Big Red Book
of Tomatoes*, which was shortlisted for the Glenfiddich Food Book of the
Year Award in 2000.

Two selections of her of her recipes from her *London Evening Standard*
column, entitled *Supper Won't Take Long* and *A Wolf in the Kitchen* are also
published by Penguin. Lindsey Bareham now works as a freelance food
writer and broadcaster.

LINDSEY BAREHAM

A Celebration of Soup

Recipes from Around the World

PENGUIN BOOKS

PENGUIN BOOKS

Published by the Penguin Group
Penguin Books Ltd, 80 Strand, London WC2R 0RL, England
Penguin Putnam Inc., 375 Hudson Street, New York, New York 10014, USA
Penguin Books Australia Ltd, 250 Camberwell Road, Camberwell, Victoria 3124, Australia
Penguin Books Canada Ltd, 10 Alcorn Avenue, Toronto, Ontario, Canada
Penguin Books (NZ) Ltd, 11 Community Centre, Panchsheel Park, New Delhi
Penguin Books (South Africa) (Pty) Ltd, 24 Sturdee Avenue, Rosebank 2196, South Africa
Penguin Books Ltd, Cnr Rosedale and Airborne Roads, Albany, Auckland, New Zealand

Penguin Books Registered Offices: 80 Strand, London WC2R 0RL, England

www.penguin.com

First published by Michael Joseph 1993
Published in Penguin Books 1994

8

Contents

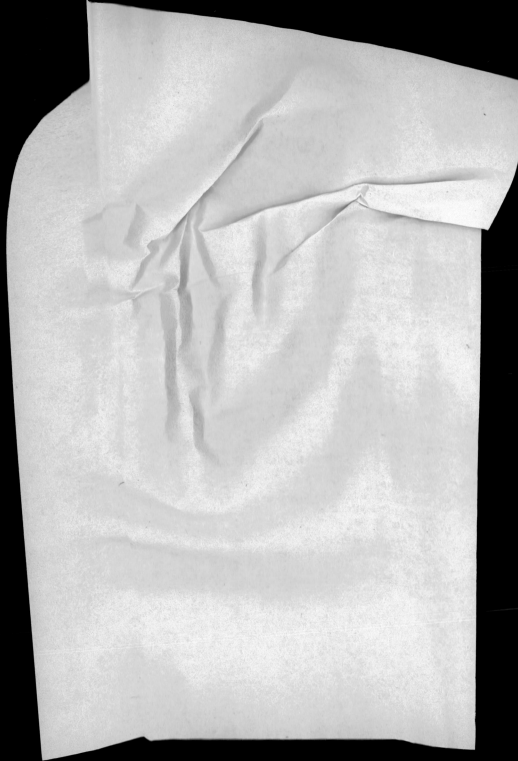

Beautiful soup, so rich and green,
Waiting in a hot tureen!
Who for such dainties would not stoop?
Soup of the evening, beautiful soup!
Beautiful soup! Who cares for fish,
Game, or any other dish?
Who would not give all else for two
Pennyworth only of beautiful soup?

(Lewis Carroll, *Alice's Adventures in Wonderland*, 1865)

Acknowledgements

The difficulty with this book has been knowing when to stop. Friends and acquaintances have showered me with recipes and I am beginning to wish I had a penny for every time I've heard someone say, 'I could live on soup.' Credits appear throughout the book for specific recipes but there are a number of people I would like to thank for their more general contribution. Many chefs had their brains picked and shared a wealth of technique, recipes and ideas. Simon Hopkinson of Bibendum, Shaun Hill of Gidleigh Park, Gary Rhodes of the Greenhouse, Raymond Blanc of Le Manoir aux Quat' Saisons, David Dorricott of SAS Portman Hotel, Rick Stein of the Seafood Restaurant, Bruno Loubet of Four Seasons, Inn on the Park, Michel and Albert Roux, Sally Clarke of Clarke's, Nico Ladenis of Nico at Ninety, Antony Worrall-Thompson of 190 and Dell' Ugo, Anton Mosimann of Mosimann's and David Eyre of the Eagle PH were especially helpful. Lorna Wing, who agreed to an interview and ended up providing all manner of support, ideas and advice, deserves special thanks. Tom Jackson, supplier of old cookery books, and the staff of Books for Cooks were immensely helpful in my search for obscure material. Special thanks also to my children Zachary and Henry, to Lindsay Stewart, my mother Jean Bareham, Liz Moscrop, Dudley Payne, Tessa de Mestre, Eva and Joseph Berkmann, Joy Davies, Jenny Dereham, Richenda Todd, and Bruce Hunter, who all contributed greatly to this book in one way or another.

Most particularly I would like to thank my cherished friend the late Elizabeth David, whose written word is always a joy and an inspiration, and who filled in all sorts of gaps. And, most importantly of all, thank you to Andrew Payne and HP.

Preface

'The great fashion is to place four fine
soups at the four corners with four dish
stands between each two, with four salt-
cellars placed near the soup tureen.' (Nicolas de Bonnefons, *Délices de la Campagne*,
1652, describing a banquet during Louis
XIV's reign)

Soup has been the cornerstone of my diet for as long as I can
remember. When I first began writing about restaurants some
twenty-odd years ago I always ordered the soup, believing, and it *is*
true, that a good way to 'read' a restaurant is by the quality of its
soup.

That's not to say I was looking for grand or complicated soups.
Quite the contrary. I am a great believer in Escoffier's dictum: *'Faîtes
simple'*, or, as Elizabeth David puts it, knowing when to leave well
alone. The point is that any soup, of any style, has to be carefully
and sensitively made if it is going to be any good.

Some of my most memorable restaurant meals have included soup,
and over the years I have been inspired to recreate some of the best
ones at home. Bouillabaisse at a restaurant overlooking the Côte
d'Azur, red onion and red wine broth at a pub in Clerkenwell, tomato
and red pepper gazpacho garnished with oysters at a small chef/
patron restaurant in the Cotswolds, chickpea and langoustine purée
at a Michelin-standard hotel in deepest Devon, and a chilli-laced
Vietnamese noodle stew at a modest café in Lewisham are a tip of
that iceberg.

I love the versatility of soup, and the endless variety of possibilities
that it presents for the home cook. I get carried away with all the
complementary trimmings that can go with it. Good bread, and the
gamut of bits and pieces that can be added to the soup during the
cooking or at the table, all interest me as much as the broth itself.
Similarly I like to extend the 'theme' or inspiration of a soup to the
rest of the meal, and in so doing, to raise its profile.

Inevitably, then, once I began working on a book about soup, the
project expanded sideways. I stuck to my original intention of
researching an international anthology of classic soup recipes. These,
and hundreds of newer combinations, form the bulk of the book.

However, the more I worked at the project, the more I found it essential to cover the basic ground rules of soup-making, and to differentiate between the key types of soup styles.

Thus the book is conceived on various levels and is intended to appeal equally to the novice and the experienced cook. Stock-making, for example, which is the mysterious key to so many soups, is covered in exhaustive detail and includes recipes from top chefs as well as advice on making the best possible use of what's on hand in the kitchen. The myriad ways to thicken and enrich soup are covered in terms of what is appropriate for a particular style of soup.

As so much soup-making is grounded in using up leftovers, there are hundreds of ideas for markedly improving such soups with judicious use of garnish and embellishment. Home-made *salsas*, dumplings, seasoned butters, creams and yoghurts, and unusual ways with croûtons, can transform, upgrade or expand even the most modest soup.

Above all this is a book intended to inspire and demystify. And it is dedicated to the memory of Alexis Soyer, whose words, compounded by the expanding market for convenience soups, are just as true today as they were in 1809:

> '... perhaps you are not aware of the reason why the great majority of the people in this country [England] are opposed to, and even accused of not liking, soup; the simple reason is, that every receipt described in most cookery books, is so complicated and expensive, that they cannot afford either the money, time or attention to prepare it.' (*A Shilling Cookery for the People*)

LINDSEY BAREHAM
London, November 1992

The History of Soup

'... on a mountain, all of grated Parmesan cheese, dwell folk that do nought else but make macaroni and ravioli, and boil them in capon's broth, and then throw them down to be scrambled for.' (Boccaccio, *The Decameron*, 1350)

Soup, from the French word *soupe*, meaning a liquid food made with various vegetables and/or meat, and often incorporating grains, pulses and fruits, is widely regarded as man's oldest food, since it must have developed about the time that boiling was discovered to be a way of cooking. The earliest recorded soup recipe, for barley soup, appears in the first true cookery book, published at the end of the fifteenth century and written by the Roman epicurian Apicius.

In ancient Rome, this national gruel was made by cooking a mixture of barley, pounded with toasted cereals called puls or pulmentus (pulses), and cooked with water to make a porridge-like soup. This and other liquid foods were called *potus*, from the verb *potare*, meaning to drink. Hence the start of numerous derivative soup names such as *potées*, *potages*, and *pot-au-feu*.

The biblical story of Esau selling his birthright to his twin brother for a 'mess of pottage' refers to a lentil version of the Apicius recipe made with lentils grown by Jacob. For centuries this was the daily fare of the ordinary people of the ancient empires of Egypt, Greece and Rome.

Later, small amounts of meat were added. The myth of the endless stock-pot is founded in medieval times, when the pot was constantly replenished with beef, veal, mutton and marrow bones, to become the precursor of *pot-au-feu* and *poule-au-pot*. Those early soups, really a by-product of cooking the meat, were thin and meagre food for the peasants, and were ladled over thick pieces of bread known as 'soppes' and 'trenchers' and eaten without the help of a spoon. If you were lucky, there then followed a slice of meat or poultry, cut from the communal pot with a dagger.

By the end of the fifteenth century, soups were produced from meat, poultry or fish in their own right and seasoning and colouring became more refined.

Terminology became more exact. The difference between the words '*soupe*' and '*potage*' appeared for the first time in 1693 and was confirmed in 1773 by the Dictionary of Trevoux; 'The word "*soupe*" is French, but quite middle-class; those who speak well should say "*servir le potage*", but not "*servir la soupe*".' That original definition, which classified (thick) soup as the everyday 'fuel' of the working classes, and (thin) *potage* as a delicate 'entrée' at the beginning of a banquet, is no longer valid. These days, when soup terminology is far more complicated and suggestive than exact, anything goes. What remains is the habit of serving soup at the beginning of a meal.

The vogue for thin *potages* led to the invention of 'veal glue', the forerunner of the bouillon cube, later to be renamed pocket, portable or traveller's soup. This was used by Captain Cook for his world voyage in 1772. At the turn of the century the first manufactured canned soups were made, almost simultaneously in France, by Nicolas Appert, and by Donkin and Hall in England. In 1847, Davidson and Symington took out British Patent 11,947 covering the manufacture of dried soup.

Which just about brings us up to date.

> 'Of soup and love, the first is the best.'
> (Thomas Fuller, 1608–61)

Soup as a Healthy Way of Life

∽

'Venite ad me, vos qui stomacho laboratis
et ego restaurabo vos.' (M. Boulanger,
1765)

This joke in culinary Latin was inscribed on a sign above a bouillon-maker, or soup-vendor, in Rue Bailleul, Paris, a premises later to be recognized as the first ever restaurant. By calling his restorative broths 'restaurants', M. Boulanger inadvertently entered the word into the international vocabulary before the thing itself.

Chefs and herbalists throughout the ages have recognized the restorative powers of broth. One of the earliest records is, 'Pottage is made of the lyquor in whych flesshe is sodden in, with puttyng to chopped herbes and oatmeal and salt', from Andrew Boorde's *The Breviarie of Health* (1598). Antonin Carême, the greatest chef of all time, and founder of *haute cuisine*, summed it up thus: 'There is a whole world of health and eating pleasure in soup. I cannot understand how to have a dinner without a few spoons of good soup because the soup is the beloved of the stomach.'

Soup and health are the subject of hundreds of old wives' tales and proverbs, including 'Who soups long, lives long' (German), and 'It's soup that makes us live, not precious conversation' (Molière, 1622–73).

Soup is soothing to swallow, quells hunger quickly and is easy to digest. The nourishing properties of a soup obviously depend on its ingredients. Whether it be thick or clear, at least 90 per cent of its bulk must be water. If that water has first been prepared as a stock, either made with flesh and bones or from vegetables or pulses, it will have some nutritive value. Adding extra protein, in the form of bread, vegetables, chicken, fish, eggs or cheese, can be done at the last minute in the form of thickeners or embellishments.

It is as well to remember that flavour and energy-value have nothing to do with each other.

'Soup is probably the finest promoter of digestion in the culinary lexicon.' (Martin Lederman, *The Slim Gourmet's Soup Book*, 1946)

SOUP IS THE SOLUTION TO A DIETER'S PRAYERS
'I never worry about diets. The only carrots that interest me are the

number you get in a diamond.' (Mae West, *The Wit and Wisdom of Mae West*, 1967)

Not only is a diet that revolves around soup a healthy diet, it is also the perfect solution for people who wish to lose weight.

Drinks with Soup

∽

'If the soup had been as warm as the claret . . .
If the claret had been as old as the chicken . . .
If the chicken had been as fat as our host . . .
It would have been a splendid meal.'
(Donald McCullough, *After Dinner Grace*, 1960)

To drink with soup, or not. That is the question. The traditional view is that the drinking begins after the soup is finished. Wine, it is generally held, is not served with soup. In many cuisines, most notably those of the Far East and parts of Asia, soup is regarded as the drink, with the double purpose of moistening other dishes. In Japan soup is served at the end of the meal to refresh the palate, aid digestion and quench the thirst.

There is more tradition linked with putting alcohol into soup than with serving it separately. Throughout France there is a custom of tipping half a glass of wine into the last dregs of the soup. In America, beef consommé is livened up with a measure of vodka to become a bullshot, and countless consommés are coloured and flavoured with fortified wine.

Matching wine with soup is exactly the same as matching it to any other food. Robust, strong-flavoured soups need full-bodied wines, and delicate, subtle broths need light, elegant wines. The type and style of a soup, be it a rough-and-ready stew or a finely balanced consommé, are also important considerations. Creamy soups go well with light, dry and fruity Sauvignon, Chardonnay and Riesling-style wines; light vegetable soups and many fish soups are well matched with Beaujolais and other light, dry red wines; meaty stews and robust vegetable hot-pots need stronger, full-bodied red wines such as Côtes-du-Rhône, Chianti, Cabernet Sauvignon and Merlot. Champagne and sweet white wines tend to go well with fruit soups and chilled soups. Well-spiced and chilli soups are good with powerful red wines and fortified wines.

Small drinks have obvious advantages as a match for soup. There is less liquid, for a start, and a shot of something strong – say flavoured vodka, a dainty glass of Madeira or a fine old sherry – solves other problems too.

Serving soup with a complementary drink, such as a flask of warm sake with Japanese or clear soups, or a bottle of Chianti with

minestrone, makes more of an event of soup. Some ingredients, however, such as eggs, globe artichokes and asparagus, are hopelessly
difficult to match. A predominance of either will give wine a metallic
flavour.

See also 'Alcohol' (pages 59–60).

Conversion Tables

〜

'The dangerous person in the kitchen is the one who goes rigidly by weights, measurements, thermometers, and scales'. (Marcel Boulestin, *What Shall We Have Today?*, 1931)

Soup-making rarely relies on precise measurement and exact quantities. However, this is a chart of the metric and imperial measures used throughout this book. All these are approximate conversions, which have either been rounded up or down. Never mix metric and imperial measures in one recipe; stick to one system or the other.

WEIGHTS		VOLUME	
½ oz	15 g	1 fl oz	25 ml
1 oz	25 g	2 fl oz	50 ml
2 oz	50 g	3 fl oz	75 ml
3 oz	75 g	5 fl oz (¼ pt)	150 ml
4 oz	110 g	10 fl oz (½ pt)	275 ml
5 oz	150 g	15 fl oz (¾ pt)	400 ml
6 oz	175 g	1 pt	570 ml
7 oz	200 g	1¼ pts	700 ml
8 oz	225 g	1½ pts	900 ml
9 oz	250 g	1¾ pts	1 litre
10 oz	275 g	2 pts	1.1 litres
11 oz	310 g	2¼ pts	1.3 litres
12 oz	350 g	2½ pts	1.4 litres
13 oz	375 g	3 pts	1.75 litres
14 oz	400 g	3¼ pts	1.8 litres
15 oz	425 g	3½ pts	2 litres
1 lb	450 g	3¾ pts	2.1 litres
1¼ lb	550 g	4 pts	2.3 litres
1½ lb	700 g	5 pts	2.8 litres
2 lb	900 g	6 pts	3.4 litres
3 lb	1.4 kg	7 pts	4 litres
4 lb	1.8 kg	8 pts (1 gallon)	4.5 litres
5 lb	2.3 kg		

MEASUREMENTS	
¼ in	0.5 cm
½ in	1 cm
1 in	2.5 cm
2 in	5 cm
3 in	7.5 cm
4 in	10 cm
6 in	15 cm
7 in	18 cm
8 in	20.5 cm
9 in	23 cm
10 in	25.5 cm
11 in	28 cm
12 in (1 ft)	30.5 cm

OVEN TEMPERATURES		
275° F	140° C	Gas Mark 1
300° F	150° C	Gas Mark 2
325° F	170° C	Gas Mark 3
350° F	180° C	Gas Mark 4
375° F	190° C	Gas Mark 5
400° F	200° C	Gas Mark 6
425° F	220° C	Gas Mark 7
450° F	230° C	Gas Mark 8
475° F	240° C	Gas Mark 9

PART ONE

∽

The Foundations of Soup-making

Equipment

✍

There are very few utensils that are absolutely essential for soup-making, either in the preparation or the cooking. Much of what you need, or will find useful, is in general use anyway.

Vital, though, are several **cook's knives**. I would recommend building up a set of the best quality you can afford. Look after them and they will last a lifetime. I always wash mine immediately after use, and sharpen them little and often with a professional steel.

After years of using carbon steel knives, which sharpen beautifully but are time-consuming to look after, my favourite knives are now Victorinox stainless steel. They are beautifully weighted and balanced and a joy to hold. For vegetables I use an 8-cm/3½-in and a 16-cm/6-in straight-edged blade; for poultry a 10-cm/4-in curved-edge blade, and for boning, a thin, curved 12-cm/5-in blade. Other favourites are a 30-cm/12-in Japanese carbon-steel **cleaver**, which allows surprising dexterity, and a pair of razor-sharp kitchen scissors.

A sturdy and large chopping board and one or two smaller boards are vital. So too is a user-friendly **potato peeler**; my current favourite is a steel swivel blade. I never seem to have enough **wooden spoons** or **rubber spatulas** and could do with more than 2 **wire balloon whisks**.

One of the most useful gadgets for soup-makers is a large size **mouli-légumes** food press, which comes with folding feet that can clamp over saucepans and bowls to hold it steady. It's really a sophisticated sieve with a masher and comes with 3 different sized metal discs for puréeing. Its relative the **mouli-julienne** comes with 5 interchangeable blades of varying sizes for slicing and grating. The advantage of these 2 pieces of equipment over an electrical equivalent is that they are remarkably cheap to buy and can't break down. It is also easier to control the final texture.

I tend to use my ancient **Kenwood Chef** or **Magimix** only when I'm pressed for time, but I wouldn't be without either. I find my hand-held **mixer**, with various attachments, far more useful, not least of all because it's less hassle to wash up afterwards.

For many sieving jobs I use a close-holed **steel colander**, the sort with a handle like a saucepan, and then a 15-cm/6-in **steel sieve**. For very fine sieving and puréeing I use a **nylon mesh drum sieve**, known by its French name, **tamis** (drum). Although it looks fragile, the tamis is remarkably sturdy and food is worked through with the back of a wooden spoon or a specially designed wooden mushroom called a **champignon**. I also regularly use a large **conical sieve/chinois**, with so fine a mesh, woven in a twill of tinned steel wire, that it is as efficient as straining through fine muslin and far less of a palaver.

For years I made my stock in a not very suitable, thin, large, aluminium, lidded stew-pot with several **wire mesh simmer mats** for protection, but when that was irretrievably burnt dry I bought a proper, tall and narrow, heavy-bottomed **stock-pot**, with side handles and a tight-fitting lid. I usually make and serve all my soups in a collection of various-sized vitreous-enamelled cast-iron Le Creuset **casserole dishes**. Occasionally I use an earthenware **marmite**; I particularly like it for soups, like onion and grated cheese, that need to be finished in the oven or under the grill.

It is as well, too, if you get bitten by the stock and soup bug, to lay in plenty of various-sized **polythene bags** for deep-freezing the excess.

If you need to buy any equipment for the kitchen I would recommend you buy professional rather than replicas of professional utensils. Nisbett's, a trade supplier, will send a copy of their excellent catalogue and deliver within twenty-four hours: Unit 1 Waterloo Street, Old Market, Bristol (tel: 0272-555843).

The most authoritative and readable book on kitchen equipment is *The Cook's Companion*, the complete manual of kitchen implements, how to use them and what they look like, by Susan Campbell, published by Chancellor Press.

Stock-making

ॐ

'If you are serious about cooking, good
stock is essential.' (Albert and Michel Roux,
The Roux Brothers, Channel 4, 1990)

It is tempting to tinker with this quote and change it to: 'If you are
serious about soup, good stock is essential.' Stock is the body and
soul of most soups. It is invariably the 'secret' ingredient that makes
so many soups rich, complex in flavour and full-bodied. It is also one
of those cooking 'mysteries' – on a par with pastry-making or cooking
rice, soufflés and gravy – that sends many competent cooks into a
tizz. Cooks of all ages, types, nationality and interest, I discovered
whenever I talked about writing this book, divide into those that do
and those that don't make stock.

I'm grateful to my mother that I grew up in a household where
the stock-pot was an inevitable consequence of roast chickens, ham
bones and vegetable trimmings. She was, and remains, a great
advocate of the pressure-cooker, in which she makes stocks quickly.
Although I took no particular interest in such goings-on, when I left
home and started providing for myself my diet revolved around the
stock-pot. It saved me a fortune, because it was usually filled with
end-of-the-day leftovers from my local street market, and also provided the foundation for imaginative and spontaneous cooking. In
retrospect I think that to understand about the stock-pot is the single
most useful piece of information for a novice cook.

Like my mother, I found myself incapable of chucking out a chicken
carcass without first boiling it up. I hadn't, however, been sufficiently
attentive to notice all the other tricks of the trade that my mother
deployed to make her stock better than an enriched but greasy and
cloudy liquid. Years went by before I understood that successful
stock-making relies on a set of commonsense rules.

There is nothing difficult about stock-making. It requires no
particular skills, and doesn't rely on exotic ingredients or mysterious
cooking techniques. It doesn't have to take hours to make, doesn't
have to fill the house with rank smells, and once some initial and
undemanding preparation has been done, it cooks itself.

Stock can be made from virtually any meat, fish, vegetable, herb
or spice. Its variations are limitless. At its most basic, stock is the
liquid you've cooked the vegetables in. At its most complex it is a

subtle balance of ingredients that complement each other to give what Albert Roux calls 'a marriage of flavours'. Perfect stock is crystal-clear and, when chilled, sets to a jelly.

The basic method, whether you are using meat, poultry, fish or vegetables, is always the same. The ingredients are put into cold water and simmered very gently until all the flavours are extracted. The length of time that takes will depend on the type of stock required and the ingredients used. The flavour is enriched and adjusted by the addition of aromatic vegetables and, perhaps, a bundle of mixed herbs. At the beginning of cooking the broth is skimmed, at the end it is cooled and strained. Surplus fat can be skimmed with a folded paper towel or scooped off in solidified form after a couple of hours in the fridge.

Stock, in some form or other, has a vital role in every cuisine. In classical French cooking, where its catch-all phrase is *fonds de cuisine*, a range of stocks really is the foundation. These *fonds*, usually in reduced and thus strengthened form, are the basis of all sauces. Small quantities are used to embellish stews and vegetable dishes. Reduced stocks are called *glace de viande*.

In such restaurant kitchens, the stock-pot is the nerve-centre of the operation. Serious restaurants prepare several stock-pots every day. These are left to simmer overnight, and one of the first jobs each day is to strain off the liquid and begin the process again. At the three-Michelin-starred Le Gavroche, in London's Mayfair, one commis chef is employed exclusively to look after the stock-pot. At the Waterside Inn at Bray, Britain's only other three-Michelin-starred restaurant, they get through 300 lb of veal bones a week.

Stock-making in French country cooking revolves around the *pot-au-feu* or the *poule-au-pot*, a dish in which a joint of beef or chicken is simmered with vegetables and herbs. The broth is served as a soup, with leftovers forming the base of a different soup, followed by the meat and vegetables. Bones from roast meats or bones that are roasted first form the base of brown stocks.

In Italy the stock-pot plays a different role from that in France. Italian *brodo* tends to be light and quickly made, and rarely includes bones. In Hungary, where the soups are simple and taste exactly of their ingredients, and often include meat, stock-making isn't considered essential. When stock is deployed it's a basic chicken and vegetable broth.

In Oriental cuisines, stock is the key to the subtle flavour of many dishes, particularly soups. It's regarded as a delicate base or a background to other more prominent flavours. Consequently stocks are made with chicken, or pork, and sometimes with both. Chinese stocks rely on the parts of the chicken that might ordinarily go to waste: backs, necks, feet, carcasses, bones, gizzards and trimmings – nothing gets wasted. Flavouring, usually leek or green (spring) onion, celery and carrot, is normally pretty basic but sometimes includes fresh root ginger. Such stocks, flavoured with aromatics such as lemon grass, galangal and sweet basil, are used in Thai cooking. Fish or fish concentrate is never used in Chinese stocks but the Thais, who make wonderful seafood soups, use a combination of a *fumet* made with fish and shellfish bones and heads, mixed with a light chicken stock.

Beef is rarely used in Far Eastern cuisines and never in the stock-pot. It occasionally appears in Korean and Vietnamese soups. In Japan, soup bases are more like infusions than stocks. Usually they are quickly made with fish and seaweeds and the liquid is called *dashi*.

In the Middle East, stock-making echoes French classical techniques. Calf's or sheep's feet are added for their gelatinous quality and marrow bones are used for richer stocks. Stock enrichment is often via the thickening agent: beaten egg-yolks and lemon in chicken stocks, and egg-yolk with vinegar in fish stocks.

At home very few kitchens can generate all the necessary bits and pieces to make a first-class stock on spec. However, some ideal stock-making materials, such as chicken and game bones and vegetable cooking water, are generated all the time in most domestic kitchens.

It is tempting to view the stock-pot as a dumping ground for leftovers. The resulting stock is then dull-looking and dull-tasting and does nothing towards making a fresh-flavoured soup. Cooked vegetables, for example, have no goodness left and can make the liquid bitter. Gravy made with flour, which would seem like a good addition, will make the stock cloudy and ruin the flavour. Bread, potatoes, pulses and milk will make the stock cloudy. Never add leftover salad, even if you've washed off the dressing, or bones from curried meats.

Many of the soups in this book advocate using a light chicken or vegetable stock. These are the stocks that can be basic, makeshift affairs, which add sufficient body to markedly improve soups that rely mainly on the flavour of the key ingredients. At a pinch, stock-cubes will do. But once you've tasted the difference between home-made stock-based soups and those made with a cube, I'd wager that stock-cubes will be relegated to the emergency section of the store-cupboard. A far better stock-standby is a can of any consommé.

However, a high proportion of recipes, and all the consommés, either rely on a good stock or will be transformed by the right one.

THE DOS AND DON'TS OF STOCK-MAKING

1. Any large lidded pan will suffice, but the best stock-pot, known as *faitouts* in France, is heavy-bottomed with a tight-fitting lid and side handles, necessary because the pot is very heavy when full. Traditionally the shape of a stock-pot is tall and narrow, to

avoid evaporation. As a guideline a 9-litre (2-gallon 40-cup) pan will serve 30; 4.5 litres (1 gallon 20 cups) will serve 15; 2.5 litres (5 pints 12½ cups) will serve 10, and 1.75 litres (3 pints 7½ cups) will serve 6.

2. The proportion of water to ingredients is never exact. As the object of the exercise is to produce a broth that is rich in flavour, don't drown the ingredients – remember, though, that there will be some evaporation during cooking. As a guideline, the closely packed ingredients should be covered by 50 mm (2 in) of water.

3. Use fresh, good-quality ingredients. Your stock will be as good as what you put in it, or, as Alice Waters of Chez Panisse puts it, 'A broth that is made with garbage will taste like garbage.'

4. Trim meats of fat. If using raw bones, rinse them well under cold running water. Pack the bones closely together before adding cold water. Some people advocate bringing the water to the boil and skimming before adding the vegetables. This makes the skimming easier because the vegetables float and get mixed up with the gunk. The *bouquet garni* is added last.

5. Bring the water to the boil very slowly, uncovered, without stirring. This will take about 1 hour. When meat and meat bones are heated in water it causes the albuminous proteins to coagulate. This forms a frothy grey scum on the surface of the water which should be spooned off to avoid clouding the liquid. Pour in a cup of cold water (chefs use crushed ice) to encourage more scum to collect. Remove the second lot of dirty scum, return to the boil and repeat until the froth is white.

6. Once a simmer has been established the surface of the liquid should merely tremble. Boiling or vigorous simmering causes solids to disintegrate, which makes the stock muddy, and the liquid to evaporate. Boiling also causes some of the fat in the meat to break down and form a stable emulsion. This will make the stock greasy, and no matter how much straining and skimming you do, it will be impossible to remove the greasy flavour.

7. Now add vegetables, and last of all the *bouquet garni*. Bring back to the boil and remove any further scum. Adjust the simmer, partially cover, and check again that the surface merely trembles. The stock-pot can now be left unattended.

8. There are 2 schools of thought about seasoning. Some cooks add a generous pinch of salt to the stock-pot and sprinkle in a few peppercorns. Others, and I'm one of them, prefer to adjust the seasoning when the soup is made. This is because salt intensifies in flavour during cooking and if the stock is reduced the saltiness may become overpowering. Peppercorns contribute to a cloudy stock.

9. Do not stir the pot during cooking. This could cloud the broth.

10. As a guideline, meat and bone stocks require 6 hours cooking in total; chicken broths between 2 and 3 hours; fish and vegetable stocks take a maximum of 40 minutes. The process can be speeded up by using a pressure-cooker (20 minutes for a chicken stock) and by chopping the ingredients into tiny pieces.

11. At the end of cooking, strain the liquid through a fine sieve (called a tammy cloth, or *étamine* in French) or through a colander lined with a doubled square of muslin (old-fashioned muslin nappy-liners are ideal!) into a suitable bowl. Never force the liquid through by pressing the stock ingredients, and be sure that the sieve doesn't touch the strained liquid in the container.

12. Let the broth cool, and skim the surface for fat globules with a folded kitchen towel. Alternatively, chill the cooled stock in the fridge overnight and scrape off the layer of fat that will form at the top. The ideal container is tall and narrow, so that the fatty area to be skimmed will be small, thick and quick to remove. If a wide-mouthed container is used the surface area of fat will be enormous, is likely to break up, and will be tricky and time-consuming to deal with.

13. Covered, the broth will keep for a few days in the fridge; after 3 days it should be boiled before using. Stock freezes well.

A STOCK-POT FLAVOUR GUIDE

The key to making good stocks is knowing and understanding your ingredients. Many soups don't rely on a complicated stock that has required thought and special buying, but will be improved by using flavoured rather than ordinary water. Use this flavour guide as a foundation for building stocks as well as an inspiration for making the best of what you might otherwise throw away.

Remember: a stock will be as good as the quality of the ingredients.

SEASONINGS

SALT

Beware or be wary of salting stock; its flavour is intensified during cooking, greatly if the stock is reduced. Sea salt is best. Alternatives to use are *miso*, *tamari* and soy sauce. All these fermented soy products, widely used in Japanese and Chinese cooking, can be used instead of salt. They also enrich and heighten flavours but add a powerful dimension that we associate with Japanese food.

PEPPERCORNS
These give an acrid taste and make the stock cloudy.

BUTTER AND OIL

Stocks and soups are enriched, their flavour enhanced, and colour improved if vegetables are first softened in butter or oil. Such cooking releases their flavours more quickly and speeds up vegetable stocks. Depth of colour can be added to a stock by first caramelizing onions (sauté gently in oil or clarified butter until dark brown) before adding water and other ingredients. Fats can be removed from the stock at the end of cooking.

TO CLARIFY BUTTER

Melt the butter in a small pan over a low heat. When the liquid bubbles, remove from the heat and skim off the froth. Allow to cool slightly and pour through muslin, cheesecloth or coffee filter paper into a storage jar, leaving the milky solids behind. The impurities that make butter go rancid are now removed and the ghee, as it is called in India and the Middle East, will keep indefinitely.

HERBS AND AROMATICS

BAYLEAVES

Powerful aromatic flavour that dominates mild-flavoured stocks. Use with discretion: 1 whole bayleaf is enough for meat-based stocks; half is ample for fish and vegetable stocks.

BASIL

Delicate but pungent, lemony, clove-like aroma and flavour that add a different dimension to vegetable stocks. Sweet basil, much evident in Thai cooking, has a more pronounced flavour in the stock-pot. (See page 325.) Also good with chicken and fish stocks.

CHERVIL, MARJORAM AND OREGANO

Used fresh, a few sprays give a lift to light chicken and vegetable stocks and transform tomato-based broths. Mild, sweet and softly aromatic.

CURRY LEAVES

Mild curry flavour that adds an interesting twist to any stock. Use with discretion in light stocks.

DILL

Mild aniseedy flavour is good in fish stocks and can add an agreeable sharpness to vegetable stocks.

GARLIC

Unpeeled and uncut garlic adds a surprisingly mellow sweetness. It deepens flavour without adding heat or sharpness.

FENNEL FRONDS
Its powerful aniseedy flavour complements fish, so a couple of fronds are commonplace in a *bouquet garni* for fish stock.

KAFFIR LIME LEAVES
Much used in Thai cooking to impart a sharp, pronounced, aromatic, lemon-zest flavour. Good in chicken and fish stocks.

LEMON GRASS
Popular in Thai cooking, imparting a pungent, delicate lemon flavour. Use with discretion; a couple of lightly crushed stalks or leaves will add an Oriental twist to a fish stock.

LOVAGE
Looks rather like flat-leaf parsley and tastes like celery. Use its strong-flavoured stalks in place of celery.

PARSLEY
Its stalks are a key component of all *bouquets garnis* and add a delicately piquant flavouring. Flat-leaf or Cyprus parsley has a milder flavour than the more common curly variety.

ROSEMARY
Pungent, strong-flavoured and to be used with discretion in lamb stocks. Otherwise too overpowering.

TARRAGON
Its fresh, lemony-aniseed flavour is a good complement to fish stocks and also works well with chicken.

THYME
A spray is often used in a *bouquet garni* for meat, poultry and game stocks. Used with discretion, it greatly enhances most vegetable stocks.

BOUQUET GARNI

'*Bouquets garnis* should be tailor-made for each stock,' says Albert Roux. Making up a bundle of aromatic herbs that will complement and improve a stock or flavoured water is a satisfying part of the stock-making procedure. Use the flavour guide for ideas, but the following are classic combinations.
Poultry: 1 stick of celery cut in half and used as a shell for a few parsley stalks, a couple of sprays of tarragon, 1 bayleaf, a sprig of thyme and leek trimmings.
Game: 1 spray of rosemary, ½ an onion, 7.5 cm (3 in) of orange peel and a sprig of thyme.

Fish: A couple of fennel stalks or outer leaf, spray each of chervil and tarragon, and leek trimmings.
Meat: 1 clove of unpeeled garlic, parsley stalks, 1 bayleaf, ½ an onion studded with a few cloves and a sprig of thyme.

Tie the bundle together with cotton or fine string, add to the stock, and discard at the end of cooking.

Commercial *bouquets garnis*, made with dried herbs, have a noticeable dusty effect on the flavour of the stock and consequently on the soup.

CITRUS FRUIT

Dried pieces of orange, lemon or tangerine peel have a powerful aromatic effect and add a subtle and haunting flavour particularly associated with Provençal dishes.

VEGETABLES

Many vegetables give a more robust flavour to the stock if they've been grilled, baked or stewed in oil before adding to the pot. To enrich the colour of a stock, begin by caramelizing the onions (cut them into chunks and cook them slowly in butter or oil until brown and soft) before adding the other ingredients and the water.

ASPARAGUS
Add trimmed stalks to asparagus cooking water and reserve for use in asparagus and pea-based soups. A delicious, subtle and quick soup can be made by cooking peeled, chopped potatoes in asparagus water before seasoning and blending.

AUBERGINES/EGGPLANT
Give body and a mild, meaty flavour to stock. Young plants can be used whole, older plants should be sliced and salted first to draw out their bitter juices. Whole aubergines that have been grilled until their skin chars add an agreeably smoky flavour. It's essential, though, to pierce their skins after cooking and drain off the bitter juices.

BRUSSELS SPROUTS, CABBAGE AND SPRING GREENS
Use with caution – their dominating cabbagey flavour easily overpowers the stock-pot.

CARROTS
Integral to most stocks because they sweeten and add good colour. Choose medium-sized and large carrots which tend to have the most flavour. Always peel and slice into chunks.

CAULIFLOWER AND BROCCOLI
Reserve the cooking water or use the outer leaves in mixed vegetable stocks.

CELERY
Gives body and sweetness. Use the outer stems and bright green leaves for stock, saving the small shoots and hearts for other dishes.

CHARD AND KALE
Their thick stems and trimmings add an earthy, very slightly lemony flavour to the stock-pot.

CORNCOBS
Reserve the corn cooking water, split the discarded kernels and continue to cook for 20 minutes. This sweet, milky liquid is the perfect base for a vegetable stock (or corncob-based soup) but needs onions, tomatoes and sharp herbs to cut its sweetness.

FENNEL
Add the bruised outer leaves and woody trimmings to any stock; adds a distinctive sharpness and mild aniseedy flavour.

GREEN BEANS
Reserved cooking water lends flavour to bean-based soups but contributes a sharp earthiness to all summer vegetable stocks. Tough old beans and trimmings can be added to all stock-pots.

LEEKS
A delicate alternative to onions; carefully washed outer green stalks and root ends are perfect for the stock-pot and are the cornerstone of vegetable stocks.

LENTILS
Add a surprisingly dense, meaty flavour. Use no more than a handful. Lentil cooking liquid provides a good base for vegetable stocks.

LETTUCE
Suitable in all vegetable stocks, imparting an intense yet delicate flavour. Use the stems and outer leaves, saving the hearts and perfect leaves for salads. Bolted lettuces are ideal.

MUSHROOMS
All edible mushroom varieties can be used in the stock-pot, and give noticeable body and meaty flavour. The strongest and richest flavour comes from fresh field mushrooms, the least from button and other closed, cultivated varieties. Make use of trimmings, parings, stalks and broken pieces in a mixed stock; for an intensely flavoured pure

mushroom stock, sauté whole mushrooms in butter or oil and then simmer in water.

Dried mushrooms – *porcini* or *cèpes*, morels, *shiitake*, chanterelles and the various Chinese varieties – have intensified flavours, and a few added to the stock-pot will contribute a distinctive earthy flavour that is quite different from that of fresh mushrooms.

NETTLES

One of the most available and nutritious free foods. When boiled in water their sting is eliminated and they produce a robustly flavoured, intensely green broth that can be turned into delicious soups. A gloved-handful adds a hearty flavour to all stocks.

ONIONS

Integral to all stocks, and all varieties are interchangeable. Spring onions, and their relative the leek, give the most delicate flavour; red onions are the sweetest, and shallots the most pungent. Caramelized onions (cooked slowly in butter or oil until brown) give colour and intensified flavour. Onion skins should be removed. Although they colour the liquid dramatically, too many impart a bitter, acrid taste.

POTATOES

As most of the nutrients and vitamins in potatoes are just below the skin, well-scrubbed thick peelings give the most flavour. All varieties give a pronounced earthy flavour to stock, the drawback being that they make the stock cloudy.

TOMATOES

Tomatoes, either ripe fresh, or tinned, add flavour and sharpness to stock. The skins can be left on – if grilled first, the charred skins give a smokiness to the stock.

Stock Recipes

༄

'Personalized soup making has become easy, once the drudgery of stock-making is eliminated, and creativeness gets free rein.' (Martin Lederman, *The Slim Gourmet's Soup Book*, 1946)

VEGETABLE STOCKS

'One of the joys of cooking soups and stews is working with the produce itself. When the vegetables first begin to cook, their colors are astonishingly pure and brilliant; then this luminescent beauty fades as its vitality is transformed into broth and sustenance. Each time I see this phenomenon I think that it's one of the privileges of cooking.' (Deborah Madison, *The Savoury Way*, 1990)

Vegetable stocks are quick to make and appeal to resourceful cooks. The cooking water from most vegetables and combinations of vegetable trimmings, and from pulses, is a useful base for all but the most particular vegetable stocks. The 'Stock-pot Flavour Guide' (pages 9–14) is a useful beginner's guide on how to build up vegetable- and herb-flavoured stocks, but almost anything goes. The skill is to enhance the flavour of your soup without dominating it. Even simple vegetable stocks will vary and improve the flavour of your soups.

Always use clean, fresh vegetables. Root vegetables should be peeled or scraped. It doesn't matter a jot how neatly you chop your vegetables – because they will be discarded at the end of cooking – but aim for similarly sized pieces. The smaller you or your food processor chop the pieces the faster they will flavour the water and the quicker the end result will be. When the vegetables, or a *mirepoix*, are cooked first in oil or butter it enriches the stock's colour and flavour. It can then be called a brown vegetable stock (*fond de légumes brun*).

ALL STOCKS MUST BE SKIMMED FOR FAT BEFORE USE.

Quick Vegetable Stock

MAKES APPROX. 570 ML/1 PT

50 g/2 oz butter
1 onion, peeled and diced
1 carrot, peeled and diced
1 stick of celery, with leaves,
  chopped
trimmings from any of the
  following: mushrooms,
  fennel, leeks, green beans,
  lettuce, asparagus or broccoli

a few parsley stalks
1 sprig each of thyme, basil,
  marjoram, fennel (optional)
salt and pepper

Melt the butter in a decent-sized pan and stir in the vegetables. Sweat, covered, over a low heat for 10 minutes before adding the herbs. Cover with 900 ml/1½ pts of water. Bring to the boil, partially cover and simmer for 15 minutes. Strain and season.

Vegetable Peelings Stock

MAKES APPROX. 1.75 LITRES/3 PTS

450 g/1 lb washed vegetable
  peelings and trimmings
  (avoid Brussels sprouts,
  cabbage and cauliflower)
2 onions, peeled and roughly
  chopped
1 head of celery, including
  leaves, chopped

a few dried mushrooms,
  rinsed
a handful of soaked lentils,
  chickpeas or any dried beans
1 bayleaf
6 stalks of parsley
1 sprig of thyme
salt and pepper

Put all the ingredients in a large pan and cover with water – approximately 2.3 litres/4 pts. Bring to the boil and simmer gently for 1 hour. Strain.

All-purpose Vegetable Stock

MAKES APPROX. 2 LITRES/3½ PTS

110 g/4 oz onions
110 g/4 oz leeks
75 g/3 oz cabbage
75 g/3 oz fennel
75 g/3 oz tomatoes
30 g/1¼ oz butter

bouquet garni *made with*
  4 parsley stalks, 1 strip of
  lemon peel, 1 bayleaf,
  1 clove, 3 sprigs of tarragon,
  1 leek leaf, 1 tsp fennel seeds
  and 4 peppercorns
salt and pepper

Finely chop all the vegetables. Soften the onions and leeks gently in the butter for 5 minutes, then add the remaining vegetables and sweat for a further 10 minutes. Add 2·3 litres/4 pts of water and the *bouquet garni* and bring to the boil. Simmer gently for 20 minutes. Strain and season.

Oriental Vegetable Stock

MAKES APPROX. 900 ML/1½ PTS

25 g/1 oz dried shiitake or Chinese black mushrooms
4 carrots, peeled and roughly chopped
8 spring onions, roughly chopped

6–8 outer lettuce leaves, sliced
2 tsp sesame oil (optional)
¼ tsp sugar
1 tsp Chinese soy sauce
salt

Rinse the mushrooms, cover with 275 ml/½ pt of hot water and leave for 30 minutes. Reserve the strained water and roughly chop the mushrooms. Put the mushrooms and their water with the carrots, onions and lettuce in a large pan with 2 litres/3½ pts of cold water. Bring to the boil, cover and simmer for 30 minutes. Strain carefully, add the oil, sugar and soy sauce, return to the heat and boil down to approximately 900 ml/1½ pts. Season with salt.

Indian Vegetable Broth/Akhni

MAKES APPROX. 1.4 LITRES/2½ PTS

3 tbsp ghee (clarified butter) or light vegetable oil
2 small unpeeled onions, quartered
1 carrot, peeled and chopped
1 large clove of garlic, crushed
5-cm/2-in piece of fresh ginger, chopped

1 tsp cumin seeds
2 tsp coriander seeds
7.5 cm/3 in cinnamon stick
3 black or 6 green cardamom pods
8 cloves
1 tsp black peppercorns
1 tsp coarse salt

Heat the ghee or oil in a large pan, and add all the other ingredients. Fry the vegetables and spices over a medium heat for 10 minutes, or until the onions are wilted and begin to brown. Add 2 litres/3½ pts of cold water and bring to the boil. Lower the heat, partially cover and simmer gently for at least 1 hour, preferably 2. Cool, strain, skim for fat and season with salt.

This recipe is adapted from Julie Sahni's *Classic Indian Cooking*.

Dried Mushroom Stock

MAKES APPROX. 1.75 LITRES/3 PTS

25 g/1 oz dried cèpes or
* porcini*
1 small onion, diced
1 tbsp vegetable oil
150 g/5 oz leeks, finely sliced
110 g/4 oz each of carrots
* and fennel, chopped*
2 sticks of celery, sliced

2 tomatoes, ripe fresh or
* tinned, chopped*
1 tbsp green lentils
6 stalks of parsley
2 sprigs of tarragon
1 tsp tomato purée
salt and pepper

Thoroughly rinse the mushrooms and soak them in 275 ml/½ pt of hot water for 30 minutes. Strain and reserve the liquid. Rinse the mushrooms again – they are usually gritty – and chop. Gently sauté the onion in the oil for a couple of minutes before adding the rest of the vegetables and the lentils. Cook for a further 10 minutes then add the herbs, tomato purée, mushroom liquid and a further 1.75 litres/3 pts of water. Bring to the boil and simmer, partially covered, for 30 minutes. Strain through a fine sieve and season with salt and pepper.

Celery Stock

MAKES APPROX. 1.75 LITRES/3 PTS

2 heads of celery, including
* leaves, chopped*
2 leeks, chopped

8 stalks of parsley
½ bayleaf
salt

Put all the ingredients, except the salt, in a large pan with 1.75 litres/3 pts of cold water. Bring to the boil and simmer, partially covered, for 30 minutes. Strain and season.

Garlic Stock

MAKES APPROX. 1.75 LITRES/3 PTS

2 large heads of garlic,
* cloves separated and*
* peeled*

bouquet garni *made with*
* 4 stalks of parsley, 1 bayleaf*
* and 2 sprigs of thyme*
salt

Put the garlic and *bouquet garni* into a large pan and cover with 2 litres/3½ pts of cold water. Bring to the boil, cover, and simmer very slowly for 2 hours. Strain and season.

CHICKEN STOCKS

'Poultry is for the cook what canvas is
for the painter.' (Jean-Anthelme Brillat-
Savarin, *La Physiologie de Gout*, 1825)

This is the most useful of all stocks. Its flavour is delicate and
unobtrusive, yet it gives body and nutritive value to all soups – so
much so that many chefs will use a light chicken stock in fish soups
and sauces.

Chicken stock is relatively quick to make, and can be made from
raw or cooked carcasses and bones, and from a whole bird or bits of
it. Traditionally a *fond blanc de volaille* is made with onions, carrots,
celery, parsley, thyme and a bayleaf. But there is plenty of room for
experimentation. Leeks, garlic, tomatoes, fennel, mushrooms, white
wine, and black and white peppercorns all enrich the stock differently.
A stock made with cooked carcasses will produce a light stock that
can be enriched but shouldn't be overpowered by vegetables and
aromatic herbs. It can also have its flavour and strength bolstered by
the addition of a small proportion of raw veal or beef.

The stock will be stronger if it is made with raw carcasses. It will
have a more developed flavour and be darker in colour if the bones
are browned first for 20 minutes in a hot oven. It is then known as
fond brun de volaille. A richer and more gelatinous chicken stock is
made by adding a veal knuckle or pork trotter.

Poached chicken dishes create stock as a by-product – *poule-au-pot*
is the classic example – but when buying a whole chicken to make
stock, always buy a boiling fowl. The double advantage of old stewing
hens is that they are full of flavour and cheap.

ALL STOCKS MUST BE SKIMMED FOR FAT BEFORE USE.

Cooked Carcass Chicken Stock

MAKES APPROX. 1.75 LITRES/3 PTS

1 chicken carcass, winglets,
  bones, giblets, and any skin,
  meat and jelly
1 onion, peeled and chopped
1 leek, chopped
2 carrots, peeled and chopped
6 outer lettuce leaves,
  shredded

1 clove of garlic, peeled
½ a bayleaf
1 sprig of thyme
6 sprigs of parsley
6 peppercorns
salt

Put all the ingredients except the salt in a large pan, cover with cold
water (approx. 2.3 litres/4 pts) and bring to the boil. Skim if necessary
and simmer gently, uncovered, for 2 hours. Strain, remove the fat,

and season. It is a mistake to think that this stock will improve with longer cooking.

This is the lightest of all the chicken stock recipes but is well balanced and gives body. Ideal for delicately flavoured soups, including seafood soup recipes.

Pressure-cooker Chicken Stock

MAKES APPROX. 1 LITRE/1¾ PTS

50 g/2 oz butter
2 mushrooms, chopped
1 onion, peeled and studded
  with 3 cloves
1 carrot, diced
1 raw chicken carcass,
  winglets, giblets (but not
  liver) and any bones

bouquet garni made with a
  few parsley stalks, a couple
  of sprays of tarragon, 1
  bayleaf, 1 sprig of thyme and
  leek trimmings, bundled
  inside 1 halved stick of
  celery
salt and pepper

Melt the butter and sweat the vegetables over a low heat, covered, for 10 minutes. Add the carcass, cover with water (approx. 1 litre/¾ pts) and bring to the boil. Skim, and add the bouquet garni. Cover and cook at pressure for 20 minutes. Drain, cool and season with caution.

Without a pressure-cooker this stock should simmer for 2 hours with the water brought up to 1.4 litres/2½ pts.

This produces a well-flavoured, aromatic stock that is suitable in all soups that call for a light chicken stock.

Michel Guérard's Cuisine Minceur Chicken Stock

MAKES APPROX. 1 LITRES/1¾ PTS

1 kg/2¼ lb crushed chicken
  carcasses and giblets
1 clove of garlic, crushed
100 g/3½ oz mushrooms,
  thinly sliced
100 g/3½ oz carrots, thinly
  sliced
1 shallot, chopped

1 leek, sliced
1 small stick of celery
7 tbsp dry white wine
50 g/2 oz onion, whole,
  studded with 1 clove
bouquet garni made with
  4 stalks of parsley, 1 sprig of
  thyme and 1 bayleaf

Put the crushed carcasses in a pan with the garlic and all vegetables except the onion. Add the wine, bring to the boil, and cook until it has almost evaporated. Add 2 litres/3½ pts of cold water, the onion and the bouquet garni and simmer gently, uncovered, for 3 hours, skimming frequently. Strain the remaining stock.

This makes a delicate chicken stock that is both understated yet packed with subtle flavour.

Michel Guérard's restaurant at the health spa Eugénie-les-Bains holds 3 Michelin stars.

Basic Brown Chicken Stock

MAKES APPROX. 1.1 LITRES/2 PTS

900 g/2 lb chicken winglets, carcasses or giblets (not liver), or combination
110 g/4 oz each of diced carrot, onion and celery
2 tomatoes, chopped

6 peppercorns
bouquet garni *made with 6 stalks of parsley, 1 sprig of thyme and 1 bayleaf*
salt

Spread the bones out on a roasting-pan and cook in a hot oven – 400° F/200° C/Gas Mark 6 – for 15 minutes. Pour off and wipe away as much fat as possible and add the vegetables. Roast for a further 5 minutes and transfer the lot to a large pan. Deglaze the roasting-pan with 275 ml/10 fl oz of boiling water and pour over the bones and vegetables. Add a further 1.1 litres/2 pts of cold water to the pan and bring to the boil. Reduce to a simmer, skim, add the *bouquet garni* and continue cooking for 2 hours. Strain and salt.

This produces a richly-coloured but essentially chicken-flavoured stock. It can be let down with water in recipes that require a light chicken stock.

Giblet Chicken Stock

MAKES APPROX. 1.75 LITRES/3 PTS

2 tbsp vegetable oil
2 carrots, peeled and chopped
2 onions, peeled and chopped
2 sticks of celery, chopped
2 mushrooms, chopped
450 g/1 lb giblets (excluding liver) or chicken necks

bouquet garni *made with 6 sprigs of parsley, 1 sprig of thyme and 1 bayleaf sandwiched in ½ a leek, split lengthways*
6 peppercorns
salt

Heat the oil in a large pan and add the vegetables. Sweat gently, stirring occasionally, for 10 minutes. Add the giblets and 2.3 litres/4 pts of cold water. Bring to the boil, skim, add the *bouquet garni* and peppercorns and simmer gently for 2 hours. Strain and taste for salt.

This makes a fragrant, aromatic and delicately flavoured stock, ideal in all recipes that call for a light chicken stock.

Boiling Fowl Chicken Stock

Boiling fowl are tough old birds that are usually egg-layers past their prime. They look scrawny and unappetizing, but their tough, year-old flesh and mature bones are rich in flavour and gelatine. The bird can be used whole or jointed. Always remove the fat that will have accumulated in the body cavity and any partially formed eggs. They are usually sold with their feet, and sometimes heads, intact but with their giblets removed.

MAKES APPROX. 2.3 LITRES/4 PTS

1 boiling fowl (they average
  1.4 kg/3 lb)
2 onions, peeled and halved
2 carrots, peeled and chopped
2 sticks of celery, chopped

bouquet garni *made with*
  6 stalks of parsley, 1 sprig of
  thyme and 1 bayleaf
salt and pepper

Rinse the bird under running water, and remove excess fat. Cover with cold water (approx. 2 litres/3½ pts) and bring to the boil. Skim to remove all the grey gunk before adding the vegetables and *bouquet garni*. Leave to simmer gently for 2 hours. Remove the chicken and strain the liquid. Season with salt and pepper.

Cool and skim. The flesh of the boiling fowl is delicious eaten warm in well-buttered doorstep sandwiches liberally seasoned with salt, pepper and freshly chopped parsley and chives.

Using a whole bird in the stock-pot greatly enriches the end product. The chicken flavour comes through strongly in this simple recipe. The stock will be gelatinous.

Chinese Chicken Stock

MAKES APPROX. 2.3 LITRES/4 PTS

2 kg/4½ lb chicken carcasses,
  feet, winglets, etc.
700 g/1½ lb chicken wings
5 cm/2 in fresh ginger, peeled
  and chopped

2 spring onions, chopped
2 cloves of garlic, peeled
salt

Cover the chicken bones and pieces with 2.3 litres/4 pts of cold water and bring to the boil. Adjust to simmer, skim, and add the ginger, onions and garlic. Continue simmering very gently for 3½ hours. Strain and season with salt.

The stock will be rich and full-bodied, lightly seasoned by the spring onions and aromatic garlic but with a hint of ginger. Ideal for all Chinese soups, most other Oriental soups, and provides an unusual background to vegetable soups.

Chinese Chicken and Pork Stock

Follow preceding recipe but add 700 g/1½ lb raw pork bones.

Japanese Chicken Stock

MAKES APPROX. 1.1 LITRES/2 PTS

450 g/1 lb chicken giblets, necks, winglets and carcasses
4 spring onions, chopped

5-cm/2-in piece of fresh ginger root, peeled and chopped
salt

Put all the ingredients except the salt into a large pan and cover with 1.4 litres/2½ pts of water. Bring to the boil, skim, and simmer gently for 1 hour. Strain and season with salt.

This makes a very light stock with a pure, clear flavour. Use in place of *dashi* (see page 45) in all Japanese soups.

TURKEY STOCKS

'Turkey boiled is turkey spoiled
And turkey roast is turkey lost
But for turkey braised
The Lord be praised.'
(Anonymous quote in *Food* by Waverley Root, 1980)

We are not great turkey eaters in my household. In fact, if we have one at all, it will be at Christmas. When we do have turkey, however, the aspect that I enjoy most is the marvellous stock that the carcass provides. Any of the chicken stock recipes can be deployed for turkey, but the end product will be stronger in flavour. Because a turkey carcass is so much larger than a chicken's, it provides the ideal excuse to make up a large batch of stock.

ALL STOCKS MUST BE SKIMMED FOR FAT BEFORE USE.

Turkey Carcass Stock

MAKES APPROX. 4.5 LITRES/8 PTS

1 turkey carcass, broken into pieces (any skin, wings, jelly and giblets should also be included)
2 onions, peeled and halved
1 large stick of celery
2 large carrots, peeled and chopped

4 cloves of garlic, peeled
6 black peppercorns
bouquet garni made with a generous spray of thyme, 6 stalks of parsley and 1 bayleaf
salt

Using your largest stock-pot, or dividing the ingredients equally between 2 pots, cover all the ingredients except the *bouquet garni* and salt with water (approx. 5.1 litres/9 pts) and very slowly bring to the boil. Skim, turn down to a low simmer, and leave, partially covered, for 2 hours. Add the *bouquet garni* and cook for a further hour. Strain and season with salt.

This produces the lightest of all the turkey stock recipes, but although similar to light chicken stocks, it has a more intrusive flavour and is not suitable for soups made with delicately flavoured ingredients.

Brown Turkey Carcass Stock

MAKES APPROX. 4.5 LITRES/8 PTS

1 raw turkey carcass, giblets, feet and winglets
1 large carrot, peeled and chopped
1 onion, peeled and chopped
1 stalk of celery, chopped
1 leek, trimmed and halved

1 ripe fresh or tinned tomato
bouquet garni made with 4 sprigs of thyme, 6 stalks of parsley and 1 bayleaf
2 cloves of garlic, peeled
6 peppercorns
salt

Break up the bones and roast in a moderate oven (400° F/200° C/ Gas Mark 6) for 20 minutes. Strain off any fat, then stir the vegetables into the bones and turn any unbrowned bones face up. Return to the oven for a further 15 minutes. Using a slotted spoon, transfer the ingredients to the stock-pot, cover with water (approx 5.1 litres/9 pts) and bring to the boil. Skim repeatedly to remove all the grey scum, then add the *bouquet garni*, garlic and peppercorns. Simmer, partially covered, for 2 hours. Strain and season with salt.

This produces a dark stock with a rich flavour and is suitable for all soups that require a robust stock.

Turkey Giblet Stock

MAKES APPROX. 900 ML/1½ PTS

1 tbsp vegetable oil
1 onion, peeled and chopped
2 sticks of celery with leaves,
  chopped
the giblets and neck of the
  turkey

bouquet garni *made with*
  1 sprig of thyme, 4 sprigs of
  parsley and ½ a bayleaf
1 clove of garlic, peeled
4 peppercorns
salt

Warm the oil and sweat the onion for 5 minutes before stirring in the celery and the giblets. Cover with 1.1 litres/2 pts of cold water and bring to the boil. Add the *bouquet garni*, garlic and peppercorns and simmer gently for 1½ hours. Strain and season with salt.

This is making-do rather than premier-league stock. It will add body and enrichment and is particularly recommended for mixed vegetable purée soups.

GAME STOCKS

'The quail is of all game the most delicate and the most agreeable. A good, fat quail pleases equally by its taste, its shape and its colour. You show your ignorance whenever you serve it otherwise than roasted or *en papillote*, for its savour is extremely volatile and every time the animal is put in contact with liquid, it dissolves, evaporates and perishes.' (Jean-Anthelme Brillat-Savarin, *La Physiologie du Gout*, 1825)

It would take several quail and a good deal more carcasses to contribute body, flavour and nutrition to the stock-pot. But that's not to dismiss this tiny game bird, as Brillat-Savarin does, on the grounds of impropriety. Quail make marvellous stock, as do all game birds, but, for most of us, such stocks are an expensive luxury.

Feathered game – grouse, partridge, snipe, woodcock, pigeon, pheasant, quail and wild duck – is associated with consommé, in which the whole bird is used to create the crystal-clear soup that is regarded as the pinnacle of soup-making. The pronounced 'gamey' flavour of stock made with all game, be it furred or feathered, makes it unsuitable as an all-purpose stock. However, the carcass, bones and trimmings left over from a roasted bird or filleted rabbit or hare can be transformed into rich, robust stocks, known as *fonds de gibier*, that require very little to make them into hearty, luxurious soups.

During the game season, raw game bones can usually be scrounged from the fishmonger. It is worth bagging and freezing cooked game carcasses until you have a minimum of 4 to make stock-making worthwhile.

Juniper berries and red wine or brandy are ideal seasonings for all game stocks.

ALL STOCKS MUST BE SKIMMED FOR FAT BEFORE USE.

Game Stock

MAKES APPROX. 1.4 LITRES/2½ PTS

1 kg/2 lb 4 oz raw trimmings, carcasses, giblets, etc. from any game, either the same variety or a mixture
2 tbsp groundnut oil
1 onion, diced
1 carrot, peeled and chopped
1 stick of celery, chopped
570 ml/1 pt full-bodied red wine

6 juniper berries
6 coriander seeds
bouquet garni *made with 7.5 cm/3 in of orange peel, 1 sprig of rosemary and 1 bayleaf*
2 cloves of garlic, peeled
salt

Chop the game carcasses and trimmings into small pieces. Heat the oil in a large pan and brown the game pieces all over. Lower the heat, stir in the vegetables and sweat, covered, for 10 minutes. Pour on the red wine and let it boil and reduce by half. Add 1.4 litres/ 2½ pts of cold water, bring back to the boil, skim, and simmer gently for 15 minutes. Add the juniper berries, coriander seeds, *bouquet garni* and garlic. Leave to simmer very gently, partially covered, for 2½ hours. Strain and season with salt.

Carcass Game Stock

MAKES APPROX. 1.75 LITRES/3 PTS

Carcass, bones and trimmings from any roasted game (not worth making with less than 2 pheasant or 4 grouse, partridge and pigeon)
4 shallots or 1 onion, peeled and diced
1 carrot, peeled and diced
4 cloves of garlic, peeled

1 stick of celery, finely sliced
2 tomatoes, quartered
dregs from the previous night's red wine (optional)
1 bayleaf
1 sprig of rosemary
4 peppercorns
salt

Break up the bones and roast them in a hot oven (400° F/200 °C/Gas Mark 6) for 15 minutes. Mix in the shallots or onion, carrot, garlic, celery, tomatoes and red wine and cook for a further 5 minutes. Tip the bones and vegetables into a large pan, deglaze the roasting-pan with 275 ml/½ pt of boiling water and add to the pan. Add 1.75 litres/3 pts of cold water and bring to the boil. Reduce the heat, skim, tuck the bayleaf, rosemary and peppercorns around the bones and cook very gently, uncovered, for 2½ hours. Strain and season with salt.

Goose or Duck Stock

MAKES APPROX. 1.4 LITRES/2½ PTS

1 cooked or raw goose or duck carcass, rinsed under boiling water, plus any bones, winglets, giblets and trimmings
1 onion, peeled and chopped
2 carrots, peeled and chopped

2 sticks of celery, chopped
2 (or more) glasses of red wine
1 bayleaf
1 sprig of sage
6 peppercorns
salt

Break up the carcass and roast it and the other bones for 15 minutes at 400° F/200° C/Gas Mark 6. Mix in the onion, carrots and celery and cook for a further 10 minutes. Transfer to a stock-pot and deglaze the roasting-pan with the wine. Pour this and 1.75 litres/3 pts of cold water into the pan and bring to the boil. Skim, then add the bayleaf, sage and peppercorns. Simmer gently for 2 hours. Strain and season with salt.

Oriental Duck Stock

MAKES APPROX. 1.75 LITRES/3 PTS

900 g/2 lb duck bones, chopped
6 spring onions
5-cm/2-in piece of fresh ginger, sliced

6 peppercorns
1 star anise
dash of sherry

Put all the ingredients in a large pan and cover with 2.3 litres/4 pts of cold water. Bring to the boil, skim and simmer gently for 2 hours. Strain.

VEAL STOCKS

'Veal is at once succulent and anonymous.
Veal stock could be likened to an unfinished
portrait, its background laid in, the essential
volumes and harmonies defined, before the
details of particular features are imposed
on the abstract structure.' (Richard Olney,
French Menu Cookbook, 1985)

Not without reason is veal stock the linchpin of the classical French
repertoire. It is both rich and mellow yet has no overpowering
character. It is the perfect vehicle for other flavours and, when
reduced with other ingredients, it is used to make the brown sauces
that are the pride and joy of French restaurant kitchens.

However, producing restaurant-quality veal stock in a domestic
kitchen is unlikely to become a weekly habit. Unlike chicken stock,
which can be made with leftover carcasses supplemented by cheap or
free scraps from the butcher, veal stock is serious. A good veal stock
relies on a high proportion of bones and meat and very little else. It is
cooked in a comparatively small amount of liquid and reduces during
cooking to give a relatively small return. The best veal stocks are
made with meat from the hard-working muscles – flank, shank,
breast or neck – and they need to be bought in large pieces. This is
essential because only with long, slow cooking can the gelatinous
juices be extracted. Under such conditions, small pieces and trimmings would disintegrate and cloud the broth.

Veal knuckle, split and chopped by the butcher, is the best bone. It
too is rich with gelatine. Very few butchers give away such bones.
However, if you are lucky enough to have a local butcher who
deserves your loyalty, he may be happy to keep you supplied with
veal bones.

There are two kinds of veal stock. Golden, brown or dark veal
stock, known as *fond brun de veau*, is made with bones that are
browned in the oven before going into the pot. White veal stock,
known as *fond blanc de veau*, is made with bones and meat that go
directly into the water. It too is rich with gelatine. Both types require
long, slow cooking – up to 24 hours is normal in restaurant kitchens
– to extract all the goodness and provide the smooth, mellow body
that characterizes veal stock.

Because veal stock takes such a long time to make, any vegetables
can be left whole or coarsely chopped. This is handy because they
can be easily fished out of the strained stock debris and the bones
returned to the pot to make second stock. Garlic should not be
peeled.

To achieve a crystal-clear stock the liquid must never boil and
never be stirred during cooking. A further precaution is to place a

small grid at the bottom of the stockpot to avoid the meat getting stuck to the pan. It also means that the inevitable deposit of gunk can settle and remain undisturbed under the grid. When the stock has finished cooking, to avoid disturbing the debris and thus clouding the stock, it is wise to remove the bones individually and then to decant the stock with a ladle rather than tip up the pan.

Despite the fact that veal stock is relatively expensive to make and takes a long time to produce, it is worth doing every now and again. It freezes successfully and is invaluable to have stashed in small quantities in the freezer. When veal stock is reduced by half its original quantity it is known as *demi-glace*, when reduced by three-quarters it is called a *glace* or meat glaze. Such nuggets of flavour can be used to bolster watery stocks and to enrich chicken stocks.

Similarly, a veal knuckle added to a chicken stock will give it body without noticeably affecting the flavour.

Veal stock keeps for up to 10 days in the fridge, up to a month in the freezer.

ALL STOCKS MUST BE SKIMMED FOR FAT BEFORE USE.

White Veal Stock

MAKES APPROX. 2.1 LITRES/4 PTS

1.8 kg/4 lb chopped veal knuckle
1.3 kg/3 lb raw veal shank meat
2 carrots, peeled
2 onions, peeled and studded with 2 cloves

2 sticks of celery
2 unpeeled cloves of garlic
bouquet garni *made with*
1 sprig of thyme, 6 stalks of parsley and 1 bayleaf

Blanch the bones and meat in boiling water for 5 minutes. Rinse and put in a large pot with 4 litres/7 pts of cold water. Bring to the boil and skim, then add all the other ingredients. Simmer, uncovered, for 4–5 hours. Strain.

A less powerful but equally good veal stock can be made by omitting the veal shank.

Second Veal Stock

Rinse the bones from any of the veal stock recipes and return them to a clean pan without seasoning or vegetables. Cover with water and simmer gently for several hours. This will make a light stock which will give body to soups that should have a distinct flavour of their own.

Elizabeth David's Quick Veal Stock

MAKES APPROX. 900 ML/1½ PTS

225 g/8 oz chopped stewing
  veal
1 small carrot, peeled and
  chopped
1 small onion, unpeeled

1 clove of garlic
1 tomato, chopped
bouquet garni of any fresh
  herbs
a pinch of salt

Cover everything with 1 litre/1¾ pts of cold water and bring to simmering point. Skim and transfer to a low oven (300° F/150° C/Gas Mark 2) for about 1 hour. Strain through a fine sieve.

This will give body and richness without overwhelming other flavours.

Nico Ladenis's Veal Stock

MAKES APPROX. 1 LITRE/1¾ PTS

1 kg/2½ lb veal bones
  (knuckles and marrow bones
  are best), finely chopped
200 ml/7 fl oz clarified butter
  (see page 10)
2 tbsp clear honey
2 tbsp pure groundnut oil
100 g/4 oz onion, peeled and
  coarsely chopped
100g/4 oz carrots, coarsely
  chopped
1 small leek, white part only, cut
  in half and washed thoroughly

2 shallots, finely chopped
2 cloves of garlic, finely sliced
225 g/8 oz can of whole
  Italian tomatoes, rinsed to
  remove pips and juices, and
  finely chopped
1 sprig of thyme
1 sprig of parsley
1 bayleaf

Brush the veal bones lightly with the clarified butter and honey. Roast them in a hot oven (425° F/220° C/Gas Mark 7) for about 45 minutes until the bones are evenly browned. Heat the oil in a heavy bottomed stock-pot and fry the vegetables, garlic and tomatoes gently without burning. Add the bones to the stock-pot and deglaze the roasting-pan with water. Top up the water to clear the bones by a good 10 cm/4 in – approx. 3.4 litres/6 pts – and bring to the boil. Skim thoroughly and simmer gently for 2½ hours before adding the herbs. Cook on for 2 more hours, skimming if necessary. Strain. Return to a clean pot and reduce slightly.

This produces a rich, well-rounded stock with a beautiful caramel colour, obtained by the combination of coating the bones with honey and the addition of ripe tomatoes.

Pressure-cooker Veal Stock

MAKES APPROX. 1.1 LITRES/2 PTS

1 kg/2½ lb veal bones,
  chopped small
1 onion, peeled and chopped
1 carrot, peeled and chopped
½ a swede, peeled and chopped
½ a turnip, peeled and chopped

For second cooking
bouquet garni *made with*
  6 sprigs of parsley, 1 sprig of
  sage or thyme and 1 bayleaf

Wash the bones and put in the open pressure-cooker with 570 ml/ 1 pt of cold water. Bring to the boil and remove the scum. Add the vegetables and another 275 ml/10 fl oz of cold water. Close the cooker, bring to pressure, and cook for 45 minutes. Reduce the pressure and strain. Allow to cool and skim for fat before adding the *bouquet garni* and 570 ml)1 pint of cold water. Bring up to the boil and reduce slightly.

BEEF STOCKS

'Beef is the soul of cooking.' (Antonin Carême, *Le Cuisinier Parisien*, 1828)

Beef stock is made from marrow bones, the inexpensive muscular cuts of meat such as shin, flank and skirt, or a combination of the two. In all cases, to extract the maximum goodness from the bone and its rich and fatty marrow, and all the flavour from the meat, beef stock requires long slow cooking. An ox-foot or a small quantity of ox-tail adds gelatine.

The end result is a clear, strongly flavoured, nutritious liquid (called broth when meat is involved) which is a good basis for many invalid soups (see pages 346–8) and restorative beef tea. In France, beef broth is a by-product of *pot-au-feu*, when a joint of beef is slow-cooked with root vegetables. The British edition is boiled beef and carrots, and the Italian relative, which uses other meats too, is *bollito misto*. Boiled tongue also yields a rich, strong stock. Recipes for these and other similar dishes can be found on pages 283–9.

Subtle flavours make little impact on beef stock, so seasoning with vegetables and aromatics is traditionally done using onion and carrot augmented by celery and other root vegetables. The classic *bouquet garni* includes parsley, thyme, garlic and bayleaves. Italian *brodo*, always made with meat and rarely with bones, generally includes tomato.

When using marrow bones, be sure that they are sawn into manageable pieces by the butcher. There is controversy about whether to leave in the marrow – a great source of flavour but also of fat – or remove it first and save it for other uses such as frying croûtons and making biscuits (see pages 125–6). If the marrow is left intact, be sure to save the thick layer of fat that will form at the top of the resultant jellied stock. The advantage of pressure-cooked bone stocks is that they reduce the cooking from many hours to 45 minutes.

British beef tripe, these days all treated, blanched and bleached and cooked within a couple of hours, doesn't stand up to the long slow cooking that used to yield marvellous stocks. I have, however, included a recipe for a tripe stock with a pig's trotter that yields a richly flavoured gelatinous stock and is almost a soup in itself.

ALL STOCKS MUST BE SKIMMED FOR FAT BEFORE USE.

Basic Beef Stock

MAKES APPROX. 1.75 LITRES/3 PTS

1 kg/2½ lb marrow bones, cut into 7.5-cm/3-in pieces
700 g/1½ lb shin, skirt, flank or other cheap muscular cut of beef, left in a large piece
2 onions, halved and each stuck with 1 clove
2 sticks of celery, halved
8 peppercorns
bouquet garni *made with* 2 sprigs of thyme, 1 bayleaf, 5 cm/2 in of orange peel and 1 unpeeled clove of garlic

Place the bones with the beef balanced on top in a large pan. Cover with 2.8 litres/5 pts of cold water and bring slowly to the boil. Remove the grey scum that will form and turn the heat down low. When only a small amount of white scum is left, add the vegetables, peppercorns and *bouquet garni*. Partially cover the pan, but be sure that the liquid merely ripples rather than bubbles furiously. Continue cooking for 3 hours and remove the meat. Cook on for a further 1–2 hours to get the maximum goodness from the marrow bones. Strain.

The fat that coagulates at the top of the chilled stock will be rich with marrow fat and will be delicious for roasting potatoes or parsnips. The beef is good sliced thickly and served warm in sandwiches made with crusty bread, served with plenty of mustard and/or pickles.

This stock is rich and meaty with a pronounced flavour. It needs little embellishment to transform it into a good broth-style soup.

Second Beef Stock

MAKES APPROX. 1.75 LITRES/3 PTS

1 pig's trotter, veal knuckle
  and/or 450 g/1 lb chicken
  winglets or carcass
beef bones from basic beef
  stock recipe (see page 32)
1 onion, halved
2 carrots, peeled and sliced

3 unpeeled cloves of garlic
bouquet garni made with
  6 sprigs of parsley, 1 sprig of
  thyme and 1 bayleaf, bundled
  inside 1 halved stick of
  celery
6 peppercorns

Put the pig's trotter, veal knuckle and/or chicken in a pan and cover with 2.3 litres/4 pts of cold water. Bring slowly to the boil and skim before adding the beef bones. Turn the heat down so that the liquid simmers gently and cook for 30 minutes before adding the vegetables, garlic, *bouquet garni* and peppercorns. Continue cooking for 2 hours. Strain. This stock will be nowhere as richly flavoured as the basic beef stock recipe, but the addition of a pig's trotter, veal knuckle and/or chicken wings produces a light stock with a surprising amount of body.

Pressure-cooker Beef Stock

MAKES APPROX. 1.75 LITRES/3 PTS

1.4 kg/3 lb (approx.) beef
  marrow bones, cut into 7.5-
  cm/3-in pieces
1 onion, peeled and roughly
  chopped
1 carrot, peeled and roughly
  chopped

1 stalk of celery, roughly
  chopped
1 bayleaf
1 sprig of thyme
8 stalks of parsley
4 black peppercorns

Pack the bones into the pressure-cooker and cover with 1.75 litres/3 pts of cold water. Bring to the boil and remove all the grey scum that will form. Tuck the vegetables and bayleaf in among the bones and drape the thyme and parsley over the top. Add the peppercorns. Put on the lid, bring up to pressure, and, using the 6.75-kg/15-lb weight, cook for 45 minutes. Reduce the pressure and strain.

The fat that will form on the surface of this intensely flavoured stock can be saved and used later. The stock can be extended by up to 1.1 litres/2 pts depending on whether the soup recipe calls for a strongly-flavoured or a light beef stock.

Quick Beef Stock

MAKES APPROX. 1.1 LITRES/2 PTS
450 g/1 lb lean beef, minced
* or chopped*
1 carrot, peeled and diced
1 leek, white part only, diced
1 onion, peeled and chopped
1 stick of celery, diced
6 stalks of parsley

4 drops of caramel (made by
* melting 50 g/2 oz sugar*
* slowly until it turns deep*
* gold, then adding 150 ml/*
* 5 fl oz of cold water and*
* boiling hard until the sugar*
* dissolves)*

Place all the ingredients except the caramel in a stock-pot with 1.1 litre/2 pts of cold water. Bring slowly to the boil, stirring every now and again, then reduce the heat, partially cover the pan, and let the mixture simmer gently for 1 hour. Strain and add the caramel to give the stock colour. Another way of adding colour is to use 2 shallots or other small onions in place of the onion specified, browning them in their skins by dry-sautéing in a non-stick pan before adding them to the stock-pot.

Italian Beef Stock/Brodo

MAKES APPROX.1.4 LITRES/2½ PTS
310 g/11 oz lean beef (shin
* and leg, chuck and blade,*
* skirt/stew meat and*
* flank/shank) or 1 kg/2½ lb*
* assorted beef bones and meat*
* scraps*
1 carrot, peeled

1 onion, peeled
1 stick of celery
1 very ripe fresh or 1 canned
* plum tomato, or 2 tsp*
* tomato purée*
4 sprigs of parsley

Put the meat and/or bones into a stock-pot and cover with 2.3 litres/ 4 pts of cold water. Bring slowly to the boil, turn down the heat so that the stock simmers gently, and skim off the scum that rises to the surface. Add the vegetables, tomato and parsley and simmer gently for 3 hours. Strain and, if necessary, return to a clean pot and boil fiercely to reduce the stock to the required amount.

Strengthening and Clarifying Second Beef Stock

MAKES APPROX. 1 LITRE/1¾ PTS
1 egg-white and shell
1 carrot, peeled and diced
1 small onion, peeled and
* diced*
1 stick of celery, diced

110 g/4 oz lean beef, finely
* minced*
6 white peppercorns
1 litre/1¾ pts beef stock,
* chilled*

Crush the egg-shell and whisk it with the egg-white. Mix it with the carrot, onion, celery, meat and peppercorns in the stock-pot. Add the cold stock and whisk continually until the liquid reaches boiling point. At this point a white crust will form. Turn down the heat and leave the stock to simmer very gently for 1 hour to extract all the goodness from the ingredients. Have ready a bowl set with a sieve lined with a tea-towel or with several layers of muslin wrung out in cold water. Break a hole in the centre of the crust and ladle out the stock. The wet cloth will filter out any stray bits from the crust.

Jellied Brown Beef Stock

MAKES APPROX. 2.8 LITRES/5 PTS

2 tbsp beef dripping or unflavoured cooking oil
1 ox-foot, split
1 marrow bone, chopped into small pieces
1 beef shin bone, chopped into small pieces
1 large onion, halved

2 large carrots, peeled and roughly chopped
bouquet garni made with 8 stalks of parsley, sprig of thyme, 1 unpeeled clove of garlic and 1 bayleaf, bundled inside 1 halved stick of celery

Heat some of the dripping or oil in a frying-pan and brown the bones in batches. Transfer the bones to a large stock-pot, packing them as closely together as possible, and cover with 3.4 litres/6 pts of cold water. Bring to the boil and skim until no more grey scum rises to the surface. Turn down the heat so that the liquid simmers gently. Tuck the vegetables and bouquet garni into the bones, partially cover, and leave the pot to simmer undisturbed for 3 hours. Strain.

The stock will be a rich golden brown and lightly jellied. The fat on the top, which contains marrow fat, can be saved for other use. A lighter second stock can be made with these bones and a fresh mixture of vegetables. The browning stage should be omitted.

Tripe Stock

MAKES APPROX. 1.75 LITRES/3 PTS

1 pig's trotter or calf's foot, split
1 veal knuckle, split
1 tbsp beef dripping
1 onion, peeled and coarsely chopped
2 carrots, peeled and coarsely chopped
2 unpeeled cloves of garlic
50 g/2 oz mushrooms, diced

1 kg/2½ lb beef tripe, washed, scraped free of fat and cut into 5-cm/2-in pieces
bouquet garni made with 6 stalks of parsley, 1 sprig of thyme and 1 bayleaf bundled up inside 1 halved stick of celery
4 black peppercorns

Rinse the pig's trotter or calf's foot and the veal knuckle and place in a pan with sufficient cold water to cover. Bring to the boil and allow to cook for 5–10 minutes while you remove the scum that will form. Chuck away the water and reserve the trotter/foot and knuckle. Melt the beef dripping in the stock-pot and gently brown the onion until it colours but doesn't burn. Stir in the carrots and garlic and, after 10 minutes, the mushrooms. Mix in the tripe, add all the other ingredients, and cover with 2.3 litres/4 pts of cold water. Bring to the boil and remove any scum – the blanching will have eliminated a good deal of it – and turn the heat down so that the liquid simmers gently. Leave, partially covered, to cook for 3 hours. Strain.

LAMB AND MUTTON STOCKS

'Of all wild or domesticated animals . . . the lamb is . . . without exception the most useful to man as food.' (Mrs Isabella Beeton, *The Book of Household Management*, 1861)

Lamb and mutton (the name of meat from mature sheep) produce a rich but intrusive and very fatty stock. Consequently both are eschewed as a universal stock, but either or both provide an irreplaceable component of many classic, particularly British, soups. Mutton broth, for example, is the traditional foundation of Scotch broth, the Scottish edition of the French *pot-au-feu*, where mutton replaces beef. These days, when sheep are slaughtered young and small, it is rare to find the stronger-flavoured mutton.

For stock-making purposes, whether the sheep used is lamb or mutton, the best cuts and bones to use are identical. Choose the inexpensive bony cuts, such as neck, shoulder, scrag end and breast. Flavouring, with vegetables and herbs, should be kept basic and left to the main soup ingredients. The addition of marigold petals to the *bouquet garni* adds a whiff of fresh hay! Body and enrichment can be added to the stock by the addition of a split veal knuckle. The effect of browning the bones is more to do with enriching the colour than the flavour.

I would recommend allowing all lamb and mutton stocks to be refrigerated overnight so that the fat sets on top of the stock. It can then be easily lifted off with a spoon: this will be delicious for cooking roast potatoes or lining the pot for an Irish stew.

ALL STOCKS MUST BE SKIMMED FOR FAT BEFORE USE.

Basic Lamb or Mutton Stock

MAKES APPROX. 2 LITRES/3½ PTS

1.4 kg/3 lb mutton or lamb neck, shoulder or breast bones
2 onions, peeled and halved
2 carrots, peeled and roughly chopped

bouquet garni *made with 6 stalks of parsley, 1 sprig of thyme, 2 bayleaves, and if possible 1 tbsp dried or fresh marigold petals*
8 black peppercorns

Cover the bones with 2.8 litres/5 pts of cold water and bring slowly to the boil. The bones will throw off lots of brown/grey scum which should be skimmed carefully. Turn the heat down to a simmer and cook, uncovered, for 30 minutes. Skim again (there will now be pools of liquid fat), add the vegetables, peppercorns and *bouquet garni*, and cook for 2 hours. Strain.

Brown Lamb Stock

MAKES APPROX. 1 LITRE/1¾ PTS

1 kg/1¼ lb neck, shoulder or breast lamb bones
1 onion, peeled and chopped
1 carrot, peeled and chopped
1 stick of celery, peeled and chopped

bouquet garni *made with 4 stalks of parsley, 1 sprig of thyme and 1 bayleaf*
6 peppercorns

Spread the bones out in a roasting-pan and brown, turning to cook evenly, for 20 minutes. Drain off the fat and put the bones in the stock-pot. Brown the vegetables, turning them around so they don't burn, for 5 minutes and add to the stock-pot. Deglaze the roasting-pan with 275 ml/½ pt of boiling water and add this and a further 1.75 litres/3 pts of cold water to the stock-pot. Bring to the boil, skim, turn down the heat and simmer gently, partially covered, for 1 hour. Add the *bouquet garni* and peppercorns and continue cooking for 1½ hours. Strain.

Indian Lamb Stock

This aromatic version is inspired by Julie Sahni's recipe for *yakhni* (meat broth) in her authoritative book *Classic Indian Cooking*. It is a fine example of how stock can be radically affected by varying the flavourings. These fine tunings provide the 'mystery' of inventive soup-making.

MAKES APPROX. 1.4 LITRES/2½ PTS

1.4 kg/3 lb lamb bones or a combination with chicken bones, chopped into 7.5-cm/3-in pieces
1 small onion, quartered
1 large unpeeled clove of garlic, crushed

0.5-cm/¼-in piece of fresh ginger
8 whole cloves
½ tsp black peppercorns
1 bayleaf

Place all the ingredients in the stock-pot and cover with 2.3 litres/ 4 pts of cold water. Bring to the boil over a medium heat. Lower the heat so that the liquid is barely simmering and skim off the quantities of scum that will rise to the surface. Partially cover the pot and simmer for 3 hours.

HAM AND PORK STOCKS

'The swine, because it parts the hoof and is cloven-footed but does not chew the cud is unclean to you; of their flesh you shall not eat, and their carcasses you shall not touch.' (Leviticus 1:4, 1000 BC)

'Pig. This is the king of unclean beasts; whose empire is most universal, whose qualities are least in question: no pig, no lard and consequently no cooking, no ham, no sausages, no *andouilles*, no black pudding, and finally no pork-butchers.' (Grimod de la Reynière, *Calendrier Gastronomique*, 1804)

... And no delicious, strongly-flavoured ham, gammon and bacon stocks that are vital in the making of rich unctuous versions of pea, lentil, cabbage and potato soups. And no mildly sweet, delicate and beautifully textured port stocks that provide the perfect backdrop for all manner of unusual couplings with fruit, and even shellfish.

Pork, whether it is fresh, salted or smoked, is not a great source of stock. Pork and ham stocks aren't often made specially or frequently in the way that most other stocks are. They are usually the by-product of a boiled ham or a poached pork joint. In both cases, if the bone is intact, two stocks can be made, first from the initial cooking liquid and secondly – with some bolstering – by boiling up the leftover bone. All these stocks benefit greatly by being cooked with plenty of carrots and onion, a bayleaf or two, and pungent herbs and spices like thyme, sage, rosemary, allspice and juniper berries.

The inexpensive cuts of pork, such as the hand and spring – also known as the shoulder, and hock or knuckle – make rich, gelatinous stocks that provide a distinctive base for robust winter soups made with dried beans, bacon and vegetables. The pig's trotter, which is rich in natural gelatine, is most often used to enrich other stocks (see page 19) rather than as the *raison d'être* of a broth. Cooked up on its own it makes a good home-made aspic. Pig's tails, chopped and added to the stock-pot, are also a good source of gelatine.

The Chinese, who are great pork eaters, use pork neck bones (spare ribs) to make a watery but recognizably Oriental stock. Even more common is the combination of pork and chicken bones to make a multi-purpose stock (see page 23).

ALL STOCKS MUST BE SKIMMED FOR FAT BEFORE USE.

Ham, Gammon and Bacon Stock

Pork that has been cured, by salting, brining or smoking, is referred to as ham, gammon or bacon. All cures, and there are many refinements, make the meat very salty. Whole hams and large cuts need to be soaked for 24 hours in cold water before any cooking begins. Smaller joints (under 2.3 kg/5 lb) can bypass the all-night soak by being placed in cold water and brought slowly to the boil. This water is then chucked out and the cooking proper begun.

All cuts, with or without bone, should be immersed in cold water, brought to the boil and simmered for 25 minutes to the 450 g/1 lb.

MAKES APPROX. 2.8 LITRES/5 PTS

2.8 kg/6 lb gammon or bacon joint (middle-cut, collar, corner or slipper)
8 peppercorns
2 onions, peeled
3 carrots, peeled

bouquet garni *made with 4 sprigs of thyme, 1 sprig of sage and 1 bayleaf bundled inside 1 halved stick of celery*

Immerse the joint in 3.4 litres /6 pts of cold water and bring slowly to the boil. Empty out the water, rinse off any scum, and refill the pan with cold water. Add the peppercorns and surround the meat with the vegetables. Bring slowly to the boil and skim repeatedly until all the froth is removed. Add the *bouquet garni* and cook at a gentle simmer for 3 hours. Remove the ham and strain the liquid. Taste for saltiness and bear this in mind if you want to reduce and thus strengthen the stock, and when you use the liquid in a soup recipe. If the stock is very salty, return the liquid to the pan with 2 peeled and halved potatoes. Simmer gently for 30 minutes and strain.

Ham Bone Stock

MAKES APPROX. 1.75 LITRES/3 PTS

1 ham bone, cracked
1 onion, peeled and stuck with
* 2 cloves*
2 carrots, peeled
1 large potato, peeled
1 parsnip, peeled
1 leek, washed and halved

bouquet garni made with
* 6 stalks of parsley, 2 sprays*
* of thyme and 1 bayleaf,*
* bundled inside 1 halved stick*
* of celery*
4 black peppercorns

Put all the ingredients in a large pan and cover with 2.8 litres/5 pts of cold water. Bring to the boil, skim if necessary, cover and turn down the heat so that the liquid simmers gently. Cook for 3 hours. Fish out the bone and strain the stock.

Pork Stock

MAKES APPROX. 1.75 LITRES/3 PTS

900 g/2 lb pork neck bones
* (spare ribs)*
1 pork hock, split
1 onion, peeled and halved
1 leek, washed and halved
2 carrots, peeled
4 black peppercorns

bouquet garni made with
* 6 stalks of parsley, 2 sprays*
* of thyme and 1 bayleaf,*
* bundled inside 1 halved stick*
* of celery*
salt

Cover the pork bones and hock with 2.8 litres/5 pts of cold water and bring to the boil. Skim repeatedly until no froth remains. Turn down the heat, add the onion, leek, carrots and peppercorns and simmer gently, uncovered, for 1 hour. Add the *bouquet garni* and simmer for a further 2 hours. Strain, return to a clean pot and boil fiercely to reduce slightly. Season with salt.

This will produce a fatty but eventually gelatinous stock. Chill and refrigerate overnight to let the fat coagulate before removing.

Chinese Pork Stock

MAKES APPROX. 1.75 LITRES/3 PTS

450 g/1 lb scraps of cheap,
* lean pork*
450 g/1 lb pork neck bones
* (spare ribs)*

5-cm × 2.5-cm/2-in × 1-in
* piece of fresh ginger*
salt

Cover the pork meat and bones with 2.3 litres/4 pts of cold water, place over a medium heat and bring to the boil. Skim the surface with a slotted spoon to remove the scum. Turn down the heat and simmer slowly, uncovered, for 1 hour. Add the ginger and partially cover the stock-pot. Continue cooking for a further 2 hours. Strain the stock and season with salt.

FISH STOCKS

'To make a good fish soup, you need four things: stock, roots, thickening and fish balls.' (Professor Knut Faegri, in Alan Davidson, *North Atlantic Seafood*)

Fish stock is quick and cheap to make. It takes 20 minutes to cook, and the main ingredient can be scrounged from the fishmonger. Most of its goodness and flavour comes from the bones and trimmings of fish. Heads and skins are particularly good – cod's head especially – and the addition of a small cleaned whiting or red mullet enriches the stock greatly.

All white fish and most crustaceans make satisfactory fish stocks, but oily fish, such as mackerel, herring, sprat and sardine, aren't suitable, except in special circumstances, and give a bitter, greasy stock. Sole, whiting, turbot and monkfish or angler-fish, which are among the few fish that yield substantial amounts of gelatine, provide stocks with the most body. Different combinations of fish and shellfish can give marked differences in flavour but the *crème de la crème* combination is held to be the combination of sole (Dover in particular), turbot or halibut bones, head and tail, with cod trimmings.

Shrimp and prawn heads and tails give a surprising amount of flavour. These and the shells of lobster and crab, which are cooked and then ground, give body and colour as well as flavour to the group of soups called bisques.

Traditionally, fish stocks are seasoned with finely diced onion, carrot, leek and a *bouquet garni* of parsley, thyme and half a bayleaf. Because fish stocks cook quickly, the vegetables should be finely sliced or diced to release the flavour in the shortest possible time. Delicacy and subtle body can be introduced by using leeks in place of onion, and white wine in place of part or most of the water. Flavour is often enriched with mushroom parings, fennel and celery, but care should be taken not to unbalance the whole.

Court-bouillon, a seasoned, acidulated liquid used to poach fish and shellfish, provides the perfect base for fish stock. Similarly, a wonderful idea would be to poach a whole split lobster, crayfish or langoustine, in, say, minestrone. The soup could be served as an hors-d'oeuvre, with the shellfish to follow.

When a fish stock is reduced it becomes a fish *fumet, glace de poisson* or *demi-glace de poisson*, and small quantities of this essence can be used to enrich a 'used' *court-bouillon* and underpowered fish stock.

Fish stock is never as clear as meat and vegetable stocks, but the clearest stocks are made from very fresh bones and trimmings. To get a clean, fresh-tasting broth it is essential to use fresh, good-quality carcasses and to use them immediately. They should be thoroughly washed under running water, and the gills, viscera and roe, which give a bitterness to the cooked stock, should be removed. Day-old fish bones are improved by blanching (cover with hot water, bring to the boil, strain and refresh in cold water). The carcass should be chopped across the backbone into 5-cm/2-in pieces.

Incidentally, fish stock is not improved by increasing the length of cooking. In fact, overcooking will cause bitterness and make the liquid very cloudy.

Fish stock should be stored covered, and will keep for a few days in the fridge, but the flavours begin to fade after 12 hours. It can be kept successfully for up to 1 month in the freezer.

Basic Fish Stock

MAKES APPROX. 1.4 LITRES/2½ PTS

900 g/2 lb carcasses, heads, tails and trimmings of non-oily fish
150 ml/5 fl oz dry white wine
1 onion or 2 shallots, finely diced
1 carrot, peeled and finely sliced

1 stick of celery, finely sliced
bouquet garni *made with*
1 sprig of thyme, 6 stalks of parsley and 1 sprig of fennel
4 black peppercorns, crushed
salt

Wash fish carcasses and heads under running cold water for 1 hour, removing the gills and viscera. Pack all the ingredients, except the salt, into a stock-pot and cover with 1.75 litres/3 pts of cold water. Bring to the boil, then simmer for 30 minutes. Strain and season with salt.

Court-bouillon

MAKES APPROX. 1.1 LITRES/2 PTS

150 ml/2 fl oz wine vinegar
1 carrot, finely sliced
1 onion, peeled, halved and finely sliced
1 stick of celery, finely sliced

12 peppercorns
1 bayleaf
½ a lemon, sliced
1 tbsp oil
1 tsp salt

Cover all the ingredients with 1.1 litres/2 pts of cold water and bring to the boil. Simmer for 20 minutes and cool before use.

This basic *court-bouillon* is used for poaching fish. After use it can be strained and used in place of water, or combined with white wine, in a fish stock. If used in a stock beware of reduction, because the salt will become saltier.

Nage

MAKES APPROX. 1.4 LITRES/2½ PTS

25 g/1 oz butter
2 carrots, peeled and finely sliced
1 leek, white part only, finely sliced
½ a stick of celery, finely sliced
½ a fennel stalk, trimmed and finely sliced
4 button mushrooms, halved and finely sliced

1 clove of garlic, peeled
50 ml/2 fl oz white wine vinegar
275 ml/10 fl oz dry white wine
bouquet garni made with 4 stalks of parsley and ½ a bayleaf
1 tsp black peppercorns, crushed
25 g/1 oz sea salt

Melt the butter in a large pan, stir in the vegetables and garlic, cover and sweat gently for 10 minutes. Add all the other ingredients and 1.4 litres/2½ pts of cold water. Bring to the boil, then immediately turn down to a simmer and cook for 20 minutes.

This *court-bouillon*, called a *nage* when used to poach shellfish, is infused with a balance of delicate flavours and gives more body to a fish stock than the classic *court-bouillon* (page 42). If used in a stock beware of reduction, because the salt will become saltier.

Gay Bilson's Fish Stock

MAKES APPROX. 2 LITRES/3½ PTS

900 g/2 lb heads and bones of good white fish (turbot, sole, conger, etc.)
50 g/2 oz butter
½ an onion, diced
1 leek, white part only, finely chopped
50 g/2 oz mushrooms, chopped

2 glasses of dry white wine
bouquet garni made with green of leek, sprig of thyme, 4 stalks of parsley and ½ a bayleaf
1 piece of dried orange peel
1 stick of vanilla

Leave the bones and heads to soak in cold water for 3 hours. In a stock-pot, melt the butter and sweat the vegetables gently until they are cooked but not browned. Add the heads and bones (chopped up), heat through, then add the wine. Reduce on a fierce heat, then cover with 2.3 litres/4 pts of cold water, bring to the boil and skim well. Add the *bouquet garni*, orange peel and vanilla, and simmer for 25 minutes. Strain.

Gay Bilson is the chef/proprietress of Berowra Waters in Sydney.

Shellfish Stock

MAKES APPROX. 1.1 LITRES/2 PTS

150 ml/5 fl oz cheap shrimps, or 275 ml/10 fl oz (minimum) heads and bodies of shrimps or prawns used in another recipe
juice of ½ a lemon
150 ml/5 fl oz dry white wine

1 small onion, peeled and diced
1 clove of garlic
bouquet garni *made with 4 stalks of parsley, 1 sprig of thyme and ½ a bayleaf*
4 peppercorns, crushed
salt

In a mortar, lightly pound the shellfish and transfer to a stock-pot. Cover with the lemon juice and white wine and boil fiercely for 2 minutes. Add all the other ingredients except the salt, and pour in 1.1 litres/2 pts of cold water. Bring to the boil, skim, and simmer for 15 minutes. Strain and season with salt.

Steamboat Stock

MAKES APPROX. 4.5 LITRES/8 PTS
50 ml/2 fl oz sesame oil
2 raw chicken carcasses and any skin or trimmings
2 cloves of garlic, peeled and crushed
5-cm/2-in piece of fresh ginger, crushed

2 stalks of celery, chopped
5 spring onions, chopped
6 peppercorns, crushed
350 g/12 oz prawn or shrimp heads and shells
salt

Heat the sesame oil and when nearly smoking fry the chicken bones and skin, the garlic and the ginger. Cook, stirring around, for 3 minutes before adding the celery and spring onions, and cook for a further 3 minutes. Cover with 4.5 litres/8 pts of cold water and bring to the boil. Skim, add the peppercorns, and lower the heat to cook the broth at a simmer for 1 hour. Stir in the prawn shells and heads and cook for a further 30 minutes. Strain and season with salt.

This delicious Oriental-style stock is the perfect base for the many Thai soup recipes. It can be adjusted with lemon grass, curry leaves, etc. using the 'Stock-pot Flavour Guide' on pages 9–14.

Dashi 1/Japanese Stock

MAKES APPROX. 1.1 LITRES/2 PTS
10 g/⅓ oz kombu *seaweed*   soy sauce
15 g/½ oz bonito flakes

Add the *kombu* to 1.1 litres/2 pts of cold water and bring slowly to the boil. Just before the water comes to the boil, remove and reserve the *kombu*. Add the bonito flakes, bring the water up to a full boil and immediately remove from the heat. Allow the flakes to settle, then strain through a muslin-lined sieve, reserving the flakes. Season with soy. The once-used *kombu* and bonito flakes can be re-used to make *dashi 2*.

This light *dashi* has a subtle yet distinctive flavour and is suitable for clear soups.

Kombu, also called *konbu*, kelp and laminaria, is a large-leaved, brownish-green seaweed commonly used in Japanese cooking. Dried *kombu*, sold in neat sheets, is available in some health food stores, and in Japanese and other Oriental food shops.

Bonito, a member of the mackerel family, is filleted, smoked, dried and fermented until it looks like a piece of orange-coloured wood. Its salty, concentrated flavour is used as a seasoning in soups and it is one of the basic ingredients of *dashi*. Bonito flakes – *hana-gatsuo* – are sold in small packets or large bags.

Dashi 2

MAKES APPROX. 1.1 LITRES/2 PTS
10 g/⅓ oz kombu *seaweed*   *10–15 g/⅓–½ oz dried bonito*
15 g/½ oz bonito flakes   *flakes*
  reserved from making dashi 1

Add the reserved *kombu* and bonito flakes to 1.75 litres/3 pts of cold water and bring to the boil. Simmer for 20 minutes, uncovered. Add the dried bonito flakes and immediately remove from the heat. Allow the flakes to settle and strain.

Dashi 2 is used in soups that require a stronger-flavoured stock.

Stock-pot Information

᧥

CLARIFICATION

Stock that is made carefully, using good fresh ingredients, and thoroughly skimmed and strained (see basic guidelines on pages 7–9) will be relatively clear and fresh-tasting. Most of the time perfect clarity is not important in a stock. Far more important is making sure that all the fat has been removed. Some soups, however, demand a stock that is crystal-clear, and to that end the liquid has to be clarified. This involves a second cooking with other ingredients which 'catch' the impurities that cloud the liquid.

Egg-white and egg-shell are the most effective clarifying agents and can be used to clear any stock. Usually, however, in soup-making, this second cooking is only bothered with if the end result is a consommé (the French term for a clear soup), where the egg is combined with other ingredients that help to create the flavour of the finished soup.

There is more information about clarification in the 'Clear Soups' section on page 309, but this basic recipe can be applied, with varying degrees of success and without affecting flavour, to any stock. See page 32–5 (basic beef stock and strengthening and clarifying second beef stock).

Basic Clarification

NB: 1 egg-white and egg-shell are sufficient to clarify up to 1.1 litres/ 2 pts of stock.

MAKES 1.4 LITRES/2½ PTS
2 egg-whites and their shells *½ a stick of celery, diced*
½ a small onion or leek, diced *1.4 litres/2½ pts cold stock*
1 small carrot, diced

Rinse the egg-shells and crush. In a stock-pot mix together the egg-whites, egg-shells, onion, carrot, celery and 1 ice-cube or 1 tbsp of very cold water (the clarification mixture works better if it is well chilled). Pour in the cold, meticulously skimmed and strained stock, and stir or whisk continuously till the mixture comes to the boil, when the egg-whites and other ingredients will form a white crust. At this point turn the heat down so that the stock merely simmers, and leave for 20 minutes so that the crust can 'collect' all the particles in the stock.

Have ready a bowl set with a fine sieve lined with a linen tea-towel or several layers of muslin previously wrung out in cold water. Clear a hole in the middle of the crust and, taking care not to break it up and disturb the liquid, ladle the stock into the sieve.

KEEPING STOCK

'From a food hygiene point of view the use of a stock-pot is not one of the best practices, particularly if you don't maintain a fairly high temperature. To have a stock-pot which is continually on the go or being reheated and cooled down is inconsistent with our normal advice that you use something once or only reheat it once at the very most.' (Mike Jacob, Chief Environmental Health Officer, Department of Health, September 1991)

One of the effects of the Food Safety Act 1990, the biggest overhaul of British food safety laws since the war, has been a highlighting of the inherent dangers of the stock-pot. The main problem is the time it takes for stock to cool down to a temperature that allows the liquid to be refrigerated. In the hours it can take to cool, the liquid passes through temperature changes that encourage maximum bacterial growth. If the stock is properly re-heated, most of the bacteria will be killed but, according to Mike Jacob, 'the main risk in a stock-pot is with *clostridium perfringens*. That is the sort of organism which has been found in a number of institutional outbreaks of food poisoning ... simply because of the reheating factor.' *If* they wish to continue making their own stocks, professional kitchens must either invest in a blast chiller – which costs anything from £3,000 to £4,500 – or change their stock-making routines.

In a domestic kitchen, where quantities are far smaller and cooling is much faster, the risks are almost negligible. However, Mike Jacob's comments highlight two important points: always cool stock quickly and thoroughly before refrigerating, and be vigilant about the length of time stock is kept in the fridge.

Stock keeps for up to 3 days in a well-chilled fridge. After that, to be on the safe side, it should be boiled up daily and cooled before returning to the fridge. It should be skimmed of fat, covered, and kept in a plastic, glass or ceramic container. Never store unstrained.

To save space in my often overcrowded fridge I usually boil down my stock by at least a quarter, sometimes half, the quantity. This reduction has the effect of concentrating the stock and intensifying the flavour. It can be brought back up to quantity by adding water. Bones should always be removed and the stock thoroughly sieved before reducing.

Glaze is the culinary term for meat stock reduced down to a syrupy consistency. It is more commonly referred to by its French culinary name, *glace* (*de viande*). The fish equivalent is *glace de poisson*. *Glace* cools to a jellied rubbery state and can be used like a stock-cube and brought up to quantity with water when needed. Jellied stock keeps longer, up to a week in the fridge, but freezes well and stays in near perfect condition for up to 3 months.

When reduced stock is frozen it is essential to make a note of the reduction ratio on the label. It's useful to freeze stock and *glace* in different-sized containers. Polythene bags, old yoghurt pots, ice-cream containers and ice-cube trays (freeze and then turn out into polythene bags) are ideal for small quantities. Bags should be supported inside a deep-sided receptacle while you ladle in the broth. Be sure to dry the exterior of the bags so that they don't stick together when frozen.

The deep freeze is also useful for building up a collection of potential material for stock, especially poultry, game carcasses and giblets, and lean trimmings from raw beef and lamb.

FACTORY-MADE LIQUID STOCK

Some high-class food stores and delicatessen have sold German and Scandinavian bottled stock for years. Sales, I suspect, aren't particularly high because the importation costs make them an extravagant alternative to home-made stock or stock-cubes.

In 1989 David Chambers, the chef of Piccadilly's Oak Room, Le Meridien Hotel, decided the time was right to go into production with a double-concentration, professional kitchen-style range of stocks. He called it Fonds de Cuisine, and devised a way of pasteurizing the stock in disposable pots that kept it fresh for 28 days; it was also suitable for home freezing.

The range was well marketed and sold too well, too quickly. In mid-1991 the under-developed company folded.

Chambers and his partner, Anton Edelmann, chef of the Savoy, approached various large catering concerns and in the end Baxters of Scotland, one of the largest producers of ready-made soups, bought the name. Part of the deal was that the chefs had to sign an undertaking not to get involved in a similar venture.

In November 1991 Sainsbury, who used to sell Fonds de Cuisine, introduced their own range of fresh stocks on a trial basis. Like Fonds de Cuisine, they contain no additives or added salt, and are thoroughly skimmed for fat. At an average £1 for 285 ml/approx. ½ pt, they are an expensive way of making soup but they do give good results. Other multiples have followed suit.

STOCK-CUBES

'... the jelly grow of a gluish substance ...
Put it into little sweetmeat pots till it is
quite cold; then you may take it out and
wrap it in flannel and afterward in paper
and it will keep many years. A piece the
bigness of a nutmeg will make half a pint of
broth. The whole leg of veal, unless very
large, will not make a piece of glue bigger
than your hand. It is made into broth by
pouring hot water on it.' (A. Blencowe, *The
Receipt Book*, 1694)

These early attempts at the stock-cube, known as veal glue and later
as pocket, portable or traveller's soup, were made by evaporating
meat broth to the consistency of thick glue. Today, nearly three
centuries later, their commercial equivalent, the powders, pastes and
cubes sold under the Knorr, Oxo, Friggs, Morga, Maggi, Hugli and
Vecon labels, rely extensively on preservatives, stabilizers and flavour
enhancers, and don't bear comparison with the real thing.

All of them, and we all have our preferences, noticeably affect the
flavour of soup to a lesser or greater degree. The most troublesome
ingredient is monosodium glutamate (MSG), a widely used and very
efficient flavour-enhancer. Although it works by intensifying other
flavours and has no taste of its own, its cloying tang is easy to detect.
Some people have violent reactions against MSG, and small quantities
can produce a condition known as Chinese restaurant syndrome.
Maurice Henssen, author of *E For Additives*, describes the symptoms
as 'heart palpitations, headaches, dizziness, muscle tightening,
nausea, weakness of the upper arms, pains in the neck and symptoms
similar to migraine'. Salt, both a preservative and a flavour-enhancer,
is almost always present.

However, the catering giants – Nestlé, Brooke Bond, Caterplan,
Book Fitch, Dohler UK, Major International and Italbrokers – who
produce dehydrated stocks have the technology to produce bouillons
which rely less on flavourings and other additives, but are reluctant
to do so. The problem is that to make stocks with higher ratios of
meat, fish, poultry and vegetables would push prices skyward. Ironically, it is the temperature control laws introduced by the Food
Safety Act 1990, which affect all commercial kitchens, that could
lead to a 'clean-up' of dehydrated stock-cubes, granules and powders.

The law specifies that hot food has to be kept at or above 63° C
and cold food at below 8° C. Large quantities of liquid – and many
restaurants prepare stock in 20–50 gallon batches – take a long
time to cool and provide the perfect incubation conditions for organ-
isms that cause food poisoning. (See 'Keeping Stock', pages 47–8.)

Consequently there is a move, started by institutional kitchens and followed by large hotel groups, away from the stock-pot and its potentially inherent health risks, towards stock products. The bottomless stock-pot – *la marmite perpetuelle* – will definitely become a thing of the past. Hopefully, those restaurants who reduce or eliminate their own stock-making will demand dehydrated equivalents that have a natural taste, and these will eventually hit the domestic market.

The increasing trend towards vegetarian cooking and the growing popularity of salt-free and lower-salt products has already had a marked effect on the contents of the stock-cube. Nevertheless, there isn't one I can wholeheartedly recommend.

GETTING BY WITH STOCK-CUBES

Stock- or bouillon-cubes can't replace home-made stock, but they are a handy stand-by when used with caution. A small amount of chicken or vegetable stock made with a cube, added at the end of cooking, can 'beef-up' a weak home-made stock or water-based soup. When used in place of stock, they should always be diluted with more liquid than specified. Salt should never be added until the end of cooking. Using vegetable cooking water instead of plain water, adding a splash of wine, and/or simmering with a finely chopped carrot, onion, celery stalk and sprig of parsley, will work wonders for the ubiquitous manufactured flavour of all stock-cubes. Tom yam Thai stock-cubes, sold by Oriental grocers, are good enough to pass as a soup when beefed-up with a few spices and scraps of shell-fish or chicken.

WATER INSTEAD OF STOCK

'The chief thing to remember is that all these soups – unless otherwise specified – must be made with plain water. When made with the addition of stock they lose all character and cease to be what they were intended to be. The fresh pleasant taste is lost owing to the addition of meat stock, and the value of the soup from an economical point of view is also lost.'
(Marcel Boulestin, *What Shall We Have Today?*, 1931)

Many of the soups in this book, soups of all types, don't need stock to bolster their deliciousness. Some, as Boulestin so aptly pinpoints, would lose their character and become an entirely different soup.

PART TWO

⌇

The Embellishment
of Soup

'Do not be afraid of simplicity. If you have
a cold chicken for supper, why cover it with
a tasteless white sauce which makes it look
like a pretentious dish on the buffet table at
some fancy dress ball?' (Marcel Boulestin,
Simple French Cooking for English Homes,
1923)

The Embellishment of Soup

This section of the book is about the things that can be added to or served with a finished soup to alter its being. These additions, or embellishments, come in the form of thickeners, fortifiers, garnishes and accompaniments.

Their role can be twofold: many make more of a soup, yet embellishment is also the fun side of soup-making that gives plenty of scope for imagination.

Artful and intelligent use of embellishment, as opposed to gilding the lily, can transform the same soup beyond recognition. For example, curried parsnip soup is wonderful served garnished with a scattering of crisped bacon fragments, croûtons, freshly chopped parsley, and a swirl of cream, but it is just as good on its own, or with just one of these garnishes. Equally, this rich and robust soup is scrumptious when garnished with deep-fried parsley or celeriac crisps or accompanied by well-buttered garlic bread served hot from the oven.

Embellishment can make a meal of an otherwise insubstantial soup. Eggs, for example, can be used to change the texture, to flavour and to give richness to most soups. The most common use, not just in soup-making, is when raw egg yolks are whisked with cream to enrich and thicken. Eggs can give body and interest to a simple soup in other ways. They can be poached in the soup just before serving, or cooked as an omelette or pancake and sliced finely to be sprinkled into the soup as a garnish. They are also a key ingredient in many different dumplings and can be used as a vehicle for accentuating or complementing a soup's flavour.

In many instances – bread is the most versatile example – the embellishment can fulfil all manner of other functions. For example, dried breadcrumbs can be used to thicken, bread crusts feature frequently as sops and toppings, and when cubed and sautéed, bread becomes the ubiquitous croûton. As an accompaniment, bread can be made specially or tailored to suit particular soups. The style of bread served as an accompaniment also alters the perception of the soup it accompanies. For example, wafer-thin Melba toast, crusty ciabatta, and pan-fried, slightly sweet, bright yellow corn bread all bring a different dimension to the presentation, flavour and texture of the same soup. A secondary aspect of garnish is the embellishment of the breads and toasts served with the soup.

However, there should always be a point to all the ingredients used in the making of a soup. If, for example, you are making a subtly balanced soup, its delicacy would be ruined by a strongly-flavoured stock. And the same is true of the myriad ways that a soup can be decorated and enriched.

Part of the joy of soup-making is the opportunity the finished 'canvas' provides to turn even the most modest soup into a minor work of art. Zen and the art of soup decoration has unlimited potential. Almost anything goes so long as the embellishment relates in some way to the taste and/or the aroma, as well as the visual appeal, of the soup.

For example, a simple broth can be dramatically changed with a garnish of peeled and diced fresh tomato and a scattering of freshly chopped parsley or mint. Similarly, a smooth, rich, puréed soup looks stunning when garnished with a swirl of a contrasting coloured purée. Texture could be introduced with a 'hair' of deep-fried pasta, vegetables or crisps, balanced on a dollop of cream or yoghurt. Equally, a selection of complementary garnishes can be served at the table for guests to make up their own 'compositions'.

A small amount of a luxury ingredient, such as a julienne of pan-fried scallops, an oyster, or a few grains of caviare, can be used to transform humble soups and add interest to a clear intensely-flavoured soup.

Garnish is also a way of giving drama and surprise to a soup. The latest visual shock tactic, currently fashionable in foodie circles and sure to filter down to the dinner-party circuit, is the use of edible gold leaf as a garnish. Imagine, for example, the impact of a large square of gold in the middle of snowy-white congee, the Chinese rice-based gruel.

The Orient, and Japan in particular, has a highly developed visual sense about food presentation. Japanese soups, particularly the clear soups called *suimono*, are composed like a picture, with scraps of food and sprays of herbs suspended in a clear liquid. Such elegance and precision negates the need for other embellishment.

It is fun, too, to echo this Japanese technique by creating picture soups like Rock Pool, devised by Antony Worrall-Thompson for his restaurant, 190 Queensgate, near Hyde Park. In the pool (a lightly jellied consommé made from smoked lobster shells and fish stock) 'swim' baby clams, mussels and crayfish. From the depths rises a miniature rock pool, draped with seaweed, where sits, and I kid you not, a baby octopus dangling his legs in the pool.

Many soups that feature in the main body of the recipes here incorporate their own embellishments, with recipes that inter-relate to the soup ingredients. You may wish to try out different garnishes – my selection of ideas and recipes is merely a drop in the ocean.

Embellishment to Go in Soup

*'That's hotch-potch – and that cocky-leeky
– the twa best soups in nature. Broon soup's
moss-water – and white soup's like scauded
(scalded) milk wi' worms in't. But see, Sirs,
hoo the ladle stauns o'isel in the potch.'
(Noctes Ambrosianae, 1822)*

THICKENERS

*'. . . besides, there is a great art in thicken-
ing, and many nice dishes have been spoilt
owing to cooks being ignorant of the proper
method.' (Cassell's Shilling Cookery, edited
by A. G. Payne, 1902)*

My first attempts at soup-making were ruined by a lack of understanding of the need to get rid of fat from stock, and by not knowing how
to thicken the broth without ending up with globs of rubberized flour
clinging to the vegetables.

Plenty of soups don't need thickening, and many, including most
vegetable purées and minestrone-style stews, generate their own
viscosity.

Often, though, a soup needs something to pull it together, to bind
the solids and liquids to make a liaison. The liaison gives the soup an
even consistency, ensures smoothness of texture and holds the
ingredients in suspension. Without it the soup would separate and
some ingredients would settle at the bottom of the tureen.

The liaison can be made at any stage in the soup-making process –
it may need to happen more than once – and different techniques
apply at different times, and for different types of soup.

The most commonly used thickeners are flour and eggs, often used
together. These and many of the alternatives, including bread,
pounded nuts and pulses, also add nutritive value and give body to a
soup. They also affect the flavour.

Puréed vegetables, particularly potatoes, are a useful alternative to
flour-based liaisons, especially in low-calorie soups. But to a certain
extent, the type of thickener used is dictated by the style of the soup.
For example, using a potato to thicken a clear soup will make the
broth cloudy, whereas an egg and cream liaison will give it a velvety

sheen. However, arrowroot or *kuzu/kudzu* will thicken without colouring, and give a glossy finish.

Also see 'Butters, Creams, Yoghurt and Eggs' (pages 61–8).

REDUCTION

Soups that don't contain cream, yoghurt, or egg can be effectively thickened by reduction. Merely simmer the liquid, uncovered, for 20–30 minutes, keeping an eye on progress. Don't forget that boiling also concentrates the flavour and intensifies the effects of salt. Saltiness can be corrected by adding a couple of peeled, halved, uncooked potatoes and simmering, covered, for 15–30 minutes; remove the potatoes before serving the soup.

Soups made with a high proportion of starchy foods such as root vegetables, chickpeas, lentils and other pulses will thicken naturally if allowed to stand for a few hours; ideally leave them overnight.

PURÉEING

A thin soup with meat, fish and/or vegetables in it can be transformed and thickened at the same time by puréeing. Either pass the whole lot through a fine sieve or whizz it up in the blender.

Puréed root vegetables, mashed without butter, cream or milk, are an effective thickener in some soups. The most widely used is potato; either raw, when a medium-sized potato is blended with 1 litre/1¾ pts of water or stock, or cooked and puréed, in which case a couple of tablespoons can be whisked into the soup at any point during the soup-making process. 1 tbsp of instant mashed potato to 570 ml/1 pt of hot soup has the same effect.

Plantains can be grated and cooked in stock as a thickener; they impart a sweet starchiness.

GRAINS, CEREALS AND FLOURS

Any flour, be it from grain or cereal, can be used in different ways to thicken liquid. The important thing to remember is that the flour must be thoroughly cooked: either before it goes into the soup, or after it has been added to the soup, in which case the liquid must be brought to the boil and cooked for at least 5 minutes. Otherwise the soup will taste starchy and dull.

Different flours have different thickening abilities: 1 tsp of potato flour or arrowroot, or 2 tsp of cornflour or rice flour, have the thickening power of 1 tbsp of wheat flour.

As a general rule, use the same proportion of flour as fat. If you are using flour to take up the fat used at the beginning of cooking (to sweat or sauté the vegetables), make sure the mixture is thoroughly incorporated and allow it to bubble up before you whisk in a little, and then the bulk, of the liquid. This is a variation on making a roux, where flour is blended into melted butter then mixed carefully and smoothly with a little liquid.

ROUX

To make a roux, take equal quantities of butter and flour; 25 g/1 oz is sufficient to thicken 1 litre/1¾ pts. Melt the fat, then draw the pan aside from the heat and blend the flour smoothly with the fat. Reheat and cook slightly, being careful not to let the mixture overheat and become oily, or to let it colour if it is required for a white soup. With the pan away from the heat add 275 ml/10 fl oz/½ pt of liquid gradually, stirring it in gently (or the soup will be lumpy), and boil for at least 7–10 minutes. Overcooking brown roux will make the starch change chemically and lose some of its thickening property; the fat separates from it, rising to the surface, giving a thin and greasy soup.

A nuttiness of flavour and colour can be achieved by first lightly roasting the flour.

BEURRE MANIÉ AND CRÈME MANIÉE

The same result, but giving extra velvetiness and flavour, comes from using a *beurre manié* or *crème maniée*, where uncooked butter or thick cream is mixed with flour and added in little bits to a simmering liquid. This is usually introduced at the end of cooking; go on adding small amounts, whisking thoroughly, until the desired thickness is achieved.

To make a *beurre manié*, take 1/3 flour to 2/3 butter, and using your fingertips (cold hands are best), work the flour into the chilled butter.

To make a *crème maniée*, take 1/3 flour to 2/3 double cream or *crème fraîche*, and using a wooden spoon, blend the flour into the cream.

POTATO FLOUR (FÉCULE)

Potato flour (*fécule*), which is rather like cornflour, is most chefs' favourite uncooked starch liaison because it has no flavour. Allow between 2 and 8 tbsp of the flour dissolved in cold water or white wine to every 1 litre/1¾ pts of liquid, depending on the desired thickness of the soup. Gradually add to the simmering liquid and cook gently for 2–5 minutes.

GROUND RICE/RICE FLOUR

These can be stirred directly into a hot liquid without it going lumpy.

ARROWROOT

This is the starch from the cassava plant. It has no flavour and should be added to soups at the end of cooking because it breaks down after prolonged cooking and ceases to thicken. Like *cornflour* or *cornstarch*, which it resembles, it should be slaked in a little water, then added to hot liquid and stirred in while thickening. The result is slightly glutinous but clearer than a flour-thickened soup.

KUZU/KUDZU

This starch is processed from the root of the *kudzu* vine and is much used in Japan where the plant grows wild. It is interchangeable with arrowroot.

BREAD

Breadcrumbs made with stale bread can be used as a thickener, as they will hold a small amount of fat in suspension. They are extensively used in Tuscan and Spanish soups, and are more effective when mixed into the yolk of an egg before adding to the soup. Similarly, ground almonds, hazelnuts and walnuts are used to thicken soups in Spain and Mexico.

EGGS AND CREAM

Egg-yolks mixed with stock, vinegar, milk, or cream are added to the soup just before it is served. Sufficient heat is necessary to coagulate the egg albumen and to form the liaison, but the soup must not be at boiling point when it is added, or allowed to boil afterwards, or it will curdle. Add 1–2 egg-yolks stirred into 50 ml/2 fl oz of liquid for every 570 ml/1 pt of soup.

LIQUIDS

'Nobody has ever been able to find out why the English regard a glass of wine added to a soup or stew as a reckless foreign extravagance and at the same time spend pounds on bottled sauces, gravy powders, soup cubes, ketchups and artificial flavourings. If every kitchen contained a bottle each of red wine, white wine and inexpensive port for cooking, hundreds of store cupboards could be swept clean for ever from the cluttering debris of commercial sauce bottles and all synthetic aids to flavouring.' (Elizabeth David, *French Country Cooking*, 1951)

This section is about the liquids, not just alcoholic ones, that give soups a lift. Some, like those in the 'Sauces, Salsas, Pestos and Pastes' section (pages 68–75), are stretching the liquid definition to the limit, but all can be poured, whisked or stirred into the soup at some point during the cooking, or just before serving, or at the table.

All these additions are about enriching, giving body and distinctiveness to soups of all types. Some – flavoured butters are a good example – alter its texture and thicken at the same time. Ways of thickening broth are explored in their own section.

ALCOHOL, VINEGAR AND OLIVE OIL

ALCOHOL

Alcohol added to soup will pep it up for two reasons – the flavour and the alcohol content. The smell will also change, but that's a consequence, not a reason. Sometimes it is added to soup partly for reasons of colouring – Madeira in consommé is the classic example.

Some recipes specify adding a measure of wine or fortified wine just before serving. If you want to cook out the alcohol first, quickly bring it to the boil and let it bubble for a moment; the flavour of the wine will remain intact, in fact the essence is softer. Adding spirit that won't be boiled for several minutes during the soup's cooking process is usually intentional; bullshots, for example, wouldn't be the same without their alcoholic kick.

WINE AND CIDER

'Après le potage un coup de vin vole un écu du médecin (After the soup, a glass of wine robs the doctor of a fee)' is a French saying that is manifested as *faire le chabrol*: this is when the last few mouthfuls of hot broth are diluted with a half a glass of wine. Sometimes the wine is poured into the bowl before the soup; this is called making a *chabrol*, and is the reason why so many Frenchmen drink, rather than spoon, their soup from the bowl.

Wine usually gets incorporated into my soups on an entirely *ad hoc* basis – if I happen to be holding a glass when I'm cooking the soup and/or if I think it will improve the end result. Some recipes in this book specify particular wines in specific soups, but generally speaking, discretion is the better part of valour; the style and colour of the wine will be reflected in the taste and look of the soup. Remember that because alcohol has a higher boiling point than water it needs to bubble away in soup for several minutes to burn off the alcohol.

If a recipe specifies marinating meat or deglazing a pan with wine, this will enrich the finished soup but no alcohol will remain when the soup is finished.

If using cider in your soup, remember not to use an iron or tin pan – it will turn the cider black and your soup an odd colour.

FORTIFIED WINE

Madeira, sherry and marsala, and sometimes port, are used as flavour-enhancers and to give a rich amber colour to many clear soups and consommés. When added to jellied consommé the wine is whisked in when the jelly is nearly cold. In this case, the proportion of wine to soup is important: ½ a glass of wine to each 1 litre/1¾ pints of jelly.

I found the following recipe in Dorothy Hartley's *Food In England*: 'At the end of August, fill a wide-necked bottle with basil and cover with sherry. Cork and stand for ten days, drain off the sherry, and refill the bottle with fresh basil till the sherry is well impregnated. A spoonful of this sherry should be put into mock turtle soup just before serving.'

Chilli Sherry

This recipe was concocted when a surfeit of chillis and the dregs of a sherry bottle happened at the same time.

150 ml/¼ pt sherry   *4 dried red chillis*

Leave the chillis to soak in boiling water for 10 minutes. Drain, poke into a small bottle or jar, and top up with sherry. Use with discretion.

SPIRITS
A measure of vodka poured into a cup of consommé is the perfect pick-me-up. Make your own flavoured vodkas by steeping herbs/and or spices in the vodka. Leave to infuse for at least one month.

VINEGAR
One of my favourite tales in Elizabeth David's book *An Omelette and a Glass of Wine* centres on a quasi-French restaurant in London in the late 1950s. Mrs David keeps coming back to the question of the salad's dressing, and it isn't until the end that we discover that its 'secret' is malt vinegar. Since those days much has changed in our eating habits and in our expectations of food. Vinegar, once something the British put on chips and beetroot, is now a specialized subject. Wine vinegar, the first exotic type, has gone varietal, but has been upstaged by sherry vinegar, balsamic vinegar, and fruit-, spice- and herb-flavoured vinegars. Then there is the Oriental range of vinegars: the various rice vinegars which range from mellow to acidic and from colourless to deep brown.

The word 'vinegar' comes from the French *vin aigre* – sour wine. Without going into great detail, that is exactly what vinegar is. It is also made from hops (malt vinegar), fermented apples (cider vinegar) and fermented rice. Its culinary use has crossed all cultural boundaries and it is one of the earliest forms of seasoning and of preserving food. While raspberry vinegar, balsamic vinegar and rice vinegar distilled with grated ginger may be new to our kitchens, they've all been around for centuries.

In soup-making, vinegar can be used to great effect as a last-minute seasoning. It evaporates when vigorously boiled and, used with discretion, doesn't leave a sharp, acidic taste.

Without getting too rarified, a splash of flavoured wine or cider vinegar (malt vinegar is usually unsuitable) will give an edge and hint of flavouring that can lift a soup in the same way as wine.

Proprietary brands of flavoured vinegars tend to be expensive, but there is no mystery to making fruit, herb and spice vinegars at home. Fruit vinegars are made by steeping soft fruit (raspberries, strawberries, blackcurrants and pears) in wine or cider vinegar for 4 days in a covered bowl. The vinegar is then strained off, boiled for 10 minutes, re-bottled in sterilized bottles and sealed. There will be some loss by evaporation. Herb vinegars are even easier: just push a few branches of your chosen herb – rosemary, tarragon and thyme are most popular – into the bottle, and leave for at least a week before using.

OLIVE OIL

A swirl of olive oil stirred into soup at the end of cooking will give it a rich, thick and full-bodied flavour. It also adds to the nutritive value of the soup. Any olive oil will make a difference; the better quality you use, the better the result.

My greatest indulgence is olive oil flavoured with lemon. A couple of years ago I was given a bottle as a gift and I'm now hooked – despite the exorbitant price – on Granverde Colonna from Principe Francesso Colonna's estate in the Molise hills of central Italy. It comes in a corked and sealed thin square bottle and has a golden olive-green colour. It's made from hand-picked olives and untreated lemons that are processed together without the use of heat or pressure, and it is nectar. A slosh of Granverde Colonna transforms dull lentil or vegetable soups; in fact it works like magic on most vegetables, salads and pulse-based dips. For a list of stockists and for mail order inquiries, contact The Oil Merchant, 47 Ashchurch Grove, London W12 9BU.

BUTTERS, CREAMS, YOGHURT AND EGGS

BUTTERS

A knob of good, unsalted butter stirred into a water-based vegetable soup will enrich it beyond belief. When you want to enrich and enhance, or add flavour, a quick, easy solution is to place a spoonful of flavoured butter at the bottom of the tureen, or bowl, before you pour over the soup. These compound butters, made by mixing one or more puréed or chopped substances into uncooked butter, can also be whisked into a soup just before serving, and act as the final liaison. Savoury butters are also a way of boosting or injecting colour, and of reinforcing the soup's flavours with the same but uncooked ingredient/s.

These butters can be made when the various herbs and leaves are in season and frozen for out-of-season use.

Butters made with onions, garlic and chives should be made as required, because these ingredients eventually turn butter rancid.

Almond Butter

75 g/2½ oz blanched and   150 g/5 oz butter, softened
  washed almonds

Pound the almonds to a fine paste, using a few drops of cold water to prevent them turning into oil. Cream into the softened butter, and rub through a fine sieve.

Sweet Garlic Butter

Despite its high proportion of garlic, this butter is so called because when garlic is boiled, rather than sautéed or used raw, its flavour is softened and sweetened. This particularly good recipe comes from Greens Restaurant in San Francisco. Make it from fresh, new garlic and stir it into a water-based vegetable soup just before serving. It loses its mild fresh quality if overcooked, and its delicacy if kept for longer than 8 hours.

12 cloves of garlic, peeled   ¼ tsp white wine vinegar
salt and pepper   a pinch of ground cayenne
5 tbsp unsalted butter,
  softened

In a small saucepan, parboil the garlic for 1 minute. Discard the water, return the garlic to the pan and cover with water. Add ¼ tsp salt and simmer gently for 20 minutes, or until the water has almost entirely evaporated and the garlic is soft.

Transfer the garlic to a bowl and mash to a paste. Add the butter, vinegar, cayenne, a pinch of salt and one of pepper. Mix well, transfer to a small bowl, cover tightly and store in a cool place until needed.

Lemon Butter

110 g/4 oz butter, creamed   rind of ½ a lemon, finely
salt and white pepper   grated

Cream the butter, season with salt and pepper and mix in the lemon rind.

Herb Butter

The following is a favourite combination, but you can mix and match your herbs according to what you have available. Keep approximately the same proportions of herb to butter.

1 dsp marjoram, finely
 chopped
1 dsp thyme, finely chopped
2 tbsp flat-leaf parsley, finely
 chopped
¼ tsp lemon peel, finely
 grated

1 shallot, finely chopped
1 small clove of garlic,
 minced
1 tsp lemon juice
110 g/4 oz unsalted butter,
 softened

Work all the ingredients into the softened butter. Cover and refrigerate.

Lime Butter

110 g/4 oz butter
4 tsp lime juice
4 tsp lime peel, finely grated

2 tsp chives, chopped
a pinch of grated fresh ginger
a pinch of powdered thyme

Cream the butter and beat in the flavourings.

Pimiento Butter

This is one of my favourite butters and is a standby used in all manner of soups. I like the smoky flavour of oven-baked peppers, but you can soften them in butter if it's more convenient. This recipe also works well with bottled or canned pimiento. It can be livened up with a touch of chilli pepper paste stirred in at the end.

2 sweet red or yellow peppers
2 large cloves of garlic,
 unpeeled

110 g/4 oz unsalted butter,
 creamed

Pre-heat the oven to 475° F/240° C/Gas Mark 9 and bake the peppers for 20 minutes (the skin will blister and go black but the flesh will be soft). After the first 10 minutes put the garlic in the oven as well. Peel, core and de-seed the peppers, peel the garlic, and pound or liquidize both to a purée. Drain in a sieve before blending the purée into the butter.

Printanier Butter

This can be made with any lightly cooked green vegetables and is a good way of using up trimmings. Always use equal quantities of butter and vegetables.

50 g/2 oz asparagus tips　　　*50 g/2 oz green beans*
50 g/2 oz fresh green peas　　　*150 g/6 oz butter, softened*

Cook the vegetables in salted water, drain, and dry. Pound the vegetables to a pulp, rub through a fine sieve, and mix the vegetable paste into the butter.

CREAM

The golden rule when using cream in soup-making is never to allow the soup anywhere near boiling point once the cream has been added. If you do, the cream will split and curdle.

The exceptions to this rule are those creams with a high fat content – clotted cream (minimum 55%), double cream (48%) and *crème fraîche* (minimum 35%). Even so, these are best added off the heat and then the soup brought slowly back to the boil.

Cream is more stable in a liquid when it is mixed with eggs and/or flour before it is introduced. Creams in the middle band of fat content, with at least 8%, can be stabilized with a cornflour solution (see later), but I'm not sure the end results are worth the effort. It is, though, a useful rescue recipe and works on other low-fat cultured products including yoghurt.

Double cream (minimum 48%) and *crème fraîche* (minimum 35%) can be boiled without curdling and are interchangeable in most soup recipes. *Crème fraîche* has a mildly sour, slightly nutty flavour that gives it a richer and more complex taste. In the days before pasteurization, the French used to leave their cream to mature naturally, giving the lactic acids and natural ferments time to thicken and flavour the cream. These days this effect is simulated by re-introducing a ferment to the cream after pasteurization. *Crème fraîche* is widely available in Britain but there are various ways to make a close approximation. The most authentic, which can also be boiled and keeps refrigerated for 1 week, is by mixing 1 tbsp of sour cream to each 275 ml/10 fl oz of double cream. Heat the mixture to lukewarm, pour into a jar, cover with muslin and leave to stand in a warm place (the airing cupboard is ideal) for 6–8 hours. Stir, cover and refrigerate until needed.

Whipping cream (minimum 35%) is so called because it contains the minimum quantity of fat for whipping ability. It is the perfect vehicle for fresh herb garnishes and can also be used as a float for other garnishes. *Single cream* (18%), *half cream* (12%) and *smetana* (10%) are best used at the end of cooking; a swirl topped with, say, a garnish of fresh herbs gives richness without loading on the calories.

Soured cream (18%) is single cream that has been thickened and its flavour sharpened by the introduction of bacterial cultures. It can be simulated instantly by mixing equal quantities of single or double cream with yoghurt. Another way is to mix together 1 tsp of fresh lemon juice to each 150 ml/5 fl oz of single or double cream, depending on how rich you want it.

Smetana (10%) is the single cream equivalent of soured cream. It's a mixture of single cream and skimmed milk, cultured to give a mild sourness.

To make a cornflour solution for saving cream sauces, dissolve 1 tbsp of cornflour in 1½ tbsp of cold water for each 570 ml/1 pt of soup. Stir a small amount of the hot soup into the cornflour solution before whisking into the remainder. Bring gently up to simmer and, stirring occasionally, cook for at least 10 minutes. The cornflour will suspend the tiny grains of the curdled cream, giving the right appearance. The texture will be slightly grainy and the flavour of the soup will be blander.

Garlic Purée

10–12 garlic cloves
200 ml/8 fl oz light chicken stock

150 ml/5 fl oz thick cream
salt and white pepper

Peel the garlic and simmer, covered, in the stock until tender (about 15–20 minutes). Remove from the heat, and pound or work to a paste in a food processor. Amalgamate with the cream and adjust the seasoning.

Saffron Cream

This is a beautiful golden colour if you use powdered saffron, or streaked with fuzzy lines of orange-yellow if you use saffron strands. The subtle flavour of saffron works well with potato and seafood soups. It can be used as a garnish, or stirred into the soup before serving.

15 g/½ oz saffron powder or strands (softened in hot water)

100 ml/4 fl oz double cream

Mix the saffron into the cream and leave for 10 minutes before stirring again and serving.

Red or Yellow Pepper Cream

1 red or yellow pepper,
  quartered and de-seeded

50 ml/2 fl oz single or double
  cream
salt and pepper

Grill the pepper until the skin blisters and begins to blacken. Slip into a plastic bag, seal and leave to sweat for 10 minutes – this makes peeling easier, but isn't essential. Pull off the skin, purée, and sieve the flesh into the cream. Season lightly.

Fresh Herb Cream

This recipe adapts to any fresh herb or young leaf; what you choose will complement the flavours of the soup. For example, basil or parsley would go well with a tomato-based soup; thyme, mint or chives with potato; watercress with watercress; chervil with carrot, and dill or sorrel with fish. It is also a good way of effectively using a mixture of fresh herbs – equal amounts of, say, parsley, sorrel, salad burnet, and chives. Go easy on tarragon (aniseedy), borage (pronounced cucumber taste), rosemary and thyme, which have strong flavours.

150 ml/5 fl oz thick cream
salt and white pepper

3 tbsp fresh marjoram, very
  finely chopped

Whip the cream until thick but not stiff. Season with a pinch of salt and white pepper, and stir in the marjoram. Float spoonfuls of the marjoram cream on top of individual servings.

YOGHURT

Some people think that the healthy alternative to cream is yoghurt. That is all very well until the food needs to be cooked. To heat yoghurt at all is a dodgy business, because even the richest, creamiest yoghurts made from full fat milk contain nowhere near the minimum fat content that allows a dairy product to tolerate boiling. It can be done, however, either by stabilizing (by whisking in 1 tsp of cornflour per 150 ml/5 fl oz of yoghurt) or by introducing the yoghurt into a hot liquid quickly, but a little at a time, almost as if you are shocking it into not realizing that, theoretically, it should split and curdle.

Yoghurt cannot be whipped in the same way as cream but it can be thickened by straining off the watery whey that has sometimes already separated in bought yoghurt. Any yoghurt can be strained, but doing so concentrates its flavour as well as thickening it; this is handy to know if you make your own yoghurt. To strain yoghurt, tip it into a sieve lined with a double square of muslin. Knot the 4 corners together, suspend over a bowl or the sink, and leave the yoghurt to drip for 3–4 hours to arrive at a creamy, spoonable texture.

The creamiest yoghurt, unless you make your own with full fat Jersey milk, is Greek yoghurt made with sheep's milk (8%). Even creamier is strained Greek yoghurt made from sheep's milk (10%), which really does taste concentrated and rich. Either is ideal to use in place of cream as a garnish, introduced at the last moment, before serving the soup. Not only does it contain half the fat of cream, but its slightly sour, acidic flavour is sometimes a more appropriate garnish to an already rich, full-flavoured soup.

Home-made Yoghurt

Any milk, even re-constituted powdered skimmed milk, can be made into yoghurt. It is a simple, foolproof procedure that requires no specialist equipment other than a cooking thermometer and a milk saver (both useful anyway) and a wide-necked insulated jar. The object is to boil then reduce some milk (this bit isn't essential but it will produce a much firmer yoghurt), allow it to cool, then add some bought yoghurt and leave the mixture for a few hours to metamorphose. It is vital to use meticulously clean equipment and to add the yoghurt culture to milk that is neither too hot (130° F/54° C) nor too cold (115° F/46° C). You can use some of the new yoghurt to start the next batch, and so on for about 3 months, after which the yoghurt is likely to turn out rather thin and watery and it is time to start afresh with a carton of commercial yoghurt.

MAKES APPROX. 400 ML/15 OZ YOGHURT

*570 ml/1 pt milk (the
creamier the milk, the
creamier the yoghurt)*

*1 generous tsp good quality,
natural, unsweetened
yoghurt*

Before you heat up the milk, be sure the pan is thoroughly clean, then scald with boiling water to be on the safe side. Place the milk and the milk saver (this is a small glass disc that stops milk boiling over) in the pan and bring the milk to the boil very slowly, then turn down the heat and leave to simmer for about 20 minutes until the milk has reduced to a little under three-quarters of the original amount. Remove from the heat, pop in the thermometer, and when the milk reaches 120° F/49° C, pour a little of it into the insulated jar/s and thoroughly mix in the (generous) teaspoon of yoghurt. Top up with the rest of the milk, stir again and screw on the lid. Leave undisturbed overnight, or for no less than 6 hours, and transfer to the fridge.

EGGS

The yolk of a fresh egg, first mixed with a little hot broth, whisked into soup just before serving, will thicken, enrich and emulsify it. The yolk can also be used as a vehicle to introduce other flavours to the soup or increase its richness. For example, it can be mixed with vinegar or lemon juice, and with double cream to make a velvet-smooth velouté-style soup (when the proportion could be 6 egg-yolks to 100 ml/4 fl oz of cream in 1.1 litres/2 pts of soup). Whole eggs can be poached or baked in the broth, to thicken and enrich slightly differently, and are delicious whisked and dropped into the soup to form threads (see page 162), or beaten together with breadcrumbs and Parmesan to flavour and thicken (see page 77).

Once the egg has been added, don't let the soup boil.

SAUCES, SALSAS, PESTOS AND PASTES

Many of the recipes mentioned here are seasonal, but proprietary brands are available all the year round. It goes without saying that home-made is best, and home-made in season with fresh, ripe ingredients is best of all.

Rouille

This is the fiery-hot Provençal sauce that is the traditional accompaniment to bouillabaisse and other fish soups. It is served separately in small bowls, to be spread on croûtons and dunked in the soup or stirred directly into individual servings. It is also very good with potato and tomato soups.

SERVES 6–8; APPROX. 175 ML/6 FL OZ

2 sweet red peppers, cored, de-seeded and quartered lengthways

1 thick slice of white bread, crusts removed, soaked in water or, to make a lighter sauce, 1 egg-yolk

2 large or 3 medium cloves of garlic, skinned

1 small red chilli, cored and de-seeded (optional, for those who like it hot)

¼ tsp salt

a few grindings of black pepper

110 ml/4 fl oz olive oil

Grill the peppers until the skin chars and blisters. Peel off the skin. Squeeze the water out of the bread. Pound or process the peppers, bread, garlic, chilli and seasoning to make a paste, and gradually incorporate the oil to make a smooth, thick, shiny sauce. If using an egg-yolk, incorporate it just before adding the oil and increase the oil by 50 ml/2 fl oz.

Transfer to a bowl and cover with clingfilm, to stop a crust forming, if not using immediately.

Ginger and Chilli Sambal

Half a teaspoonful of this hot, sour paste from Indonesia provides a good contrast to sweet or mild-flavoured soups. It will keep for several weeks stored in an airtight jar in the fridge.

SERVES 8–10

8–10 fresh or dried red chilli peppers, cored and de-seeded
2 cloves of garlic, peeled
1-cm/½-in piece of fresh ginger, peeled

3 tbsp white vinegar
1 tbsp brown sugar
1 tsp salt

Put all the ingredients in the blender, or pound manually, to make a smooth paste.

Romesco Sauce

This is Jane Grigson's recipe for the famous Spanish sauce that originates from the province of Tarragona, where the small hot Romesco peppers are grown. Its success relies on using authentic ingredients grown in hot climates, not watery tomatoes and chilli powder. A refined version of this sauce, which uses 1 thick slice of white bread fried in 2 tbsp of olive oil rather than the 200 ml/8 fl oz in this recipe, is also good.

2 large, ripe tomatoes
3 cloves of garlic, peeled
24 hazelnuts, blanched, or 12 each almonds and hazelnuts
2 dried red chillis, de-seeded and soaked in warm water for 30 minutes, or ½ tsp chilli purée

salt and pepper
1 tbsp flat-leaf parsley
200 ml/8 fl oz olive oil
2 tbsp dry sherry vinegar or 1 each wine vinegar and dry sherry

Bake the tomatoes and whole peeled garlic in a moderate oven for about 15 minutes. After 10 minutes add the nuts and chillis. Transfer to the blender, scraping the tomato pulp from its skin and cutting out the core, and blend to a purée, adding the seasoning, parsley and olive oil – gradually – to make a smooth sauce. Finally stir in the vinegar or vinegar and sherry, and correct the seasoning.

Onion and Tomato Compôte/Sofregit/Sofrito

In Spanish cookery, sofregit or sofrito is the basis of all manner of stews and slow-cooked dishes. The combination of onions cooked slowly to accentuate their sweetness, combined with full-flavoured tomatoes and a hint of garlic, is a versatile soup base. It is a good mixture to make with a glut of over-ripe tomatoes and is best suited to being made with large, mild Spanish onions.

75 ml/3 fl oz (approx.) olive oil
900 g/2 lb onions, finely chopped
2 fat cloves of garlic, crushed and chopped

450 g/1 lb ripe tomatoes, skinned, de-seeded and chopped

Cover the bottom of a large, heavy-bottomed pan with olive oil. Heat the oil, and cook the onions, stirring every now and again, on the lowest heat. When they've turned a reddish brown (this takes about 1 hour), turn up the heat and add the garlic. Cook for a minute to introduce the flavours, then add the tomatoes. Stir everything around and cook gently until all the water in the tomatoes has evaporated.

Fresh Tomato and Chilli Sauce

This is quick to make: aromatic, and a delicious mixture of sweet, sour, hot and mild. It is very good stirred into light summer soups, such as a cucumber and yoghurt mixture, then garnished with fresh coriander or mint. It is best used the same day but will keep, covered, in the fridge for a couple of weeks.

SERVES 8–10
450 g/1 lb very ripe tomatoes
1–3 fresh or dried red chillis
2 cloves of garlic, peeled
1-cm/½-in piece of fresh ginger, peeled

1 tbsp brown sugar
1 tsp salt
1 tbsp lemon juice

Scald the tomatoes in boiling water and peel off the skins. Put all the other ingredients in the food processor and process the mixture to a paste. Core the tomatoes and add to the blender; process quickly, just enough to combine paste and tomato.

Saffron Mayonnaise

2 cloves of garlic, roughly chopped
½ tsp salt, preferably coarse sea salt
1 egg-yolk, room temperature
110 g/4 fl oz light olive oil

½ tsp cayenne pepper
a pinch of saffron threads, dissolved in 1 tbsp hot water
lemon juice or vinegar to taste

Pound the garlic with the salt to form a smooth paste. Add the egg-yolk and pound/stir for 60 seconds. Whisk in the oil, drop by drop to begin with, until it is all thoroughly incorporated. Stir in the cayenne and dissolved saffron; season to taste with the lemon juice or vinegar.

Adjust the consistency by stirring in a little warm water.

Ginger Salsa

225 g/8 oz baked tomato
  sauce (below)
2 tsp grated fresh ginger
2 tbsp spring onion or
  shallots, finely chopped
1 tbsp fresh red chilli peppers,
  cored, de-seeded and finely
  chopped

2 tbsp fresh coriander,
  chopped
2 tbsp fresh lemon juice
salt and pepper

Mix all the ingredients together. Serve chilled.

Cucumber Salsa

10 cm/4 in cucumber, peeled
  and cored
salt
450 g/1 lb ripe, firm
  tomatoes
½ a small red onion, finely
  diced

4 tbsp coriander leaves, finely
  chopped
3 cloves of garlic, peeled and
  finely chopped
2 bottled/canned jalapeño or
  serrano chillis, finely diced
a splash of rice wine vinegar

Finely dice the cucumber, transfer to a colander and dredge with salt. Leave while you scald the tomatoes in boiling water. Peel off their skins, core, and squeeze out the seeds. Finely chop the flesh and mix with all the other ingredients. Rinse the salt off the cucumber, drain and add to the mixture. Chill before serving.

Baked Tomato Sauce

This is worth making when you have a glut of beautifully ripened, good-flavoured tomatoes. It freezes successfully.

900 g/2 lb ripe tomatoes
2 tbsp olive oil
½ a small onion, finely
  chopped

salt
sugar

Bake the tomatoes in a pre-heated oven at 400° F/200° C/Gas Mark 6 for 10 minutes. When cool enough to handle, core the tomatoes and slip off their skins. Roughly purée the tomatoes in a blender or food processor or pass through a mouli-légumes. Meanwhile, heat the oil and gently sauté the onion until soft and translucent. Cook the puréed tomatoes and onions together over a medium heat until they have thickened and the excess liquid has evaporated. Taste and season with salt and if necessary with a pinch of sugar.

The sauce is subtly seasoned with a smoky flavour if the tomatoes are grilled over wood or charcoal.

Nuoc Nam

This Vietnamese chilli-fish sauce is used as a relish and flavour-enhancer.

3 red chillis, chopped
3 cloves of garlic, peeled and
  chopped
25 ml/1 fl oz vinegar

a dash of white wine
1 tbsp sugar
juice of 3 limes
110 ml/4 fl oz fish stock

Pound the chilli and garlic until smooth, incorporating the vinegar, white wine and sugar. Stir in the lime juice and fish stock. Stir thoroughly.

Richard Shepherd's Anchovy Sauce

At Langan's Brasserie this sauce, served with individual spinach soufflés, is one of the most famous items on the menu. Each soufflé is made to order and when it arrives at the table, the waiter makes a hole in the centre and pours in a little of the sauce. The sauce, also made with eggs but perfectly cut by the anchovies and a touch of lemon, offsets the spinach soufflé a treat. The combination translates easily into a marvellous soup combination but this unusual sauce is also particularly good with tomato and potato soups.

1 small can anchovy fillets,
  rinsed under cold water to
  remove oil
3 egg-yolks
1 tsp fresh lemon juice

225 g/8 oz unsalted butter,
  clarified (see page 10) and
  warmed
a pinch of cayenne

Begin the sauce by pounding or processing the anchovy fillets with 2 tsp of water, and transfer them to a bowl. Whisk the egg-yolks in a small pan with 1 tbsp of cold water and the lemon juice. Cook over a gentle heat, whisking continuously, and slowly, bit by bit, add the warm butter. When all the butter is incorporated, season with a pinch of cayenne. Whisk the egg mixture into the anchovies until the two are thoroughly mixed. Pass through a fine sieve into a clean pan and re-heat without boiling.

Fresh Mint Relish

225 g/8 oz mint leaves
2 green chillis, cored and de-
* seeded*
3 tbsp onions, finely chopped
* or minced*

¾ tsp grated fresh ginger
1½ tbsp lemon juice
1 tsp sugar
1 tsp salt, preferably sea salt
3 tbsp water

Put all the ingredients in a food processor and blend until reduced to a fine, smooth purée. You will probably need to scrape the sides of the container from time to time. Cover and chill thoroughly before serving.

This recipe is adapted from one given by Julie Sahni in her book *Classic Indian Cooking*. It is supposed to have the consistency of a thick *pesto* and keeps for up to a week in the refrigerator. It freezes successfully but, because the liquid separates from the pulp, it needs a thorough stirring before use.

Pistou

Pistou, a hot, pungent paste made by pounding garlic and basil leaves, mixed with Parmesan and olive oil, and sometimes with pine-nuts, is integral to a minestrone-style soup devised in Nice called *soupe au pistou* (see page 267). It is similar to, and served in much the same way as *pesto*, the famous Italian sauce.

It can either be put in the bottom of a hot tureen with the soup poured over it 10 minutes before serving, or served separately for people to help themselves.

2–4 cloves of garlic, peeled
4 tbsp pine-nuts, (optional)
a large bunch of basil leaves,
* finely chopped*

50 g/2 oz Parmesan, freshly
* grated*
175 ml/6 fl oz olive oil

Pound the garlic in a mortar, add the pine-nuts and continue pounding. Add the basil, and keep pounding, and then the Parmesan. When you have worked it to a paste, stir in the oil gradually, a few drops at a time, until everything has amalgamated into a cohesive sauce.

This, and other similar sauces, can be made quickly and easily in a food processor or blender (see next recipe) but the results won't be so good. In this case you would also miss out on the marvellous, heady aroma from the pounded basil.

Pesto

This is Giuliano Bugialli's recipe from his superb and beautifully illustrated book *The Taste of Italy*. Also see page 261 for minestrone Genovese style.

6 walnuts, shelled	2 medium cloves of garlic,
1 tbsp pine-nuts	peeled
1 tbsp butter	175 ml/6 fl oz olive oil
a large bunch of fresh basil	110 g/4 oz Parmesan, freshly
leaves	grated
2 heaped tbsp drained, boiled	salt and pepper
spinach	

Put the walnuts, pine-nuts, butter, basil, spinach, garlic and 50 ml/ 2 fl oz of the oil in a blender or processor and work to a smooth paste. Add the remaining oil and blend until very smooth. Transfer to a bowl, mix in the Parmesan, salt and pepper, and mix thoroughly.

Parsley Pesto

2 cloves of garlic	3 tbsp olive oil
¼ tsp sea salt	3 tbsp Parmesan, grated
8 tbsp flat-leaf parsley, stalks	red wine vinegar
removed and finely chopped	

Begin by pounding the garlic to a paste with the salt. Add 1 tbsp of the parsley and work it vigorously into the garlic; then stir in the olive oil, cheese, and remaining parsley. Add the vinegar to taste, and season with more salt if necessary.

Dill Pesto

1 large bunch of dill, stems	1 tbsp lemon juice
removed and finely chopped	110 ml/4 fl oz olive oil
1 clove of garlic, crushed	salt and pepper

Blend the dill and garlic together in a food processor. Add the lemon juice and slowly, little by little, add the olive oil to make a thick paste. Season.

The same recipe works well with marjoram, tarragon, and a mixture of fresh herbs to include parsley, chives, mint, thyme and basil, when it becomes a variation on the classic *salsa verde* (see opposite).

Salsa Verde

*4 tbsp flat-leaf parsley, finely
  chopped
3 tbsp mixed fresh herbs, e.g.
  thyme, chervil, rocket, dill,
  tarragon, basil, marjoram
  and mint, finely chopped*

*1–2 tbsp capers, rinsed and
  chopped (optional)
grated peel of 1 lemon
lemon juice to taste
150 ml/¼ pt olive oil
salt and pepper*

To retain the bright green colour of this sauce, it needs to be mixed
just before serving. Whizz all the ingredients and 1 tbsp olive oil in
the processor. When you have made a thick paste, add the rest of the
olive oil in a slow trickle until you have a thick green mayonnaise-
like sauce. It will suffer no harm if all the ingredients are mixed in
advance, covered and stored in the fridge, with the lemon juice
stirred in just before serving.

Bagnet Verde

A traditional accompaniment to *bollito misto*.

SERVES 10

*1 large bunch (175 g/6 oz)
  flat-leaf parsley, finely
  chopped
1 small bunch (25 g/1 oz)
  mint, finely chopped
3 anchovies, rinsed under
  running water and finely
  chopped
1 tbsp capers, finely chopped*

*4 small pickled cucumbers,
  finely chopped
4 tbsp fine breadcrumbs
2 hard-boiled egg-yolks
2 cloves of garlic, minced
2–3 tbsp vinegar
1 tbsp sugar
salt and pepper
150 ml/¼ pt olive oil*

Mix the chopped parsley and mint in a bowl. Using a pestle and
mortar, or a second bowl and a wooden spoon, cream together the
anchovies, capers, pickled cucumbers, breadcrumbs and hard-boiled
eggs. Mix this into the parsley and mint, adding the garlic, vinegar,
sugar, salt and pepper. Finally, beat in the olive oil as in the recipe
for *salsa verde* (above).

POACHED EMBELLISHMENTS

The majority of the recipes in this section are for tasty morsels that are poached in the finished broth or soup immediately before serving. Most, and that includes the last-minute addition of staples such as pearl barley, tapioca, rice, dried pasta and noodles, are a means of bulking-out the soup. They are also a way of providing texture and interest and varying the soup from one day to the next.

Other recipes, such as the many I have included for the ubiquitous ball or dumpling, are a means of providing bulk as well as of introducing interesting textures and flavours. Depending on the ingredients, and that goes for ravioli too, dumplings can be comfort food or a vehicle for injecting some exotic flavours into an otherwise bland broth.

With the exception of pasta, which needs to be boiled fast in order to expand the starch granules to make them tender to the bite, the poaching liquid should be brought to a gentle simmer before cooking begins.

WHOLE GRAINS

BARLEY
Allow 40 g/1½ oz for each 1.1 litres/2 pts
Wash the barley in tepid water; blanch it for 5 minutes in boiling water and poach in lightly simmering soup for 2 hours.

RICE
Allow 40 g/1½ oz for each 1.1 litres/2 pts
Wash the rice several times and cook first in water in your usual way. Strain, rinse under cold running water, and throw the rice into the soup 5 minutes before serving. Rice that is cooked in the soup needs to be cooked initially at boiling point and then simmered for 20 minutes. Brown and wild rice take 40 minutes.

SEMOLINA
Allow 50 g/2 oz for 1.1 litres/2 pts
Simmer gently for 12 minutes.

TAPIOCA
Allow 65 g/2½ oz for 1.1 litres/2 pts
Simmer gently for 25 minutes.

DUMPLINGS

> 'My housekeeper will have these in her new
> fashion, although I tell her that when I was
> a young man, we used to keep strictly to

> my father's rule, "No broth no ball; no ball
> no beef", and always began dinner with
> broth and white suet dumplings boiled in
> the broth with the beef, and then the meat
> itself . . .' (Cranford, from *Food in England*,
> Dorothy Hartley, 1954)

Quantities for the number and size of cooked dumplings can be only
an approximate guideline because their size will depend on your
lightness of hand (or otherwise). Size and shape of dumplings can be
varied according to whim but relies slightly on the consistency of the
dumpling mixture.

BREAD DUMPLINGS

Parmesan 'Dumplings'/Passatelli

According to Marcella Hazan, a doyenne of Italian cooking, *passatelli*
is native only to the Romagna section of Emilia, a narrow strip of
territory east of Bologna, bordering on the Adriatic Sea. The
Romagnoli, she goes on to explain, want their food to be satisfying
but simple and delicate in taste.

The *passatelli*, which are worm-like dumplings made from a stiff
dough of Parmesan, breadcrumbs and eggs, with a hint of nutmeg,
are a traditional accompaniment, cooked briefly in the soup before
serving, to make more of a home-made meat broth. They are only
worth making with Parmesan grated freshly for the occasion.

Some cooks include the peel of a lemon, very finely grated, but my
favourite recipe, from Ms Hazan's indispensable book, *The Classic
Italian Cookbook*, does not. See page 83 for the meat version.

SERVES 6

75 g/2½ oz freshly grated Parmesan	¼ tsp nutmeg
40 g/1½ oz fine dry breadcrumbs	2 eggs

Before you begin preparation, have the broth at simmering point.

On a pastry board combine the grated Parmesan, breadcrumbs
and nutmeg. Make a mound with a well in the centre. Break the eggs
into the well and knead all the ingredients together. You should end
up with a firm paste with a granular consistency; if it is too sloppy,
add more Parmesan and breadcrumbs in equal quantities.

Assemble your mouli-légumes with the disc with the largest holes,
and press the paste through the mouli so that the 'worms' fall directly
into the broth. Cook at a slow boil for a minute or two. Turn off the
heat and allow to stand for a few minutes, ladle into soup plates and
serve with a bowl of freshly grated Parmesan.

Austrian Bread Dumplings/Knockerl

MAKES APPROX. 10 WALNUT-SIZED DUMPLINGS

100 g/4 oz day-old bread
15 g/½ oz butter or lard
150 ml/5 fl oz milk
1 large egg
75 g/3 oz flour

1 tbsp parsley, marjoram, dill,
thyme or chervil, or a
mixture
salt and pepper

Dice the bread, fry it lightly in the butter or lard and tip into a mixing bowl. Whisk the milk and egg together and mix into the bread. Sift the flour into the egg, milk and bread mixture, add the herbs and season with salt and pepper. Mix thoroughly and leave for 30 minutes. If the mixture seems too dry and crumbly, add more milk; if too wet, add a little more flour.

With wet hands, quickly form into marble-sized balls and carefully drop into lightly salted simmering water, or directly into the soup. They will be ready after about 10 minutes and will pop up to the surface.

Austrian Savoury Dumplings with Bacon/Serviettenknödeln

MAKES APPROX. 20 DESSERTSPOON-SIZED DUMPLINGS

4 soft white rolls or baps with
dark crusts removed
50 g/2 oz melted butter
200 ml/7 fl oz milk
salt and grated nutmeg

3 egg-yolks
1 tbsp parsley, chopped finely
4 rashers of smoked streaky
bacon, rind removed, diced
3 egg-whites, stiffly whisked

Roughly chop the bread and mix with the butter, milk, a generous pinch of salt and nutmeg, the egg-yolks and the parsley. Leave to macerate while you fry the bacon until crisp in its own fat. Mix the bacon and its fat into the main mixture and leave for a further 30 minutes before folding in the egg-whites. Drop spoonfuls of the mixture into the simmering broth and test for doneness after 10 minutes.

This mixture is traditionally formed into one large dumpling which is folded into a buttered cloth, poached in water, sliced and then fried in butter until golden.

SUET DUMPLINGS

Suet dumplings need to be boiled in a covered pan rather than lightly poached in simmering liquid.

Suet and Parsley Dumplings

MAKES APPROX. 16–20 SMALL WALNUT-SIZED DUMPLINGS
110 g/4 oz self-raising flour *50 g/2 oz suet*
¼ tsp salt *15 g/½ oz curly parsley,*
freshly ground black pepper *finely chopped*

Sift the flour into a mixing bowl and mix in the salt and a few twists of black pepper. Stir in the suet and parsley and add just enough cold water to make a pliable yet stiff but not too sticky dough. With floured fingers form the dough into marble-sized balls. Drop into lightly boiling broth, cover, and test one after 15 minutes.

Suet and Mushroom Dumplings

MAKES APPROX. 16–20 WALNUT-SIZED DUMPLINGS
110 g/4 oz self-raising flour *50 g/2 oz mushrooms, very*
¼ tsp salt *finely chopped*
freshly ground black pepper *1 small onion or shallot,*
50 g/2 oz suet *peeled and minced*

Sift the flour into a mixing bowl, add the salt and a little pepper, and stir in the suet. Thoroughly incorporate the mushrooms and onion before stirring in just enough cold water to form the mixture into a firm, pliable dough that leaves the sides of the bowl clean. With floured fingers form the dough into marble-sized balls. Drop into lightly boiling broth, cover, and test one after 15 minutes.

Suet and Horseradish Dumplings

MAKES APPROX. 16–20 MARBLE-SIZED DUMPLINGS
110 g/4 oz self-raising flour *1 small onion or shallot,*
¼ tsp salt *peeled and minced*
freshly ground black pepper
50 g/2 oz suet
25 g/1 oz fresh or preserved
  grated horseradish, chopped
  finely

Sift the flour into a mixing bowl, add the salt and a little pepper, and stir in the suet. Mix in the horseradish and onion and stir in just enough cold water to form the mixture into a stiff but elastic dough. With floured fingers form the dough into small balls. Drop into lightly boiling broth, cover, and test one after 15 minutes.

POTATO DUMPLINGS

It is worth noting that potato dumplings are very absorbent. For this reason you may prefer to poach them first in boiling water before adding them to the soup.

Gnocchi

MAKES APPROX. 25–30 × 2.5-CM/1-IN GNOCCHI

900 g/2 lb floury-variety   *275 g/10 oz plain flour*
 potatoes   *1 egg*
salt, pepper and a pinch of   *1 dsp olive oil*
 nutmeg

Boil the potatoes in their skins in well-salted water. Cool and skin. Dry mash, season, and pile the potatoes on to a floured board. Make a well and add a small amount of the sifted flour, then the egg, and sprinkle on the olive oil. Quickly work the mixture to incorporate the flour, adding more as you do so. You will end up with a soft, light, yet firm dough that is easy to mould. Leave to rest for 20 minutes, while you put on a large pan of water to boil.

Divide the mixture in half and roll each half into a long thin sausage. Chop into 2.5-cm/1-in pieces. Carefully roll each gnocchi round the prongs of a fork to make a slight curl. Poach the dumplings in small batches in lightly simmering water. They are done when they pop up to the surface, which takes about 5 minutes. Scoop them out with a slotted spoon, drain, and slip into a soup tureen or into individual serving dishes.

Potato and Horseradish Dumplings

MAKES APPROX. 12 MARBLE-SIZED DUMPLINGS

15 g/½ oz semolina   *1 tbsp parsley, finely chopped*
225 g/8 oz floury-variety   *1 tbsp creamed horseradish*
 potatoes, boiled, peeled and   *salt and pepper*
 mashed   *½ beaten egg*
25 g/1 oz butter   *25 g/1 oz flour*
25 g/1 oz onion, finely chopped

Sift the semolina into the potato. Melt the butter and sweat the onion until transparent. Mix into the semolina/potato mixture, then add the parsley, horseradish and seasoning. Slowly incorporate the egg and enough flour to make a soft, cohesive dough. Form into small dumplings and poach in salted water for 7–10 minutes. Remove with a slotted spoon, drain and proceed.

Beef and Potato Dumplings/Locsei

MAKES APPROX. 12–15 WALNUT-SIZED DUMPLINGS

2 large potatoes, peeled and grated	1 egg, whisked
	1 tbsp flour
225 g/8 oz good-quality lean beef, ground to a paste	1 tbsp semolina
	salt and pepper

Rinse and pat dry the potatoes and mix with the meat, egg, sifted flour and semolina, and a generous pinch of salt and pepper. When thoroughly mixed, form into small balls. Poach, covered, in gently simmering salted water for 25 minutes. These dumplings must be cooked immediately they are made, otherwise the potato will start to turn black. The starch in the potatoes helps the dumplings to gel.

FLOUR AND GRAIN DUMPLINGS
See also 'Pasta and Soup Noodles' (pages 87–101).

Green Dumplings

This particularly delicious recipe comes from Bill Neal's unusual book, *Southern Cooking*. It is only worth making with fresh basil.

MAKES APPROX. 20 × 7.5-CM/3-IN DUMPLINGS

175 g/6 oz flour	2 tbsp basil, finely chopped
2 tsp baking powder	2 tbsp parsley, finely chopped
1 tsp salt	4 tbsp spring onion, finely chopped
1 tsp sugar	
1 egg, well beaten, with enough milk added to make 200 ml/7 fl oz	

Sift the flour, baking powder, salt and sugar together twice. Make a well in the centre of the dry ingredients and quickly stir in the liquid. Gently fold in the herbs and onion.

Drop large spoonfuls of the mixture into the simmering broth. Cover immediately and reduce the heat so that the liquid does not boil. Cook for 10 minutes.

Matzo Dumplings/Maceszgombóc

MAKES APPROX. 15–20 GOLFBALL-SIZED DUMPLINGS

50 g/2 oz butter	salt and pepper
½ a small onion, chopped	a pinch of ginger
finely	110 g/4 oz matzo biscuits
1 egg	(approx. 2 and a bit
1 egg-yolk	crackers), crumbled
1 tbsp parsley, chopped finely	

Melt a little of the butter and gently fry the onion. Beat the rest of the butter until frothy, then cream with the whole egg and egg-yolk. Mix in the parsley, salt, pepper and ginger, and the cooled onion. Add 1 tbsp of cold water, beat thoroughly with a wooden spoon or whisk and, finally, mix in the matzos. Leave the mixture to rest for 30 minutes. Form into dumplings and poach gently, covered, for 25 minutes.

Rice Dumplings with Marjoram/Majorannás Rizsgombóc

MAKES APPROX. 25–30 WALNUT-SIZED DUMPLINGS

110 g/4 oz rice or millet	200 ml/8 fl oz hot beef broth
1 tsp goose fat	2 tbsp butter
½ an onion, finely chopped	1 egg
salt and pepper	3 egg-yolks
1 tbsp marjoram, finely chopped	50 g/2 oz flour

Soak the rice or millet in warm water for 15 minutes to soften. Drain. Meanwhile heat the goose fat in a pan and gently sauté the onion until transparent. Mix the onion into the rice and season with salt, pepper, and marjoram. Pour in the hot beef broth and simmer until the rice is tender and has absorbed all the stock. Finally, whisk together the butter, egg, egg-yolks, and sifted flour and mix well with the rice. Form into small dumplings and poach in gently simmering beef broth. Test one after 5 minutes.

MEAT DUMPLINGS

Beef Marrow-bone Dumplings/Quenelles à la Moelle

MAKES APPROX. 15–20 ELONGATED WALNUT-SIZED DUMPLINGS

110 g/4 oz uncooked beef bone	110 g/4 oz fine breadcrumbs
marrow	salt
3 eggs	1 tbsp flour

Mash the marrow and rub it through a sieve until smooth. Incorporate the eggs, one by one, stirring all the time; when quite smooth, add the breadcrumbs little by little and season with salt.

Flour a board, lay out the mixture and roll it lightly. Make elongated balls about the size of a walnut and poach them, covered, in gently simmering broth for 20 minutes.

Chinese Beef Balls

MAKES APPROX. 20 MARBLE-SIZED BALLS

225 g/8 oz finely minced beef	*1 small onion, minced*
2 water-chestnuts, finely chopped	*½ a beaten egg*
	salt and pepper

Mix all the ingredients evenly to form a firm 'dough'. Form into small balls and poach in gently simmering broth for 25 minutes.

Beef and Parmesan 'Dumplings'/Passatelli

This is the meat version of the recipe given on page 77. It comes from Marcella Hazan's sequel to *The Classic Italian Cookbook – The Second Classic Italian Cookbook.*

SERVES 6

150 g/5 oz beef fillet	*¼ tsp salt*
25 g/1 oz beef marrow or butter	*¼ tsp grated nutmeg*
	1 egg
40 g/1½ oz freshly grated Parmesan cheese	*50 g/2 oz fine, dry breadcrumbs*

Remove any skin or membrane from the beef fillet, and cut the meat into small pieces. Put the meat and the marrow or butter in the food processor and process to a soft, almost creamy consistency. Transfer to a bowl, and add the Parmesan, salt, nutmeg, egg and breadcrumbs. Mix thoroughly and form into a ball.

Assemble your mouli-légumes using the disc with the largest holes, and press the paste through the mouli so that the 'worms' fall directly into the simmering broth. Cook at a slow boil for a minute or two, then turn off the heat and allow to stand for a few minutes before serving.

Meat *passatelli* are traditionally served with a rich capon broth, but are good with a home-made chicken or beef broth.

Devonshire Chicken Dumplings

MAKES APPROX. 20–25 WALNUT-SIZED DUMPLINGS
225 g/8 oz cooked chicken   *225 g/8 oz breadcrumbs*
1 chicken liver, fried in butter   *1 tsp curly parsley, finely*
stewed giblets   *chopped*
2 rashers of bacon, fried to a   *salt and pepper*
crisp in their own fat   *2 eggs, whisked*

Mince finely and mix together the chicken, its liver, scraps from the giblets and the bacon, with its rind removed. Stir in the breadcrumbs, parsley, a pinch of salt and few grinds from the peppermill, and the eggs. The mixture should be stiff, so add extra breadcrumbs if necessary. Form into walnut-sized balls and poach in gently simmering broth. They will pop up to the surface after 15 minutes, when the soup will be ready to serve.

This recipe is a good way of using up the remains of a roast chicken. The carcass and the picked-over giblets can go into the stock-pot and could provide a broth in which to cook the dumplings.

Lamb's Liver Dumplings

MAKES APPROX. 12 MARBLE-SIZED DUMPLINGS
2 tbsp plain flour   *1 onion, minced*
1 egg, beaten   *2 tbsp parsley, finely chopped*
110 g/4 oz lamb's livers,   *¼ tsp ground nutmeg*
minced or finely chopped   *salt*

Sift the flour into the egg and stir in all the other ingredients. With wet hands, form the mixture into small balls and poach gently for 6–8 minutes.

Turkish Lamb Meatballs

MAKES APPROX. 16 MARBLE-SIZED BALLS
225 g/8 oz lamb, finely   *½ tsp fresh mint, finely*
minced   *chopped*
1 small onion, grated   *salt and black pepper*

Mix all the ingredients thoroughly, form into small balls and poach for 15 minutes. These tasty dumplings are integral to the Turkish hot yoghurt soup on page 185.

Stuffed Lettuce Leaves/Lattughe Ripiene

This recipe, found in Arabella Boxer's marvellous *Mediterranean Cookbook*, originates from Genoa and though fiddly to make is well worth the effort. The bundles are cooked and served in a good beef broth accompanied by a dollop of hot *ragú bolognese*.

MAKES 8 BUNDLES: ENOUGH FOR 4

8 large lettuce leaves
50 g/2 oz soft breadcrumbs
a little milk
40 g/1½ oz butter
1 small onion, minced
1 clove of garlic, finely
  chopped
1 stalk of celery, finely
  chopped
½ a carrot, finely chopped
1 stalk of parsley, finely
  chopped

200 g/7 oz veal, minced
50 g/2 oz calf's brains,
  blanched (optional)
50 g/2 oz sweetbreads,
  blanched (optional)
1 tbsp flour
150 ml/5 fl oz veal or chicken
  stock
1 egg-yolk
2 tbsp Parmesan, grated
½ tbsp marjoram, chopped
salt, pepper and nutmeg

Blanch the lettuce leaves for 2 minutes in boiling water and drain. Cover the breadcrumbs with milk and leave to soak for 10 minutes, then squeeze out the excess milk. Soften the butter and gently stew the onion, garlic, celery, carrot and parsley. Add the chopped meats and stir around until they are pale golden (about 2–3 minutes), then add the flour and 150 ml/5 fl oz of stock. Cook gently for 15 minutes or until the stock is completely absorbed. Put the contents of the pan in a food processor, or pound in a mortar, and process until smooth. Add the soaked breadcrumbs, egg-yolk, Parmesan, marjoram, a generous pinch of salt, a few twists of black pepper and a pinch of grated nutmeg. Process or pound into a smooth cream. Place a mound like a small egg on each lettuce leaf, roll up and tie with fine string.

10 minutes before you are ready to serve the soup, poach the bundles in lightly simmering broth. Lift them out with a perforated spoon, untie the string, and serve in soup plates, 2 per person.

Chicken Mousse/Budino di Pollo

SERVES 6

175 g/6 oz raw chicken
  breast
75 ml/3 fl oz chicken stock
4 eggs, beaten

50 g/2 oz Parmesan, freshly
  grated
salt and pepper
nutmeg

Pound or purée the chicken breast with the chicken stock and push through a sieve so that you end up with a fine cream. Strain the beaten eggs into the chicken cream and mix thoroughly. Stir in the cheese and season with salt, pepper and nutmeg. Butter 6 ramekins and half-fill with the chicken mixture. Cover with foil, pierced a few times to let the steam out, and place the pots in a pan filled with sufficient water to come half-way up the pots. Cook gently for 15 minutes, or until the chicken mixture is firm. Turn each one out into a soup-plate and cover with chicken stock and you have *budino di pollo in brodo*.

This superb recipe comes from the Pappagallo restaurant in Bologna, courtesy of Elizabeth David's *Italian Food*.

SEAFOOD DUMPLINGS

Fish and shellfish dumplings tend to be integral to a fish soup and are rarely made on spec or to eke out a seafood broth. The recipes here can be modified to suit whatever fish or shellfish you have on hand; other recipes are included with their complementary soup in the main text of recipes.

Salmon Quenelles

MAKES APPROX. 16–20 DESSERTSPOON-SIZED QUENELLES

175 g/6 oz soft white breadcrumbs	½ tsp salt
150 ml/5 fl oz milk	¼ tsp ground white pepper
350 g/12 oz salmon, filleted and cut into chunks	a generous pinch of ground nutmeg
175 g/6 oz butter, diced	2 eggs
	1 dsp chives, chopped

Leave the breadcrumbs to soak in milk while you pound or purée the salmon in a food processor. Squeeze any excess milk from the breadcrumbs and add to the fish. Pound or process, incorporating the butter, the seasoning and then the eggs, one at a time, until you have made a smooth, pale paste. Finally, mix in the chives and chill in the fridge for 30 minutes. Using a dessertspoon, form into quenelles and poach in fish broth or soup for 15 minutes.

Ginger Flounder Dumplings

MAKES APPROX. 10 WALNUT-SIZED DUMPLINGS

225 g/8 oz flounder fillets	a few drops of fresh ginger juice
1 small onion, minced	50 g/2 oz flour
¼ tsp salt	

Pound or use a food processor to grind the flounder to a paste. Add the onion, salt, ginger juice and enough of the sifted flour to hold the mixture together. Form into small balls and poach in simmering liquid for 15 minutes.

LARGE DUMPLINGS

Another way to stretch soup is to poach what the French call *le farci*. This is a single large dumpling, formed into a ball and wrapped in cabbage leaves, which is poached in the soup for 30 minutes before serving. The tureen is brought to the table, complete with *le farci*, where the dumpling is removed, then carved, and each person is served a slice before the soup is ladled over it. The recipe can be varied, but the one that follows, which will provide 4–6 servings, originates from the Gascony region of France. *Le farci* is sometimes cooked inside or alongside a chicken in recipes for *poule-au-pot*. Like its beef equivalent, *pot-au-feu*, the broth is served first, followed by the chicken, various root vegetables and slices from the dumpling (see page 290).

Le Farci

2 or 3 large cabbage leaves	1 shallot or small onion,
110 g/4 oz fresh breadcrumbs	peeled and chopped
3 tbsp stock	1 clove of garlic, peeled and
110–150 g/4–5 oz pork or	chopped
lean bacon chopped finely	2 egg-yolks, beaten
2 tbsp flat-leaf parsley, finely	salt and pepper
chopped	

Begin by blanching the cabbage leaves in boiling water for a few minutes. Remove and drain them while you soak the breadcrumbs in a little stock. Squeeze out the excess liquid and mix thoroughly with all the other ingredients. Form into a ball. Wrap the cabbage leaves around the ball and tie in place with some thin string, leaving a long loop so that it can easily be fished out of the soup. Bring the soup up to simmering point and gently lower the ball into it. Bring back to a simmer and cook gently for 30 minutes. Remove the string before slicing. Put a slice in each soup-plate and ladle over the broth.

PASTA AND SOUP NOODLES

See also 'Flour and Grain Dumplings' (pages 81–6). Adding pasta to clear soup is a quick, easy and satisfying way of both personalizing the dish and stretching it. For example, a combination of green with regular white or transparent noodles, perhaps flecked with fresh herbs if the noodles are home-made, will look and taste a lot more interesting than just adding lengths of spaghetti.

Whether you are using a ready-made pasta or one you've made yourself, it is important that it is cooked in vigorously boiling liquid.

It may be preferable to cook the pasta first in boiling salted water – drained and rinsed in cold water – before adding it to the soup-pot.

If using different-sized pasta pieces in the same soup, be sure to adjust the cooking times appropriately. When using packet pasta, shorten the cooking time by 5 minutes, so that the final cooking is done in the soup.

Pasta or noodles, made with wheat, rice, buckwheat, and bean or yam threads, come in many forms in China, Japan and South-east Asia, and feature widely in soups. Most are available in Oriental foodshops and, increasingly, in large national supermarket chains. Many of these pastas are interchangeable with Italian-style equivalents. Less familiar are rice noodles, which are white, slightly glutinous, and almost tasteless. Buckwheat noodles, particularly popular in Japan, have a nutty flavour and are a speckled brownish-grey colour. The most common Japanese soup noodles, called *udon*, are made with bleached white wheat flour and no eggs.

The Chinese equivalent of ravioli is called wonton and the dough (a similar mixture of flour, egg and salt, and sometimes cornflour) is sold ready-cut into wonton squares or skins in Oriental foodshops.

Ravioli Paste

This is Elizabeth David's quick and easy recipe, from *Italian Food*, requiring no eggs.

SERVES 2–4: APPROX. 450 G/1 LB DOUGH
50 g/2 oz butter   *a pinch of salt*
225 g/8 oz flour   *boiling water*

Cut the butter into small pieces and rub into the flour. Season, and add enough boiling water (approx. 175 ml/6 fl oz) to form a stiff dough. Knead for 5 minutes and divide into 2 or 4 parts depending on the size of your floured board. With a floured rolling-pin, roll out the paste very thin, using more flour to prevent sticking. Cover with a cloth to prevent drying out while you roll the rest of the paste. To cook the finished ravioli, poach in gently simmering water or broth for about 4 minutes.

Egg Pasta Dough

SERVES 4–6: APPROX. 700 G/1¾ LB DOUGH
400 g/14 oz flour   *4 large eggs, beaten*
a pinch of salt

Sift the flour and salt into a bowl. Make a well in the middle and pour in the eggs. Work the flour into the eggs and continue with your hands until the ingredients are well mixed, adding 1 tablespoon or more of flour if necessary, so that the mass holds well together.

Knead for 10–15 minutes until the dough is smooth and elastic, adding a little more flour if it is too sticky. Wrap in clingfilm and leave to rest for 30 minutes at room temperature before rolling out.

Divide the dough into 2 balls for easier handling. On a lightly-floured surface with a lightly-floured rolling-pin, roll each ball out as thinly as possible, working from the centre outwards. This job can be speeded up and made easier with the help of a manual or electric pasta machine.

Leave to dry for 20 minutes before cutting. Cook the pasta in a large pan of boiling water for 5 minutes. A splash of olive oil will help prevent the pasta from sticking together, or to the pan.

This is Claudia Roden's foolproof recipe from her marvellously user-friendly book, *The Food of Italy*. It can also be used to form the basis for the following recipes.

Herb Pasta

Mix 50 g/2 oz finely chopped fresh herbs with the eggs before making the dough.

Mushroom Pasta

Mince 25 g/1 oz of fresh or dried and reconstituted mushrooms very finely. Knead into the dough.

Saffron Pasta

Beat 25–50 g/1–2 oz saffron powder into the eggs.

Tomato Pasta

Beat 2 tbsp tomato purée into the eggs and knead into the mixture.

Green Pasta

SERVES APPROX. 6
200 g/7 oz fresh spinach or   *400 g/14 oz flour*
   100 g/3½ oz frozen   *a pinch of salt*
3 eggs, beaten

If using fresh spinach, discard the stalks, rinse under cold running water, and sweat gently in a covered pan until limp. Drain and squeeze dry, then purée and mix into the eggs.

Sift the flour into a bowl with the salt and make a well in the centre. Pour the egg mixture into the flour and gently work into a soft dough that holds together well. Knead for 15 minutes, cover with clingfilm or foil, and leave to rest for 30 minutes. Proceed as for the egg pasta recipe.

Wholemeal Pasta

400 g/14 oz wholemeal flour   *5 eggs, beaten*
100 g/4 oz semolina   *2 tbsp olive oil*
1 tbsp salt

Sift together the flour, semolina and salt into a bowl. Make a well in the middle and gently, using your fingertips, work the eggs into the dough while gradually incorporating the olive oil. Knead until you have worked a dry but elastic dough. If it is too sticky, sift in a little more flour. Cover the dough with clingfilm or foil, and leave to rest for 2 hours. Cut the dough into 2 or 4 pieces and proceed as for the egg pasta.

Buckwheat Pasta

200 g/7 oz wholemeal flour   *5 eggs, beaten*
200 g/7 oz buckwheat flour   *1 tbsp salt*
100 g/4 oz semolina   *2 tbsp olive oil*

Follow the wholemeal pasta recipe above.

Egg Pasta with Milk

SERVES 6–8
450 g/1 lb plain flour   *2 eggs, beaten*
a pinch of salt   *150 ml/5 fl oz milk, warmed*

Sift the flour into a bowl and stir in the salt. Make a well in the middle and, using the tips of your fingers, mix in the eggs. Gradually incorporate the milk, a little at a time, to make a firm dough. Knead well for 10–15 minutes until you have a smooth, elastic dough. Wrap in clingfilm and leave in a warm place for at least 30 minutes. Divide in half or quarters and roll as thin as you can.

Hungarian Soup Noodles/Laskatesszta Levesbe

SERVES APPROX. 4–6
1 egg   *salt*
50–75 g/2–3 oz strong,
  white flour

Whisk the egg in a bowl and tentatively sift in the flour with a pinch of salt to make a firm dough. Knead thoroughly and, on a floured board, roll out the dough very thin and cut into vermicelli noodles. Cook the noodles in a large pan of salted boiling water for 3 minutes. Drain and rinse with cold water. The noodles are now ready to be added to the soup. This same mixture can be rolled and cut into different shapes. The same ingredients are also used to make the following recipe.

Hungarian Pinched 'Dumplings'/Csipetke/Galuskas

MAKES APPROX. 20 'PINCHES'

See preceding recipe for ingredients and dough-making method. Leave the kneaded dough to rest for 15 minutes before cutting it into 6 pieces. Roll each piece to finger thickness and, with floured fingers, pinch off little bits into simmering soup or salted water. Poach for 5 minutes.

Ribelli

SERVES 4–6
150 g/5 oz plain flour   a pinch of salt
1 egg, beaten

Sift the flour into the egg, season and mix thoroughly to make a thick paste. Leave to dry out slightly for 30 minutes, then grate on a flat grater into lightly simmering broth. Cook for a couple of minutes and serve.

STUFFED PASTA

The quickest and easiest way to make a quantity of ravioli is to roll out 2 sheets of pasta at a time; one for the base and the second for the topping. Cover one sheet with a damp cloth and brush the other with egg wash. Using a teaspoon, place equal amounts of your chosen filling on the egg wash sheet, approx. 5 cm/2 in apart, and cover with the second sheet of pasta. Press around the mounds of filling to seal the ravioli. Using a sharp knife or a ravioli cutter, cut out the ravioli and place on a tray dusted with flour. Place a sheet of greaseproof paper between the layers.

Potato and Garlic Ravioli

This is my version of Sally Clarke's version of Alice Waters's original recipe devised for her restaurant Chez Panisse in San Francisco. It is often on the menu at Sally's restaurant, Clarke's, in Kensington, where she serves it dusted with Parmesan or with a fresh tomato concassé made with black pepper, olive oil and finely chopped thyme, lightly reduced with cream.

MAKES APPROX. 30 RAVIOLI
450 g/1 lb washed spinach
a pinch of salt
6 large egg-yolks
450 g/1 lb strong flour
900 g/2 lb floury-variety
  potatoes

150 ml/¼ pt double cream
4 big cloves of garlic, chopped
a few sprigs of fresh thyme,
  finely chopped

Begin by making the ravioli. First sweat the spinach in a covered pan with a little salt. When cooked, squeeze dry, chop, and whisk in the food processor with the eggs. Mix the egg and spinach into the flour, add a pinch of salt, and knead until you have a firm, smooth and elastic dough. Wrap in clingfilm and leave to rest for at least 15 minutes.

Meanwhile, boil the potatoes in their skins and at the same time put the cream and garlic on to simmer very gently for 20 minutes. Dry mash the peeled potatoes while still hot and whisk in the cream and garlic until the potatoes fluff. Add the finely chopped thyme and leave to cool.

On a lightly floured surface roll out the pasta into wafer-thin sheets. Cut out circles (a cookie cutter is perfect for this), and pipe or spoon on enough of the potato mixture to make moon-shaped pasties. Brush the edges with an egg wash or beaten milk and pinch together. Leave on a rack to dry for 20 minutes and then plunge into boiling water for 30–40 seconds. Remove the pasties with a slotted spoon and slip them into the soup tureen a few minutes before serving.

Potato and Garlic Purée

MAKES APPROX. 40 RAVIOLI
2 heads of garlic
900 g/2 lb floury-variety
  potatoes
3 tbsp flat-leaf parsley, finely
  chopped

2 tbsp butter
salt and black pepper
6 tbsp cream

Separate the garlic cloves, remove their husks, and halve. Peel the potatoes, and slice thinly using a mandoline. Put the garlic, potatoes, parsley and butter in a small saucepan and add water to cover by 5 cm/2 in. Bring to the boil, season with a generous pinch of salt, lower the heat, and simmer, partially covered, until the potatoes and garlic are soft and the water cooked away. This takes about 25 minutes.

Pass the potatoes and garlic through a mouli-légumes or mash by hand; do not be tempted to use a food processor because this will reduce the purée to a gluey glop. Whisk in the cream to make a firm purée and season to taste with salt and pepper. Chill.

Using either bought wonton skins or 5-cm/2-in squares cut from sheets of one of the fresh pasta recipes (pages 87–90), place 2–3 tsp of the purée in the centre. Brush the edges with water, milk or an egg wash and cover with a second wonton skin, gently stretching over the filling. Press the skins tightly with your fingers and run a pastry wheel round the edges to seal. Dust with flour and cover with a cloth while you continue.

Poach for 3–5 minutes in gently simmering salted water, then remove with a slotted spoon, drain and slip into the soup.

Pumpkin Purée 1

SERVES 6–8 ; APPROX. 24 LARGE RAVIOLI

110 g/4 oz butter
450 g/1 lb pumpkin, peeled
  and cut in 2.5-cm/1-in
  squares
225 g/8 oz thick cream
2 tbsp sage, minced or
  chopped finely

2 tsp thyme leaves, minced or
  chopped finely
½ a bayleaf
2 eggs, beaten
salt and white pepper

Heat half the butter in a sauté pan, and when it begins to froth, add the pumpkin and cook, stirring frequently to stop it from sticking and burning, until it flops into a purée. Turn the purée into a saucepan, add half the cream and half the herbs, and cook very gently, stirring occasionally, for up to an hour, until the mixture is a thick purée with no trace of liquid. Remove the bayleaf, add the rest of the butter, and whisk in the beaten eggs. Leave to rest for 10 minutes, whisk again, season to taste and leave to cool.

On a floured board, roll out thin sheets of one of the pasta doughs on pages 87–90 and stuff the ravioli using the method described on page 91. Poach the ravioli for 5 minutes in boiling, salted water. Remove with a slotted spoon, drain, and slip into the soup.

Pumpkin Purée 2

This recipe for pumpkin purée is a speciality of Mantua, famous for its sweet and tasty pumpkins, and is traditionally served stuffed in *tortelli* squares on Christmas Eve. The dish doesn't satisfactorily translate in this country because of the quality of the pumpkins available, but also because of a key ingredient, *mostarda di frutta*, also known as *mostarda di Cremona*, an unusual fruit preserve flavoured with mustard oil. In her exhaustive and illuminating book *Italian Food*, Elizabeth David charts the 'dishonourable travesty of that ancient and beautiful preserve so often noted by travellers in Italy, from Michel de Montaigne in the 1580s and the Reverend John Ray FRS in the 1660s down to the 1950s when I myself was so beguiled by its shining appearance in those big wooden pails in the Milan provision stores'. Since the 1970s, she goes on, when a Cremona firm began exporting a brand of the preserve that radically changed the original fruit content (which was whole pears, cherries, little oranges, figs, plums, apricots, and slices of melon and pumpkin) and added corn syrup and a range of certified colour and preservatives, *mostarda di frutta* sold away from its origins is barely recognizable.

Mostarda di frutta, of Cremona, is clearly one of the many specialities of Lombardy to bring home. It is generally eaten as an accompaniment to cold boiled meats and ham, and does much for cold turkey.

SERVES 10–12

1.4 kg/3 lb piece of pumpkin
2 eggs, beaten
110 g/4 oz fine breadcrumbs
110 g/4 oz amaretti
    (miniature sweet almond
    macaroons), crushed
110 g/4 oz Parmesan, freshly
    grated
peel of ½ a lemon, grated
    finely

¼ tsp nutmeg, grated
salt
110 g/4 oz mostarda di
    Cremona, finely chopped
    (optional; if tempted to
    experiment with alternatives,
    be sure to use mustard
    essence in the mixture and
    not ordinary mustard)

Peel the pumpkin, remove the seeds and bake, wrapped in foil, at 400° F/200° C/Gas Mark 6, for 1 hour. Mash to a purée, beat in the eggs, then mix in the breadcrumbs, macaroons, Parmesan, lemon rind, nutmeg and salt, and the *mostarda di Cremona*. Stir thoroughly and leave to chill before using.

Ricotta and Parmesan Paste

SERVES 6–8

700 g/1½ lb fresh spinach,
    with stems removed, or
    450 g/1 lb frozen
1 tbsp butter
½ an onion, minced
2 tbsp Parmesan, freshly
    grated

1 tsp salt
pepper
nutmeg
275 g/10 oz ricotta

Rinse the spinach under running water and sweat gently until the leaves are wilted. Drain, squeeze out remaining juice, and chop finely. Meanwhile melt the butter, gently sauté the onion until soft, then add the spinach and stir around for a couple of minutes. Tip the mixture into a bowl, add the Parmesan, salt, pepper, and a generous pinch of nutmeg, and stir in the ricotta. Mix thoroughly and chill before using.

Caprese Paste

SERVES 6–8

110 g/4 oz Parmesan, freshly grated
175 g/6 oz Caciotta, Provolone or Gruyère, freshly grated
3 eggs, beaten

2 tbsp basil or marjoram or both, finely chopped
¼ tsp nutmeg, freshly grated
salt and pepper
150–200 ml/6–8 fl oz milk

Mix the cheeses into the eggs, fold in the herbs and seasonings, and add the milk little by little, to form a firm, pliable mixture. Cover and chill until needed.

Cappelletti

This is the traditional filling for *cappelletti* (little ravioli) from Perugia, where *cappelletti in brodo* is the traditional Christmas Eve dish. It will not spoil the recipe to omit the veal brains, and the stuffing is delicious made with all pork instead of the mixture of veal and pork.

MAKES APPROX. 40 CAPPELLETTI

25 g/1 oz butter
175 g/6 oz lean pork, chopped
175 g/6 oz lean veal, chopped
50 g/2 oz piece of ham, chopped
50 g/2 oz veal brains, cleaned, soaked for 1 hour in cold water and drained

5-cm/2-in piece of celery, finely chopped
1 small carrot, peeled and diced
50 ml/2 fl oz Marsala
1 egg
50 g/2 oz Parmesan, grated
¼ tsp nutmeg
salt and pepper

Melt the butter and gently sauté the meat, brains, celery and carrot together for about 5 minutes. Add the Marsala and cook for a further 20 minutes. Tip into a food processor and mince finely before adding the egg, cheese and seasoning. Allow the mixture to cool before using.

To make *cappelletti*, roll out 2 approximately equal-sized sheets of pasta dough (see pages 87–90). Cover one with a damp cloth and brush the other with an egg wash or beaten egg-yolk. Working quickly, put teaspoons of the paste at 3.5-cm/1½-in intervals on the painted sheet, cover with the second sheet, press round the stuffing and cut out to make small rounds, about 3.5 cm/1½ in. Cappelletti take approx. 4 minutes to poach and can be cooked directly in boiling broth.

Any leftover *cappelletti* can be fished out of the broth and warmed through in cream, or served hot from the broth, smothered in Parmesan and butter.

Korean Beef Dumplings

This recipe comes from Jennifer Brennan's book *One-Dish Meals of Asia*. The ravioli-style dumplings are a feature of a robust, Orientally-flavoured beef-based soup called *man too*.

SERVES 8–10: APPROX. 24 LARGE RAVIOLI

2 tbsp vegetable oil
225 g/8 oz lean beef, pounded
 to a paste
1 medium onion, minced
1 tbsp sesame seeds, toasted
 in a dry frying-pan until pale
 brown and then ground
2 cloves of garlic, minced
4 small mushrooms, finely
 chopped

2 tbsp finely chopped tender
 cabbage leaves
50 g/2 oz beansprouts with
 tails removed, washed,
 drained and finely chopped
3 tbsp pine-nuts
2 tbsp soy sauce
¼ tsp black pepper

Heat the oil in a large frying-pan or wok and sauté the beef, onion, ground sesame seeds, and garlic until the meat has uniformly changed colour. Stir in all the remaining ingredients and stir-fry for a further minute or two. Transfer to a bowl, mix thoroughly, cover and leave to cool.

To make the dumplings, use one of the pasta doughs on pages 87–90 and break off 2.5-cm/1-in dough balls. On a floured board, roll the balls into 7.5-cm/3-in discs. Place 1 tablespoon of the mixture on the lower half of the circle, paint the edge with an egg wash or egg-yolk, and fold over to make a moon-shaped patty. Crimp and press the edges to seal.

Poach for 3–4 minutes in simmering broth.

Wontons

Wonton, which means 'swallowing the cloud', is the Oriental equivalent of ravioli and is folded from a square, into a triangle with two edges crimped together. The final result looks like a large ear of corn. The dough, made from flour, cornstarch, egg, water and salt, can be bought ready made in Oriental supermarkets, sometimes cut into the usual 7.5-cm × 10-cm/3-in × 4-in squares or rounds. Any of the pasta dough recipes on pages 87–90 can be used.

Chicken and Shrimp Filling

SERVES 6: APPROX. 30 WONTONS

110 g/4 oz chicken breast, minced
110 g/4 oz shrimps or prawns, shelled, de-veined and minced
2 spring onions, finely chopped
2.5-cm/1-in piece of fresh ginger, grated
2 tbsp parsley, finely chopped
1 tbsp vegetable oil
2 tsp cornflour
½ tsp sugar (optional)
2 tsp soy sauce
a pinch of salt and pepper

Mix all the ingredients together thoroughly – use a food processor if you have one. Cover and chill. If using round wonton skins, place 1 tsp of the mixture in the centre of a skin, moisten the edges, cover with a second skin and crimp the edges. If using square skins, place a skin in a diamond shape on your left hand. Put a spoonful of the mixture just below the middle of the square, and moisten the 2 left-hand edges with beaten egg. Fold the moist edges together to make the square into a triangle. Next, fold the two corners of the triangle in the centre and 'glue' in place with egg wash.

Parboil the wontons by dropping them a few at a time in boiling salted water. Cook for 6–8 minutes until they float to the surface. Remove with a slotted spoon, then cook for a further 5–6 minutes in the soup.

Chicken and Mushroom Filling

Jew's Ear mushrooms have a distinctive crunchy yet gelatinous texture and are available in most multiples and in any Oriental food store.

SERVES 6–8

175 g/6 oz chicken leg, minced
2 tbsp dried Jew's Ear or other wood-ear mushrooms (soaked in warm water for 20 minutes), finely chopped
1 tbsp grated fresh ginger
1 tbsp soy sauce
1 tbsp sesame oil
1 egg, beaten
1 tbsp spring onion, finely chopped

Mix all the ingredients together. Cover and chill before use.

Pork, Prawn and Mushroom Filling

MAKES 40–50 WONTONS

225 g/8 oz pork, minced
225 g/8 oz prawns, peeled,
  de-veined and chopped
2 tbsp spring onions, finely
  chopped
25 g/1 oz Chinese dried black
  mushrooms (previously
  soaked in warm water for 20
  minutes), finely chopped

2 tsp rice wine or dry sherry
1 tsp light soy sauce
1 tsp sesame oil
1½ tsp sugar
½ tsp salt
freshly ground black pepper to
  taste

Mix all the ingredients together. Cover and chill before use.

VEGETABLES

Duxelles

My ancient edition of *Larousse Gastronomique* neatly describes duxelles as a kind of mushroom hash. Its robust and meaty flavour is a good standby for putting body into lack-lustre soups.

25 g/1 oz butter
2 shallots, peeled and finely
  diced
110 g/4 oz mushrooms,
  chopped very finely

1 tbsp parsley, finely chopped
  (optional)
salt and pepper
nutmeg

Heat the butter and lightly brown the shallot. Add the mushrooms, parsley, salt, pepper and nutmeg and stir-fry over a medium flame so that any surplus moisture left in the mushrooms is evaporated, and at the same time everything is thoroughly cooked.

La Fricassée

One way to bolster the flavour of a vegetable soup is to sauté a couple of tablespoons of the vegetables used in the soup and add them to the pot just before serving. Vegetables best suited to this treatment are onions, leeks, carrots, turnips, parsnips and tomatoes. If the cooking fat is 'taken up' with flour, it is also a way of thickening the soup.

1 tbsp butter, lard or oil
2–3 tbsp of a combination of
  onion, leek, carrot, turnip,
  parsnip and tomato, diced

2 tbsp flour
a little stock from the soup

Heat the fat and begin by cooking the onion, then add the other vegetables and cook for a few minutes before stirring in the flour. Let it bubble up and then stir in a little stock. Cook for 5 minutes and pour into the soup.

FRIED EMBELLISHMENTS

BALLS AND PATTIES

Hungarian Soup Peas/Rántott Borsó

In Hungary, I learn from George Lang's *The Cuisine of Hungary*, they have special equipment for making dough peas. I have experimented with a holed draining-spoon but agree with Lang that a colander is the best improvised implement. It is important to make the peas in batches and to keep them on the move with a wooden fork or spatula to avoid them sticking and clumping together. They can be made in advance and crisped up in the oven just before serving.

SERVES 6–8
50 g/2 oz flour　　　　　　*a pinch of salt*
1 egg　　　　　　　　　　*65 g/2½ oz lard or chicken*
75 ml/3 fl oz milk　　　　　　*fat*

Sift the flour and mix with the egg, milk and salt until smooth. Heat the lard in a large frying-pan and just before it starts to smoke, turn the heat right down. Little by little drip the batter through the colander into the frying-pan, making sure the drops are evenly distributed. Cook them till golden brown all over and drain on absorbent paper. Place some 'peas' in each plate and serve the soup on to them.

Italian Meatballs/Polpetti

MAKES APPROX. 30 WALNUT-SIZED BALLS
3 slices stale bread　　　　　　*1 tbsp flat-leaf parsley, finely*
a little milk　　　　　　　　　*chopped*
450 g/1 lb lean beef, minced　　*1 clove of garlic, crushed*
2 eggs, whisked　　　　　　　*salt and pepper*
2 tbsp Parmesan, freshly　　　*olive oil for frying*
grated

Cover the bread with milk and leave to soak for 10 minutes. Squeeze the bread to remove all the liquid and mix with the meat, eggs, cheese, parsley, garlic and seasoning. Flour your hands and a board, and form the mixture into little balls. Flatten slightly and fry on both sides in olive oil. Drain on absorbent paper and add to the soup.

Rouzole

SERVES 4–6

125 g/4½ oz streaky bacon,
 finely diced
125 g/4½ oz raw ham,
 chopped
2 eggs, beaten
3 cloves of garlic, finely
 chopped

75 g/3 oz dried breadcrumbs
1 sprig of mint, chopped
salt and pepper
goose fat, lard or oil for frying

Mix all the ingredients together. Heat sufficient fat or oil to cover a large non-stick frying-pan. When hot, spread the mixture evenly in the pan to form a large pancake. Brown on both sides. When the rouzole is cooked through, cut into slices, squares or bite-sized pieces to add to the soup 10 minutes before the end of cooking. It is especially good with broad bean and pea soups.

Chinese Shrimp Balls

One of my best discoveries is the back room at Soho's oldest Chinese supermarket, Loon Fung (42–44 Gerrard Street; open 10a.m.–7p.m. daily). This is where I load up with freshly made *dim sum* for my deep-freeze, stock up with dried mushrooms and seaweeds, and where I have spent hours pondering over the hundreds of edible curiosities. One of Loon Fung's best bargains is their 500 g/1 lb boxes of quick-frozen raw prawns, or shrimps as the Chinese call them. It's after such visits that I might make these delicious prawn-heavy balls, adapted from a recipe in Doreen Yen Hung Feng's book, *The Joy of Chinese Cooking*, published in 1952. They will transform a bowl of chicken broth, and have been the centrepiece of all manner of impromptu 'Chinese' soups.

The balls can be varied with the addition of lightly chopped fresh flat-leaf parsley or coriander, but I prefer to add other seasonings as a last-minute garnish.

It is worth making a big batch, as they freeze perfectly. Alternatively, halve the ingredients – either way, try to get someone to help you shape the balls before frying begins.

Incidentally, Loon Fung sell various ready-made prawn balls which are good but not a patch on these. Another room there is full of Chinese soup-bowls, steamers and cooking equipment; they are probably the cheapest source in Chinatown.

MAKES APPROX. 40 WALNUT-SIZED BALLS

1.4 kg/3 lb raw prawns   *1 tsp salt dissolved in 1 tbsp*
  (shrimps)   *cold water*
110 g/4 oz pork fat (lard)   *vegetable oil*
4 egg-whites
110–175 g/4–6 oz self-
  raising flour

Rinse the prawns, remove their black central vein, and drain. Mince or process to a pulp and transfer to a large mixing-bowl. Cut the lard into pieces and, using your hands, cream together with the prawn pulp. In a separate bowl whisk the egg-whites and gradually whisk in the sifted flour and the salt and water mixture. Blend the two lots of ingredients by stirring with the hand in one direction. After 15–20 minutes, pick it up and throw it back against the bowl. Continue stirring and throwing until the mixture is quite stiff and the prawns have turned from grey to white to slightly pinkish. By now the mixture should have acquired a natural adhesive quality; this can be tested by squeezing a little lump of mixture into a bowl of cold water. If the lump holds its shape well and does not begin to disintegrate or become sticky and shapeless when lightly touched by the fingers, it is ready for deep-frying.

Heat at least 1 cm/½ in of clean vegetable oil. Have a bowl of cold water next to the prawn mixture, dip your left hand into the water, take a mass of mixture and squeeze a generous lump through the hollow between your thumb and the base of your index finger. Shape into balls and drop carefully into the hot vegetable oil. Fry until the balls have puffed to double their size and are a golden colour. Drain, and serve whole or sliced into the soup.

Thai Fried Prawn Balls

MAKES APPROX. 15–20 MARBLE-SIZED BALLS

450 g/1 lb raw prawns   *½ tsp peppercorns, ground*
4 cloves of garlic   *salt*
1 tbsp coriander root or   *oil for deep-frying*
  leaves, finely chopped

Wash, de-vein and finely mince the prawns. Pound or process the garlic, coriander, peppercorns and salt and work into the prawns until you have a malleable paste. Rinse your hands in cold water and shape into small balls which can be rolled in flour or breadcrumbs. Deep-fry the balls for about 5 minutes until they are golden brown. Drain and add to soup.

Garnishes

Drawing the line between what is a garnish and what would be
better classified as an enrichment added towards the end of cooking
proved very difficult. In the end, after much indecision, I made the
division on the basis that a garnish is anything that is added at the
last moment and *isn't necessarily* an embellishment. There is, nevertheless, some cross-over with most of the sections within the 'Embellishment to Go in Soup' section (pages 55–101).

To garnish means to decorate, and when it comes to soup-garnish-
ing the only boundaries are your imagination. It isn't, however,
compulsory, and most of my garnishes, like my soups, reflect what I
have to hand at that moment.

Garnishing can be simple or elaborate but should always link in
with the soup in some way as well as looking attractive. It can reflect
the soup's flavour or be in direct contrast with it. It can provide the
only texture, and be the only fresh ingredient. The garnish can be
the trump card that transforms a bland soup, or the joker playing a
visual trick.

However elaborate or simple the garnish, always pay attention to
the shape, the colour and the texture of any ingredients you use in
relation to the type of soup it will adorn. What you are aiming at is
visual interest that tastes good too. Don't be afraid to experiment and
to use combinations of garnishes.

Unless otherwise specified, the quantities given in these recipes
provide sufficient garnish for 4–6 servings.

HERBS AND FLOWERS

'A bowl filled with sprigs of parsley, chives,
mint, dill, cress, coriander, tarragon or any
herb which happens to be available will
normally be found on the table at a Persian
meal. According to an ancient belief,
women who eat the herbs at the end of the
meal with bread and cheese will have no

difficulty in keeping their husbands.'
(Michelle Berriedale-Johnson on Ancient
Persian cookery in *The British Museum Cook-
book*)

If you are serving a soup with a particular herb seasoning, add a
generous handful of that herb just before you purée or serve the
soup. This will provide a fresher flavour. Fresh herbs sprinkled on to
the soup or mixed in with cream or yoghurt have the same effect.
Parsley is the commonest herb garnish because of its availability but
also because of its bright green colour and adaptability. Chives, which
have a far stronger oniony flavour than some people realize, should
be used with discretion. Flowering Chinese chive has a delicate but
pronounced garlicky flavour. Other herbs should be used to complement ingredients in the soup, but you will have to discover what you
like. Basil, for instance, is especially good with tomatoes; mint with
peas, potatoes and cucumber; rocket, dill and thyme with potatoes;
and coriander with spicy soups.

The flowers of most herbs, notably mint, borage, oregano, thyme
and fennel, can also be used as a garnish. See also 'A Stock-pot
Flavour Guide: Herbs and Aromatics' (pages 10–11).

Dried herbs are not suitable for garnishing.

Edible flowers and their leaves can provide an appropriate garnish,
but most have powerful flavours. Lavender, rose petals, pansy,
jasmine, Japanese chrysanthemum leaves, geranium leaves and
flowers, marigold petals and nasturtium leaves and flowers are all
usable.

SEAWEEDS AND VEGETABLES

Next to herbs, leafy vegetables are the most universally common
soup garnish. Unless the leaves are very young, small or thin, they
need to be blanched for a couple of minutes in boiling water if the
soup is to be served immediately. Rather than chop the leaves, roll
them like a thick cigar and slice them into ribbons. Sorrel, which will
add a tart lemony flavour, and spinach are ideal leaf garnishes; so
too are Chinese *pak choi* and Chinese kale. Flavour is more intrusive
with most types of cabbage, with regular curly kale, beetroot tops,
peppery turnip tops, celery and celeriac leaves, and watercress.

Slicing vegetables into interesting or unlikely shapes, thicknesses
and strands is a neat form of garnish much deployed in Japanese
soups. Marco Pierre White, the talented chef of Harveys, is keen on
serving mounds of courgette and carrot 'spaghetti' as a garnish to
just about every savoury dish except soup – with which it works very
effectively.

Small quantities of raw, blanched or lightly sautéed vegetables
held back from the main soup can be used alone or as part of a
garnish. For instance, asparagus spears with an asparagus soup;

small fresh, minted peas with a pea soup; sliced mushrooms, perhaps a different variety, with a mushroom soup; florets of watercress with a watercress soup, and so on.

Spaghetti of Carrot

2 large, fat carrots   large knob of butter

Trim the ends of the carrots and peel them. Trim the edges of the peeled carrots so that they have the shape of a thick wedge. Then cut the wedges into 2-mm/⅛-in slices. Turn the slices so that they are layered on top of one another and cut them again into 2-mm/⅛-in strips. The strips should resemble spaghetti.

Put the carrot strips in a pan, add enough water to cover generously, and add the butter. Bring to the boil and simmer until the carrot strips are tender but still firm. Drain.

Cauliflower and Broccoli Stems

The stems of cauliflower and broccoli can be skinned and diced or shaped into small barrels to be blanched for a couple of minutes in boiling salted water. They make a pretty and tasty garnish to a white soup.

Toasted Seaweed

The dark green, paper-thin laver that the Japanese call *nori* (much used to wrap vinegared rice and raw fish) and the Koreans call *kim* can be flash-grilled and used as a garnish.

1 sheet of nori per person   sesame oil

Nori is sold in packets of sheets; brush both sides of each sheet lightly with sesame oil and place it under a hot grill, or wave it in front of a low flame for 30 seconds until crisp. Using scissors, cut the *nori* into squares and then into thin strips.

CREAMS, YOGHURTS AND BUTTERS

Pouring cream and thin yoghurt can be swirled on the top of individual servings at the last minute. To create a marbled effect, pour the cream from the centre, round and out to the sides, then draw a fork through the cream.

Other garnishing and embellishment ideas using creams, yoghurts and butters are given on pages 61–8.

CHEESE

Unless a soup recipe specifies the use of a particular cheese, the only one I use as a soup garnish is Parmesan.

It is expensive, but I regard it as a necessity and always buy a piece (kept wrapped in foil at the bottom of the fridge) which goes on the table for people to grate for themselves. This comment from Marcella Hazan, author of numerous Italian cook books, is spot on: 'Do not under any circumstances use ready-grated cheese sold in jars. Even if this commercially grated cheese were of good quality, which it is not, it would have lost all its flavour long before getting to the market. It is of no interest whatever to Italian cooking' . . . or soup garnishing.

FRIED GARNISHES

All successful frying depends on using an appropriate fat or oil heated to the right temperature.

Ordinary butter is not suitable for the pan-fried dishes in this section because it burns at a low temperature, turns brown, smokes and ruins the food. Mixed with a little oil (2–4 tsp of oil to 50 g/2 oz butter) it can reach a higher temperature without burning; the same is true of rendered bacon fat. If a recipe demands butter it should be clarified. This is a simple and worthwhile chore, but ready-made clarified butter is widely available in Indian and Middle Eastern food shops, where it is called ghee.

To clarify butter: Melt any amount of butter in a frying-pan over a low heat. When the whole surface is bubbling, remove from the heat and allow it to cool slightly before you pour it through muslin or cheesecloth into a storage jar. The impurities that make butter go rancid are now removed and the ghee will keep indefinitely.

To render bacon fat: Bake or fry streaky bacon or thick fatty rinds until the fat begins to run. This takes 10–15 minutes. Strain through muslin and store.

To render raw fat: Chop the fat into 1-cm/½-in pieces and simmer for 20 minutes in a covered saucepan with 275 ml/½ pt water to draw the fat out of the tissues. Uncover the pan and boil slowly to evaporate the water. When the spluttering is finished you will end up with a pale yellow liquor dotted with globules. Strain and reserve.

Dripping: Chicken, beef and pork fat, known as dripping, can be collected during and after cooking for later use. Always strain the fat to remove specks of meat, etc. that will turn it rancid. Lamb fat, which has a far stronger flavour, is less useful.

Cooking oils: Olive oil imparts a rich, fruity flavour to fried foods. The following, provided they are kept free of impurities, won't flavour the food: groundnut, arachide or peanut oil, sunflower oil, vegetable oil, soya oil, corn or maize oil.

BATTERS, OMELETTES AND PANCAKES

Egg Strands

3 large eggs
2 tsp vegetable oil

a generous pinch of salt

Gently but thoroughly beat the egg with the salt and 3 tsp of water. Brush a non-stick frying-pan (18–20 cm/7–8 in) with oil and heat over a medium flame. When hot, but not smoking, remove from the heat and pour in a quarter of the egg mixture, just enough to make a thin layer on the bottom of the pan. Tilt the pan to get an even covering before the mixture sets. Using a flexible spatula, ease the omelette loose and either flip it over or cover the pan with a plate, turn it upside down and slip the omelette back into the pan. Return to the heat for a couple more seconds. Remove to a plate, cool, roll and slice into strands.

Pancake Strips

50 g/2 fl oz flour
salt
1 egg, whisked

6 tbsp milk or soda water, or
a mixture of both
oil for frying

Sift the flour and a tiny pinch of salt into the egg and gradually add the milk to form a smooth batter. Heat 1 tbsp of oil until it smokes, then remove the pan from the heat. Have ready in a cup 2 tbsp of batter; pour and quickly swirl around in the pan before returning it to the heat. Cook for a couple of minutes and turn with the help of a slice. The object is to end up with thin pancakes that can then be rolled and cut into thin slices. Sprinkle on to the soup just before serving, or serve separately for people to help themselves.

Buckwheat Pennies

175 g/6 oz buckwheat flour
110 g/4 oz flour
salt and pepper
2 tbsp oil
1 small onion or shallot,
  minced or finely diced

1 tsp mixed fresh herbs of
  your choice
oil for frying

Mix the flours, a pinch each of salt and pepper, and the oil. Stir in the onion and herbs and enough water to form the mixture into a soft dough. Knead well for 5 minutes and roll into a log of your chosen diameter – 1 cm/½ in is ideal. Cut in 0.5-cm/¼-in slices and deep-fry until golden.

CROÛTONS

Croûtons are made from thin slices of stale, firm-crumbed bread fried in oil or butter. Their success depends on even cooking at a very low temperature.

Traditionally the bread is cut into small squares, which is why different-shaped croûtons, which require a bit more effort, are so special. For example, lozenge, triangular or diamond shapes, those the French call *dents de loup* (wolves' teeth), batons or crests and hearts, give extra visual interest.

Flavour can be introduced via the cooking fat, but remember that some fats and oils could swamp the flavour of the soup. Goose, chicken, marrow, and *foie gras* fat give the richest and most intrusive flavour; olive oil is suitable for robustly flavoured soups, while butter or an unobtrusive vegetable oil are best for delicate soups. Similarly, garlic, cheese, most herbs and some spices are also widely used to flavour croûtons and should be chosen to complement particular soups.

Croûtons aren't always made from bread. For example, more unusual, and more work-intensive, are the pale yellow croûtons made from ground maize (polenta).

Croûtons will keep without deterioration for up to a week. Store in an airtight tin or sealed greaseproof bags.

Instructions for clarifying fresh fat and butter can be found on page 141.

Croûtons

50 g/2 oz any stale, close-grained white bread	*2 tbsp oil or 50 g/2 oz butter, lard or fat*

Remove the crusts and cut the bread into 0.5-cm/¼-in squares or batons, or stamp into shapes with a special cutter. Heat the oil, fat or butter until smoking (if using unclarified butter do not let it brown) and sauté the croûtons, tossing and stirring so that they colour evenly. Remove to absorbent kitchen paper to drain.

Croûtes

Large croûtons are usually called croûtes, but the term also applies to toasted and oven-dried sliced bread. Unless the croûtes are first sealed by frying, they are generally served as an accompaniment (see page 123) because they quickly become waterlogged in soup.

Any of the recipes for croûtons can be used for croûtes. Croûtes provide a useful 'float' for other garnishes.

6 thin slices from a narrow,   2 tbsp oil or 50 g/2 oz butter,
  stale French loaf   lard or fat
½ a clove of garlic (optional)   salt

Follow the recipe for croûtons, previous page. If using garlic, rub one side of each croûte with the cut surface of the garlic clove.

Anchovy Croûtons

50 g/2 oz day-old white   6 anchovy fillets, rinsed under
  bread, crusts removed   running water
4 tbsp olive oil   ½ tsp lemon juice

Cut the bread into approximately 0.5-cm/¼-in dice. Gently heat the oil in a small frying-pan and stir-fry the anchovies until the fillets disintegrate. Add the bread squares, stirring constantly until they become golden brown and crisp. Sprinkle over the lemon juice. Transfer to absorbent kitchen paper to drain.

Bacon Croûtons

50 g/2 oz day-old wholemeal   1–2 tbsp vegetable oil
  bread, crusts removed
2–4 rashers smoked streaky
  bacon

Cut the bread into 1-cm/½-in dice. Heat 1 tbsp of the oil and gently fry the bacon until crisp and all the fat has run out. Remove the bacon to drain and cool, then add the bread squares to the pan. Turn frequently, adding the rest of the oil if necessary, until the croûtons are crisp and evenly browned. Drain on absorbent paper. Crumble or chop the bacon and mix in with the croûtons.

Cheese Croûtons

½ a day-old ciabatta loaf   2 tbsp olive oil
15 g/1 oz freshly grated
  Parmesan

Slice the loaf thinly and dice. Heat the oil and gently sauté the bread until it is golden and crisp all over. Remove from the pan, sprinkle with Parmesan and grill for a couple of minutes. Drain on absorbent paper.

Garlic Croûtons

3 slices of stale processed   1 large clove of garlic, peeled
  bread, crusts removed   and chopped
3 tbsp olive oil

Cut the bread into 0.5-cm/¼-in dice. Gently heat the oil and before it
begins to smoke add the garlic. Stir-fry the garlic for a couple of
minutes, and remove with a slotted spoon before it turns nut-brown.
Add the bread squares to the pan and sauté, tossing the pan occasionally and stirring the bread around to cook it uniformly. Drain on
absorbent paper.

To make *very* garlicky croûtons: chop the garlic very finely and set
aside while you cook the bread. Just before the end of cooking, mix in
the garlic so that it browns and clings to the croûtons.

Polenta Croûtons

225 g/½ lb fine grain maize   ¼ tsp salt
  flour (polenta)   25 g/1 oz butter
570 ml/1 pt water   olive oil for brushing

Put the flour into a large pan (it needs space to 'grow', and constant
stirring) with the water and salt. Stir thoroughly and bring to the
boil, stirring all the while. Cook for 30 minutes, stirring frequently,
whisk in the butter, and pour into a well-oiled deep dish. Leave to set
rock hard, which will take around 30 minutes, then slip out of the
dish and cut into small squares or batons. Brush the croûtons with
oil and grill until lightly browned on both sides so that all edges and
surfaces are sealed. This prevents them being waterlogged in the
soup.

CRISPS, FLAKES, LEAVES AND HAIRS

Pan- and deep-fried herbs and vegetables provide spectacular, surprising and delicious garnishes. They can be 'floated' on cream or butter
garnishes, will sit happily on thick puréed soups, and will resist
getting waterlogged for some time if they are thoroughly cooked.
Replenishments can be served in a separate dish.

Crisps can be prepared in advance, but to retain their crunchiness
they must be carefully drained on absorbent paper before being dried
out in a warm, dry place (your oven at its lowest temperature, or an
airing cupboard, are both ideal) for an hour or so. The crisps can
then be successfully stored in an airtight tin or greaseproof bag.

Pan-fried Sage

50–75 g/2–3 oz clarified   24 sage leaves
  butter

Heat the butter until it begins to fizz but not smoke. Remove from the heat and cook the leaves in batches so that they are evenly covered with hot fat. Allow to sizzle for a few seconds, turn and repeat. Take care not to add the leaves to fat that is too hot, or to leave them in the pan too long. Remove and drain.

Pan-fried Parsley

6–12 attractive sprays of   75 g/3 oz clarified butter
  parsley

Wash and dry the parsley, trim the stalks and proceed as for pan-fried sage.

Hair of Ginger

2 × 5-cm/2-in pieces fresh   2 tbsp olive oil
  ginger

Peel the ginger and slice lengthways into matchstick juliennes. Heat the oil until a light haze rises from the surface. Lower the heat and stir in the ginger, twisting it around the pan to crisp evenly; this will take about 60 seconds. Remove and drain.

Hair of Leek

1 leek, white part only   2 tbsp olive oil

Cut the leek lengthways into the thinnest possible juliennes, about 7.5–10 cm/3–4 in long. Follow the instructions for hair of ginger though the cooking time will be shorter.

Hair of Parsnip

2 small parsnips   2 tbsp olive oil

Peel, core and slice the parsnips lengthways into matchstick juliennes. Follow instructions for hair of ginger.

Beetroot Crisps

4 raw beetroots   oil for deep-frying

Peel and trim the beetroots. Cut them in half, slicing horizontally, and shave each half into thin slices. Pat dry, and deep-fry in hot oil (375° F/190° C) in batches so that the crisps can cook evenly. Be sure to bring the oil back up to temperature between batches. Drain on absorbent paper.

Celeriac Crisps

1 small celeriac (about   oil for deep-frying
  450 g/1 lb)

Follow the recipe for beetroot crisps, above.

Green Plantain Crisps

Plantains, also known as green bananas, are generally baked or boiled and eaten as a filler vegetable. Their starchy, slightly sweet flesh makes them a good foil to spicy foods; with soups they are particularly good served deep-fried as crisps or chips.

Unlike bananas, plantains cling tightly to their skins and need to be peeled with a sharp knife, cutting through the skin in lengths and peeling off sections. For crisps or chips choose yellowing plantains, and peel into salted or acidulated water until required.

1 or 2 green plantains   oil for deep-frying

Peel the plantains, removing all the green skin. Using a sharp knife or a mandoline, cut the plantains into wafer-thin rounds and soak in iced water for 30 minutes. Pat dry, and deep-fry at about 350° F/ 180° C until golden. These can also be pan-fried in clarified butter. In Jamaica they are sometimes dusted with ground cinnamon, and in India with ground turmeric, before frying.

Potato Crisps

2 medium-sized floury   oil for deep-frying
  potatoes

Peel the potatoes and cut them into wafer-thin slices, using a sharp knife or a mandoline. Put them immediately into a big bowl of cold water. Swirl around to get rid of the starch, rinse again and dry in a cloth.

Deep-fry in small batches in very hot oil (375 °F/190 °C) for 2 minutes. Drain.

Lotus Root Crisps

The pretty lacy effect is as much an attraction as the nutty flavour of these crisps, made from the underwater rhizome of the lotus flower. Unlike most crisps, these crisp up as they cool and are best not served directly from the pan.

lotus root (it looks like a string   oil for deep-frying
*   of fat sausages)*

Peel the lotus root and cut into wafer-thin slices, using a mandoline or a very sharp knife. Drop into acidulated water, to prevent discoloration, pat dry, and deep-fry in batches in very hot oil (375° F/190° C) for a couple of minutes until golden brown. Drain.

Coconut Flakes

flesh from a fresh coconut

Cut the coconut flesh into flakes and pan-fry (or toast) in a non-stick pan over a medium heat. Coconut has a high fat content and burns easily.

Almond Flakes

50 g/2 oz almonds   15 g/½ oz clarified butter

Heat the butter and stir-fry the almonds until lightly golden all over. Remove them immediately from the pan and wrap in absorbent paper to drain.

For a nuttier flavour, toast the almond flakes under a hot grill. Other nuts and seeds, including hazelnuts, pine-nuts, pistachios, sunflower seeds, caraway seeds, dill, fennel and melon seeds can be treated in the same way.

Pumpkin Strips

½ a small pumpkin   olive oil
flour, seasoned with salt and
* pepper*

Peel and de-seed the pumpkin. Cut it into thin slices and leave in a sieve sprinkled with salt for a couple of hours – this helps get rid of excess moisture. Rinse under cold water, pat dry, dip the strips into seasoned flour and fry over a medium heat until both sides are golden brown. Drain.

Crisped Onions

2 medium-sized onions, peeled   *vegetable oil for shallow-frying*

Cut the onions in half lengthways and then slice each half into very thin half rings. Leave the onions sandwiched between several layers of absorbent kitchen paper for 30 minutes. Heat sufficient oil to give a depth of 1 cm/½ in. When the oil is hot, stir in the onions. Continue stir-frying, taking care the onions don't burn, until all their moisture has evaporated and the onions have cooked to a deep brownish colour. The process is likely to take at least 20 minutes. Remove the onions with a slotted spoon and spread out on absorbent paper. Once cooled, they will turn very crisp.

This recipe can be adapted by adding a little chopped garlic, fresh ginger, and/or fresh coriander towards the end of cooking. In Asian cooking, where these onions are a ubiquitous garnish, they are often served with yoghurt.

The onions can be frozen in small batches.

Gold Leaf and Gold Dust

Gold is the ultimate power garnish. It has no flavour, costs loads of money, but looks stunning, specially in candlelight. Gold dust can be sprinkled on home-made noodles used for garnish, and squares of gold leaf can be floated on to soup. Buy from goldsmiths or serious artist's material shops.

Caviare, Salmon Roe/Keta and Lumpfish

A little caviare used as a soup garnish goes a long way. It is especially good in jellied consommé. Cheaper alternatives are the larger, bright red salmon roe known as *keta* in Japan, and Swedish lumpfish roe which is sold dyed red or black.

Embellishment to Go with Soup

'He caused some biscuit and cakes to be
dipped into the pot and softened with the
liquor of the meat which they called brewis
and gave everyone some to stay their stom-
ache.' (Daniel Defoe, *Robinson Crusoe*)

BREAD, BREAD ROLLS AND PIZZA

'We have become a very food-conscious
people during the past few years. Ever more
cookery books pour from the presses, mille-
feuille pastry and shark fin soup, crêpes su-
zette and boeuf Stroganoff, quiche lorraine
and bouillabaisse and Linzertorte no longer
hold any mysteries for us. How about
putting the horse in front of the cart and
having a crack at baking a decent loaf of
bread?' (Elizabeth David, *Sunday Times*, 25
March, 1956 – in 1979 Mrs David was to
produce the definitive tome on bread-
making, *English Bread and Yeast Cooking*)

A good crusty loaf, fresh from the oven, is the classic accompaniment
to a bowl of steaming soup. Since Mrs David's paean on the paucity
of a decent loaf, things have greatly improved. Most supermarkets
now stock at least one olive-oil loaf, fancy stuffed breads, a decent
approximation of an authentic baguette, a brioche loaf, soda bread
and ready-to-roll pizza dough.

My selection of bread recipes is chosen for variety, ease of preparation and deliciousness.

Ciabatta

A fruitless search for a domestic recipe for the now ubiquitous Italian
flat-bread called ciabatta resulted in this painless version. It is a
collaboration between Giorgio Rocca of the restaurant Da Felicini in
Monforte d'Alba, and the English cookery writer Lynda Brown. It is
quick and easy to make in a food processor, doesn't require kneading,

and keeps for up to 5 days. This bread, with its slightly chewy texture, air-bubble dough and thick, crisp crust, is wonderful with soup.

Quantities can be scaled up to make more loaves at the same time; but the quality of the loaf is radically altered by the length of fermentation. Ms Brown discovered that 'a fermentation time of 3–6 hours produces a light puffy ciabatta; 12-hour fermentation deepens the flavour, producing the elusive background sweetness; 24 hours produces the more complex flavour that bread buffs relish'.

MAKES 1 × 18-CM/7-IN LOAF

3.5 g/⅛ oz fresh yeast or
1 × 2.5 ml tsp easy blend
dried yeast (following packet
instructions)

225 g/8 oz unbleached white
bread flour
3–5 tbsp extra virgin olive oil
a pinch of salt

Fit a dough blade to the food processor. Blend the dried yeast briefly with the flour, add the oil and salt, and pour between 200–240 ml/ 7–8 fl oz of hand-warm water gradually through the funnel with the motor running. Process for a minute or so, using just enough water to form a thick batter. Scrape down any batter from the lid, cover if you are using a food processor (put in the funnel, to form an airtight seal) and leave for a minimum 3–6 hours. The dough should be puffy and sticky.

Scrape the dough gently into a non-stick shallow pan and leave in a warm place for 30–40 minutes.

Bake in a pre-heated oven, at 425° F/220° C/Gas Mark 7, for 30–40 minutes until golden.

Focaccia

Focaccia, like ciabatta, is an Italian flat-bread made with olive oil. It is rich and aromatic and usually garnished with rosemary, thyme or sage leaves. Shape the dough into a square, round or oval.

MAKES 2 × 20.5-CM/8-IN SQUARE LOAVES

25 g/1 oz dried yeast, or
50 g/2 oz fresh
approximately 475 ml/18 fl oz
hand-warm water
½ tsp sugar

1 kg/2 lb 4 oz unbleached
white flour or a mixture of
whole wheat and white
coarse salt
150 ml/5 fl oz olive oil
2 sprigs of sage, rosemary or
thyme

Dissolve the fresh yeast in a little of the warm water, adding the sugar to activate it. Meanwhile sift the flour into a large bowl, mix in the salt, and when the yeast mixture is bubbling away, stir it into the flour. Add 4 tbsp of the olive oil and enough of the remaining warm water to make a soft dough. Remove it to a floured surface and knead thoroughly for several minutes until the dough is smooth and shiny.

Wash and dry the bowl and oil it with a little of the olive oil. Return the dough to the bowl, brush the top with olive oil, cover with clingfilm or a damp cloth, and leave it in a warm place for about an hour, when it will have doubled in size.

Punch it back and knead again for a couple of minutes. Cut the dough in half and shape it with a rolling-pin into 2 1-cm/½-in thick pieces. If desired, slash the top to make decorative indentations and brush the bread generously with olive oil. Sprinkle with coarse sea salt, and the rosemary, thyme or sage leaves. Transfer to a well-oiled baking-sheet and leave to prove for 30 minutes. Pre-heat the oven to 450° F/230° C/Gas Mark 8 and bake for 20–30 minutes.

Khubz/Pizza

This is Caroline Conran's recipe, from an excellent idiot's guide to understanding the principles of bread-making written for a book called *Masterclass*, expert lessons in kitchen skills. *Khubz* is a flat, disc-shaped bread that is simple to make and delicious to eat. It is a suitable dough for pizzas.

1 tsp salt	1 tbsp fresh yeast or ½ tbsp
350 g/12 oz plain flour	dried
	1 level tbsp sugar

Mix the salt into the flour in a large bowl. Mix the yeast with the sugar in 125 ml/4 fl oz of hand-warm water, whisk and leave in a warm place. Sift the flour into a bowl and add the yeast mixture, kneading thoroughly until you have a smooth dough. Allow it to rest while you wash the bowl, then knead lightly on a floured surface for a few minutes. Replace in the bowl, cover with clingfilm, and put the bowl somewhere warm until the dough has risen to more than double its original size. (It should take 45–60 minutes.) Remove to a floured board and roll out to 0.5 cm/¼ in thick. Make into one large round or cut out several small ones with a saucer. Place on a greased baking-tray, prick the top here and there with a fork, and prove for 15 minutes, covered. Pre-heat the oven to 375° F/190° C/Gas Mark 5 and bake for 30 minutes until golden. Brush the top with melted butter and serve while still warm.

Corn Bread/Broa

Broa is the name of the pale yellow, crusty bread made in Portugal. It has a sweetish flavour, dense dough and is perfect for making bruschetta (see page 124).

MAKES 2 LARGE OVAL LOAVES

100 g/4 oz fresh yeast or
  50 g/2 oz dried
1 tsp sugar
600 ml/1 pt hand-warm
  water

450 g/1 lb cornmeal
1 kg/2 lb strong white flour
salt
2 tbsp corn oil

Cream the yeast with the sugar and a little of the warm water (if using dried yeast, follow the instructions for fermentation). Sift the cornmeal, flour and salt into a bowl and pour in the creamed yeast. Sprinkle a little flour over the surface, and leave in a warm place for about 15 minutes or until the yeast has started working.

Using your hands, work the flour into the yeast liquid then add the rest of the warmed water and the corn oil until you have made a sticky dough. Remove to a well-floured surface and knead the dough vigorously until you have lost the stickiness and the dough is smooth and elastic.

Stretch a piece of clingfilm over the bowl and leave in a warm place for a couple of hours until the dough has doubled in size. Knock back the dough, cut in half, and knead each piece into a fat oval or round. Transfer each piece to a well-oiled baking-sheet, slip into a plastic carrier bag, and leave for about an hour to double its size.

Pre-heat the oven to its very highest temperature – mine is 475° F/ 240° C/Gas Mark 9 – and place a shallow tray of boiling water on the base of the oven (the steam gives the bread its thick, brown crust; a trick that can be used for any bread requiring a good crust). Bake for 25 minutes, then lower the temperature to 400° F/200° C/Gas Mark 6 for a further 10 minutes. Transfer to a wire rack to cool and eat the bread warm.

Brioche

This is a double recipe from Jane Grigson's *European Cookery* which gives ingredients for sufficient dough to make a brioche loaf and a bacon-stuffed brioche that will feed 6. With soup, serve toasted.

450 g/1 lb plain flour or bread
  flour
1 packet Harvest Gold dried
  yeast
2 level tsp salt
3 eggs

100 g/3½ oz butter, melted
150 ml/¼ pt milk
275–350 g/10–12 oz piece
  fat smoked streaky bacon
beaten egg to glaze

Sift the flour into a bowl and add the yeast and salt. Beat or process together the eggs, butter and half the milk in a warmed bowl. Tip in the flour and work into a dough, using the remaining milk if needed.

The dough should be soft, slightly waxy, and yellowish: if it is a bit tacky don't worry. Tie the bowl into a plastic bag and leave in a warm place for 1½–2 hours or until it has risen and doubled in size.

Meanwhile, dice the bacon and fry it in its own fat until nicely browned, but not hard or crisp. Drain and cool.

Punch down the dough and put one half into a warmed, buttered loaf tin. Mix the bacon pieces into the other half, kneading them well in. Put into another (buttered) loaf tin, or a fluted brioche tin, or make into a ring and put on a baking-sheet if the dough is not too soft. Tie into plastic bags and leave for 30–40 minutes to prove.

Pre-heat the oven to 400° F/200° C/Gas Mark 6 and bake for 40 minutes. Check after 25 minutes and brush the tops with beaten egg. Put back in for a further 5 minutes at least, out of the tins, to give the sides a chance to bake crisp.

Garlic Naan Bread

Indian flat-bread naan can be treated like pizza and topped or stuffed with nuts, herbs and sultanas. Its slight sweetness makes it a good foil for spicy soups, but I particularly like it with lentil and other pulse soups. The dough can be fashioned into any size or shape you like; reduce the cooking time if you decide on miniature naan.

If made in advance, naan can be stored between sheets of greaseproof paper in an airtight container. To revitalize, pop in a warm oven for a couple of minutes or under a hot grill.

MAKES 12 × 15-CM/6-IN ROUND PIECES

1 packet of dried yeast
1 tsp sugar
275 ml/5 fl oz hand-warm
  water
700 g/1½ lb unbleached plain
  flour
1½ tsp salt

150 ml/5 fl oz natural
  yoghurt
2 tbsp olive oil
2 tbsp sunflower oil
16 cloves of garlic, peeled and
  cut into slivers

Sprinkle the yeast and sugar into the warm water, whisk, and leave for about 10 minutes until frothy. Warm a china mixing-bowl and sieve into it the flour and salt. Stir in the yeast mixture, yoghurt and olive oil and work into a soft dough, using your hands. Remove to a floured surface and knead for 5–10 minutes until you have a smooth, elastic dough. Shape into a ball, return to the bowl, cover and leave in a warm place for about 1 hour until the dough has doubled in size.

Meanwhile heat the sunflower oil in a small sauté pan and stir-fry the garlic for a couple of minutes until softened but not coloured. Drain on absorbent kitchen paper.

Punch back the dough and knead again, adding more flour to prevent sticking if necessary. Divide into 12 pieces. Shape each into a smooth ball. Flatten each ball and stretch with your fingertips to make a 15-cm/6-in round.

Pre-heat the oven to 475° F/240° C/Gas Mark 9, heat several oiled baking-trays, and place 2 or 3 pieces of dough on each tray. Press some of the garlic into each round, brush with water or more yoghurt, and bake for 7 minutes until puffed and golden brown. Remove from the oven, cool slightly and serve.

To make stuffed naan, roll into even-sized pieces, spread 5 cm/¼ in of the chosen filling (cooked chopped potato laced with coriander or cumin is very good) on one piece, brush its rim with water and cover with a second piece. Pinch the edges together and bake as above.

Quick Wholemeal Loaf

This loaf is also known as the Grant loaf, so called because the recipe was devised by Doris Grant, one of the founders of the wholefood movement forty years ago. It needs no kneading or second proving, which is why the loaf never rises above the level of the tin.

MAKES 1 × 900-G/2-LB LOAF

1 tsp dried yeast or 15 g/½ oz fresh
1 tsp salt

1 tsp sugar (or, to make the scrumptious version served at Ballymaloe, Myrtle Allen's famous restaurant near Cork, use 1 tbsp black treacle)
450 g/1 lb wholemeal flour

If using fresh yeast, cream it with a little warm water; if using dry yeast activate it by whisking with 100 ml/4 fl oz of hand-hot water, and add the sugar. When the liquid has developed a good froth, pour into the flour, which you have first warmed in the oven with the salt. Stir in a further 200 ml/8 fl oz of hand-hot water and mix thoroughly, first with a wooden spoon and then with your hands. This dough should be soft, floppy and too wet to knead; depending on the absorbency of the flour, you may need to add more water. When the dough is smooth, transfer it to a well-greased 1-kg/2-lb bread tin. Cover with clingfilm and leave in a warm place to rise to within 2.5 cm/1 in of the rim. Pre-heat the oven to 400° F/200° C/ Gas Mark 6, sprinkle the loaf with flour, and bake on the middle shelf for 35–40 minutes. Remove the loaf from its tin and return it to the oven for 5–10 minutes to crisp up the bottom.

Soda Bread

Indescribably good eaten hot from the oven, soda bread is easier to slice if left to cool and 'set' for 3–4 hours.

MAKES 1 LARGE ROUND LOAF

450 g/1 lb coarse wholemeal
flour
175 g/6 oz plain white flour
1 rounded tsp bicarbonate of
soda

1 tsp salt
400 ml/15 fl oz buttermilk

Preheat the oven to 400° F/200° C/Gas Mark 6. Mix the dry ingredients in a mixing-bowl and stir in enough buttermilk to form a soft dough. Turn on to a floured work surface and knead lightly until the dough is smooth. Form into a circle about 3.5 cm/1½ in thick and place on a greased or well-floured baking-sheet. Slash the top with a deep cross, dust with flour, and bake for about 45 minutes or until the bread is browned and sounds hollow when tapped on the base. Cool the bread wrapped in a tea-towel if you want to keep the crust soft.

Potato Bread

Potato loaves are light, distinctively delicious, toast and last well, and make exceptionally good croûtons and sandwiches. Use only floury, mealy varieties of potato, and always cook them in their skins, dry thoroughly and mash without fat or liquid. This is Dr A. Hunter's recipe, first published in 1805 in his book *Receipts in Modern Cookery; with a Medical Commentary*. Elizabeth David cites it in *English Bread and Yeast Cookery* as her favourite potato bread recipe.

MAKES 1 LARGE LOAF

450 g/1 lb plain white flour
20 g/¾ oz salt
15 g/½ oz fresh yeast
275 ml/10 fl oz mixed milk
and water

110 g/4 oz dry mashed
potato

Have the flour and salt ready sifted in a bowl, the yeast creamed with a little water, and the milk and water warm in a jug. When your potatoes are cooked, peeled, sieved and weighed, mix them with the flour as if you were rubbing in fat, so that the two are very thoroughly amalgamated. Then add the yeast and the warm milk and water. Mix the dough as for ordinary bread. Leave until it is well risen (in a warm place, covered for about 2 hours), knead lightly, shape and put into a 1.5 litres/2–2½ pt capacity tin. Cover with a damp cloth and leave until the dough reaches the top of the tin. Bake in a moderately hot oven (425° F/220° C/Gas Mark 7) for 45 minutes.

To get a fresh, sweet flavour, bake this bread in wet, then well-buttered, thoroughly clean clay flowerpots.

To make potato rolls, form into your chosen shape, slash the tops and paint with egg wash if desired, and bake at 400° F/200° C/Gas Mark 6 for 20 minutes.

To flavour/season and decorate the rolls, paint with water and sprinkle on poppy, sesame, dill or caraway seeds before baking.

Thousand-layer Rolls

MAKES 10 ROLLS

275 g/10 oz plain white flour	*a pinch of salt*
10 g/¼ oz dried yeast	*275 ml/10 fl oz hand-hot water*
1 tbsp groundnut or corn oil	*1–2 tbsp sesame oil*
1 tbsp sugar	

Follow the method for Chinese steamed buns/Bao (see page 122). After the dough has risen, place it on a well-floured board and knead lightly for 60 seconds. Pinch off 30 equal pieces. Roll out 20 of the pieces into 6-cm/2½-in rounds; the dough will spring back about 1 cm/½ in. Next, roll the remaining 10 pieces of dough into rounds of 8.5–10 cm/3½–4in; they too will shrink back. Take 3 of the smaller rounds and brush the tops of each lightly with sesame oil. Stack the three together and wrap them in a larger round, tucking the edges under. Brush the top and bottom with sesame oil and place on a square of waxed paper. Steam for about 10 minutes as directed on page 122.

Quick Rolls

MAKES 10 MINIATURE ROLLS

225 g/8 oz plain flour	*salt*
1 heaped tsp baking powder	*150 ml/5 fl oz milk*

Mix the flour, baking powder and a generous pinch of salt, and add the milk gradually to make a stiff dough. Cover the dough with a dusting of flour and knead for a couple of minutes. Divide into 10 pieces, and form either into balls or into short sausages. Place on a greased baking-sheet, slash the tops and brush with milk or egg wash. If liked, decorate with poppy seeds.

Bake at your highest oven temperature for 12 minutes.

Chinese Steamed Buns/Bao

These buns look like shiny-smooth giant white marshmallows. They have a curious, slightly chewy texture and are usually sold stuffed (with a pre-cooked lamb or barbecued pork filling) and eaten as a snack or part of a *dim sum* meal. They can be bought ready made, steamed or ready-for-steaming, in Chinatown and freeze perfectly. To prepare from freezing, unfreeze and then steam until heated through. Once the dough is made, they take only 10 minutes to cook.

MAKES 12–15 BUNS
10 g/¼ oz dried yeast
275 ml/10 fl oz hand-hot
  water
1 tbsp sugar

1 tbsp groundnut or corn oil
a pinch of salt
275 g/10 oz plain white
  flour

Sprinkle the yeast into the warm water with the sugar, stirring until dissolved. Leave for a few minutes for the yeast to activate. Add the oil and salt and gradually sift in the flour, stirring with a wooden spoon to make a rubbery dough. Knead the dough for a few minutes until smooth but still springy. Form into a ball and cover with clingfilm or a damp tea-towel. Leave somewhere warm for an hour or two until the dough has doubled in size. Remove to a floured surface and knead lightly a few times. Pinch off 12–15 pieces of equal size. Roll each into a 10-cm/4-in round about 0.5 cm/¼ in thick, and place on a square of waxed or rice paper. If filling the buns, make an indentation in the centre, pop in the filling, and pull the pastry up and over, twisting the edges and pressing to seal. Turn the buns upside down and place on a square of waxed or rice paper.

Leave the buns for 30 minutes to rise, then place them, uncrowded, in the steamer and steam for 10 minutes only when they will be glossy.

WAYS WITH BREAD AND DOUGH

Bread Tartlets

This idea is quick, easy, tasty and impressive. Any processed bread can be thus transformed.

6 slices of processed bread　　　*50 g/2 oz butter, melted*

Cut the crusts from the bread. Roll the slices with a rolling-pin until they are thin and leathery. Cut out 7.5-cm/3-in circles (an upturned wineglass is a perfect cutter), paint both sides with melted butter and fit into a buttered tartlet tray. Bake in a hot oven (375° F/190° C/Gas Mark 5) for 15 minutes, or until the cases are nicely crisped.

The cases, now sealed, can be loaded with any savoury or sweet filling. This method is also useful for canapé bases; in which case cut out squares, triangles etc.

Croûtes

These are thin, whole slices of baguette-type bread dried to a crisp in a slow oven or under the grill and served as an accompaniment. If placed in the soup they would disintegrate instantly. They can be made in advance and stored in an airtight tin.

Cheese Croûtes

1 day-old stick loaf   25 g/1 oz Parmesan, freshly
25 g/1 oz butter, melted   grated

Slice the loaf thinly. Grill to pale golden on one side, then turn and paint the uncooked sides with butter and sprinkle lightly with Parmesan. Return to the grill.

Garlic Croûtes

1 day-old stick loaf or   ½ a clove of garlic, peeled
ciabatta   olive oil (optional)

Slice the loaf thinly and lay out the slices on an oven tray. Bake in a slow oven (200° F/100° C/Gas Mark 4) until the croûtes are dry but not browned. Rub one side of the croûtes with garlic. For a richer flavour dribble olive oil over them.

Meat Glaze Croûtes

Paint oven-dried croûtes with reduced meat glaze. If appropriate, sprinkle with blanched, shelled and crushed pistachios, pan-fried pine-nuts or almonds.

Marrow-fat Croûtes

Spread oven-dried croûtes with a thin layer of cooked marrow-fat and garnish with finely chopped parsley.

Bruschetta and Crostini

These are Italian names for thick slices of toasted or oven-browned country bread. Bruschetta is rubbed with garlic and drenched with olive oil and served topped with anything and everything, while crostini is the Italian equivalent of the French croûte.

Bruschetta

thick slices from day-old   ½ a clove of garlic, peeled
country-style bread   olive oil

Either toast the bread on both sides, rub one side with garlic and dribble generously with olive oil, or drench with olive oil before toasting, then rub one side with garlic.

The Provençal equivalent of bruschetta is *pain à l'aillade*.

Garlic Bread

Crisp butter- and garlic-drenched hot bread goes well with most soups. Any crusty loaf will do, but a stick-shaped loaf is usual; it is the perfect use for a stale French baguette. Other herb butters (see pages 61–4) can be used in the same way; olive oil can be substituted for butter.

110 g/4 oz butter   4–8 cloves of garlic, minced
                                         or finely chopped

Pre-heat the oven to 400° F/200° C/Gas Mark 6. Melt the butter with the garlic and set aside. Using a sharp knife, make diagonal incisions about 2.5 cm/1 in apart, as if you were slicing the loaf but without cutting right through. Take a sheet of silver foil large enough to parcel the loaf, and place the loaf in the middle. Using a spoon or pastry brush, paint the garlic butter on to both sides of each slice, pouring any left over on the top of the loaf. Close the parcel and bake for 10 minutes.

Melba Toast

Melba toast, made by cutting stale bread into thin slices and toasting it into curls, is thought to have been the invention of Madame César Ritz. It is most easily made by toasting medium-cut processed bread in a toaster, removing the crusts, then slicing the toast horizontally through the middle to make 2 thin slices. Cut these into triangles and toast the uncooked side briefly under a hot grill, allowing the toast room to curl.

Cool on a rack. Melba toast can be stored in airtight containers; heat through in a warm oven before serving, with or without flavoured butters.

Polenta Cakes

Follow the recipe for polenta croûtons on page 109, but cut the set polenta into 5-cm × 1-cm/2-in × ½-in chips, or use a pastry cutter to make other shapes. Brush with oil, and grill or bake until golden.

BISCUITS AND PASTRIES

BISCUITS

Cheese Straws

MAKES APPROX. 20 STRAWS

450 g/1 lb frozen puff pastry or Delia Smith's quick flaky pastry (see page 128)

175 g/6 oz Parmesan, freshly grated

Pre-heat the oven to 350° F/180° C/Gas Mark 4. Roll out the dough into a 50-cm × 60-cm/20-in × 24-in rectangle. Sprinkle half the Parmesan over the dough, pressing the cheese into the pastry with the rolling-pin. Fold the dough in half crosswise and roll out again back to its original size. Sprinkle on the remaining cheese. With a sharp knife cut the dough into 1-cm/½-in strips and twist into corkscrews. Arrange the twists on an ungreased baking-tray so that they touch each other; this stops them untwisting. Bake for about 15 minutes until the straws are puffed and golden. Remove, cut them apart and cool on a rack.

Potato Sticks

MAKES APPROX. 20 PIECES

1 egg-yolk
100 g/4 oz butter or margarine
100 g/4 oz flour
150 g/5 oz mashed potato

salt
1 dsp of any of the following: coarse sea salt, oatflakes, caraway, dill, poppy or celery seeds

Pre-heat the oven to 375° F/190° C/Gas Mark 5. Cream the egg and butter, sift in the flour and work in the mashed potato. Season with salt. On a floured surface roll the dough about 1 cm/½ in thick and cut it into 5-cm x 1-cm/2-in × ½-in sticks. Brush the top with water or milk and sprinkle with salt, oatflakes or seeds. Transfer to a greased and flour-dusted baking-sheet, leaving a little space between each stick, and cook for 15–20 minutes.

Parmesan Biscuits

MAKES 12 × 2.5-CM/1-IN TRIANGLES

100 g/4 oz self-raising flour
salt and pepper
50 g/2 oz butter

1 egg-yolk
50 g/2 oz Parmesan, freshly grated

Pre-heat the oven to 300° F/150° C/Gas Mark 2 and butter and flour a baking-tray. Meanwhile sift the flour into a mixing-bowl and season with a generous pinch of salt and a little pepper. Cut the butter into small pieces and work into the flour. Work in the egg-yolk and Parmesan to make a stiff dough; if the mixture seems too dry add a little milk. Roll out the pastry 1 cm/½ in thick and cut into 2.5-cm/1-in triangles, squares or circles. Bake for 20 minutes and serve hot, dusted with Parmesan.

Parmesan Tuiles

MAKES APPROX. 18

50 g/2 oz flour
75 g/3 oz almond flakes
75 g/3 oz Parmesan, freshly grated

40 g/1½ oz butter, melted
1 egg-white, beaten

Pre-heat the oven to 400° F/200° C/Gas Mark 6. Sift the flour into a bowl and mix in the almond flakes, Parmesan and melted butter. When thoroughly incorporated, fold in the egg-white and form into a dough. Flour a suitable surface and roll the dough into a very thin sheet. Cut into 7.5-cm/3-in rounds and lay out on a well-greased baking-sheet. Bake for 6–8 minutes and, if liked, while still warm curl round a clean broom-handle or shape round a cup to form the traditional shape.

PASTRIES

In Russia they are called *piroshkis*, in Argentina and Mexico *empanadas*, in India *samosas* and *batis*, in Turkey *böreks*, and in Great Britain we call stuffed pastry 'turnovers' *pasties*. The type of pastry, shape of the bundle and style of cooking may vary, but these 1-, 2- or 3-bite pastries can be tailor-made for hundreds of soups. Puréed vegetables, laced with the fresh herbs that you are using in the soup garnish; complementary cooked vegetables, sliced or diced, held in a thick sauce made with the soup; lightly sautéed sliced mushrooms; and chopped hard-boiled egg mixed with grated Gruyère, Feta or Mozzarella that will melt into the pastry, are particular favourites.

Keep 225-g/½-lb batches of ready-made pastry, either your own or shop-bought, in the deep-freeze and bring up to room temperature before using; allow at least 1 hour.

Sour Cream Pastry

MAKES 225 G/½ LB PASTRY

175 g/6 oz flour
1 tsp salt
50 g/2 oz butter or
  margarine

1 egg, beaten, or a little milk
4–6 tbsp sour cream

Sift the flour and salt together. Cut the fat into small pieces and quickly rub it into the flour to make a mixture that looks like breadcrumbs. Work the beaten egg with the sour cream, and add a little at a time, stopping when the dough forms a cohesive mass. Chill until needed.

Shortcrust Pastry

MAKES 450 G/1 LB PASTRY

150 g/5 oz butter or lard
290 g/10½ oz plain flour,
  sifted

60 ml/2½ fl oz cold water

Cut the butter into pieces and quickly work into the flour. Using a knife or spoon, stir in the water, a little at a time, until the mixture looks like big breadcrumbs and clings together. Knead quickly and leave to rest until you're ready to use it. Always make pastry with cold hands and touch it as little as possible.

Potato Pastry

Potato pastry is light and moist to eat and is a good use for leftover potato. It can be used instead of short pastry.

MAKES 225 G/½ LB PASTRY

75 g/3 oz butter or lard
110 g/4 oz plain flour

110 g/4 oz mashed potato

Rub the butter or lard into the flour until it resembles breadcrumbs.

Mix in the potato, kneading firmly, and adding a little water – sufficient to make a stiff dough. Leave to rest for 15 minutes before use.

Delia Smith's Quick Flaky Pastry

This is a heaven-sent alternative to puff pastry, which takes ages to make.

MAKES APPROX. 450 G/1 LB PASTRY

175 g/6 oz butter or block margarine	salt
225 g/8 oz plain flour	cold water, to mix

Wrap the fat in foil and freeze for 30–45 minutes. Meanwhile sift the flour and salt into a mixing-bowl. When you take the fat out of the freezer hold it in the foil, dip it into the flour, then grate it on a coarse grater placed in the bowl over the flour. Keep dipping the fat down into the flour to make grating easier. At the end you will be left with a lump of grated fat in the middle of the flour. Using a palette knife (not your hands), work the fat into the flour to make a crumbly mixture. Now add enough water to form a dough that leaves the bowl clean, using your hands to bring it all gently together. Pop the dough into a polythene bag and chill it for 30 minutes in the fridge before use.

Filo/Phyllo Pastry

Filo is fragile, wafer-thin pastry made without fat. It is widely available sold in a roll of sheets and can be kept indefinitely deep-frozen, and if you don't use it all in one go it can be re-frozen repeatedly. When you are using it, remember that it dries out very quickly, needs to be painted with oil or melted butter, and should be kept under a damp tea-towel.

Batis

MAKES APPROX. 30 WALNUT-SIZED BALLS

225 g/8 oz shortcrust or flaky pastry	1 tsp cumin seeds
	½ tsp chilli powder
For the filling	1–2 tbsp fresh coriander leaves, finely chopped
2.5-cm/1-in piece fresh ginger, peeled and finely chopped	225 g/8 oz mashed potato
	salt

To make the filling, mix the ginger, cumin, chilli and coriander into the mashed potato and season with a generous pinch of salt.

Roll the pastry into approx. 7.5-cm/3-in circles (an upturned wineglass is ideal) and place a pile of the filling in the centre. Fold the dough around the mixture, pinch together in whatever way is easiest, and glue with water or egg wash. Paint with egg wash and place the balls on a greased baking-sheet. Pre-heat the oven to 350° F/180° C/ Gas Mark 4 and bake for 15 minutes until the balls are crisp and golden.

Böreks

MAKES 16 LARGE CORK-SHAPES
4 sheets filo pastry
50 g/2 oz melted butter

For the filling
50 g/2 oz butter
75 ml/3 fl oz milk, scalded

450 g/1 lb mashed potato
2 spring onions, finely sliced
2 tbsp each of parsley and dill,
 finely chopped
salt and pepper

If you are using cold mashed potato, first melt the butter in the hot milk and stir it into the mash before you mix in the onion, herbs and seasoning. Cool while you cut out the pastry.

You are aiming to end up with cork-shaped pastries, but because filo pastry is so fragile and breaks easily you may find you have to adapt the size and shape of your *böreks* or use more filo. Use melted butter as a glue. Carefully lay out all the sheets on top of each other and cut in 4, so that you end up with 16 rectangles measuring approximately 25 × 13 cm/10 × 5 in. Brush all over with the melted butter before the pastry goes brittle. Place a dessertspoon of the filling in the centre of each piece of filo, fold round the pastry and seal it with melted butter. Pre-heat the oven to 350° F/180° C/Gas Mark 4 and bake the *böreks* on greased baking-sheets for approximately 20 minutes, when they will be crisp and golden.

Empanadas

MAKES APPROX. 20 × 6-CM/2½-IN PASTIES
450 g/1 lb short pastry

For the filling
225 g/8 oz best-quality
 minced lamb or beef
2 medium-sized potatoes,
 finely diced

1 shallot or small onion,
 finely chopped
3 tbsp good meat stock
salt and pepper

Pre-heat the oven to 400° F/200° C/Gas Mark 6 and grease a couple of baking-trays. Mix all the filling ingredients in a bowl and leave

and roll out to a thin sheet. Cut out 10 12-cm/5-in circles. Make
while you attend to the pastry. Flour a surface, take half the pastry
small piles of the mixture in the middle of the lower half of the circle,
damp the edges, fold over the empty half of the circle and crimp the
edges together. Brush with milk or egg wash and punch a few
airholes with a fork. Repeat.

Place on the baking-tray and cook for 10 minutes, then lower the
heat to 325° F/170° C/Gas Mark 3 and cook for a further 15 minutes.

Filo Triangles

MAKES 24 PASTRIES
12 sheets filo pastry
110 g/4 oz unsalted butter,
  melted

For the filling
110 g/4 oz Feta cheese
2 large hard-boiled eggs,
  peeled

4 tbsp parsley, finely chopped
2 tbsp fresh dill, finely
  chopped
2 spring onions, finely
  chopped
salt and pepper

Pre-heat the oven to 350° F/180° C/Gas Mark 4 and butter a baking-
tray (or 2). Mix and gently mash all the filling ingredients together,
tasting before adding salt and pepper.

Work with 2 sheets of filo at a time, keeping the rest covered with
a damp cloth. Have the melted butter, a pastry brush and the filling
mixture at hand. Cut the 2 sheets lengthways into 4 strips approx.
7.5 cm/3 in wide. Tuck the strips under the damp cloth, and take out
one at a time. Brush it all over with butter and place a heaped
teaspoon of the mixture at one end of the strip. Fold one corner over
the mixture, nudging it down to make a triangle. Continue to fold,
using up the entire length of double filo, making a multi-layered
triangle cushion. Brush all over with butter and place, seam side
down, on the baking-tray. Continue with the remaining strips. Bake
for 35 minutes until golden.

Piroshkis

These are the traditional accompaniment to borscht and other Russian soups and are often made with scraps of meat from the stock
mixed with a little of the puréed soup.

MAKES APPROX. 15 PASTIES OR SQUARES
225 g/8 oz flaky or shortcrust   *milk or beaten egg to glaze*
pastry

For the filling
15 g/½ oz butter
1 small onion, grated or finely
  chopped
50 g/2 oz mushrooms,
  minced or finely chopped
225 g/8 oz cooked chicken,
  turkey or other meat, minced

1 egg, hard-boiled and minced
1 tsp each parsley and dill,
  finely chopped
salt and pepper
2–3 tbsp stock or soup

Melt the butter and gently sauté the onion until soft. Add the mushrooms, then the meat, egg, herbs and seasoning. Stir-fry for a few minutes, adding the liquid if the mixture seems too dry.

Pre-heat the oven to 425° F/220° C/Gas Mark 7. Grease a baking-tray. Roll out the dough and use the floured rim of a wineglass to cut out rounds of pastry. Place a heaped teaspoon of the cooled filling in the middle, run a wet finger round the edge, fold over, and crimp the edges so that no filling can escape during the cooking. Paint with milk or beaten egg, place on the baking-tray and cook for about 20 minutes until the little *piroshkis* are golden.

Samosas

MAKES 16 SAMOSAS
450 g/1 lb Delia Smith's
  quick flaky pastry (see
  page 128)

For the filling
a little cooking oil
3-cm/1½-in piece fresh
  ginger, peeled and grated
2 tbsp ground coriander seeds
1 large onion, finely chopped
2 cloves of garlic, finely
  chopped

1–2 fresh chilli peppers, de-
  veined and finely chopped
salt
450 g/1 lb potatoes, boiled
  and diced
1 tbsp fresh mint, chopped
4 tbsp coriander leaves,
  chopped
1 tbsp garam masala
1 tsp salt
oil for deep-frying

To make the filling, heat a little cooking oil and sauté the ginger and ground coriander. Add the onion and after a couple of minutes the garlic, chillis and salt. Stir-fry gently, and when the onion is softened but not browned add the potatoes, mint and a little water if the mixture is very dry. Continue cooking over a low flame for 10 minutes or until the potato is cooked, then mix in the coriander leaves and garam masala. Remove from the heat and leave to cool.

Divide the dough into 8 balls and roll each ball into a 23-cm/9-in circle. Cut the circles in half and curl each half into a cone. Fill the cone with the cooled potato mixture and attempt to fashion a triangle by fixing the edges with water. Heat the oil until very hot

(375° F/190° C) and drop in 3 or 4 samosas. This will lower the oil temperature, which you should maintain. The pasties will puff and blister; they are ready after about 10 minutes, when they will be golden brown. Drain on absorbent paper. The pasties can be re-heated in a warm oven.

CROQUETTES AND PANCAKES

The shapes and sizes of these recipes can be adjusted according to whim. They serve approximately six people.

Broad Bean Croquettes

900 g/2 lb broad beans   50 g/2 oz fresh breadcrumbs
salt and pepper   oil for deep-frying
2 eggs, beaten

Shell the beans and plunge them into fast boiling water for a couple of minutes; drain, cool and slip off their skins. Return to the pan and cook, covered, in simmering salted water until the beans are tender. Drain and push through a sieve. Season to taste with salt and pepper and cool. Shape into 3.5-cm/1½-in squares, dip each one in beaten egg and breadcrumbs and deep-fry until golden. Drain on absorbent paper before serving.

Latkes

'Latke' is the Yiddish for pancake, but a good latke is thin and crisp. They can be made in advance and kept warm in a low oven but are best made immediately before eating; if practicable, have two frying-pans on the go. Serve with wedges of lemon, or with sour cream and/or a tart apple sauce if appropriate.

1 small onion (optional)   salt and pepper
450 g/1 lb potatoes   olive oil
2 eggs, beaten
50 g/2 oz matzo meal,
  chickpea or chestnut flour (for
  a nutty flavour), or plain flour

If including an onion, grate it first and then the potatoes. Rinse the potatoes, drain, and dry in a tea-towel. Mix the potatoes, onion, eggs, flour and seasonings to make a thick batter. Heat 1 cm/½ in of oil and drop about 1 tbsp of the mixture per latke into the pan. Quickly spread the mixture round with the back of the spoon and cook for a few minutes on each side. Drain on absorbent paper, and keep them warm in the oven while you finish the rest.

PART THREE

❧

Types of Soup

'The making of a good soup is quite an art, and many otherwise clever cooks do not possess the *tour de main* necessary to its successful preparation. Either they over-complicate the composition of the dish, or they attach only minor importance to it, reserving their talents for the meal itself, and so it frequently happens that the soup does not correspond to the quality of the rest of the dishes; nevertheless, the quality of the soup should foretell that of the entire meal.' (Madame Seignobos, *Comment on Forme une Cuisinière*, 1903)

Types of Soup

Deciding how to arrange the hundreds of soup recipes that I decided to include in this never-ending project gave me plenty of sleepless nights. Initially I'd planned to annotate them seasonally, but the combined forces of our increasingly blurred seasons and the widespread availability of imported and forced produce seemed to make a nonsense of that.

So many people, I discovered, think of soup in terms of type: 'Will you be including cold soups? . . . quick soups? . . . whole meal soups? . . . bread soups? . . . and will you bother with consommé?' became almost daily questions. So that is what I've done – I've carved up the recipes into eight categories that encompass thick soups, thin soups, soups for delicate constitutions and the jaded palate, everyday soups and soups for parties and special occasions.

The selection is, of course, the tip of the iceberg. Many recipes are classics of their type or variations on a theme, others are inspirations borne out of what lurks at the bottom of the fridge and in the recesses of the larder. These recipes, used in conjunction with the extensive section on 'Garnishes' and 'Embellishment to Go with Soup', give infinite scope to personalize the recipes.

135

Quick Soups

'I do not pretend to show you how to prepare broth from meat in ten minutes ... In order to prepare bouillon [from your preferred stock-cube] pour three-quarters of a pint of boiling water into a saucepan. Add a teaspoonful of liquid meat extract [stock-cube]. Let it boil for a few minutes in order to dissolve the extract completely. Salt. Add a tiny piece of butter. Let it melt. Serve in two teacups.' (Édouard de Pomiane, *Cooking in Ten Minutes*, 1948)

'We never eat dinner off trays, but we do have lunch while watching TV because the kids can't see us breaking our rule. This could be one of those tins of soup that looks posher than it tastes ...' (Tony Robinson (Baldrick in *Blackadder*), 'My TV Dinner', *Sunday Telegraph Magazine*, 1990)

All the soups here take under 15 minutes to prepare and cook, and some take far less. Some rely on tins and frozen foods and others are worth making only if you have some decent stock on hand.

ALMOST AN A-Z OF QUICK SOUPS

∽ AUBERGINE, TOMATO, GARLIC AND ∽ COCONUT MILK SOUP

This is an easy and delicious soup of no real origin but with South-east Asian overtones. The coconut milk, which is rich, mild and nutritious, combined with the quickly cooked vegetables, and fire from the garlic and chilli, provide a good balance of textures and flavours. The recipe is adapted from one in *Ken Hom's Vegetable and Pasta Book*, which is full of good ideas.

SERVES 4–6

400 g/14 oz aubergine	1 fresh chilli pepper, cored,
225 g/8 oz tomatoes	de-seeded and finely chopped
900 ml/1½ pts chicken or	2 large cloves of garlic, finely
vegetable stock	chopped
400 ml/14 fl oz tinned	1 tsp salt
coconut milk	a generous pinch of white
2 tbsp groundnut oil	pepper
2 small onions, finely chopped	a pinch of sugar

Peel and cut the aubergine into 1-cm/½-in cubes. Blanch the tomatoes in boiling water for 60 seconds, peel and chop into small chunks.

Bring the stock and coconut milk to simmering point in a large pan. While they are simmering, heat a wok or large frying-pan and add the oil. When hot, stir-fry the onions, chilli, garlic and aubergine at a high heat for about 4 minutes until nicely browned. Drain on absorbent paper, then add to the soup. Add the seasoning, adjusting to taste. If necessary add a little sugar.

✑ BANANA CURRY SOUP ✑

'This recipe came from an Estonian woman who used to work with us at the Hole in the Wall in Bath. She had moved all over Europe during the war, finally ending up in Bath. This always seemed such a strange combination for an Eastern European to come up with. But she was a very good cook, and this was one of her best recipes.'
(Joyce Molyneux of The Carved Angel)

SERVES 6

25 g/1 oz butter	350 g/12 oz ripe,
1 small onion, chopped	unblemished bananas, peeled
½ tsp curry powder	and chopped
700 ml/1½ pts light chicken	2 tbsp lemon juice
stock	salt
	150 ml/5 fl oz single cream

Melt the butter in a pan and sweat the onion for 5 minutes. Stir in the curry powder and cook for a further 30 seconds or so. Add the stock, bananas, lemon juice, and salt to taste. Bring to the boil, cover and simmer gently for 15 minutes. Process the soup in a processor or blender and stir in the cream. Taste and adjust the seasonings, then return the soup to the pan and re-heat to serve.

✑ BEANCURD AND CHINESE LEAVES SOUP ✑

This is a light, pure and nutritious Chinese soup that can be made successfully with spinach-like *pak choi*, Chinese flowering cabbage and Chinese water spinach, or with Chinese kale which looks like a bolted English lettuce, as well as the more commonly available creamy-coloured Chinese leaf.

SERVES 4–6
1 litre/1¾ pts vegetable stock
225 g/8 oz Chinese leaves,
  cut in 2.5-cm/1-in strips
  across the width

¼ tsp salt
450 g/1 lb beancurd, cut into
  2.5-cm/1-in cubes

Heat the stock to boiling, turn down to a low simmer and add the Chinese leaves and salt. Cover and cook for 3 or 4 minutes. Tip in the beancurd, stir and heat through, uncovered, for 60 seconds. Serve in shallow bowls.

✑ BEANSPROUT AND SESAME SEED SOUP ✑

Kong na-mool kook is a classic from Korea. It is worth going to the trouble of dry-roasting the sesame seeds, which intensifies their nuttiness and interest.

SERVES 6–8
1 level tbsp sesame seeds
2 tbsp sesame or vegetable oil
6 spring onions, finely sliced
1 stick of celery, finely sliced
1 clove of garlic, finely sliced
1½ tsp salt

½ tsp black pepper
¼ tsp sugar
8 tbsp soy sauce
450 g/1 lb fresh beansprouts,
  blanched
2.3 litres/4 pts boiling water

Begin by heating a small non-stick frying-pan and stir-frying the sesame seeds over a moderate heat for a couple of minutes. Set aside. Heat the oil in a pan large enough to hold the finished soup, and over a low heat gently stir-fry the white part of the spring onions, the celery and the garlic and cook until soft but not browned. Add the salt, pepper, sugar, the prepared sesame seeds and half the soy sauce. Simmer for 4 minutes. Add the beansprouts and stir-fry for 2 minutes. Add the boiling water and the rest of the soy sauce, stir, and leave to simmer gently for 2–3 minutes. Stir in the green slices of spring onion, simmer for 1 minute, taste for seasoning and serve.

✑ BROCCOLI AND CHEESE SOUP ✑

At the height of the London restaurant boom in the early eighties there was a brief appearance by a café specializing in the food of the deep South. Hominy grits and scratch chicken did not catch on, but I have fond memories of a thick gloppy soup made with melted processed cheese slices and overcooked broccoli. This is a refined version. The cheese acts as a thickener and makes the soup very filling.

SERVES 6–8

25 g/1 oz butter
1 medium onion, chopped
1 spray of fresh tarragon,
  finely chopped
2 large potatoes, peeled and
  grated or finely chopped and
  well rinsed
salt and pepper

1.75 litres/1½ pts vegetable
  stock
700 g/1½ lb broccoli
175 g/6 oz farmhouse
  Cheddar, grated
1 tbsp finely chopped parsley
  (optional)

Melt the butter and soften the onion. Add the tarragon, potatoes and seasoning. Stir thoroughly and pour in sufficient stock to cover. Bring to the boil, turn down to simmer, cover and leave for 10 minutes. Meanwhile chop the broccoli into small pieces and boil, covered, in the rest of the stock. Liquidize the potatoes and broccoli together and return to a clean pan. Taste for seasoning, remembering that the cheese will be quite salty, then stir in the grated Cheddar and most of the parsley. Heat through without boiling and serve garnished with a little more parsley.

✑ BREAD SOUP ✑

Acorda is the most basic of the many Portuguese and Spanish bread soups. It is simple and very quick to make but the quality of the ingredients, few as they are, must not be compromised. It must be made with good bread, not the processed variety; in Portugal it would be the cornmeal bread called *broa* (see page 116), which has a golden colour, dense dough and a sweet flavour. This is a soup for garlic-lovers; the flavours are pungent and fiery. It is often served with poached eggs, which enriches and softens the soup. For a sweet, mild garlicky soup, see page 222.

A pleasantly dull English version of this soup can be made with 1.1 litres/2 pts of stock to 225 g/8 oz of breadcrumbs, seasoned with salt and pepper. Such a combination is a vehicle for open-ended embellishment – finely chopped fresh herbs at the very least.

SERVES 6–8

225 g/8 oz stale bread, crusts removed
6 cloves of garlic
1 tbsp fresh coriander, finely chopped

1 tbsp flat-leaf parsley, finely chopped
salt
4–5 tbsp olive oil
1.1 litres/2 pts boiling water

Cut the bread into cubes the size of lump sugar. Crush the garlic and herbs and pound to a paste with a little salt and some water – this can be done in seconds in a processor. Put in a warm tureen with the olive oil and bread cubes. Pour on the boiling water and stir to mix all the ingredients into a lumpy cream, adding a little more water if necessary. Taste for seasoning and serve.

∽ CARROT SOUP ∽

Potage Crécy is a classic French soup. This is a speedy, healthy version; for a richer soup substitute 50 g/2 oz of butter for the vegetable oil and sift in 1 tbsp of flour before adding the stock. For a very rich version add 150 ml/¼ pt of double cream 2 minutes before the end of cooking.

SERVES 4–6

a splash of vegetable oil
1 onion, finely diced
1 leek, finely sliced, tough outer green leaves discarded
salt and pepper
450 g/1 lb carrots, peeled and grated

1.1 litres/2 pts chicken or rich vegetable stock
150 ml/5 fl oz natural yoghurt
1 tbsp chives

In a non-stick lidded pan heat the oil and stir in the onion and leek. Season with ¼ tsp of salt, stir again and cover. Leave to sweat for 3 minutes and then stir in the carrots. Cover and cook for a further 5 minutes. Meanwhile bring the stock to the boil and pour over the vegetables. Cover and simmer vigorously for 6–7 minutes, by which time all the vegetables should be cooked.

Liquidize, return to a clean pan, re-heat and taste for seasoning. Remove from the heat and stir in most of the yoghurt and most of the chives. Ladle into bowls and garnish with a blob of yoghurt, a few snips of chives and a twist of black pepper.

᥉ CARAWAY AND BEETROOT SOUP ᥉

This is a sure winner from Hungary. It isn't worth making without the essential flavouring of the caraway seeds.

SERVES 6

275 g/10 oz beetroot,
  preserved in vinegar
1 tsp caraway seeds, tied in a
  muslin bag
1.4 litres/2½ pts water

275 ml/½ pt sour cream
1 level tbsp flour
1 egg-yolk
salt and sugar

Drain the vinegar from the beetroot. Push half of it through a fine sieve (or liquidize) and dice the other half into small cubes. Bring the sieved beetroot to the boil with the caraway seeds in the water and turn down to simmer. Meanwhile stabilize 2 tbsp of the cream by mixing it with a glass of water and the flour. When you've made a smooth paste, stir the mixture into the simmering soup. Add the diced beetroot, bring back to a simmer, and cook for 10 minutes. Fish out the muslin bag with the caraway seeds.

Tip the egg-yolk into a tureen, mix with the rest of the cream and gently stir in the hot soup. Taste for salt and/or sugar. Serve with croûtons or polenta chips.

᥉ COURGETTE SOUP WITH PARSLEY AND BASIL ᥉

SERVES 6

2 tbsp olive oil
1 small onion, finely chopped
5 medium courgettes, grated
salt and pepper
1.4 litres/2 pts light chicken
  stock

2 tbsp flat-leaf parsley, finely
  chopped
2 tbsp basil, finely chopped
2 eggs
4 tbsp Parmesan, freshly
  grated

Using a pan that can hold the finished soup, heat the olive oil. Sauté the onion until it is soft but not browned and stir in the courgettes, ½ tsp of salt and a little pepper. Cover and sweat, stirring a couple of times, for 5 minutes. Add the stock, bring quickly to the boil and simmer, covered, for 10–12 minutes. Liquidize, and return the soup to a clean pan. Beat the herbs into the eggs and stir in the Parmesan. Bring the soup up to a simmer, remove from the heat, and beat in the herb, egg and cheese mixture. Taste for seasoning and serve.

∽ Dill and Cucumber Soup ∽

The feathery leaves of the hardy dill weed have a distinctive strong aniseedy flavour. In Hungary it is used to flavour everything, in the same way as we use parsley. This recipe can be made without the cucumber, when it is known as *kaporleves*.

SERVES 4

20 g/¾ oz bacon dripping
20 g/¾ oz flour
2 heaped tbsp fresh dill leaves,
  finely chopped
400 ml/¾ pt cold water
½ a cucumber, peeled, grated,
  salted and left to drain

150 ml/¼ pt milk, scalded
salt
150 ml/¼ pt sour cream
1 egg-yolk

Heat the bacon dripping and stir in the flour to make a thick roux. Remove from the heat, stir in half the dill leaves and, pouring slowly, add about half the water. Bring up to the boil, stirring all the while, and cook for 60 seconds. Remove from the heat and stir in the rinsed and drained cucumber and the rest of the water. Bring back to the boil, then simmer gently for 10 minutes before adding the hot milk. Taste for seasoning.

Mix together the sour cream, egg-yolk and the rest of the dill in a tureen (or divide between individual bowls) and pour on the soup, stirring as you do so.

Serve with croûtons fried in bacon fat.

∽ Frisée or Curly Endive and ∽
Cannellini Bean Soup

This is a good wheeze for using the bitter, outer leaves of curly endive. It is a very successful mix of textures, and of sharp and mild flavours.

SERVES 4

350 g/12 oz curly endive
1 litre/1¾ pts chicken stock
3 cloves of garlic, finely
  chopped
1 small red chilli pepper,
  chopped

3 tbsp olive oil
salt and pepper
225 g/8 oz can white
  cannellini beans

Wash the leaves and boil them in salted water for a couple of minutes – this tones down their bitterness. Drain and chop finely. Bring the stock to the boil while you pound the garlic with the chilli pepper, 1 tbsp of the oil, a generous pinch of salt and a little water. Heat a pan and stir-fry the garlic paste for a couple of minutes.

Tip the curly endive, paste and beans into the stock and simmer for a couple of minutes. Taste for seasoning, stir thoroughly and serve, giving each bowl a splosh of the remaining olive oil. Accompany with bruschetta, and Parmesan to be grated into the soup.

✑ GARLIC SOUP WITH EGGS ✑

This is the version of *aigo boulido* with eggs and is rich with the heady Provençal mixture of olive oil, tomatoes, garlic and thyme.

SERVES 4–6

6 tbsp olive oil
1 medium mild onion, finely
  chopped
3 leeks, finely sliced
3 cloves of garlic, chopped
225 g/½ lb sun-ripened
  tomatoes, skinned and
  chopped
1.4 litres/2½ pts boiling
  water

salt and pepper
½ a bayleaf
2 sprigs of thyme
a pinch of saffron
12 thin slices oven-toasted
  French bread
1 egg per person, poached

Heat the oil and gently soften the onion. Add the leeks and cook for a few minutes before stirring in the garlic and tomatoes. Stir well and leave to stew for 5 minutes. Add the boiling water, salt, black pepper, bayleaf, thyme and saffron and boil fast for a good 10 minutes. Warm the soup-bowls and use a slotted spoon to divide the solid part of the soup between the bowls. On this lay the bread, topped with a poached egg. Ladle the soup liquid over the eggs.

You may find this soup easier to serve from a tureen.

✑ GARLIC SOUP WITH CHEESE ✑

This is the French recipe for garlic soup, *aigo boulido*, which is similar to the Portuguese/Spanish bread soup *acorda* (see page 139) but prepared quite differently, with spectacularly milder results. Paul Bocuse does a version which has 2 cloves, 3 fresh sage leaves instead of thyme, omits the bayleaf, doubles the cheese, and uses 15 cloves of garlic to 1.75 l/3 pts of water.

SERVES 4

10 slices dry French bread	1 clove
40–50 g/1½–2 oz cheese:	½ a bayleaf
Gruyère, Emmenthal or	2 tsp salt
Parmesan, grated	black pepper
12 cloves of garlic, peeled and	1.2 litres/2 pts water
left whole	1 tbsp olive oil
1 sprig of thyme	

Pre-heat the oven to 300° F/150° C/Gas Mark 2. Meanwhile lay the bread slices on a baking-sheet and cover with cheese. Put the whole garlic cloves, thyme, clove, bayleaf, salt and a few grinds of black pepper in a pan with the water. Bring to the boil, partially cover and simmer at a brisk roll for 15 minutes.

5 minutes before the soup is ready, bake the bread slices – just sufficiently for the cheese to melt. Rinse out a tureen with hot water, load in the bread and sprinkle with the olive oil, then pour on the soup through a strainer. Cover for 5 minutes before serving.

✍ GARLIC SOUP WITH POTATOES ✍

This is my favourite of all the garlic soups; the egg, tomato and potato combines with all the other ingredients to give a marriage made in heaven.

SERVES 4–6

6 tbsp olive oil	salt and pepper
1 medium mild onion, finely	3 medium potatoes, peeled,
chopped	thickly sliced and rinsed
3 leeks, finely sliced	½ a bayleaf
3 cloves of garlic, chopped	2 sprigs of thyme
225 g/½ lb sun-ripened	a pinch of saffron
tomatoes, skinned and	2 tbsp flat-leaf parsley, finely
chopped	chopped
1.4 litres/2½ pts boiling	1 egg per person, poached
water	

Follow the recipe for garlic soup with eggs (see page 143), adding the potatoes with the water and seasonings. Omit the bread and sprinkle the parsley over the potatoes before laying on the poached eggs. Pour over the soup liquid and serve.

✌ GARLIC SOUP WITH MINT ✌

This is an Albanian recipe called *mehudehra*; the mint is the ingredient that gives it its charm.

SERVES 6

40 mg/1½ oz butter
6 cloves of garlic, peeled and crushed
2 level tsp paprika
1.75 litres/3 pts vegetable stock or water
75 g/3 oz vermicelli, broken into 2.5-cm/1-in pieces, part-cooked if necessary

1½ tsp salt
¼ tsp black pepper
1 tbsp fresh mint, finely chopped
1 tbsp parsley, finely chopped
1 tbsp coriander, finely chopped

Heat the butter and fry the garlic over a gentle heat for a couple of minutes. Stir in the paprika and the stock or water and bring to the boil. Add the vermicelli, salt and pepper. Stir in the mint and simmer for 2 minutes. Serve liberally garnished with parsley and coriander.

✌ HERB SOUP WITH SOUR CREAM AND EGG ✌

This is an exquisite, delicate soup created by Hungarian master chef Gyula Vasvary in 1820. I found it in George Lang's *The Cuisine of Hungary*, a marvellous book for soup-lovers.

SERVES 4–6

1 tsp fresh marjoram leaves
1 tsp fresh thyme leaves
1 tsp apple mint
40 g/1½ oz butter
1 tbsp 2.5-cm/1-in lengths of chives
1 tbsp flour

1.4 litres/2½ pts water
1 tsp salt
pepper
3 egg-yolks
1 tbsp sour cream
3 hard rolls, cut into halves and toasted

Chop the marjoram, thyme and apple mint. Melt 25 g/1 oz of the butter in a small pan and stir-fry the marjoram, thyme, apple mint and chives. Sprinkle in half the flour and stir-fry for a couple of minutes. Set aside while you bring the water up to simmer with the salt and a few grinds of pepper. Mix the egg-yolks with the sour cream, the remains of the butter and the rest of the flour. Stir a little hot water into the egg mixture before whisking it into the soup. Continue stirring over a low heat until it thickens, add the herbs, and simmer for 60 seconds. Place half a toasted roll in a soup plate and ladle the soup over it.

⸛ HERB SOUP WITH POTATOES ⸛

This is a Bavarian recipe traditionally served on Easter Thursday. It can be adapted to almost any combination of fresh herbs, but with a predominance of 3 herbs. In Germany chervil is usually the dominating flavour.

SERVES 4

50 g/2 oz butter
1 medium onion, finely
  chopped
450 g/1 lb fresh herbs, such
  as chervil, watercress,
  parsley, sorrel, marjoram

salt and pepper
1 large floury-variety potato,
  peeled, diced and rinsed
1.1 litres/2 pts boiling water
  or vegetable stock

Melt the butter and gently soften the onion without browning. Stir in the herbs, a generous pinch of salt and a little pepper, cover and leave to sweat for a couple of minutes. Add the potato and 275 ml/ ½ pt of the boiling liquid. Cover and simmer for 5 minutes before adding the rest of the liquid. Simmer for a few minutes until the potato can be mashed into the soup. Stir around, taste for seasoning, and serve with hot croûtons fried in bacon fat.

⸛ JERSEY ROYAL AND MINT SOUP ⸛

This is one of my all-time favourite soups.

SERVES 4

6 spring onions
40 g/1½ oz butter
450 g/1 lb new season Jersey
  Royal potatoes
40 g/1½ oz flour

1.4 litres/2½ pts light
  chicken stock or water
6 sprigs of mint, finely
  chopped
salt and pepper

Discard the root and any tough outer leaves and finely slice the spring onions. Sweat in the butter until the onions soften and then add the potatoes which have been scraped, rinsed and finely sliced. Coat the potatoes with the butter, mixing around to prevent sticking, and continue cooking for 5 minutes.

Next, stirring all the time, sift in the flour to take up the fat. Allow to bubble up and add the stock. Add half the finely chopped mint, bring back to the boil, and turn down to simmer for approximately 10 minutes until the potatoes are cooked but not collapsed. Season and sprinkle with the remaining chopped mint.

∽ LAMB, LEMON AND MINT SOUP ∽

This is a surprisingly satisfying soup and distantly related to the Greek/Cypriot *avgolemono*. If you want to make more of the soup, boil 50 g/2 oz of quick-cook rice in water and add to the soup before the lemon and egg mixture.

SERVES 6–8

1.75 litres/3 pts lamb stock	1 heaped tsp allspice
salt and pepper	2 heaped tsp cinnamon
4 egg-yolks	2 generous tbsp fresh mint,
3 tbsp lemon juice	finely chopped
2 heaped tsp paprika	50 g/2 oz butter

Bring the lamb stock to the boil, taste and adjust the seasoning, and turn down to simmer while you mix the egg-yolks and lemon juice in a large bowl or tureen. Work the paprika, allspice, cinnamon and fresh mint into the butter.

Whisk the hot soup into the egg mixture, stir, and leave to stand for 3 minutes. Stir in the herb butter and serve. This is good with garlic bread.

∽ LETTUCE SOUP ∽

To be at its most succulent, sweet and delicate, the lettuce should be just-picked; it is an ideal way of using bolted lettuce. The soup can be varied by using a mixture of watercress and lettuce or grated courgette, by leaving out the mint, or by complementing the lettuce with other fresh herbs such as parsley, chervil or marjoram. Chives would be too powerful.

SERVES 4

1 large lettuce, or equivalent	1 tbsp potato flour
25 g/1 oz butter	1 litre/1¾ pts chicken or
1 shallot or 4 spring onions,	vegetable stock
finely chopped	1 egg-yolk
1 tbsp fresh mint	110 g/4 oz single cream
salt and pepper	

Finely shred, wash and drain the lettuce. Soften the butter in a heavy-bottomed pan, stir in the onions and cook until soft but not browned. Mix in the lettuce, half the mint, ¼ tsp of salt and a few grinds of black pepper. Cover and sweat over a low heat for 5 minutes, stirring occasionally. Remove the lid and boil hard for 30 seconds to get rid of some of the liquid. Sift the flour on to the lettuce and quickly stir it around to take up the fat. Barely cover with hot stock and bring up to the boil, stirring vigorously. Add the rest of the stock and simmer gently for 10 minutes. Add the rest of the mint and liquidize for a full 3 minutes.

Return to a clean pan and bring back to simmer. Meanwhile whisk the egg-yolk into the cream with a little of the hot soup and whisk the liaison into the soup. Simmer gently, taking care not to let it boil. Taste for seasoning and serve.

This is a pretty pale green soup flecked with darker green specks.

∽ LETTUCE AND PEA SOUP ∽

SERVES 4–6

450 g/1 lb fresh peas in their
  pods
1 Cos lettuce
1.1 litres/2 pts water
100 g/4 oz butter

salt and pepper
275 ml/½ pt single cream
several sprays of chervil for
  garnish

Shell the peas and remove the outer leaves from the lettuce. Put them in a pan with the water, cover and simmer for 10 minutes. Strain off most of the liquid and reserve. Liquidize the lettuce and pea-pods with the remaining liquid. Push the purée through a sieve into the reserved stock and discard the pulp.

Meanwhile melt the butter in a small pan with a tight-fitting lid and sweat the peas and shredded lettuce heart for 10 minutes. Tip the pea mixture into the hot soup, bring up to a simmer and cook for 5 minutes. Liquidize and strain into a clean pan. Bring back to a simmer, taste for seasoning, remove from the heat and stir in the cream. Serve with a spray of chervil and Melba toast.

∽ LEMON GRASS, GINGER AND SWEETCORN SOUP ∽

The pungent, dry/sour lemony flavour of the lemon grass and the freshness of the ginger give this sweet, creamy soup a South-east Asian edge. I like to serve it with a chilli-based relish, stirred in at the table so people can control their own heat-threshold.

SERVES 6

50 g/2 oz butter
2 shallots, finely chopped
1 medium onion, finely sliced
1 tbsp fresh root ginger, peeled
  and grated
1 whole lemon grass, chopped
  into 2.5-cm/1-in chunks
salt and pepper

4–6 cobs of corn
1 litre/1¾ pts chicken stock
50 ml/2 fl oz single cream,
  mixed with 50 ml/2 fl oz
  milk, or 100 ml/4 fl oz
  coconut milk
1 tbsp coriander leaves

Using a sizeable pan, melt the butter over a slow heat and stir in the shallots, onion, ginger and lemon grass. Season with a generous pinch of salt, cover, and cook for a couple of minutes. Slice the corn off the cob with a sharp knife, add to the pan, stir it around and pour in the stock. Bring the soup to a simmer and cook, covered, for 5 minutes.

Fish out the lemon grass (it doesn't matter if you don't find it all) and liquidize the soup in batches, keeping the motor running for a full 3 minutes. Pour and push through a sieve into a clean pan. Add the cream/milk and taste for seasoning; depending on the age of the sweetcorn, you may need a little sugar as well as salt and pepper. Bring back to simmer but don't allow the soup to boil.

Serve sprinkled with the coriander leaves and with a tomato-based chilli salsa (see page 70) or a bottle of Tabasco for people to help themselves.

⌇ MUSHROOM SOUP ⌇

This is Egon Ronay's recipe, adapted slightly to fit the 15-minute deadline, from *The Unforgettable Dishes of My Life*.

SERVES 4

50 g/2 oz stale white bread	1 medium clove of garlic,
milk (enough to moisten	finely chopped
bread)	2 tbsp parsley, finely chopped
450 g/1 lb button	nutmeg, salt and pepper
mushrooms, rinsed under	570 ml/1 pt chicken stock
running water	100 ml/4 fl oz double cream
50 g/2 oz butter	

Moisten the bread with the milk and leave to soak while you finely chop or mince the mushrooms.

Melt the butter and stir in the mushrooms, cover and leave to stew for 4 minutes. Squeeze surplus milk from the bread and tear into pieces. Stir into the mushrooms, adding the garlic, parsley, a generous pinch of nutmeg and the chicken stock. Bring to the boil, turn down the heat immediately, cover and simmer gently for 10 minutes.

Liquidize, return to the pan, adjust the seasoning and bring back to the boil. Stir in the cream and serve. Phew.

⌇ NETTLE SOUP ⌇

You'll need to wear washing-up gloves to prepare this soup. Use only the tops of young stinging-nettles and wash thoroughly in cold water.

SERVES 4–6

1 leek or 4 spring onions, finely sliced	25 g/1 oz flour
25 g/1 oz butter	1.1 litres/2 pts light chicken stock, hot
450 g/1 lb stinging-nettles	1 egg-yolk
salt and pepper	50 ml/2 fl oz creamy milk

Sweat the leek or onions in the butter until limp, stir in the nettles, season with ¼ tsp of salt, cover, and cook for 5 minutes. Remove the lid and boil hard for 30 seconds before sifting in the flour. Stir thoroughly as you pour in the hot stock. Simmer for 5 minutes and purée in batches. Return to a clean pan, scoop out a little of the broth and mix it with the egg and milk, and stir back into the soup. Simmer gently for 30 seconds, taste for seasoning and serve with croûtons fried in bacon fat and crisp bacon pieces.

Nettle soup is complemented by pearl barley, which takes too long for inclusion here, and is very good with bread and bacon dumplings (see page 78).

∽ NORI AND MISO SOUP ∽

SERVES 4

1 dsp vegetable oil	1 tbsp brown miso
1 medium onion, finely sliced	1 carrot, peeled and cut into matchsticks
1 clove of garlic, crushed	
½ tsp ground coriander	1.1 litres/2 pts vegetable stock
½ tsp ground ginger	2 sheets nori seaweed
1 dsp tomato purée	1 dsp chives, chopped

Heat the oil in a heavy-bottomed pan and fry the onion and garlic. Mix in the spices, tomato purée and *miso* to form a gunge, then stir in the carrot. Cook over a low heat for 5 minutes, adding a little stock if it gets too dry. Meanwhile bring the stock to the boil. Lightly toast the sheets of *nori* by placing under a grill for 30 seconds a side. Add it, torn into shreds, to the stock and stir in with the chives. Tip the carrot mixture into the soup and simmer for about 10 minutes. Taste for seasoning and serve.

∽ OKRA SOUP ∽

This is an unusual Bulgarian recipe that relies on using small fresh okra; larger ones tend to be woody and fibrous. Okra is far more delicate than it looks, disintegrates easily and then becomes slimy. Take care not to cut into the pods.

SERVES 6

1 tbsp groundnut or sunflower oil	450 g/1 lb small fresh okra
1 onion, finely chopped	3 large ripe tomatoes, blanched, peeled and chopped
1 clove of garlic, crushed	1 egg
3 tsp flour	150 ml/5 fl oz yoghurt
2 tsp paprika	1.75 litres/3 pts water or vegetable stock
1½ tsp salt	2 tbsp parsley, finely chopped
¼ tsp black pepper	

Heat the oil in a large pan and add the onion. Stir in the garlic and cook for about 3 minutes, taking care not to brown either. Sift in 2 tsp of the flour, the paprika, salt and pepper and stir-fry for 2 more minutes. Gradually stir in the liquid and bring to the boil. Simmer for a couple of minutes, slide in the okra and tomatoes and cook for 8–10 more minutes.

Meanwhile in a small bowl mix the egg and yoghurt with 1 tsp of flour dissolved in a little water. Remove the soup from the heat, stir in the egg/yoghurt mixture, reduce the heat to very low and simmer for a couple of minutes. Serve garnished with a pinch of paprika and the parsley.

Serve with crusty bread for dunking.

∽ PARSLEY SOUP ∽

One day a couple of years ago David Dorricott, the chef of the SAS Portman Hotel, London, was busy preparing the 'Hotelier of the Year' dinner when *TV am* came on the 'phone demanding a quick and easy soup recipe for simultaneous broadcast. David happened to be gazing at a particularly fine bunch of parsley, and so this soup was devised. Just like that. It occasionally appears on the menu at Truffles, where it is likely to be garnished with a blob of yoghurt topped with caviare set in a basket woven out of potato, or with a heart-shaped lidded feuilletée filled with caviare.

The secret of its vibrant colour and fresh flavour is to cook and liquidize the soup quickly.

SERVES 1

3–4 handfuls of flat-leaf parsley	salt and pepper
175 ml/6 fl oz boiling water	a large knob of butter
	1 tbsp double cream

Pile the parsley into the lightly seasoned boiling water. Stir in the butter and cream, liquidize quickly, and pour into a warmed serving dish.

Seared scallops or pan-fried chicken nuggets would be a good 'garnish' for this thick soup. Salmon roe (keta) is a dynamic, and cheaper, alternative to caviare; lumpfish is not in the frame.

See also page 227.

✐ PEA SOUP WITH PARMESAN CROÛTONS ✐

This *zuppa di piselli* is a very delicious soup devised by Bartolomeo Stefani for his book *L'arte de ben cucinaire*, published in 1662 and updated by Michelle Berriedale-Johnson.

SERVES 6

700 g/1½ lb fresh or good-
   quality frozen peas
1 large onion, finely chopped
2–3 large cloves of garlic,
   chopped
1.3 litres/2¼ pts good chicken
   or veal stock
25 g/1 oz toasted pine-nuts
15 g/½ oz sugar

juice of 1 lemon
salt and freshly ground white
   pepper
6 slices fine-grain brown
   bread
approx. 6 tbsp olive oil
approx. 50 g/2 oz Parmesan,
   freshly grated

Cook the peas with the onion and garlic in the stock for 15 minutes, and purée. Meanwhile, coarsely pound the pine-nuts with the sugar and lemon juice, using a pestle and mortar or a blender. Mix into the soup and taste for seasoning.

To serve the soup, fry the slices of bread in the olive oil until they are crisp and brown on both sides. Place a slice of the bread in the bottom of each heated serving bowl and sprinkle liberally with Parmesan. Re-heat the soup and pour it over the bread. Serve with more freshly grated Parmesan.

✐ POTATOES WITH PEAS ✐

This is Frances Bissell's terrific combination, especially good if made with tasty new potatoes.

SERVES 4

450 g/1 lb potatoes
1 litre/1¾ pts chicken or
   vegetable stock
110 g/4 oz fresh shelled peas

salt and pepper
1 tbsp skimmed milk powder
12 large basil leaves

Peel and finely dice the potatoes and cook in the stock. Purée half the mixture until smooth and return to the pot, reserving 2 tbsp of stock. Bring back to the boil and add the peas. Simmer for 2 minutes before seasoning.

Meanwhile blend the skimmed milk powder with the reserved stock and add this to the soup. Just before serving tear the pungent basil leaves into shreds and stir these into the boiling soup.

Frances Bissell is cookery writer for *The Times*.

ᵥ *PEA SOUP WITH BACON SANDWICHES* ᵥ

Peas and ham are a wonderful and particularly English combination. This is Jane Grigson's recipe. Ideally it should be made when you have cooked a piece of smoked bacon in a stock slaked with a glass of white wine.

SERVES 6

175 g/6 oz potato, peeled and diced
110 g/4 oz butter
2 medium leeks, trimmed and finely sliced
450 g/1 lb shelled peas
1.75 litres/3 pts smoked bacon stock
pepper
6 slices cooked, smoked bacon, cut in strips
12 thin-cut slices light-textured brown or granary bread, buttered

Sweat the potato for 5 minutes in half the butter. Stir in the leeks, then the peas, and add enough stock to cover the vegetables easily. Simmer until tender (about 10 minutes), purée in a blender, and put through a sieve back into the rinsed-out pan.

Taste and adjust the seasoning; if the soup is too salty, add more water. Leave to simmer gently while you make the sandwiches with the bacon and buttered bread. Cut them into triangles and toast under the grill. Serve with the soup.

ᵥ *RED PEPPER AND TOMATO SOUP* ᵥ

SERVES 4

400 g/14 oz can red pimientos, drained
450 g/1 lb sun-ripened fresh tomatoes, blanched and peeled
570 ml/1 pt boiling light chicken or vegetable stock
salt and pepper
1 tbsp flat-leaf parsley or basil, finely chopped

Strain the pimentos and liquidize with the tomatoes and half the hot stock. Pour and push through a sieve into the rest of the stock. Stir thoroughly while you bring the soup up to a simmer, cook gently for 5 minutes, season, and stir in the chosen herb just before serving.

∽ SAFFRON SOUP WITH FRESH HERBS ∽

This is a beautiful golden colour and is really an onion-flavoured, creamy, runny potato purée.

SERVES 4–6

225 g/½ lb onions, finely
　chopped
450 g/1 lb potatoes, peeled
　and finely chopped
1 chicken stock-cube,
　crumbled

1.1 litres/2 pts milk
½ tsp saffron strands
salt and pepper
570 ml/1 pt double cream
1 tbsp flat-leaf parsley, chives
　and tarragon, finely chopped

Put the onions, potatoes and crumbled stock-cube in a pan with the milk. Simmer gently for about 10 minutes until the potatoes are cooked. Liquidize or purée, then rub through a sieve into a clean pan. Stir in the saffron strands, taste for seasoning, and stir in the cream. Bring back to a simmer, fold in the herbs and serve.

Serve with crostini or garlic croûtons; as an exceptionally delicious alternative, garnish with whipped cream laced with caviare.

∽ SORREL SOUP ∽

Sorrel grows wild in the English countryside, and 2 handfuls sweated in butter (it liquidizes itself) with stock or milk make a delicious soup that tastes like delicate spinach, laced with lemon. Its tart acidity is beautifully complemented by cream or a velouté liaison, but when combined with onion and potato and a knob of butter it becomes a delicious, easily digestible soup best made with water.

Incidentally, sorrel is rewarding to grow. It comes up without fail in February and grows vigorously until the first frost; it is worth searching out some French plants, which produce a larger leaf with a superior flavour.

This is Margaret Costa's fine recipe, slightly adapted for the sake of speed, from her marvellous *Four Seasons Cookery Book*. Because the sorrel is barely cooked – it is boiling that dulls its vibrant colour – the soup is bright green with a fresh flavour.

SERVES 6

40 g/1½ oz butter
½ a medium onion, finely
　chopped
2 medium potatoes, peeled and
　finely chopped or grated
1.1 litres/2 pts good chicken
　stock

2 handfuls (approx. 225 g/
　8 oz) of sorrel, washed and
　coarse stems removed
salt, pepper and nutmeg
a pinch of sugar
150 ml/¼ pt double cream

Melt the butter and cook the onion until soft but not browned. Add the potatoes, stirring them up with the onion, then the stock. Season and simmer until the potatoes are tender (5–10 minutes). Put batches of soup into the blender or food processor with some of the raw sorrel. Switch on at top speed and whizz until amalgamated, repeating until all the soup is done.

Re-heat without boiling, taste for seasoning, and decide if the soup needs thinning with water or more stock. Stir in 4 tbsp of the cream. Serve with a swirl of cream, a grating of nutmeg, and croûtons.

∽ SWEETCORN SOUP ∽

This is a recipe for the occasion when you have freshly picked corn on the cob; it is a purist recipe adapted from Paul Bertolli and Alice Waters's *Chez Panisse Cooking*. The results will be surprisingly sweet, rich and full of flavour.

SERVES 6

50 g/2 oz unsalted butter
1 medium onion, diced
1.4 litres/2½ pts water

5 cobs of corn, the kernels
    stripped with a sharp knife
salt and pepper

Melt the butter in a pan that can hold the finished soup and add the onion and 275 ml/½ pt of water. Cover and simmer for 10 minutes. Add the remaining water and bring to the boil. Add the corn kernels and simmer for 5 minutes.

Purée the soup in batches in a blender, allowing the blender to run a full 3 minutes for each batch. Press the purée through a coarse sieve, one that will catch the fibres and skins but will permit the starchy juice to pass through. Season with ½ tsp of salt and a few grinds of pepper, and taste for adjustments.

Gently re-heat the soup, divide it among heated bowls, and garnish each with a dollop of garlic butter (see page 62).

Alice Waters is the chef/proprietor of Chez Panisse in San Francisco.

∽ TOMATO SOUP ∽

SERVES 4

1 medium onion, finely diced
50 g/2 oz butter
700 g/1½ lb ripe tomatoes,
    peeled and chopped
salt, pepper and sugar
570 ml/1 pt light stock,
    chicken, vegetable or veal

2 tbsp chervil, basil or chives,
    chopped
1 tbsp fresh mint and/or
    parsley, finely chopped

Gently cook the onion in half the butter. When soft add the tomatoes. Season with ¼ tsp of salt and a few twists of black pepper and simmer briskly for 5 minutes. Pour on the stock, previously heated, and simmer for 15 minutes. Pass through a sieve to collect the pips, core, etc. Return to the pan, warm through and taste for seasoning; you may need a little sugar if the tomatoes are tart. Stir in the chervil, basil or chives and serve strewn with the mint or parsley and a small knob of butter.

For a creamy tomato soup, whisk in 100 ml/4 fl oz of single cream with the first lot of herbs.

∽ TOMATO AND BREAD SOUP ∽

Pappa al pomodoro is a Tuscan stalwart made with coarse country bread, proper tomatoes and fruity olive oil. If you can't replicate these ingredients, don't bother with this soup.

SERVES 4

*200 g/7 oz country bread,
  sliced and crusts removed*
*1 litre/1¾ pts light chicken
  stock*
3 cloves of garlic, crushed
4–5 tbsp olive oil

*750 g/1½ lb very ripe
  tomatoes, peeled and cut into
  chunks*
salt and pepper
*10 leaves of basil (at least),
  shredded*

Pop the bread into a cool oven and leave to dry but not colour. Bring the stock to the boil. Fry the garlic in a little of the olive oil until it begins to colour. Add the tomatoes and the toasted bread, broken into chunks, stirring until the bread flops and merges in with the tomatoes. Slowly stir in the hot stock, a little at a time, to make a thick mush. Season to taste, with plenty of black pepper, add the basil and simmer gently, stirring every now and then, for 10–15 minutes.

Serve with a sloosh of olive oil, with more on the table.

∽ TOMATO SOUP WITH LEMON GRASS ∽

SERVES 4

*1.1 litres/2 pts chicken or
  vegetable stock*
1 lemon grass stalk
1½ tsp salt
2 tsp sugar
1 tbsp lemon juice
4 spring onions, finely sliced

1 red chilli pepper, finely sliced
*1 tbsp coriander, finely
  chopped (reserve a bit for
  garnish)*
450 g/1 lb fresh tomatoes
1 egg-white
2 tsp sesame oil

Put the stock on to simmer while you peel the lemon grass stalk and finely chop the tender inside shoot. Put this with the salt, sugar, lemon juice, spring onions, chilli and coriander in the simmering stock and stir well. Add the tomatoes and stir well and simmer for 3 minutes. Whisk the egg-white with the sesame oil in a small bowl. Pour the mixture in a slow dribble into the soup, using chopsticks or a fork to pull the egg strands as they hit the soup; experienced Oriental chefs recommend drawing a figure-of-eight. Garnish with the reserved coriander leaves and serve.

∽ WALNUT SOUP ∽

This French soup comes from Elizabeth David's *Summer Cooking* and only competes for inclusion in this section if it is made with the help of a food processor. The stock has to be incorporated into a paste made with the garlic and walnut, which would take longer than 15 minutes by hand. It is particularly special when made with fresh 'green' walnuts.

SERVES 6

175 g/6 oz walnuts, as fresh as possible
1 large clove of garlic

1.1 litres/2 pts light stock
150 ml/¼ pt single cream
salt and pepper

Crush the walnuts and garlic to a paste with a little of the stock. Incorporate the rest of the stock slowly until the mixture is the consistency of single cream. Pour the soup through a sieve into a pan, and bring to the boil. Remove from the heat and add the cream. Taste for seasoning and serve.

∽ WATERCRESS, BEANSPROUT AND ∽ BEANCURD SOUP

SERVES 4

1.1 litres/2 pts chicken or duck stock
1 bunch of watercress
225 /½ lb beansprouts
lemon juice

soy sauce
salt and black pepper
275 g/10 oz block of beancurd

Heat the stock to boiling while you trim away the stalks and chop the watercress. Simmer for 2 minutes before adding the beansprouts. Simmer for 3 more minutes, then add lemon juice, soy sauce, salt and black pepper to taste.

Divide the beancurd into 16 equal cubes, share between the soup-bowls and ladle over the soup.

✑ CREAM OF WATERCRESS SOUP ✑

SERVES 4

1 onion, finely chopped
40 g/1 ½ oz butter
1 medium potato, peeled and
  chopped
2 bunches watercress,
  shredded

salt and pepper
400 ml/¾ pt milk
275 ml/½ pt vegetable stock
4 tbsp double cream

Gently fry the onion in the butter, and when limp add the potato and watercress. Season with ¼ tsp of salt, cover and sweat for 5 minutes. Add the milk and stock, cover and simmer for 10 minutes. Add the cream, bring back to the boil, liquidize and serve.

QUICK SOUPS WITH MEAT

✑ BEEF, TOMATO AND CHILLI BROTH ✑

Chupi is an Argentinian soup that is a glorious mess. It is a slight cheat to include it here; it really needs 20 minutes simmering and has to be cooked in 2 cooking pans to meet the deadline.

SERVES 6

3 tbsp cooking oil
1 large onion, finely chopped
1 clove of garlic, finely
  chopped
1 red pepper, cored, de-seeded
  and finely diced
2 fresh red chilli peppers,
  cored, de-seeded and finely
  chopped
3 tomatoes, blanched, peeled
  and chopped

450 g/1 lb best minced beef
1 large potato, peeled and
  finely diced
2 carrots, peeled and finely
  diced
1 tbsp finely chopped flat-leaf
  parsley
1.2 litres/2 pts beef stock
salt and pepper

Heat the oil in a large heavy pan and fry the onion, adding the garlic when the onion is limp and golden. Add the pepper, chillis and tomatoes and simmer for 5 minutes. Stir in the beef, smashing down any lumps with a fork, then the potato, carrots and parsley. Pour on the stock, previously brought up to the boil, season with ½ tsp of salt and some pepper, bring back to the boil, and simmer, covered, for 15–20 minutes.

Serve with a chilli sauce (see page 70) and bread for mopping.

∽ BEEF DUMPLING SOUP ∽

Breadcrumbs, suet or flour mixed with herbs, cheese, egg, bacon or meat, and then formed into dumplings or balls, are described in detail on pages 76–87. Ideas for matching them appear in 'Clear Soups' (pages 309–27).

Among the quickest dumplings to cook are the Hungarian *majorannás rizsgombóc*, in which fresh marjoram is bound with rice, flour, onion, egg and beef broth. The dumplings are poached in seasoned beef broth.

SERVES 6
1.75 litres/3 pts good beef broth
salt and pepper
25–30 rice dumplings with marjoram (see page 82)

1 tbsp fresh marjoram, roughly chopped

Bring the broth to the boil and taste for seasoning. Poach the dumplings in the broth and check after 5 minutes.

Serve the hot soup garnished with fresh marjoram.

∽ CHICKEN AND CHINESE MUSHROOM SOUP ∽

This is an aromatic, garlicky and peppery-hot soup seasoned with salty, pungent *nam pla* Thai fish sauce.

SERVES 4
3 cloves of garlic, chopped
1 tbsp coriander root
8 black peppercorns
1 tbsp vegetable oil
1.1 litres/2 pts chicken stock
5 dried Chinese mushrooms, soaked in hot water, stemmed and cut in ribbons

225 g/8 oz raw breast of chicken
1 tbsp nam pla (Thai fish sauce)
skin of 1 small cucumber
4 spring onions, cut diagonally into 2.5-cm/1-in pieces

Pound the garlic, coriander root and peppercorns into a paste and stir-fry in the hot oil for 60 seconds. Add the chicken stock, Chinese mushrooms, the chicken meat cut into bite-sized pieces and the fish sauce. Bring to the boil, reduce immediately to a low heat, and leave to simmer for 15 minutes.

Meanwhile use a small sharp knife to fashion 12 leaf-shapes from the cucumber. Float these and the spring onions in the soup and simmer for a further 60 seconds before tasting for seasoning. Add more *nam pla* if necessary.

◇ CHICKEN, COCONUT AND GALANGAL SOUP ◇

Gai tom ka is a spicy, rich and tasty soup that brings together the uniquely Thai flavourings of mild coconut milk spiked with pungent aromatic galangal, lemon grass, chilli and fresh coriander. It is one of my favourite combinations. This is the recipe of Vatcharin Bhumichitr, who runs the delightful restaurant Chiang Mai in London.

SERVES 2–4

425 ml/16 fl oz chicken stock
2 lime leaves
5-cm/2-in piece of lemon grass, chopped
2.5-cm/1-in piece of galangal, split lengthways into several pieces
60 ml/2½ fl oz nam pla (Thai fish sauce)

50 ml/2 fl oz lemon juice
110 g/4 oz raw chicken breast, finely sliced
150 ml/5 fl oz coconut milk
2 small red chilli peppers, lightly crushed
1 tbsp coriander leaves

In a pan heat the stock and add the lime leaves, lemon grass, galangal, fish sauce and lemon juice. Stirring thoroughly, bring to the boil. Add the chicken and the coconut milk. Continue to cook over a high heat, stirring constantly, until the meat is cooked through (about 2 minutes). Add the crushed chillis for the last few seconds. Pour into small bowls and garnish with coriander leaves.

Thais would eat this as part of a meal or with a bowl of rice, taking a spoonful at a time to season the rice.

◇ CURRIED SWEETCORN SOUP WITH CHICKEN ◇

This hybrid soup originates from Ken Hom's book *Chinese Cookery* but is slightly adapted. It is an extremely good use for a tin of creamed sweetcorn, which softens the impact of the curry powder.

SERVES 6

1.1 litres/2 pts chicken stock
225 g/8 oz raw chicken
  breasts, skinned and boned
1 egg-white
1 tsp cornflour
1 tsp salt
1 egg
1 tsp sesame oil

275 g/10 oz can creamed
  sweetcorn or 450 g/1 lb
  fresh corn on the cob
1 tbsp dry sherry or rice wine
1 tbsp curry powder or paste
1 tsp sugar
4 spring onions, finely sliced

Bring the stock to the boil while you begin the preparations. Thinly slice the chicken breasts into fine shreds about 7.5 cm/3 in long. Mix these shreds with the egg-white, cornflour and salt in a small bowl and set aside. Beat the whole egg and sesame oil together in a small bowl and set aside. Open the can of sweetcorn, or remove the kernels from the cob with a sharp knife if using fresh corn.

Blanch the chicken shreds in boiling water for 20–30 seconds until they turn white. Drain. If using fresh corn, cook it in the boiling stock for 10 minutes and then add the sherry or rice wine, curry powder, salt and sugar. If using canned corn, add it to the boiling stock with the sherry or rice wine, curry powder, sugar, and salt if needed. Bring back to the boil, then simmer gently for 5 minutes. Add the blanched chicken shreds and then slowly pour in the egg and sesame oil mixture in a steady stream, stirring all the time. Transfer the soup to a tureen and serve sprinkled with spring onions.

৩৮ CHICKEN AND WATERCRESS SOY SOUP ৩৮

This is a light, elegant Chinese soup that relies on decent chicken stock. It can also be made with Chinese leaves or sorrel and can be made more of by adding 3 or 4 shrimp balls (page 100) per serving.

SERVES 4–6

1.1 litres/2 pts chicken-based
  stock
2 bunches of watercress,
  stems trimmed
175 g/6 oz raw chicken breast

2 tbsp light soy sauce
1 tsp sugar
4 spring onions, finely
  chopped

Bring the stock up to simmering point. Blanch the watercress in a pan of boiling water for a few seconds. Refresh immediately in cold water to prevent further cooking. Slice the chicken into thin slices about 5 cm/2 in long, and blanch them in a little of the boiling stock for 2 minutes.

Add the blanched watercress and chicken to the stock, then add the soy sauce and the sugar. Bring back to simmer, tip in the spring onions and serve with Chinese steamed buns (see page 122).

∾ CHICKEN AND PORK HOT AND SOUR SOUP ∾

This is a Szechuan recipe that is a meal in itself, with far more and spicier ingredients than is usual in Chinese soups.

SERVES 4–6

1.1 litres/2 pts chicken or chicken and pork stock
175 g/6 oz chicken breast, cut into slivers
175 g/6 oz lean pork, cut into slivers
25 g/1 oz dried prawns, soaked and drained
225 g/8 oz beancurd, cut into small cubes
50 g/2 oz dried Chinese mushrooms, soaked in hot water for 5 minutes and cut into strips
75 g/3 oz tinned bamboo shoots, cut into thin strips

2 tbsp light soy sauce
2 tbsp vinegar
1½ tsp salt
1½ tsp freshly ground black pepper
2 tsp cornflour, mixed with 1 tbsp water
3 eggs, beaten
3 spring onions, finely sliced
2 tbsp coriander leaves, chopped
2 green chilli peppers, de-seeded and finely chopped
lemon quarters

Bring the stock up to a simmer. Stir in the chicken, pork and prawns and simmer for 5 minutes. Then add the beancurd, mushrooms, bamboo shoots, soy sauce, vinegar, salt and pepper. Simmer on for 5 minutes. Mix the cornflour solution into the eggs and pour it into the soup in a thin stream, while you paint a figure-of-eight with a fork or chopstick. Keep stirring until the egg has set. Serve garnished with the spring onions, coriander and green chilli peppers, and with lemon quarters separately for people to squeeze into their soup.

∾ HAM AND BEANSPROUT SOUP ∾

This is a fresh, light yet filling soup. Cellophane noodles, made with ground mung bean flour, need to be soaked for 15 minutes in warm water before quick cooking in boiling liquid. They absorb about 4 times their weight in liquid. An alternative is one of the many types of rice noodles, rice vermicelli or rice sticks. They too need pre-soaking.

SERVES 4–6

50 g/2 oz cellophane noodles
75 g/3 oz fresh beansprouts
1.1 litres/2 pts chicken stock
1 tbsp light soy sauce
75 g/3 oz lean finely sliced
  English smoked bacon,
  Parma ham or similar,
  shredded

2 spring onions, finely
  chopped
2 tbsp fresh coriander, finely
  chopped

Put the noodles to soften in warm water, which will take most of the 15 minutes. If you can be bothered trim the beansprouts so they look like fat, white worms. Bring the stock to a simmer. Add the drained noodles, chopped into 5-cm/2-in lengths, and the soy sauce, and simmer for 2 minutes. Add the bacon or ham, the spring onions and half the coriander, and simmer for 30–60 seconds (depending on the thickness of the bacon). Finally, add the beansprouts. Cook for a further 30 seconds, sprinkle on the rest of the coriander and serve with soy sauce and a chilli condiment on the side.

ᵔ PORK AND CHINESE WATERCRESS SOUP ᵔ

Chinese watercress, also known as melon seed plant on account of the shape of its leaves, has a slightly vinegary flavour. Unlike English watercress, its leaves are fleshy.

SERVES 6

50 g/2 oz pork, minced
1 tsp cornflour
½ tsp sugar
½ tsp pepper
1 tbsp soy sauce
1 tbsp vegetable oil
5-cm/2-in piece fresh ginger,
  peeled and grated

1 dsp salt
1.75 litres/3 pts boiling
  water
450 g/1 lb Chinese
  watercress/gwaah jee choy
2 eggs, well beaten

Mix the minced pork with the cornflour, sugar, pepper, soy sauce and half the vegetable oil. Heat the remaining oil in a heavy-bottomed pan and stir-fry the ginger and salt for 30 seconds. Pour on the boiling water, bring back to the boil, and toss in the washed and trimmed Chinese watercress. Cover the pot and simmer for 6–7 minutes. Add the meat mixture, cover the pot and boil for 5 minutes. Remove the pan from the heat and leave to stand, covered, for a couple of minutes. Just before serving stir in the beaten eggs gently, and when they are slightly set, serve the soup.

✧ PORK AND RICE SOUP ✧

Kao dom or *khao tom moo* is an easily digestible and nutritious Thai soup and a quick-cook variation on the Chinese congee (see page 255). Preserved radish and 2 fried cloves of garlic are often included. It provides an interesting way of using leftover cooked rice to good effect, and is a standard Thai breakfast and food for invalids.

SERVES 4

1.1 litres/2 pts chicken stock
4 tbsp pork, minced
200 g/7 oz cooked rice
2 tbsp nam pla (Thai fish sauce)
1 small egg for each serving
1 tbsp minced fresh ginger
1 tbsp dried onion flakes, fried until golden and drained

3 spring onions, finely chopped
1 dried red chilli pepper, finely chopped (optional)
1 tbsp coriander leaves, chopped

Bring the chicken stock up to a simmer, sprinkle in the minced pork and add the cooked rice. Simmer for 2 minutes, stirring around to break up the pork. Season with the fish sauce. Break an egg into each serving bowl and divide the ginger, onion flakes, spring onions, red pepper and coriander leaves between the bowls. Ladle on the soup and serve.

QUICK SOUPS WITH SEAFOOD

Some recipes call for salting the fish before cooking; this helps to firm up the flesh but is more effective if the salt remains for up to 1 hour.

✧ CLAM SOUP ✧

This is Alexandre Dumas's recipe, translated by Elizabeth David, from his *Grand Dictionnaire de Cuisine* (1873). A variation would be to omit the tomato, marjoram and celery and replace it with 2–3 tbsp of coriander and flat-leaf parsley; an idea I pinched from the chef at Odins in London, one of my favourite restaurants, where the art is as good as the food.

SERVES 6

48 vongole *or small clams (mussels or cockles would be just as good)*
¾ bottle of dry white wine

1 clove of garlic, peeled and left whole or sliced (see method)
1 litre/1¾ pts fish stock

1 leek, white part only
1 small onion or shallot,
  finely chopped
1 tbsp olive oil

1 tomato, peeled and chopped
3 sprays of marjoram
a few leaves of celery
salt and pepper

Put the clams in a pan with the white wine and cook over a fierce heat until they have all opened. Drain them, saving the liquid, and remove the empty half shells. Meanwhile sauté the leek and onion or shallot in the oil, adding the clove of garlic, then the liquid from the clams and the fish stock. Add the tomato, marjoram and celery and let it bubble away for 10 minutes. Remove the garlic (optional; I prefer to slice it and leave it in) and marjoram, stir in the clams, taste, adjust seasoning with salt and pepper, and pour into a tureen. Serve separately small croûtons of bread fried in olive oil.

If making this recipe with coriander and parsley, add half with the garlic and the rest just before serving.

∽ SOUP OF COCKLES, PRAWNS AND SCALLOPS ∽

Fish soup and the lamentable lack of any British fish soup tradition was one of Elizabeth David's obsessions, aired frequently over the years. This is one of several soups she devised, using Italian techniques, that are made with ingredients easily obtainable in England: 'being boneless, they will be more to English taste than most of the Italian fish stews.'

For purposes of speed I've replaced fresh peas with frozen.

SERVES 4–5

1 small onion or shallot, finely
  sliced
3 tbsp olive oil
2 tomatoes, peeled and
  chopped
450 g/1 lb frozen peas
salt and pepper
4 or 5 whole mint leaves
900 ml/1½ pts boiling fish or
  light chicken stock
225 g/½ lb filleted brill, sole
  or other white fish, cut into
  pieces

150 ml/¼ pt shelled, boiled
  cockles, thoroughly rinsed
  under running water to
  remove sand and grit
6 scallops, sliced into 2
  rounds, and coral, separate
110 g/4 oz shelled prawns
3 tbsp parsley, finely chopped
1 clove of garlic

Slice the onion and let it turn faintly golden in 1 tbsp of olive oil; add the chopped and skinned tomatoes, and after a minute or two the peas. Season with salt, pepper, and the mint leaves. Pour over the hot stock and simmer until the peas are cooked. Add first the white fish and after 5 minutes the cockles, then the scallops, then their orange corals, then the prawns.

Have ready a sauce made by pounding the parsley with the garlic Stir the sauce into the soup just before serving. Provide hot crusty bread.

∽ GREEN FISH SOUP ∽

I first came across Marion Jones, who devised this recipe, when she and her husband Robin were running an excellent and very idiosyncratic restaurant in a converted dairy in urban Battersea. In the late seventies they moved out to Malvern Wells and opened the Croque-en-Bouche. This down-to-earth recipe is foolproof, impressive and delicious and typical of her style at the Croque.

SERVES 8

½ a large onion, thinly sliced
1 small leek, thinly sliced
25 g/1 oz unsalted butter
25 g/1 oz flour
1 litre/1 ¾ pts hot fish stock,
 flavoured with fennel and a
 grating of nutmeg
salt and pepper

450 g/1 lb skinned and
 filleted haddock, whiting,
 hake or conger eel, cut into
 chunks
350 g/12 oz sprouting
 broccoli or calabrese
150 ml/¼ pt double cream

Sweat the onion and leek in the butter until soft without letting it brown. Off the heat stir in the flour and cook again gently for a few minutes, stirring all the while. Remove from the heat again and stir in most of the stock. Bring up to a simmer and cook for 10 minutes, taste for seasoning, and add the fish. Cook for 1 minute and allow to cool slightly before processing, blending at top speed or sieving until smooth.

Meanwhile, peel the broccoli or calabrese stalks, cut off some of the flowering heads for a final garnish, and chop the rest. Cook the chopped part in just enough lightly salted water to cover. Drain, keeping the liquor, and refresh under cold water. Mix with some of the liquor and sieve into the fish soup, blending again if necessary. Dilute to taste with the remaining fish stock and broccoli liquor. Reheat until just below boiling point, add the cream, check the seasoning and serve garnished with the steamed broccoli flowers.

ﾟ SMOKED HADDOCK SOUP ﾟ

Cullen skink is a rich soup from the Moray Firth, the home of the
Finnan haddock. If Finnan is unavailable, use any smoked haddock
but avoid those bright yellow fish that have been dyed.

SERVES 4–6

1 large onion, chopped
50 g/2 oz butter
450 g/1 lb Finnan haddock,
  filleted
570 ml/1 pt water

225 g/8 oz potato, mashed
570 ml/1 pt fish or light
  chicken stock, or milk
salt and pepper
1 tbsp parsley, finely chopped

Soften the onion in the butter in a large pan and then add the fish,
cut into large pieces. Cover with the water and simmer for 10
minutes. Remove the fish to cool, and go over it for bones before
flaking the flesh off the skin. Stir the potato into the cooking liquid,
and when it's nicely incorporated add the stock or milk and then the
fish. Simmer for 10 minutes, taste for seasoning, and serve with a
slosh of cream and a generous sprinkling of parsley.

ﾟ MUSSELS WITH SORREL AND CREAM ﾟ

Moules à la poulette, in this case with sorrel, is one of the many
refinements of *moules marinières* when all the mussels are taken out
of their shells. Strictly speaking, *'poulette'* means previously cooked
ingredients which are then bound with a velouté sauce made with
eggs and cream.

SERVES 4

1.1 litres/2 pts mussels,
  scrubbed and rinsed in
  several changes of water
1 onion, finely chopped
1 tbsp parsley, finely chopped
1 tsp fresh thyme, finely
  chopped
½ a bayleaf

a couple of glasses of white
  wine or cider
40 g/1½ oz butter
salt, pepper and cayenne
a pinch of cayenne pepper
50 ml/2 fl oz double cream
a handful of sorrel, finely cut
  into ribbons

Put the cleaned mussels in a large pan with the onion and herbs.
Pour over the white wine, cover the pan, and put it over a fierce heat
so that the shells open quickly. As soon as the shells open, take the
pan off the heat and quickly pinch out the mussels into a warmed
tureen. Discard the shells. Strain the mussel liquor/white wine
through a fine sieve into a clean pan. Add the butter, season generously with black pepper and cayenne but cautiously with salt, and

stir in the cream and sorrel. Bring briskly to the boil and pour it over the mussels in the tureen. Serve with very small croûtons of brown bread lightly fried in butter.

∽ OYSTER VELOUTÉ ∽

Any oysters are suitable for this delicate *potage aux huîtres*. If your fishmonger opens the molluscs for you, be sure to transport them home carefully because the water in the shells (added to the stock through muslin or a fine sieve) will improve the soup.

SERVES 4

25–50 g/1–2 oz butter,
  depending on the number of
  oysters
12 or more oysters
2 tsp fresh herbs such as
  parsley, dill, chives and basil,
  chopped

1.4 litres/2½ pts fish stock
2 egg-yolks
a pinch of saffron
juice of 1 lemon

Heat the butter in a pan that can hold the finished soup. Gently fry the oysters for 10 seconds, flip and fry the other side. Add the herbs and then the stock, previously brought up to the boil. Simmer very gently for 5 minutes. Beat the egg-yolks in a tureen, adding the saffron and lemon juice. Whisk in a little of the hot soup, then pour on the rest, stirring all the time. Serve with croûtons fried in butter.

∽ SOUR SHRIMP SOUP ∽

Tom yam goong is a refreshing, pungent and chilli-hot Thai soup, often cooked at the table in a steamboat (see pages 296 and 300). To moderate the heat threshold, adjust the number of chillis and leave out the chilli paste.

SERVES 6

1.4 litres/2½ pts water or
  light chicken stock
3 stalks lemon grass, tender
  part only, cut into 5-cm/2-in
  lengths
5 kaffir lime leaves
150 g/5 oz small mushroom
  caps or straw mushrooms
40 ml/1½ fl oz nam pla
  (Thai fish sauce)
6 dried red chilli peppers

10 ml/½ fl oz chilli paste
225–450 g/½–1 lb raw
  shrimps or prawns, shelled
  and de-veined
4 spring onions, chopped into
  2.5-cm/1-in pieces
6 or 8 sweet basil leaves
100 ml/3½ fl oz lime juice
2 tbsp coriander leaves, finely
  chopped

Bring the water or stock to the boil and add the lemon grass, lime leaves, mushrooms, fish sauce and chillis. Boil for 2 minutes and then add the chilli paste, prawns, spring onions, sweet basil and lime juice. Cook until the shrimps or prawns turn pink, and serve flecked with coriander leaves.

WHAT'S-IN-THE-CUPBOARD SOUPS

These are the quick soups that get conjured out of store cupboards and will rarely be repeated exactly the same.

∽ BAKED BEAN SOUP ∽

The best way to stretch a can of beans between 4.

> 4 rashers streaky bacon
> 1 small onion, finely diced
> 400 g/14 oz can baked beans
>
> 900 ml/1½ pts chicken stock
> Worcestershire sauce, salt and
>   pepper

Grill the bacon or fry it slowly in a non-stick pan. When it is crisp and most of the fat has been released, put the bacon to one side and gently sauté the onion. When the onion is soft but not browned, transfer it to a suitable pan and tip in the beans and chicken stock. If you like your beans spiced, season with Worcestershire sauce and/or a chilli condiment, and with salt and pepper. Bring up to the boil, stir, and heat the beans through. Just before serving mix in the crumbled bacon. Serve with chunky croûtons fried in bacon fat or, if ravenous, doorstep toasted bacon sandwiches.

∽ BRUSSELS SPROUT SOUP ∽

This is the perfect use for leftover cooked sprouts, and has been devoured with relish by people who claim they can't eat them.

> SERVES 4
> 16–20 cooked Brussels
>   sprouts
>
> 900 ml/1½ pts light chicken
>   stock
> salt and pepper

Liquidize the sprouts with 275 ml/½ pt of the stock. Pour into a pan with the rest of the stock, bring up to the boil and simmer gently for 10 minutes. Season to taste with salt and pepper. Serve with cream, crisp grilled bacon pieces and toasted cheese croûtons, separately (page 108).

∽ CARROT AND ORANGE SOUP ∽

SERVES 6

50 g/2 oz butter
1 large onion, peeled and
  grated
700 g/1½ lb carrots, peeled
  and grated
1 large potato, peeled, grated
  and thorougly rinsed

salt
1 large sweet orange
1 small orange, peeled and
  sliced into thin segments
1 tbsp parsley, finely chopped

Melt the butter in a large pan. Stir-fry the onion for a couple of minutes, then add the carrots and potato, season with ½ tsp of salt, stir thoroughly and cover. Leave to sweat for 5 minutes. Meanwhile grate 2 tbsp of peel from the large orange, then cut the orange in half and extract all its juice. Stir the peel into the vegetables and cover with boiling water. Bring back to the boil and simmer at a brisk roll, covered, for 10 minutes. Liquidize the soup, return to the pan and add the orange juice. Check the seasoning and, if necessary, thin the purée with water. Bring back to the boil and serve garnished with the orange segments and parsley.

∽ CHICKPEA SOUP WITH MINT AND GARLIC ∽

Sopa de panela, a Spanish chickpea, garlic and mint soup, is at its finest when enriched with good quality olive oil. I use a slosh of my much-prized Granverde Colonna, a delicious olive oil matured with lemons (see page 61).

SERVES 4

2 400 g/14 oz cans
  chickpeas
2 fat cloves of garlic, roughly
  chopped
6 tbsp olive oil
2 tbsp lemon juice

salt and pepper
2 tbsp fresh mint leaves, finely
  chopped
2 tbsp flat-leaf parsley, finely
  chopped

Drain the liquid from the chickpea can into a measuring jug and make up the amount to 900 ml/1½ pts. Purée this liquid with the chickpeas, garlic, olive oil and lemon juice and season to taste with salt and pepper. Turn into a pan and stir in most of the mint and parsley. Heat through, taste and adjust the seasoning.

Serve garnished with the rest of the mint and parsley and, if liked, a swirl of olive oil, and with triangular croûtons (see page 107) and lemon wedges on the side.

∽ CORN, POTATO AND CHEDDAR CHEESE SOUP ∽

Lorna Wing's recipe is more of a thick glop than a soup but is a delicious, filling comfort-feed; an ideal 'morning after' lunch.

SERVES 4

25 g/1 oz butter
1 small onion, finely diced
1 large (225 g/½ lb) potato,
  peeled and diced
25 g/1 oz flour
a splash of white wine
  (optional)

275 ml/½ pt milk
1 medium-sized tin sweetcorn
50–75 g/2–3 oz Cheddar,
  grated
few sage leaves, chopped
400 ml/¾ pt double cream
chopped chives

Melt the butter, soften the onion and potato and sift in the flour. Stir round to take up the fat and make a smooth roux with the wine, if using, or a little milk. Stir in the rest of the milk, bring up to the boil and turn down immediately to simmer. Drain the sweetcorn and add it, the cheese, sage and cream to the pan. Simmer-stir until the cheese melts and you achieve a suitable gloppy consistency. Serve sprinkled with chives.

∽ CORN, CHILLI AND CHICKEN SOUP ∽

Sopa de elote is a spicy/sweet Mexican soup that puts a small amount of chicken to good use. If using uncooked chicken, sauté it gently with the onion before adding the other ingredients. A Chinesey version of this soup is made by omitting the chillis and tomato paste and using 2 finely chopped spring onions in place of the small onion. Season with 1 tbsp of soy sauce.

SERVES 4

25 g/1 oz butter
1 shallot or small onion,
  finely chopped
25 g/1 oz flour
1 litre/1¾ pts chicken stock,
  or bouillon-cube with water
4 tbsp tomato juice or 1 tbsp
  tomato purée thinned with
  3 tbsp water

110 g/4 oz cooked chicken
275 g/10 oz can sweetcorn,
  drained
2 fresh red chilli peppers, de-
  seeded and finely chopped
salt and pepper

Heat the butter in a pan that can accommodate the completed soup. Gently stir-fry the onion without browning. Sift in the flour, stirring vigorously to avoid lumps, and make a smooth paste with a little of the stock. Allow to bubble for a minute before stirring in the tomato juice, chicken, sweetcorn, chilli peppers and the rest of the stock. Bring to the boil quickly and turn down immediately. Leave to simmer for 10 minutes. Taste for seasoning. Serve with quick rolls (see page 121) or garlic croûtes (see page 123).

↶ PARMESAN, EGG AND PARSLEYED CHICKEN BROTH ↶

Stracciatella is a classic Italian quick soup but does rely on decent stock.

SERVES 4–6

2 large eggs
1 tbsp Parmesan, freshly
 grated
1 tbsp parsley, finely chopped

1.1 litres/2 pts rich chicken
 stock
salt and pepper

Whisk the eggs, cheese and parsley with a little of the hot stock. Meanwhile season and heat the remaining stock and when it comes almost to the boil, pour in the egg mixture, stirring constantly. Bring almost to the boil again and transfer to a warm tureen. Serve with crusty bread.

↶ PARMESAN, EGG AND LEMON CHICKEN BROTH ↶

Minestra d'uova is another Italian classic. When Parmesan, egg, lemon and breadcrumbs are formed into a dough which is then grated into the broth, this soup becomes *Passatelli in brodo* (see page 319) or *Milli fanti/Soupe niçoise*.

SERVES 6

1.75 litres/3 pts rich chicken
 stock
4 eggs
50 g/2 oz fine dry
 breadcrumbs

50 g/2 oz Parmesan, freshly
 grated
50 ml/2 fl oz lemon juice
grated rind of 1 lemon
salt and pepper

Bring the stock to the boil. Blend the eggs, breadcrumbs, cheese, lemon juice and rind together in a bowl. Season with salt and pepper.
 Turn off the heat under the broth and whisk in the egg mixture. Bring the soup back to the boil, stirring continuously. Serve immediately.

∽ PEA AND PEAR SOUP ∽

Out of the blue one day I had a telephone call from Sonia Stevenson, whom I'd never met but whose restaurant, now under different ownership, used to be one of the best in the country. She'd heard on the grapevine that I was writing a book on soup and offered to send me some recipes. Our talk turned to quick soups and she reminisced about this one, first mentioned by one of her customers and then to become a favourite at the Horn of Plenty.

In summer, when made with ripe pears and young peas, the results are quite different. Either way the mint undercuts any sweetness, and the soup can be served hot or cold.

SERVES 4

450 g/1 lb frozen peas
2 × 400 g/14 oz cans
  unsweetened pears

2 tbsp fresh mint, finely
  chopped, or mint jelly
salt and white pepper

Cook the peas in salted water for a few minutes. Meanwhile pour the liquid from the cans of pears into a measuring jug and make up to 900 ml/1½ pts with cold water. Drain the peas and liquidize with the pears and liquid. Pour into a pan, add the mint and cook through. Season to taste with salt and white pepper.

∽ MINT AND PEA SOUP ∽

There are various versions of this soup, but I've chosen Simon Hopkinson's because it is almost instant and almost entirely storecupboard. It is not on the menu at his restaurant, Bibendum. The cream can be replaced by milk or reconstituted milk. It is good hot or cold.

SERVES 6

900 g/2 lb frozen peas
900 ml/1½ pts chicken stock,
  or 1 chicken stock-cube and
  570 ml/1 pt water

1 tsp concentrated mint sauce
salt and pepper
275 ml/½ pt single cream
a pinch of sugar

Cook the peas in the stock or water plus cube, with the mint and a pinch of salt and pepper, covered, for 10 minutes. Pour into a liquidizer and strain through a sieve, pushing through as much as possible. Return to a clean pan with the cream and bring back to the boil. Remove immediately and adjust the seasoning, adding a pinch of sugar if you like. Serve with croûtons.

∽ POTATO, ONION AND FETA CHEESE SOUP ∽

SERVES 4

2 large potatoes, peeled, grated
 and rinsed
40 g/1½ oz butter
2 medium onions, finely
 chopped

salt
2 eggs, whisked with 150 ml/
 5 fl oz water
50 g/2 oz Feta cheese, grated
chives (optional)

Cover the potatoes with salted water and cook, covered, for 5 minutes. Meanwhile melt the butter, gently stir-fry the onions until coated, then season with salt, cover the pan, and cook for 5 minutes. Mix the onions into the potatoes, top up with 275 ml/½ pt of water, bring up to the boil and simmer for 5 minutes. Stir a spoonful of the hot potato broth into the egg mixture before returning it to the pot. Serve with croûtons sprinkled with the Feta cheese and, if you have some, a sprinkling of chives.

∽ TOMATO RICE SOUP ∽

SERVES 4

50 g/2 oz quick-cook rice
15 g/½ oz butter
1 onion, finely diced
15 g/½ oz flour
400 g/14 oz can tomatoes,
 roughly chopped
2 tbsp tomato purée

2 tbsp parsley, finely chopped
salt and pepper
1 tbsp lemon juice
900 ml/1½ pts chicken stock
 or equivalent using stock-
 cubes
1 tbsp chives, chopped

Begin by cooking the rice according to the packet instructions while you heat the butter and gently sauté the onion. Sift in the flour to take up the fat, and stir in the tomatoes, purée and 1 tbsp of the parsley. Boil hard for a minute or two. Season with salt and pepper and stir in the lemon juice before adding the stock. Bring up to the boil and simmer for 5 minutes before liquidizing. Pass through a sieve to get rid of the plethora of pips and return to the pan. By now the rice will be cooked. Drain and tip into the soup. Check the seasoning and stir in the chives and the rest of the parsley.

∽ RICE, EGG AND LEMON BROTH ∽

Avgolemono soupa is a classic Greek soup made with fish or chicken stock, and is sometimes served with meatballs, in which case the rice is left out. To meet the 15-minute deadline and avoid stock evaporation, this version relies on quick-cook rice, cooked in boiling water.

SERVES 4
40 g/1½ oz quick-cook rice
*1.1 litres/2 pts chicken or fish
  stock*
2 eggs

*juice of 1 large lemon (3–4
  tbsp)*
salt and pepper

Begin by getting the rice under way, according to the packet instructions. Next bring the stock up to the boil. Meanwhile beat the eggs with the lemon juice. Drain the rice and stir it into the broth. When it comes back to the boil stir a little of the boiling soup into the egg/lemon mixture. Turn down the heat as low as possible and whisk the egg/lemon mixture into the soup. Continue to whisk, without allowing it to boil, for a couple of minutes. Remove from the heat, taste for seasoning and serve.

∽ WHITE BEAN SOUP ∽

SERVES 4
1 scant dsp cooking oil
1 medium onion, finely diced
1 fat clove of garlic, chopped
*2 × 400 g/14 oz cans white
  beans, rinsed*
*900 g/1½ pts chicken stock
  or equivalent using stock-
  cubes*

salt and pepper
1 tbsp parsley, finely chopped
*1 peperoni sausage, finely
  sliced*

Heat the oil and gently sauté the onion until soft but not brown. Add the garlic and the drained beans and stir around before adding the stock. Bring up to the boil, season generously, and liquidize half the soup. Return to the pan, stir in the parsley and peperoni, simmer for 3 minutes and serve with chilli croûtons.

∽ NICHOLAS HASLAM'S QUICK BISQUE ∽

Quite the most ingenious cookery book I came across during my soup research is *The Slim Gourmet's Soup Book*: 500 soups from 5 cans. This amazing book, published in 1956, takes 5 starting points – tinned tomato, consommé, vegetable, chicken and mushroom soup – to create 'wheel' charts of soup cocktails. None, though, could match this recipe in Caroline Blackwood and Anna Haycraft's book *Darling, You Shouldn't Have Gone to So Much Trouble*, concocted from Nicholas Haslam's larder.

SERVES 6–8

2 cans lobster or crabmeat
1 can turtle soup
1 can condensed tomato soup
1 can pea soup
1 can beef bouillon or
  consommé

1 tsp dried onions,
  reconstituted with a very
  little hot water
1½ cartons of cream
brandy

Heat all the ingredients, adding the cream and brandy at the very end. Served with croûtons, this is a meal in itself.

✎ RAY PARKES'S SPINACH AND PISTACHIO SOUP ✎

At the height of the swinging sixties and into the early seventies Ray Parkes ran one of London's most fashionable restaurants. Parkes was camp, glamorous, fun, and his food indulgent. Nobody knew that it was a kitchen that ran largely on tins. This is one of the enduring successes.

SERVES 4

400 g/14 oz can cream of
  chicken soup
225 g/½ lb frozen spinach
50 g/2 oz pistachios, peeled
  and toasted

½ tsp nutmeg, freshly grated
275 ml/½ pt sour cream
Tabasco
salt and pepper

Heat the chicken soup and pass through a sieve to remove the chicken pieces. Add the frozen spinach and bring to the boil. Add the pistachios and simmer for 5 minutes before stirring in the nutmeg and most of the cream.

   Meanwhile stir a few drops of Tabasco with the rest of the cream. Serve with a dollop of the Tabasco cream.

Thick Soups

〜

'I have never cooked seriously either for myself or for anyone else. In the days when I was too poor to eat in restaurants and was besieged by acquaintances even nearer to starvation than I, the most I ever did was to take a saucepan which had been used for a variety of purposes without ever being washed, fill it with water and bring it to the boil. The result was known as Workhouse Soup. As, naturally, very little of this brew was consumed, on subsequent occasions I added to it anything that came to hand. The more "acquired" (nasty) the flavour became, the more distant the places in which I said the recipe had originated. When a consistency of cake and a state of uneatability was reached, I described the dish as Tibetan.' (Quentin Crisp on Tibetan Workhouse Soup, from Caroline Blackwood and Anna Haycraft, *Darling, You Shouldn't Have Gone to So Much Trouble*)

This enormous category of soups includes fresh and dried vegetable purées, shellfish bisques, cream and egg-bound soups, and a gamut of soups including some bread, onion, potato, rice and bean soups whose ingredients collapse in the cooking and thicken themselves. Such soups the French call *potages liés*.

CREAM AND VELOUTÉ SOUPS

Much soup terminology is confusing and its interpretation, even to classically trained chefs, is open-ended. *Cream* soups, for instance, aren't necessarily made or garnished with cream. Often cream is used to describe the consistency of the finished soup, and several feature in the *purée* and *bisque* selection. Many such soups, though, are made from vegetables, fish, shellfish, or poultry sweated in butter or oil, then thickened with flour, or by adding a cream-based

179

béchamel and then thinning with stock. At the end of the cooking the soup is then thickened again with egg-yolk, sometimes mixed with cream. Such soups are also called *velouté*.

For the purposes of this book, all the soups in this selection are finished with an egg liaison, usually mixed with cream.

It is important not to allow any of these soups to boil once the egg has been added. Soups that have been cooked with cream should be served in hot bowls. For more information about egg and cream liaisons see page 58.

✑ ALMOND CREAM SOUP ✑

An elegant and subtle soup refined by Roger Vergé and served at his restaurant Le Moulin de Mougins, Mougins, France.

SERVES 4
20 g/⅔ oz butter
*1 leek, white part only, cut
  into fine rounds*
*1 litre/1½ pts light chicken
  stock*
*12 g/½ oz round-grain
  Carolina rice, rinsed*

110 g/4 oz ground almonds
275 ml/½ pt thick cream
2 egg-yolks
salt

Soften the butter with 1 tbsp of water and cook the leek for 5 minutes. Add the stock, bring up to the boil and stir in the rice and ground almonds. Turn the heat right down, cover, and simmer very gently for 25 minutes. Meanwhile, whisk the cream and egg-yolks together in a large bowl. Liquidize the soup and pour it, whisking as you do so, into the egg and cream. Return everything to a clean pan and gently re-heat. Season with salt and strain through a fine sieve. Serve in hot soup-cups or bowls, with parmesan tuiles (see page 126).

✑ CREAM OF ASPARAGUS ✑

This is Marcel Boulestin's recipe, without the 2 lumps of sugar he adds at the beginning of cooking.

SERVES 4–6
570 ml/1 pt water
1 tsp salt
½ a bundle of asparagus
*2 floury-variety potatoes,
  peeled and chopped*
*2 small onions or 3 shallots,
  finely chopped*

50 g/2 oz butter
*900 ml/1½ pts light chicken
  or veal stock*
25 g/1 oz flour
1 egg-yolk
50 ml/2 oz thick cream

Put the water on to boil, then add the salt, asparagus, potatoes and onions and cook for 5 minutes. Drain the vegetables but reserve the cooking liquid. Soften half the butter in a pan and add the well-drained vegetables. Smear a little butter on a piece of greaseproof or foil paper and cover the vegetables, and cook very slowly for a few minutes, making sure that the vegetables don't brown. Remove the paper, slice the tips off a few of the asparagus and set aside. Pour in the reserved cooking liquid and the stock. Bring up to the boil and simmer gently for 30 minutes.

Meanwhile rub the flour into the rest of the butter. Liquidize the soup and strain into a clean pan. Add the floured butter in small lumps and stir thoroughly while you bring the soup up to the boil. Cook for 5 minutes until the flour is cooked and the soup thickens.

Remove from the heat and stir in the egg mixed together with the cream. Serve decorated with the reserved asparagus spears and croûtons fried in butter.

∽ BEAN AND BACON SOUP ∽

A perfect winter warmer; the ubiquitous bean and bacon combination is given an unusual twist in this Romanian recipe, which is seasoned with vinegar and dill and enriched with sour cream and egg-yolks.

SERVES 6

225 g/8 oz haricot, pinto or butter beans
2 litres/3½ pts water
100 g/4 oz piece smoked bacon
1 Cos lettuce, washed and shredded

salt and pepper
2 egg-yolks
150 ml/¼ pt soured cream
1 tbsp vinegar (see page 60)
a small bunch of fresh dill

Soak the beans in cold water overnight. The next day drain the beans and put them in a large pan with the 2 l/3½ pts cold water. Cube the bacon and add it to the pan. Bring the water up to the boil, skim, partially cover and simmer gently for a couple of hours until the beans are very soft; depending on the type and age of the beans, they may require more cooking and/or more water.

Mash the beans slightly to help them flop, then stir in the lettuce and a few grinds of black pepper and cook for a further 5–10 minutes. Mix the egg-yolks with the cream and vinegar and stir into the hot soup, taking care not to let it boil again. Remove from the heat, taste for seasoning, and stir in most of the dill, keeping a few fronds for garnish. Serve with plenty of crusty bread for dunking and scooping.

∾ FRENCH BEAN AND ALMOND SOUP ∾

This is a simple but exquisite soup when made with prime beans and good stock. Pounded almonds thicken the broth, and the egg-yolks enrich it. The recipe comes from Elizabeth David's *Summer Cooking*.

SERVES 4

350 g/12 oz French beans
1.4 litres/2½ pts mild-
flavoured stock (chicken is
best)
salt and pepper

50 g/2 oz skinned almonds,
lightly browned under the
grill or pan-fried in a little butter
lemon juice
2 egg-yolks

Top, tail and string the beans, and cut them in half. Bring the stock up to the boil, add ½ tsp of salt, and cook the beans. Meanwhile, pound the almonds roughly in a mortar and 2 minutes before the beans are ready, stir the paste into the soup. Adjust the seasoning with a little lemon juice, salt and pepper. Beat the egg-yolks with 2 tbsp of broth, stir into the soup and re-heat without boiling.

Serve with Parmesan biscuits (see page 126).

∾ CAULIFLOWER SOUP WITH SOUR CREAM AND ∾
TINY DUMPLINGS

SERVES 4–6

450 g/1 lb bite-sized
cauliflower florets
1 small onion, finely diced
50 ml/2 fl oz clarified fat
from smoked streaky bacon
1 large carrot, peeled and
diced

1 tbsp flour
salt and pepper
1 egg-yolk
75 ml/¼ pt sour cream

Put the cauliflower florets in a spacious pan and cover with boiling water. Add ½ tsp of salt and parboil for 5 minutes. Drain the florets but reserve the liquor, making it up to 1.4 litres/2½ pts in total.

Meanwhile sauté the onion in the rendered bacon fat until transparent but not browned. Add the diced carrot and sweat, covered, for 5 minutes, stirring occasionally. Sift and stir in the flour, and add a little of the hot cauliflower broth to make a smooth cream. Let it bubble up and season with salt and pepper. Stir in the rest of the cauliflower liquor and continue stirring while you bring the liquid up to the boil. Turn down the heat to a simmer and add the cauliflower florets. Simmer for 5 minutes. Mix the egg-yolk with the sour cream and stir into the soup.

5 minutes before the soup is ready, poach 5 or 6 *csipetke* (see page 91) per serving in boiling water and add them to the soup. Serve garnished with chopped parsley and crumbled bacon.

∽ CREAM OF CHERVIL SOUP ∽

Chervil has a delicate flavour, rather like flat-leaf parsley perfumed with aniseed, which combines well with eggs and cream. Its pale green lacy leaves are fragile, and its flavour and colour fade quickly once the herb is picked. So this is a gardener's soup. Folding in uncooked leaves just before serving refreshes the flavour as well as the colour of this very special soup.

SERVES 6

50 g/2 oz butter
175 g/6 oz spring onions, finely chopped
350 g/12 oz chervil, stripped from the stalks and finely chopped
1.4 litres/2½ pts boiling water
salt and pepper
570 ml/1 pt milk
1 tbsp potato flour or similar (see page 57), slaked in a little cold water
2 egg-yolks
50 ml/2 fl oz double cream

Melt the butter and sweat the onions until limp but not browned. Stir in 275 g/10 oz of the prepared chervil and cook gently, stirring all the time, for a couple of minutes until the chervil has wilted. Pour on the boiling water, season, whisk thoroughly and leave to simmer, uncovered, for 25 minutes. Purée the soup and return to a clean pan. Add the milk, bring up to a simmer and stir in the potato flour mixed with a little water. Continue stirring with a whisk until the soup is thick and smooth.

Have ready the egg-yolks mixed with the cream and stir a little of the hot soup into the mixture. Remove the pan from the heat and whisk the liaison into it. Return to the heat and whisk a few more times, taking care that the soup does not boil, then stir in most of the rest of the chopped chervil.

Serve in hot bowls, garnished with a blob of whipped cream laced with the last of the chervil. A few croûtons provide a good texture contrast.

∽ GREEN SUMMER SOUP WITH TOMATO AND PARSLEY ∽

The mixture of three distinctive herbs – chervil, tarragon and watercress – matched with cucumber and cut by a fresh tomato and parsley garnish is an interesting balance of flavours. Mrs Beeton's version of this, called 'Good Woman's Soup', replaces the watercress with 1 white-heart lettuce, and the greens are shredded rather than puréed; that version is good with bacon-based dumplings and a garnish of fresh parsley. This is not the same as *potage bonne femme* (see page 228), a cream of potato, carrot and leek, seasoned with parsley or chervil, and enriched with cream and butter.

SERVES 4

12 sprigs of chervil
5 sprigs of watercress
2 sprigs of tarragon
½ a small cucumber, peeled
15 g/½ oz butter
salt and white pepper
570 ml/1 pt jellied chicken
 stock

75 ml/3 fl oz milk
2 egg-yolks
75 ml/3 fl oz double cream
2 ripe tomatoes, peeled, cored
 and the flesh diced
1 dsp parsley, finely chopped

Chop the chervil, watercress and tarragon with their stalks. Roughly chop the peeled cucumber. Melt the butter and stir in the chopped greens, season with ½ tsp of salt, cover and sweat over a very low heat for 5 minutes. Stir once or twice. Meanwhile bring the stock up to the boil, add half the milk and pour over the greens. Bring back to a simmer, cook for a couple of minutes and then purée. Pour and press through a fine sieve into a clean pan. Whisk the egg-yolks with the cream and the rest of the milk, and pour the liaison slowly into the soup, whisking all the time. Continue cooking, without allowing the soup to boil, until slightly thickened. Pour into warmed bowls and garnish with the diced tomatoes and chopped parsley. Serve with hot garlic bread scattered with more parsley.

∽ CUCUMBER AND SORREL CREAM ∽

SERVES 6

50 g/2 oz butter
6 spring onions, finely sliced
2 cucumbers, peeled and
 chopped
salt and white pepper

a handful of sorrel leaves
1.4 litres/2½ pts good stock
2 egg-yolks
275 ml/½ pt thick cream

Melt the butter and sweat the spring onions for a couple of minutes before adding the cucumber and ½ tsp of salt. Stir it around to cook evenly for 5 minutes before adding the sorrel, reserving a few of the best leaves for the garnish. Let everything cook to a flop without browning and then pour on the stock. Bring the soup up to the boil and simmer gently for 30 minutes. Purée the soup but let it retain some texture; I prefer to use a mouli rather than a liquidizer for this soup. Return to a clean pan and taste for seasoning. Bring the soup up to a simmer and have ready the egg-yolks beaten with half the cream. Whisk the liaison into the soup, taking care not to let it boil, and stir thoroughly before removing from the heat.

Pour the soup into heated bowls and garnish each serving with croûtons hidden by a spoonful of whipped cream laced with finely shredded fresh sorrel, or chopped chives.

✑ TURKISH MINT AND YOGHURT SOUP ✑

Authenticity demands dried, not fresh, mint for this everyday Turkish soup called *yayla corbasi*. It is best made with thick, rich and creamy Greek yoghurt (see directions for making your own, page 67). The addition of chickpeas and paprika, added before the yoghurt liaison, makes the soup more substantial and is a matter of taste.

SERVES 6

110 g/4 oz long-grain rice
1.75 litres/3 pts rich chicken
  or lamb stock
salt and pepper
2 egg-yolks

570 ml/1 pt strained Greek
  yoghurt
2 tbsp dried mint
50 g/2 oz butter
2 tsp paprika

Boil the rice in the stock until soft. Season with salt and pepper to taste, and remove the pan from the heat. Beat the egg-yolks into the yoghurt, then add a little of the hot stock, stirring until evenly incorporated. Slowly pour the yoghurt liaison into the soup, stirring all the while. Mix in half the mint, return the pan to the heat, and continue cooking without allowing the soup to boil, until the soup thickens.

Turn off the heat and allow to stand while you melt the butter, stir in the paprika and the rest of the mint and let the mixture sizzle for a few seconds. Drizzle the mixture over the soup, before serving with lightly oiled hot pitta bread cut into wedges.

✑ CHARENTAIS ONION SOUP ✑

One of the legacies of my family's first French camping holiday is a disproportionate affection for the apéritif Pineau des Charentes, a brandy-laced wine. For my parents, coping with four children aged between eight and eighteen, the discovery of this local speciality proved an essential *aide de vacances*. This delicious but cholesterol-laden local recipe uses the dregs of the bottle to very good effect.

SERVES 6–8

25 g/1 oz butter
200 g/8 oz onion, finely
  chopped
salt and pepper
a pinch of cayenne
1 bayleaf
1.4 litres/2½ pts light veal or
  jellied chicken stock

4 egg-yolks
approx. 100 ml/4 fl oz Pineau
  des Charentes Blanc
275 g/10 oz Gruyère, grated
several thin slices of French
  bread, dried in the oven
8–10 freshly shelled walnut
  halves

In a large heavy-bottomed pan melt the butter and gently stir-fry the onion with ½ tsp of salt for about 10–15 minutes until soft. Add a pinch of cayenne pepper and 1 bayleaf. Pour on the stock, bring slowly to the boil and simmer at a gentle roll for 10 minutes. Taste for seasoning.

Meanwhile beat the 4 egg-yolks together with the Pineau and stir in the grated cheese. Remove the soup from the heat and gradually beat in the Pineau, egg and cheese mixture. Return to a very low heat and keep on beating until the soup is thickened, but on no account let it boil. Place the oven-dried croûtes in the serving dishes, top with some walnuts and pour on the soup. Serve with more croûtes or with Melba toast (page 124); anything else would be too rich.

✑ MADEIRA ONION SOUP ✑

Sopa de cebola a Madeirense, a similarly rich but more unusual onion soup from Madeira, is subtly scented with cloves, sweetened with sultanas and perked up with cayenne pepper and dry Madeira. The recipe is adapted from the authoritative and evocatively written *The Food of Portugal* by Jean Anderson. Like many soups, and onion ones in particular, this soup will be mellower if it is cooled, covered and chilled for 24 hours. In this case, stop the cooking before adding the egg liaison.

SERVES 6

50 g/2 oz butter
2 tbsp olive oil
1 kg/2½ lb Spanish or other
  mild onions, thinly sliced
6 whole cloves
1 tsp paprika
2 tbsp seedless sultanas

1.4 litres/2½ pts beef stock
275 ml/½ pt water
½ tsp salt
⅛ tsp black pepper
4 large egg-yolks, lightly
  beaten
50 ml/2 fl oz dry Madeira

Heat the butter and oil in a heavy-bottomed pan and sauté the onions for about 30 minutes, stirring occasionally, until limp and golden and lightly touched with brown. Add the cloves, paprika, sultanas, stock and water. Cover and simmer for 60 minutes, then uncover and simmer for a further 30 minutes. Taste and season with salt and pepper. Mix a little of the hot soup into the egg-yolks and stir the mixture into the soup. Simmer gently for a few minutes before adding the Madeira.

Serve with *broa* (see page 116) or another crusty bread.

✑ IRANIAN ONION SOUP ✑

An unusual aromatic sweet and sour onion soup seasoned with lemons, sugar, dried mint and cinnamon, and tinted yellow with turmeric.

SERVES 6

50 g/2 oz butter	*1 tsp turmeric*
3 medium onions, thinly sliced	*juice of 2 lemons or 1 lime*
	2 tbsp sugar
25 g/1 oz flour	*1 tbsp dried mint*
1.75 litres/3 pts water	*½ tsp cinnamon*
salt and pepper	*2 eggs, beaten lightly*

Melt the butter and gently stir-fry the onions until they flop and begin to turn golden brown. Sift the flour into the onions, stirring to take up the fat, and let it bubble away for a few seconds. Stir in a little of the water to make a smooth cream of the flour and then stir in the rest of the water. Add 1 tsp of salt, 1 level tsp of black pepper and the turmeric and bring slowly up to the boil. Turn the heat right down and simmer, covered, for 30 minutes. Stir in the lemon or lime juice, then the sugar, and simmer for 10 more minutes. Stir in the mint and cinnamon and remove from the heat.

Mix a little of the hot soup into the eggs and stir the mixture into the soup. Serve with mild, bland flat-bread *khubz* (see page 116), and a bowl of fresh herbs such as parsley, chives, mint, basil, coriander and tarragon.

✑ LE TOURIN ✑

Le tourin, a famous thin French onion soup, is made by sweating very finely sliced onions in fat, stewing them in water, and just before serving, thickening the soup with egg-yolks. The finished soup is then poured on to slices of oven-dried French bread. Every south-west region of France claims to have invented *le tourin*, or *torril*, *tourri*, or *ouliat*, and it varies slightly according to the type of fat, quantity of onions, number of eggs and seasonings used. For example, the Bordelais version is made with pork dripping and seasoned with vinegar; a Toulousain version adds garlic, tomatoes and aniseed grains, and a Périgord version is enriched with garlic, tomatoes and wine. Another includes chopped solidified egg-white.

Le tourin is an immensely comforting soup that is easy to digest.

SERVES 6

50 g/2 oz lard, duck or goose dripping	*1.75 litres/3 pts cold water*
3 large mild onions, sliced in the thinnest possible rounds	*2 or 3 egg-yolks*
	a few drops of vinegar
salt	*6 or more slices of French bread, dried in the oven*

Melt the dripping in a large, heavy-bottomed pan and stir in the onions, stirring until they begin to soften. Season with ½ a teaspoon of salt and leave to cook gently for 30–45 minutes until the onions are a pale golden, creamy pulp. Pour on the water (to make a thicker soup, stir in 1–2 tbsp of flour before adding the water) and bring slowly to the boil. Simmer gently for 10–15 minutes. Meanwhile beat the egg-yolks with a few drops of vinegar and a ladleful of hot soup, and pour it slowly into the soup, stirring all the time. Allow the soup to simmer, but not boil, until it thickens. Divide the dried bread slices between the bowls and pour on the soup.

∽ ONION AND GARLIC SOUP ∽

SERVES 4

225 g/8 oz onions, finely sliced	*salt and pepper*
	½ tsp thyme buds or tiny leaves, finely chopped
50 g/2 oz butter	
900 ml/1½ pts good stock	*a few drops of vinegar*
bouquet garni *made with 1 bayleaf, 4 branches of thyme and 6 sprays of parsley*	*1 egg-yolk, beaten with a splash of milk*
1 head of garlic, cloves removed from their skins	

Gently sweat the onions in the hot butter and cook until soft and mushy. At the point when they are beginning to brown, add the stock, *bouquet garni* and garlic. Season well. Bring slowly to the boil and simmer gently, partially covered, for 30 minutes. Fish out the *bouquet garni*, adjust the seasoning and add the thyme leaves. Mix the vinegar into the egg and milk, add a little of the hot soup, and stir the mixture back into the soup. Heat through without boiling.

Serve with hot crusty bread.

∽ Fresh Green Pea Soup ∽

This is a light, elegant summer soup.

SERVES 4

25 g/1 oz butter	black pepper
1 shallot, 2 spring onions or ½ a small onion, finely chopped	1 sprig of mint
	approx. 150 ml/¼ pt water
	50 g/2 oz boiling double cream
25 g/1 oz ham, cut into strips	juice of 1 lemon
	2 eggs
225 g/8 oz shelled young peas	900 ml/1½ pts boiling light veal or chicken stock
½ tsp salt	1 dsp parsley
½ tsp sugar	

Heat the butter and soften the shallot or onion without letting it brown. Stir in the ham and the peas and stir around a few times before seasoning with the salt, sugar, a few grinds of pepper, and the sprig of mint. Pour on just enough hot water to cover and simmer until the peas are soft. Pour on the boiling cream and remove from the heat.

Whisk the lemon juice into the eggs and stir into the soup. Return to the heat and warm through without letting the soup boil. Pour the boiling stock into the soup, stirring constantly. Serve immediately, garnished with a few leaves of parsley.

∽ Potato Cream ∽

This is a master recipe for a smooth potato soup finished with an egg liaison. Its permutations for variety are limitless. It can be made with water (most of the potato's nutritional value is just under its skin), any stock, or milk, or a combination of 2 or all of them. The flavour of the soup will also be affected by the variety of potato, and the time of year. When cooked or garnished with dried or fresh herbs, or spices, such soups are surprisingly different. The potato can stand up to spicy ingredients, and to curry spices and chillies, yet it reflects subtle flavours like mushrooms, truffles and saffron.

Garlic and onions will change the soup's flavour quite differently depending on how much are used and how they are cooked. The type of cooking fat or oil will also subtly change the soup's taste.

The potato is a stunningly hospitable host to other flavours. It is a delicious match with almost any vegetable you care to name. For soups within this category it is particularly good puréed with leeks, carrots, apples, fresh peas, artichokes, pumpkin, and swedes; the proportion is a matter of taste. A potato purée is wonderful laced with blanched and shredded sorrel, spinach, watercress, and tomatoes. Matched with smoked haddock it is a marriage made in heaven. And a potato cream is subtly lifted by freshly grated Parmesan and other cheeses, stirred in just before serving; specially when a few cloves of garlic have been simmered in the soup.

Favourite garnishes are parsley, mint, chives, coriander, thyme, chervil and marjoram. Use the 'Embellishment' recipes (pages 51–132) for ways of introducing texture and other flavours, and for using the soup as a canvas for additional ingredients. Also see 'Purées' (pages 203–42).

SERVES 6

50 g/2 oz butter
1 small onion or shallot, or 3 or 4 spring onions, chopped
salt and pepper
900 g/2 lb potatoes, peeled (optional) and chopped
25 g/1 oz flour (optional)
a small bunch of herbs of your choice

1.75 litres/3 pts light chicken stock (or any stock, water or milk diluted with water or stock)
2 egg-yolks
150 ml/¼ pt double cream

Soften the butter, stir in the onion and season with ½ tsp of salt. Cover and sweat gently for 5 minutes. When the onion is softened but not browned stir in the potatoes. Cover and sweat gently, stirring every so often, for a further 5 minutes. If using flour sprinkle it in at this point and stir carefully into the vegetables, making sure it takes up the fat and doesn't form lumps. If you wish to flavour the potato with your chosen herb, add it at this point, either chopped or left in a spray to remove at the end of cooking. Pour on the chicken stock and bring up to the boil. Simmer gently for 10 minutes or so, until the potatoes are soft – length of cooking will depend on the size of the pieces and the type of potato.

Fish out the bunch of herbs and purée the soup. Return to the pan and adjust the seasoning. Mix the egg-yolks with the cream and stir into the soup. Cook for a couple of minutes without boiling. If you haven't already put the herbs into the soup, stir them in now, reserving a little for a garnish. Serve with garlic bread or croûtons.

∽ SALSIFY CREAM WITH EGG CLOUDS ∽
AND PISTACHIOS

Salsify, a spindly white root vegetable covered with a thick brown skin, is subtly flavoured and is undervalued in this country. This soup is a real winner.

Once peeled, salsify discolours easily.

SERVES 6

4 roots salsify, washed and
  scraped (like a carrot)
25 g/1 oz butter
1 shallot, 4 spring onions or
  ½ a small onion, finely
  chopped
salt and pepper
25 g/1 oz flour

1.1 litres/2 pts light chicken
  stock
1 tbsp parsley, finely chopped
2 eggs, separated
275 ml/½ pt double cream
25 g/1 oz chopped pistachio
  nuts

Begin by chopping the salsify and putting it immediately into cold water, acidulated with a splash of vinegar or lemon juice. Heat the butter and gently soften the onion. Add the drained salsify, stirring it around to coat with some of the butter. Season with ½ tsp of salt, cover, and sweat for several minutes, stirring occasionally. Sift in the flour and stir thoroughly before pouring on the chicken stock. Bring up to the boil, cover, and simmer over a low heat for 30–45 minutes until the salsify is quite soft. Purée and press through a sieve into a clean pan. Stir in the chopped parsley and adjust the seasoning.

Beat the egg-yolks into the cream, mix in a ladleful of the hot soup and pour the liaison back into the soup. Carefully heat through almost to simmering point but don't let it boil. Meanwhile whisk the egg-whites to a stiff cloud.

To serve, pour the very hot soup into heated bowls. Float spoonfuls of the stiffly beaten egg-whites on to the surface of the soup, and sprinkle over the chopped pistachio nuts.

✑ SPINACH CREAM WITH PARMESAN ✑

SERVES 6

700 g/1½ lb spinach
40 g/1½ oz butter
salt and pepper
a pinch of nutmeg
1.75 litres/3 pts chicken or
  well-balanced vegetable stock

5 tbsp Parmesan, freshly
  grated
2–4 egg-yolks

Pick over the spinach, removing any discoloured leaves and the hard stems. Wash and pat it dry, then shred it, cutting across the width of the stem; this is simply done by rolling several leaves together like a duff cigar. Melt the butter and add the spinach, pressing it down. Sprinkle in ½ tsp of salt and a pinch of nutmeg. Cover and sweat, turning the leaves around occasionally, until the spinach has flopped. Meanwhile bring the stock up to the boil. Pour the hot stock over the spinach and bring up to a simmer.

Stir the Parmesan into the egg-yolks, thinning with a ladleful of the hot stock. Remove the pan from the heat and beat the Parmesan liaison into the soup. Return the pan to the heat and cook very gently for a minute or two.

Serve with focaccia (see page 115), or another crusty olive oil bread, warm from the oven.

✑ TOMATO AND COURGETTE SOUP WITH GARLIC, ✑
TOMATO AND BASIL MAYONNAISE

Soupe Menerboise, a great favourite from Elizabeth David's *Summer Cooking*, is reminiscent of the more familiar Provençal summer vegetable soup, *soupe au pistou*. Both are made with young vegetables and both rely on fresh basil for the accompanying sauce.

In this version, where the sauce is a kind of mayonnaise, it is important to the final flavours to grill the tomatoes used in the mayonnaise. Without this smokiness the soup loses part of its charm.

SERVES 4–6

3 tbsp olive oil
2 onions, finely sliced
225 g/8 oz courgettes, diced
450 g/1 lb tomatoes, peeled and cored
2 small potatoes, peeled, diced and rinsed
1.1 litres/2 pts hot water
110 g/4 oz shelled and peeled broad beans

40 g/1½ oz pasta or broken-up spaghetti
salt and pepper
3 cloves of garlic
a small bunch of basil
2 egg-yolks
2 tbsp Parmesan, freshly grated
1 tbsp flat-leaf parsley, finely chopped

Heat the olive oil, stir in the onions and 'let them melt but not fry'; this will take at least 15 minutes. Add the diced courgettes and continue cooking very gently for 10 minutes. Meanwhile, peel, core and roughly chop all but 2 of the tomatoes and add them to the pot. When these are softened, add the cubed potatoes and the hot water. Bring up to the boil and simmer gently for 10 minutes until the potatoes are nearly cooked, then add the broad beans, the pasta, ½ tsp of salt and several grinds of pepper.

Meanwhile grill the reserved tomatoes, skin them and remove their seeds. Pulverize the garlic cloves, adding the tomatoes and basil. Add the egg-yolks, to make a sauce that resembles a thin mayonnaise.

When the pasta is cooked, stir a ladleful of the soup into the egg sauce, then another. Pour the mixture slowly back into the soup, stirring all the time, and without letting the soup boil. Just before serving, stir in the Parmesan.

Garnish with the chopped parsley, have more Parmesan on the table and serve with crusty bread.

∽ CREAM OF WATERCRESS ∽

SERVES 6

50 g/2 oz butter	½ tsp salt
6 spring onions, chopped	40 g/1½ oz flour
225–350 g/½–¾ lb fresh watercress, tough stems removed, washed and dried in a cloth	1.4 litres/2½ pts boiling chicken stock
	2 egg-yolks
	150 ml/¼ pt thick cream

Heat the butter over a low heat and gently cook the spring onions until soft and translucent. Set aside a handful of the watercress for use later. Stir the bulk of the watercress into the onions. Season with salt, cover, and sweat slowly, stirring occasionally, for several minutes until the watercress is a wilted tangle.

Sift in the flour, stirring around to make a paste and let it bubble for a couple of minutes. Pour on the boiling chicken stock, slowly at first to take up the flour paste, and simmer for 5 minutes. Purée through a mouli-légumes (or process lightly in a liquidizer so the soup isn't too smooth), and return to a clean pan. Taste and adjust the seasoning.

Beat the egg-yolks and cream together and add a little of the hot soup. Return the mixture to the soup, stirring all the while, and heat through without boiling.

To garnish the soup, drop the reserved handful of watercress leaves into boiling water for 60 seconds. Refresh in cold water, drain and dry. Either chop the leaves very finely and fold them into the soup before serving, or decorate the top of the soup with the whole leaves.

∽ WATERCRESS AND CHICKEN CREAM WITH ∽ WATERCRESS ISLANDS

Antony Worrall-Thompson is one of London's most exciting chefs, always ahead of trends and fashions in food. This recipe, quite out of keeping with his current style of rustic Mediterranean cooking, and adapted slightly, is a survivor of his *nouvelle cuisine* days. The quick cooking of the watercress stops its colour fading.

SERVES 4–6

900 ml/1½ pts strong chicken stock
1 chicken breast, boned and finely diced
3 bunches of luxuriant watercress, washed and
stalks removed
275 ml/½ pt double cream
salt and white pepper
4 egg-whites
2 egg-yolks

Bring the stock to the boil and add the chicken. Simmer for 5 minutes. Add 2½ bunches of watercress leaves and most of the cream, and cook for 60 seconds. Liquidize the soup in batches and return to a clean pan. Taste for seasoning. Meanwhile dip the remaining watercress leaves in boiling water, refresh in cold water and pat dry. Chop finely. Whisk the 4 egg-whites, with a pinch of salt added, to stiff peaks. Fold in the chopped watercress. Have ready a pan of boiling water and quickly poach spoonfuls of egg-white, turning once. Remove and drain on absorbent paper.

To complete the soup, beat the egg-yolks with the last of the cream and whisk it back into the warmed soup. Re-heat gently and don't let it boil.

Serve the soup in warmed bowls with the watercress islands floating on top.

CREAM AND VELOUTÉ SOUPS WITH SEAFOOD

ᔒ CLAM SOUP WITH MUSHROOMS ᔒ

SERVES 4

2 tbsp olive oil
36 clams, scrubbed and rinsed in several changes of water
40 g/1½ oz butter
1 shallot or small onion, finely chopped
225 g/8 oz mushrooms, thinly sliced
275 ml/½ pt chicken stock
275 ml/½ pt warm water
1 tbsp potato flour, arrowroot or similar (see page 57)
150 ml/¼ pt milk
3 egg-yolks
salt and pepper

Choose a heavy-bottomed, lidded pan and heat the olive oil with the clams. Cook over a brisk heat and remove once the shells have opened. Tip the clams into a bowl set with a colander. Remove the clams from their shells and dip them into the drained juices to rinse off any sand. Chop the clam meat and set aside. Carefully strain the reserved clam juices; if they are sandy, let the sand settle and then gently pour the liquor through a coffee filter or a double thickness of absorbent kitchen paper.

Heat half the butter in a small frying-pan and soften the shallot. Add the mushrooms with a generous pinch of salt and a little pepper, then turn up the heat and sauté for 3–4 minutes.

Bring the chicken stock and water up to the boil and add the clam juices, the contents of the frying-pan and the clams. Return to a simmer. Meanwhile, in a soup tureen or serving pan, slake the potato flour with the milk and beat into the egg-yolks. Pour the hot soup into the egg and milk mixture, stirring vigorously all the time. Taste and adjust the seasoning. Serve with crostini (see page 124).

COCKLE CREAM WITH BACON, TOMATOES AND POTATOES

SERVES 4

2.3 litres/4 pts cockles	2 tomatoes, peeled, cored and
900 ml/1½ pts water	sliced
25 g/1 oz butter	2 potatoes, peeled and diced
50 g/2 oz lean bacon, diced	salt and pepper
1 small leek, finely sliced	juice of 1 lemon
1 stick of celery, finely	2 eggs
chopped	chopped parsley

Wash the cockles thoroughly in several changes of water. Cover the cleaned cockles with the water and boil fast for about 10 minutes until they have opened. Place a colander over a large bowl and strain, reserving the liquid. Pick the cockles out of their shells and put to one side. Heat the butter in a pan that can hold the entire soup, and sauté the bacon, stirring in the leek, celery and tomatoes. Season and sweat gently until the mixture begins to flop. Pour on the strained cockle liquor, taking care not to let any sand into the soup. Add the potatoes and simmer gently until soft, then add the shelled cockles.

Taste for seasoning. Whisk the lemon juice into the eggs, stir in a little of the hot soup, and return the liaison to the pan, stirring as you do so. Heat through but don't let the soup boil. Serve sprinkled with parsley and with triangular croûtons, fried in rendered bacon fat, in a separate dish.

CRAB, SAFFRON AND CREAM SOUP

During my stint writing about restaurants for *The Sunday Telegraph*, one of my discoveries was Soanes, a home-from-home restaurant in Petworth, on the edge of the West Sussex Downs. My lunch began with this soup, a favourite of Carol Godsmark, the talented self-taught chef/patron.

The crabmeat could be replaced by pre-cooked mussels, lobster, scallops or monkfish.

SERVES 4

25 g/1 oz butter
2 shallots, finely chopped
1 large carrot, peeled and
  diced
1 leek, finely chopped
2 cloves of garlic, finely
  chopped
2.5-cm/1-in piece fresh
  ginger, peeled and grated
1.1 litres/2 pts well-reduced
  fish stock, made with Dover
  sole bones or red mullet (see
  page 42)
570 ml/1 pt dry white wine
275 ml/½ pt double cream

1 tsp saffron threads
1 small red chilli pepper
½ tsp star anise
salt and pepper
2 egg-yolks mixed with 150 ml/
  ¼ pt double cream
1 leek, cut in very fine
  5-cm/2-in juliennes
1 medium carrot, peeled and
  cut in very fine 5-cm/2-in
  juliennes
110 g/4 oz fresh white
  crabmeat
1 dsp chopped parsley or
  coriander

Gently heat the butter in a large pan and sweat all the diced and chopped vegetables and the garlic and ginger until soft but not browned. Add the fish stock and white wine and reduce by half. Add the 275 ml/½ pt of double cream, the saffron, and the chilli ground with the star anise, and simmer gently until the flavours develop. Season to taste with salt and pepper. Strain. Stir a ladleful of the hot soup into the egg and cream liaison and then slowly, stirring all the time, pour it back into the soup. Stir or whisk for a couple of minutes without letting the soup boil. Turn off the heat, cover and leave while you attend to the garnish.

Steam the julienne of leek and carrot for a couple of minutes so that it retains its bite but isn't raw; if there's room steam the crabmeat at the same time. Divide the crabmeat between warmed bowls, pour on the soup, and decorate the top with the julienne of leek and carrot. Sprinkle on the chopped parsley or coriander and serve.

Serve with Melba toast (page 124); almost anything else would be too rich.

～ OYSTER SOUP ZEPHIR ～

This is an elegant soup for a special occasion, best made when oysters are plentiful. If your fishmonger is opening the oysters for you, be sure he reserves the liquid inside the shell.

A dry white wine can be used in place of champagne. Zephir, or zephyr, is a French culinary term for creating a froth.

SERVES 4

16 oysters	1 egg-yolk, mixed with 100 ml/
15 g/½ oz butter	4 fl oz double cream
1 small shallot, finely	salt and pepper
chopped	1 tbsp dill or chervil, snipped
275 ml/½ pt good fish stock	for garnish
150 ml/¼ pt Champagne	

Remove the oysters from the shell, trimming away any tough tendons, and reserving the oyster liquor. Heat the butter and gently stir-fry the shallot until transparent. Pour in the fish stock, Champagne and strained oyster liquor. Bring to the boil and reduce by half. Slip the oysters into the hot stock and remove almost immediately. Cover to keep warm and then whisk the egg liaison into the stock. Return to the heat to warm through, but don't allow to boil. Remove from the heat and whisk like mad to get up a good froth (you can do this in a liquidizer), return the oysters and taste for seasoning.

Pour the soup into warmed bowls, giving each serving 4 oysters, and garnish with little sprays of dill or chervil. Serve with very thin brown bread and butter or Melba toast (see page 124).

∾ HAMBURG EEL SOUP ∾

No book on soup would be complete without this famous dish. The seemingly bizarre and long list of ingredients produces a surprisingly delicious and subtle soup. It is a meal in itself.

SERVES 6

450 g/1 lb eel, skinned and	1 sprig of tarragon
cut into 5-cm/2-in pieces	1 sprig of sage
350 g/¾ lb pears, peeled,	1 onion, quartered
cored and sliced	dash of wine vinegar
150 ml/¼ pt dry white wine	1 bayleaf
1 strip of lemon peel	approx. 200 g/7 oz canned or
½ a small cauliflower, divided	bottled petits pois
into small sprigs	salt and pepper
1.4 litres/2½ pts beef stock	1 egg-yolk
1 sprig of thyme	

Sprinkle the eel pieces with salt and leave for 2 hours.

Meanwhile put the pears in a pan with the white wine and lemon peel and simmer. Cook the cauliflower sprigs in the stock, seasoned with the thyme, tarragon and sage. Rinse and dry the eel and put it in a pan with the onion, vinegar and bayleaf and enough water to cover. Bring up to the boil and simmer for about 15 minutes. Strain the cooking liquor into the stock and ease the eel flesh off the central bone. Put the fillets into a warmed soup tureen and cover. Strain the pear cooking liquid into the stock and put the pear slices with the eel in the tureen.

Simmer the soup for 10 minutes to marry the flavours, stir in the drained peas, and taste for seasoning. Fish out the sprigs of thyme, tarragon and sage.

Mix a little of the hot soup into the egg-yolk and stir it back into the soup. Cook gently without boiling for a couple of minutes and pour the hot soup over the eel and pears.

Serve, making sure everyone gets some eel and pear.

∽ BILLI BI ∾

The qualifying ingredients in this much abused soup are mussels, dry white wine, saffron and an egg and cream liaison. To my mind it should be a rich velvety, pale yellow soup, thick with plump mussels.

Recipes vary enormously: some allow for half a dozen mussels per serving, others for double that quantity. Some specify leaving the mussels on the shell, others favour removing them. Personally I prefer a high proportion of mussels, removed from their shells.

SERVES 4

50 g/2 oz butter	400 ml/¾ pt good fish stock
2 large shallots, finely chopped	½ tsp saffron threads
400 ml/¾ pt dry white wine	2 egg-yolks, mixed with 150ml/ ¼ pt double cream
1 kg/1¾ pts mussels, scrubbed and washed in several changes of water	salt and pepper
	2 tbsp flat-leaf parsley, chopped

Melt the butter and soften the shallots. Pour on the white wine and let it bubble up before adding the mussels. Cover and cook over a fierce heat, shaking the pan a few times, until the mussels open. Place a colander over a bowl and tip on the mussels. Remove the mussels from their shells and set aside (chuck out the shells).

Strain the liquid into a pan, add the fish stock and bring up to a simmer. Stir in the saffron, remove from the heat and carefully whisk in the egg and cream liaison. Return to the heat, warm the soup through without boiling and add the mussels. When the soup has thickened, taste for seasoning. Pour into warmed bowls, sprinkle on the parsley and serve with plenty of crusty bread for dunking.

ᴄ SCALLOP AND POTATO CREAM WITH CORAL ᴄ

Scallops and potatoes are a marvellous combination in almost any form. This soup, made with a purée of potatoes, laced with chopped milk-poached scallops then garnished with slivers of bright orange coral, is a sort of liquid *coquilles St-Jacques*.

It is easy and quick to make and unbelievably delicious.

SERVES 4

50 g/2 oz butter	*4 large cleaned scallops with*
2 small shallots, finely	*their coral (total weight*
chopped	*approx. 350 g/12 oz)*
450 g/1 lb potatoes, peeled	*275 ml/½ pt milk*
and diced	*2 egg-yolks*
salt and pepper	*75 ml/3 fl oz double cream*
570 ml/1 pt hot fish stock	*1 tsp chives, snipped*

Heat 40 g/1½ oz of the butter and soften the shallots. Stir in the diced potato, season with ½ tsp of salt and a few grinds of black pepper, cover and sweat for 5 minutes. Stir thoroughly, return the lid and cook for a further 10 minutes. Pour on the hot fish stock, stir, cover and simmer gently for 10 minutes. When the potatoes are soft, purée the contents of the pan. Pour and press through a fine sieve into a clean pan.

Meanwhile rinse the scallops and trim away any tough bits and the pinky/grey frilly gills. Cut off the coral and set aside. Dice the white meat and put it in a pan with the cold milk and a generous pinch of salt. Bring up to a simmer and cook for a couple of minutes. Tip the chopped scallops and their cooking milk into the potato purée and whisk thoroughly. Bring back to a simmer, adjust the seasoning and remove the pan from the heat.

Beat the egg-yolks into the cream, add a ladleful of the soup, then another, and stir the liaison into the pan. Return the pan to the heat and warm through without boiling. Just before serving, melt the remaining butter and gently sauté the scallop coral, either whole, halved or chopped.

Pour the soup into warmed bowls and garnish with the coral and a few snips of chives.

✑ SCALLOP CREAM WITH LIME AND DEEP-FRIED ✑
CHERVIL

This is an exciting fresh-flavoured soup devised by David Dorricott, the talented chef of the SAS Portman Hotel. The acidity from the lime zest is in perfect conflict with the rich mixture of chicken and fish stock, and the egg and cream liaison. The combination is a delicious foil for the very lightly 'cooked' scallops.

SERVES 4
25 g/1 oz butter	275 ml/½ pt fish stock
150 g/5 oz scallop trimmings	8 scallops
zest of 2 limes	3 egg-yolks
a small bunch of chervil	150 ml/¼ pt double cream
275 ml/½ pt chicken stock	salt and pepper

Heat the butter and stir-fry the scallop trimmings for 3–4 minutes. Add the lime zest, chervil stalks, and the chicken and fish stocks. Simmer for 15 minutes. Strain.

Meanwhile trim the scallops, slice them into thin rounds, and arrange in soup-plates. Mix the egg-yolks with the cream and add to the hot strained stock, whisking all the while. Return to the heat and warm through without boiling. Taste for seasoning. Pour the soup on to the scallops and garnish with deep-fried chervil sprigs (see page 109).

✑ SCALLOP AND ARTICHOKE SOUP ✑

This is another favourite scallop soup made with potatoes. It comes from Margaret Costa's *Four Seasons Cookery Book*, one of the most original and relevant cookery books despite the fact that it was written 20-odd years ago.

SERVES 6
50 g/2 oz butter	1 litre/1¾ pts well-seasoned
1½ Spanish onions, finely chopped	chicken stock
	salt and pepper
700 g/1½ lb Jerusalem artichokes, peeled and chopped	4 large or 6 small scallops
	275 ml/½ pt milk
	2 egg-yolks
2 medium potatoes, peeled and chopped	6 tbsp cream
	1 tbsp parsley, finely chopped

Heat the butter and cook the onions until soft and transparent. Stir in the artichokes, then the potatoes, making sure everything is coated with butter. Cover and cook gently for 15 minutes. Pour on the chicken stock, cover, and simmer for about 20 minutes until all the vegetables are soft. Purée and return to a clean pan. Taste and adjust the seasoning with salt and pepper.

Now the scallops. Cut off the pink coral and set aside. Chop the white part into dice, put in a pan with the milk, and simmer gently for a couple of minutes. Add the scallops and the milk in which they were cooked to the artichoke soup, and cook through. Beat the egg-yolks into the cream, and pour this back into the soup, stirring thoroughly as you do so. Just before serving, stir in the uncooked scallop corals, cut into 2 or 3 pieces. Scatter lavishly with chopped parsley and serve.

∾ SHRIMP SOUP ∾

An exquisite, delicately flavoured soup, made with stock from the shrimp shells, thickened with breadcrumbs, and given a velvety finish with an egg and cream liaison.

SERVES 2–4

570 ml/1 pt cooked shrimps, pink or brown	900 ml/1½ pts water
225 g/8 oz any white fish, with skin	3 tbsp white breadcrumbs
1 small onion, chopped	50 g/2 oz butter
2.5-cm/1-in piece of lemon peel	juice of ½ a lemon
small bundle of herbs suitable for a fish stock (see page 41)	a pinch of nutmeg
	1 egg-yolk
	150 ml/¼ pt double cream
	salt and pepper
	parsley or chervil

Shell the shrimps and put their shells, the white fish, onion, lemon peel, and herbs into a pan with the cold water. Bring up to the boil and simmer for 20 minutes. Strain the liquid and stir in the white breadcrumbs.

Meanwhile pound or blend the shrimps with the butter, adding the lemon juice and a pinch of nutmeg. Turn the purée into a pan and whisk in the shrimp stock thickened with the breadcrumbs. Simmer for 5 minutes and then press through a fine sieve into a clean pan. Beat the egg-yolk with the cream, stir in a ladleful of the hot soup, and slowly whisk the liaison back into the pan. Taste for seasoning.

Pour into warmed bowls and garnish with a spray of chervil or a little minced parsley.

✑ CREAM OF PUMPKIN AND SHRIMP SOUP ✑

This is an unusual but successful coupling. The recipe comes from
French Provincial Cooking by Elizabeth David. The soup will spoil if it
isn't eaten within 24 hours of making.

SERVES 6

900 g/2 lb slice of pumpkin,   salt and pepper
  peeled and diced   100 g/4 oz peeled prawns or
1 stick of celery, chopped   shrimps
900 ml/1½ pts milk, boiled   ½ tsp lemon juice
570 ml/1 pt mild stock or water   50 g/2 oz butter

Put the pumpkin and celery in a heavy-bottomed pan with the milk
and stock, and season with salt and pepper. Leave to simmer for
about 30 minutes until the pumpkin is tender. Purée and sieve into a
clean pan.

Meanwhile pound the prawns or shrimps with the lemon juice,
diluted with a little of the pumpkin purée, and add this back to the
soup. Simmer gently for 10 minutes, sieve again, adjust the seasoning
and stir in the butter.

✑ NORTH SEA FISH SOUP ✑

This is Gidleigh Park's celebrated fish soup, a wonderful combination
of flavours and textures refined by its chef Shaun Hill. The fish bones
and trimmings, and the shellfish debris, are used to create the stock,
despite which it is a relatively quick soup to make and requires no
fiddly technique.

As is the case with all good soup recipes, the ingredients listed are
only a guideline. If you can't get or don't like the fish listed, use
different ones, or increase the quantity of one and leave out another.
Aim for different textures and bear in mind that different fish cook
more quickly than others.

SERVES 4

1 small bunch of parsley,   900 ml/1½ pts cold water
  immersed in cold water and   2 shallots, chopped
  drained   juice of 1 lemon
75 g/3 oz sea bass fillet   salt and pepper
75 g/3 oz hake fillet   2 egg-yolks
75 g/3 oz haddock fillet   2 tbsp double cream
4 scallops   2 tomatoes, blanched, peeled
75 g/3 oz whole prawns   and quartered
50 g/2 oz butter   croûtons (see page 107)
65 ml/2½ fl oz dry white wine

Cut the stalks from the bunch of parsley. Wash the bones and trimmings from the fish, the red scallop corals, and the prawns under cold running water. Melt half the butter and sweat the bones, scallop corals, prawns in their shells, and washed parsley stalks. Add the wine and the cold water, which should just cover everything; if it doesn't, use a different-shaped pan. Bring up to the boil and simmer for 10 minutes. Strain the stock, which will have reduced slightly, into a clean pan. Fish out the whole prawns and set aside. Add the shallots, bring the stock back to the boil, and simmer for a few minutes.

Cut each piece of fish, and each scallop, into 4 pieces and turn them briefly in the lemon juice. Season them with salt and pepper and then add them to the stock; first sea bass, then hake, then haddock, and lastly the scallops. The whole process should take no more than 2 minutes, and the scallops no more than 30 seconds; remember that they continue to 'cook' until eaten. The minute the soup returns to boiling point turn off the heat. Beat the egg-yolks into the cream, stir in a ladleful of the soup, and stir it back into the soup, taking care not to break up the fish. Taste for seasoning, and if necessary add lemon juice as well as salt and pepper.

To complete the soup, scoop out and discard the seeds from the tomatoes and dice the tomato flesh. Transfer to the soup tureen with croûtons, the reserved prawns and the chopped parsley. Pour over the soup and serve.

PURÉES

All the soups in this section have been forcibly puréed. This can be done in a blender, a food processor, a mouli-légumes, occasionally with a ricer or masher, or by pouring and pushing the food through a fine sieve. All types of equipment have their advantages and drawbacks; the electric machines are quick but reduce all ingredients to the same processed smoothness; the mouli-légumes is harder work and messier but makes it easier to control the degree of purée. The fine sieve, perhaps used in conjunction with a pestle and mortar, is very hard work but gives spectacular results without bashing up the food.

To get the right result it is sometimes essential to use a sieve, often in conjunction with either a processor or a mouli-légumes.

DOUBLE SOUPS

The enthusiasm for double soups at some of America's trend-setting caterers, most notably Alice Waters's restaurant Chez Panisse, and the New York delicatessen Silver Palate, has been slow to catch on over here. Double soups – when two soups are served together in one bowl – can only be made with puréed soups. Not only must the flavours complement each other, but the soups must be of exactly the same consistency. They are a fuss and a fiddle to get right but look spectacular.

An obvious combination is red and yellow peppers, but a match of soups made with, say, more starch or fibre in one partner can be adjusted with cream or thinned with stock or water. It is important to measure out quantities before pouring out portions and to pour them at the same time.

Various double soups matches are highlighted in this section, while others appear in 'Cold, Jellied and Uncooked Soups' (pages 328–45), and 'Soups for Parties' (pages 354–62).

ᘓ JERUSALEM ARTICHOKE SOUP ᘓ

These are the small knobbly tubers which, like their namesake the globe artichoke, have a delicate but haunting flavour. They have no connection with the Holy Land: 'Jerusalem' is an anglicized distortion of 'girasol' – girasolem – the name of plants whose flowers follow the sun. That explains why artichoke soup is often called Palestine soup; a more appropriate name is f'artichoke soup. This is one of the best soups I know.

Small, young artichokes need only be scrubbed; bigger ones need peeling, and there is inevitable wastage. Once peeled, drop them into acidulated water (a dash of lemon juice or vinegar) as they discolour instantly.

SERVES 6

110 g/4 oz butter
1 large onion, chopped
1 clove of garlic, chopped
900 g/2 lb Jerusalem
 artichokes, peeled and
 chopped
½ a stick of celery, chopped

salt and pepper
1.1 litres/2 pts light chicken,
 turkey, or vegetable stock, or
 water
275 ml/½ pt milk, or half
 milk and half double cream
 (optional)

Heat half the butter in a large pan and soften the onion, then stir in the garlic, artichokes and celery. Season with ½ tsp of salt, cover, and leave to sweat for a couple of minutes. Pour on the stock, bring up to the boil, turn down to simmer, cover partially, and leave to cook until all the vegetables are soft. Purée, then return to a clean pan and add the milk or milk and cream mixture if using. Bring up to a simmer, taste and season, adding more liquid if the soup is too thick. Whisk in the last of the butter.

Serve scattered with toasted, chopped almonds (see page 112) or hazelnuts, crisply fried bacon pieces, or bacon croûtons, with a sprinkling of parsley or chives. Artichoke crisps (see page 109), served separately, make more of an occasion of the soup.

∽ ALMOND SOUP WITH FRESHLY ROASTED ∽ CHICKEN

Nico Ladenis, who produces exquisite and intensely flavoured French food at his two-Michelin-starred restaurant Nico at Ninety, is famous for his attention to detail. This is one of his finest soups, worthy of a special dinner for two preceded by a light appetizer and followed by cheese and/or dessert, yet only worth the trouble with tip-top ingredients.

SERVES 2

1 free-range chicken (approx.
  1.6 kg/3½ lb)
1 medium carrot, peeled and
  cut lengthwise into quarters
1 medium onion, skinned and
  stuck with 2 or 3 cloves
1 stick of celery, chopped
1 small leek, white part only,
  split
bouquet garni

a few peppercorns
570 ml/1 pt water
150 ml/¼ pt dry white wine
knob of butter
225 g/8 oz almonds
1 tbsp clear honey
coarse salt and pepper
40 g/1½ oz Basmati rice
200 ml/7 fl oz double cream

Remove the legs from the chicken and chop them into pieces. Place them in a pan with the carrot, onion, celery, leek, *bouquet garni* and a few peppercorns. Cover with the cold water and bring slowly to the boil. Turn the heat down very low, cover the pan and simmer for 1½ hours. Strain and slowly reduce by half. Add the wine and turn off the heat.

Meanwhile, pre-heat the oven to 350° F/180° C/Gas Mark 4. Place a knob of butter on a baking tray, let it melt in the oven, and pour on the almonds. Flick them around so they are evenly coated with butter and bake them for about 10 minutes, while the oven warms up, until they are golden. When the oven has reached the correct temperature, brush the breast of the chicken with the honey, sprinkle over a little salt and a few grinds of black pepper, and roast for 40 minutes. Remove the chicken and let it rest in a warm place. While the chicken is cooking, boil the rice according to packet instructions (about 10 minutes). Drain, rinse and set aside.

Liquidize the chicken stock with the almonds and double cream. Pour into a clean pan with the rice and cook gently for 10 minutes. Taste and adjust the seasoning.

To serve, remove each chicken breast with a small sharp knife. Pour the soup into two soup plates and 'garnish' with a chicken breast. Sprinkle with freshly ground black pepper.

∽ APPLE SOUP ∽

> 'Nym appeles sethe hem frete hem throue
> an her sieve – cast it on a pot and caste
> thereto good fat broth, and sugar and
> safron (and on fisshe days almond mylke
> and oile of olive), and boile hit mease and
> caste onto good pouder and gif forth.'
> (Manuscript recipe 1400)

A delicious and unexpected soup.

SERVES 6

75 g/3 oz pearl barley
1.75 ml/3 pts beef stock
450 g/1 lb cooking apples,
 peeled, cored and chopped

½ tsp ginger
¼ tsp white pepper
lemon juice

Soak the barley for 20 minutes in cold water, then simmer gently in
275 ml/½ pt of the beef stock. Meanwhile bring the rest of the beef
stock up to the boil, add the apples and simmer until soft. Purée and
sieve (to remove any scraps of core), then season with the ginger and
pepper. Mix in the cooked pearl barley and taste, adjusting the flavour
with a little lemon juice if necessary.

∽ ASPARAGUS SOUP ∽

It is not an extravagance to make soup with asparagus. Quite the
reverse, for it is the only time that the whole stem is used without
any wastage: the woody stalk goes in the stock, the tough middle
section is puréed, and the tips are used for garnish.

SERVES 4–6

450 g/1 lb bunch of
 asparagus
50 g/2 oz butter
225 g/½ lb leeks, white part
 only, sliced
salt and pepper
1 tbsp parsley, chopped

1.4 litres/2½ pts vegetable or
 light chicken stock
100 ml/4 fl oz double cream
½ tsp grated lemon peel
2 tbsp Parmesan, freshly
 grated

Trim off the woody part of the asparagus stems and bring up to the
boil in the stock. Simmer for 15 minutes then strain.

 Heat the butter and soften the leeks, stirring around as necessary.
Cut off the tips of the asparagus and set aside. Cut the middle sections
into chunks and stir them into the leeks with a generous pinch of

salt and the parsley. Cook for a couple of minutes and then pour in the strained stock. Bring up to the boil and simmer for about 10 minutes until the asparagus is tender. Purée and then press through a fine sieve to remove the fibrous bits. Return to a clean pan, pour in the cream, season to taste and stir in the lemon peel. Leave to simmer gently while you drop the asparagus tips into boiling water and cook for a couple of minutes.

Pour the soup into warm bowls, sprinkle generously with Parmesan and lay the asparagus tips on top.

✑ PROVENÇAL SOUP WITH SAFFRON MAYONNAISE ✑

Olive-oil-smeared oven-roasted aubergines, red peppers, tomatoes, and onions are sweated with garlic, bayleaves and thyme, then puréed with a basil-seasoned stock, to make a rich aromatic soup. Sharpened with lemon juice and served with saffron mayonnaise, it is a truly winning combination, redolent of the South of France. The recipe is adapted from the marvellous *Greens Cookbook*, recipes from the San Francisco restaurant.

SERVES 4–6

700 g/1½ lb aubergines, cut lengthways
4 tbsp olive oil
1 tsp salt
pepper
1 large red onion, halved but not peeled
1 large or 2 medium red peppers, halved and de-seeded

2 large ripe tomatoes
5 branches of thyme
1 bayleaf
2 cloves of garlic, chopped
1 tsp dried basil
2 tbsp fresh basil, chopped
1.75 litres/3 pts vegetable stock or water
juice of 1 lemon

Pre-heat the oven to 400° F/200° C/Gas Mark 6. Brush the surface of the split aubergines with olive oil and season with salt and pepper. Lay on a baking-tray and cook for 20 minutes. Brush the onion, both sides of the peppers, and the tomatoes with olive oil and put in the oven for a further 20 minutes. Remove the vegetables and allow to cool. Skin the tomatoes, the onion, and what you can of the pepper. Roughly chop all the vegetables. Gently heat 2 tbsp of olive oil with the thyme, bayleaf, garlic and dried basil. Stir-fry for a couple of minutes before adding the chopped vegetables, 1 tsp of salt and 1 tbsp of chopped basil. Pour on the stock or water. Bring to the boil, cover, and simmer gently for about 30 minutes.

Purée the soup in a mouli or at a slow speed in the processor, preserving some of the texture and flecks of black aubergine and red pepper skin. Return to a clean pan, taste and season with the lemon juice, and perhaps more salt.

Heat through, adding more liquid if the soup is too thick. Serve with croûtons (see page 107) and saffron mayonnaise (see page 70), and a sprinkling of fresh basil leaves.

ᕤ AUBERGINE SOUP WITH RED PEPPER CREAM ᕤ

Grilling the aubergine first gives it a mellow, nutty dimension that enriches its subtle flavour.

SERVES 4

700 g/1½ lb approx.
  aubergines
1 tbsp olive oil
1 shallot, finely chopped

1 fat clove of garlic, chopped
salt and pepper
900 ml/1½ pts hot chicken
  or lamb stock

Lay the whole aubergines out on a baking-tray and grill, turning regularly, until the skin is blistered and the aubergines are beginning to sag. Remove to a colander set over a bowl. Make slashes down the length of the aubergine so that the bitter juices can run out. Peel the skin off in strips, scraping any flesh that clings inside the skin.

Meanwhile heat the olive oil and soften the shallot, adding the garlic a couple of minutes later. Mash the grilled aubergine into the shallot, season with salt and pepper, and continue cooking until the aubergine is completely soft. Pour on the hot stock, simmer for 5 minutes and purée. Taste and adjust the seasoning. Serve with a dollop of red pepper cream (see page 66), croûtons and a few snips of chives.

ᕤ BLACK BEAN SOUP WITH TOMATO SALSA ᕤ

This is a Caribbean recipe, from Cuba. The cayenne and garlic give the soup a kick which is echoed in the *salsa*. It is a lovely mix of textures too.

SERVES 4–6

2 tbsp oil
1 medium onion, chopped
2 fat cloves of garlic, peeled
  and crushed
1 stick of celery with leaves,
  chopped
225 g/8 oz black beans,
  soaked overnight in cold
  water

2.3 litres/3 pts vegetable
  stock or water
2 tsp salt
¼ tsp black pepper
½ tsp cayenne pepper
juice of 1 large lemon
3 tbsp dry sherry
tomato salsa (see page 70)

Heat the oil in a large pan. Soften the onion, then add the garlic and celery, stirring frequently. Mix in the drained beans and pour in the stock or water. Bring to the boil, lower the heat, cover the pan and simmer gently for about 2 hours, until the beans are soft. Use a slotted spoon to fish out about half the beans. Blend them to a purée with some of the hot stock. Stir the purée back into the soup, season with the salt and the two peppers, and simmer for 10 minutes, stirring constantly. Just before serving stir in the lemon juice and sherry.

Serve with a covering of freshly grated Cheddar, and hand the tomato *salsa* separately.

This soup is also delicious garnished with chopped hard-boiled eggs and savory or celery leaves.

✎ BROAD BEAN SOUP WITH ROUZOLE ✎

Broad beans and bacon are a scrumptious combination. A bacon-based dumpling (see page 78) would be delicious in this soup, but *rouzole*, a bacon, breadcrumb and garlicky patty seasoned with mint, is particularly special.

SERVES 6

450 g/1 lb young broad beans in the pod
2 potatoes, peeled, diced and rinsed
1 leek, finely sliced
1.4 litres/2½ pts water
½ tsp sugar
salt and pepper

100 ml/4 fl oz milk or 50 ml/ 2 fl oz single or double cream
25 g/1 oz butter
rouzole (see page 100)
2 tbsp savory or parsley, chopped

Put the whole beans in a large pan with the potato and leek, cover with the water, and season with sugar, salt and pepper. Simmer for 45 minutes. Strain the beans, reserving the cooking water, and purée with some of the liquid. Push the purée through a fine sieve into a clean pan and stir in the reserved cooking water, which should be about 1.1 litres/2 pts. Add the cream or milk, reheat and adjust the seasoning. Whisk in the butter, then the chopped *rouzole* and serve with a sprinkling of chopped savory.

The following is a richer version, ideal for when young broad beans aren't available:

900 g/2 lb broad beans
a few lettuce leaves, shredded
2 tbsp savory or parsley, chopped
3 spring onions, sliced

900 ml/1½ pts light veal or chicken stock
50 ml/2 fl oz single or double cream
salt and pepper

Remove the beans from the pod. If they are very old it would be advisable to blanch the beans in boiling water, then slip off their outer skins (which can be tough and will turn the soup a dull colour) before proceeding with the recipe. Cook the beans, lettuce, savory or parsley, and spring onions in salted water, until the beans are tender. Purée the beans with about 275 ml/½ pt of the cooking liquid. Reheat with the stock, simmer for a few minutes before adding the cream, then the butter, and seasoning.

∽ BLACK BEAN SOUP WITH PRAWNS ∽

A lovely recipe from Mexico.

SERVES 4

150 g/5 oz black beans, soaked overnight
⅛ tsp cumin, ground
¼ tsp dried oregano
1 bay leaf, or 2 avocado leaves
700 ml/1¼ pts water
2 tbsp olive oil
1 medium onion, finely chopped
1 clove of garlic, chopped
1 medium tomato, blanched, peeled, cored and chopped
salt and pepper
570 ml/1 pt chicken stock
225 g/½ lb peeled raw prawns, cut into 1-cm/½-in pieces
4 tbsp dry sherry
snipped chives

Wash and pick over the pre-soaked beans, then put them in a pan with the cumin, oregano, bayleaf and water. Bring slowly to the boil, then cover, turn the heat right down, and simmer gently for about 2½ hours until the beans are very soft. Fish out the bayleaf and leave to cool slightly while you heat the oil and gently sauté the onion and garlic until soft but not brown. Add the tomato and simmer for a few minutes. Season, and tip the mixture into the beans. Purée the contents of the pan and pour into a clean pan. Stir in the chicken stock, bring up to a simmer and then stir in the prawns. Cook for 2 minutes, turn off the heat and stir in the sherry.

Serve decorated with a sprinkling of chives.

∽ FLAGEOLET BEAN SOUP WITH CHICKEN LIVERS ∽
AND CROÛTONS

A velvety and beguiling soup, well worth the fiddle of splitting the cooked beans. Adapted from a recipe in Nouvelle Cuisine by Jean and Pierre Troigros.

SERVES 4

160 g/5½ oz dried flageolet
  beans, or 350 g/12½ oz
  fresh flageolet beans in their
  pods
30 g/1¼ oz butter
3 leeks, finely sliced

10 chicken livers
1.4 litres/2½ pts poultry
  stock
5 tbsp single cream
salt and pepper

If you are using dried beans, soak them in warm water for a minimum of 2 hours, then simmer gently for 2 hours; shell fresh beans and cook them in boiling water, uncovered, for 25 minutes.

Heat 25 g/1 oz of the butter and soften the leeks. Meanwhile, put aside 3 of the chicken livers, cut the others in half and add them to the softened leeks. Cook for about 10 minutes until the livers are firm. Pour on the stock, cover the pan, and simmer gently for 25 minutes.

Split 24 of the beans in half lengthways and put to one side. Add the rest of the beans to the soup. Heat through, and then purée the soup. Return it to a clean pan, add the cream, heat through and taste for seasoning.

Cut the reserved chicken livers into (approximately) 1-cm/½-in squares. Heat the last scrap of butter and sauté the livers, seasoning with salt and pepper.

Divide the livers and split beans between the soup-plates, and pour on the soup. Serve croûtons separately, to be floated on the soup at the last minute.

✑ TUSCAN BEAN SOUP WITH PARSLEY ✑

This soup is especially delicious when made with fresh cannellini beans (in which case reduce the cooking time), and good-quality olive oil.

SERVES 4–5

350 g/12 oz cannellini beans,
  soaked for at least 3 hours
1.1 litres/2 pts cold water
salt and pepper

3 tbsp olive oil
2 fat cloves of garlic, chopped
4 tbsp parsley, chopped

Cover the soaked beans with the water and bring slowly to the boil. Simmer gently for about 60 minutes, until the beans are quite soft but not collapsed. Purée about half the beans with a little of the cooking liquid, and return to a clean pan with the whole beans and the rest of their liquid. Season well with salt and pepper.

Heat the oil and gently cook the chopped garlic, taking care not to let it burn. When pale golden, stir in the parsley and cook for a couple of seconds. Stir into the soup, leave to stand, covered, for 4 or 5 minutes, and serve.

∽ BEETROOT CREAM ∽

SERVES 6

450 g/1 lb raw beetroot
1.7 litres/3 pts chicken stock
4 sprigs of parsley
6 peppercorns
8 coriander seeds
½ tsp fennel seeds
1 leek, chopped
2 celery stalks, chopped

2 carrots, peeled and chopped
4 shallots, finely chopped
1 clove of garlic, peeled and
  chopped
salt and pepper
150 g/5 oz strained Greek
  yoghurt (see page 67)
1 tbsp snipped chives

Scrub the beetroot but do not peel or cut it. Place it in a pan with the chicken stock, and add the parsley, peppercorns, coriander and fennel seeds bundled up in a muslin bag. Bring to the boil, lower the heat, partially cover, and simmer gently for 60 minutes. Add the chopped leek, celery, carrots, shallots and garlic, and cook on for a further 20 minutes.

Remove the pan from the heat. Fish out the beetroot and leave to cool, remove and discard the muslin bag. Rub off the skin of the beetroot and trim the ends. Transfer to a processor or blender and purée with the other vegetables and the stock. Sieve into a clean pan, re-heat, taste and season.

Serve the soup with a dollop of yoghurt garnished with chives.

∽ BRAZIL NUT AND LEMON SOUP ∽

This idea comes from Joyce Molyneux's *The Carved Angel Cookbook,* and is perfect for using up a glut of Brazil nuts left over from Christmas.

SERVES 6

25 g/1 oz butter
1 medium onion, sliced
salt
1.2 litres/2 pts chicken stock
100 g/4 oz Brazil nuts,
  shelled

zest of 1 lemon, cut into thick
  strips
65 ml/2½ fl oz single cream

Melt the butter, stir in the chopped onion, season with a generous pinch of salt and sweat, covered, for 15 minutes. Add the stock, nuts and lemon zest. Bring up to the boil, then turn down the heat, cover and simmer for 20 minutes. Purée until smooth. Return to a clean pan, taste and adjust the seasoning, stir in the cream, re-heat and serve.

∽ BROCCOLI SOUP WITH CASHEW NUTS ∽ AND CRUDITÉS

An unusual idea from Jean Conil's book *Cuisine Fraîcheur*.

SERVES 3–4

1 medium onion, chopped	150 g/5 oz cashew nuts
1 tbsp sunflower oil	1 clove of garlic, peeled
400 ml/15 fl oz water	1 tbsp chopped watercress
225 g/8 oz broccoli, stalk cut into thin slices, florets left whole	50 g/2 oz tofu or fromage frais
	salt and pepper

Soften, but don't brown, the onion in the oil. Add the water and broccoli and simmer, covered, for 7 minutes until almost tender. Add the cashew nuts, garlic, watercress and tofu or fromage frais. Cook for 4 more minutes, then liquidize to a thick purée. Taste and season. Serve in individual soup bowls with an assortment of crudités: radishes, carrots, celery and fennel sticks.

∽ BROWN WINDSOR SOUP WITH HORSERADISH ∽ DUMPLINGS

This is the forebear of the ubiquitous 'brown soup' that was the standard pre-and post-war bill of fare at hotels and boarding houses throughout the British Isles – and largely responsible for giving British soups a bad name. Made properly it is rich and sustaining; rather like liquid stew.

SERVES 4

25 g/1 oz butter	1.4 litres/2½ pts beef stock
1 small onion, finely chopped	bouquet garni with 4 stalks of parsley, 1 spray of thyme, ½ a bayleaf and 1 clove of garlic (optional)
green of 1 leek, chopped	
1 small carrot, peeled and diced	
salt and pepper	
350 g/12 oz stewing steak, trimmed and diced	16 or more horseradish dumplings (see pages 79–80)
1 tbsp flour	1 tbsp parsley, chopped

Melt the butter, stir in the onion and cook for a couple of minutes before adding the leek and carrot. Season with a generous pinch of salt and pepper, cover, and sweat for 5 minutes. Add the beef and brown it all over. Sift in the flour, stirring and scraping to mix it in well. Pour on a little of the stock, stirring thoroughly to take up the flour, and then pour on the rest. Bring to the boil, turn down the heat, add the *bouquet garni*, cover and simmer very slowly, stirring occasionally, for 2 hours. Remove the remains of the *bouquet garni* and liquidize the soup, adding a little more stock or water if it is too thick. Taste for seasoning and serve with the cooked dumplings and a sprinkling of parsley.

∽ CABBAGE AND BACON SOUP ∽

SERVES 4–6
25 g/1 oz butter
1 small onion, chopped
100 g/4 oz smoked bacon,
  rinds removed and diced
450 g/1 lb cabbage, cored and
  shredded

1 medium potato, peeled and
  diced
1.1 litres/2 pts chicken or
  turkey stock
salt and pepper
3 tbsp single cream

Melt the butter and soften the onion with the bacon, cooking until the onion is limp and the bacon is beginning to crisp. Stir in the cabbage, then the diced potato, stirring around so everything is nicely mixed up. Cook for a couple of minutes before pouring on the stock. Season lightly with salt and generously with pepper. Bring up to the boil, turn down the heat and cover the pan. Cook gently for 30 minutes or until the cabbage is tender. Liquidize. Return to a clean pan, re-heat and adjust the seasoning. Serve with a swirl of cream and croûtons.

∽ CAULIFLOWER SOUP ∽

SERVES 4–6
40 g/1½ oz butter
1 medium onion, chopped
1 clove of garlic (optional)
salt and pepper
1 large cauliflower
570 ml/1 pt water
1 large potato, peeled and
  chopped

1 sprig of thyme
900 ml/1½ pts chicken or
  vegetable stock
100 ml/4 fl oz cream or milk
  (optional)

Heat the butter, add the onion and garlic, a generous sprinkling of salt, stir and cover. Leave to sweat for a few minutes while you attend to the cauliflower. Chop off the leaves and stems, cut them into manageable pieces and boil up in the water. Cut the cauliflower into small florets and stir into the onion, adding the diced potato and thyme. Cover and continue cooking over a low heat for 10–15 minutes, stirring occasionally. Strain the cauliflower-stem water into the vegetables, top up with the chicken or vegetable stock and bring slowly up to the boil. Turn down to simmer, cover, and cook for about 20 minutes until the cauliflower is completely soft. Remove the thyme and purée. Return to a clean pan, re-heat, taste and adjust the seasoning. Stir in the cream or milk, re-heat and serve.

Cauliflower soup can be radically altered by its garnish. It is lovely matched with watercress or mint cream (see page 66), or simply embellished with toasted almonds, crisp bacon or croûtons, or with fresh parsley, coriander or chives. Peeled, seeded and chopped ripe tomatoes, mixed with chopped fresh parsley and stirred in just before serving, provide a fresh contrast of colour, texture and flavour. For a change try serving a green *salsa* (see page 75) separately for people to help themselves. For a more substantial soup, stir in freshly grated Parmesan just before serving.

✑ CRÉCY SOUP ✑

This is a classic carrot soup, so named after either Crécy-en-Ponthieu or Crécy-en-Brie, two small towns in France which both produce good root crops and both lay claim to the title.

The basic recipe can be adapted by omitting the rice and upping the quantity of onion, and stirring in 100 ml/4 fl oz of fresh orange juice just before serving. Garnish this carrot and orange soup with grated orange zest.

SERVES 4

75g/3 oz butter	25 g/1 oz rice
225 g/8 oz carrots, peeled and sliced	1 sprig of thyme
1 medium onion or 2 small shallots, finely chopped	700 ml/1¼ pts light veal or chicken stock
salt and pepper	fresh parsley, chives or chervil

Soften 50 g/2 oz of butter and stir in the carrots and onions. Season with a generous pinch of salt and cover. Sweat, stirring occasionally, for 10 minutes without letting the vegetables brown. Add the rice and thyme and pour on the stock. Bring up to the boil, turn down the heat and simmer gently for about 30 minutes. Fish out the thyme and purée the soup. Re-heat, adjust the seasoning, whisk in the last of the butter and serve with croûtons and a sprinkling of fresh parsley, chives or chervil.

✑ CELERY CREAM SOUP ✑

This is Simon Hopkinson's recipe, which is rich, very thick and full of flavour. It is just as good with less cream but the colour will be sludgier.

Celery soup is deliciously enhanced with Parmesan; stir in a couple of tablespoons, freshly grated, just before serving.

SERVES 4

*1 lovely head of celery with
  leaves
110 g/4 oz butter
1 onion, finely chopped
570 ml/1 pt light chicken
  stock*

*1 tsp celery seed
570 ml/1 pt double cream
celery salt and pepper*

Remove all the green leaves from the celery. Set aside. Roughly chop and wash the stalks. Melt the butter and sweat the onion and celery together very slowly for at least 45 minutes in a covered pan, stirring occasionally. Add the stock, celery seed, a pinch of celery salt (take care, it contains MSG) and a generous grinding of pepper. Simmer for 20 minutes. Coarsely chop the reserved celery leaves and add to the soup. Liquidize very thoroughly to break down the fibrous flesh, push and pour through a sieve and return to a clean pan. Stir in the cream, re-heat and adjust seasoning.

✑ CELERY AND DANISH BLUE CHEESE SOUP ✑

SERVES 4

*50 g/2 oz butter
1 medium head of celery,
  chopped
2 medium onions, chopped
25 g/1 oz flour*

*1.1 litres/2 pts chicken stock
salt and pepper
50 g/2 oz Danish blue cheese
1 tbsp parsley, chopped*

Soften the butter and gently sweat the celery and onions in a covered pan for 15 minutes. Stir occasionally to prevent them browning or sticking. Sift in the flour, stirring thoroughly, moisten with a little stock, and season generously with pepper but go easy on the salt because celery seems to produce salt when it cooks. Pour on the rest of the stock, cover and simmer for 45 minutes. Purée and return to a clean pan. Re-heat and check the seasoning. Meanwhile mash the cheese to a cream and whisk it gradually into the hot soup. Take care not to let it boil. Taste again for seasoning, stir in the parsley and serve with croûtons.

✑ CHESTNUT SOUP ✑

SERVES 4

225 g/8 oz chestnuts
40 g/1½ oz butter or rendered
    bacon fat
2 small onions or shallots,
    finely chopped

1 small carrot, peeled and
    diced
1 stick of celery, chopped
1.4 litres/2½ pts good stock
salt and pepper

Chestnuts are a pain to peel. Their shells come away easily enough
once they are cooked but the inner skin clings tight. The job is best
done directly from the oven while still hot; score their skins and bake
at 300° F/150° C/Gas Mark 2 for 15 minutes, allow them to cool
slightly, squeeze the shell, then use a small sharp knife to lever off
both shell and skin.

Meanwhile, melt the butter or bacon fat and stir in the onion,
carrot and celery. Stir-fry for a few minutes then add the chestnuts
and seasoning. Add the stock, bring to the boil, then turn down the
heat to simmer for about 40 minutes until the chestnuts have collapsed. Purée, re-heat the soup and taste for seasoning. Serve with
croûtons.

✑ CHESTNUT AND LENTIL SOUP ✑

A beautiful autumn soup with subtle flavouring.

SERVES 6

350 g/12 oz chestnuts,
    cooked and shelled (see
    previous recipe)
4–5 tbsp olive oil
1 tsp marjoram, chopped
4 branches of thyme
¼ tsp fennel seeds, ground
100 ml/4 fl oz dry white
    wine
1 tbsp tomato paste
110 g/4 oz lentils, rinsed
2.3 litres/4 pts water

1 medium carrot, peeled and
    diced
1 stick of celery, finely diced
½ a small onion, finely
    chopped
1 large clove of garlic, finely
    chopped
1 bayleaf
4 sprigs of parsley
salt and pepper
1 tbsp parsley, chopped

Chop the cooked chestnuts into small pieces. Heat 2 tbsp of the olive
oil and stir in the chestnuts, the marjoram, thyme and fennel. Stir-fry
for a few minutes, then add the wine and tomato paste. Let everything
simmer together for a few minutes and set aside while you attend to
the lentils. Put them in a pan with 2.3 litres/4 pts of water and bring
to the boil. Cook at a gentle roll for 5 minutes, skim and add the

carrot, celery, onion, garlic, bayleaf, and 4 sprigs of parsley. Turn down the heat and simmer very slowly for about 30 minutes until the lentils are done.

Fish out the parsley and bayleaf, and purée half the lentils with a little of the cooking liquid. Pour the puréed lentils and the rest of the lentils and their liquid into the chestnut mixture. Heat through, taste and adjust the seasoning. Serve with croûtons, a sprinkling of parsley and a swoosh of your finest olive oil (see page 61). This lovely recipe is adapted from Deborah Madison's *The Savoury Way*.

∽ CREAMED CHICORY SOUP WITH BACON ∽

Another all-time favourite soup: a haunting and intriguing mix of flavours. It is Simon Hopkinson's recipe, and often on the menu at Bibendum, the restaurant he owns with Terence Conran.

SERVES 6

110 g/4 oz butter
6 large heads of chicory, coarsely sliced
1 large onion, peeled and chopped
1 clove of garlic, peeled and bashed
juice of 1 lemon
glass of dry white wine
1 medium floury potato, peeled and chopped
1 bayleaf
1.4 litres/2½ pts chicken stock
110 g/¼ lb piece of smoked streaky bacon
salt and pepper
150 ml/¼ pt double cream
6 thin rashers of bacon
chopped parsley

Melt the butter in a large pan, allow it to brown slightly, then throw in the chicory. Stir around and allow it to take on a golden colour before you stir in the onion. Turn down the heat, cover and cook gently until the onion is soft. Stir in the garlic and lemon juice, then the wine. Allow it to bubble up, to burn off the alcohol, then add the potato, bayleaf and stock. Lob in the piece of bacon, season with ¼ tsp of salt and several grinds of pepper, cover and simmer for approx. 1 hour.

Remove the bayleaf, fish out the bacon and liquidize the soup. Pass it through a fine sieve, return to a clean pan, and reheat with the cream. Remove the rind from the bacon, dice the meat into small pieces and return to the soup. Taste and adjust the seasoning. Meanwhile, grill the thin rashers of streaky bacon, cool and crumble.

Serve with croûtons, the crumbled bacon and a generous sprinkling of chopped parsley.

∽ CHICKPEA SOUP WITH FRIED EGGS ∽

A simple, surprising and delicious soup.

SERVES 6

225 g/8 oz chickpeas, soaked overnight in cold water
4 tbsp olive oil
1 medium onion, finely chopped
2 cloves of garlic, finely chopped

1 tbsp mint leaves, finely chopped
700 ml/1¼ pts chicken or beef stock
salt and pepper
juice of ½ a lemon
6 eggs

Cover the chickpeas with fresh water, bring slowly to the boil, then simmer gently for at least 1 hour until quite soft. Drain, reserving 275 ml/½ pt of the cooking liquid. Heat 2 tbsp of the olive oil and soften the onion and garlic. Transfer to a blender or food processor, add the mint leaves and 150 ml/¼ pt of the stock, and purée. Add the chickpeas with the reserved 275 ml/½ pt of cooking liquid, and purée. Return to a clean pan, add the rest of the stock and simmer for 5 minutes, stirring well. Taste and season with salt, pepper and lemon juice. Just before serving, heat the rest of the olive oil and fry the eggs. Pour the soup into bowls, and slip a fried egg into each bowl.

Provide good bread for dunking and mopping.

∽ CHICKPEA AND LANGOUSTINE SOUP ∽

This is an unbelievably good soup that doesn't rely on langoustine for its deliciousness. The langoustine, or quickly seared scallops, are a pleasant diversion but it is the rich, creamy flavour and texture of the chickpeas that makes this soup. I have experimented a lot with chickpea soups and Shaun Hill, the chef of Gidleigh Park, who devised this one, is right: chickpeas need to soak for 2 days in cold water to fulfil their flavour potential.

SERVES 4

225 g/8 oz chickpeas, soaked in cold water for 48 hours
1.6 litres/2¾ pts water
salt and pepper
4 tbsp extra virgin olive oil
1 large onion, peeled and sliced

2 large cloves of garlic, peeled and sliced
1 tsp coriander seeds, crushed
4 langoustines or 4 scallops (optional)
juice of ½ a lemon

Drain the chickpeas and bring to the boil in 1.3 litres/2¼ pts of the water, seasoned with a pinch of salt. Turn down the heat and simmer very gently for at least 2 hours, or until the chickpeas are quite soft. Purée the chickpeas with the cooking liquor.

Meanwhile heat 2 tbsp of olive oil and fry the onion with the garlic until soft and they start to colour. Add the crushed coriander seeds and the langoustines or scallops (if using). Cook for a couple of minutes (turning the scallops after 60 seconds), pour in 275 ml/½ pt of water and bring to the boil. After 2 minutes lift out the langoustines (or scallops), remove and set aside their tail meat. Return the bones and debris to the pan and cook for a further 5 minutes. Strain this liquor into the chickpea purée (I have made this soup without the shellfish but by adding the onion slop to the chickpea purée for more processing). Adjust the balance of flavour with the lemon juice, black pepper and a little more salt. If the soup is too thick, thin it with a little more water or stock.

Serve the soup in warmed bowls garnished with the chopped shellfish, and a generous swirl of your finest olive oil.

ᴄᴏ CUCUMBER AND COCONUT CREAM WITH HOT ᴄᴏ
PEPPER AND CHIVES

SERVES 4–6

1½ large cucumbers, peeled and grated	1 tsp fresh fennel leaves, chopped
1 onion, finely chopped	½ a wineglass of sherry
700 ml/1¼ pts rich chicken or ham stock	1 tbsp chives, chopped
50 g/2 oz butter	salt and pepper
400 ml/¾ pt thick coconut cream	½ a green chilli pepper, de-seeded and chopped

Place the grated cucumber, onion, stock, butter and coconut cream in a pan and simmer gently, uncovered, for 20 minutes. Purée, return to a clean pan and bring up to simmer with the fennel and sherry. Cook for 8 minutes, taste for seasoning and serve garnished with chives and a sprinkling of chilli pepper.

ᴄᴏ COURGETTE AND MINT SOUP ᴄᴏ

This is my favourite courgette soup, devised by trial and error after eating a similar version at the Serpentine Restaurant, when run by Prue Leith. The quick cooking of the courgette and the last-minute addition of the mint and parsley give the soup a sharp, fresh flavour. It's a very pretty pale green with darker green flecks.

SERVES 6

50 g/2 oz butter
1 small onion, finely diced
1 shallot, finely diced
900 g/2 lb courgettes,
  chopped
1 cooked potato, diced

salt and pepper
1.75 litres/3 pts chicken stock
2 tbsp mint, freshly chopped
2 tbsp flat-leaf parsley, freshly
  chopped

Soften the butter and gently sweat the onion and shallot until transparent. Stir in the chopped courgettes and potato, season generously, cover and cook for 5 minutes, stirring a couple of times. Add the stock, bring to the boil, turn down the heat and simmer for 5 minutes. Liquidize with the mint and parsley. Return to a clean pan, reheat, taste for seasoning and serve.

∽   CUCUMBER AND MUNG BEAN SOUP   ∽

An Indian recipe in which shreds of cucumber, potato and onion are bound together in a thick bean purée and seasoned with cumin, coriander and lemon juice. The recipe is adapted from Julie Sahni's excellent *Classic Indian Cooking*.

SERVES 6

150 g/5 oz split mung beans,
  soaked for 3–4 hours in cold
  water
⅛ tsp turmeric
1.1 litres/2 pts water
175 g/6 oz grated potatoes
110 g/4 oz onions, thinly
  sliced
2 large cucumbers, peeled and
  grated

1½ tsp coarse salt
4 tbsp ghee or light vegetable
  oil
¾ tsp cumin seeds
¼ tsp black pepper
juice of ½ a lemon
2 tbsp coriander leaves, finely
  chopped

Drain the beans and put them in a pan with the turmeric and 570 ml/1 pt of cold water. Bring quickly to the boil, reduce the heat and simmer, partially covered, for about 30 minutes or until the beans are tender. Purée the beans with their cooking water and make the liquid up to 1.1 litres/2 pts. Add the potatoes, onion, cucumber and salt, and bring to the boil, stirring constantly. Reduce the heat to simmer and cook uncovered for 5 minutes.

Meanwhile, heat the ghee or oil in a small pan and when very hot add the cumin and black pepper and stir-fry for 5 seconds until the cumin turns dark brown. Remove from the heat and tip into the soup. Add the lemon juice and coriander, mix thoroughly, taste and adjust the seasoning. Serve with a garnish of fresh coriander, and with hot naan or another flat-bread (see page 116).

☙ CREAM OF FENNEL SOUP ☙

This is a luxurious soup, with a high proportion of fennel to liquid and much fortification from cream, butter, white wine, and Pernod. For a lighter version – fennel, leek and potato soup – increase the stock by 570 ml/1 pt, omit the alcohol and cream, and use the white part of 1 leek and 1 potato (peeled and chopped) instead of the onions.

SERVES 6

110 g/4 oz butter
2 onions, chopped
4 large heads of fennel, coarsely chopped
1 glass of dry white wine
1 tsp fennel seeds

900 ml/1½ pts light chicken stock
large measure of Pernod
275 ml/½ pt whipping cream
salt and pepper

Melt the butter and sweat the onions and fennel over a very low heat, covered, until thoroughly wilted and soft. Stir occasionally; this will take about 30 minutes but the longer and slower, the better. Add the white wine and fennel seeds and simmer gently, uncovered, for 10 minutes. Add the chicken stock and simmer, covered, for a further 30 minutes. Liquidize and pass through a fine sieve into a clean pan.

In a small pan, heat the Pernod and ignite. When the flames subside, stir into the soup, followed by the cream. Re-heat but don't allow to boil. Taste and correct the seasoning with salt and pepper. Serve.

☙ SWEET GARLIC SOUP ☙

This is mild, aromatic and soothing.

SERVES 4–6

1 whole head of garlic, peeled
2 large sweet onions, sliced
1.1 litres/2 pts light chicken stock
salt and pepper

2 tbsp rendered bacon fat
1 tbsp parsley, chopped
1 tbsp flour
1 tbsp chives, chopped
2 tbsp dill leaves, chopped

Put the garlic and onions in a pan with the stock and season lightly. Bring to the boil, cover, and simmer gently for 15 minutes.

In another pan, heat the bacon fat and stir in the parsley. Sift in the flour, stirring to form into a thick roux, and gently allow to brown. Pour a ladleful, and then another, of the hot broth into the roux and let it bubble up while you stir to form a thick sauce. Pour the sauce into the soup, bring up to the boil and simmer for 10 minutes. Liquidize and return to a clean pan. Taste and adjust the seasoning. Stir in the chives and dill and re-heat. Serve with croûtons.

✍ FRESH GINGER AND LETTUCE SOUP ✍

SERVES 4

2 onions, finely chopped
2 carrots, peeled and finely
  chopped
25 g/1 oz butter
1 Iceberg lettuce, shredded
4 slices of fresh ginger, peeled
  and grated

6 or 8 parsley stalks
1 tbsp flour
1 litres/1 ¾ pts boiling chicken
  stock
salt and pepper
1 tbsp parsley leaves, chopped
50 ml/2 fl oz single cream

Sauté the onions and carrots in the butter until soft but not coloured. Turn up the heat and quickly sauté the lettuce, ginger and parsley stalks until they wilt, then sift in the flour, stirring thoroughly. Pour on the hot chicken stock, simmer for 5 minutes, then purée. Pour through a fine sieve into a clean pan. Taste and adjust the seasoning. Serve with parsley and a swirl of cream, and with croûtons.

This is Nerys Roberts's recipe from Y Bistro, Llanberis.

✍ LEEK SOUP ✍

Leeks are the national emblem of Wales; this is a St David's Day soup.

SERVES 4

25 g/1 oz butter
4 rashers of bacon, chopped
4 large leeks, chopped
450 g/1 lb potatoes, peeled
  and chopped

salt and pepper
900 ml/1 ½ pts light stock or
  water
150 ml/¼ pt milk
1 tbsp parsley, chopped

Melt the butter and sauté the bacon. Stir in the leeks, cover, and sweat for a couple of minutes before adding the potatoes. Season with salt and pepper, pour on the stock and bring up to the boil. Lower the heat and simmer gently for 30–40 minutes. Liquidize, return to a clean pan and add the milk. Reheat, taste for seasoning and serve sprinkled with the parsley.

∽ SPICED LENTIL SOUP ∽

SERVES 6–8

½ tsp ground ginger
½ tsp ground black pepper
½ tsp ground turmeric
½ tsp ground fenugreek
¼ tsp ground cloves
2 tsp ground cumin
1 tsp ground cinnamon
grated rind of 1 lemon
4 tbsp olive oil
1 large onion, chopped
3 cloves of garlic
175 g/6 oz brown lentils

2 stalks of celery, chopped
350 g/12 oz tomatoes,
 blanched, cored, peeled and
 chopped
1.4 litres/2½ pts light stock
 or water
2–3 tbsp lemon juice
large bunch of flat-leaf parsley
 or coriander, chopped
salt
¼ tsp ground chilli

Mix all the spices, except the chilli, with the lemon rind. Heat the oil in a large pan and soften the onion. Stir in the spices and stir-fry for a couple of minutes. Add the garlic and lentils, stirring around to make sure they are coated with spices and oil. Mix in the celery and tomatoes and sweat for a couple of minutes before pouring on the stock. Bring up to the boil, then turn the heat down so that the soup cooks at a low simmer for about 60 minutes, or until the lentils are tender.

Purée the soup, adding more liquid if it seems too thick. Stir in the lemon juice and parsley or coriander, adjust the seasoning and serve with a sprinkling of ground chilli.

Alternatively, garnish with fried onion and garlic (see page 113) in place of the ground chilli. Serve toasted pitta bread, torn into scraps for DIY garnishing, separately.

Adapted from Jill Norman's *The Complete Book of Spices*.

∽ MASOOR DAL SOUP ∽

SERVES 4–6

185 g/6½ oz Egyptian red
 split lentils (masoor dal),
 picked over, washed and
 drained
2 litres/3½ pts water
10 whole cloves
2 bayleaves

1 tsp whole black peppercorns
½ tsp ground turmeric
1¼ tsp salt
1 tbsp lime juice
⅛ tsp cayenne pepper
1 tbsp coriander, chopped

Put the lentils in a large pan with the water, bring to the boil and remove any scum. Meanwhile bundle the cloves, bayleaves and peppercorns in a piece of muslin. Drop the bundle and the turmeric into the pan. Turn the heat down very low, almost cover the pan and simmer very gently for 1½ hours. Discard the bundle and purée the soup in batches. Return to a clean pan and stir in the salt, lime juice and cayenne. Stir, taste and adjust the seasoning.

Strew with coriander and serve some croûtons separately.

CREAM OF MUSHROOM SOUP

SERVES 4

3 shallots
1 clove of garlic (optional)
50 g/2 oz butter
700 g/1½ lb field
  mushrooms, trimmed and
  roughly chopped
juice of ½ a lemon

1 tbsp flour
1.1 litres/2 pts light chicken
  stock
110 g/4 fl oz double cream
salt and pepper
a pinch of nutmeg

Over a low heat sweat the finely chopped shallots and garlic in the butter for 5 minutes until they are soft but not browned. Stir in the mushrooms and lemon juice and sweat until their juices begin to run. Sift in the flour and cook thoroughly, stirring to avoid lumps. Pour on the hot stock, bring up to the boil, and simmer gently for 35 minutes.

Liquidize the soup to make a slate-grey thick liquid flecked with dark grey. Return to the pan, add the cream and re-heat. Taste and adjust the seasoning with salt, pepper and nutmeg; the soup will have lightened considerably and will be rich and delicately flavoured.

NETTLE, ONION AND GARLIC SOUP

SERVES 6

110 g/4 oz butter
450 g/1 lb onions, finely
  sliced
salt and pepper
4 large cloves of garlic,
  chopped

225 g/½ lb young nettle tops,
  washed
1.75 litres/3 pts water
150 ml/5 fl oz cream

Melt the butter and stir in the onion. Season with ½ tsp of salt, cover, and sweat, stirring from time to time, for 10 minutes. Add the garlic and cook until both are a soft, golden mass. Stir in the nettle leaves, season with black pepper, and add the water. Bring up to the boil and simmer for 5 minutes.

Liquidize the soup and return it to a clean pan. Re-heat and adjust the seasoning. Pour into soup-bowls and sprinkle on a few croûtons. Whisk the cream lightly and spoon a dollop over the croûtons. Serve with slices of well-buttered soda bread.

This recipe is adapted from the even richer nettle soup served at Dunworley Cottage Restaurant, Bandon, County Cork.

✎ FIVE ONION SOUP WITH CHIVE CREAM ✎

SERVES 4–6

75 g/3 oz butter
2 medium onions, sliced
salt and pepper
3 large leeks, white part only,
  sliced
3 shallots, diced
4 spring onions, trimmed and
  sliced

1 medium floury potato,
  peeled, diced and rinsed
1 sprig of thyme
1 bayleaf
4 cloves of garlic, peeled
1.1 litres/2 pts good stock
100 ml/4 fl oz double cream
2 tbsp chives, chopped

Heat the butter in a spacious, lidded, heavy-bottomed pan. Stir in the onions, and after a couple of minutes, season with ½ tsp of salt and add the leeks, shallots and then the spring onions and potato. Stir everything around, cover, and leave to sweat over a very low heat for 30 minutes. Stir occasionally. Add the thyme, bayleaf and garlic, and several grinds from the peppermill. Pour on the stock, bring slowly to the boil, then reduce the heat and cook, partially covered, for 20 minutes.

Strain the liquid into a clean pan, fish out the bayleaf and thyme sprig, and purée the onion mixture with a ladleful of the broth. Reheat and adjust the seasoning. Just before serving, lightly whisk the cream and stir in the chives. Garnish the soup with croûtons and spoon on a dollop of the chive cream.

✎ OX-TAIL SOUP ✎

This, I think, is the definitive ox-tail soup and is a refinement of Gary Rhodes's superb ox-tail stew served at the Greenhouse in Mayfair. No flour is used, and the vegetables form the thickening. It is rich, full-flavoured and a substantial dish. To make it into a complete meal, increase the quantity of meat and serve with suet dumplings (see page 78), miniature mashed potato mounds or potato gnocchi (see page 80). This soup gets even better with a 24-hour delay between making and eating. Once chilled it will be possible to skim off some of the fat, making it less unctuous, although that is part of its charm.

SERVES 4

8 pieces of ox-tail	1 bayleaf
2 onions, finely chopped	275 ml/½ pt Guinness (red
2 carrots, peeled and diced	wine would be just as good
1 leek, finely chopped	but different)
3 sticks of celery, finely	1.75 litres/3 pts veal, beef or
chopped	oxtail stock
2 cloves of garlic (optional)	salt and pepper
8 whole tomatoes	chopped parsley
4 sprigs of thyme	

Fry the ox-tail until it is browned all over and a lot of fat has been released. Set aside. Reserve 1 tbsp of the fat and stir-fry the onions, carrots, leek and celery, then add the garlic, tomatoes, thyme and bayleaf. When they have started to brown return the ox-tail to the pan with the Guinness or wine, and the stock. Bring up to the boil, turn down the heat, cover and simmer very gently for at least 1½ hours, stirring occasionally, until the meat is tender.

Remove the pieces of ox-tail and set aside. Pour the soup through a fine sieve, push the vegetables through, and discard the tomato skins and fibrous debris. Pick the meat from the ox-tails, add it to the soup and re-heat. Taste and adjust the seasoning.

Garnish with parsley and serve triangular croûtons separately.

∽ PARSLEY SOUP ∽

The secret of the vibrant green colour and rich flavour of this soup is the high proportion and slow cooking of the leeks with the parsley stalks, before the parsley leaves are added. A third bunch of parsley is merely blanched, refreshed in cold water and liquidized with the rest of the soup at the end of cooking. This is Simon Hopkinson's recipe, and sometimes on the menu at Bibendum in South Kensington.

SERVES 6

110 g/4 oz butter	900 ml/1½ pts light chicken
3 large leeks, green parts	stock
removed, sliced	salt and pepper
3 big bunches of flat-leaf	275 ml/½ pt double cream
parsley, stalks removed	
2 medium floury potatoes,	
peeled and chopped	

Melt the butter in a stainless steel or enamelled pan and sweat the leeks and all the parsley stalks gently, uncovered, for 20 minutes. Add the potatoes, chicken stock and salt and pepper and simmer for a further 20 minutes.

Coarsely chop the leaves of 2 bunches of parsley and add to the soup. Simmer for 2 minutes. Meanwhile blanch the leaves of the third bunch of parsley in fiercely boiling water for 30 seconds. Refresh immediately under running cold water and gently squeeze dry in a tea-towel.

Liquidize the soup at full throttle together with the blanched parsley to make a vivid green purée. Pass through a fine sieve into a clean pan, add the cream, re-heat and adjust the seasoning.

✑ PEANUT SOUP ✑

SERVES 6

25 g/1 oz butter
1 medium onion, finely
  chopped
110 g/4 oz toasted peanuts,
  finely ground
450 g/1 lb potatoes, boiled
  and chopped

1 litre/1¾ pts chicken or beef
  stock
150 ml/¼ pt single cream
salt and pepper
2 tbsp chopped chives

Soften the onion in the butter. Pour the contents of the pan into a blender or food processor, and add the peanuts, potatoes and a little of the stock. Blend to a smooth purée. Pour into a pan, add the rest of the stock, and simmer gently, covered, for 15 minutes. Stir in the cream, season with salt and pepper and re-heat without boiling. Pour into warmed soup-bowls and cover with chopped chives.

✑ POTAGE BONNE FEMME ✑

An old-fashioned French soup, and probably the one most frequently cooked all over France. The addition of carrots is not essential but adds colour; the parsley or chervil and cream are refinements.

SERVES 4

40 g/1½ oz butter
2 large leeks, finely sliced
3 carrots, diced
450 g/1 lb potatoes, peeled,
  diced and rinsed
1.1 litres/2 pts water

salt and pepper
½ tsp sugar (optional)
50 ml/2 fl oz single cream
1 tbsp parsley or chervil,
  chopped

Melt the butter and gently sauté the leeks and carrots. When thoroughly coated with butter, add the potatoes, the water, a generous pinch of salt and ½ tsp of sugar. Simmer gently for 30 minutes. Purée and pass through a fine sieve. Adjust the seasoning, serve with a swirl of cream and a flourish of chopped parsley or chervil.

∽ CURRIED PARSNIP SOUP ∽

This is Jane Grigson's famous recipe, made up for an *Observer* article in 1969, and loved by everyone who tastes it. The colour is deep saffron, the texture is thick, fluffy and creamy, the flavour subtle and not obviously parsnip. I usually omit the cream and flour, have made it just as successfully with water and without potato, and have greatly increased the proportion of parsnip. The key to its success seems to be the combination of lightly sautéing the parsnip with the onion and garlic, the curry powder, and the slow simmering until the parsnips are soft, before puréeing the soup.

SERVES 6–8

1 medium onion, chopped
1 large clove of garlic, split
1 very large parsnip, peeled
  and chopped
1 medium floury potato,
  peeled and diced
2 heaped tbsp butter
1 level tbsp flour (optional)
1 rounded tsp curry powder
  (the original recipe specified
  1 tbsp of the following
  mixture: 1 rounded tsp
  ground turmeric, ¼ tsp
  ground fenugreek, ½ tsp
  chilli flakes or 1 dried red
  chilli, 1 level tsp cumin seed,
  and 1 heaped tbsp coriander
  seeds, pounded together and
  bottled. In all subsequent
  recipes it was replaced by the
  curry powder)

1.1 litres/2 pts beef stock
570 ml–1.1 l/1–2 pts water
salt and pepper
150 ml/¼ pt single cream
1 tbsp chopped chives or
  parsley

Cook the onion, garlic, parsnip and potato gently in the butter, covered, for 10 minutes. Stir in the flour and the curry powder. Cook for 2 minutes, giving the whole thing a turn round from time to time. Pour in the stock gradually. Leave to cook. When the parsnip is really tender, purée and dilute to taste with the water. Correct the seasoning. Re-heat, add the cream and a sprinkling of chives or parsley, and serve with bacon croûtons and crusty bread with plenty of good butter.

✑ CREAM OF POTATO, LEEK AND ONION WITH ✑
BUTTERED ONION FLOP

Soups made with the combination of leek, onion and potato, as this one is, can't fail to be delicious whatever the proportions and final finish. When puréed and chilled this combination becomes vichysoisse (see page 339). These purées are delicious served piping hot with a tablespoon of *salsa*, *pesto* or paste (see pages 68–75) stirred just before serving. In this version, the vegetables are simmered until soft then puréed, and 'garnished' with strands of onion softened in butter. *Minestrina tricolore* is a similar Italian soup, with chopped carrot and celery stirred into a potato purée, flavoured with Parmesan and milk, and garnished with parsley.

SERVES 4–5

2 large onions
1 large leek, chopped
225 g/½ lb potatoes, peeled
  and chopped
4 sprigs of parsley

1.1 litres/2 pts water
salt and pepper
25 g/1 oz butter
75 g/3 oz single cream
1 tbsp parsley or chives

Peel and chop one of the onions and put it in a pan with the leek, potatoes and parsley sprigs. Cover with the water, and add a generous pinch of salt and pepper. Cook until the vegetables are soft. Purée and return to a clean pan, adjust the seasoning, and reheat.

Meanwhile, slice the second onion very finely. Heat the butter and gently soften the onion until soft and golden. Tip the contents of the pan into the soup and simmer very gently for 10 minutes. Just before serving, bring the cream to boiling point and pour in a pattern on top of the soup. Serve garnished with parsley or chives.

✑ POTATO AND WATERCRESS SOUP ✑

SERVES 4–6

900 g/2 lb potatoes, peeled,
  diced and rinsed
2 onions, sliced
1.1 litres/2 pts water
salt, pepper and nutmeg or
  mace to taste
275 ml/½ pt milk

2 raw tomatoes, peeled,
  quartered, seeds and cores
  removed
2 bunches of watercress,
  leaves finely chopped
dash of white wine

Boil the potatoes and onions in the salted water until soft. Purée, return to the heat, and add the milk, plenty of pepper and a scraping of nutmeg or mace. Taste and adjust the seasoning.

Dice the tomato. When ready to serve, stir in the chopped watercress leaves, the diced tomato, and the wine.

᧬ PUMPKIN AND CHEESE SOUP ᧬

It was the pumpkin gnocchi at Riva in Barnes that began a recent obsession with pumpkin soup. On the way home, my lunch date, who happened to be Elizabeth David, recalled a pumpkin soup made by one Raymond Blanc, at his newly opened (1977) Les Quat' Saisons in Oxford. When she got home from that meal, Mrs David devised the recipe that follows, which is her version of the young turk's soup. As she pointed out, the original is unlikely to have contained Fontina, an Italian cow's milk cheese reminiscent of Gruyère but sweeter and more buttery.

My own file on pumpkin soups now stands at 21 distinctly different versions, and that doesn't include several others made with squashes.

It matches well with root vegetables, pulses and seafood, and can take spicy seasoning or sweet ones. Crisp bacon and croûtons, or any fresh herb, make suitable garnishes.

At its simplest, pumpkin soup is made by simmering the peeled and chopped flesh in water or stock, to be puréed and diluted with milk and cream. More elegant and diverse versions include Elizabeth David's embellishment of 100 g/4 oz of shrimps pounded with lemon juice; a cinnamon, clove, sugar and wine vinegar seasoning (*Kuerbissuppe* from Germany) and puréed with apricots; the addition of an equal weight of tomatoes and potatoes, plus onions and a velouté finish; and more dramatically, cooked with oysters (Wolfgang Puck), and mussels (Sophie Grigson), and garnished with nutmeg gnocchi (Bruno Lubet). Raymond Blanc's latest pumpkin soup is flavoured with white wine, kirsch, cream and nutmeg, garnished with croûtes loaded with Gruyère, cream, egg-yolk and kirsch, and grilled to a light brown.

Incidentally, that was also the day that Mrs David told me she had more respect for Simon Hopkinson than for anyone else cooking today.

SERVES 4

550 g/1¼ lb pumpkin flesh	150 ml/¼ pt double cream
900 ml/1½ pts water	salt
570 ml/1 pt approx. mild chicken or clear vegetable stock	100 ml/4 oz Fontina cheese, or other cheese with quick melting properties

'Cut the pumpkin flesh into small pieces, and simmer them in the water until quite soft, adding extra water if necessary. Push all through a fine sieve. Return the resulting purée to the rinsed saucepan or casserole, thin with the chicken or vegetable stock – or water if you have neither – and reheat, adding the cream gradually and seasoning with salt.

To serve the soup have ready 4 wide ovenproof soup-bowls, and cut the cheese into dice. Heat the oven, pour the hot soup into the bowls, scatter diced cheese on to each, transfer them to the oven and heat until the cheese melts. Serve straight from the oven, without delay.'

∽ Pumpkin Soup with Garlic and Chilli ∽

This is Sally Clarke's interesting version garnished with oven-crisp pumpkin seeds, from the ingenious *The Women Chefs of Britain*, a compilation of recipes by Absolute Press, and sometimes on the menu at Clarke's in Kensington.

SERVES 6

1 medium pumpkin
  (preferably a green-skinned
  variety)
75 ml/scant 3 fl oz olive oil
6 cloves of garlic, crushed
1 tbsp sage, chopped
1 large onion, roughly
  chopped
1 leek, roughly chopped
2 sticks of celery, roughly
  chopped

½ a fennel bulb, roughly
  chopped
2 small red chilli peppers,
  chopped very fine, with seeds
approx. 1.75 litres/3 pts
  water
2 tsp salt
vegetable oil and salt for
  roasting pumpkin seeds
1 tbsp parsley, finely chopped
1 tbsp virgin olive oil

Cut the pumpkin into quarters, scoop out the seeds and reserve. Peel the pumpkin and cut into approximately 2.5-cm/1-in cubes.

Heat the 75 ml/3 fl oz of olive oil and stir-fry the garlic and sage until aromatic, but don't let it burn. Add the onion, leek, celery, fennel, pumpkin and chillis, and increase the heat slightly, stirring around until the vegetables begin to soften. Cover with the water and bring to the boil, then simmer gently, half-covered, until all the vegetables are soft. Purée to a smooth consistency. Pass through a medium-fine sieve into a clean pan, adjusting consistency and taste by adding water and salt if and as necessary. Re-heat.

Meanwhile, wash the pumpkin seeds under a cold running tap to release the strings of flesh. Lay the cleaned seeds on a baking tray, drizzle with a little vegetable oil and sprinkle generously with salt. Bake for 10–15 minutes in a medium to hot oven (375° F/190° C/ Gas Mark 5 to 425° F/220° C/Gas Mark 7), turning with a spoon occasionally, until they are golden brown and crisp to the bite.

Serve in warm soup-plates sprinkled with the seeds and garnished with parsley and a drizzle of virgin olive oil.

⌒ SWEDE SOUP WITH PARSLEY CREAM AND ⌒
POLENTA CHIPS

Swedes come very low in the vegetable pecking order, but their sweet honey-coloured flesh is perfect soup material. This is a mild, delicate soup.

SERVES 4–6

75 g/3 oz butter
2–3 shallots, finely chopped
a small bunch of parsley
450 g/1 lb swede, peeled and
  diced

salt and pepper
1.1 litres/2 pts good stock
100 ml/4 oz double cream
polenta chips (see page 125)

Heat the butter and soften the shallots. Stir in the parsley stalks and the diced swede, making sure everything gets thoroughly coated with butter. Season with a generous pinch of salt, cover, and leave to sweat, stirring occasionally, for 15 minutes. Pour on the stock, bring to the boil and simmer gently for 30 minutes. Purée, return to a clean pan, adjust the seasoning and re-heat.

Meanwhile chop the parsley leaves finely. Just before serving whisk the cream lightly and fold in the parsley. Pour the soup into bowls and serve with a spoonful of parsley cream and grilled polenta chips on the side.

⌒ RED PEPPER CREAM ⌒

There are two good ways of making red or yellow pepper soups. The first is to peel, core and dice the peppers, and simmer them with butter and enough water to cover, before puréeing and sieving, then blending with other ingredients. The other, which gives a fresher, lighter flavour, is to cook the peppers by scorching their skins under the grill or in the oven. Either way the soup will be sweet, and true to the pepper's colour.

SERVES 4

4 large sweet red peppers
1 tbsp light oil
1 medium onion, finely
  chopped

700 ml/1¼ pts chicken stock
275 ml/½ pt tomato juice
salt and pepper
lemon juice

Pre-heat the grill. Lay out the peppers, a few inches from the heat, and grill them, turning frequently until their skin is blackened and blistered all over. Pop them into a plastic carrier bag, seal the opening, and leave to sweat for about 20 minutes. This makes them easier to peel; merely rinse away the flaky skin under running water. Pull away their cores and seeds. Chop the flesh into chunks and transfer to a food processor or blender.

Meanwhile, heat the oil and soften the onion. Add it to the pepper flesh with about 275 ml/½ pt of chicken stock, and purée. Push through a fine sieve, to catch any scraps of skin, into a clean pan, and add the tomato juice and the rest of the stock. Stir while you bring the soup up to a simmer, then lower the heat and cook, covered, for about 10 minutes. Taste and season with salt, pepper and lemon juice.

This soup looks stunning topped with a blob of whipped cream.

❧ SPICY RED PEPPER SOUP ❧

A thick, spicy, rich and aromatic 'stew', and a recipe developed by Greens of San Francisco from Elizabeth David's recipe for the Catalan soup, *Mayorquina*. *Ancho* is the name for the dried pod of a particular kind of *poblano*, the universal name for green chilli peppers used in Mexican cooking. *Ancho* tend to be a brick-red colour and are pretty hot.

SERVES 6

1–2 ancho *chillis*
3 tbsp olive oil
½ tsp finely chopped mixed
  marjoram, thyme and savory
2 bayleaves
2 cloves
4 cloves of garlic, chopped
1 medium red onion, sliced
1 leek, white part only, sliced
450 g/1 lb pimientos or red
  bell peppers, seeded and
  roughly chopped

1 tsp salt
450 g/1 lb ripe tomatoes,
  peeled, cored, seeded and
  chopped, juice reserved
1.4 litres/2½ pts water
225 g/8 oz Savoy cabbage,
  shredded
1 tbsp parsley or marjoram,
  chopped

Remove the stems, seeds and veins from the chillis. Chop them into large pieces and cover with water. Bring to the boil and simmer for 20 minutes, then purée in a blender.

Meanwhile heat the olive oil, stir in the marjoram, thyme, savory, bayleaves and cloves and cook gently until they are aromatic. Add the garlic and stir-fry for 30 seconds without letting it brown, then stir in the onion, leek, peppers and salt. Stir well, cover the pot and leave to sweat for 15 minutes, adding a little water if the vegetables seem dry. Add the tomatoes, 4 tbsp of the chilli purée, and the water. Bring to the boil, lower the heat, and turn down to a low simmer. Add the cabbage, cover, and cook as slowly as possible for 40 minutes.

Let the soup cool briefly then purée in batches, letting each batch process for at least 60 seconds. Return to a clean pan, re-heat, taste and adjust the seasoning with salt and more chilli.

Serve garnished with fresh parsley or marjoram.

～ SPICED SPINACH SOUP WITH ONION FLAKES AND ～ YOGHURT

This is an Indian-inspired recipe. The soup can be given Caribbean overtones by omitting the spices and rice and cooking 25 g/1 oz of grated creamed coconut with the spinach. For spinach and coconut soup, use a chicken stock and finish the soup with double cream.

SERVES 4–6

3 tbsp clarified butter
1 large red onion, sliced
1 clove of garlic
salt and pepper
110 g/4 oz rice
4 cloves, the 'ball' part only
1 tsp cumin seeds
¼ tsp freshly grated nutmeg
1.4 litres/2½ pts vegetable
  stock

450 g/1 lb spinach, washed,
  stems removed and yellowing
  leaves discarded
grated peel and juice of 1
  lemon
100 ml/4 fl oz single cream
100 ml/4 fl oz strained Greek
  yoghurt (see page 67)
onion flakes (see page 113)

Heat the clarified butter and soften the onion with the garlic and salt. Stir in the rice. Grind the cloves and cumin seeds and sprinkle on to the rice with the nutmeg. Stir-fry for 5 minutes. Add 275 ml/½ pt of stock and simmer for 10 minutes. Press the spinach into the pot, cover, and when the leaves have wilted pour on the rest of the stock. Bring up to the boil, turn down immediately, and simmer for 5 minutes. Purée, re-heat, stir in the lemon peel and cream, re-heat very gently and season to taste with the lemon juice, pepper, and more salt if needed.

Serve with croûtons, a dollop of creamy Greek yoghurt and a topping of crisp onion flakes. Complete the Indian theme with naan bread (see page 118).

～ SWEET POTATO SOUP ～

To my mind, Elisabeth Lambert Ortiz is one of the most trustworthy cookery writers in print. When I happened upon this Brazilian recipe, *sopa de batata doce*, in *Latin American Cooking*, described as 'the most delicious soup I have ever had', that was good enough for me. The ingredient list belies its subtlety, 'a lovely tart hint of tomato flavour balancing the slight sweetness of the potato'. Boniato, the right variety of sweet potato for this soup, has pink or brownish skin and white flesh. The soup will be a golden-yellow colour.

SERVES 6

450 g/1 lb boniatos (sweet potatoes)
50 g/2 oz butter
1 medium onion, finely chopped

4 medium tomatoes, peeled, cored and chopped
900 ml/1½ pts beef stock
salt and pepper

Peel the sweet potatoes, slice thickly, cover with cold salted water and bring to the boil. Simmer, covered, for about 20 minutes. Drain and chop coarsely.

Heat the butter and sauté the onion until soft. Squash in the tomatoes, stir around and cook for 5 minutes. Tip the sweet potatoes, the tomato mixture and about 275 ml/½ pt of the stock into a blender or food processor, and reduce to a smooth purée. Pour into a pan with the rest of the stock. Re-heat, season and serve.

∽ TURNIP SOUP WITH CARDAMOM AND TURNIP ∽ GREENS

Use very young turnips for this recipe, or, better still, the French variety called *navet* that is white, tinged with a purple edge. This lovely, surprising soup was served to me at my agent's house, cooked by his friend Belinda Timbers; I pinched the turnip green idea from the enterprising *Greens Cook Book*.

SERVES 6–8

900 g/2 lb young turnips or navets
75 g/3 oz butter
2 medium onions, sliced
2–3 cloves of garlic, peeled and squashed
salt and pepper

2.5 cm/1 in root ginger, peeled and chopped
peel of ½ a lemon, sliced
4–6 cardamom pods
1.1 litres/2 pts light chicken stock

Peel the turnips thinly (don't bother if using *navets*), roughly chop them and reserve their greens. Heat 50 g/2 oz of the butter and gently sauté the onion and garlic with a generous pinch of salt. Add the ginger, lemon peel, whole cardamom pods and turnips. Give everything a good stir, cover, and leave to sweat for 10 minutes. Pour on the stock, bring to the boil, turn down the heat and simmer gently until the turnips are soft. Fish out the cardamom pods and purée. Return to a clean pan, re-heat and adjust the seasoning.

Meanwhile, melt the remains of the butter and sauté the turnip greens for a few minutes on each side. Shred with a sharp knife and stir into the soup just before serving. Alternatively, shred the greens before cooking and sauté at a high temperature to cook to a crisp.

∾ YELLOW PEPPER SOUP ∾

SERVES 4

4 large yellow peppers
25 g/1 oz butter
1 medium onion, finely
  chopped
1 leek, white part only, sliced

1 small potato, peeled, diced
  and rinsed
1.1 litres/2 pts chicken stock
salt and pepper

Pre-heat the grill. Lay out the peppers, a few inches from the heat, and grill them, turning them frequently until their skin is blackened and blistered all over. Pop them into a plastic carrier bag, seal the opening, and leave to sweat for about 20 minutes. This makes them easier to peel; merely rinse away the flaky skin under running water. Pull away the cores and seeds. Chop the flesh into chunks and transfer to a food processor or blender.

Meanwhile, heat the butter and soften the onion, leeks and potatoes. Add to the pepper flesh with about 275 ml/½ pt of chicken stock, and purée. Push through a fine sieve, to catch any scraps of skin, into a clean pan, and add the rest of the stock. Stir while you bring the soup up to a simmer, then lower the heat and cook, covered, for about 10 minutes. Taste and season with salt and pepper.

Serve this as a double soup with red pepper soup (see page 000), though it is delicate and delicious on its own, simply garnished with coriander or chives.

∾ CREAM OF TOMATO SOUP ∾

Two pounds of sun-ripened tomatoes stewed and puréed with a litre of good vegetable or light chicken stock, then finished with a little cream and seasoning, will produce an exquisite cream of tomato soup for 4. If the tomatoes are grilled first the flavour will be smoky; if they are sautéed in butter or oil, the flavour will be richer, and if they are added to a *mirepoix* of celery, carrot and onion or leek, the taste will be fortified. Light cooking gives a fresher taste, and lengthy stewing (and consequent reduction) intensifies the flavour. Garlic, thyme, basil, parsley, chives, dill and coriander all complement tomato soups, as do lemon and orange juice and zest, ginger and cumin.

This is my basic recipe but it varies depending on the quality of tomatoes; removing the skins before cooking is a matter of preference – they will be caught, along with the pips and cores, in the sieve.

SERVES 4

25 g/1 oz butter
3 shallots, or 4 spring onions,
  finely chopped
1 clove of garlic, smashed and
  peeled
700 g/1½ lb ripe tomatoes,
  skinned and roughly chopped
bouquet garni made from 4
  stalks of parsley, 1 branch of
  thyme, and ½ a bayleaf

salt and pepper
1.1 litres/2 pts light chicken
  stock
100 g/4 oz double cream
2 tomatoes, skinned, cored
  and flesh cut into dice
1 tbsp snipped chives

Heat the butter and soften the shallots or spring onions and garlic, but don't let them brown. Add the tomatoes, *bouquet garni*, a generous pinch of salt and a little pepper. Leave to simmer gently, stirring occasionally, until the tomatoes have turned to a mush and most of the liquid has evaporated. Add the stock, bring to the boil, partially cover the pan and simmer gently for 20 minutes. Fish out the *bouquet garni*. Purée, pass through a fine sieve (this is important to catch the pips, core and skin), and return to a clean pan. Re-heat, pour in the cream, simmer for a couple of minutes and adjust the seasoning with salt and pepper and, perhaps, a little sugar.

Serve with croûtons, a few raw tomato dice and chives. It is also delicious with shredded fresh basil leaves and a spoonful of *pesto* or *pistou* (see pages 73–4).

✎ INDIAN CREAM OF TOMATO SOUP ✎

I love the hot, sweet sour flavour of Madhur Jaffrey's recipe, discovered in one of my favourite cookbooks, *Eastern Vegetarian Cooking*. I leave out the butter and flour emulsion.

SERVES 4–6

700 g/1½ lb ripe tomatoes,
  chopped
1 tbsp chopped lemon grass
1 or 2 curry leaves
5-cm/2-in piece of fresh
  ginger, peeled and chopped
1¼ tsp salt
110 ml/4 fl oz water
4 tbsp unsalted butter (optional)
2 tbsp white flour (optional)

110 ml/4 fl oz single cream
570 ml/1 pt milk
½ tsp ground roasted cumin
  seeds
⅛ tsp ground black pepper
⅛ tsp cayenne pepper
2 tsp lime or lemon juice
1 tbsp chopped coriander
  leaves

Put the tomatoes, lemon grass, curry leaves, ginger, salt and the water in a pan and bring to the boil. Lower the heat, cover, and simmer gently for 15 minutes. Uncover, increase the heat and simmer more aggressively for 15 minutes. Purée and sieve; you should end up with about 400 ml/¾ pt of thick tomato juice.

Meanwhile, if including the flour and butter liaison, heat the butter, stir in the flour and cook on a low heat for a couple of minutes. Pour in the hot tomato juice, stirring all the time. If not, proceed directly to adding the cream, milk, cumin seed, black pepper, cayenne pepper and lime or lemon juice. Stir thoroughly and re-heat without boiling. Serve garnished with the freshly chopped coriander.

BISQUES

A bisque is a thick soup or purée made with shellfish and a highly seasoned *court-bouillon*. Most often, though, it refers to a shellfish soup thickened and/or flavoured with its own shell. Shrimps and prawns, in particular, have a great deal of flavour in their shells. There is also carotenoid pigment in the shell and it is this, combined with browned vegetables, that gives a bisque its characteristic burnt umber colour. Careful sieving is vital for a successful bisque; for crab, lobster and other harder-shelled shellfish, a heavy metal conical sieve (chinoise) and a tapered wooden pestle, to pound the meat and shell through, are vital.

See also 'Cream Soups with Seafood' (pages 194–203) and 'Quick Soups' (pages 164–170).

✑ CLAM BISQUE ✑

SERVES 4–6

36 clams, scrubbed and washed in several changes of water	1.1 litres/2 pts fish stock
	salt and pepper
1 onion, sliced	1 tbsp flour
1 carrot, peeled and diced	1 tbsp butter
1 bayleaf	150 ml/¼ pt double cream
2 sprigs parsley	150 ml/¼ pt Madeira

Put the washed clams in a casserole with the onion, carrot, bayleaf, parsley and stock. Half-cover the pan and simmer very slowly for 1 hour. Strain, return to a clean pan and season with salt and pepper. Work the flour into the butter and whisk a little at a time into the simmering soup. Stir in the cream and cook on for 5 minutes. Add the Madeira, bring back to a simmer and serve.

↶ CRAB BISQUE ↷

These days Richard Shepherd is rarely to be found behind the range at Langan's Brasserie but his bisque lives on.

SERVES 4

100 g/4 oz each of onion, leek, celery and carrot, cut into small dice
50 g/2 oz butter
450–700 g/1–1½ lb crab (with 'fingers' removed and shell and claws broken into smaller pieces)
bouquet garni made with bayleaf, thyme, parsley stalks and peppercorns

50 g/2 oz tomato purée
4 tbsp Cognac
4 tbsp dry white wine
570 ml/1 pt white stock
570 ml/1 pt fish stock
50 g/2 oz rice
salt and pepper
50 g/2 oz double cream

Sweat the vegetables in the butter with the crab pieces until the vegetables are tender. Add the *bouquet garni*, tomato purée, Cognac, wine and stock. Then add the rice and simmer for 45 minutes.

Strain off the liquid and discard the large, tough piece of crab shell, but pulverize the remainder into a paste. Pass the crab paste through a sieve to remove any sharp pieces of shell, then add the liquid. Return the soup to the heat and bring to the boil again. Check the seasoning and consistency, which should be fairly thick. If it is too thin, add *beurre manié* (1 dsp each of flour and butter mashed together, whisked into the soup, a little at a time). Serve with a swirl of cream.

↶ LOBSTER BISQUE ↷

SERVES 6–8

1 small boiled lobster
110 g/4 oz butter
1 large carrot, diced
1 medium onion, chopped
bouquet garni made with parsley, thyme and a bayleaf
50–110 g/2–4 oz rice
150 ml/¼ pt white wine

1.75 litres/3 pts fish or chicken stock, or half and half
salt and pepper
cayenne pepper
110 g/4 oz double cream
1 glass of brandy

Remove the cooked lobster meat from the shell and set aside. Put the shell in a carrier bag, or between sheets of newspaper, and smash it with a wooden rolling-pin. Heat half the butter, and sauté the vegetables, stirring around until they brown and begin to soften. Add the *bouquet garni*, rice (how much will depend on whether you are eking out the lobster), the lobster shell, wine and stock. Bring to the boil and simmer for 20 minutes until the rice is cooked.

Remove the big pieces of shell and the *bouquet garni* from the pan. Put the rest of the butter, any coral from the lobster, the lobster meat (reserving one chunk for garnishing) and the contents of the saucepan into a liquidizer, or through a mouli. Strain carefully into a clean pan. Re-heat, and correct the seasoning with salt, pepper and cayenne. Slice the reserved lobster meat, stir it into the soup with the cream and brandy, heat through and serve very hot.

✍ LOBSTER BISQUE (ECONOMICAL) ✍

A perfectly acceptable bisque can be made from the lobster debris and shell. It seems appropriate to use Lillian Beckwith's recipe from *Hebridean Cookbook*; after all, the Scots produce marvellous lobsters, and we're a canny lot. Alternatively, follow the preceding recipe omitting the lobster meat.

SERVES 6

1 or 2 lobster shells	25 g/1 oz butter
1.1 litres/2 pts water	25 g/1 oz flour
salt and pepper	150 ml/¼ pt single cream
a pinch of sweet basil	

'Pound the lobster shell into small pieces and put into the cold water along with the salt and pepper and sweet basil. Bring to the boil and simmer for 1½–2 hours. Sieve the liquid carefully so that no pieces of shell remain. Meanwhile melt the butter in a saucepan. Stir in the flour until it begins to froth. Add the lobster stock slowly, stirring continuously. Cook for 10 minutes. Remove from the heat and stir in the fresh cream.'

✍ SHRIMP BISQUE (LAZY METHOD) ✍

SERVES 6

1 litre/1¾ pts uncooked shrimps	2 cloves of garlic, peeled and crushed
310 g/11 oz potatoes, peeled, diced and rinsed	1 litre/1¾ pts milk, chicken or beef stock
200 g/7 oz tomatoes, blanched, peeled and chopped	salt and pepper

Simmer everything, uncovered, for 60 minutes. Liquidize thoroughly, then pass through a fine sieve. Re-heat, thinning with more liquid if necessary, adjust the seasoning, and serve with croûtons and a sprinkling of parsley.

∽ SHRIMP BISQUE (ZEALOT'S METHOD) ∽

This is a superlative version from Alice Waters of Chez Panisse, San Francisco.

SERVES 4

2 tbsp unsalted butter
40 g/1½ oz each of onion,
  carrot, celery and fennel, cut
  into small dice
1 large clove of garlic, sliced
50 g/2 oz red bell pepper,
  diced
1 bayleaf

75 g/3 oz diced tomato
350 g/12 oz shrimps
50 ml/2 fl oz water
1.1 litres/2 pts fish stock
110 g/4 oz soft white
  breadcrumbs
⅛ tsp salt
⅛ tsp ground cayenne

In a large pan brown half the butter and sauté the vegetables, garlic, red pepper and bayleaf, stirring occasionally, for 10 minutes, until lightly browned. Add the tomato and reduce the heat to very low.

In a sauté pan brown the rest of the butter. Add the shrimps (in their shells) and sauté over a high heat, turning often, for about 4–5 minutes, or until the shells are browned all over and encrusted with bits of butter. Transfer the shrimps to the bowl of a food processor. Deglaze the sauté pan with the water and add it to the vegetables. Process the shrimps to a coarse paste and add the paste to the vegetables. Add the fish stock, bring to a simmer, and cook for 10 minutes.

Pour the soup through the mouli, or process again, then sieve, pushing through as much of the shrimp and vegetables as possible; the harder you work at this the better the texture and flavour of the finished soup will be. Re-heat the broth very gently, stirring in the breadcrumbs. Leave for 10 minutes while you wash out the food mill and fit it with the medium blade. Pass the bisque through the food mill. Taste, and adjust the seasoning with salt and cayenne. Re-heat and serve.

Stews, Gumbos, Chowders, Minestrones and Potages

ᗡ

> 'Minestrone, that hefty, rough-and-ready, but nutritionally sound traditional midday soup of northern Italian agricultural and manual workers, features frequently in such publications. Often the readers are told that it can be made with some such ingredients as a bouillon cube, a tin of chicken noodle soup, and a few frozen French beans ... Knowledge in the case in point helps one to discriminate in the matter of deciding what is or is not an acceptable substitute or alternative in a recipe.' (Elizabeth David, *Italian Food*, introduction to the US edition, 1963)

This is the group of soups that most of us make most of the time; the bits-and-pieces soups that don't have an exact recipe but depend on using up and padding out. These are the minestrones (*minestre*) of Italy, the *potage*, and the *potée* or 'peasant soups' of France, the chowders of America and gumbos of Creole. What these soups lack in finesse they make up for in robusticity. These are the soups that simmer away on the back burner for hours. They are rough-and-ready stews made with easily digestible and nutritiously sound ingredients that will fill you up and build you up. They are seasonal soups that rely on good, fresh produce eked out with pulses, dried beans and pasta and stale bread. Sometimes they turn into an everlasting soup, to be topped up and totally changed over a number of days. Some such soups are lip-smackingly good but impossible to reconstruct exactly the same, and others need plenty of help from embellishment and garnish to make them edible.

Some of the best combinations, like the French staple *potage bonne femme*, a water-based stew of leek, potato and sometimes carrot, are so good that they have become a national institution. Others – minestrone is a classic example – have been universally adopted and diluted almost out of recognition from their origins.

This, then, is a collection of the best. See also 'Quick Soups' (pages 136–78), 'Thick Soups' (pages 179–242) 'Whole Meal Soups' (pages 283–308).

243

∾ ASHE TORSH ∾

Ashe is the Persian name for soup, and this is a splendid version combining meatballs, dried fruit, chickpeas and rice, seasoned with cinnamon and dried mint.

SERVES 6

50 g/2 oz rice
2.3 litres/4 pts water
3 tsp salt
2 tbsp butter
1 small onion, finely chopped
110 g/4 oz dried prunes
4 tbsp parsley, finely chopped
50 g/2 oz walnuts, chopped
110 g/4 oz dried apricots
50 g/2 oz ready cooked
  chickpeas (canned will do)
100 ml/4 fl oz mild vinegar

40 g/2½ oz sugar
1 tbsp dried mint
¼ tsp cinnamon
¼ tsp pepper

For the meatballs
225 g/8 oz minced beef
1 small onion, chopped
¼ tsp cinnamon
¼ tsp pepper
¼ tsp salt

Begin with the meatballs. Pound the beef to a pulp and mix with the grated onion and seasonings. Form into balls the size of small walnuts and set aside. Cook the rice in the water with 1 tsp of salt for 15 minutes.

Meanwhile heat the butter and sauté the onions until they change colour but are not burnt. Add the prunes to the water and rice, and cook for a further 15 minutes. Then add the parsley, chopped walnuts and meatballs and simmer gently for 20 minutes. Add the apricots, chickpeas, vinegar and sugar and simmer on for a further 15 minutes. At the end of cooking, rub the dried mint between the palms of your hands to make it powdery and stir it, the cinnamon, 1 tsp of salt, and the pepper into the soup. Taste: you may need to add some or all of the last tsp of salt.

∾ AQUACOTTA ∾

Tomato and bread soup is one of Tuscany's oldest. It evolved from a peasant broth, usually made with garlic, stale bread, and onion, and is now most often made with tomatoes and celery and served with a poached egg. Other variations include added mushroom, red peppers, and spicy grilled sausage, and leeks in place of onion with a seasoning of red chilli pepper. Some people fry the bread in olive oil first. In Portugal this soup is called *sopa de tomate e cebola*; the Parmesan is omitted and the finished soup is served garnished with parsley, and the butter-fried croûtes are served separately.

SERVES 4

4 tbsp olive oil
2–3 large onions, finely
  chopped
5 sticks of celery with leaves,
  finely chopped
1 red pepper, cored and diced
700 g/1½ lb ripe tomatoes

salt and pepper
1 litre/1¾ pts boiling water
8 slices country-style stale
  bread, dried out in the oven
4 eggs
Parmesan

Heat the oil in a large pan and gently sauté the onion until it begins to flop and change colour. Stir in the celery, pepper and tomatoes, season well with salt and pepper and cook for 20 minutes. Pour on the boiling water, stir, and leave to simmer for 30 minutes. Line the base of a fireproof serving dish with the bread. Pour on the soup and carefully break the 4 eggs, evenly spaced, into the soup. The soup is ready when the eggs have set. Serve with freshly grated Parmesan.

SHIN OF BEEF SOUP WITH POTATO-HORSERADISH DUMPLINGS

SERVES 6

50 g/2 oz oil
50 g/2 oz butter
450 g/1 lb shin of beef, finely
  sliced
1.75 litres/3 pts beef stock
  (see page 32)
450 g/1 lb carrots, cut into
  chunks

450 g/1 lb leeks, sliced
salt and pepper
potato-horseradish dumplings
  (see page 80)
110 g/4 oz broad beans,
  shelled, blanched and peeled

Heat the oil and butter and quickly sauté the beef until all sides have changed colour. Drain on absorbent paper and simmer very gently with the beef stock for 40 minutes. Add the carrots and leeks and cook for a further 20 minutes until everything is tender. Adjust the seasoning.

Have ready the poached potato-horseradish dumplings and the broad beans. Add both to the pot. Serve with a pot of English mustard and a bottle of Worcestershire sauce on the table for people to help themselves. This is a refinement and variation on the British stalwart boiled beef with onions, devised by the caterer Lorna Wing.

∽ BORSCHT ∽

Originally from the Ukraine, borscht has become the most popular soup in Russia. There are many different versions, always with beetroot and finished with soured cream, but proportions of beetroot and other ingredients vary enormously. Light, summer versions can be made with water, while a mushroom borscht is based on a dried mushroom stock (see page 18). This is a traditional beef broth borscht.

SERVES 6

50 g/2 oz butter
350 g/12 oz beetroot, peeled and diced
1 carrot, peeled and diced
1 medium onion, peeled and sliced into fine rings
2 tomatoes, peeled and chopped
1 tbsp wine vinegar
1 tbsp sugar
2 litres/3½ pts beef stock (see page 32)

½ medium cabbage, chopped
salt
2 medium potatoes, peeled and diced
6 cloves of garlic, crushed
½ tsp black pepper
1 medium beetroot, unpeeled
150 ml/5 fl oz soured cream
1 tbsp fresh dill

Melt the butter and stew the beetroot and carrot, stirring everything around to get it evenly coated with butter. Add the onion, tomatoes, vinegar and sugar and moisten with a little of the meat stock. Simmer gently for 15 minutes. Add the cabbage, cover, and cook on for a further 20 minutes. Pour on the rest of the stock, give it a good stir and add ½ tsp of salt. Add the potatoes, garlic and pepper and bring back to a simmer, cooking on until the potatoes are tender.

Ten minutes before the end of cooking, peel and grate the remaining beetroot. Mix it and its juices into the soup; this will freshen up the colour and flavour. Leave to stand for 10 minutes before serving with a dollop of sour cream, a sprinkling of dill and buttered black bread.

∽ SOUPE AUX BROUTES ∽

A version of *potage bonne femme* with spring cabbage shoots and lots of garlic. Simple, cheap, delicious and a joy to behold. This is Pierre Koffmann's version, from his delightful book *Memories of Gascony*, and *not* on the menu at his two-Michelin-starred restaurant, La Tante Claire, in London.

To turn this into a complete meal, serve with *mique* or *le farci* (see page 87), a breadcrumb and herb patty which cooks in the soup, doubles in size and is served in thick slices. The soup is then called *soupe aux miques et aux choux*.

SERVES 6–8

1 kg/2¼ lb young spring cabbage shoots or leaves
2 litres/3½ pts light chicken stock or water
salt and pepper
700 g/1½ lb potatoes, peeled and cut into chunks
200 g/7 oz carrots, cut in thick slices

6 leeks, thickly sliced
5 cloves of garlic, sliced lengthways
bouquet garni made with thyme, celery, bayleaf and parsley

Cut out the central core and stems of the cabbage leaves, slice into thick ribbons, and blanch in the boiling stock or water for 2 minutes. Lift out with a slotted spoon.

Season the stock with salt and pepper and simmer all the other ingredients (*not* the cabbage) for approx. 60 minutes until the potatoes are on the point of collapse. Add the cabbage 10 minutes before the end of cooking. Adjust seasoning.

✍ GREEN BEAN SOUP WITH MINT ✍

SERVES 6

3 tbsp olive oil
2 medium onions, peeled and chopped
1 large clove of garlic, minced
2 medium waxy-variety potatoes, peeled, chopped and rinsed
1.1 litres/2 pts chicken stock

275 ml/½ pt water
450 g/1 lb young green stick beans, trimmed into 1-cm/½-in pieces
½ tsp salt
pepper
2 tbsp mint, chopped

Heat the oil and stir-fry the onions and garlic for about 5 minutes until limp. Add the potatoes, continue stirring, and cook for a further 4 or 5 minutes until the potatoes take on a little colour. Pour on the stock, bring to the boil, then turn down low, cover and simmer for 40 minutes by which time the potatoes will be on the point of collapse.

Meanwhile salt the water and cook the beans until very tender. Drain the liquid into the soup, keeping back the beans. Give the soup a quick whizz in the processor or blender, or push through a mouli. Return to a clean pan, add the beans, taste and adjust the seasoning with salt and pepper. Stir in the mint.

∽ EGG BOUILLABAISSE WITH PEAS ∽

SERVES 6–8

6 tbsp olive oil
2 leeks, or 6 spring onions
  and 1 small onion, sliced
2 large ripe tomatoes, peeled,
  cored and chopped
6 new potatoes, scraped and
  sliced
5 cloves of garlic, peeled,
  halved and crushed
1 sprig of fennel

5 cm/2 in dried orange peel
a pinch of saffron strands
2 litres/3½ pts boiling water
450 g/1 lb shelled peas
salt and pepper
1 egg per person
1 tbsp parsley, chopped
6 slices oven-dried French
  bread

For maximum ease of cooking and serving you need a large, low ovenproof dish for bouillabaisse. Heat the oil and lightly sauté the leeks or onion and spring onion. Add the tomatoes, potatoes, garlic, fennel, orange peel and saffron, stirring everything together thoroughly. Turn up the heat as high as possible and add the boiling water, the peas, ½ tsp salt and several grinds of black pepper. Boil hard for about 10 minutes, or until the potatoes are almost cooked. Turn down the heat and poach the eggs in the soup (you may find it easier to poach the eggs separately, slipping them into the tureen or individual bowls at the last moment). Sprinkle lavishly with chopped parsley. The soup is served over a slice or 2 of oven-dried bread.

∽ RED CABBAGE SOUP WITH GARLIC AND ∽ ROSEMARY OIL

SERVES 8–10

4 tbsp olive oil
1 medium onion, chopped
1 small clove of garlic,
  chopped
25 g/1 oz thinly shredded
  pancetta (Italian streaky
  bacon)
450 g/1 lb red cabbage,
  coarsely shredded
1 large stick of celery, chopped
110 g/¼ lb pork rind,
  blanched for 60 seconds and
  sliced into thin strips
3 tinned plum tomatoes,
  drained, cored and chopped

1 sprig of thyme
1.75 litres/3 pts beef stock
salt and pepper
225 g/8 oz luganega or
  another pure pork sausage
approx. 450 g/1 lb canned or
  150 g/5 oz soaked and
  cooked cannellini or other
  white beans, drained

For the flavoured oil
3 medium cloves of garlic,
  crushed
4 tbsp olive oil
½ tsp rosemary leaves,
  chopped

Heat the olive oil and sauté the onion, garlic and *pancetta* until the vegetables start to colour. Add the shredded cabbage, celery, pork rind, tomatoes and thyme. Stir everything around thoroughly and leave to sweat, giving the odd stir, until the cabbage is tender. Add the stock, 2 tsp of salt and ¼ tsp of black pepper, cover the pan, and cook over the lowest possible heat for 2 hours. Remove the pan from the heat and skim away as much of the fat that will have settled on the surface as possible.

Meanwhile, cook the sausage in a small non-stick pan, taking care to brown all sides, and transfer to the pot. Purée half the cooked beans into the soup and simmer for 15 minutes before adding the other half. Taste the soup and adjust the seasoning, and if it seems too stew-like, add more stock or water.

To make the flavoured oil, put the crushed garlic cloves and the oil in a small pan and stir-fry over a medium heat until the garlic is golden. Add the chopped rosemary, turn off the heat, and stir. Pour the oil through a sieve into the soup pot. Simmer for 15 minutes. Serve with good crusty bread.

This is an adaptation of Marcella Hazan's *zuppa di cavolo nero*, from her *Classic Italian Cookbook*.

✑ CALDO VERDE ✑

This, Portugal's national dish, is a thick cabbage soup made with a kale-like cabbage called *couve gallego*. The closest equivalent we have is kale, but collards, turnip greens or Savoy cabbage will do. In the markets of Portugal you see the women stacking the leaves and rolling them into fat cigars, then shaving them into the finest shreds with razor-sharp knives. *Caldo verde* originated in Minho province but is now everywhere, regardless of season or temperature. To be truly authentic it should contain a slice of *chouriço* (a garlicky sausage). This recipe comes from Jean Anderson's definitive book *The Food of Portugal*.

SERVES 8

4 tbsp olive oil
1 large onion, finely chopped
or minced
1 large clove of garlic, finely
minced
6 large potatoes, peeled and
chopped
2.3 l/4 pts cold water
175 g/6 oz spicy dried pork
sausage, thinly sliced

2½ tsp salt
¼ tsp freshly ground black
pepper
450 g/1 lb kale, collards or
the most fibrous cabbage
available

Heat 2 tbsp of the oil and sauté the onion and garlic for a couple of minutes, until they begin to colour. Add the potatoes and stir-fry for 2–3 minutes. Pour on the water and boil until the potatoes are mushy. Meanwhile, in a different pan, fry the sausage over a low heat in 1 tbsp of oil until most of the fat has run out, and drain.

When the potatoes are soft, remove the pan from the stove and, using a potato masher, mash the potatoes right into the soup mixture. Add the sausage, salt and pepper, cover, and return to the heat for 5 minutes.

Wash the greens, trimmed of coarse stems, slice them filament thin, and add to the soup with the last tablespoon of olive oil. Cover and cook to your preferred doneness. Check the seasoning and ladle into large soup dishes. Serve with the Portuguese cornbread called *broa* (see page 116).

∽ CHAO THIT BO ∽

A favourite Vietnamese soup that is an exquisite marriage of textures, flavours, and visual interest. My recipe is adapted from *The Foods of Vietnam* by Nicole Routhier.

SERVES 4–6

225 g/8 oz ground lean beef
1 small onion, minced
4 tbsp nuoc nam
  (Vietnamese fish sauce) or
  the Thai equivalent, nam pla
black pepper
15 g/½ oz cellophane noodles
2 tbsp vegetable oil
1 tsp grated fresh ginger
75 g/3 oz uncooked long-
  grain rice

1.5 litres/2¾ pts water
1 tbsp sugar
1½ tsp salt
2 large cloves of garlic,
  minced
1 tbsp lemon grass bulb,
  minced
2 spring onions, finely sliced
1 tbsp coriander, shredded
2 tbsp roasted peanuts (not
  salted variety), crushed

Begin by marinating the beef, onion, 1 tbsp of *nuoc nam* and a little black pepper in a soup tureen. Mix thoroughly, cover with clingfilm, and refrigerate. Soak the noodles in warm water for 20 minutes, then drain, chop into 5-cm/2-in lengths and set aside.

Heat 1 tbsp of the oil in a large pan and stir-fry the ginger and rice for about 60 seconds or until the rice begins to turn milky white. Add the water and bring to the boil. Reduce the heat and simmer, partially covered, for about 20 minutes, or until the rice is very tender. Stir in the remaining *nuoc nam*, the sugar and the salt.

Heat the remaining 1 tbsp of oil in a small pan and stir-fry the garlic and lemon grass for about 60 seconds until they are aromatic and golden. Stir this into the soup, add the cellophane noodles and bring to the boil. Stir again and pour over the meat, breaking it up as you do so with a fork.

Sprinkle the spring onions, coriander, a few grinds of black pepper and the ground peanuts over the soup before serving.

∽ CHICKEN SOUP WITH MATZAH BALLS ∽

'Chicken soup, prepared and eaten on Shabbat and holidays, was made by cooking all of the chicken parts and innards, excluding the head and lungs, in a pot of water, with onions, carrots and salt. The feet of the chicken were added to the soup to give it a rich flavour. When cooked in water, the skin of the feet came off, settled on the bottom of the pot, and gave the soup a nice colour and rich flavour. If an extra piece of meat or chicken were available, it would be added to the soup. Often the skin from the neck of the bird was filled with fat, flour, raw chopped potatoes, cooked potatoes, or cooked grains. Each end was sewn together and the neck was cooked in the soup. The heart was also added to the soup. In the summer, various fresh vegetables, such as parsley root or parsley leaf, might be added. Some women added millet or other grains, or even something special, such as farfl, lokshn, or cooked rice. If extra ingredients were added to the basic soup, they would be added from the onset of the cooking.' (Amy Snyder, Columbia University Master's thesis on the cooking of a Jewish lady from Lagev, Poland)

SERVES 6

1 small boiling chicken or 1 chicken quarter plus a chicken carcass (all uncooked)
2.3 litres/4 pts beef stock
2 carrots, grated or chopped
2 medium onions, chopped

2 stalks of celery, sliced
2 sprigs of parsley
salt and pepper
50 g/2 oz vermicelli (lokshn)
matzah/matzo balls (see page 82)

Put the chicken and bones in a pan with the beef broth. Bring to the boil, cook for 10 minutes, skim and lower the heat. Add the carrots, onions, celery, parsley and salt and pepper. Simmer slowly, covered, for 50 minutes. Strain, strip the meat from the chicken quarter, or the equivalent from the boiler, and return to the soup. Add the vermicelli and cook for 10 minutes. Poach the matzah balls in the soup and serve.

∽ CHICKEN GALANGAL HOPKINSON ∽

Simon Hopkinson, the chef of Bibendum, is crazy about Thai food. This is his definitive recipe.

SERVES 6

For the stock
900 g/1½ pts water
2 chicken legs with thigh
1 stick of lemon grass, coarsely chopped
2 lime leaves, torn
2.5 cm/1 in galangal, unpeeled and chopped
4 cloves of garlic, unpeeled and crushed
6–8 Thai shallots (deep pink) or ordinary shallots
stalks from 1 bunch of coriander
1 tbsp nam pla (Thai fish sauce)
2 small fresh serrano chillis, chopped
1 tom yam stock-cube, from Oriental food stores (perks up the soup)

For the soup
1 large tin thick coconut milk
bulb and bottom 2.5 cm/1 in of a stick of lemon grass
1 cm/½ in galangal, peeled and finely diced
2 lime leaves, cut in thin strips
leaves from 1 bunch of coriander
10 mint leaves, chopped
2 spring onions, finely sliced
1 tbsp nam pla
juice of 1 lime
1 tsp sugar
2 small serrano chillis, de-seeded and chopped
150 ml/¼ pt double cream

Put all the stock ingredients in a pan, bring to the boil, skim, and simmer, half covered, for 60 minutes. Remove the chicken legs from the pan and leave to cool.

Strain the stock through a sieve into another pan. Add the coconut milk and all the other soup ingredients except the cream. Bring to the boil, then turn down the heat and simmer gently for 5 minutes. Meanwhile skin the chicken legs and dice the flesh coarsely. Add to soup with the cream, re-heat, and serve.

∽ CHICKEN AND ANDOUILLE GUMBO ∽

Andouille, its New Orleans name, is a highly seasoned sausage made of ground lean pork and beef. It originates from Poland and can be bought here as *kielbasa*. To make this into a complete meal, add cooked rice.

SERVES 6–8

1 small chicken, cut into
  pieces
	110 g/4 oz each of onion, red
	  onion, spring onion and green

1 tsp minced garlic	bell peppers, finely chopped
½ tsp salt	75 g/3 oz celery, finely chopped
½ tsp cayenne pepper	2 litres/3½ pts chicken stock
½ tsp Tabasco	225 g/½ lb highly-seasoned
2–3 tbsp flour	pork and beef sausage (Polish
2–3 tbsp vegetable oil	kielbasa)

Marinate the chicken pieces for 60 minutes in a mixture made with the garlic, salt, cayenne and Tabasco. Dredge the chicken pieces with 1–2 tbsp of flour and sauté the pieces in the hot oil for about 10 minutes, stirring in the marinade juice. Put the chicken aside, add a little more oil to the pan, and stir in the vegetables. Stir-fry for 10 minutes and sift in 1 tbsp of flour. Keep on stirring, letting the flour darken, and mix in a little stock to make a smooth, thick vegetable stew. Slowly incorporate the rest of the stock and add the sausage. Simmer gently, stirring frequently, for 45 minutes.

Meanwhile cut the chicken into small dice and return to the soup. Taste and adjust the seasoning if necessary.

∽ CANJA ∽

A Portuguese chicken, mint, and lemon soup with seed-shaped pasta that looks like rice.

SERVES 6

1 whole chicken breast (225–310 g/½–¾ lb)	40 g/1½ oz mint, chopped
	40 g/1½ oz risi, seme di

1 medium onion, cut in thin
  wedges
	melone *or* semi di peperone
	  or other pastina, cooked as

4 sprigs of parsley	per packet instructions
4 strips lemon zest,	salt
5 cm × 1 cm/2 in × ½ in	⅛ tsp white pepper
2.3 litres/4 pts rich chicken	1 lemon, edges serrated and
stock	cut into 6 slices
1 tbsp lemon juice	6 sprigs of mint

Simmer the chicken breast with the onion, parsley, and lemon zest in the chicken stock over a low heat for about 40 minutes. Remove the chicken breast and cool. Strain the broth, return to a clean pan, and boil uncovered for 8–10 minutes to reduce it slightly. Meanwhile skin and bone the chicken breast, cut the meat into large juliennes, and add to the broth along with the lemon juice, chopped mint and pastina. Season to taste with salt and add the pepper. Heat through for a couple of minutes. Ladle into soup-bowls and float on each portion a slice of lemon topped with a sprig of mint.

∽ CHORBA WITH HARISSA ∽

This is the Yugoslav version of a beef or lamb stew/soup that features throughout the Middle East. It is a lighter version of *harira*, the food eaten at sundown each day during the fasting month of Ramadan, and is eaten all the year round. Vegetables are puréed or left as a slop, and the usual mix of tomatoes, peppers, celery, onion and aromatics is sometimes enriched with chickpeas and/or lentils and vermicelli, but then it becomes *harira*. *Harissa*, a chilli-hot cocktail, is cooked in the soup and can be served as a supplement at the table so people can adjust their own heat threshold. The vinegar and egg liaison adds an intriguing sour flavour.

SERVES 6

900 g/2 lb lamb shoulder or fillet, cut in small pieces
1.2 litres/2 pts water
1 bayleaf
3 stalks of parsley
celery leaves from a head of celery, chopped
1 medium onion, chopped
1 tomato, skinned and chopped
1 small chilli pepper, de-seeded and finely chopped

1 green pepper, cut in chunks
2 tsp sea salt
25 g/1 oz butter
1 tbsp flour
½ tsp paprika
3 tbsp white wine vinegar
2 eggs, beaten
150 ml/¼ pt sour cream
2 tbsp chopped coriander
lemon wedges

Cover the meat with the water and bring to the boil. Skim away the white foam, adding a little more cold water, skim again. Add the bayleaf, parsley, celery leaves, onion, tomato, chilli, green pepper and salt. Bring back to the boil, lower the heat, and simmer gently for 1½ hours. Fish out the pieces of meat and set aside. Discard the bayleaf. Using a perforated spoon, lift the vegetables out of the soup and purée. Strain the soup liquid through a sieve into a bowl. Melt the butter in a pan that can hold the finished soup. Stir in the flour and paprika and cook for 60 seconds, then the puréed vegetables, stirring until everything is merged. Slowly add the soup liquid to the pan, stirring to avoid any lumps, and simmer for 4 or 5 minutes. Add the meat and continue cooking while you make the liaison. Beat the vinegar into the eggs and stir in a ladleful of the hot soup. Pour this back into the soup, stirring, but taking care that the soup doesn't boil. Turn off the heat, add the sour cream, stir, leave to settle for a minute then serve garnished with coriander and lemon wedges.

∽ CONGEE ∽

Congee is the Chinese equivalent of chicken noodle soup. The skill is to let the rice cook very slowly so that the starch is released gradually, thickening the soup yet without the grains disintegrating. The 'porridge' is made with water or stock, and flavoured with duck or chicken, pork, Chinese sausages, meat or fishballs, preserved vegetables, or beancurd. Coriander, spring onions and flat-leaf parsley are sometimes used as a garnish. It is a great beginning to a *dim sum* meal and is far more delicious than sounds possible.

SERVES 6

2.3 litres/4 pts boiling water	bones, lower legs, wings and
3 pieces dried scallops or	neck of one roast duck or
Chinese mushrooms (from	225 g/8 oz pork loin, finely
Chinese foodstore)	chopped
1 small piece dried tangerine	1 small piece root ginger,
skin (gwaw pay)	peeled and grated
165 g/6 oz short-grain rice	6 Chinese shallots or spring
2 tbsp sesame oil	onions
1 dsp salt	3 tbsp coriander, chopped

Bring the water to the boil with the dried scallops or mushrooms and the tangerine peel. Wash the rice, drain and stir-fry in the hot oil with the salt. When the rice begins to turn milky-looking add the boiling water and the duck debris. Bring back to the boil then turn down low, cover, and simmer very gently for 30 minutes.

Stir the soup and add the ginger, reheat and simmer for 1½–2 hours. Taste for salt, fish out the bones and return to the pan any scraps of meat you can strip from them. Sprinkle the surface with chopped spring onions and coriander and serve.

✍ FASOULADA ✍

Fasoulada or fassolada, is a simple Greek bean and vegetable soup that varies from house to house.

SERVES 6

*450 g/1 lb dried white beans,
soaked overnight*
2.3 litres/4 pts water
*2 large tomatoes, peeled and
chopped*
1 large onion or leek, chopped
*1–2 carrots, peeled and
chopped*
*2 potatoes, peeled and
chopped*

*3 sticks of celery with leaves,
chopped*
*2 cloves of garlic, peeled and
split*
4–5 tbsp olive oil
salt and pepper
2 tbsp flat-leaf parsley
black olives

Drain and rinse the beans. Cover with the water, bring to the boil and skim away the froth that rises. Simmer, covered, for 30 minutes. Add the tomatoes, onion, carrots, potatoes, celery, garlic and olive oil and continue to simmer for 1½–2 hours, or until the beans are quite tender. If necessary top up with more water so that all the ingredients are submerged. Season to taste with salt and pepper. Stir in the parsley and a few black olives, and simmer for a few more minutes before serving with Greek bread, more olives, sliced celery, radishes, cucumber and lemon wedges.

✍ GWAYTIO WITH CHILLI-VINEGAR SAUCE ✍

A typical Thai noodle soup.

SERVES 6–8

*1 tbsp dried red chilli flakes,
or 2 small red chillis,
de-seeded and finely chopped*
2 tbsp white vinegar
2 tbsp peanut oil
*225 g/8 oz lean beef, cut in
1-cm/½-in strips*
5 cloves of garlic, chopped
110 g/¼ lb minced beef
*2 sticks of celery, obliquely
sliced into 2.5-cm/1-in
pieces*
2 spring onions, finely sliced

*1.75 litres/3 pts beef stock
(see page 32)*
1 tsp black pepper
½ tsp ground cinnamon
*3 tbsp nam pla (Thai fish
sauce)*
*350 g/¾ lb wet noodle sheets
(gwaytio), cut into strips*
*150 g/5 oz beansprouts,
blanched in boiling water for
60 seconds*
*1 tbsp coriander leaves,
chopped*

Mix the chilli flakes into the vinegar in a small serving bowl, and set aside.

Heat the oil and quickly stir-fry the beef slices, browning all over. Remove and set aside. Stir the garlic into the pan and cook until golden before adding the minced beef, celery and onions. Stir-fry until the beef has changed colour. Pour in the stock and season with the pepper, cinnamon and fish sauce. Bring up to the boil, simmer a couple of minutes, taste and if necessary adjust the seasoning. Add the noodles and bring back to the boil. Add the beansprouts and serve topping each serving with beef strips and coriander leaves. Accompany with the chilli vinegar for those who like it hot.

⌘ GARBURE ⌘

This is one of those catch-all terms that refers to French meal-in-a-pot stew-soups. Another is *potée*, a rustic soup that evolves out of whatever is in season and to hand, but often involves pork. *Garbure* tends to mean a special *potée*, often made with cabbage and preserved goose, and is traditional in the Landes, Béarn and the Pyrenees. This is Richard Olney's recipe from *Simple French Food*. In Béarn, the soup would be made in a *toupin*, a squat earthenware casserole that narrows at the top.

SERVES 4

1 small, green, crinkly-leaved cabbage
3 tbsp goose fat
2 carrots, diced
2 turnips or navets, diced
1 large onion, halved and finely sliced
1 large leek, white part finely sliced crosswise
bouquet garni made with a celery branch, leek greens, a bayleaf, parsley and 4 sprigs of thyme

salt and cayenne
2.3 litres/4 pts water
450 g/1 lb fresh or 225 g/ ½lb cooked dried white beans
350 g/12 oz potato, peeled and cubed
350 g/12 oz pumpkin, seeded, peeled and cubed
1–2 pieces preserved goose (1 per person if serving as a complete meal)
slices of stale country bread

Quarter, core, de-rib and shred the cabbage coarsely. Par-boil for 10 minutes in boiling salted water, then drain well, pressing gently.

Heat the goose fat and gently stew the carrots, turnips, onion, and leek, stirring regularly, adding the drained cabbage after 15 minutes. Cook on for another 10 minutes, and add the *bouquet garni*, ½ tsp of salt and a pinch of cayenne. Pour on the boiling water, stir in the beans, potatoes, and pumpkin and cook, uncovered, at a slow simmer for about 40 minutes. Stir occasionally to check that nothing is sticking and top up with water if you think it necessary.

Submerge the pieces of goose in the soup and cook for another 30 minutes. If you are serving the meat as a separate course, remove them from the pot. Otherwise strip the meat from the bone and keep warm or return to the pot. Line individual dishes with dried bread and ladle over the soup, giving each serving some goose.

∽ LAMB AND BARLEY BROTH WITH BREAD DUMPLINGS ∽

SERVES 6

450 g/1 lb scrag end of neck of mutton or lamb, sliced
2 onions, sliced
2 leeks, sliced
4 carrots, diced
1 small turnip or swede, neatly diced
1 small stick of celery, chopped

110 g/4 oz pearl barley
1.75 litres/3 pts lamb stock (see page 37)
salt and pepper
bread dumplings (see page 78)
2 tbsp parsley

Put the meat, onion, half the leeks, the carrots, turnip or swede, celery and pearl barley, in a pan with the stock. Bring to the boil, turn down the heat and simmer gently for 1 hour. Taste and adjust the seasoning with salt and pepper and perhaps a pinch of sugar. Add the rest of the leeks and the dumplings. Serve garnished with parsley and chunks of well buttered brown bread.

∽ HUNGARIAN TARRAGON LAMB SOUP WITH PARSLEY DUMPLINGS ∽

SERVES 4

225 g/8 oz lean lamb, cubed
150 g/5 oz mixed chopped onion, celery and carrot
1.4 litres/2½ pts rich lamb stock (see page 37)
25 g/1 oz flour
25 g/1 oz butter
1 tbsp lemon juice
150 ml/¼ pt double cream

1 tbsp tarragon vinegar
2 tbsp tarragon leaves
a pinch of sugar
parsley dumplings (see page 79)
salt and pepper
50 ml/2 fl oz sour cream
1 egg-yolk
paprika

Cover the lamb and mixed vegetables with the stock. Bring to the boil and simmer until the meat is half cooked. Rub the flour into the butter and whisk small pieces into the soup to thicken it. Add the lemon juice, double cream, tarragon vinegar, tarragon leaves and a pinch of sugar. Simmer for 10 minutes before adding some tiny parsley dumplings. Simmer for a further 10 minutes, taste and adjust the seasoning. Just before serving mix the sour cream into the egg-yolk, add a ladleful of hot soup and pour back into the soup. Heat through but take care not to let it boil. Serve with a dusting of paprika.

ᵔ CHINESE LEEK AND NOODLE SOUP ᵔ

This is a typical Chinese noodle soup. Similar versions can be made with spinach, any of the Chinese cabbages, cucumber, cress, celery, beans, lettuce, mushrooms, and tofu. (For Thai *gwaytio*, Vietnamese *pho* and Japanese *udon* noodle soups, see pages 256, 266, 88.)

SERVES 6

1 tbsp cooking oil
1 clove of garlic, crushed
15 g/½ oz dried mushrooms, soaked in warm water for 30 minutes
350 g/12 oz leeks or Chinese spring onions, trimmed, finely sliced and carefully washed

225 g/8 oz carrot, sliced
1.75 litres/3 pts vegetable, light chicken or pork and chicken stock (see page 23)
1 tbsp soy sauce
110 g/4 oz vermicelli-type noodles
2 tbsp fresh coriander

Heat the oil and stir-fry the garlic and mushrooms for 60 seconds. Add the leeks and carrot, and stir-fry for 2 more minutes. Pour on the stock and soy sauce and bring to the boil. Turn down the heat, add the noodles and simmer for 10 minutes. Taste for seasoning and serve sprinkled with fresh coriander.

ᵔ POTAGE ESAU ᵔ

My favourite lentil stew-soup.

SERVES 4

2 tbsp olive oil
4 slices smoked streaky bacon, chopped
2 onions, diced
2 carrots, chopped
2 cloves of garlic, chopped
1 leek, chopped

2 tbsp parsley, chopped
1 bayleaf
salt and pepper
225 g/8 oz green lentils
glass of dry white wine
1.4 litres/2½ pts ham or gammon stock

Heat the oil and stir-fry the bacon, adding the onions, carrots, garlic, leek, 1 tbsp of parsley and the bayleaf. Stir everything around, season with pepper and a little salt and add the lentils. Cover, and sweat, stirring a couple of times, for 10 minutes. Pour in the glass of wine and allow it to bubble up before you add the stock. Simmer until the vegetables are tender. Purée a quarter of the soup (remove the bayleaf), return to the pan and re-heat. Check the seasoning and stir in the last of the parsley. Serve with a wedge of lemon and a swirl of your best olive oil.

∽ LONDON PARTICULAR ∽

' "This is a London particular . . . A fog, miss," said the young gentleman.' (Charles Dickens, *Bleak House*). Subsequently a dense London fog became known as a 'pea-souper'.

SERVES 6–8

50 g/2 oz butter	2.4 litres/4 pts cold water
3 rashers smoked streaky bacon, chopped	1 ham knuckle or 2 pig's trotters
1 large onion, sliced	salt and pepper
450 g/1 lb split green peas, soaked overnight	2 tbsp Worcestershire sauce

Melt the butter and gently sauté the bacon. Stir in the onion and sweat together for 5 minutes. Add the drained, soaked peas and stir well to coat in the fat. Pour on the water, add the ham knuckle or pig's trotters, season with pepper and bring to the boil. Skim, cover, and simmer for about 2 hours or until the peas are mushy.

Remove the ham knuckle or pig's trotters and purée the soup. Pick out any meat from the bones and return to the soup. Adjust the seasoning with Worcestershire sauce and serve.

∽ LOCRO ∽

In Ecuador, where this soup comes from, they use annatto to give the distinctive piney, peppery flavour and deep orange-yellow colour of this delicious soup. Paprika is the closest equivalent. It is a lovely slop of a soup, heaven for potato fans.

SERVES 6–8

50 g/2 oz butter	275 ml/½ pt milk
1 rounded tsp ground annatto	150 ml /¼ pt single cream
1 medium onion, finely sliced	225 g/8 oz Cheddar, grated
1.1 litres/2 pts water	salt and pepper
1.8 kg/4 lb potatoes, peeled, sliced and rinsed	2–3 avocados, peeled and sliced

Use a large, heavy-bottomed pan that can hold all the ingredients. Melt the butter and stir-fry the annatto for a few seconds. Add the onion and sauté gently until it begins to flop. Pour on the water and bring to the boil. Add the potatoes, bring back to the boil then turn down to simmer very slowly. Stir occasionally but leave until the potatoes are cooked but still holding their shape. Stir in the milk and cream and cook on until the potatoes begin to disintegrate. Stir in the cheese, season with salt and pepper to taste, and serve immediately with freshly cut slices of avocado separately.

✑ *MINESTRONE* ✑

The variations are limitations. According to season, almost any vegetable can be added to minestrone – peas, beans, spinach, leeks, small courgettes – and rice can be substituted for the pasta. Minestrone is often served lukewarm, turned into a complete meal with smoked Milan sausages (*minestrone alla milanese*), and leftovers form the basis for another famous Italian soup, *ribollita*. Serve with *pesto* (see page 74) and you have *minestrone alla genovese*. This is Elizabeth David's recipe.

SERVES 6

110 g/4 oz dried haricot
 beans
2 carrots, peeled and diced
2 small potatoes, peeled, diced
 and rinsed
1 small turnip, diced
1 stick of celery, chopped
½ a small cabbage, cored and
 shredded
2 onions, finely chopped
olive oil
2 cloves of garlic, chopped
2 rashers of bacon, chopped

2 tbsp herbs, made up of one
 or a mixture of marjoram,
 thyme, basil, etc.
4 tomatoes, peeled and
 chopped
1 small glass of red wine
50 g/2 oz broken-up macaroni
 or spaghetti or small pasta
 shapes
1.75 litres/3 pts hot water
2 tbsp Parmesan
salt and pepper

'Put the haricot beans to soak overnight. Next day prepare all the vegetables, and melt the sliced onions in the oil, adding 2 cloves of garlic, the bacon cut into pieces, and plenty of herbs, and the chopped tomatoes. Pour in the red wine, let it bubble a minute or two, then add the drained haricot beans; cover them with 1.75 litres/3 pints of hot water and let them boil steadily for 2 hours. Now put in the carrots and about 15 minutes later the turnip and potatoes. Ten minutes before serving, add the celery, the cabbage cut into strips, and the pasta. See that the soup is properly seasoned, stir in 2 tbsp of grated Parmesan, and serve more Parmesan separately.' (Elizabeth David, *Italian Food*)

∽ MINESTRONE VERDE ∽

SERVES 6

50 g/2 oz dried haricot beans
a few bacon rinds
2 cloves of garlic, crushed
salt and pepper
2 tbsp olive oil
2 leeks, sliced into thin rounds
2 large tomatoes, chopped
4 tbsp parsley, chopped
2 tbsp chives, snipped
10 leaves of basil, or other
fresh herb, shredded

225 g/8 oz stick beans,
chopped into 1-cm/½-in
lengths
1 medium potato, peeled, diced
and rinsed
1.75 litres/3 pts hot water
50 g/2 oz noodles, broken up
into small lengths
Parmesan

Soak the haricot beans overnight. Next day generously cover them with water and bring them to the boil with the bacon rinds and 1 garlic clove. Boil for 2½ hours, topping up with water if necessary, adding salt at the end of cooking.

Heat the oil and stir in the leeks, tomatoes, the second crushed garlic clove, 2 tbsp parsley, 1 tbsp chives and half the basil. Season with salt and pepper and gently stew until the tomatoes are cooked down to a pulp. Add the stick beans and the potato. Cook for a few more minutes, then pour in the hot water. Bring quickly to the boil, boil fast for 10 minutes, then add the broken up noodles, the haricot beans and their liquor (but not the bacon rinds), and simmer for 10 more minutes.

Before serving stir in the remaining parsley and other fresh herbs. Serve Parmesan separately.

∽ MULLIGATAWNY ∽

This is a legacy from the British days of the Raj, a soup created 2 centuries ago by local cooks in the south of India for their English masters. What was a highly and delicately spiced broth has changed radically over the years. The version served in many Indian restaurants up and down Britain has earned mulligatawny a reputation as a dreary, greasy soup spiced up with curry powder and garnished with apple instead of mango. This is Julie Sahni's recipe from *Classic Indian Cooking*.

SERVES 6

450 g/1 lb mixed diced
vegetables (onions, carrots,
celery, parsnip and
mushrooms)

1.4 litres/2½ pts rich chicken
stock (see page 19)
1 tsp finely chopped garlic
1 sprig of coriander leaves

¼ tsp black pepper
2 tbsp ghee (clarified butter,
  see page 10) or light
  vegetable oil
1 medium-sized onion, finely
  chopped

4 tsp curry powder
3 tbsp plain flour (optional)
110 g/4 fl oz double cream
2 tbsp coriander leaves, finely
  minced

Put the mixed diced vegetables in a pan with the stock, garlic, sprig of coriander and black pepper. Bring to the boil, turn down the heat, cover and simmer for 45 minutes or until the vegetables are soft. Cool slightly and purée in batches, then pass through a fine sieve. Re-heat and simmer gently while you heat the ghee or oil and stir-fry the finely chopped onion for about 10 minutes, or until it turns golden brown. Stir in the curry powder, and the flour if using, and cook for 60 seconds without burning. Whisk this dry mixture into the soup and simmer until the soup is thickened. Stir in the cream and the minced coriander leaves, salt to taste, re-heat and serve.

⟡ SOUPE À L'OIGNON ⟡

Don't stint on the slow cooking of the onions in butter and/or olive oil. This, followed by a long, slow simmering for their flavours to merge with the stock, is what gives this soup its rich sweet savour.

SERVES 6–8
1 tbsp olive oil
40 g/1½ oz butter
700 g/1½ lb onions, thinly
  sliced
1 tsp salt
pepper
a generous pinch of sugar
40 g/1½ oz flour
150 ml/¼ pt dry white wine
  or dry white vermouth

2 litres/3½ pts boiling brown
  turkey, chicken, veal or beef
  stock, or stock and water
3 tbsp Cognac (or brandy)
rounds of hard-toasted French
  bread
110–225 g/¼–½ lb Swiss
  cheese or Parmesan, grated

Heat the oil and butter in a large, heavy-bottomed pan with a lid. Stir in the onions, cover, and sweat very gently, stirring every now and again, for 15 minutes. Uncover, turn up the heat, stir in the salt and a generous pinch of sugar (slight caramelization helps develop a good colour). Cook for 30–45 minutes, stirring regularly, until the onions are a deep golden colour but not burnt. Sprinkle on the flour and stir-fry for 3–4 minutes. Pour in the dry white wine or vermouth, stir thoroughly while it bubbles up, and slowly add the boiling stock, taking care to avoid lumps. Bring up to the boil then simmer, covered, for 30–40 minutes.

Just before serving, stir in the Cognac. Pour into a soup tureen and serve the croûtes and cheese separately.

✑ *SOUPE À L'OIGNON GRATINÉE* ✑

Follow the method for Soupe à l'Oignon, previous page, but make it either in an ovenproof casserole or decant into individual ovenproof dishes. *For 6–8 servings*, slice 50 g/2 oz of Gruyère or Emmenthal into wafer-thin slivers and stir into the finished soup with 1 tbsp of grated raw onion. Float 12–16 slices of hard-toasted French bread on top of the soup and cover with 110–175 g/4–6 oz of grated Swiss or a mixture of Swiss and Parmesan cheese. Bake for 20 minutes in the oven and finish under a hot grill to brown the top lightly.

✑ *SOUPE À L'OIGNON AVEC SOUFFLÉ* ✑

Follow method for Soupe à l'Oignon on page 263. Pour the finished soup into individual oven proof bowls, leaving a 5-cm/2-in gap at the top of the bowl. *For 6 servings*, make a soufflé mix with 2 egg-yolks, 225 ml/8 fl oz of thick béchamel sauce, 2–3 tbsp of grated Gruyère cheese and 3 stiffly whisked egg-whites. Cover the hot soup with slices of well-dried toast as in the main recipe. Sprinkle this 'platform' with a little grated cheese, spoon the prepared soufflé mixture on top, and bake immediately at 400° F/200° C/Gas Mark 6 for 8–10 minutes until the soufflé is risen and golden.

✑ *GRATINÉE NORMANDE* ✑

Cider gives the classic French bistro soup a mellower flavour *and* makes it more digestible. This recipe is also very good made with double the quantity of onions, a beef broth and red wine. Thick croûtes are rubbed with garlic and arranged in layers with the onions, topped with broth and finished with Parmesan. The whole lot is baked for 60 minutes and served with additional onion broth.

SERVES 8

75 g/3 oz butter	4 tsp flour
700 g/1½ lb onions, ideally purple Breton variety	1.4 litres/2½ pts chicken stock
bouquet garni *made with 3 sprigs of parsley, ½ a bayleaf and 1 sprig of thyme*	salt and pepper
	150 ml/¼ pt double cream
570 ml/1 pt medium sweet cider	16 slices dry-toasted French bread
	50 g/2 oz Gruyère, grated

Melt 50 g/2 oz of the butter and stir in the onions. Sweat, covered, over a very low heat until limp. Add the *bouquet garni*, pour on 400 ml/¾ pt of the cider and simmer, uncovered, for 10 minutes. In a separate small pan melt the remaining 25 g/1 oz of butter, stir in the flour to make a smooth roux and incorporate a little of the chicken stock. Cook gently for 5 minutes and pour into the onions. Stir in the rest of the stock, bring up to the boil, turn down the heat and simmer for 15 minutes. Season to taste with salt and pepper.

Pre-heat the grill. Divide the remaining cider between 6 serving bowls, pour in the soup, add a slosh of cream and top with the toasted bread. Sprinkle over some grated Gruyère, and place under the hot grill until the cheese is melted and golden.

∽ PASTA E FAGIOLI ∽

A thick peasant soup made with fresh or dried beans and one or several different miniature pasta shapes, stewed in a beef broth thick with tomatoes, a little *pancetta*, and served with Parmesan. A Neapolitan variation omits the onion, is cooked in water not stock, and substitutes 100 ml/4 fl oz of olive oil for the butter and bacon.

SERVES 4–6

40 g/1½ oz pork fat
50 g/2 oz pancetta or
  streaky bacon, chopped
1 small onion, chopped
1 clove of garlic, chopped
1 stick of celery, chopped
175 g/6 oz dried beans,
  soaked overnight
2 litres/3½ pts beef stock (see
  page 32)

450 g/1 lb ripe (or tinned)
  tomatoes, peeled, cored and
  chopped
salt and pepper
110 g/4 oz short pasta or
  small pasta shapes
3 tbsp parsley, chopped
Parmesan

Heat the fat and sauté the *pancetta* or bacon until it begins to colour. Stir in the onion, garlic and celery and cook for a couple of minutes. Add the soaked and drained beans and the stock. Simmer, covered, for 1 hour. Add the tomatoes, ¼ tsp of salt and several grinds from the peppermill. Simmer, covered, until the beans are tender. Depending on the age and quality of the beans, this could take up to 3 hours. As beans absorb an enormous amount of liquid in their cooking you may need to top up with stock or water.

Scoop out some of the beans and purée them. Return to the pot and add the pasta and half the parsley. Boil hard, uncovered, until the pasta is cooked – because of reduction, you may prefer to wholly or partly cook the pasta before adding it to the soup. Check the seasoning, stir in the rest of the parsley, and leave to stand for 5 minutes before serving. Provide Parmesan for people to help themselves.

∽ JAMAICAN PEPPERPOT SOUP WITH MATZO ∽
DUMPLINGS

A highly spiced West Indian hot-pot made with flesh, fish or fowl, but most often with crab, and sometimes salt-fish, tripe or beef. Callaloo, the spinach-like leaves of the root vegetable dasheen, can be replaced by chard, Indian kale or spinach.

SERVES 6–8

225 g/½ lb shin of beef
225 g/½ lb pig's tail or salt
  beef
2.8 litres/5 pts water
225 g/½ lb callaloo, finely
  chopped
12 okra pods
225 g/½ lb yam, peeled and
  sliced

225 g/½ lb coco or pumpkin,
  peeled and sliced
1 chilli pepper, de-seeded and
  sliced
700 ml/1¼ pts coconut milk
2 spring onions, crushed
matzo dumplings (see page
  82)
salt and pepper

Put the beef and the pig's tail or salt beef in a pan with the water and callaloo and simmer, uncovered, for about 2 hours or until the meat is tender. Add all the other ingredients and simmer for about 30 minutes more until everything is tender and the soup is thick. Add the dumplings 15 minutes before the end of cooking.

∽ PHO ∽

Pho is the Vietnamese word for soup but is also a collective term for substantial noodle-based soups. This is a typical recipe. The chicken (and stock) could be replaced by any meat.

SERVES 4–6

50 g/2 oz rice noodles
small piece of ginger root
1 clove of garlic, crushed
4 spring onions, chopped
3 tbsp nuoc nam
  (Vietnamese fish sauce), or
  nam pla, the Thai
  equivalent
1 stalk lemon grass, chopped
1.75 litres/3 pts light chicken
  stock

110 g/4 oz raw chicken,
  sliced into strips
1 red chilli pepper, finely
  sliced
50 g/2 oz beansprouts,
  blanched in boiling water
25 g/1 oz ginkgo nuts,
  crushed
2 tbsp fresh coriander,
  chopped
1 lime

Cook the noodles in boiling salted water for 4 minutes. Strain and set aside. Sauté the ginger on a low heat for 15 minutes, cool and slice. Add the ginger, garlic, spring onions, *nuoc nam* and lemon grass to the stock and simmer for 45 minutes. Strain. Add the chicken pieces to the strained stock and simmer for 10 minutes.

Re-heat the noodles by covering with boiling water. Drain and divide between the soup-bowls. Pour over the soup and garnish each bowl with some of the sliced chilli, beansprouts, nuts, coriander and a wedge of lime. Serve more *nuoc nam* separately for those who like it.

⁓ Soupe au Pistou ⁓

The French equivalent of a mixture of *minestrone alla genovese* and the Neapolitan *pasta e fagioli*, a stew of diced vegetables and white haricot beans seasoned with an aromatic paste made by pounding basil, garlic and Parmesan with olive oil.

SERVES 6–8

110 g/4 oz flageolet or haricot beans, pre-soaked and part-cooked for 60 minutes in unsalted water

110 g/4 oz shell pasta

110 g/4 oz carrots, scraped and diced

110 g/4 oz celeriac or celery, diced

110 g/4 oz leeks, white part only, or spring onions, chopped

75–100 g/3–4 oz potatoes, peeled, diced and rinsed

2 tomatoes, peeled and chopped

75–110 g/3–4 oz young turnips, peeled and diced

3 sprigs of basil, chopped

pistou *(see page 73)*

approx. 2.1 litres/3¾ pts boiling water

salt and pepper

Put all the ingredients except the pasta and *pistou* in a large pan and cover generously with boiling water. Simmer for 30 minutes, then add the pasta. Cook until the pasta is tender but retains a slight bite. Adjust the seasoning.

Serve the *pistou* separately, for people to stir a dollop into their soup or mix it into the soup before serving, and provide some Parmesan or Gruyère.

⁓ La Potée ⁓

A simple rustic soup, and the traditional daily food of the peasants of eastern France, made with fresh vegetables and home-cured bacon. Quantities are flexible, but the vegetables should be in approximately equal quantities, cut into similar-sized pieces, and added to the pan in order of cooking time. To turn the *potée* into a main meal, double the quantity of meat, perhaps adding 450 g/1 lb of boiling sausage. Also see Garbure (page 257).

SERVES 6–8

450-g/1-lb piece of bacon, trimmed of fat
2.3 litres/4 pts water
12 small potatoes, peeled, chopped and rinsed
6 small onions, chopped
12 small carrots, scraped and chopped
6 small French turnips (navets), chopped

450 g/1 lb peas
450 g/1 lb French stick beans, chopped, or shelled broad beans
heart of 1 young cabbage, cut in strips
pepper

Cover the piece of bacon with the water and bring to the boil. Skim and leave to simmer, half covered, for 30 minutes. Add the potatoes, onions, carrots and turnips, cover, and simmer for 30 minutes. Add the peas and the stick beans or broad beans, and cook for a further 20 minutes. Taste and adjust the seasoning with pepper; you may not need salt. 5 minutes before serving add the cabbage. Fish out the bacon, cut it into small pieces, return to the pan and serve.

∽ RIBOLLITA ∽

Ribollita is an Italian word meaning to re-heat. In Tuscany *ribollita* is the name of a soup made with the remains of the day's minestrone re-heated with cabbage, served on bread and garnished with olive oil. If you start from scratch, make the minestrone 24 hours in advance. In Tuscany they use a purplish cabbage called *cavolo nero*; chard is the best substitute.

Another way of reviving leftover minestrone is to mix it with an equal quantity of water (450 ml/¾ pt for 4 servings) and boil it with 100 g/3½ oz of Arborio (risotto) rice. Simmer, covered, for 10 minutes. Check for salt and ladle into soup-bowls. Stir in Parmesan (35g/1 oz in total) and 2 shredded basil leaves per bowl. Leave to cool and serve at room temperature.

SERVES 6

minestrone (see page 261)

24 hours later
450 g/1 lb chard or green cabbage

6–8 slices stale rustic bread
olive oil, the best possible

Cook the chard or green cabbage in boiling salted water. Drain and chop coarsely. Have ready 6 warmed soup-plates, each lined with a thick slice of bread, and pile in the cooked cabbage. Ladle the reheated minestrone over the bread. Serve the olive oil separately for people to pour over their soup.

SEAFOOD STEWS AND FISHERMEN'S SOUPS

'Surely it is curious that this island, with its vast fishing industry, has never evolved a national fish soup?' (Elizabeth David, *Italian Food*, introduction to the US edition, 1963)

Most coastal nations have a tradition of regional seafood soups and stews cooked at sea, by the fishermen, in one pot.

Chowder, the American name for a rough-and-ready soupy stew, usually containing seafood and potatoes, is thought to be an anglicization of the French word *chaudière*. This is the old name for the iron cauldron (*chaudron*) used by Breton fishermen off Newfoundland and Iceland to make their soup. In France such soups are often called *chaudrée*, but are most similar to the soups called *cotriade*; refined versions are *migourée*, from the French *mijoter*, to simmer. Like all the other soups in this grouping, recipes are flexible and more of 'a stated principle, not a detailed plan of construction', as Jane Grigson put it.

In the case of chowders, there is one qualification: New England-style chowders tend to be made with milk, New York-style chowders with tomatoes and water. All these soups could be classified as complete meal soups and their recipes can be adapted accordingly. Some, like bouillabaisse and *bourride*, two gargantuan fish soup/stews, are relegated to the 'Whole Meal Soups' section (see pages 302 and 304). Recipes for *kakavia*, the Greek equivalent of bouillabaisse, and *brodetto*, its Italian version, also appear in that section (see pages 308 and 304). See also 'Quick Soups' (pages 164–70) and 'Cream Soups' (pages 194–202).

࿓ MANHATTAN CLAM CHOWDER ࿓

'. . . clam,' Mrs Hussey hurried toward an open door leading to the kitchen, and bawling out 'clam for two.' 'Queequeg,' said I, 'do you think that we can make out a supper for us both on one clam?' However, a warm savoury steam from the kitchen served to belie the apparently cheerless prospect before us. It was made of small juicy

> clams, scarcely bigger than hazelnuts,
> mixed with pounded ship biscuits, and
> salted pork cut up into little flakes; the
> whole enriched with butter and plentifully
> seasoned with salt and pepper . . .' (Ishmael
> at Pots Inn, Nantucket, run by Mrs Hosea
> Hussey, in Herman Melville, *Moby Dick*)

In America Manhattan clam chowder will be made with giant, meaty quahog clams. These are rarely available from British fishmongers, so quantities are for small Venus, cherrystone or little neck clams. Clams can be replaced by cockles, mussels, oysters and chunks of fish.

To make a New England chowder, omit the tomatoes and use scalded milk rather than stock.

Lobster chowder is made by using the carapace, claws, etc. to make a stock and making a cream with butter, coral and a few crumbled water biscuits, which is used to thicken scalded milk flavoured with onion, mixed with the stock and the diced lobster meat.

SERVES 4–6

splash of cooking oil
110 g/4 oz streaky bacon,
  chopped
25 g/1 oz butter
1 large onion, chopped
2 sticks of celery, chopped
2 medium floury potatoes,
  chopped
2 leeks, sliced
400 g/14 oz can plum
  tomatoes

3 tbsp parsley, chopped
1 sprig of thyme
1 bayleaf
1.1 litres/2 pts fish stock
36 (at least) clams, scrubbed
  and rinsed under running
  water
1 glass dry white wine
  (optional)
salt and pepper

Heat a splash of oil and slowly sauté the bacon, increasing the heat as the fat begins to melt, and cook to a crisp. Put the bacon to one side. Add the butter and gently sweat the onion, celery and potatoes with a generous pinch of salt. When they are nicely softened, stir in the leeks, tomatoes, most of the parsley, the thyme and bayleaf. Pour on the stock and leave to simmer.

Meanwhile put the cleaned clams in a pan with the wine, or a little stock or water. Cover and cook fiercely until all the clams open (discard any that don't). Pick the clams out of their shells and put to one side; strain the cooking liquor carefully (it may contain sand) into the soup. Taste the soup, adjust the seasoning and stir the clams into the soup. Serve garnished with the last of the parsley and the crisp bacon pieces.

∽ CALLALOO ∽

Callaloo is the greenery of taro, dasheen and related plants. It is a key ingredient in this famous Caribbean soup, a rich stew of pork, crab, okra and chilli which is a speciality of Trinidad.

SERVES 6

110 g/4 oz bacon, salt pork or gammon, chopped	1.1 litres/2 pts chicken stock
1 onion, chopped	225 g/8 oz shelled crabmeat, flaked
3 spring onions, finely chopped	juice of 1 lime
1 small red chilli pepper	225 g/8 oz okra, trimmed and sliced
2 cloves of garlic, chopped	15 g/½ oz butter
450 g/1 lb callaloo leaves, shredded	salt and pepper

Simmer the bacon, onion, spring onions, chilli pepper, garlic and callaloo leaves in the stock until the meat is tender. Mix the crabmeat with the lime juice. Add the okra, and when that is almost cooked, add the crabmeat but keep back the juice. Simmer gently for 5 minutes, stir in the butter and the shellfish juice, and adjust the seasoning. Stir in the coconut milk, taking care to keep the soup at a light simmer.

Callaloo is often served with cooked plaintain pounded and rolled into balls, or with cornmeal spinners (dumplings made with 110 g/ 4 oz of cornmeal and of plain flour mixed with ½ tsp of salt and sufficient water to bind), which are poached in the soup just before serving.

∽ CLAM SOUP WITH SAUSAGE ∽

The Portuguese coupling of clam and sausage is given a spicy twist in this wonderful, gutsy soup, devised by Mark Miller of Coyote Café in San Diego.

SERVES 4–6

2 tbsp olive oil	225 g/8 oz chorizo or other hot sausage
½ a Spanish onion, chopped	
4 large cloves of garlic, sliced	570 ml/1 pt fish stock
450 g/1 lb plum tomatoes	20 small clams
1 large floury potato, peeled, diced and rinsed	¼ bunch of coriander, chopped
	4 lime wedges

Heat 1 tbsp of olive oil and sauté the onion and garlic in a covered pan for 15 minutes. Sear the tomatoes over a flame or under the grill, turning them frequently to char all the skin. Chop and add to the pan, and continue to cook slowly for a further 20 minutes.

Meanwhile, boil the potato in lightly salted water for 5 minutes. Rinse under cold water and set aside. Cut the *chorizo* into thick slices and sauté slowly in the rest of the oil, turning to make sure all surfaces are cooked; this will take about 20 minutes. Tip the sausage slices and the cooking oil into a dish, deglaze the pan with a little fish stock and add this to the sausage slices.

Add half the remains of the stock to the onion, garlic and tomato mixture and then add the clams. Cover and cook over a medium heat for 4 minutes. Add the *chorizo* and reserved juices, and the potato, and continue cooking until all the clams are open. Add the remaining stock, stir and serve garnished with coriander, with wedges of lime for squeezing into the soup.

✧ PARTON BREE ✧

'Parton' is Gaelic for crab, and 'bree' or 'brigh' means stock, juice or broth – in this case, soup. This is an update of a turn-of-the-century recipe from the *Cookery Book of Lady Clark of Tillypronie*.

SERVES 4

50 g/2 oz rice	570 ml/1 pt chicken, veal or
570 ml/1 pt milk	fish stock
1 large freshly boiled crab,	150 ml/5 fl oz single cream
yielding at least 175 g/6 oz	1 tbsp parsley, finely chopped
each of white and brown	a dash of anchovy essence
meat	salt and white pepper

Cook the rice in the milk until soft. Purée the rice and milk with the brown crabmeat, and tip into a pan with the stock. Stir gently while you bring up to a simmer, adding the white crabmeat broken into shreds and small chunks, reserving the claws. Stir in the cream, the claws and the parsley.

Taste, and season with the anchovy essence, salt and pepper. Serve with dainty slices of well-buttered brown bread.

✧ BRETON CONGER EEL SOUP ✧

SERVES 6

1½ tbsp cooking oil	400 g/14 oz can tomatoes
2 large leeks, sliced	bouquet garni
700 g/1½ lb conger eel,	700 g/1½ lb potatoes, peeled,
skinned and cut into thick	diced and rinsed
slices	salt and pepper
1.75 litres/3 pts water	1 tbsp parsley, chopped

Heat the oil and soften the leeks. Add the eel slices, turning them around to sear them on all sides. Pour on the water and bring up to the boil. Add the tomatoes, *bouquet garni* and potatoes. Bring back to the boil, turn down the heat, and simmer gently for about 45 minutes, skimming away any grey foam that forms.

Fish out the pieces of eel, remove the meat from its central bone and return to the soup. Remove the *bouquet garni*, adjust the seasoning and serve sprinkled with parsley.

❧ BRITTANY COTRIADE ❧

SERVES 6

25 g/1 oz butter	1.75 litres/3 pts water
1 onion, sliced	a generous handful of sorrel
900 g/2 lb potatoes, sliced	450 g/1 lb approx. garfish
bouquet garni	2 red mullet, filleted
salt and pepper	175 g/6 oz cod fillet

Heat the butter and soften the onion until it begins to colour. Stir in the potatoes and *bouquet garni*, season, and pour on the water. Bring to the boil and simmer until the potatoes are almost cooked. Add the sorrel, then the fish, cut in thick slices, and more water if necessary. Bring back to the boil, and simmer for about 10 minutes until the fish is cooked. Serve with crusty bread and plenty of butter.

❧ CALDILLO DE PERRO ❧

This is an Andalucian fishermen's stew. To be authentic it has to be made with small, just-caught hake (long, slim members of the cod family with sweet delicate flesh), and the juice of bitter Seville oranges. Traditionally 'dog soup' is served on an earthenware platter with sodden pieces of bread.

SERVES 4

450–700 g/1–1½ lb hake, cut in thick slices	200 ml/6 fl oz freshly squeezed bitter orange juice
2 tbsp olive oil	or sweet orange juice cut
4 cloves of garlic, crushed	with lemon juice
1 Spanish onion, sliced	salt and pepper
1.1 litres/2 pts boiling water	

Begin by salting the slices of hake; leave them for 60 minutes to stiffen (optional).

Meanwhile heat the oil and stir-fry the garlic until it begins to turn brown. Discard and stir in the onion. Before it gets a chance to brown, pour on the boiling water. Cover and simmer until the onion is quite soft. Turn up the heat and add the hake without allowing the pan to go off the boil. Cook thus for 15 minutes, then stir in the orange juice. Season. Serve with plenty of bread for mopping.

∽ PRAWN SOUP ∽

Soto udang is an elegant, fresh Thai prawn soup flavoured with root ginger and coriander. If possible use fresh prawns, shelled and deveined.

SERVES 4

1 tbsp cooking oil
2 cloves of garlic, crushed
2 shallots or small onions, finely sliced
1-cm/½-in piece of fresh ginger, peeled and finely chopped
175 g/6 oz prawns

900 ml/1½ pts light chicken stock
100 g/4 oz noodles (see pages 87–8)
1 small leek, thinly sliced
2 tbsp coriander, chopped
salt and pepper

Heat the oil and stir-fry the garlic, onions and ginger until softened. Add the prawns, stirring for a couple of minutes, then pour on the stock. Bring to the boil, then reduce the heat and simmer for 5 minutes. Add the noodles, stir well and simmer for 10 minutes. Stir in the leek and half the coriander, and cook for 2 minutes. Taste, adjust the seasoning, and serve garnished with the rest of the coriander.

∽ SHRIMP SOUP ∽

This is a Portuguese recipe, rich in flavours of onion, garlic and tomato stewed in olive oil (*sofrito*), sharpened with wine and cayenne pepper, and thick with fresh parsley and coriander. It is a fiddly business to peel 700 g/1½ lb of shrimps or prawns (either is suitable), but worth it for this recipe. In the restaurants of the seaside resorts west of Lisbon, where *sopa de camarão* is a speciality, it is eaten saturated with hunks of their dense bread called *broa* (see page 116).

A refined version of this soup is made by reducing the quantity of shrimps, and using only 1 bayleaf, which is removed before the whole soup is liquidized at high speed and then force-sieved. The soup is finished with the parsley, rather than cooked with it, the coriander is omitted, and it is warmed through with 100 ml/4 fl oz of double cream.

SERVES 6

700 g/1½ lb uncooked shrimps
   or prawns, in the shell
2 litres/3½ pts water
2 tbsp olive oil
3 medium onions, peeled and
   chopped
2 large cloves of garlic, peeled
   and minced
3 large ripe tomatoes,
   blanched, peeled, cored,
   de-seeded and chopped

3 tbsp parsley, finely chopped
2 bayleaves
50 ml/2 fl oz tomato paste
¼ tsp black pepper
½ tsp cayenne pepper
1 cup dry white wine (vinho
   verde, to be exact)
½ tsp salt
2 tbsp coriander, finely
   chopped

Cover the shrimps with the water and bring up to the boil. Drain at once, reserving the water. Heat the olive oil and sauté the onions and garlic until they begin to turn transparent. Stir in the tomatoes, parsley, bayleaves, tomato paste, black pepper and cayenne and simmer, covered, very gently for 25 minutes. Add the shrimp cooking water and the wine and simmer, covered, for 60 minutes, until the soup has reduced by about one-third.

Meanwhile, shell the shrimps and remove the black central vein. Add the shrimps and the salt to the pot, heat through and adjust the seasoning. Serve with a sprinkling of coriander and good crusty bread for dunking and mopping.

✎ SALT COD SOUP ✎

Francesco Zanchetta is the delightful young chef of Riva, a stunningly good Italian restaurant in leafy Barnes. This is his recipe. Don't be tempted to 'improve' the soup by using stock – that would make it too rich.

SERVES 6

200 g/7 oz salt cod, softened
   in water for 24 hours
1 tbsp olive oil
3 or 4 sticks of celery
½ clove of garlic
1 onion, sliced
6 plum tomatoes, chopped
1 potato, peeled, chopped and
   rinsed

2 glasses of dry white wine
4 bayleaves
10 leaves fresh basil (when
   available)
1 tbsp flat-leaf parsley
½ a clove or ¼ tsp ground
   cloves
1.4 litres/2½ pts water
salt and pepper

Begin this soup by cutting the salt cod into 5-cm/2-in squares. Heat the olive oil and fry the celery, garlic and onion until soft, then stir in the salt cod with the tomatoes and potato. When the salt cod has started to colour, splosh in the wine, bayleaves, half the basil (if using), half the parsley, and the cloves. Let everything bubble up, and mix in 275 ml/½ pt of the water. Bring up to the boil and stir in the rest of the water, then turn down the heat and simmer for 30 minutes. Taste for seasoning and serve garnished with the remaining basil (if using) and parsley.

If you like, you can keep back some big pieces of boiled salt cod, and add these just before serving.

∽ NORMAN CREAM OF FISH SOUP ∽

SERVES 4–6

275 ml/½ pt unshelled
  prawns or 1 small langouste
  tail
225 g/8 oz slice of cod or
  other white fish
1 carrot, peeled and chopped
1 onion, finely chopped
1 tomato, quartered
1 small stick of celery,
  chopped
1 clove of garlic, peeled and
  crushed

¼ of a fennel bulb
6 sprigs of parsley
2 sprigs of marjoram
1 small glass of cider
2 heaped dsp soft white
  breadcrumbs
1.1 litres/2 pts water
salt and pepper
nutmeg
150 ml/¼ pt double cream
1 tbsp parsley, chopped

Shell the prawns. Put the shells into a large pan with the white fish and its skin, the carrot, onion, tomato, celery, garlic, fennel, and sprigs of parsley and marjoram, and pour over the cider and the water. Season, bring to the boil, and simmer for 25 minutes. Strain the liquid into a clean pan, pushing the debris against the side of the sieve to get out every scrap of goodness.

Meanwhile, pound the prawns with the breadcrumbs and a little soup liquor to make a stiff paste. Beat the soup into the prawn paste and bring up to the boil, stirring as you do so. Simmer gently for 15 minutes, stirring frequently. Taste and adjust the seasoning with more salt and pepper, and nutmeg. Bring the cream to the boil and stir into the soup with half the parsley. Garnish with the rest of the parsley and serve with hot garlic bread.

∽ OKRA AND POMPANO SOUP ∽

This is a typical coastal dish from Cartagena in Colombia, and is an exotic, highly-spiced fish soup. Any firm-fleshed, non-oily white fish can be used in place of pompano – huss, cod or monkfish would be particularly suitable.

SERVES 6

1.8 litres/3¼ pts fish stock
2 medium onions, finely
  chopped
2 cloves of garlic, chopped
1 large tomato, blanched,
  peeled, cored and chopped
2 fresh chilli peppers,
  de-seeded and chopped
¼ tsp ground cumin
¼ tsp allspice
225 g/8 oz okra
4 tbsp lemon juice

450 g/1 lb small yams, peeled
  and cut into 2.5-cm/1-in
  dice
2 ripe plantains, peeled and
  sliced
25 g/1 oz butter
6 fillets of fish, cut into
  2.5-cm/1-in chunks
2 tbsp tomato paste
1 tbsp Worcestershire sauce
salt and pepper

Bring the fish stock to the boil with the onions, garlic, tomato, chilli peppers, cumin and allspice. Cover and simmer gently for 15 minutes. Plunge the okra and lemon juice in a saucepan of boiling salted water, bring back to the boil, then drain and rinse in cold water. Add the okra to the pan with the yams and plantains and cook, covered, over a very low heat for 60 minutes.

Meanwhile, heat the butter and fry the fish. Add the fish, with the tomato paste and Worcestershire sauce, to the soup. Simmer for 10 minutes, then taste and adjust the seasoning. Cook for a further 20 minutes and serve.

∾ SLICED FISH SOUP WITH SAFFRON ∾

Soupe à l'emincé de poisson, devised in the early eighties by three-Michelin-starred chef Guy Savoy at his eponymous Paris restaurant, is a refined fish stew finished in the oven.

SERVES 4

2 tbsp olive oil
1 carrot, finely diced
1 small onion, finely chopped
1 leek, white and tender green,
  finely chopped
1 ripe tomato, blanched,
  peeled, de-seeded and chopped
1.4 litres/2½ pts good fish
  stock
bouquet garni

1 clove of garlic, finely chopped
a pinch of saffron threads
50 ml/2 fl oz double cream
a pinch of dried thyme
salt and pepper
350 g/12 oz fish fillets
  (monkfish, red snapper and
  sole or whiting), cut into
  0.5-cm/¼-in strips
1 tbsp chervil leaves

Heat the oil and soften the carrot, onion and leek. Stir in the tomato and cook for another minute before adding the fish stock, *bouquet garni*, and garlic. Bring up to the boil, skim and stir in the saffron. Simmer gently for 40 minutes.

Meanwhile pre-heat the oven to 375° F/190° C/Gas Mark 5. Lay out 4 ovenproof soup-plates on a baking tray and bake until very hot.

Stir the cream and thyme into the soup, taste, and adjust the seasoning with salt and pepper. Ladle 225 ml/8 fl oz (about a cupful) of soup into each bowl and evenly distribute the sliced fish among the bowls. Return to the oven for 2 minutes. Top up with the rest of the soup, sprinkle on the chervil leaves and serve.

∽ SHCHI WITH SORREL AND SPINACH ∽

Shchi is a famous Russian soup usually made with fresh or salted cabbage. This version, from the terrific international recipe selection at the back of Alan Davidson's *North Atlantic Seafood*, uses sorrel and spinach instead.

SERVES 4

*275 g/10 oz sorrel, trimmed
  of stalks
275 g/10 oz spinach,
  trimmed of stalks
25 g/1 oz butter
1 onion, finely chopped
1 carrot, finely chopped
2 tbsp flour
900 ml/1½ pts hot water
bouquet garni with 1
  bayleaf*

*4 black peppercorns
salt and pepper
450 g/1 lb white fish, cut into
  bite-sized chunks
1 tbsp cooking oil
150 ml/¼ pt sour cream
2 hard-boiled eggs, chopped
2 spring onions, finely sliced*

Rinse the sorrel and spinach in cold water and sweat it, covered, until it flops and makes a purée. Heat the butter and soften the onion and carrot, then sift in half the flour, stirring around to take up the fat. Pour in a little of the water and stir to make a smooth paste, then add the rest with the spinach and sorrel purée, *bouquet garni*, peppercorns and a generous pinch of salt. Bring to the boil, turn down and simmer while you prepare the fish.

Turn the fish pieces in flour, salt and pepper and fry them in the hot oil. Divide them among 4 soup-bowls and pour over the soup, fishing out the *bouquet garni* and bayleaf first. Serve with a dollop of sour cream, the chopped hard-boiled egg and the chopped spring onion.

Rinse the fish and place the pieces in a pan with the water. Bring to the boil, remove any scum, add a pinch of salt and simmer for 3–4 minutes. Using a slotted spoon remove the fish and cover. Meanwhile, heat the butter and soften the onions. Add the tomato purée. Add the gherkins to the fish stock, then the onion mixture, capers, bayleaf and peppercorns. Bring to the boil and simmer gently for 10 minutes. Return the fish pieces and reheat, adjusting the seasoning if necessary.

To serve, place a portion of fish in each bowl with a couple of slices of lemon and some olives, pour over the soup, and sprinkle with chopped parsley.

∽ THAI FISH SOUP ∽

SERVES 4

1.1 litres/2 pts fish stock
2.5-cm/1-in piece of galangal,
  cut in quarters
2 stalks of lemon grass, sliced
  and smashed
3 kaffir lime leaves
4 spring onions, sliced
1 tsp ground chilli

3 tbsp lime juice
2 tsp nam pla or nuoc nam
  (Thai or Vietnamese fish
  sauce)
450 g/1 lb firm white fish
  fillets, cut into chunks
1 tbsp coriander, chopped

Bring the stock to the boil with the galangal, lemon grass and lime leaves. Simmer for 15 minutes and strain. Add the spring onions, ground chilli, lime juice and fish sauce, then the fish pieces. Simmer gently for 5 minutes and serve garnished with the coriander.

∽ ELIZABETH DAVID'S CUCUMBER FISH SOUP ∽

SERVES 3–4

50 ml/2 fl oz olive oil
1 small onion, sliced
3 cloves of garlic, chopped
2 tbsp parsley, chopped
½ a small cucumber, peeled
  and cut into small dice
225 g/8 oz tomatoes,
  blanched, peeled, cored and
  chopped
salt and black pepper

a pinch of cayenne pepper
a pinch of mace
1 glass of dry white wine
approx. 150 ml/¼ pt water
225 g/8 oz smoked cod fillet
225 g/8 oz halibut, cut into
  thick slices
2 fillets of lemon sole, cut into
  thick slices
50 g/2 oz shelled prawns

Heat the olive oil, melt the sliced onion, and then add the garlic, half the parsley, the cucumber and tomatoes. Season with salt, black pepper, cayenne and mace and give the stew a good stir. Add the white wine, let it bubble up, then add the water. Simmer gently for 20 minutes, thinning with more water if you feel it necessary.

Lay on the fish, starting with the cod, and 5 minutes later the halibut, then the lemon sole, adding the prawns only for 2 or 3 minutes at the end of cooking. Sprinkle on the rest of the parsley. Serve with thin slices of oven-dried French bread rubbed with garlic.

∽ CLAM AND OKRA CHOWDER ∽

SERVES 6

*50 g/2 oz salt pork or
unsmoked streaky bacon
1 large onion, chopped
2 red bell peppers, cored and
chopped
3 large tomatoes, cored, peeled
and chopped
225 g/8 oz okra*

*⅓ tsp curry powder
900 ml/1½ pts fish stock
1 tsp arrowroot, slaked in a
little cold water
salt and pepper
24 clams (at least),
thoroughly washed*

Gently sauté the salt pork or bacon, increasing the heat as its fat runs out, then add the onion. When lightly browned, add the peppers, tomatoes and okra. Sprinkle on the curry powder, stir it around, then add the stock. Simmer gently for 15 minutes, then stir in the arrowroot slaked in water. Cook for 5 minutes, then taste and adjust the seasoning.

Meanwhile, put the clams in a pan over a fierce heat, cover, shake the pan a couple of times, and cook until they are all open. Pick the clams out of their shells, leaving a few in situ for effect. Tip into the chowder with their liquor, heat through and serve.

Whole Meal Soups

*

'Now just such a mess of delicious hot pottage
Was smoking away when they entered the cottage
And causing a truly delicious perfume
Through the whole of an ugly old ill-fashioned room.
Poor Blogg when seeing the reeky
Repast placed before, scarce able to speak, he
In ecstasy muttered, "By Jove, Cockaleeky!"'
(Richard Harris Barham, British clergyman and poet,
1788–1845)

Many of the soups in other sections teeter on the brink between
being complete meals and fulfilling Brillat-Savarin's dictate, laid down
in *Physiologie du Goût* in 1825: 'The correct order of foods is starting
with the heaviest and ending with the lightest.' Those annotated
here, though, are the soups that provide a main meal as well as a
soup course. These might, like *pot-au-feu* and cock-a-leekie, be served
separately, while others, such as bouillabaisse and steamboat 'soups',
are soup and main course all in one.

See also 'Thick Soups' (pages 179–242) 'Soup Stews' (pages 243–
82) and 'Soups for Parties' (pages 354–62).

BEEF

* POT-AU-FEU *

'In France, the *pot-au-feu* is the symbol of
family life . . . A good *pot-au-feu* will always
be a comfortable and thoroughly bourgeois
dish which nothing may dethrone.' (Auguste Escoffier, 1845–1935)

There can never be too much *pot-au-feu*. Leftover broth provides the
basis for a fine consommé and is perfect stock. And the beef can be
eaten cold. In *French Provincial Cooking* Elizabeth David suggests *salade
parisienne*, a potato salad with a highly seasoned dressing with parsley
and shallots. The cold beef is also good hashed.

Adding cabbage is optional, and it should always be blanched first in boiling water before adding to the soup. In France the knuckle bone would be picked over and served as an appetizer with a vinaigrette.

SERVES 8–10

1.4 kg/3 lb rump steak, topside, silverside, neck or chuck
1 veal knuckle bone
700 ml/1¼ lb top ribs
450 g/1 lb chopped marrow bones
4.5 litres/8 pts water
4 medium carrots, peeled
1 medium onion, topped and tailed but skin intact, and stuck with 4 cloves
6 medium leeks, trimmed

bouquet garni made with 1 stick of celery, 1 clove of garlic, 1 bayleaf, 2 sprigs of thyme and several parsley stalks
25 g/1 oz salt
8 peppercorns
2 medium parsnips, peeled and halved lengthways
2 medium onions, peeled and quartered
½ small cabbage, boiled in water for 8–10 minutes

Put the beef, veal knuckle and bones in a huge pan and cover with the water. Bring slowly to the boil (this will take at least 60 minutes), and remove all the white scum that will form. Pour in a large cupful of water and skim again (see page 8). Partially cover the pan and simmer gently for 45 minutes. Add 1 carrot, the onion stuck with 4 cloves, 2 leeks cut in half, the bouquet garni, salt and peppercorns, and continue cooking for about 3 hours. Remove the meat to a plate while you fish out the vegetables and bouquet garni.

Strain the broth through a cloth-lined colander. Skim with several sheets of absorbent kitchen paper, one after the other, to remove any fat, and return the broth to a clean pan. Add the meat, the parsnips, 4 leeks cut into 5-cm/2-in lengths, 3 carrots chopped into thick slices and the 2 onions cut into quarters. Bring back to a simmer and cook for 20 minutes. Add the boiled cabbage, if using, 5 minutes before serving.

There is a choice of ways to serve the pot-au-feu.

Method 1: remove the meat and, using a very sharp knife, cut several slices. Lay these over a layer of croûtes (oven-dried French bread) and pour over the broth and vegetables. Serve accompanied by gherkins, vinegar pickles, mustard, coarse salt, a piquant sauce, or horseradish.

Method 2: serve the strained broth first with a few sliced vegetables, then follow with the carved meat, more vegetables and relishes.

✑ PETIT MARMITE ✑

This is exactly the same as *pot-au-feu*, with a young chicken, or a chicken carcass and its giblets, added 1 hour after the meat. The soup is served with the carrots, turnips, leeks and scraps of chicken, and accompanied by croûtes spread with marrow from the marrow-bones, or cheese croûtons (see page 108). The beef, cut into cubes, is then served with the cabbage (blanched for 8–10 minutes in boiling water, cooled, then heated in the broth) on a separate plate but at the same time. Parmesan should be served separately.

✑ BELGIAN HOT-POT ✑

This is one of the oldest dishes in the Belgian repertoire and a variation on *pot-au-feu*. It produces a rich, gelatinous broth that cannot be satisfactorily skimmed for fat unless it is cooled overnight; the solidified fat is removed, and *le hoche-pot* re-heated the next day. It can be arrested thus before the second lot of vegetables is added. The pig's trotters and ears can be eaten separately; two brasserie ideas, serving them in a garlicky vinaigrette or breadcrumbed with a mustard dressing and grilled, are particularly good.

SERVES 8–10

450 g/1 lb brisket of beef
450 g/1 lb shoulder of lamb
225 g/½ lb breast of lamb
2 salted pig's ears or 110 g/4 oz salt pork belly
2 pig's trotters, split and blanched
4.5 litres/8 pts water
1 tsp salt
4 onions, peeled, 1 left whole, the others chopped
4 leeks, trimmed and cut into 5-cm/2-in lengths

4 carrots, peeled, 1 left whole, the rest sliced
450 g/1 lb potatoes, peeled, cut into chunks and rinsed
2 turnips, peeled and chopped
2 sticks of celery, sliced
1 small cabbage, sliced and blanched in boiling water
450 g/1 lb small pork sausages or bacon and herb dumplings (page 78)

Cut the meat into fair-sized chunks and place in a huge pan with the pig's ears or belly and the trotters. Cover with the water, add the salt, and bring slowly to the boil (this will take about 1 hour). Skim, throw in a cupful of cold water and skim again. Add the whole onion, 1 leek and the whole carrot. Adjust the heat so that the pan barely simmers, cover, and simmer for 2–3 hours until the meat is tender. Remove the vegetables and discard. Skim the surface with several sheets of absorbent paper, sheet after sheet, to remove the fat.

Now begin cooking the vegetables that will be eaten with *le hoche-*

pot. Start with the vegetables that take the longest – potatoes, then turnips, carrots and celery, ending up with the cabbage.

When everything is cooked, take out the meat and vegetables and put them on a large warm platter. Cover and keep warm. Bring the soup back to boil, and poach the sausages or bacon and herb dumplings in the soup for about 10 minutes. Arrange these with *le hoche-pot*. Serve the soup first, then bring on the main course and provide mustard and horseradish with it.

✑ BOLLITO MISTO WITH BAGNET VERDE ✑

A tradition in northern Italy, a stupendous dish of boiled meats – always beef and chicken – which varies from region to region. *Gran bollito misto* has seven different meats; in Lombardy there are likely to be calf's or pig's feet; in Emilia-Romagna, sausages and other pork products; and in Verona, which is the regional capital of *bollito*, the most common combination is sausage or chicken stuffed with bread and herbs. This party version can be scaled down, or simplified; use it as ground rules.

Traditionally *bollito* is served with a green sauce (see page 75), *mostarda di Cremona* (see pages 93–4) and/or other interesting relishes, pickles and olives.

SERVES 20

1.4 kg/3 lb approx. ox tongue
1 pig's trotter or calf's foot, scrubbed and blanched (this will give the broth a rich, gelatinous quality)
2 carrots, cut into chunks
2 stalks of celery, cut into chunks
2 onions, cut into chunks
1 kg/2¼ lb brisket, topside or silverside of beef

900 g/2 lb boneless veal
1 tbsp salt
1.4 kg/3 lb approx. boiling chicken
a selection of root vegetables (potatoes, carrots, turnips) and onions
1 cotechino (coarse-cut boiling sausage), pre-cooked

Place the tongue, pig's trotter or calf's foot in a huge pan with the vegetables. Cover with plenty of boiling water and bring briskly back to the boil. Skim, throw in a cup of cold water and skim again, removing all the white froth that rises to the surface. Add the beef, which must also be submerged, bring back to the boil, cover and simmer gently for 60 minutes. Skim again, then add the veal and 1 tsp of salt. Cover, cook for 30 minutes, then add the chicken and simmer for a further 90 minutes. Taste for seasoning. Fish out the tongue, which has to be skinned, and remove all the vegetables. In the meantime, cook the selection of vegetables – potatoes, carrots, baby turnips and onions – separately.

Serve in individual bowls, giving everyone a thick slice of each meat, a slice of *cotechino* and some vegetables, and cover with broth. Alternatively, slice the meats in thick pieces, lay them out on a platter surrounded by vegetables and moistened with the broth, and serve the bulk in a separate tureen. Serve with *bagnet verde* (see page 75) or another spicy sauce, pickles and olives.

∽ BOGRÁCSGULYÁS WITH GALUSKAS ∽

Hungarian goulash soup with flour dumplings; also see the consommé version, *gulyás erőleves* (page 312) and the lamb version called *palócleves* (page 297).

SERVES 6–8

50 g/2 oz lard
225 g/8 oz onion, finely chopped
900 g–1.4 kg/2–3 lb shin of beef, cut in 3.5-cm/1½-in cubes
1 tsp paprika
½ tsp caraway seeds
2 cloves of garlic, crushed
2 sweet peppers, red, yellow or green, cored, de-seeded and sliced

3 red chilli peppers
2 ripe or canned tomatoes, chopped
900 g/2 lb potatoes, peeled and cubed the same size as the meat
salt and pepper
galuskas *(see page 91)*

Melt the lard and gently sauté the onion until it begins to turn transparent. Mix in the pieces of meat, stirring to cover them evenly with fat and to brown on all sides. Sprinkle in the paprika, remove the pan from the heat, and stir thoroughly. Return to the heat and stir-fry for a couple of minutes. Add the caraway seeds and the crushed garlic. Moisten with water, stir to incorporate and then add a little more water, stirring thoroughly. Simmer gently, with the meat just covered by water, for 15 minutes.

Add the sliced peppers, chilli peppers, tomatoes and the cubed potatoes to the pan. Mix thoroughly and add enough water to cover, remembering, as Fred Macnicol puts it in *Hungarian Cookery*, that 'this is meant to be a soup with everything else included, rather than a stew which has become somewhat wet'. Simmer until the potatoes are cooked and the meat tender. Taste and adjust the seasoning, removing the chilli peppers if the taste is getting too fiery. Meanwhile cook the *galuskas* in boiling salted water, drain them and add to the *gulyás*.

Serve with bread door-steps.

✑ MEXICAN POT-AU-FEU WITH SALSA ✑

This is a spiced-up, highly seasoned version of *pot-au-feu* with a chilli-hot relish and an accompaniment of rice, chickpeas, carrots and courgettes. The adaptation is based on a recipe from Patricia Quintana's *The Taste of Mexico*, and originates from a high plateau in the state of San Luis Potosi, famous for its prickly pear cactus, Indian figs and pirul trees. There the stew is served with a tomatillo/garlic and chilli paste. Tomatillos are a tiny green vegetable with a tart flavour akin to green plums or rhubarb. Green tomatoes are often given as an alternative but there is no real substitute; hence the *salsa* alternative. This dish needs to be started 24 hours in advance.

SERVES 10

bouquet garni *made with 2 sprigs of mint, 6 bayleaves, 4 sprigs of thyme and 4 sprigs of marjoram*
2 turnips, peeled and chopped
2 onions, chopped
1–2 heads of garlic, sliced in half
small bunch coriander
small bunch flat-leaf parsley
5.6 litres/10 pts boiling water
1 kg/2¼ lb beef bones, chopped into sections
1 kg/2¼ lb beef shin, chopped into sections
1.5 kg/3½ lb beef neck or chuck, cut in 5-cm/2-in cubes

1 tsp salt
6 carrots, peeled and cut into large chunks
2 large chayote/christophene squashes, peeled and quartered
3 ears of corn, sliced into 3 pieces
6 courgettes, cut into large chunks
6 spring onions, finely sliced
225 g/8 oz long-grain white rice, cooked
225 g/8 oz chickpeas, cooked
50 g/2 oz green chilli peppers, chopped
1 large bunch of coriander, chopped
cucumber salsa *(page 71)*

Add the *bouquet garni*, turnips, onions, garlic and small bunches of coriander and parsley to the boiling water. Return to the boil and add the beef bones, shin and neck or chuck and the salt. Bring to the boil over a medium heat. Skim thoroughly. Turn the heat to low and simmer for 2½ hours, skimming whenever necessary. Remove the vegetables, herbs and bones and leave the beef to cool in the broth overnight. The next day skim off the fat that will have formed.

Re-heat the broth 30 minutes before you are ready to eat. Add the carrots and squash and simmer for 25 minutes. Half-way through the cooking add the pieces of corn, and 8 minutes before serving add the courgettes.

To serve, pour the broth into a soup tureen. Arrange the beef in the centre of a large heated platter, garnish with the cooked vegetables, and scatter with chopped spring onion. Serve the rice, chickpeas, chillis, chopped coriander and salsa in separate dishes for diners to garnish their own stew. Serve with tortillas or a crisp flatbread (see page 116).

✑ MENUDO DE RABO ✑

Philippine ox-tail soup stew, a glorious variation on the British version (page 226) from Jennifer Brennan's book *One-Dish Meals of Asia*.

SERVES 4–6

4 tbsp ghee (clarified butter, see page 10) or lard
900 g/2 lb ox-tail segments, washed and patted dry
3 large carrots, scraped and cut into 2.5-cm/1-in pieces
1 large onion, peeled and coarsely chopped
2.3 litres/4 pts water
1 large onion, peeled, quartered and the quarters halved

4 medium tomatoes, peeled and chopped
1 sweet green pepper, cored, de-seeded and cut into thick strips
2 large potatoes, peeled, cut into chunks and rinsed
2 spicy Portuguese sausages, sliced
110 g/4 oz cooked chickpeas
approx. 1 tbsp soy sauce
½ tsp black pepper

Heat 2 tbsp of ghee or lard and lightly brown the ox-tail segments all over. Add the carrots and the coarsely chopped onion, stir-frying until the onion becomes translucent. Remove the carrots and put them aside for later.

Pour on the water (there must be sufficient water to cover the ox-tail by 5 cm/2 in) and quickly bring up to the boil. Reduce the heat to a simmer, skim repeatedly, cover and cook until the meat is tender (this could take up to 4 hours) and virtually falling off the bone. Strain the stock into a bowl (there should be 1.75 litres/3 pts) and reserve the ox-tail segments. Skim the surface of the stock with several sheets of absorbent paper, one after the other, until all the surface fat is removed.

Heat the remaining 2 tbsp of ghee or lard in the pot and stir-fry the onion segments until golden. Add the tomatoes, reserved carrots, green pepper, pieces of ox-tail, potatoes and sausages. Stir-fry for about 10 minutes until the tomatoes have flopped. Reduce the heat so the stew merely simmers, then cover and cook for 10 minutes. Uncover and pour in the stock, the cooked chickpeas, soy sauce and pepper.

CHICKEN AND GAME

∽ COCK-A-LEEKIE ∽

One of Scotland's finest dishes, first recorded in 1598. Its simplicity, using leek-and prune-flavoured beef or beef broth to slow-simmer an old cockerel, belies its depth of flavour. It is also a striking dish to look at: the bright green of the leeks, pearly white of the fowl and jet black of the prunes against a clear, rich broth. By tradition cock-a-leekie is served in bowls, each with a slice or two of chicken and beef, a few prunes and some leek, plus some broth. 'Potage coky-lecky' was described by Escoffier in *Ma Cuisine* as 'a very popular soup in England where it is served at shooting luncheons'; he used a veal stock, sautéed finely sliced leeks before adding them to the pot, and suggested an optional prune compôte!

SERVES 8–10

1.4 kg/3 lb capon, boiling cock
  or good quality roaster
900 g/2 lb piece stewing beef,
  tied up, or 2.3 litres/4 pts
  good beef stock
900 g–1.4 kg/2–3 lb leeks,
  trimmed

salt and pepper
450 g/1 lb prunes, soaked
  overnight and stoned
parsley

Put the fowl, breast side down, into a large pot with the beef, if used, and cover with the stock or equivalent amount of water. Bring slowly to the boil and skim repeatedly until all the froth is gone – adding a little cold water speeds this up.

Meanwhile, slice half the leeks in slanted rings and tie the rest in a bundle. Add the bundle to the soup-pot with ½ tsp of salt. Simmer for approximately 2 hours, until the meat is almost cooked. Fish out the bundle of leeks, add the prunes, cook for 20 minutes and adjust the seasoning. Add the sliced leeks and simmer for 10 minutes. To serve, remove the chicken and beef. Serve everything together in a soup-bowl, or season the broth with pepper and serve it as a first course, to be followed by thick slices of chicken and beef with leek and prunes, moistened with a little broth. Garnish both with parsley.

∽ POULE-AU-POT ∽

Poularde Henri IV is another name for this famous dish, in which a chicken, stuffed with a well-seasoned mixture of chicken livers, garlic, shallots, ham and breadcrumbs, and sometimes accompanied by a meaty stuffed cabbage (*chou farci*) and/or 'green' sausages (*boudins verts*) and a large dumpling (*farcidure*), is cooked in its own broth and

To make the *milhas*, bring the milk to the boil and sprinkle in the cornmeal, stirring thoroughly as you do so. Simmer as it thickens, adding the butter and seasoning after 5 minutes.

To serve, remove the chicken, cabbage, *farcidure* and vegetables from the pan, draining carefully. Serve the soup in a tureen at the beginning of the meal, or place it on the table together with a large platter, or two, of the chicken cut up into thick slices arranged with the vegetables, the cabbage cut into sections and the *boudins verts*. Serve the *milhas* separately, and the *farcidure*, cut and served like bread.

∽ BUN SAO VIT ∽

A subtle soup that combines mint with cucumber, fresh coriander, lettuce, pickled bamboo shoot, vermicelli and duck, with a seasoning of pungent *nuoc nam* – all flavours that characterize Vietnamese cooking. Because duck is so fatty, it is essential to prepare the stock 24 hours in advance so that you can easily skim (and save) all the fat.

SERVES 6–8

1 duck, approx. 1.8 kg/4 lb
225 g/8 oz vermicelli noodles
225 g/8 oz pickled bamboo
  shoot, soaked for 20 minutes
  in warm water
4 tbsp nuoc nam
  (Vietnamese fish sauce)
1 tsp salt

black pepper
1 Iceberg lettuce, shredded
1 cucumber, peeled, cored and
  cubed
3 tbsp coriander leaves,
  chopped
3 tbsp mint leaves, chopped

Place the duck in a large deep saucepan and add water to cover by 7.5 cm/3 in. Bring slowly to the boil, then lower the heat and simmer very gently for 90 minutes, until the duck is tender. Remove the duck, cover with foil and set it aside to drain well. Refrigerate the stock overnight.

Next day, skim the fat and reduce the stock by boiling to approximately 2 litres/3½ pts. Cook the noodles in boiling water for 3–5 minutes. Drain, rinse under cold water and drain again. Set aside. Add the prepared pickled bamboo shoot, *nuoc nam*, salt and pepper to the stock and simmer for 15 minutes. Meanwhile, remove the skin from the duck and chop the flesh into large chunks. Arrange on a platter with the lettuce, cucumber, coriander and mint leaves. Pour boiling water through the noodles (in a colander) and divide between the soup-bowls, topping each bowl with the duck stock. Serve with the platter of goodies so that guests can flavour and build their soup as they wish.

ÎLE-DE-FRANCE CHICKEN AND BACON POTTAGE

This is one of many variations on *poule-au-pot*, and my favourite. The chicken can either be flavoured with tarragon or stuffed with a tarragon-seasoned stuffing. The soup that results is a delicious marriage of beef broth seasoned with the tarragon chicken; the bacon, cooked separately, provides a second stock for another soup. The garnishing, also cooked separately, is a selection of springtime vegetables: peas, baby carrots, white and purple turnips (*navets*) and spring onions. They can be simply boiled in salted water or stock, or glazed (cut into olive shapes, glazed in butter and sugar and simmered in stock).

SERVES 6–8

1 large chicken

Stock
approx. 900 g/2 lb rib of beef
  soup meat
3 carrots
3 onions, 2 stuck with a clove
1 small leek
2 bouquets garnis (see page
  31)
4.1 litres/7 pts warm water
450 g/1 lb piece boiling
  bacon

Stuffing
40 g/1½ oz butter
the chicken liver
a splash of brandy or white
  wine
salt and pepper
4 tbsp white breadcrumbs

2 tbs tarragon, chopped
1 tbsp chervil, chopped
1 egg

**Flavouring, if not using
  stuffing**
the chicken liver
2 sprigs of tarragon
50 g/2 oz butter

Vegetables
450 g/1 lb frozen petits pois
  or shelled small, young, fresh
  peas
450 g/1 lb small new carrots
10–12 spring onions or small
  onions
350 g/12 oz small, white and
  purple turnips (navets)
2 tbsp parsley, finely chopped

Get the stock under way by putting the beef bones, 2 carrots, 2 onions (1 stuck with a clove), leek and *bouquet garni* in a pan with the warm water. Bring to the boil, skim, add a little cold water and skim again. Turn down the heat and simmer for 90 minutes. Put the bacon joint in a second pan with the remaining carrot and onion and cover with cold water. Bring to the boil, skim as for the beef, turn down the heat, cover and simmer for about 60 minutes. Turn off the heat and leave covered.

Meanwhile, prepare the stuffing. Heat the butter and sauté the chicken liver for a couple of minutes. If using brandy or wine, pour it in, let it bubble up, then ignite it. Season with salt and pepper, stir in the breadcrumbs and process or mash it to form a cohesive crumbly mass. Work in the chopped herbs and bind with the egg. Season the inside of the chicken and stuff; sew it up securely at both ends. (If flavouring, rather than stuffing the chicken, push all the flavouring ingredients into the cavity and sew at both ends.) Put the chicken on a greased baking tray.

15 minutes before the beef stock is ready, put the chicken into a pre-heated oven, 350° F/180° C/Gas Mark 4, and bake for 15 minutes. Blot dry. Fish out the *bouquet garni* from the stock and replace it with a fresh one. Add the chicken and simmer for 60 minutes.

To co-ordinate with the end of cooking, cook the garnishing vegetables; these will take approximately 15 minutes if glazed, half the time if boiled.

To assemble, remove the chicken from the stock and carve into serving portions or thick slices. Decorate with slices or nuggets of stuffing. Put these at one end of a large serving platter, and arrange the sliced ham and beef pieces from the stock at the other. Load on the vegetables and moisten everything with a little broth, serving the rest in a tureen. Sprinkle with freshly chopped parsley.

LAMB

∽ CAWL ∽

Cawl is Welsh for soup but is synonymous with the mutton broth cum vegetable stew that is virtually the national dish of Wales. The first published recipe is thought to be Lady Llanover's in 1867 in *Good Cookery*, but in the mutton-rearing hills and valleys of Wales it has a long history. Like so many stew soups it is all the better for being re-heated, and is an ever-lasting soup that can be added to and altered. Leeks are integral, but any winter vegetables are suitable. It is generally eaten as a one-dish meal but it can be split in two; the broth first with the finely sliced and lightly cooked leeks, and then the meat with the stewed vegetables. There is a tradition too, of eating cawl with a special hand-fashioned deep, round-bowled wooden spoon, often to be found on sale at ye olde crafte shoppe.

SERVES 6–8

900 g/2 lb best end of neck
50 g/2 oz pearl barley
225 g/8 oz carrots, peeled and
 sliced
2 onions, sliced
1 swede, peeled and chopped
900 g/2 lb leeks, 1 left whole,
 the rest sliced

salt and pepper
1 sprig of thyme
1 bayleaf
900 g/2 lb potatoes, peeled
 and cut into big chunks, or
 new potatoes left whole
1 tbsp parsley, chopped

Trim the meat of any big chunks of fat and put in a deep pan with plenty of water to cover. Bring to the boil slowly, skim, splash in a little cold water and skim again. Add the pearl barley, carrot, onions, swede and the whole leek, trimmed of its coarse green end. Bring back to the boil, add ½ tsp salt and several grinds of pepper, the thyme and the bayleaf, and simmer gently for 2 hours. Fish out the whole leek, add the potatoes and simmer on for 20 minutes. Taste for seasoning. 5 minutes before the end of cooking add the sliced leeks.

To serve, remove the meat, cut it into chops, and give each serving a chop and a share of the vegetables with plenty of the almost raw leeks on top. Garnish with parsley. Accompany with a toothsome chunk of bread and a piece of Caerphilly.

∽ SCOTCH BROTH ∽

The recipe for Scotch Broth is almost interchangeable with that for Cawl. Adjust the quantity of leeks by half, omit the potatoes and add other root vegetables. Add 110 g/4 oz of dried green peas (soaked overnight) at the start of cooking, and half a shredded cabbage or a sliced celery heart towards the end. Stir the parsley into the soup and serve with oatcakes and/or a dish of boiled potatoes.

∽ HOTCH POTCH ∽

In this variation on Cawl and Scotch Broth, the neck of mutton (900 g/2 lb) is cooked with 6 young carrots, 6 young turnips, 6 small onions, 900 g/2 lb shelled peas, 1 small cauliflower, and 1 small lettuce, added in that order after the meat has simmered for 1 hour. Season and serve as for Cawl.

∽ MONGOLIAN HOT-POT ∽

The simplicity of this dish belies its rich flavouring. By the time the broth is drunk, usually 1½ hours after the meal has begun, the soup is fresh from constant replenishment yet rich after poaching the wafer-thin slices of lamb. After the initial thrill of using chopsticks to quick-poach the slivers of meat has worn off, the soup is enriched by adding part-cooked egg noodles and *pak choi*, as well as meat. Spicy dipping sauces (pages 68–75) should be provided in small saucers.

For this recipe you will need an Oriental steamer known as a steamboat. It is fuelled by its own burner and looks like a funnel surrounded by a moat.

SERVES 6

2.8–3.4 litres/5–6 pts lamb
  broth
1.8–2.8 kg/4–6 lb lean lamb,
  sliced into wafer-thin strips
  or squares

350 g/12 oz egg noodles,
  part-cooked
900 g/2 lb pak choi or other
  Chinese cabbage, torn into
  manageable pieces

Get the steamboat burner under full blaze. Pour 1.1 litres/2 pts of broth into the moat, and when it has settled at a rolling boil the meal can begin. Give everyone a pile of meat and of cabbage, and set placings with chopsticks and a soup-bowl. Have more stock to hand (you will need to replenish the moat as the meal progresses), and serve the noodles in a couple of central bowls. Give everyone their own saucer of dipping sauce.

✑ PALÓC SOUP ✑

The mutton or lamb version of Hungarian goulash (see page 287), seasoned with paprika and caraway, and 'disguised' with quickly cooked 2.5-cm/1-in lengths of stick beans.

SERVES 8

110 g/4 oz smoked streaky
  bacon, diced
1 medium onion, finely
  chopped
1 tbsp paprika
1.4 kg/3 lb boned lean lamb,
  cut into small dice
1 tsp salt
pepper
1 clove of garlic, minced
a pinch of caraway seeds

450 g/1 lb potatoes, peeled,
  diced and rinsed
450 g/1 lb young green stick
  beans, cut into 2.5-cm/1-in
  lengths
1 bayleaf
1 dsp flour
275 ml/½ pt sour cream
1 tbsp flat-leaf parsley and/or
  1 tbsp dill leaves, chopped

Gently fry the pieces of bacon until its fat runs out, then increase the heat slightly and stir-fry the onion. Sprinkle in the paprika, stirring around to take up the fat, and then add the cubed lamb. Season generously with salt, pepper, the garlic and caraway seeds. Moisten with a little water, increasing to about 275 ml/½ pt, stirring around to make a thick mixture. Simmer very gently until the meat seems tender, topping up the water whenever necessary.

Meanwhile cook the potatoes and beans separately in boiling salted water, with barely enough water to cover the vegetables. When they are done, add them both with their cooking liquids to the pot. Add the bayleaf and more water if it seems necessary. Simmer for 10 more minutes, taste and adjust the seasoning with salt and pepper.

Stir the flour into the sour cream, pour into the soup and simmer for 5 minutes. Sprinkle on the parsley and/or dill leaves and serve.

✑ Provençal Pot-au-feu ✑

Lamb, and sometimes veal and a chicken, is cooked with the beef to make a Provençal *pot-au-feu*. The meal is quite different: it is always prepared 24 hours in advance so that the broth may be properly skimmed, and the cold meats are eaten dressed with olive oil, chopped parsley and shallots, and served with olives, capers, *aïoli* and a salad of chickpeas. This marvellous meal can be expanded with potatoes, beetroot, sweet red peppers, etc. – whatever is available.

Use the method for basic *pot-au-feu* on page 283. Proportions for 8–10 servings are: 1.2 kg/2½ lb of flank of beef, 1.2 kg/2½ lb of shoulder, middle neck or breast of lamb, and 450 g/1 lb of shin of veal. Ask the butcher to roll and tie the meats, and cook them with their bone. Cook with 2 carrots, 2 leeks, 2 onions and 2 tomatoes, and tie a garlic clove into the *bouquet garni*.

The chickpea salad is made while the chickpeas are still hot – dress it generously with olive oil, sliced onion, garlic, minced parsley and a little vinegar.

PORK

✑ Gulartsoppa/Arter Med Flask ✑

Both Denmark and Sweden claim yellow pea soup as a national dish. Recipes vary, but yellow peas and a smoked pork product are the vital ingredients.

SERVES 8

275 g/10 oz yellow split peas, soaked
2.5 litres/4½ pts water
salt and pepper
450 g/1 lb piece smoked or streaky bacon, or salt pork
small celeriac, peeled and diced, or 4 sticks of celery, chopped
3 leeks, trimmed and sliced, or 2 bunches of spring onions, trimmed and sliced in chunks

225 g/8 oz carrots, diced
450 g/1 lb potatoes, peeled, diced and rinsed
8 small onions, peeled
small bunch of thyme sprigs, tied together
8 gammon chops, green or smoked
boiling sausage and/or 4 frankfurters

Cook the soaked peas very slowly in half the water, without salt, for about 2 hours or until very tender. Sieve or process and then season with salt and pepper. At the same time set the piece of bacon or pork to simmer in the remaining water. After 1 hour of cooking, add the vegetables and thyme. When the water returns to a decent simmer, add the chops and the boiling sausage. Cook for another hour.

Remove the bacon or pork, the chops and the boiling sausage from the pan. Slice, arrange them on a large platter, and keep warm. Stir the pea purée into the bacon pan, adding more water if it seems necessary. Correct the seasoning and add the boiling sausage or the frankfurters cut into slices. Cook for 5 minutes. Serve the soup, then bring the meat to eat on side plates, with a second helping of soup.

✑ POTÉE LORRAINE ✑

Or boiled ham with vegetables. A variation on this soup is known as grape-pickers' soup and/or *potée champenoise*.

SERVES 6

1 tbsp lard	1 sprig savory or celery
2 onions, sliced	leaves
4 leeks, sliced	6 pure pork sausages
450 g/1 lb ham hock	200 g/7 oz green beans,
4 large carrots, peeled and	trimmed
chopped	200 g/7 oz broad beans,
2 small turnips, chopped	shelled
110 g/4 oz haricot beans,	200 g/7 oz peas, shelled
soaked overnight	6 medium potatoes, peeled,
2 cloves	halved and rinsed
1 bayleaf	salt and pepper
4 cloves of garlic, crushed	a pinch of nutmeg
225 g/8 oz piece lean smoked	
bacon	

Melt the lard in a huge pan, gently soften the onions, then stir in the leeks. Lay the ham over the vegetables and cover generously with water. Bring up to the boil, skim, turn down the heat and simmer, covered, for 1 hour.

Add the carrots, turnips, haricots, cloves, bayleaf, garlic, bacon and savory or celery. Cook for 90 minutes then add the sausages, green beans, broad beans, peas, potatoes, cabbage and more water if necessary. Taste to see if the stew needs salt, and add plenty of pepper and a pinch of nutmeg. Cook for a further 30 minutes.

Slice the meat and serve with the vegetables preceded by the soup.

∾ STEAMBOAT 'HAPPY FAMILY' ∾

Unlike most steamboat meals, a high proportion of this one is cooked separately in the kitchen, but everything comes together to be served at the same time.

SERVES 6

1.75 litres/3 pts seasoned
  chicken stock
2 slices ginger root, each 5 ×
  2.5 × 0.25 cm/2 × 1 × ⅛ in
1 tbsp sherry, gin or vodka
20 steamed pork or beef balls
  (see page 83)
20 steamed shrimp balls (see
  page 100)
6 dried scallops, soaked
  overnight and simmered in
  sufficient water to cover for
  60 minutes
15 g/½ oz dried grass
  mushrooms, soaked in warm
  water for 20 minutes
6 or 12 button mushrooms
  (tinned or fresh)

½ a medium bamboo shoot,
  cut into fine shreds
50 g/2 oz Virginia ham,
  shredded
1 poached chicken breast,
  shredded
2 cooked chicken gizzards,
  sliced wafer-thin (optional)
50 g/2 oz gingko nuts
50 g/2 oz snow peas or
  mangetout, trimmed
1 tbsp cornflour slaked in
  2 tbsp cold water (optional)
110 g/4 oz tinned abalone,
  finely sliced

When the steamboat is fully fired put on the stock with the ginger root and the sherry, gin or vodka. When it boils, turn the heat down so that it simmers gently. Add the prepared pork, chicken and prawn balls, and the scallops, grass mushrooms, button mushrooms and bamboo shoot. Simmer for 5 minutes. Add the ham, chicken strips and sliced cooked gizzards if using. Cook for 2 minutes, just enough to heat them through, then add the gingko nuts and snow peas. Simmer for 5 minutes.

Turn up the heat and add the cornflour mixture, if using, and turn off the heat the moment the soup thickens. At the last minute add the abalone slices.

Serve with soaked bean-thread or rice noodles.

VEGETABLES

৩ *VEGETABLE POT-AU-FEU WITH HARISSA* ৩

Not a lot of people know that before Michel Guérard opened a health
spa with its (now) three-Michelin-starred restaurant at Eugénie-les-
Bains, he ran a modest bistro called Le Pot-au-feu in a Paris suburb.
He went on to devise *cuisine minceur*, an innovative gourmet health
and diet regime, and the subject of a book by the same name. Last
year the sequel, *Minceur Exquise*, was published. This recipe, which
comes from the book, is clever and simple. The result is stunning to
behold and delicious to eat.

Harissa, a chilli-hot paste and powder common in North Africa
and the Middle East, can be bought tinned. It is easy to make by
pounding small chilli peppers with garlic, olive oil, a pinch of cayenne,
and cumin.

SERVES 4

*4 red onions, trimmed but
 unpeeled*
*4 small white onions or
 shallots, trimmed but
 unpeeled*
8 cloves of garlic, unpeeled
2.3 litres/4 pts boiling water
4 carrots, peeled and trimmed
*1 celery heart, washed and
 quartered*
*4 leeks or 8 spring onions,
 white part only, with a cross
 cut into the green end*
bouquet garni
*1 piece of cinnamon stick,
 5 cm/2 in long*

sea salt and black pepper
*½ a cauliflower, divided into
 4 large florets*
*110 g/4 oz stick beans,
 trimmed*
*2 courgettes, peeled and
 quartered lengthways*
½ tsp harissa
*110 g/4 oz frozen petits pois,
 de-frosted*
*4 ripe tomatoes, blanched,
 peeled and quartered, with
 core and seeds pinched out*

Put the red and white onions and the garlic in a pan with half the
boiling water. Cook for 20 minutes, turn off the heat and leave
covered. Add the carrots, celery, leeks, *bouquet garni* and cinnamon
to a second pan, with 1 tsp salt and the remaining boiling water.
After the water has come back to the boil, cook on for 5 minutes.
Add the cauliflower and cook for 10 minutes. Add the stick beans
and courgettes and cook for 4 minutes longer.

Remove from the heat, and add the *harissa* and 1 litre/1¾ pts of
the onion stock. Cover the pan and keep warm. Remove the onions
and garlic with a slotted spoon, refresh in cold water, peel carefully
and add to the other vegetables. Quickly bring the soup up to the

boil, throw in the peas and tomatoes, and boil hard for 60 seconds. Pour the soup into a tureen and serve.

You may prefer to squeeze the garlic on to croûtes already spread with olive paste or tapenade, to serve separately with the soup.

SEAFOOD

✐ AIGO-SAU ✑

A Provençal fish soup which, unlike bouillabaisse, its more famous relative which must have certain fish to be authentic, *aigo-sau* is more relaxed. It is cooked and served in exactly the same way.

SERVES 6–8

*1 kg/2½ lb mixed white fish
 (sea bass, bream, John Dory,
 monkfish, grey mullet, etc.)
4–6 medium potatoes, peeled,
 sliced and rinsed
1 onion, finely sliced
3 tomatoes, skinned and
 chopped
2 cloves of garlic, minced*

bouquet garni *made with
 bayleaf, fennel, thyme, celery
 leaves and parsley*
salt and pepper
4 tbsp olive oil
slices of French bread dried in
 the oven
rouille *(see page 68) or* aïoli

Rinse the fish, and cut the larger ones into big pieces. Put them in a pan on top of the potatoes, onion, tomatoes and garlic, and tuck in the *bouquet garni*. Season with salt and pepper and pour on the olive oil. Pour on 2 litres/3½ pts of water, bring quickly to the boil, and boil fast for 20 minutes.

Serve as it is, or separate the broth into a tureen. Pour over slices of dried French bread and serve the fish and vegetables on a large platter. Accompany with *rouille* or *aïoli* and croûtes.

✐ BOUILLABAISSE ✑

'Bouillabaisse is only good because cooked
by the French, who, if they cared to try,
could produce an excellent and nutritious
substitute out of cigar stumps and empty
match boxes.' (Norman Douglas, *Siren Land*,
1911)

Bouillabaisse, name after a method of cooking – *bouillon-abaisse*, meaning broth rapidly boiled to reduce – started out as a fishermen's soup made with the fish left behind in the nets. It is thought to have originated in Marseille, perhaps introduced by colonizing Greeks who make an almost identical dish called *kakavia*, but there are versions of it all along the Mediterranean coastline.

Bouillabaisse caught the imagination of housewives and, in turn, restaurateurs, and has developed into a soup of romance and mystery surrounded by legend and hearsay. To be authentic it must be made with a variety of non-oily firm and soft-fleshed fish, tiddlers and big 'uns alike. It must include rascasse. The fish are quickly boiled in water or fish stock with onions, garlic, tomatoes, parsley and saffron, often potatoes too, and the whole dish is served with *rouille* and croûtes. Normally the fish and vegetables are eaten separately from the broth, which is poured over the croûtes.

SERVES 7–8

2.3–2.8 kg/5–6 lb mixed fish, at least 6 different types chosen from: rascasse, wrasse, red mullet, weever fish, little shore crabs, crawfish and rock lobster, shrimps and prawns various, conger eel, bream, sea bass, John Dory, monkfish, whiting
3 medium onions, finely sliced
2 leeks, white part only, finely sliced
4–6 potatoes, peeled, sliced and rinsed
2 very large tomatoes, peeled, cored and chopped
4–6 cloves of garlic, chopped
1 bunch flat-leaf parsley, coarsely chopped

1 piece of dried orange peel
1 branch each of thyme and fennel
1 bayleaf
2–3 cloves
12 black peppercorns
1 dried chilli pepper
275 ml/½ pt olive oil
1 tbsp sea salt
3.4 litres/6 pts boiling water (or fish stock for a stronger-flavoured broth)
3 pinches of saffron filaments
rouille *(page 68)*
14 or more slices of over-dried French bread (in Marseille it would be marette, *specially made for the purpose, perhaps fried in olive oil and rubbed with garlic)*

Rinse the scaled and gutted fish, and cut the large ones into 7.5-cm/3-in pieces. Put the onions, leeks, potatoes, tomatoes, garlic, parsley, orange peel, thyme, fennel, bayleaf, cloves, peppercorns and chilli pepper in a large pan. Lay on the firm-fleshed fish, on top of any crustacea, pour on half the olive oil and sprinkle with the sea salt. Pour on the boiling water and boil fast, covered, for 7 minutes. Add the soft-fleshed fish with the rest of the olive oil and the saffron, previously soaked in a little warm water, and boil for another 7 or 8 minutes.

Lift the fish out of the pot, lay on a warm platter with the vegetables, pour the soup into a tureen and serve both at the same time with the *rouille* and croûtes in separate dishes.

∽ BOURRIDE OF SALT COD WITH BOILED POTATOES ∽

'If the bouillabaisse is sombre, bourride is blonde, more vigorous, more meaty and abundant, with a robust perfume.' (*Le Gourmande Vagabond Promenades Gastronomiques*, 1928)

SERVES 4

50 ml/2 fl oz olive oil
2 medium onions, chopped
1 leek, chopped
3 cloves of garlic, chopped
1 strip of orange peel
1 tomato, chopped
2 stalks of parsley
1 bayleaf
1 sprig of thyme

570 ml/1 pt fish stock
350 g/12 oz salt cod, soaked
  for 36 hours
110 g/4 oz aïoli
1 tbsp parsley, chopped
garlic croûtes (see page 123)
900 g/2 lb waxy potatoes,
  boiled and sliced

Heat the olive oil and gently soften the onions, leek and garlic. Add the orange peel, tomato, and herbs and let everything bubble up for a couple of minutes before you add the stock. Simmer for 10 minutes. Cut the fish into 4 pieces and poach them for 5–10 minutes (depending on thickness), remove and keep warm. Strain the cooking liquor through a sieve into a second pan.

Pour a ladleful of the hot broth on to the *aïoli* and whisk it thoroughly, and then whisk the mixture back into the soup. Warm through as you whisk and the soup thickens but on no account let it boil. To serve, put a piece of fish into a warmed soup-plate, pour over the soup and serve sprinkled with parsley, with the garlic croûtes and potato slices separately.

∽ BRODETTO ∽

Meaning 'little broth', *brodetto* is anything but and is a speciality of the Adriatic coast. There are many versions of this fine dish but the variety and number of fish are regarded as a measure of quality. The same procedure is followed whatever the fish, and this is what sets it apart from other similar fish stews. Its base is a fish stock, seasoned with pounded garlic, parsley, tomatoes, oregano and a little vinegar, which cooks to a deep red-brown colour. Parsley and garlic are pounded then fried in olive oil, and added to a thick sauce made with fresh tomatoes. If squid is included, and it often is, that is cooked for 30 minutes before the other fish, cut into big pieces, are cooked on top. The fish and broth, with croûtes, are served at the same time.

Along the Tuscan coast *brodetto* is called *cacciucco*, in Sicily it is known as *casola*, and in Sardinia, *ziminu*. *Burrida*, the Genoese version, is seasoned with dried mushrooms, 2 or 3 chopped anchovy fillets and a little basil. This recipe is also very good made entirely with squid, clams and mussels.

SERVES 10

150 ml/¼ pt olive oil
3 onions, finely chopped
2 cloves of garlic, skinned and
  crushed
700 g/1½ lb tomatoes,
  peeled, de-seeded and chopped
4 tbsp flat-leaf parsley,
  chopped
salt and pepper
2 chilli peppers, de-seeded and
  chopped (optional)
250 ml/8 fl oz white wine

700 g/1½ lb squid or
  cuttlefish, cut into rings, and
  with tentacles coarsely
  chopped
1.8 kg/4 lb assorted white
  fish, cleaned and scaled
700 g/1½ lb mussels or
  clams, washed, steam-cooked
  to open and removed from
  their shells, with juices
12 crostini (see page 124)

Heat the oil and gently soften the onions with the garlic until they turn golden brown. Add the tomatoes, half the parsley, salt, pepper and chilli peppers (if using). Stir, letting everything merge and sweat. Pour in the wine and let it bubble up for a couple of minutes, then add the stock. Stir as it comes up to the boil. Add the fish in layers with the squid or cuttlefish first, the firmer-fleshed fish 5 minutes later and the delicate fish 2 minutes later, and the mussels and clams last. Sprinkle on the last of the parsley.

In Italy the soup is ladled on to the bread, but I prefer to serve the *crostini* separately.

∽ CALDILLO DE PESCADO ∽

This is a typically robustly flavoured Spanish fish soup. An Andalucian version, *Caldillo de Perro*, or dog soup, is made by frying big pieces of hake in garlicky oil, boiling water and fresh bitter orange juice (see page 273). Bread is added when the soup is served.

SERVES 6–8

1.4 kg/3 lb skinned, filleted
  cod, cut into big pieces
50 ml/2 fl oz lemon juice
50 ml/2 fl oz olive oil
2 medium onions, finely
  chopped
1 fresh red or green chilli
  pepper, finely chopped
1 red pepper, de-seeded and
  diced

2 cloves of garlic, crushed
900 g/2 lb small new or
  waxy-variety potatoes, sliced
  wafer-thin and rinsed
½ tsp oregano or 1 tsp fresh
  chopped marjoram
275 ml/½ pt dry white wine
1.1 litres/2 pts fish stock (see
  page 42)
fresh chopped herbs to garnish

Season the pieces of cod with salt and pepper and sprinkle with the lemon juice. Heat the oil and gently fry the onions, chilli and red pepper until soft. Add the garlic, the cod, and after a couple of minutes pile in the potatoes. Sprinkle on the herbs and pour on the wine and fish stock. Bring quickly to the boil, turn down to a simmer, and cook, covered, for 15 minutes or until the potatoes are cooked. Serve sprinkled with the garnishing herbs.

∽ LAKSA ∽

One of the most scrumptious meals I know; a perfect combination of mild, chilli-hot, rich and delicate flavours, and crunchy, soft and milky textures. A speciality of Malaysia, this is a favourite version from Rafi Fernandez's book *Malaysian Cookery*.

SERVES 4–6

6 tbsp oil
900 ml/1½ pts prawn stock and/or simmer the prawn heads and tails in water for 15 minutes
350 ml/12 fl oz thick coconut milk
225 g/8 oz large fresh prawns, shelled and de-veined (reserve shells and heads)
6 fried beancurd cakes, cut in half diagonally
24 fish or prawn balls (page 101)
salt and pepper
450 g/1 lb rice vermicelli, soaked in hot water until soft
450 g/1 lb beansprouts, tailed, rinsed and blanched in boiling water
½ a cucumber, peeled, seeded and cut into juliennes

4 spring onions, chopped
1 tbsp coriander (optional)
lemon wedges

Ingredients to be ground together

2 stalks of lemon grass, white part only
2 cloves of garlic
2.5-cm/1-in piece of fresh ginger, peeled
5 candlenuts or 12 almonds
1 stock-cube-sized piece blacan (fermented shrimp paste, similar to Vietnamese nuoc nam and Thai nam pla)
6 dried chillis (de-seeded for milder flavour)
1 tsp turmeric powder
1 large onion, finely chopped

Heat the oil and stir-fry the ground ingredients until aromatic. Add the prawn stock and bring to the boil. Turn down to a simmer and whisk in the coconut milk, stirring constantly to prevent curdling. When it is simmering gently add the prawns, beancurd and fish or prawn balls, and season with salt. Simmer until the prawns are done.

Drain the vermicelli in a colander and pour boiling water over. Divide between warmed soup-bowls, top with the beansprouts, and pour on a generous serving of hot soup. Garnish with the cucumber, spring onion and coriander. Serve with the lemon wedges.

✍ MIZUTAKI ✍

In Japan, fondue or steamboat meals that combine soup and the main course are called *nabemono*. As is traditional in Japan, and essential to this type of cooking, the soup is drunk at the end of the meal.

SERVES 6–8

3.4 litres/6 pts water
1 tsp salt
450 g/1 lb udon *noodles (white or wheat flour)*
4 whole chicken breasts, skinned, boned and cut into 1-cm/½-in slices
16 raw medium-sized prawns, shelled and de-veined
6 leaves of pak choi or other Chinese cabbage, cut in strips
12 mushrooms
1 bunch of watercress, trimmed and separated into sprigs
1 small daikon (oriental white radish), peeled and sliced into 5 cm × 7.5-cm/ 2 in × 3-in thin slabs

2 red peppers, cored and de-seeded and cut in strips
2 × 10-cm/4-in slabs of pressed beancurd cut into 2.5-cm/1-in cubes, fried golden and drained
1.75 litres/3 pts chicken stock
10-cm/4-in square of kombu
ponzu dipping sauce (lemon, soy and seaweed marinated liquid, available in all Oriental stores)

Bring the water to the boil, add salt and cook the *udon* noodles for 10 minutes, stirring occasionally to stop them sticking. Drain and rinse under cold running water. Set aside in a large, shallow serving dish. Blanch the chicken pieces in a little more boiling water and set aside.

Now begin forming a decoration over the noodles with all the ingredients that will be cooked by the guests in the chafing pot. Begin with the prawns, and working inwards, the cabbage, mushrooms, watercress, radish slices and red peppers. Pile the beancurd cubes in the centre.

When the steamboat is under full steam, pour in the chicken stock and add the square of dried *kombu*. Bring to the boil over a moderate heat and whisk out the *kombu* the moment the liquid boils. Add the chicken pieces and their liquid and bring the broth back to a simmer.

To serve, provide everyone with chopsticks, a decent-sized bowl and their own dish of *ponzu*. The meal begins with the shrimps, chicken and vegetables, then the noodles are tipped into the broth to conclude the meal.

⟋ KAKAVIA ⟋

The simplified Greek version of bouillabaisse (see page 302).

SERVES 6–8

2 onions, finely sliced	salt and pepper
450 g/1 lb ripe tomatoes, peeled, cored and chopped	1 tsp oregano
	275 ml/½ pt olive oil
900 g/2 lb Cyprus potatoes, peeled, sliced and rinsed	2.3 litres/4 pts hot water
	1.8–2.3 kg/4–5 lb small fish, mixed varieties
a handful of celery leaves, chopped	juice of 2 lemons

Lay the vegetables in a large pan and season with salt, pepper and oregano. Pour on the olive oil and cover with the water. Bring quickly to the boil, boil hard for 10–15 minutes until the potatoes are cooked, then add the fish (either whole or cut into similar-sized chunks) and continue cooking for 7–8 minutes.

Squeeze over the lemon juice and serve.

Clear Soups

∾

'My ideal menu might begin with a small
clear soup . . .' (Nico Ladenis, chef/patron
of Nico at Ninety)

Nico probably had an intensely flavoured consommé in mind when
he made that remark, quoted in his book *My Gastronomy* – a few
spoonfuls of a crystal-clear liquid made by the slow, careful cooking
of a finely balanced, ingredient-heavy stock. It will have been
strained, all fat removed, and clarified into a delicately golden, bright,
sparkling consommé. Nico's clear soup is likely to be what is called a
double consommé, in which a key ingredient of the stock is reinforced
in the clarification. It might have been made with one or two whole
game birds or perhaps he was referring to his exquisite *consommé de
champignons au Madère aromatisé aux feuilles de coriandre* (page 318),
in which the stock is made with a 1.4-kg/3-lb maize-fed chicken, and
foie gras, onions, tomato purée and 450 g/1 lb of mushrooms are
sautéed for 60 minutes before the clarification begins.

Such soups are the stuff of banquets, and classically-minded chefs
at restaurants like Nico at Ninety. For the domestic cook they are
inordinately time-consuming to make, and very expensive to produce
in terms of what you end up with. They are not designed to stay
hunger, but to tickle the palate and leave room for a meal of many
rich courses. However, full details of clarification are given on
page 46.

The golden rules are: remove all fat from the stock; stir in the
clarification ingredients and keep stirring until the soup begins to
tremble; keep the liquid at a light simmer and stir until the egg-white
forms a sort of crust. Don't stir again. Take care not to disturb the
crust when you strain off the consommé. For clarification you will
need two egg-whites for up to 2.3 litres/4 pts of liquid.

Not all clear soups are such hard work. They do, though, tend to
need a good, well-balanced stock. This is because what goes into the
soup is generally a last-minute addition, quickly cooked, and does
little to affect the flavour of the finished soup. In effect, the stock
provides a nutritious background to show off or complement the
flavours of the dumplings, ravioli, noodles, wonton, or vegetables
that give the finished soup its name.

The Italians are past-masters of the clear soup, particularly variously-formed pasta in *brodo* (see page 319). France, Britain, Germany, Austria and other mid-European countries have a tradition of flour, breadcrumb, suet, meat and liver dumplings served in thick as well as in clear soups. The Oriental countries tend to mix protein-rich dumplings, sometimes noodles too, with quick-fried or lightly poached vegetables in a light chicken or chicken and pork stock. The Japanese use *miso*, seaweed and dried fish flakes (bonito) to make almost instant stock for their minimalist soups.

There is an infinite variety of clear soups possible. Use the flavour guide to build a stock and dip into the 'Garnish' and 'Embellishment' sections for ways of turning it into a unique soup. See also 'Quick Soups' and 'Restorative Soups'.

∽ TO MAKE A PASTRY SOUP-LID ∽

'*Soupe aux Truffes Elysées*. Stew small diced carrots, onions, celery and mushrooms in butter. Put two tablespoons of this mixture in deep individual ovenproof soup bowls. To eat add sliced truffles, sliced *foie gras* and half a cup of chicken consommé to fill two-thirds of the bowl. Roll out a thin layer of flaky pastry, brush edges with beaten egg-yolk, tightly sealing each dish. Put bowls into a very hot oven. When pastry has risen and crisp, crack open.' (Paul Bocuse, *Great Chefs of France*, edited by Anthony Blake and Quentin Crewe, 1978)

A pastry topping is a dramatic way to serve any soup but is particularly suited to the concentrated bouquet of consommé. Be sure to use ovenproof soup-bowls, to 'glue' the lid thoroughly to the sides of the bowl, and not to fill them too full.

MAKES ENOUGH FOR 6–8 LIDS
500 g/1 lb pastry (page 127)
1 egg-yolk, whisked with a splash of milk or water

1 egg-white, whisked to a froth

Roll out the pastry 5 cm/¼ in thick and cut into circles about 5 cm/2 in wider than the top of the soup-bowls. Paint a 2.5-cm/1-in band of egg-white round the outer rim of each bowl. Take a circle of pastry and carefully place it, without stretching, across the top of the bowl. Seal down the sides. Paint the entire pastry lid with the egg-yolk solution.

Pre-heat the oven to 425° F/220° C/Gas Mark 7 and bake the soup-bowls for 10–15 minutes. They are ready when the pastry is slightly risen, crisp and golden.

✑ CLEAR MULLIGATAWNY ✑

SERVES 6

cooked chicken or game
 carcass and bits of meat
 picked from the bones,
 shredded
1.1 litres/2¼ pts veal or beef
 stock
2 large onions, sliced
1 large cooking apple, cored
 and sliced

1 tbsp desiccated coconut
1 dsp curry powder
2 large egg-whites
salt, pepper and cayenne
lemon juice
50 g/2 oz boiled rice

Break up the carcass and put in a pan with the stock, onions, apple, desiccated coconut and curry powder. Cover and simmer very gently for 45–60 minutes. Strain and skim the surface with damp absorbent paper to remove any grease.

Whisk the egg-whites into the stock, return the pan to a moderate heat, and keep on whisking until a white sludge forms on the surface. Leave to simmer for 5 minutes, break a hole in the sludge and ladle out the clear broth through a muslin-lined strainer. Taste and adjust the seasoning with salt and pepper, then bring out the flavours with lemon juice and, if liked, a pinch of cayenne. Throw in the rice and the shredded meat. Re-heat and serve.

✑ MAURITIAN HOT SPICY SOUP ✑

A spicy, hot and unusual recipe from Pomegranates, a truly international restaurant in London's Pimlico.

SERVES 5

110 g/4 oz tamarind
1 tbsp cooking oil
5 g/⅛ oz aniseed
2 cloves of garlic
2 tbsp curry powder
4 red chilli peppers, cored and
 chopped
½ a medium onion, finely
 chopped

4 medium tomatoes, blanched,
 peeled, cored and chopped
900 ml/1½ pts chicken stock
 (see page 19)
salt and pepper
¼ of a cooked chicken breast,
 finely shredded
25 g/1 oz coriander leaves,
 chopped

Dilute the tamarind in 200 ml/8 fl oz of hot water. Meanwhile, heat the oil and crush/fry the aniseed with the garlic and curry powder over a low heat. Stir in the chopped chillis and onion and cook until the onion is soft. Add the tomatoes and cook for a further 5 minutes. Strain the chicken stock and tamarind water into the mixture and simmer gently, stirring occasionally, for 15 minutes. Taste for seasoning. Put the shredded chicken and chopped coriander in a tureen and pour over the soup. Serve.

ᔕ GULYÁS CONSOMMÉ ᔕ

This is a refined, consommé version of the famous Hungarian stew called *gulyás* (herdsman), usually translated as goulash. The key flavourings are caraway, sweet capsicum peppers and paprika. *Bográcsgulyás*, the original soupy stew, eaten with *galuskas* ('pinched' dumplings), appears on page 287.

SERVES 6

1 tbsp bacon fat	salt and pepper
1 large onion, finely chopped	1.75 litres/3 pts water
½ a clove of garlic, finely	a few parsley leaves, chopped
chopped	a few celery leaves, chopped
½ tsp caraway seeds	2 egg-whites
25 g/1 oz paprika	2 tomatoes, blanched, cored
700 g/1½ lb lean beef (500 g/	and diced
1 lb cubed, 225 g/8 oz	1 sweet green pepper, diced
minced)	1 sweet red pepper, diced

Melt the bacon fat and gently sweat the finely chopped onion and garlic, stirring in the caraway seed and paprika. Add the *cubed* beef, season well with salt and pepper, and stir in a couple of tablespoons of cold water. Bring to the boil, cover, then turn the heat down as low as possible. Leave to simmer, stirring occasionally, until the meat is almost cooked.

Pour on the rest of the water, add the chopped parsley and the celery leaves, and bring back to the boil. Simmer until the meat is quite tender. Strain, and skim off the fat. Set aside the meat.

Whisk the egg-whites and mix with the *minced* beef, one tomato and a little water. Add the strained broth to the mixture, stirring all the time, and bring slowly to the boil. Leave to simmer for 60 minutes. Remove from the heat and leave to rest for 10 minutes. Line a sieve with muslin and carefully pour the consommé through. Skim for fat, and adjust the seasoning.

To serve, divide the meat, diced peppers and remaining tomato between the soup-bowls, and pour on the boiling consommé.

∽ GREEN CONSOMMÉ ∽

SERVES 6

6 level tbsp diced, cooked green
   beans
6 level tbsp frozen peas
1 ripe avocado pear, peeled,
   diced and tossed in the juice
   of 1 lemon

salt and white pepper
1.75 litres/3 pts well-
   flavoured beef stock (see page
   32)
Tabasco or chilli essence
1 tbsp chervil leaves

Mix the green beans and frozen peas with the lemon-tossed avocado, and season with salt and white pepper. Bring the stock up to the boil, season with a few drops of Tabasco, pour over the vegetables and serve decorated with chervil.

∽ CONSOMÉ DE POLLO À LA MEXICANA ∽

SERVES 6

4 spring onions, finely sliced,
   or 2 tbsp chives, chopped
2 ripe avocado pears, peeled,
   diced and tossed in the juice
   of 1 lemon
2 tomatoes, blanched, peeled,
   cored and diced
10 sprigs of coriander, finely
   chopped

3 fresh red or green chilli
   peppers (serranos if
   possible), cored and chopped
225 g/8 oz Mozzarella,
   grated
1.75 litres/3 pts well-
   flavoured and seasoned
   chicken or chicken and veal
   stock (see page 19)

Put the prepared onions, avocado, tomatoes, coriander, chilli and Mozzarella in a tureen and pour over the boiling stock.

∽ CLEAR BEETROOT CONSOMMÉ ∽

SERVES 4

900 g/2 lb uncooked beetroot,
   peeled and chopped small
2 carrots, peeled and chopped
2 young turnips or navets,
   trimmed and chopped
2.3 litres/4 pts clarified beef
   stock (see page 34)

2 tsp wine vinegar
salt and pepper
100 ml/4 oz double or sour
   cream

Put the chopped vegetables in a pan with the stock. Simmer, very gently, until all the vegetables are soft and the soup is a good clear red. Strain carefully without pressing the vegetables.

Adjust the seasoning with vinegar, salt and white pepper. Serve the cream separately.

· The vegetables, which will have absorbed a lot of stock, can be puréed to form the basis of a second soup.

✑ BEEF BROTH WITH NOODLES ✑

SERVES 6

1.75 litres/3 pts marrow-   soup noodles (see page 90)
bone beef and ox-foot stock
(see page 35)

Bring the broth to the boil, turn down to simmer, adjust the seasoning and poach the *levesbe* for about 5 minutes; they are done when they rise to the surface.

Serve garnished with rounds of marrow from the marrow bones, and a sprinkling of parsley and chervil. This recipe is almost identical to the German *Spätzlesuppe*, traditionally served before the roast goose on Christmas Day.

✑ CHINESE BEEF BALL SOUP WITH SPINACH ✑

SERVES 5–6

225–350 g/½–¾ lb fresh   1.4 litres/2½ pts chicken or
spinach   chicken and pork stock (page
Chinese beef and water   23), heated
chestnut dumplings (page   salt and pepper
83)

Trim and shred the spinach. Add the dumplings to the hot stock, cook as directed on page 83, and 5 minutes before they are ready add the spinach. Season.

✑ POTAGE D'OR ✑

1.75 litres/3 pts good chicken   25 g/1 oz butter
or chicken and duck stock   2 shallots, finely chopped
(see page 19)   1 dsp turmeric
a pinch of saffron strands   salt and white pepper
10 dsp grated carrot   1 wineglass of sherry

Heat up the stock very slowly with the saffron and the grated carrot. Meanwhile melt the butter and soften the shallots. When they are almost transparent stir in the turmeric. Little by little, stir in about

275 ml/½ pt of stock and when the turmeric is completely dissolved and evenly distributed, add the rest. Bring up to the boil, taste, and adjust the seasoning. Just before serving stir in the sherry.

⌒ CELERY CONSOMMÉ ⌒

This is a delicate, intensely flavoured clear soup. For a crystal-clear finish, clarify the soup at the end of cooking.

SERVES 6

2 heads of celery, scrubbed and chopped

1.75 litres/3 pts good beef stock (see page 32)

salt and pepper

Put the chopped celery in a pan with the cold stock and bring slowly to the boil. Simmer very gently for 30 minutes. Strain, return to a clean pan, re-heat and adjust the seasoning.

Serve with some elegant biscuits (see page 125) – home-made cheese straws or Parmesan tuiles would be perfect.

⌒ THAI CUCUMBER SOUP ⌒

This is Madhur Jaffrey's vegetarian adaptation of tom yam, the marvellous Thai prawn soup (see page 324).

SERVES 4

12–16 whole stalks of fresh coriander

8 dried kaffir lime leaves

1 tbsp chopped lemon grass

900 ml/1½ pts good vegetable stock (see page 16)

salt and pepper

4 tsp lime or lemon juice

110 g/4 oz peeled, julienned cucumber

1 tbsp coriander, chopped

2 spring onions, finely sliced

1–2 hot green chilli peppers, de-veined and finely chopped

Add the coriander stalks, kaffir lime leaves and lemon grass to the stock and bring to the boil. Lower the heat, cover, and simmer gently for 20 minutes. Strain. Add the salt, lime or lemon juice and cucumber. Stir and bring back to the boil. Simmer, uncovered, for a few seconds.

Turn off the heat and check the seasoning. Pour into individual bowls and garnish with the chopped coriander, spring onions and green chillis.

✑ FENNEL SOUP ✑

This is a delicious and very easy soup from Calabria. This version is based on a recipe in *Regional Italian Cooking* by Valentina Harris.

SERVES 6

4 tbsp olive oil
4 large fennel bulbs, trimmed,
  cored and finely sliced
1 fat clove of garlic, chopped
3 tbsp parsley, chopped

sea salt and pepper
1.1 litres/2 pts cold water
6 oven-dried pieces of bread;
  preferably ciabatta or
  another rustic Italian bread

Heat the oil and stir-fry the fennel, garlic and 2 tbsp of the parsley. Season with a good pinch of sea salt, cover with the cold water, and bring slowly to the boil.

Turn the heat down very low, cover, and simmer gently for about 40 minutes, or until the fennel has almost collapsed. Adjust the seasoning, stir in the remaining parsley and pour the soup on to the bread.

✑ GARLIC SOUP ✑

SERVES 4

2 small heads of garlic
10 sage leaves
6 branches of thyme
2 cloves
1 bayleaf
a pinch of saffron strands

Parmesan
1 tbsp olive oil
1.1 litres/2 pts water
salt
1 tbsp chervil or parsley,
  chopped

Snap apart the heads of garlic, flaking off their papery skins. Squash each clove with the flat of a knife, then peel off the inner skin. Put the garlic, sage, thyme, cloves, bayleaf, saffron and olive oil in a pan with the water. Bring to the boil, turn down the heat, partially cover the pan and simmer at a gentle roll for 30 minutes. Strain, season with salt and stir in the chervil or parsley. Serve freshly grated Parmesan separately.

This soup is delicious on its own and not at all hot. The golden-coloured, aromatic and softly flavoured broth is the perfect backdrop for any number of ravioli, dumpling, pasta and vegetable embellishments (see pages 76–101). It is particularly good with potato gnocchi (see page 80), or ravioli filled with ricotta (see page 94), an idea from *The Savoury Way*, one of the best vegetarian cookbooks in print.

∽ GAME SOUP ∽

Game produces a strongly-flavoured, distinctive stock and is often the soul of an elegant consommé. The bones and debris of cooked game are also the basis of a rich clear soup. Simmered with a small quantity of beef, the flavour is more rounded.

SERVES 4–6

1.4 litres/2½ pts game stock (see page 26)
225 g/8 oz shin of beef, sliced
1 carrot, peeled and chopped
1 onion, chopped

bouquet garni
dash of port or 1 tsp redcurrant jelly
lemon juice
salt and pepper

Put the stock, beef, carrot, onion and *bouquet garni* in a pan and simmer gently until the meat is tender. Strain into a clean pan, reserving the meat. Re-heat and season with the port or redcurrant jelly, lemon juice, salt and pepper.

Serve with miniature forcemeat dumplings. Shred the beef, mix with creamed horseradish or mustard and serve on thick slices of buttered toast.

∽ LAMB BROTH WITH RICE AND MEATBALLS ∽

This is a Middle Eastern version of the thoroughly British lamb broth with barley and dumplings (see page 258). *Fata*, an Egyptian feast-day soup traditionally eaten 70 days after Ramadan and made with the sacrificial lamb, is similar. The lamb broth is poured over slices of toasted Arab bread, previously soaked with crushed garlic fried in butter, and sizzled with 4 tablespoons of vinegar.

SERVES 4–6

450 g/1 lb stewing lamb, cubed
1.75 litres/3 pts lamb stock
½ tsp ground cinnamon
50–75 g/2–3 oz rice

lamb meatballs (see page 84)
salt and pepper
3 tbsp parsley, finely chopped

Put the lamb in a pan with the stock and cinnamon and bring slowly to the boil. Skim, partially cover the pan, turn down the heat and simmer very gently until the meat is quite tender; this will take between 1 and 2 hours. Add the rice and the cooked meatballs, and simmer for a further 15 minutes. Taste and adjust the seasoning. Serve sprinkled with parsley and a dusting of cinnamon.

✥ STUFFED LETTUCE LEAVES IN BROTH ✥

A fiddly but worthwhile recipe, and a speciality of Genoa, *lattughe ripiene in brodo* is a blueprint for other stuffings; raid the dumpling recipes (see pages 76–101) for ideas. Traditionally it is served with a dollop of *ragú bolognese*. Then, when served with good bread, a salad and plenty of Parmesan, it becomes a meal.

SERVES 4

900 ml/1½ pts good veal or   Parmesan
  chicken stock (see page 29)
stuffed lettuce leaves (see page
  85)

For method see page 85.

✥ CLEAR SOUP WITH LIVER DUMPLINGS ✥

This was one of Mozart's favourite soups, acceptable for fasting days and Fridays because it was almost vegetarian. He favoured garnishing the chicken broth with chives, and drank this first, eating the liver dumplings afterwards with sauerkraut.

SERVES 6

1.75 litres/3 pts rich chicken   *lamb's liver or calf's liver*
  or beef stock (see page 21)   *dumplings (see page 84)*
chicken and its liver (see page
  84)

For method see page 84. Serve garnished with fresh herbs and pancake strips.

✥ NICO LADENIS'S CONSOMMÉ DE CHAMPIGNONS
AU MADÈRE AROMATISÉ AUX FEUILLES DE CORIANDRE

SERVES 6–8

40 g/1½ oz fresh foie gras   *450 g/1 lb button*
100 g/4 oz onion, very finely   *mushrooms, minced*
  chopped   *75 ml/3 fl oz Madeira*
1 large tbsp tomato purée   *3 egg-whites*
2 litres/3½ pts rich chicken   *salt*
  stock (see page 22)   *a few coriander leaves*

Melt the *foie gras* in a large pan, add the onion, and sauté until transparent. Add the tomato purée, chicken stock and mushrooms and simmer gently, covered, for 60 minutes. Just before removing from the heat, add 50 ml/2 fl oz of Madeira. Strain the liquid through a fine sieve, pressing the mushrooms to extract their juices but don't force them through the sieve. Discard the debris.

Allow the liquid to cool to hand-hot. Whisk the egg-whites to semi-soft, then, over the heat, whisk them into the soup. Continue whisking while the soup comes up to simmering point, and leave to simmer for 5–6 minutes to clarify. Carefully strain the soup through muslin. Add more Madeira and salt to taste. If necessary reduce slightly until the taste and colour are correct. Serve decorated with a few coriander leaves.

∾ PASTA IN BRODO ∾

There are many regional pasta-in-broth soups throughout Italy. Made with fresh pasta, they are delicate yet filling, and served garnished with fresh herbs, small leaves of spinach, rocket, or sorrel and Parmesan, they are elegant enough for formal as well as family occasions. Turn to pages 87–96 for various fresh pasta, stuffed pasta and egg recipes to add to a good broth. The following are some classic dishes.

In all cases, cook the pasta in fast-boiling liquid; some recipes specify starting the cooking in water to avoid evaporation of the stock. The broth is rarely clarified but is usually made with meat as well as bones – which is the definition of broth. See also 'Quick Soups'.

∾ PASSATELLI ∾

Passatelli is a sort of summer pasta made with breadcrumbs that is pressed through the holes of a colander or mouli-légumes (in Italy they have a special implement) into a rich broth just before serving. There are two versions, one made with Parmesan, butter and seasoning, and the other enriched with pounded beef. This is similar to *ribelli* (see page 91), which is grated into the simmering stock.

SERVES 6

1.75 litres/3 pts good beef, capon, turkey or beef broth (page 34)
cheese passatelli *(see page 77)*

meat passatelli *(see page 83)*

For method see *passatelli* recipe. Serve with extra Parmesan.

∽ CAPPELLETTI IN BRODO ∽

Cappelletti (see page 95) are little ravioli, stuffed with minced pork, veal, ham and brains, folded into a triangle and then pinched together to look like a headscarf.

∽ PASTA IN BRODO CON FEGATINI E PISELLI ∽

This is a lovely combination of fresh peas (frozen will do), short lengths of fine pasta, and quickly sautéed chicken liver. The quantities can be increased to make it more filling.

SERVES 6

110 g/4 oz fine pasta, broken
 into small pieces
1.75 litres/3 pts chicken
 stock (see page 19)
350 g/12 oz shelled young
 peas or frozen petits pois

40 g/1½ oz butter
12 chicken livers, rinsed and
 chopped or sliced
Parmesan

Pre-cook bought pasta in boiling salted water according to the packet instructions. Drain and tip into the stock with the peas. Meanwhile heat the butter and seal the chicken liver pieces, stir-frying swiftly. Transfer to the soup with their butter. Grate over some Parmesan and serve with more.

∽ PASTA IN BRODO AL PESTO ∽

Break a handful of fine pasta into small pieces and cook in boiling broth. Serve with a tablespoon of *pesto* (see page 74) stirred in at the last minute.

∽ BUDINO DI POLLO IN BRODO ∽

Pounded chicken flesh, mixed with Parmesan, egg and nutmeg (see page 85), is oven-baked in individual ramekins and turned out in the soup-plate. To serve, pour over some hot chicken broth.

∽ GNOCCHI ∽

The Italian dumpling called gnocchi (see page 80) is delicious poached in beef, veal, chicken or turkey broth. Serve with a garnish of fresh herbs reflecting the gnocchi stuffing if appropriate. Serve with Parmesan for grating into individual servings.

❧ RASAM ❧

There are many versions of *rasam*, a highly seasoned lentil broth which is a South Indian speciality. It is made by boiling lentils (*dal*) in water and using the liquid as the base for a tomato, tamarind and spice-seasoned thin soup. Because it has no suspending agent, *rasam* has a sediment and all the bits and pieces sink to the bottom. Give it a good stir before serving; it is traditionally drunk from cups, served with a spoon or mixed with rice, but is also popular served as a soup. This is Julie Sahni's version, from her marvellous *Classic Indian Cooking*. It is a good soup for a party.

SERVES 8

175 g/6 oz yellow lentils or
* yellow split peas*
1 tsp turmeric
550 g/1¼ lb ripe tomatoes,
* blanched, cored and chopped*
2 tsp garlic, finely chopped
50 g/2 oz tamarind pulp
1 tbsp ground coriander
1 tsp ground cumin
¼ tsp each red and black
* pepper*

1 tsp treacle or sugar
1 tbsp coarse salt
2 tbsp ghee (clarified butter)
* or light vegetable oil*
¾ tsp black mustard seeds
⅛ tsp ground asafetida
2 tbsp coriander leaves, finely
* chopped*

Cover the washed lentils with 1 litre/1¾ pts of cold water. Season with the turmeric and bring to the boil. Reduce the heat, partially cover, and simmer, stirring occasionally, for about 35 minutes or until the lentils are tender. Meanwhile, purée the tomatoes with the garlic and 100 ml/4 fl oz of cold water and set aside. Put the tamarind pulp in a small bowl, cover with 4 tbsp of boiling water, and leave to soak for 15 minutes. Then mash the pulp with the back of a spoon and strain, squeezing out as much juice as you can. Discard the stringy fibre.

Purée the lentils and whisk in 700 ml/1¼ pts of hot water. Leave to rest for 15 minutes. The lentils will sink to the bottom (these can be used for another dish – we need only the liquor for this recipe). Pour into a clean pan, add the tomato purée, tamarind juice, coriander, cumin, red and black pepper, treacle or sugar, and salt. Bring to the boil, then reduce the heat, partially cover the pan, and simmer gently for 15 minutes. Heat the ghee or oil and when very hot, carefully add the mustard seeds (they will splutter and pop), and a few seconds later, add the asafetida. Turn off the heat and pour the spiced butter into the lentil broth. Stir, cover the pan, and leave for 5 minutes. Check for salt, stir in the coriander leaves and serve.

∽ BOUILLON DE LÉGUMES D'EUGÉNIE ∽

A few diced or julienned vegetables cooked in a decent stock, served garnished with fresh herbs, offers endless variation. Alexis Soyer, the celebrated chef of the Reform Club who set up a soup kitchen in Ireland in 1847, gave it a twist by caramelizing the vegetables before adding the stock (see next recipe). Michel Guérard, the talented chef who devised *cuisine minceur*, cooks his version without any fat, which means it can be served hot or cold; 'Eugénie' refers to Eugénie-les-Bains, Guérard's health spa and restaurant with three Michelin stars.

SERVES 4

50 g/2 oz carrots
50 g/2 oz button mushrooms
25 g/1 oz leek, white part only
25 g/1 oz celery or celeriac
1.3 litres/2¼ pts Michel
  Guérard's chicken stock
  (page 20)

75 g/3 oz tomato pulp,
  coarsely chopped
1 sprig of tarragon, chopped
1 tsp parsley, chopped
1 tsp chervil, chopped

Chop the vegetables into fine juliennes and tip them all, except the tomato pulp, into the simmering, well-seasoned stock. Simmer for 10 minutes so that the vegetables are firm but cooked. Stir in the tomato pulp and serve garnished with the herbs.

∽ SOYER'S CLEAR TURNIP SOUP ∽

This can also be made with a combination of 225 g/8 oz of diced white turnip, Jerusalem artichoke or carrot, mixed with 50 g/2 oz each of diced onion, leek or celery.

SERVES 6

50 g/2 oz butter
225 g/8 oz white turnips or
  navets, prepared, diced and
  blanched
1 generous tsp sugar

1.75 litres/3 pts veal or light
  beef stock (see page 29)
salt and pepper
1–2 tbsp parsley, savory,
  chives or tarragon, chopped

Melt the butter and stir in the diced turnips, making sure they get thoroughly coated. Sweat gently for a couple of minutes, then sprinkle in the sugar and at the same time raise the heat. Stir until the juices turn golden-brown and the turnip slightly caramelizes, taking care not to burn the edges. Add the stock and simmer for about 15 minutes, until the turnips are tender. Skim, taste and adjust the seasoning. Stir in the herbs and serve.

CLEAR SOUPS WITH SEAFOOD

> 'But there is a way to make a soup from
> oysters that demands only oysters. Oysters
> there *must* be, and for the rest, you make
> or even pour from a tin the best beef con-
> sommé you can get, and heat it and put in
> the cold washed shell-fish. Then you put an
> unbroken egg yolk tenderly into each soup
> plate, and pour the consommé with its mul-
> titude of oysters over it, in a gentle way so
> that the yolk will cook a little and stay
> whole. That is all. It is quick, and easy, and
> it is good, too.' (M. F. K. Fisher, *The Art of
> Eating*)

With care, a fish stock will be clear, but it will never compare with
the crystal clarity of a well-nurtured meat stock. While a fish stock is
prepared quickly, the carcasses throw fine sediment that takes hours
to settle and will pass through a fine sieve. If the stock is clarified
before the sediment has settled, the process will rob the stock of most
of its flavour. Better to settle for a slightly cloudy stock than miss out
on flavour; it is only worth clarifying a strongly flavoured fish stock
or reinforcing the flavours in the clarification. See 'Cold, Jellied and
Uncooked Soups' (pages 344–5).

✑ FISH SOUP WITH CRAB AND MELON ✑

A delicate, dainty summer appetizer.

SERVES 4

1.1 litres/2 pts good fish stock
  (see page 42)
225 g/8 oz ripe and aromatic
  melon flesh
225 g/8 oz white crabmeat

4 thin slices of peeled lemon
salt and white pepper
1 dsp chervil or coriander
  leaves

Slowly reduce the fish stock by one-third while you scoop out the
melon flesh with a melon-baller or cut it into equal-sized shapes.
Divide the crabmeat and melon between 4 bowls, add a lemon slice
and pour over the reduced fish stock. Check the seasoning, and serve
garnished with chervil or coriander leaves.

∽ THAI PRAWN SOUP ∽

This is an authentic version of *tom yam* (*kung*), the 'sour', chilli-hot lemony prawn soup. It can also be made with fish cutlets (allow 110 g/4 oz of firm-fleshed fish per person) and whole cleaned baby squid.

SERVES 4

8 medium-sized raw prawns
1.4 litres/2½ pts fish stock
  (page 42)
1 stalk lemon grass, chopped
  into 2.5-cm/1-in lengths
salt
4 small green chillis, finely
  sliced in rings
1 tbsp nam pla (Thai fish
  sauce)

2 spring onions, finely
  chopped
1 tbsp fresh lime juice
3 Thai basil leaves or mint
  (see page 325)
1 tbsp coriander leaves,
  chopped
lime or lemon wedges

Shell the prawns, leaving their tails intact. Put their heads into a pan with the fish stock, lemon grass and a generous pinch of salt. Bring to the boil, simmer for 10 minutes and strain. Add 2 of the chillis. Simmer gently for 10 minutes, then add the prawns and the fish sauce. Cook for a further 5 minutes before stirring in the spring onions, the rest of the chillis, the lime juice and the basil. Taste, adjust the seasoning if necessary, and serve sprinkled with coriander leaves and a wedge of lime or lemon.

∽ JAPANESE CLEAR SOUP WITH PRAWNS AND ∽
SPINACH

SERVES 4

4 medium raw prawns
25 g/1 oz kuzu or potato
  flour (see pages 57–8)
50 g/2 oz spinach

900 ml/1½ pts dashi 1 (see
  page 45)
salt
a few slivers of lemon zest

Shell and de-vein the prawns, leaving their tails intact. Wash and pat dry. Carefully slit the back of the prawns and press them out flat. Make a lengthwise slit in the middle of each and poke the tail through the slit to make a prawn 'flower'. Salt the prawns lightly and dredge in the flour. Drop into lightly salted boiling water and cook for 2 minutes. Drain thoroughly on absorbent paper.

Wash the spinach, par-boil in lightly salted water for 2 minutes, drain and plunge immediately into cold water. Drain and roll the leaves to squeeze out the water. Slice into 5-cm/2-in rounds. Warm 4 bowls, and arrange a prawn over a mound of spinach in each. Bring the *dashi* to the boil, taste for seasoning and ladle over the prawns. Float a few slivers of lemon zest on top, and serve.

✍ THAI SQUID SOUP WITH SWEET BASIL ✍

Thai basil is pungent and minty, and its leaves are tougher and smaller than regular basil. Confusingly, Thais call it sweet basil and it is also known as holy basil. Despite being flown in from Thailand, it is cheaper than regular basil and available from foodstores specializing in Chinese, Indonesian, Thai or Malaysian produce. A mixture of mint and regular basil will give a similar flavour.

SERVES 6

1.8 litres/3¼ pts fish or prawn stock (see page 44)
2 stalks of lemon grass, roughly chopped
2 red chilli peppers
juice of 2 limes
2 tbsp nam pla (Thai fish sauce)

6 pale yellow round African aubergines, quartered (optional)
110 g/4 oz squid rings
salt and pepper
handful of Thai basil leaves
1 tbsp coriander leaves

Bring the stock to the boil and add the lemon grass and whole chillies. Simmer for 10 minutes, strain and return to simmer. Add the lime juice, the fish sauce, the aubergines (if using) and the squid. Simmer gently until the squid is tender, then taste and adjust the seasoning. Stir in the basil and cook for another 60 seconds, then sprinkle on the coriander and serve.

✍ CHINESE SHRIMP BALL SOUP ✍

SERVES 6

1.4 litres/2½ pts Chinese or light chicken stock (page 22)
Chinese shrimp balls (see page 100)

salt and pepper
4 spring onions, finely sliced
6 Cos, or similarly crisp, lettuce leaves, shredded

Bring the stock to a simmer and poach the shrimp balls for 10 minutes. Taste and adjust the seasoning. Stir in the spring onions and lettuce.

BEROWRA WATERS SHELLFISH SOUP WITH LOBSTER WONTONS

SERVES 4

2 ripe tomatoes, chopped
1 carrot, grated
1 stick of celery, finely
  chopped
1 leek, white part only, finely
  sliced
lobster shell or heads and
  shells from 225 g/8 oz
  prawns, crushed up
1.1 litres/2 pts Gay Bilson's
  fish stock (see page 43)
a pinch of saffron strands

For the wontons
225 g/8 oz lobster or prawn
  meat, finely chopped
4–6 spring onions, finely
  chopped
2.5-cm/1-in piece of fresh
  root ginger, crushed to
  extract juice (use a garlic
  press)
salt and pepper
1 packet of wonton wrappers
  (see page 96)

Put the tomatoes, carrot, celery, leek, and lobster or prawn debris into a pan with the stock, and simmer for 20 minutes and strain. Meanwhile, put the saffron in a cup with a little boiling water. Crush with the back of a spoon and leave for 10 minutes. Strain into the soup.

Make the wonton stuffing by mixing the chopped shellfish with the spring onion and ginger juice, and season with salt and pepper. Place 1 tsp of stuffing on each wonton skin, fold and seal (see page 96). Poach in the soup for 3 minutes and serve.

SHELLFISH BROTH WITH CHICKEN AND SHRIMP WONTONS

SERVES 6

chicken and shrimp wontons
  (see page 97)
1.4 litres/2½ pts shellfish
  stock or chicken stock,
  simmered for 10 minutes
  with heads and tails from
  225 g/8 oz shrimps

salt and pepper
1 small bunch of watercress,
  stalks trimmed and yellowing
  leaves discarded

Poach the wontons in the simmering broth according to the method on page 97. 2 minutes before the end of cooking, season and stir in the watercress. To make this into a complete meal, add some cooked egg noodles, beansprouts and shredded Chinese cabbage.

∽ CLEAR WHITING SOUP ∽

A delicate, beautifully balanced soup devised by Rick Stein and served at his superb Seafood Restaurant at Padstow, Cornwall.

SERVES 6

2 whole fillets from a small
  whiting, skin left on
1.75 litres/3 pts fish stock
  made with the whiting bones
  (see page 42)
2 small egg-whites
225 g/8 oz skinned whiting
  fillets, chopped
1 small tomato, chopped
½ an onion, finely chopped

4 parsley stalks
1 carrot, peeled and cut into
  4-cm/1½-in juliennes
¼ fennel bulb, cut into
  4-cm/1½-in juliennes
a few chives
juice of ¼ of a lemon
2 tbsp soy sauce
1 small spray of fennel,
  chopped

Cut the 2 whole whiting fillets diagonally across into 1-cm/½-in lozenge shapes. Poach these for 60 seconds in a little simmering stock, drain and set aside, and pour the cooking liquor back with the rest of the stock.

Whisk the egg-whites with a ladleful of stock and pour into a pan with the rest of the stock, the chopped whiting fillet, the tomato, onion and parsley stalks. Bring slowly to the boil, stirring occasionally, and give one final stir as the liquid boils. Turn down the heat, and leave to simmer very gently for 15–20 minutes until the egg-white forms a dirty, cloudy crust trapping all the debris. Carefully pour or ladle out the consommé and strain through the muslin.

Have ready the julienne of carrot and fennel, previously blanched in boiling salted water for 60 seconds, refreshed in cold water and drained. Cut the chives to similar lengths. Re-heat the consommé, season with the lemon juice and soy sauce, and stir in the carrot and fennel juliennes and the chives. Add the whiting lozenges and chopped fennel, and serve.

Cold, Jellied and Uncooked Soups

'I believe I once considerably scandalized her by declaring that clear soup was a more important factor in life than a clear conscience.' (Saki [H. H. Munro], 1870–1916)

Although soup had been an integral part of the evening meal throughout France for hundreds of years, it was Louis XIV who made it fashionable with the aristocracy. Elegant, fancy soups were served at his table, and because he trusted no one, all his food had to be tasted. By the time the soup reached the King it was inevitably lukewarm or cold. Thus the 'arrival' of the cold soup.

The most refined cold soup is a chilled consommé, jellied to within a tremble of collapse, and, perhaps, floated with cream and garnished with a delectable titbit. The jelly might be coloured with beetroot juice or Madeira, chopped and served in crystal to show off its sparkling clarity. Such soups rely on carefully made stocks rich with natural gelatine, and later clarified. Sometimes commercial gelatine or aspic is used to reinforce or speed up the setting. Such soups, which are very nutritious and easy to digest, are also served to invalids and those in need of building up.

Other countries have a tradition of very different chilled soups. In Russia and Poland many centre on the beetroot, while Hungary has a famous cold cherry soup, and Spain's most well-known soup is the often refined bread and tomato slop called gazpacho. Scandinavia has a wide repertoire of cold fruit soups, and the Middle East, Israel and Turkey all match cucumber and yoghurt, often with mint.

Vichysoisse, one of the most universally popular chilled soups, was devised in America by a Frenchman and is the inspiration for hundreds of raw and cooked puréed cold soups (see page 339).

At its simplest a chilled soup might be little more than raw vegetable juice or a glorified cocktail, like Bloody Mary soup and Jeremy Round's gin and parsley soup. These can then be frozen to a slush to make an iced-slush soup, or even an ice-cream soup; an idea developed by President Eisenhower's chef when he welcomed Mr Khrushchev on a State visit and served borscht ice-cream.

With the aid of gelatine, which becomes aspic when it is softened and diluted, modest seasonal fruits, vegetables and herbs can be suspended in dramatic-looking jellies, and served as a 'solid' chilled soup.

USING COMMERCIAL GELATINE TO MAKE ASPIC

Gelatine is sold in powder or sheet form and both are sold by weight. For a jellied soup you will need 7 g/¼ oz of gelatine for each pint of liquid. *Powdered gelatine* should be sprinkled into 150 ml/¼ pt of cold stock and left to soften for a few minutes. Stir in the rest of the stock and simmer, very gently, over a low heat, stirring until the granules are completely dissolved. *Sheet gelatine* should be soaked in cold water for 10 minutes until soft. Drain, then swirl into warm stock, stirring over a low heat, until the gelatine completely disappears.

Most liquids set within 4 hours if refrigerated; the process can be speeded up by setting the bowl on iced water or, in an emergency, by popping it into the deep-freeze for 5–10 minutes at a time. Full setting power is reached after 12 hours. Jellied soups should never set too hard – the broken lumps should hold their shape softly.

Agar, also known as agar-agar, is a vegetable gelling agent produced from some seaweed species. It is used as a thickener but also, like gelatine, dissolves in hot liquid and sets when cool. Chinese swallows, the rare Salanganes, use agar-agar in their nest building, the elusive ingredient for bird's nest soup.

TO MAKE HOME-MADE ASPIC

For home-made aspic (a well-flavoured, gelatinous stock which is clarified), see page 39.

❦ NORMANDY APPLE SOUP ❦

SERVES 6

50 g/2 oz butter
2 leeks, white part only,
  sliced
900 g/2 lb dessert apples,
  peeled, cored and chopped
2 medium potatoes, peeled,
  chopped and rinsed

1.4 litres/2½ pts light
  chicken stock
150 ml/¼ pt double cream
2 tsp Calvados
a generous pinch of cinnamon
salt and pepper
2 whole dessert apples

Melt three-quarters of the butter and stir in the leeks. Cover and sweat over a low heat for about 5 minutes. Add the apples and cook, uncovered, for 5 minutes. Add the potatoes, then the stock. Bring to the boil, then reduce the heat and simmer, covered, for 45 minutes. Purée and strain through a sieve. Stir in the cream, Calvados and cinnamon, taste and season. Cool.

Just before serving, peel, core and dice the two whole apples. Melt the rest of the butter and gently sauté the apples for about 5 minutes, until the outsides colour and the flesh is soft. Drain carefully on absorbent paper. Garnish the chilled soup with the diced apple and serve.

∽ COLD CURRIED APPLE SOUP ∽

SERVES 6

15 g/½ oz butter
1 medium onion, diced
1 level tbsp curry powder
900 ml/1½ pts light chicken
  stock
900 g/2 lb dessert apples,
  peeled, cored and chopped

salt and pepper
juice of 1 lemon
150 ml/¼ pt single cream
a few leaves of mint, chopped

Melt the butter, soften the onion and stir in the curry powder. Add the stock, the apples and a generous seasoning of salt and pepper. Bring up to the boil, cover, turn down the heat and simmer for 45–60 minutes. Purée, strain through a sieve and cool. Add the lemon juice and cream when cold. Serve garnished with chopped mint.

∽ SOPA DE AGUACATE FRÍA ESTILO ATLIXCO ∽

Atlixco is one of the most important avocado-producing areas of Mexico. This is a superb cold avocado soup, adapted from Patricia Quintana's beautiful book *The Taste of Mexico*.

SERVES 6

110 g/4 oz butter
1 medium onion, grated
2 cloves of garlic, minced
½ a leek, finely chopped
1 carrot, grated
1.65 litres/3 pts well-
  flavoured chicken stock made
  with 1 head (or several
  cloves) of unpeeled garlic and
  6 mint leaves and chilled
4 ripe avocados, peeled

200 ml/8 fl oz double cream
200 ml/8 fl oz plain yoghurt,
  beaten
salt
2 tbsp lime juice
50 g/2 oz onion, finely
  chopped
2 tbsp coriander, chopped
100 ml/4 fl oz olive oil
  (optional)

Melt the butter over a low heat and stir in the grated onion, garlic, leek and carrot with 570 ml/1 pt of the stock. Simmer for about 25 minutes, stirring occasionally, until thick and cooked. Cool. Meanwhile blend the avocados with the rest of the stock, processing until smooth. Strain through a fine sieve, stir in the cream and yoghurt and then the vegetable mixture. Taste and add salt and lime juice to taste. Cover with clingfilm and chill in the fridge for 60 minutes. Stir and pour into individual bowls with a garnish of the chopped onion and coriander and a swirl of olive oil.

∽ Chilled Dried Apricot and Lentil Soup ∽

This soup might not sound much, but is surprisingly delicious and very sustaining.

SERVES 6

225 g/8 oz brown lentils
110 g/4 oz dried apricots
1 tbsp olive oil
1 medium onion, finely
  chopped
1 clove of garlic, chopped
1.1 litres/2 pts chicken stock

salt and pepper
½ tsp ground cardamom
150 ml/5 fl oz plain, good-
  quality yoghurt
1 tbsp each mint and
  coriander, chopped

Rinse the lentils, tip them into a pan and cover them with cold water. Bring to the boil, covered, over a moderate heat. Turn off the heat and leave for 60 minutes, then drain and transfer to a bowl. Meanwhile cover the apricots with warm water and leave to soak for 30 minutes. Drain and chop.

Heat the oil in a pan that can hold the entire soup. Gently cook the onion until limp but not browned, then stir in the garlic and sauté for a further 2 minutes. Add the lentils, apricots and stock, and season with a generous pinch of salt and several grinds from the peppermill. Stir in the cardamom, bring to the boil slowly, and simmer, covered, for 45 minutes or until the lentils are on the point of collapse. Purée, taste and adjust the seasoning. Cool, stir in the yoghurt, chill, and serve garnished with the chopped mint and coriander.

∽ Chilled Broad Bean Soup with Savory ∽

SERVES 4

450 g/1 lb shelled young
  broad beans
700 ml/1 pt light chicken
  stock (see page 19)
1 tbsp savory, chopped finely

juice of ½ a lemon
salt and pepper
50 ml/2 oz double cream
50 ml/2 oz plain yoghurt
1 tbsp savory leaves

Reserve 4 broad beans and add the rest to the gently simmering stock. Cook gently for 5 minutes, purée, then sieve. Stir in the chopped savory and the lemon juice, and adjust the seasoning with salt and pepper. Chill the soup for 4 hours, then garnish with the cream and yoghurt and decorate with the fresh savory leaves and the reserved 4 beans, peeled and chopped.

✑ JELLIED BEETROOT SOUP ✑

Jellied beetroot juice is as spectacular to look at as it is delicate to eat. It can be made individually in small moulds, to be tipped on to plates before serving, or broken up with a fork and served in bowls. I like it best garnished with more grated cooked beetroot, offset with a generous dollop of sour cream, and decorated with chives, but it matches well with carrot, apple and fennel. To make a chilled beetroot soup, omit the gelatine, retain the diced beetroot and stir it with shredded lettuce leaves, sliced spring onions, diced cooked new potatoes, diced cucumber, and egg-whites if liked, into the chilled stock. Stir in the soured cream and garnish with plenty of parsley and dill.

SERVES 4

700 g/1½ lb beetroot
1.1 litres/2 pts dried
  mushroom stock (see page
  18) or jellied chicken stock
  (see page 22)
juice of 1 lemon
½ tsp sugar

a pinch of cayenne
salt and pepper
14 g/½ oz powdered or sheet
  gelatine (see page 329)
150 ml/5 fl oz sour cream
chives

Set aside 2 smallish beetroots. Peel and dice the others. Keep back 110 g/4 oz of the diced beetroot and simmer the rest in the stock for 30 minutes. Remove from the heat and add the reserved diced 110 g/4 oz to improve the colour and flavour. Strain after 45 minutes. Meanwhile cover the 2 whole beetroots in lightly salted water and boil until tender. Leave to cool.

Season the beetroot broth with the lemon juice, sugar, cayenne and salt and pepper. Measure off 275 ml/½ pt of stock, and when cool add the gelatine. When dissolved, incorporate the rest of the warm beetroot stock. Pour into 4 moulds and chill in the fridge for at least 4 hours. Just before you are ready to serve, peel the 2 boiled beetroots and grate their flesh.

To serve, dip the base of each mould in hot water and invert on to a plate. Garnish with a dollop of sour cream and chopped chives.

✑ HUNGARIAN CHERRY SOUP ✑

There are many variations of *meggyleves*, the famous sour cherry soup, but none to equal this one, which has been served for years at the Gay Hussar in Soho and was devised by its original owner, Victor Sassie. If you are unable to find wild sour cherries or morellos, use ordinary cherries, crack some of the cherry stones, simmer them gently in a little red wine and strain this liquid into the soup.

grated zest of 1 lemon
juice of 2 lemons
double measure of brandy
600 ml/1 pt soured cream

6 lb morello cherries
granulated sugar

Stone the ch... stones and stalk... cinnamon so that none of the juice is lost. Put the and simmer for 5 minutes with the sugar and wine. Bring to the boil cinnamon, and the zest and the liquid into a clean pan. Add the tip in the cherries and all the juice of the lemons. Bring to the boil and here). Bring back to the boil then (a rubber spatula is essential Cool slightly and stir in the brand... remove immediately from the heat.

Pour the soured cream into a large bowl. Slowly whisk in the soup, holding back the cherries for the moment, a little at a time, until the two mixtures have mixed nicely. Tip in the rest of the fruit, stir thoroughly and chill for ... ours before serving.

CHILLED CURRIED CARROT SOUP WITH COCONUT MILK

This is an unusual variation on the many delicious chilled carrot soups.

SERVES 6

450 g/1 lb carrots, peeled and chopped
900 ml/1½ pts chicken stock (see page 19)
15 g/½ oz butter
1 medium onion, finely chopped

1 tbsp curry powder
salt and pepper
225 ml/8 fl oz coconut milk, made by diluting creamed coconut to the consistency of milk
1 lemon

Cover the carrots with the stock, bring to the boil, cover, and simmer until the carrots are tender. Heat the butter and sauté the onion until soft but not browned. Add the curry powder and stir-fry for a couple of minutes. Purée the carrots with the onion and curry mixture and pass through a fine sieve. Re-heat, adjust the seasoning and simmer gently for 10 minutes. Cool to hand-hot and stir in the coconut milk. Chill, stir and serve garnished with peeled lemon slices.

ICED CUCUMBER AND YOGHURT SOUP

This is a refreshing, delicious combination popular in Eastern Europe and the Middle East served as a salad in India (*raita*) (Cook), and Greece (*tzatziki*). Alternative seasonings include saffron, and parsley. There is none to equal this recipe, adapted by Simon Hopkinson from an old Constance Spry one, sometimes appears on the menu at Bibendum.

SERVES

2 small cucumbers
salt
275 ml/½ pt plain yoghurt
275 ml/½ pt tomato juice
1 small clove of garlic, finely chopped

275 ml/½ pt light chicken stock (see page 19)
a small bunch of mint
275 ml/½ pt single cream
8 drops Tabasco or chilli essence

Peel, de-seed and chop the cucumbers. Sprinkle on the salt and leave to drain for 30 minutes. Mix the yoghurt, tomato juice, garlic, chicken stock and mint, (reserving a few leaves for garnish). Strain through a fine sieve. Wash the cucumber and squeeze out the excess moisture in a clean tea-towel. Stir into the strained soup along with the cream and Tabasco. Taste and adjust the seasoning. Chill until very cold, and garnish with the reserved mint finely chopped.

CHILLED CUCUMBER AND TOMATO SOUP

SERVES 6

25 g/1 oz butter
1 large cucumber, peeled and sliced
1 bunch spring onions, finely sliced
900 ml/1½ pts boiling water

350 g/¾ lb ripe tomatoes
salt and pepper
½ a lemon
sugar
1 tbsp sour cream
1 tsp chives, snipped

Melt the butter and gently stew the cucumber and spring onions. Pour on the boiling water and simmer for 30 minutes. Put the tomatoes in a different pan, half fill with boiling water, cover, and simmer for 10 minutes. Smash the tomatoes through a mouli, or purée then sieve them. Add the pulp to the cucumber, stir, and adjust the seasoning with salt, pepper, lemon juice, and possibly sugar. Stir in the sour cream. Chill. Serve garnished with chives.

∽ MINTED CUCUMBER CREAM SLUSH ∽

SERVES 6

2 large cucumbers (approx.
  900 g/2 lb
10 mint leaves

275 ml/½ pt single cream
salt
lemon juice

Peel and de-seed the cucumbers. Roughly chop, steam for 10 minutes, then purée them and force through a fine sieve. Finely shred the mint, slicing across the leaf, and stir into the purée. Cover, refrigerate, and leave for a minimum of 4 hours so that the purée is beginning to freeze. Just before serving, stir in the cream. Adjust the seasoning with salt and lemon juice.

∽ CORIANDER SOUP ∽

SERVES 6–8

4 tbsp olive oil
4 medium onions, coarsely
  chopped
2 large cloves of garlic, peeled
  and minced
4 medium potatoes, peeled and
  coarsely chopped

1.75 litres/3 pts chicken
  stock
salt
¼ tsp cayenne pepper
1 large bunch of coriander,
  coarsely chopped

Heat 3 tbsp of olive oil and gently sauté the onions and garlic for about 5 minutes. Add the rest of the oil and the potatoes, and stir-fry for 60 seconds. Add the stock, bring up to the boil, cover, and simmer for 45 minutes or until the potatoes are mushy. Purée until smooth, or force through a fine sieve. Pour the soup into a large bowl, salt to taste, and stir in the cayenne and coriander. Cover and refrigerate for 24 hours. Serve with good crusty bread.

∽ PALESTINIAN FRUIT SOUP ∽

SERVES 6

2 oranges, peeled
2 stalks of rhubarb, cut in
  chunks
4 slices of fresh pineapple
225 g/8 oz pitted cherries
225 g/8 oz strawberries

½ tsp cinnamon
2 tbsp lemon juice
2 tbsp honey
1.75 litres/3 pts water
½ tsp salt
225 ml/7 fl oz sour cream

Combine all the ingredients except the sour cream and simmer, covered, for 20 minutes. Purée and/or force through a fine sieve. Chill thoroughly and stir in the sour cream before serving.

✌ SOPA DE COCO ✌

This unusual soup was devised by chef Gabriel Gambou at the restaurant Arrecife in Manzanillo – coconut country.

SERVES 6

900 ml/1½ pts milk
75 g/2 oz fresh coconut,
  finely shredded
400 ml/¾ pt fresh coconut
  milk
400 ml/¾ pt canned coconut
  milk

40 g/1½ oz sugar
salt
150 ml/5 fl oz double cream
ground cinnamon

Bring the milk to the boil. Cool slightly, stir in the fresh coconut and simmer very gently for 20 minutes. Purée, and tip into a clean pan with the fresh and tinned coconut milk. Season with sugar and a generous pinch of salt. Bring slowly to a simmer and whisk in the double cream. Simmer gently for about 20 minutes, until the soup thickens slightly. Cool and chill. Pour into individual bowls, ideally hollowed-out coconut shells, sprinkle with cinnamon and serve.

✌ COLD LENTIL AND SPINACH SOUP ✌

SERVES 6–8

110 g/4 oz brown lentils
110 g/4 oz spinach, washed
  and sliced
2 tbsp sunflower seed oil
1 onion, finely chopped

1 fat clove of garlic, chopped
400 ml/¾ pt buttermilk
salt and pepper
½ a lemon

Rinse the lentils and cover with cold water. Bring to the boil and simmer very gently for about 45 minutes, until almost tender. Stir in the spinach and cook for 10 minutes. Meanwhile heat the oil and gently sauté the onion until it turns transparent. Add the garlic, stir-fry until golden, then tip the contents of the pan into the lentils. Purée, pour into a bowl, and cool.

When cold, stir in the buttermilk – there should be 2–3 parts soup to 1 of buttermilk. Adjust the seasoning with salt, pepper and lemon juice. Chill thoroughly before serving.

✑ *A***JO** *B***LANCO** ✑

This subtly flavoured soup is variously called almond soup, grape soup, bread soup and garlic soup, depending on the proportions of these key ingredients, and sometimes, white soup. I like a high proportion of grapes, and my recipe is based on Maite Manjon's in *Flavours of Spain* and is called chilled grape soup. It is attributed to Málaga, famous for its sweet muscat raisins and its almonds.

SERVES 6

30 whole almonds (peeled) and blanched
4 fat cloves of garlic, peeled and halved
1 tbsp olive oil
1 tbsp white wine vinegar
75 g/3 oz crustless white bread

900 ml/1½ pts water
salt
350 g/12 oz muscat grapes, peeled, halved and pips removed

Process the almonds, garlic, oil and vinegar at top speed. Add a little bread, then some water, and continue thus until the bread and water are both used up and you have created a thick white purée. Taste, and adjust the flavours with more oil, vinegar and salt, if necessary. Pour into a bowl, stir in the grapes, cover with clingfilm and chill. Serve with an ice cube in each bowl.

It will be delicious – as would other dessert fruit soups – with croûtons (or fingers of bread) fried in butter and lightly caramelized with sugar.

✑ *C***HILLED** *P***ASSION-FRUIT AND** *M***ELON** *S***OUP** ✑

A Russian version of this delicate soup omits the passion-fruit and adds 150 ml/5 fl oz of soured cream, stirred in at the end.

SERVES 4

1 ripe melon, weighing approx. 900 g/2 lb
200 ml/7 oz dry white wine
5 passion-fruit, cut in half

50–100 g/2–4 oz sugar
400 ml/¾ pt water
juice of 1 lime or lemon

Scoop out the pips of the melon, reserving some, and chop the flesh into pieces, discarding the skin. Purée the flesh with the wine and when smooth, add the flesh and pips scooped from the halved passion-fruit and process lightly. Pour into a bowl.

Meanwhile dissolve the sugar in the water over a low heat, then simmer for a few minutes. Cool. Use the sugar water and lime or lemon juice to season the soup, adding a little of each alternately until you end up with the right flavour. Chill.

Rinse the reserved pips, spread them out on a sheet of foil and toast under a slow grill. Serve separately as a garnish.

↝ PARSLEY AND GIN SOUP ↜

Before his premature death at the age of 32, in 1989, Jeremy Round was cutting a swathe through food journalism with his lively *Independent* column. In his search for the perfect Bloody Mary, Jeremy came across Ed Keeling's BM soup, served at the New Orleans Hyatt Regency. And parsley and gin soup was born.

SERVES 2–4

225 ml/8 fl oz tinned tomato
  juice
50 g/2 oz celery, chopped
75 g/3 oz onion, chopped
50 g/2 oz sweet green pepper,
  de-seeded and chopped

4 heaped tbsp parsley,
  chopped
50 ml/2 fl oz gin
salt and pepper

Liquidize. Chill. 'The greenish mush is both cooler and inflamer – best eaten in very small portions on hot, humid days by the pool.'

↝ PLUM AND TOMATO SOUP ↜

SERVES 6

1 fl oz/25 g olive oil
1 medium onion, finely
  chopped
450 g/1 lb red plums, stoned
450 g/1 lb tomatoes, peeled,
  cored and de-seeded
75 ml/½ pt tomato juice
570 ml/1 pt chicken stock

1 sprig of thyme
1 tsp caster sugar
salt and pepper
2 red plums, peeled, stoned
  and diced
1 tsp chives, snipped
1 tbsp parsley, finely chopped

Heat the oil and gently sauté the onion till soft but not browned. Stir in the plums, tomatoes, tomato juice, stock, thyme, sugar, a generous pinch of salt and a few grinds of pepper. Bring to the boil, turn down the heat, simmer gently for about 15 minutes. Leave to cool slightly, fish out the thyme, and force through a fine sieve. Check the seasoning and chill. Serve garnished with the chopped raw plums, chives and parsley.

✐ CHILLED PEA SOUP ✐

SERVES 4

1 onion, finely chopped
2 cloves of garlic, crushed
570 ml/1 pt chicken stock
225 g/8 oz frozen petits pois
8 mint leaves
¼ tsp sugar

1 small sprig of fresh
 rosemary
salt and pepper
1 tbsp lemon juice
150 ml/¼ pt soured cream

Simmer the onion and garlic in the chicken stock until tender. Add the peas, mint, sugar and rosemary and cook for a further 5 minutes. Fish out the rosemary, purée and cool. Adjust the seasoning with salt, pepper and lemon juice. Stir in the cream and chill.

✐ PEAR AND WATERCRESS SOUP ✐

SERVES 6

1 large bunch of watercress
900 ml/1½ pts light chicken
 stock (see page 19)
3 ripe pears, cored, peeled and

 sliced
salt and pepper
juice of ½ a lemon
175 ml/6 oz double cream

Trim away the watercress stalks and bring quickly to the boil in a pan with the stock, the pears, a generous pinch of salt and a few grinds of black pepper. Turn down the heat, cover, and simmer very gently for 15 minutes. Process in small batches with some watercress leaves in each batch. Pass through a fine sieve to catch the fibrous debris. Stir in the lemon juice, taste and adjust the seasoning. Cool, stir in the cream and chill.

✐ DIAT'S CRÈME VICHYSOISSE GLACÉE ✐

Leeks and potatoes are one of those culinary marriages made in heaven. Louis Diat's now ubiquitous Vichysoisse, devised when he was chef at the Ritz-Carlton in the 1920s, is a refinement of *potage bonne femme*, the simple leek and potato soup made every day in thousands of households all over France. He remembered his mother chilling theirs with milk when he was a child growing up in Vichy. Vichysoisse is his sophisticated version. Others, including the Roux brothers, have refined it further by only using cream, by altering the proportion of leek to potato and onion, by adding garlic with celeriac and reducing the leeks, and by eliminating leeks entirely in favour of cauliflower. There is even a breadfruit version in the Caribbean.

SERVES 6–8

50 g/2 oz butter	1 level tsp salt
4 leeks, white part only, washed and sliced	570 ml/1 pt milk white pepper (optional)
1 medium onion, chopped	275 ml/½ pt double cream
5 medium potatoes, peeled, diced and rinsed	1 tbsp chives, snipped
1.1 litres/2 pts light chicken stock or water	

Melt the butter and sweat the leeks and onion until soft and very lightly browned in places. Stir in the diced potatoes and cook for a couple of minutes before adding the chicken stock or water and the salt. When the potatoes are tender, purée the soup and pass through a fine sieve. It is important not to omit the sieving, in fact it may be necessary to do it twice to achieve a perfect smoothness. Add the milk, taste for seasoning and re-heat with half the cream. Sieve again, for extra smoothness, and add the remaining cream. Chill for at least 4 hours. Serve sprinkled with chives.

∽ RED PEPPER JELLY WITH YELLOW PEPPER CREAM ∽

Or vice versa.

SERVES 4

4 red peppers	salt and pepper
25 g/1 oz butter	yellow pepper cream (see page
1 onion, finely chopped	66)
1.1 litres/2 pts chicken stock	1 tbsp chives, chervil leaves
14 g/½ oz gelatine	or whole basil leaves

Core and de-seed the peppers and chop into small pieces. Melt the butter and gently sweat the onion, stirring in the peppers after a couple of minutes. Season with a generous pinch of salt, then cover and sweat for 5 minutes. Pour on the stock and simmer gently for 20 minutes. Purée, cool and add the gelatine (see page 329). When thoroughly dissolved, pass the whole soup through a fine sieve, check the seasoning and pour either into 1 bowl or 4 moulds. Leave refrigerated for at least 4 hours. To serve, either break up the jelly with a fork or turn out the individual bowls (dip the base in hot water) on to a plate. Garnish with a dollop of yellow pepper cream and the fresh herbs.

Serve with croûtes or bruschetta spread with olive paste or tapenade.

∽ CHILLED TOMATO CONSOMMÉ WITH WHIPPED ∽
CREAM CROÛTES

SERVES 6

1.75 litres/3 pts chicken or beef stock	1 sprig of thyme
900 g/2 lb ripe tomatoes, chopped	450 g/1 lb minced beef
1 spring onion, chopped	2 egg-whites, beaten till stiff
2 sprigs of parsley	sugar
	salt and pepper

Put all the ingredients in a pan and bring slowly to the boil. Leave to simmer, uncovered, very gently for 1 hour. Everything will have been trapped in the egg-white, which will now resemble grey sludge. Carefully pour or ladle out the clear broth underneath. Taste and adjust the seasoning. Chill and serve iced, with croûtes spread with whipped cream sprinkled with chives, chervil or basil; Devon or Cornish cream would be heaven.

∽ ICED TOMATO AND BASIL SOUP WITH AVOCADO ∽
CROÛTES

In 1974 one of France's most innovative chefs, Michel Guérard, whose restaurant merits three Michelin stars, published *Cuisine Minceur*. This is *haute cuisine* for slimmers. In March 1992 he published an update, *Minceur Exquise*, and this soup is his revision of fresh tomato soup with pounded basil.

SERVES 4

1 kg/2¼ lb ripe tomatoes, blanched and peeled
1 tbsp olive oil
2 onions, finely chopped
1 clove of garlic, finely chopped
1 stick of celery, finely chopped
bouquet garni *made with parsley, thyme and 1 bayleaf*
a bunch of basil *(approx. 20 leaves)*

570 ml/1 pt water
1 tsp Worcestershire sauce
salt and pepper

For the croûtes *(page 123)*
a few slices of bread
½ an avocado
juice of 1 lime
¼ tsp Tabasco
salt and pepper

Quarter the tomatoes and pull out their seeds and cores. Heat the olive oil and gently sauté the onion, garlic, celery and *bouquet garni* for about 5 minutes. Add the tomatoes, water and half the basil leaves. Bring quickly to the boil and boil for 5 minutes. Fish out the *bouquet garni* and blend the soup in batches for a full 60 seconds per batch. Pass through a fine sieve into a bowl, pressing with a wooden spoon to extract all the juice. Cool, then refrigerate for 1½ hours. Add the Worcestershire sauce, and adjust the seasoning if necessary.

Put aside 4 of the remaining basil leaves, and process the rest with a ladleful of the soup. Stir back into the soup. Just before serving prepare the croûte topping. Mash the avocado with the lime juice, Tabasco, and a little salt and pepper. Serve the soup in chilled bowls with an ice-cube or two, and a leaf of basil. Serve the croûtes separately.

∽ GAZPACHO ANDALUZ ∽

Gazpacho, a cold soup from Andalusia, is really a salad soup to be served on hot summer days and made with whatever is ripe and to hand. It generally includes tomatoes, cucumber, peppers, garlic and onion, all chopped very finely or blended to a pulp with bread, water, olive oil and vinegar. There are no exact proportions of ingredients of what is puréed and what isn't. Usually the soup is served iced, with ice-cubes, with a selection of other chopped garnishes to be added at the table. It is a dish to be played around with.

One idea is to make an entirely *green* gazpacho (grapes, avocado, cucumber, green pepper, celery, spring onions, with white grape juice, a squeeze of lime and fresh mint), and serve it with a tomato-based version as a double soup.

SERVES 6–8

700 g/1½ lb ripe tomatoes, peeled and chopped
225 g/8 oz decent (not packet sliced) breadcrumbs
1 medium cucumber, peeled, de-seeded and chopped
3 cloves of garlic, chopped
2 red peppers, cored, de-seeded and chopped
5 tbsp red or white wine vinegar
5 tbsp olive oil
1 tbsp tomato concentrate

salt and pepper
900 ml/1½ pts water

Garnishes
small croûtons fried in olive oil
hard-boiled eggs, whites chopped, yolk crumbled
spring onions, sliced
black olives
cucumber, peeled and diced
red or yellow pepper, diced

Mix together the tomatoes, breadcrumbs, cucumber, garlic, peppers, vinegar, olive oil and tomato concentrate in a large bowl. Season generously with salt and pepper. Purée in batches with a little of the water, transferring the finished purée to a second bowl. Chill for at least 4 hours. Serve with ice-cubes and a little more water stirred into the soup. Set out some or all of the garnishes in little bowls for people to help themselves.

∽ GAZPACHO WITH ROASTED CUMIN, YOGHURT, AND ∽ AVOCADO SLICES

Rick Cunningham devised this chilli-laced version for an Independence Day Dinner. I came across it in *The Open Hand Celebration Cookbook – Great (West Coast American) Chefs Cook for Festive Occasions.*

SERVES 6–8

1 tbsp garlic, minced
1 large cucumber, peeled, de-seeded and diced
1 red and 1 yellow pepper, de-seeded and diced small
3 jalapeño peppers, de-seeded and chopped
1 medium red onion, finely chopped
6 ripe large tomatoes, peeled, cored, de-seeded and diced
1.4 litres/3½ pts tomato juice

juice from 2 fresh limes
1 tbsp Worcestershire sauce
1 tsp chilli sauce
100 ml/4 fl oz olive oil
salt and pepper
2 tbsp dry pan-fried cumin seeds, finely ground
100 ml/4 fl oz plain yoghurt
2 avocados, halved, stones removed and sliced

In a large bowl, mix together the garlic, cucumber, red and yellow peppers, jalapenos, onion, tomatoes, tomato juice, lime juice, Worcestershire sauce, chilli sauce and olive oil. Purée one third of the mixture and stir back into the chopped ingredients. Season with salt, pepper and 1 tbsp of roasted cumin. Cover with clingfilm and chill for 24 hours. Stir, adjust seasoning with more salt and pepper and a scrap of cumin.

Mix the remaining cumin into the yoghurt. Ladle the gazpacho into individual bowls and garnish with an avocado slice or two and a dollop of yoghurt. Serve with chilled vodka shots.

COLD, JELLIED AND UNCOOKED SOUPS WITH SEAFOOD

∽ *ICED HADDOCK SOUP* ∽

An idea from Elizabeth David, possibly inspired by *chlodnik* or another Polish or Russian cold fish soup, and published in *Summer Cooking*.

SERVES 4

275 ml/½ pt milk, used to poach a 175 g/6 oz piece of smoked haddock
150 ml/¼ pt plain yoghurt
2 ripe tomatoes, peeled, de-seeded and chopped
1 tsp vinegar from 100 ml/4 oz cucumber pickled in dill, chopped

2 tbsp parsley, finely chopped
2 small pickled onions, chopped
½ a fresh cucumber, peeled and diced
1 tbsp capers
1 tbsp chives
black pepper

Flake the fish and mix it into the yoghurt, thin with the milk, and stir in all the other ingredients. Chill for at least 4 hours. Serve decorated with red lumpfish caviare.

∽ *CHILLED FRESH RED PEPPER AND TOMATO PURÉE* ∽
WITH OYSTERS

I can still recall the delicate balance of flavours and textures in this gazpacho-style soup, and its vivid colour off-set by 2 pearly-white oysters. The perfect soup for a hot summer's day, devised by Patrick McDonald and served at his restaurant Epicurean in Cheltenham.

SERVES 6

6 red peppers, cored and chopped
2 large beef tomatoes, peeled and chopped
2 whole cloves of garlic, peeled and chopped
½ a cucumber, peeled and chopped

4 basil leaves
1 shallot or ¼ of a medium onion, chopped
150 ml/¼ pt water
150 ml/¼ pt olive oil
25 g/1 oz Parmesan
salt and pepper
12 oysters

Put the chopped peppers, tomatoes, garlic, cucumber, basil leaves, and onion in a large china bowl. Mix thoroughly, cover and refrigerate for 24 hours. Pour on the water, olive oil and Parmesan. Liquidize and check the seasoning. Serve in chilled bowls with the oysters separately. This would also be good with pan-seared scallops or chargrilled salmon fillets.

✑ COLD BUTTERMILK SOUP ✑

SERVES 6

700 g/1½ lb shrimps or
  prawns, cooked and chopped
½ a medium cucumber, peeled
  and finely diced
1 tbsp dill, minced

1 tbsp mild mustard
1 tsp salt
1 tsp sugar
2.3 litres/4 pts buttermilk

Mix the shrimps, cucumber, dill and seasonings; stir in the buttermilk and chill thoroughly. A delicious surprise from M. F. K. Fisher's *How to Cook a Wolf*.

✑ SOUPE DE TRUITE PROVENÇALE PAUL CÉZANNE ✑

This unusual recipe, from Jean Conil's *Cuisine Fraîcheur*, originates from Conil's great-great-uncle Maxim, who was married to Paul Cézanne's sister Rose, and bears the artist's name because brother and sister were united in thinking it better than bouillabaisse.

SERVES 4

350 g/12 oz trout, skinned
  and filleted
juice of 2 lemons
juice of ½ an orange
1 tsp white vinegar
salt and pepper
50 g/2 oz stale bread,
  crumbled
2 cloves of garlic, peeled and
  chopped
4 stoned green olives
1 tbsp olive oil
1 green chilli pepper, de-seeded
  and sliced
1 red onion, peeled and
  chopped

50 ml/2 oz plain yoghurt
1 tbsp tomato purée
2 basil leaves
2 mint leaves
570 ml/1 pt water
1 tbsp parsley or coriander,
  chopped

Garnish
25 g/1 oz red pepper, de-
  seeded and diced
1 large tomato, skinned,
  de-seeded and diced
25 g/1 oz cucumber, peeled
  and diced

Rinse the trout fillets, dry and cut into tiny dice. Leave to marinate for 3 hours with the lemon and orange juice, vinegar and a pinch of salt and pepper. Meanwhile mix the bread, garlic, olives, oil, chilli, onion, yoghurt, tomato purée, basil and mint in a large bowl, add the water, cover and refrigerate for 3 hours. When ready to serve, liquidize the contents of the bowl and stir in the fish with its marinade. Add the garnish ingredients. Serve in a tureen, adding 1 ice-cube and a sprinkling of chopped parsley or coriander.

Restorative Soups

_∽

'There is a whole world of health and eating pleasure in soup. I cannot understand how to have a dinner without a few spoons of good soup because the soup is the beloved of the stomach.' (Antonin Carême, 1783–1833)

Restorative soups falls into various categories. They may be healing, reviving, cleansing or comforting. Most of all they need to be easy to digest, aromatic and enticing to look at. When possible such soups should be made without fat, and carefully skimmed.

Marrow, from beef bones, is the most light and digestible fat and is recommended for those in need of 'building up'. Gelatine, both natural and manufactured, is an aid to digestion and helps other foods to be absorbed into the body. This explains why meat and bone-intensive broths made with beef, chicken and veal are imbued with such restorative value. Such broths and jellies can be cheered up with miniature dumplings, snickets of vegetables and, if it's a heart-starter that's needed, a shot of vodka.

Many herbs and vegetables, particularly onions, garlic and seaweeds, are rich in vitamins and are easy to digest. Others, such as elderberry, beetroot, spinach, nettles, potato, and caraway have particular attributes, as you will discover from the following recipes. Beancurd, *miso* (cultured bean paste) and vegetable jelly made from dried and fresh vegetables are the vegetarian equivalents of beef and chicken broths.

See also 'Clear Soups' (pages 309–27) and 'Thick Soups' (pages 179–242).

∽ *JUS DE RÔTI* ∽

This produces an exquisite, very nourishing and intensely flavoured broth. Unlike most stocks it has no vegetable flavours, and no seasoning except salt and pepper. It can be made with any bones – game is particularly good – but they must be chopped fine. Colour can be deepened by adding ½ an onion, first seared until black in a hot non-stick pan, to the finished simmering *jus* for 10–15 minutes. Fish out the onion before serving.

SERVES 4
900 g/2 lb chicken wings   *salt and black pepper*

Lay out the chicken wings, season with salt and black pepper, and roast in a moderate oven (400° F/200° C/Gas Mark 6) until the bones turn a deep mahogany colour. Drain off the fat for at least 30 minutes, then return to the cleaned pan or a stock-pot and cover with water. Simmer very gently, partially covered – with pierced foil if using the roasting tray – for 60 minutes. Strain and skim for fat.

✑ ALEXIS SOYER'S REAL ESSENCE OF BEEF ✑

The great Reform chef (1809–58) was also famous for the soup kitchens he set up in Dublin at the time of the potato famine in 1847. He fed 26,000 people daily, and taught people the value of the broth produced by bones and lowly cuts of meat. His Nectar or Ozmazone was a precursor of the stock-cube, and was also known as Portable Soup (see also page 49). 'Take 1 lb of solid beef from the rump, a steak would be the best, cut it into thin slices, which lay upon a thin trencher, and scrape quite fine, with a large and sharp knife (as quickly as possible, or the juice of the meat would partially soak into the wood, your meat thus losing much of its strengthening quality); when like sausage meat put it into a stewpan or saucepan, and stir it over the fire five or six minutes until thoroughly warmed through, then add a pint of water, cover the pan as tightly as possible, and let it remain close to the fire or in a warm oven for 20 minutes, the pass it through a sieve pressing the meat with a spoon to extract all the essence.

'If wanted stronger, put only half instead of one pint of water; seasoning may be introduced, that is a little salt, sugar and cloves, but no vegetables.'

✑ BEEF TEA ✑

To provide its full nutritive value, beef tea is made in a china jug or bowl and cooked in a double boiler or bain-marie in the oven. The meat is trimmed of fat, and the broth must never boil. It should be crystal-clear and skimmed of all fat.

SERVES 2–3
450 g/1 lb topside   *salt and pepper*
570 ml/1 pt water

Mince the meat or scrape into shreds. Put the meat and its juices in a jug or bowl with the water and leave to soak for 60 minutes. Stand the jug or bowl in a pan of simmering water and leave to cook for 2 hours, checking that the broth never boils. Strain carefully and float a piece of absorbent kitchen paper over the top to blot up any fat. Adjust the seasoning and serve with Melba toast (see page 124).

∽ SAVOURY BEEF JELLY ∽

Proceed as for beef tea but season with 10 white peppercorns, 1 clove, 2 sprigs of parsley, 1 bayleaf, 1 blade of mace and 1 stick of celery. Cover the bowl and cook for 3 hours. Strain, cool, skim and then add the gelatine, previously dissolved (see page 329).

∽ VEGETABLE JELLY ∽

Cover a quantity of fresh, ripe, shelled beans, peas, string or small kidney beans with water. Cover tightly and simmer gently, topping up the water if necessary, until quite tender. Turn into a sieve, pressing the vegetables gently to extract all the juice. The juice makes a jelly with a very high albumen content.

∽ FAKKI ∽

This Greek fasting soup, served during Holy Week, is a well-seasoned lentil, onion and garlic stew.

SERVES 6

450 g/1 lb yellow lentils, rinsed and picked over
2.3 litres/4 pts water
2 onions, chopped
3 cloves of garlic, chopped
3 stalks of celery, chopped
450 g/1 lb approx. tinned tomatoes, chopped

3 tbsp flat-leaf parsley, chopped
1 bayleaf
salt and pepper
3 tbsp mixed oregano, basil and mint, chopped
2 tbsp wine vinegar

Cover the lentils with the water and bring to the boil. Skim, stir in all the other ingredients, and bring back to the boil. Turn down to simmer, cover, and cook gently for 2 hours, stirring occasionally. Check the seasoning.

Serve with a well-seasoned warm salad of cooked greens – spinach, nettles, chard, young dandelion, etc. – dressed with lemon juice and sesame oil, and with crusty bread. On non-fasting days use olive oil, and slosh some of it on the soup before serving.

✑ BULLSHOT ✑

Bullshots are best served hot and peppery. Use chilli vodka (see page 60) or season with a few drops of Tabasco, or similar. The ideal pick-me-up after, or during, a late party or ball and a popular picnic surprise.

SERVES 1
100 ml/4 fl oz strong beef consommé

3 tbsp vodka
salt, pepper and Tabasco

Heat the consommé, and as it reaches boiling point remove from the heat and add the vodka and seasoning to taste.

✑ FUL NABED SOUP ✑

An Egyptian convalescent soup made with the broad white beans that are popular in Egypt. It is plain, delicate and highly nutritious.

SERVES 6–8
450 g/1 lb white dried skinless beans, soaked for 48 hours
2.3 litres/4 pts water
2 tbsp olive oil

salt and white pepper
3 tbsp parsley, finely chopped
juice of 1 lemon
lemon wedges

Bring the beans to the boil with the water. Skim, turn down the heat, cover and simmer for 60 minutes or until tender. Purée the beans with the water and return to the pan. Add the oil, salt and pepper, bring back to the boil, and simmer for 10 minutes. Stir in the parsley and a squeeze of lemon, and serve with lemon wedges and fingers of toasted pitta bread.

✑ BOUILLON DE SANTÉ ✑

Flavour 1.1 litres/2 pts of strong, reduced chicken broth with ½ an onion, a handful of parsley, 1 sprig of thyme and 3 of spearmint, a little balm, 1 clove, and salt and pepper to taste. This broth, strained, was drunk by Queen Henrietta Maria every day of her life, and to it was attributed her good health. The recipe came to light in *The Closet of Sir Kenelm Digby Knight Opened*, published on his death in 1665.

❧ BEETROOT CONSOMMÉ ❧

Beetroot is low in calories and high in vitamin A, iron and phosphorus. (For recipe see page 313.)

❧ POTAGE DE SANTÉ ❧

This is Escoffier's version.

SERVES 5–6

1.4 litres/2½ pts puréed
  potato soup
50 g/2 oz sorrel, melted in
  25 g/1 oz butter

50 g/2 oz butter
1 tbsp chervil leaves

Heat the soup, stir in the melted sorrel, and just before serving add 50 g/2 oz butter and a few chopped chervil leaves.

❧ ELDERBERRY SOUP ❧

The pea-sized, tart elderberry is high in vitamins A, B, and C, and in calcium, potassium and iron.

SERVES 6–8

1 litre/1¾ pts ripe elderberries
1 litre/1¾ pts water
a 2.5-cm/1-in cinnamon stick
4 cloves
1 large lemon, sliced
570 ml/1 pt approx.
  unsweetened crabapple or
  grape juice (if using
  commercial juice, dilute to
  half strength with water and
  use less sugar)

75–150 g/3–5 oz sugar
1 tsp arrowroot
2 tbsp cold water
lemon juice
sour cream
nutmeg

Rinse the berries and simmer gently in the water with the cinnamon stick, cloves and lemon slices for 40 minutes. Push through a sieve, forcing through as much pulp as possible. Make up the soup to 2.3 litres/4 pts with crabapple or grape juice (see above), re-heat and sweeten to taste, stirring in the sugar so it doesn't catch.

Slake the arrowroot in the cold water and stir into the soup. Simmer gently until it thickens. Adjust the seasoning with sugar and lemon juice. Cool and chill for at least 4 hours. Serve in chilled bowls with a dollop of sour cream and pinch of nutmeg.

✑ GARLIC SOUP ✑

Garlic is an aid to digestion, a calmative, and if eaten regularly is thought to help build a resistance to germs. *Soupe à l'ail* or *aigo boulido* (see page 143), a simple Provençal garlic soup, is rated locally as a cure-all.

✑ MISO SOUP WITH BEANCURD AND WAKAME ✑

Miso is the salty, cultured bean paste from which soy sauce evolved. It is high in protein, minerals and lactic acid, also in calcium, iron, phosphorus, magnesium, sulphur and copper. It is common in Japanese soups and is stocked by health food stores.

Wakame is a vivid green seaweed that is popular in Japanese cookery (see also page 352).

SERVES 4

275 g/10 oz firm beancurd (tofu)
2 spring onions, trimmed and finally chopped
900 ml/1½ pts light vegetable stock (see page 16)

4 tbsp miso
4 pieces wakame, soaked for 10 minutes
1 tsp soy sauce

Cut the beancurd into 16 equal cubes and divide between warmed soup-bowls. Divide the spring onions also. Heat the stock, blend a little of it with the *miso*, and return to the pan. Bring almost to the boil and add the shredded *wakame* and the soy. Heat through gently, and serve.

✑ WINE SOUP ✑

A German and Austrian tradition, this is served before the start of a meal.

SERVES 6–8

1 bottle of white wine
1 tbsp caster sugar
2 cloves

a small stick of cinnamon
2 eggs, whisked

Bring the wine up to the boil with the sugar and spices. Strain, and pour into the whisked eggs, whisking as you do so. You may care to add a few stale breadcrumbs, first fried in butter and drained. This soup is pretty if poured over thin, quartered lemon slices first dredged with caster sugar.

∽ WAKAME SOUP ∽

Wakame, a seaweed popular in Japanese cookery, is rich in vitamins B1 and B12, and eaten regularly, will improve the quality of hair. It is reputed to help the body eliminate the effects of animal foods.

SERVES 4

1 tsp cooking oil
2 onions, finely chopped
8 pieces of dried wakame,
  soaked for 20 minutes in 1.1
  litres/2 pts warm water

tamari to taste

Heat the oil and soften the onions, cooking until a light golden colour. Meanwhile shred the *wakame* and tip it and its soaking water into the onions. Simmer for 30–40 minutes. Season with tamari.

∽ EHESTANDSKACHEN ∽

A Saxon soup for a hangover, traditionally served at lunch on the second day of ancient Saxon village celebrations.

SERVES 8

1 small chicken or boiling
  fowl
3 carrots, peeled
2 parsnips, peeled
1 celery root
3.4 litres/6 pts water
25 g/1 oz flour
50 g/2 oz butter
110 g/4 oz gooseberries

2 × 2.5-cm/1-in pieces of
  lemon peel
1 cinnamon stick
50 g/2 oz raisins
50 g/2 oz small seedless
  grapes
225 g/8 fl oz sour cream
salt and pepper
lemon juice

Put the chicken in a pan with the carrots, parsnips and celery root, and cover with the water. Simmer gently for 60–90 minutes until everything is cooked. Strain and skim the broth for fat.

Rub the flour into the butter, break off little pieces and whisk them into the soup, bringing it slowly back to the boil. Simmer for 5–10 minutes. Meanwhile attend to the chicken. Discard the skin, sinews, etc. and chop the meat into small pieces.

In a second pan, cook the gooseberries with the lemon peel and cinnamon stick in sufficient lightly salted water to cover. When the gooseberries have turned golden and are soft, push them through a fine sieve into the skimmed broth. Similarly, simmer the raisins and grapes in a little water until soft. Add them to the broth. Stir in the chicken pieces and sour cream, simmer gently, taste and adjust the flavour with salt, pepper and lemon juice.

ᴄᴏ SPRING TONIC SOUP ᴄᴏ

This soup celebrates the arrival of spring with a marriage of seasonal vegetables and herbs. Most, like sorrel, spinach and nettles, are thought to cleanse the blood. The ingredients can be adapted to whatever is available.

SERVES 4–6

1–2 tbsp olive oil
2 medium-sized new potatoes, scrubbed and diced
2 carrots, peeled and diced
1 bunch of spring onions (or 2 leeks), trimmed and chopped
1 sprig of thyme and a few thyme flowers
5 cloves of garlic, peeled
1 small bunch of parsley, leaves only

salt and pepper
1 bunch of watercress
225 g/8 oz spinach
225 g/8 oz nettle tops
225 g/8 oz sorrel leaves
1 small lettuce, chopped
a handful of rocket leaves
2 litres/3¾ pts vegetable or light chicken stock
tarragon or white wine vinegar

Heat the oil and stir in the diced potatoes, carrots, spring onions or leeks, sprig of thyme, garlic and parsley leaves. Stir everything around, sprinkle on ½ tsp of salt, cover, and cook gently for 5 minutes. Add the greens, topping up as the first ones in begin to wilt. Stir, and when everything has flopped, add the stock. Bring quickly to the boil, lower the heat and simmer gently for about 15 minutes or until the potatoes are soft. Liquidize to preferred smoothness.

Return the mixture to the pan, taste, and adjust the seasoning with a little vinegar and salt. If you think it needs it, stir in a knob of butter or a swirl of olive oil. Serve garnished with thyme leaves. This is based on a Georgian fasting day soup, which would not be made with a meat stock, and would be finished with egg-yolks whisked with lemon juice and a smattering of chopped pistachio nuts.

Soups for Parties

∽

'Cold soup is a very tricky thing and it is the rare hostess who can carry it off. More often than not the dinner guest is left with the impression that had he only come a little earlier he could have gotten it while it was still hot.' (Fran Lebowitz, *Metropolitan Life*, 1978)

Chilled soups are a very good idea to serve at parties. Apart from last-minute garnishing they require no attention. Several are included here, where all the servings are for 10 or more, and there are plenty more on pages 328–45.

Recipes throughout the book can be scaled up to feed large groups of people. Often, though, the domestic kitchen is not equipped to cook for parties and it is more practicable to follow a recipe for 6 and make it twice, or thrice. Soups can also be 'expanded' with judicious use of the 'Embellishment' (page 55) and 'Garnish' (page 102) sections. Also see 'Whole Meal Soups' (pages 283–308) – many of the recipes are for 8–12 servings.

∽ CHILLED AVOCADO, CUCUMBER AND WATERCRESS ∽ SOUP

Clare Ferguson devised this recipe for *The Sainsbury's Book of Parties*.

SERVES 40–50

6 tbsp olive oil
350 g/12 oz spring onions or leeks, trimmed and sliced
4 cucumbers, peeled, quartered lengthways and cut into chunks
8 tbsp cornmeal (polenta)
3.7 litres/6½ pts hot turkey stock (see page 24)

4 bunches of watercress, trimmed, coarser stems discarded
12 ripe avocados
1.4 litres/2½ pts low-fat natural yoghurt
salt and pepper

Heat the oil in a large heavy-based pan. Add the spring onions or leeks and soften without browning. Add the cucumber, stirring occasionally, and cook for 10 minutes. Stir in the cornmeal and pour in just under half the hot stock. Bring to the boil, stirring, and simmer for 10 minutes. Turn off the heat. Put a quarter of the watercress into a food processor with a ladleful of the soup base. Process to a green-speckled purée then transfer to a large bowl. Repeat 3 times with the remaining watercress and more ladlefuls of soup. Process the rest of the soup base on its own and return to the pan.

Remove the flesh from 4 of the avocados, chop, and put in the food processor with one-third of the natural yoghurt. Process in bursts until fairly smooth. Add one-third of the puréed soup base from the pan and process again until completely smooth. Whisk this mixture into the pan of stock. Repeat this process twice more with the remaining avocados, yoghurt and soup base.

Amalgamate the green-speckled purée with the soup mixture, and season to taste. Cover with clingfilm to prevent discoloration and chill for up to 48 hours.

Pour into cups or bowls immediately before serving; oxidation of the surface will spoil the soup's pastel green colour.

✑ BLACK BEAN SOUP FOR A CROWD ✑

A spicy, tasty soup devised for *The Savoury Way*, the sequel to *The Greens Cookbook*, food from the San Franciscan vegetarian restaurant.

SERVES 40–50

2.3 kg/5 lb black beans
5 medium onions, finely
  chopped
4 large cloves of garlic, finely
  chopped
1.8 kg/4 lb approx. canned
  plum tomatoes, chopped,
  juice reserved

3 chipotle *chilli peppers,*
  minced
2 large bunches of coriander
2 tbsp salt

Rinse and sort over the beans. Put them in a 20-litre/4-gallon pot and cover with cold water to about 10 cm/4 in from the top. Bring to the boil slowly, skim, then add the onions and garlic. Lower the heat and simmer very gently until the onions have softened (about 15 minutes), then add the tomatoes and their juices, the *chipotle* chillies and half the coriander. Occasionally give the beans a stir and simmer for 60 minutes, then add the salt and cook on for another 30 minutes or until the beans are soft. Stir in the remaining coriander, taste, and serve garnished with a blob of sour cream, a grating of firm cheese and a few finely sliced chilli peppers.

⨀ *BARLEY BROTH* ⨀

SERVES 10

2 litres/3½ pts lamb stock
 (see page 37)
75 g/3 oz pearl barley
225 g/½ lb carrots, peeled
 and diced
450 g/1 lb leeks, diced

225 g/½ lb turnips or navets,
 peeled, diced and blanched
2 onions, finely chopped
3 sticks of celery, diced
salt and pepper
3 tbsp parsley, finely chopped

Bring the skimmed and seasoned stock to the boil. Throw in the well-washed barley and simmer for 10 minutes. Add the vegetables and simmer for 50 minutes. Taste, adjust the seasoning and stir in the parsley. Serve.

⨀ *BOTVINYA* ⨀

The keynote of this cold Russian fish soup is *kvas*, a rye beer. I include a recipe, which takes 3–4 days to mature, but dry white wine or cider could be substituted. The recipe comes, courtesy of *Soups*, from the excellent *Time/Life* series master-minded by Richard Olney, from Elena Molokhovets, *Podarok Molodym Khozyaikam*. This is a soup that is guaranteed to get the party off on the right footing; it has a high alcohol content.

SERVES 12

1 kg/2½–3 lb salmon, sea
 trout or firm-fleshed white
 fish
225 g/½ lb sorrel, stemmed,
 chopped and sweated with 1
 tbsp butter until it collapses
 into a purée
450 g/1 lb spinach, parboiled,
 squeezed and finely chopped
1 cucumber, peeled, de-seeded
 and diced
4 spring onions, chopped
2 tbsp dill, finely chopped
3 tbsp parsley, chopped
salt
100 ml/4 fl oz black treacle
2.3 litres/4 pts kvas (see
 below), cider or dry white
 wine

25 crayfish tails or prawns
 (optional luxury)
grated horseradish

Kvas
2.3 litres/4 pts boiling water
225 g/8 oz stale rye bread,
 dried and broken into pieces
4 tbsp black treacle
7 g/¼ oz fresh yeast (double
 if using dried)
½ tsp malted barley flour
 (optional)
raisins

Get the *kvas* under way by pouring the boiling water over the bread. Cover with a thick cloth and leave to cool until lukewarm. Strain through a sieve lined with a muslin cloth into a second bowl; do not squeeze the cloth. Add the treacle to the strained liquid, stirring thoroughly until dissolved. Cream the yeast with the flour and a little warm liquid, and stir into the bowl. Cover and leave to stand in a warm room for 12 hours. Strain the liquid again and bottle it, adding 2 raisins to each bottle. Cork and store in a cool place. The *kvas* will be ready after 3–4 days; it must be used within 2 months.

Poach the fish in lightly salted water for 10 minutes until it flakes easily. Drain, cool, remove all the skin and bones and cut into bite-sized pieces. Put the sorrel and spinach into a cold soup tureen and add the cucumber, spring onion, dill, parsley, salt and treacle. Stir in the *kvas*, cider or dry white wine and chill thoroughly – this will take about 4 hours.

Decorate with the crayfish tails or prawns, if using, at the time of serving. Serve a bowl of grated horseradish separately.

ᴄ CURRIED MANGO AND YOGHURT SOUP ᴄ

A lovely soup which is on the menu at Chutney Mary, a charming Anglo-Indian restaurant and verandah bar close to Chelsea Harbour, in London.

SERVES 8

2 tbsp gram flour	6 green chilli peppers, chopped
200 ml/7 fl oz natural yoghurt	2 tbsp cooking oil
4 ripe mangoes, peeled and pulp puréed, or 200 ml/7 fl oz mango purée	½ tsp mustard seeds
2 litres/3½ pts cold water	1 level tsp cumin seeds
½ tsp fresh ginger, finely chopped	15–20 curry leaves (from Indian grocery)
	salt
	fresh mint

Stir the flour into the yoghurt and mix it with the mango pulp and water. Add the ginger and green chillis and bring to the boil. Turn down to simmer and continue to cook until thoroughly merged and thickened, stirring continuously. Strain.

Meanwhile heat the oil. When it begins to smoke, add the mustard seeds for a few seconds until they start to pop, then add the cumin seeds and a couple of seconds later the curry leaves. Cook for 3–5 seconds more and stir the mixture into the soup. Simmer for 10 minutes, strain, taste for salt and serve hot or chilled garnished with a sprig of mint.

∽ *CONSOMMÉ DE CAVIARE, CRÈME D'ASPERGES* ∽

The PR for Four Seasons, Inn on the Park, London, had the clever idea of inviting food writers to cook-along with Bruno Lubet and his brigade to celebrate their new custom-designed kitchen. I volunteered myself to be chief helper on this chilled, jellied consommé that preceded *artichaut à la grècque, coquilles grillées; gros raviolis de ris de veau, poireaux et champignons,* and *capuccino glace.* This consommé is neither liquid nor set and has a delicate flavour enhanced by the caviare and complemented by the fresh taste of the asparagus, which is akin to young peas. The texture is like eating Guinness.

A variation on this soup, also a Lubet speciality, is made by adding enough saffron to turn the soup yellow and poaching diamond-shaped pieces of scallop, red mullet and sea bass in the soup, to be served with a thin line of *rouille* (see page 68) running round the edge of the plate and mounds of diced cooked shallots, artichoke and tomato: *consommé de bouillabaisse.*

SERVES 10

For the stock
4 tbsp cooking oil
3 big onions, chopped
1 head of celery, chopped
900 g/2 lb leeks, chopped
4 big cloves of garlic, crushed
  in their skins
2 heads of fennel, chopped
4 carrots, chopped
a bunch of flat-leaf parsley
a small bunch of thyme
1 star anise
10 coriander seeds
2.8 kg/6 lb fish bones,
  preferably carcass and heads
  of mullet, sole, brill or other
  fish with high gelatine content
  (see page 41)
1 litre/1 ¾ pts vegetable stock
  (see page 16)

570 ml/1 pt dry white wine

For the clarification
6 egg-whites
a splash of cold water
2 handfuls of crushed ice

For the asparagus cream
5 large spears of asparagus,
  blanched in boiling water
  then held under cold running
  water to arrest the cooking
1 litre/1 ¾ pts vegetable stock,
  reduced by half
1 bunch of chervil
50 g/2 oz cream

To finish
sheet gelatine (see page 329)
caviare

Heat the oil and sweat the chopped onions, celery, leeks, garlic, fennel and carrots. Add the herbs, spices, fish bone stock and vegetable stock. Cover with water, bring up to the boil, turn down to simmer and cook for 20 minutes. Add the white wine, bring back to the boil, turn down and cook, covered, for 25 minutes. Strain off the debris. Return to a large pan with a big surface area for quick reduction and reduce by about half.

For the clarification, pour the stock into a high-sided pan. Whisk the egg-whites with a splash of cold water and 2 handfuls of ice and whisk into the soup. Leave to simmer very slowly for 30 minutes. It will start to puff up, catching all the impurities, and look like a disgusting mould. Ladle out into a bowl through a muslin-lined sieve.

Cool the consommé. Meanwhile make the asparagus topping. Chop the asparagus spears and liquidize with the reduced vegetable stock, the cream and chervil. Push and scrape the whole lot through a conical sieve: this is helped by tapping the sides hard.

Add the leaf gelatine to the cooked consommé, whisking until thoroughly incorporated. When cool, pour 2.5 cm/1 in of the soup into a dish. Add caviare and pour the asparagus cream over the back of a spoon. Decorate with sprigs of chervil.

∽ BRUSSELS SPROUT AND CHESTNUT SOUP ∽

SERVES 10

110 g/4 oz butter
225 g/8 oz onions, finely
 chopped
900 g/2 lb Brussels sprouts,
 trimmed
175 g/6 oz unsweetened
 chestnut purée
¼ tsp grated nutmeg

½ tbsp caster sugar (optional)
150 ml/¼ pt sherry
1.1 litres/2 pts chicken stock
salt and pepper
chopped fresh chestnuts
275 ml/½ pt double cream
4 tbsp minced parsley

Heat the butter and soften the onions until golden. Add the prepared sprouts with the chestnut purée, nutmeg and sugar, if using, along with the sherry. Cover with a double thickness of damp greaseproof paper and simmer gently for 40 minutes. Add the stock, bring to the boil, simmer for 10 minutes, liquidize and sieve. Taste and adjust the seasoning. Serve with a garnish of chopped fresh chestnuts, a blob of thick cream and a sprinkling of minced parsley.

∽ TRACHANAS ∽

When I revealed to my Cypriot greengrocer that I was writing a book about soup, he insisted that I bought a bag of the dried wheat and yoghurt sticks called *trachanas* that hang around his shop. *Trachanas* in Greece and *kisshik* in Cyprus and the Lebanon looks unpromisingly like dried, brown rissoles. It is made by mixing burghul (wheat) with sour milk or yoghurt that is left to ferment. It is then salted, spread out to dry and chopped into pieces for winter soups. When it is soaked and/or boiled with water or stock it transforms into an

exquisite lemony gruel-like soup that is packed with vitamins and
easy to digest.

It is traditionally enriched with slices of salty Halloumi cheese,
allowed to melt under the grill, and can be given the *avgolemono*
treatment with egg and lemon juice whisked in at the last moment.
A packet of *trachanas*, which lasts indefinitely, is a useful standby;
allow 50 g/2 oz per person mixed with 10 fl oz/½ pt of chicken stock
or water.

SERVES 10–12

450 g/1 lb bag of trachanas	*225–350 g/8–12 oz*
2.3 litres/4 pts chicken stock	*Halloumi cheese*
or water or mixture	*3 lemons cut into wedges*
3 tsp salt	*1 small bunch of flat-leaf*
black pepper	*parsley or coriander*
3 eggs (optional)	
juice of 3 lemons (optional)	

Rinse the *trachanas* thoroughly in a large sieve. Place in a heavy-
bottomed pan and cover with the correct amount of liquid. Leave
overnight, if you have time, or at least 2 hours, and break up any
remaining pieces with a potato masher. Bring it very slowly to the
boil, stirring all the time because it sticks easily. Once boiled, turn
down the heat, half-cover the pan and simmer gently for 30 minutes.
If it seems too thick, add more stock or water, the salt and some
black pepper. If you plan to avgolemonize the soup, whisk the eggs
with the juice of 3 juicy lemons and whisk the mixture into the soup.
Don't let it boil again.

Cut the cheese into thin slices and cover the surface of the soup.
Place under the grill or in a hot oven until the cheese begins to
soften. Serve with lemon wedges and a bowl of chopped flat-leaf
parsley or coriander.

∽ MELON, GINGER AND PORT SOUP ∽

This recipe comes from Gavin Lannen, the pastry chef at the Swan
Hotel, Southwold, Suffolk.

SERVES 8–10

1 ripe watermelon, peeled and	*25 g/1 oz fresh ginger, peeled*
de-seeded	*and grated*
3–4 glasses of port (being an	*icing sugar to taste*
Adnams'-owned hotel, this is	*melon balls, raspberries and*
the finest)	*yoghurt to garnish*
225 g/8 oz raspberries,	
puréed and sieved	

Purée the watermelon and sieve with the port. Mix in the raspberry purée, fresh ginger and icing sugar to taste. Cover and refrigerate for at least 12 hours.

Serve straight from the fridge in ice-cold bowls and garnish with melon balls, fresh raspberries, mint and 1 tsp per serving of natural yoghurt.

∽ SOLFERINO SOUP ∽

SERVES 10–12

110 g/4 oz tiny carrots, finely
  sliced
2.3 litres/4 pts boiling
  chicken, veal or vegetable
  stock
110 g/4 oz butter
1 large onion, chopped
4 leeks, chopped, dark green
  part discarded

700 g/1½ lb tomatoes,
  peeled, cored and chopped
700 g/1½ lb potatoes, peeled,
  chopped and rinsed
1 clove of garlic, peeled
salt and pepper
2 tbsp parsley, chopped

Cover the finely sliced carrots with a little stock and set aside. Melt half the butter and soften the onion, then mix in the chopped leeks and cook gently for about 8 minutes until both vegetables are tender. Add the tomatoes, potatoes and garlic, and the rest of the stock. Simmer gently for 30 minutes.

Meanwhile cook the carrots briefly so that they are tender but still crisp. Drain their cooking liquid into the soup. When the soup is cooked, purée it into a clean pan. Re-heat, season, add the remaining butter, the carrots and parsley.

∽ TOMATO SOUP WITH MINIATURE GREEN DUMPLINGS ∽ AND FRESH HERBS

To be made when there is a glut of tomatoes.

SERVES 12

50 g/2 oz butter
2–3 bunches of spring onions,
  trimmed and finely sliced
2 cloves of garlic, peeled
10 branches of flat-leaf
  parsley, tied in a bundle
1.4 kg/3 lb ripe tomatoes,
  peeled

2.3 l/4 pts light chicken stock
1 tsp salt
pepper
48 miniature green dumplings
  (see page 81)
2 tbsp chives, snipped
1 tbsp chervil leaves

Melt the butter and gently sweat the spring onions until they turn limp. Stir in the garlic, parsley and tomatoes. Raise the heat and cook fast for 5 minutes, then pour in 570 ml/1 pt of the stock and add the salt and pepper. Bring back to the boil, then turn down and cook at a brisk simmer for 15 minutes. Add the rest of the stock and cook for a further 15 minutes.

Remove the parsley bundle and pour the soup through a sieve to catch the pips and core. Taste and adjust the seasoning, perhaps with a little sugar. Re-heat. Poach the green dumplings and serve the soup with the chives and chervil leaves stirred in at the last moment.

∽ MILANESE TRIPE SOUP ∽

SERVES 12

*2 kg/4½ lb honeycomb tripe,
 cleaned, washed, and cut in
 10-cm/4-in squares*
*4.5 litres/8 pts tripe or beef
 stock*
1 onion, stuck with 2 cloves
2 sticks of celery
*200 g/7 oz dried white beans,
 soaked overnight and drained*
50 g/2 oz butter
*200 g/7 oz bacon, chopped
 and blanched*
*1 medium-sized onion, thinly
 sliced*
*3 leeks, white part only,
 thinly sliced*

1 celery heart, thinly sliced
4 small carrots, thinly sliced
*2 tomatoes, skinned, de-seeded
 and chopped*
*3 medium-sized potatoes,
 peeled, diced and rinsed*
*1 medium-sized cabbage,
 trimmed, blanched and
 shredded*
4 tbsp chopped prosciutto *fat
 or smoked bacon fat*
1 clove of garlic, chopped
salt and pepper
Parmesan, grated
croûtons

Put the tripe in a large pan with the stock, the onion stuck with cloves, and the celery sticks. Bring to the boil, turn down to simmer, cover, and cook for 1 hour (if the tripe is not pre-cooked, as it usually is these days, cook for 3 hours). Drain, and slice the tripe into thin strips. Strain the stock a second time through a fine sieve.

Meanwhile, in a second pot, cook the beans in lightly salted water over a low heat until tender. Melt the butter in a large pan and sauté the bacon, onion and leeks. After 10 minutes stir in the celery heart, carrots and tomatoes, stir and cook gently for another 10 minutes. Add the sliced tripe and add 3.4 litres/6 pts of the tripe liquor. Bring to the boil, turn down the heat and let the soup simmer. Add the potatoes, cover and simmer for 20 minutes. Add the cooked beans and cabbage and simmer for 2 minutes. Taste and adjust the seasoning. Cook for a couple more minutes.

Sauté the chopped *prosciutto* or bacon fat with the chopped garlic. Stir into the soup and serve the Parmesan and croûtons separately.

Correcting Soup Problems

THE EGG LIAISON CURDLES AND SPLITS
If a little hot soup has been added to the liaison first this shouldn't happen. If it does, bung the whole lot in a liquidizer, give it a high speed whizz, then pass it through a very fine sieve.

THE CREAM OR YOGHURT CURDLES AND SPLITS
This will be because there isn't enough fat content in the cream or yoghurt (see page 66). The soup can only be salvaged, not cured, and the flavour and texture will alter slightly. Slake a little potato flour (see page 57) in water, whisk into the soup, and simmer for 5 minutes. Taste and check that the flour is cooked. Liquidize in batches at high speed, then pass through a very fine sieve.

THE COCONUT MILK CURDLES
Separation of fats and solids is caused by overheating, and with coconut milk this happens naturally at very low temperatures. It won't affect the soup and doesn't matter a jot.

THE SOUP TASTES FLOURY
Cook further, at a simmer, until the flour is properly cooked.

THE SOUP IS TOO SALTY
Add a peeled potato, it will absorb the salt. Alternatively, make another batch of soup without salt and add it to the first.

THE SOUP IS TOO CHILLI-HOT
Add a pinch of sugar; also the best solution if you burn your mouth with a chilli.

THE SOUP IS GREASY
Sometimes, when a soup has settled, a thin layer of oil settles on the surface. Remove carefully with absorbent paper, sheet by sheet, until it is obvious that you are now just collecting soup. If there's time, chill the soup overnight in the fridge, then scoop off the congealed fat. Another idea is to throw ice-cubes into a hand-warm soup; the grease will collect round the ice-cubes, which you lift out and chuck.

THE SOUP IS BURNT
If soup ingredients have stuck to the bottom of the pan and been burnt, it may be possible to ladle off the top half of the soup. If it *tastes* burnt there is no salvation; chuck.

A Glossary of Soup Terminology

ACORDAS
A soupier version of a *migas*, the bread-based 'dry' soups and stews of Portugal. Also the name of a quickly-made garlic and bread soup similar to *aigo boulido*.

AQUACOTTA
Tuscan peasant soup made with bread, tomatoes, garlic and onions, usually served with an egg poached in the soup.

AIGO BOULIDO
French garlic and bread soup, sometimes served with eggs.

AIGO SAU
Provençal fish soup similar to bouillabaisse but without the fuss.

AIGO SAU D'IOU
Bouillabaisse with potatoes and poached eggs.

D'ARGENTEUIL
Soup made with asparagus.

AVGOLEMONO
Greek soup made with chicken or fish stock and rice, and finished with eggs and lemon juice; often served with meatballs. Also popular throughout the Middle East, where it is called *beid bi lamoun*.

BILLI BI
Mussel soup made with white wine, saffron and egg and cream finish.

BIRD'S NEST SOUP/YIEN WAW
Authentic bird's nest soup is made from rare sea swallow's nests, which are imbued with rich gelatinous protein, and is often served decorated with clouds of egg-white. It is available in two forms: cleaned and purified in cup-like nestlets, or cleaned and purified in dried, slightly curved chips called *loong ngaah* or dragon's teeth (25–40 g/1–1½ oz serves 6–8).

BISQUE
Thick soup or purée made with shellfish and a highly-seasoned *court-*

bouillon; hence *bisque de homard*, etc. Often used to describe a shellfish soup thickened with its shell.

BOGRÁCSGULYÁS
Hungarian beef goulash soup, usually served with flour dumplings called *galuskas*.

BOLLITO MISTO
Northern Italian dish of different meats boiled together, with the broth drunk as a soup, usually served with pickles and a green relish.

BORSCHT
Beetroot-based and -coloured stew/soup enriched with cabbage, onions, tomatoes and potatoes, and seasoned with garlic and vinegar, generally finished with soured cream. Originally from the Ukraine, but celebrated as Russia's most popular soup.

BOTVINYA
Celebrated Russian cold fish soup flavoured with *kvas*, a Russian rye beer.

BOUILLABAISSE
Provençal fishermen's soup named after a style of quick-boil cooking. Originally from Marseille but thought to be introduced by the Greeks (see also *kakavia*). Must contain rascasse, saffron and olive oil to be authentic. Usually also cooked with sliced potatoes and served with the broth first, with *rouille* and croûtes, followed by the fish and vegetables.

BOUILLI
Gascon version of *pot-au-feu*: beef, veal and a hen cooked with vegetables and 'finished' with *confit* of pork spare rib and barley.

BREWIS
A Welsh gruel made with oats or bread, a lump of bacon, seasoning and water.

BREE OR BRIGH
Gaelic for stock, broth, juice or soup.

BRODO
Light broth made by simmering vegetables, meat and bones in water and used in most Italian soups.

BROSE
Simple soup thickened with lightly toasted oatmeal.

BURRIDA
Genoese version of *brodetto*, the Italian fish stew/soup, seasoned with anchovy fillets and basil.

CACCIUCCO
Tuscan name for *brodetto*, the Italian fish stew/soup.

CALLALOO
Caribbean stew/soup made with green callaloo leaves, pork, crab and okra.

CALVO VERDE
Portugal's national dish: a thick cabbage soup with a potato base and garnished with slices of garlicky cured pork sausage.

CANJA
Portuguese chicken, mint, rice and lemon soup with seed-shaped pasta.

LA CARABACCIA
Florentine onion soup dating back to the Renaissance and very similar to French onion soup.

CAWL
Welsh mutton and vegetable stew/broth.

CHABROL
Faire chabrol – Limousin and Bordelais custom of mixing a little red wine into the last few mouthfuls of soup and drinking it directly from the bowl.

CHLODNIK
Cold Russian fish soup, traditionally made with red fish, cucumber, hard-boiled eggs, carrot and beetroot.

CHORBA
Light version of *harira*, an Arabic break-fast soup.

CHOWDER
American seafood soup, often made with clams, derived from the French fishermen's soup *chaudière*, and served in its cooking-pot. New England-style is made with milk; New York-style with tomatoes and water.

CHUPI
Argentinian beef and vegetable stew/soup.

COCK-A-LEEKIE
One of Scotland's finest dishes: a chicken cooked in a beef broth and finished with prunes and leeks.

CONGEE
Chinese equivalent of chicken noodle soup; a comforting, restorative meat-enriched rice 'porridge'.

CONSOMMÉ
Intensely flavoured clarified broth, often served jellied.

COTRIADE
Sustaining fish soup from Brittany.

COUSINETTE
A sort of salad soup from Béarn, made with greens such as Swiss chard, sorrel and curly endive (frisée).

CRÉCY
Soup made with carrots.

CULLEN SKINK
Puréed cream soup made with smoked Finnan haddock.

DOUBLE SOUP
Two separately made soups served together in one bowl. Contrasting colour is as important as complementary flavours; for instance, red and yellow peppers.

DRY SOUP
Not really a soup at all, but served between courses in a large Spanish or Mexican meal.

DUBARRY
Soup made with cauliflower.

ESAU
Lentil soup, so named after the story in the Bible.

FASOULADA
National soup of Greece made with fava beans. Also popular throughout Turkey, Kurdistan and Armenia.

GAENG CHUD
Thai name for soup.

GARBURE
A soup that is more like a stew, but also used to denote a cabbage-based soup. In Béarn, where it originates, the *garbure* is cooked in a glazed earthenware pot. Cooking begins with water and potatoes, often includes roasted chestnuts and cabbage, and is a finely tuned balancing act of ingredients and their cooking lengths. The last spoon-

fuls are often drunk with a little wine, known locally as *faire goudale*; elsewhere in France as *faire chabrot/chabrol*.

GAZPACHO
A liquid salad with pieces of bread soaked in it; once peasant food, now the most popular of all Spanish soups.

ST-GERMAIN
Soup made with peas.

GERMINY
Soup made with sorrel.

GULYÁS
Whole meal soups of Austria and Hungary.

GUMBO
Creole soup/stew containing okra; in Southern America gumbo refers to stews with tomatoes and sweet peppers.

GWAYTIO
Thai noodle soup that is really a meal, made with pieces of meat or fish, meat-balls or fishballs, and a garnish of spring onion, chilli, ground peanuts, crisp fried garlic and *nam pla*. Also the name of the rice pasta used to make wide soup noodles.

HARIRA
Stew-like lamb-based soup and the official break-fast after Ramadan, finished with egg and vinegar.

HOTCH POTCH
Variation on cawl and Scotch broth, a mutton and root vegetable stew/soup made with peas, cauliflower and lettuce.

HOT-POT SOUPS
Oriental method of poaching meat, shellfish and vegetables in a broth, in a chafing pot. The method originates from nomadic Mongolian tribes.

LA JOTA
Slow-cooked hearty bean, potato, bacon and sauerkraut soup from Trieste.

KACHEN
A cross between a soup and a stew; in fact an ancient Saxon meat and vegetable dish.

KHLODNICK
Popular Polish iced fish soup, mistakenly thought to come from Russia, where it's also popular. At its most elaborate it includes crayfish, sturgeon, *kvas* (a type of beer), beetroot tops and pickled cucumber, with hard-boiled egg sprinkled with chervil and fennel served separately.

LAKSA/SINGAPORE LAKSA
Malaysian chilli-laced coconut broth with vermicelli, sliced fish-cake, prawns, seafood, beansprouts and pickles.

LOCRO
Pink-tinged cheese and potato soup from Ecuador.

LONDON PARTICULAR
An English pea-souper; a thick pea soup.

MAYORQUINA
Catalan/Majorcan soup of garlic, onion, pimento, tomatoes, leeks, cabbage and aromatics, served over bread with olive oil garnish. Cooked in an earthenware *marmite*.

MAYERITSA
Traditionally eaten after the midnight service on Easter Saturday in the Greek Orthodox church, to break the Lenten fast. Made with the entrails of a baby lamb or kid.

MEHUDEHRA
Albanian garlic soup with mint parsley, coriander and vermicelli.

MELOKHIA
One of the most ancient Egyptian dishes, a lamb-based stew with spinach-like melokhia leaves, which give a glutinous creamy texture.

MIMOSA
Soup with hard-boiled eggs, yellow part exposed.

MINESTRE
Catch-all term for various Italian bean and vegetable soups made with basic stock; the most famous being minestrone.

MIROSHIRU
Japanese term for thick soups.

MOCK TURTLE
Soup made with stock from a calf's head, with forcemeat or egg-balls, to resemble turtle eggs.

MOURTAIROL
Patois for bread with *bouillon*.

MULLIGATAWNY
Spiced and curried vegetable soup, a relic of Anglo-Asian recipes dating back to the days of the Raj.

OLLA PODRIDA
Spanish version of *pot-au-feu*, and the national stew of Andalucia, made with beef, pork, a hen, *chorizo*, chickpeas and root vegetables. Cooked in an earthenware pot – the *olla*.

L'OUILLADE
Catalan-style *potée*, and the national soup, named after the earthenware *marmite* in which it is cooked. Key ingredients include, among others, pork, beans and cabbage.

PANADE
Bread soup.

PAPPA AL POMODORO
Tuscan bread, tomato, olive oil and garlic soup, garnished with basil.

PARMENTIER
Soup with predominance of potato.

PEPPERPOT
Highly-spiced West Indian hot-pot made with flesh, fish or fowl.

PETIT MARMITE
Tall, bulbous, lidded earthenware crock used to cook and serve soup.

PHO
Vietnamese for soup; usually stew-style and with noodles.

POTAGE
Early word for soup – pottage – and one of many French names for a country-style thick soup.

POT-AU-FEU
Beef equivalent of *poule-au-pot*.

POTÉE
French term for food cooked in an earthenware pot, but more widely used to describe a country-style soup made with fresh local vegetables and home-cured pork.

POT-POURRI

French variation on *olla podrida* (the ancestor of *pot-au-feu* devised by Menon, Louis XV's chef in the early eighteenth century), made with partridge or pheasant, lamb, beef, beef shanks, a beef or chicken stock flavoured with a ginger, coriander seed, clove and peppercorn mignonette, and root vegetables, served either from the pot or split so the soup comes first (reduced and thickened with breadcrumbs), followed by the meats and vegetables.

POULE-AU-POT

A name attributed to Henry IV that describes a chicken stuffed with a well-seasoned bread, ham and herb patty cooked in broth, sometimes with stuffed cabbage, a giant dumpling, green sausages and root vegetables, and served in separate courses as a complete meal.

À LA POULETTE

Ingredients previously cooked and then bound with a velouté sauce with eggs and cream.

POWSOWDIE

Scottish sheep's-head broth cooked with barley, pig's trotters and root vegetables.

PROVENÇAL

Soup dominated by a combination of tomatoes, garlic and onions stewed in olive oil.

PUCHERO

A stew rather than a soup, and the national dish of Argentina. In the *pot-au-feu* family; beef, calf's foot, pieces of fowl stewed with sweet and ordinary potatoes, sweetcorn, onions, pumpkin, bacon and liver sausage. Serve the meat, vegetables and soup separately.

À LA REINE

Soups dominated by chicken but thought to be derivative of dishes favoured by the wife of Louis XV, Marie Leczynska, daughter of Stanislas, deposed King of Poland who became Duke of Lorraine (and gave his name to quiche).

RIBOLLITA

Italian word meaning re-cooked, but in Tuscany it refers to re-cooking the remains of the minestrone and serving it over a pile of cabbage and bread, dressed with olive oil.

RISI E BISI

Famous classic Italian soup made with rice and peas.

SALDAS
Basque name for a very thick soup.

SCHCHI
Russian stew-like sauerkraut soup.

SCOTCH BROTH
Mutton, leek and root vegetable soup/stew with dried green peas and shredded cabbage.

SHOLEH OR ASH/E
Iranian (Persian) rice-based soup.

SHORBA/H
Arabic name for soup but also the name of a substantial slow-cooked chickpea and vegetable soup.

SOBRONADE
A peasant-style soup so richly charged with meat and vegetables that it is a meal in itself.

SOUP, LA SOUPE
Catch-all word for liquid food; sometimes refers to a compôte of fruit. Also means to enliven (soup-up); to be in the soup is to be in trouble.

SOTO AND SOP
Indonesian names for soup.

SOTO AYAM
Indonesia's most popular soup, made with chicken, garlic, crushed nuts, and chicken 'garnished' with noodles, hard-boiled eggs, spring onions, rice, carrot and lime wedges.

STRACCIATELLA
Chicken broth enriched with Parmesan, egg and parsley.

SUIMONO
Japanese term for clear soups.

TARATOR
Bulgarian yoghurt and cucumber soup; similar versions exist in Turkish and most Middle Eastern cuisines.

TEA
Beef broth; in Jamaica any non-alcoholic liquid.

TOURAINS
French patois for quick soups; also refers to soups made with onions

or garlic or tomatoes, or a combination of two or more, and often thickened or enriched with egg-yolks and vinegar and whisked egg-white.

TREMPER
To pour soup over pieces of bread.

VELOUTÉ
In soup terms, *velouté* is used to describe certain thickened soups, usually butter and flour and/or eggs and/or cream. But a widely used general term for a white sauce made with white veal or chicken stock and bound by eggs.

VICHYSSOISE/CRÈME VICHYSSOISE
Chilled and puréed leek and potato soup enriched with cream and sprinkled with chives, invented in 1920 by Louis Diat, the French-born chef of the New York Ritz-Carlton.

YAYLA CORBASI
Turkish mint and cucumber yoghurt soup.

ZIMINU
Sardinian version of the Italian fish soup *brodetto*.

ZUPPA INGLESE
Italian name for English trifle; the ultimate Italian version being *tiramisu*.

Endpiece

❧

The Story of Augustus who would not have any Soup

Augustus was a chubby lad;
Fat ruddy cheeks Augustus had:
And everybody saw with joy
The plump and hearty, healthy boy.
He ate and drank as he was told,
And never let his soup get cold.
But one day, one cold winter's day,
He screamed out 'Take the soup away!
O take the nasty soup away!
I won't have any soup today.'
Next day, now look, the picture shows
How lank and lean Augustus grows!
Yet, though he feels so weak and ill,
The naughty fellow cries out still
'Not any soup for me, I say:
O take the nasty soup away!
I *won't* have any soup today.'
The third day comes: Oh what a sin!
To make himself so pale and thin.
Yet, when the soup is put on table,
He screams, as loud as he is able,
'Not any soup for me, I say:
O take the nasty soup away!
I WON'T have any soup today.'
Look at him, now the fourth day's come!
He scarcely weighs a sugar-plum;
He's like a little bit of thread,
And, on the fifth day, he was – dead!

(From *Struwwelpeter, Merry Stories and Funny Pictures*, Heinrich Hoffman)

Bibliography

Absolute Press: *The London Restaurant Recipe Book*, 1983; *New Vegetarian Cuisine*, 1986; *The Women Chefs of Britain*, 1990.

Anderson, Jean: *The Food of Portugal*, Robert Hale, 1987.

Andreas: *Aphrodite's Cookbook*, Neville Spearman, 1977.

Aris, Pepita: *Recipes From a Spanish Village*, Conran/Octopus, 1990.

Au Yeung, Mrs Cecilia J.: *Chopsticks Recipes*, Chopsticks Publications Ltd, 1982.

Ayrton, Elisabeth: *The Cookery of England*, Penguin, 1974; *The Pleasure of Vegetables*, Penguin, 1983.

Barber, Richard: *Cooking and Recipes from Rome to the Renaissance*, Allen Lane, 1973.

Bareham, Lindsey: *In Praise of the Potato*, Michael Joseph, 1989.

Beck, Simone, Bertholle, Louisette, and Child, Julia: *Mastering the Art of French Cooking*, Penguin, 1961.

Beeton, Isabella: *Mrs Beeton's All About Cookery*, Ward Lock and Co., undated.

Benghiat, Norma: *Traditional Jamaican Cookery*, Penguin, 1985.

Berjane, J.: *French Dishes for English Tables*, Warne, 1931.

Berriedale-Johnson, Michelle: *The British Museum Cookbook*, British Museum Publications, 1987.

Bertholle, Louisette: *French Cooking for All*, Penguin, 1984.

Bertolli, Paul, and Waters, Alice: *Chez Panisse Cooking*, Random, 1988.

Bhumichitr, Vatcherin: *The Taste of Thailand*, Pavilion, 1988; *Thai Vegetarian Cooking*, Pavilion, 1991.

Bilton, Jan: *The International Dinner Party Cook Book*, Piatkus, 1985.

Binns, Brian: *Feasting with Brian Binns*, James Service, 1977.

Binstead, Raymond and Devey, James D.: *Soup Manufacture*, Food Trade Press, 1970.

Bissell, Frances: *A Cook's Calendar*, Chatto & Windus, 1985.

Blackwood, Caroline and Haycraft, Anna: *Darling, You Shouldn't Have Gone to So Much Trouble*, Jonathan Cape, 1980.

Blue, Lionel, and Rose, Jane: *A Taste of Heaven*, Darton, Longman and Todd, 1977.

Bourne, Ursula: *Portuguese Cookery*, Penguin, 1973.

Boxer, Arabella: *Arabella Boxer's Garden Cookbook*, Weidenfeld & Nicolson, 1974; *Mediterranean Cookbook*, Dent, 1981; *Arabella Boxer's Book of English Food*, John Curtis/Hodder & Stoughton, 1991.

Brennan, Jennifer: *Thai Cooking*, Jill Norman and Hobhouse, 1981; *One-Dish Meals of Asia*, Times Books, 1984.

Briggs, Desmond: *Entertaining Single-Handed*, Penguin, 1968.

Brimi, Arne: *A Taste of Norway*, Norwegian University Press, 1987.

Brissendon, Rosemary: *South East Asian Food*, Penguin, 1969.

Bryan, John E., and Castle, Coralie: *The Edible Ornamental Garden*, Pitman, 1974.

Bryant, Max: *Bush Cooking*, Kangaroo Press, 1988.

Bugialli, Giuliano: *The Taste of Italy*, Octopus, 1984.

Campbell, Elizabeth: *Encyclopedia of World Cookery*, Spring Books, undated.

Carluccio, Antonio: *A Passion for Mushrooms*, Pavilion/Michael Joseph, 1989.

Carrier, Robert: *Entertaining*, Sidgwick & Jackson, 1977; *Food, Wine and Friends*, Sphere, 1980.

Casas, Penelope: *Foods and Wines of Spain*, Penguin, 1982; *Tapas*, Alfred A. Knopf, 1989.

Castelvetro, Giacomo: *The Fruit, Herbs and Vegetables of Italy*, 1989.

Ceserani, V., and Kinton, R.: *Practical Cookery*, Edward Arnold, 1981.

Charial-Thuilier, Jean-André: *Bouquet de Provence*, BPCC Hazell Books, 1990.

Chaliand, Gérard: *Food without Frontiers*, Pluto Press, 1981.

Collins, Mary (ed.): *Spices of the World Cookbook by McCormick*, Penguin, 1964.

Conil, Jean: *Cuisine Fraîcheur*, Aurum Press, 1987.

Cooper, Terence: *Trouper Cooper's Curry Cookbook*, Collins, 1983.

Costner, Susan: *Great Sandwiches*, Crown, 1990.

Craig, Elizabeth: *Hotch Potch*, Collins, 1978.

Curtis, Denis: *Thought for Food*, Sunday Telegraph, 1982.

Daly, Dorothy: *Cooking the Italian Way*, Paul Hamlyn, 1958.

Dang Cao, Thai: *The Exotic Cookery Collection: Vietnam*, Octopus, 1987.

David, Elizabeth: *French Country Cooking*, Penguin, 1951; *French Provincial Cooking*, Penguin, 1960; *Summer Cooking*, Penguin, 1965; *English Bread and Yeast Cookery*, Allen Lane, 1977; *Italian Food*, Harper Row, 1987; *An Omelette and a Glass of Wine*, Jill Norman, 1984.

Davidson, Alan: *Mediterranean Seafood*, Penguin, 1972; *A Kipper with My Tea*, Macmillan, 1988.

Day, Harvey: *The Complete Book of Curries*, Kaye and Ward, 1967.

Del Conte, Anna: *Portrait of Pasta*, Paddington Press, 1976; *Entertaining All'Italiana*, Bantam Press, 1991.

De' Medici, Lorenza: *The Renaissance of Italian Cooking*, Pavilion, 1989.

Der Haroutunian, Arto: *Classic Vegetable Cookery*, Ebury Press, 1985.

Dimbleby, Josceline: *The Cook's Companion*, Sainsbury, 1991.

Downer, Leslie, and Youeda, Minoru: *Step by Step Japanese Cooking*, Macdonald, 1985.

Downing, Beryl: *Quick Cook*, Penguin, 1981.

Driver, Christopher: *The British at Table 1940–1980*, Chatto & Windus, 1983.

Edwards, John (trans.): *The Roman Cookery of Apicius*, Rider, 1984.

Eldon, Kathy and Mullen: *Tastes of Kenya*, Eamon, 1986.

Elliot, Rose: *Rose Elliot's Complete Vegetarian Cookbook*, Collins, 1985; *The Supreme Vegetarian Cookbook*, Fontana, 1990.

Escoffier, Auguste: *Ma Cuisine*, Hamlyn, 1965.

Eyton, Audrey: *The Complete F-Plan Diet*, Penguin, 1982.

Ferguson, Sheila: *Soul Food*, Weidenfeld & Nicolson, 1989.

Fernandez, Rafi: *Malaysian Cookery*, Penguin, 1986.

Fisher, M. F. K.: *The Art of Eating*, Collier Books, Macmillan Publishing Co, 1990.

Fitzgibbon, Theodora: *A Taste of London*, Pan, 1973.

Floyd, Keith: *Floyd on Fish*, BBC Publications, 1985; *Floyd on France*, BBC Publications, 1987.

Forbes, Leslie: *A Table in Tuscany*, Webb & Bower, 1985.

Fry, Pamela: *Cooking the American Way*, Spring Books, 1963.

Fullick, Roy (ed.): *The Elle Cookbook*, Michael Joseph, 1981; *The Second Elle Cookbook*, Michael Joseph, 1985.

Gardnier, Kenneth: *Creole Caribbean Cookery*, Grafton, 1986.

Garrett, Guy, and Norman, Kit: *The Food for Thought Cookbook*, Thorsons, 1987.

Girardet, Fredy, and Campbell, Susan (ed.): *Cuisine Spontanée*, Macmillan, 1985.

Green, Henrietta, and Moine, Marie-Pierre: *10 Minute Cuisine*, Conran Octopus, 1991.

Greenberg, Sheldon, and Lambert Ortiz, Elisabeth: *The Spice of Life*, Michael Joseph, 1983.

Grigson, Jane: *Good Things*, Penguin, 1971; *English Food*, Penguin, 1974; *Fish Cookery*, Penguin, 1975; *The Observer Guide to European Cookery*, Michael Joseph, 1983; *The Observer Guide to British Cookery*, Michael Joseph, 1984; *Exotic Fruits and Vegetables*, Jonathan Cape, 1986.

Grigson, Sophie: *Sophie's Table*, Michael Joseph, 1990; *Sophie Grigson's Ingredients Book*, Pyramid, 1991.

Guérard, Michel: *Cuisine Minceur*, Macmillan, 1976; and Coumont, Alain, *Minceur Exquise*, Pyramid, 1992.

Guermont, Claude, with Paul Frumkin: *The Norman Table*, Scribners, 1985.

Hagler, Louise: *Tofu Cookery*, The Book Publishing Co., 1982.

Harben, Philip: *The Way to Cook*, Bodley Head, 1945.

Hartley, Dorothy: *Food in England*, Futura, 1985.

Hazan, Marcella: *The Classic Italian Cookbook*, Macmillan, 1973; *The Second Classic Italian Cookbook*, Jill Norman and Hobhouse, 1978.

Hill, Shaun: *Shaun Hill's Gidleigh Park Cookery Book*, Century, 1990.

Hobhouse, Caroline: *Great European Chefs*, Pyramid, 1990.

Hodgson, Moira: *Good Food from a Small Kitchen*, Corgi, 1987.

Holt, Geraldene: *The Gourmet Garden*, Pavilion, 1990.

Hom, Ken: *Chinese Cookery*, BBC Publications, 1984; *East Meets West*, Papermac, 1987; *Ken Hom's Vegetable and Pasta Book*, BBC Publications, 1987; *The Taste of China*, Pavilion, 1990; *Fragrant Harbour Taste*, Bantam Press, 1991.

Hope, Simon: *The Reluctant Vegetarian*, Heinemann, 1985.

Horley, Georgina: *Good Food on a Budget*, Penguin, 1969.

Howard, Elizabeth Jane, and Maschler, Fay: *Howard and Maschler on Food*, Michael Joseph, 1987.

Hunt, Janet: *Simple and Speedy Wholefood Cooking*, Thorsons, 1982.

Hutchins, Sheila: *Grannie's Kitchen*, Granada, 1981.

Innes, Jocasta: *The Pauper's Cookbook*, Penguin, 1971.

Jaffrey, Madhur: *Eastern Vegetarian Cooking*, Jonathan Cape, 1983.

Jamil-Garbutt, Nina: *The Baghdad Kitchen*, Kingswood Press, 1985.

Johnston, Mireille: *The Cuisine of the Rose*, Penguin, 1982.

Jump, Meg: *Cooking with Chillies*, Bodley Head, 1989.

Kenton, Leslie and Susannah: *Raw Energy Recipes*, Century, 1985.

Koffmann, Pierre: *Memories of Gascony*, Octopus, 1990.

Kovi, Paul: *Paul Kovi's Transylvanian Cuisine*, Crown, 1985.

Ladenis, Nico: *My Gastronomy*, Ebury, 1987.

Lambert Ortiz, Elisabeth: *The Book of Latin American Cooking*, Penguin, 1969; *The Fibre Cook Book*, Jill Norman and Hobhouse, 1982.

Lampert, Junko: *The Tofu Cookbook*, Chronicle Books, 1986.

Lang, George: *The Cuisine of Hungary*, Penguin, 1971.

Langley, Andrew: *The Selected Soyer*, Absolute Press, 1987.

Larousse Gastronomique: Paul Hamlyn, 1961.

Lassalle, George: *The Adventurous Fish Cook*, Papermac, 1984; *The Fish in my Life*, Macmillan, 1989.

Lederman, Martin: *The Slim Gourmet's Soup Book*, Oldbourne, 1946.

Lee, Rustie: *Caribbean Cookery*, Collins, 1985.

Leith, Prudence, and Waldegrave, Caroline: *Leith's Cookbook*, Fontana, 1979; *Prue Leith's Dinner Parties*, Jill Norman, 1984.

Lo, Kenneth: *Cheap Chow*, Pan, 1976; *Chinese Provincial Cooking*, Elm Tree Books, 1979.

Loewenfeld, Claire: *Everything You Should Know about Your Food*, Faber, 1978.

Longacre, Doris: *More with Less Cookbook*, Lion Publishing, 1977.

Luard, Elisabeth: *European Peasant Cookery*, Bantam Press, 1986; *European Festival Food*, Bantam Press, 1990.

Lytton Toye, Doris: *Contemporary Cookery*, Vogue Receipts, Conde Nast Publications, 1947.

Mabey, David: *The Guiltless Gourmet*, Mitchell Beazley, 1985.

Macnicol, Fred: *Hungarian Cookery*, Penguin, 1978.

Madison, Deborah: *The Greens Cookbook*, Bantam Press, 1987; *The Savoury Way*, Bantam, 1990.

Manjon, Maite, and O'Brien, Catherine: *Spanish Cooking at Home and on Holiday*, Penguin, 1973.

Mennell, Stephen: *All Manners of Food*, Blackwell, 1985.

Michaels, L. D.: *The Complete Book of Pressure Cooking*, Mayflower, 1977.

Millau, Christian: *Dining in France*, Sidgwick & Jackson, 1986.

Miller, Mark: *Coyote Café*, Ten Speed Press, 1989.

Millon, Marc and Kim: *A Taste of Britain*, Webb & Bower, 1985.

Mitchell, Paulette: *The New American Menu Cookbook*, Rodale Press/Century, 1984.

Molyneux, Joyce: *The Carved Angel Cookery Book*, Collins, 1990.

Moore, Henry (introduction by): *The Artist's Cookbook, Colourful Recipes from the RCA*, Macdonald Orbis, 1987.

Mosimann, Anton: *Cuisine à la Carte*, Northwood Books, 1981; *Cuisine Naturelle*, Macmillan, 1985; *Anton Mosimann's Fish Cuisine*, Macmillan, 1988; *Cooking with Mosimann*, Macmillan, 1989; *The Art of Anton Mosimann*, Waymark, 1990; *Anton Mosimann – Naturally*, Channel 4/Ebury Press, 1991.

Nash, S. Elizabeth: *Cooking Craft*, Pitman, 1944.

Nathan, Joan: *Jewish Holiday Kitchen*, Schocken Books, 1979.

Neal, Bill: *Bill Neal's Southern Cooking*, Chapel Hill, 1985.

Nicol, Ann: *Pick Your Own Cookbook*, Threshold Books, 1987.

Nilson, Bee (ed.): *W. I. Diamond Jubilee Cookbook*, Pan, 1977.

Norman, Jill: *The Complete Book of Spices*, Dorling Kindersley, 1990.

Olney, Richard: *Simple French Food*, Penguin, 1981; *The French Menu Cookbook*, Dorling Kindersley, 1986.

Parker, Audrey: *Cooking for Christmas*, Faber, 1970.

Perry, Karin: *The Fish Book*, Chatto & Windus, 1989.

Pertwee, Ingeborg: *For Starters*, World's Work, 1984.

Pettigrew, Jane: *The Festive Table*, Pavilion, 1990.

Pirbright, Peter: *Off the Beeton Track*, Binnacle Books, 1946.

Puck, Wolfgang: *The Wolfgang Puck Cookbook*, Random House, 1986.

Quintana, Patricia: *The Taste of Mexico*, Stewart Tabari and Chang, 1986.

Reekie, Jenny: *The Raw Food Cook Book*, Kingswood Press, 1986.

Roden, Claudia: *A Book of Middle Eastern Food*, Penguin, 1968; *Claudia Roden's Picnic*, Penguin, 1981; *Mediterranean Cookery*, BBC Publications, 1987; *The Food of Italy*, Chatto & Windus, 1989.

Rogers, Jenny (ed.): *The Taste of Health*, BBC Publications, 1985.

Ronay, Egon: *The Unforgettable Dishes of My Life*, Victor Gollancz, 1989.

Root, Waverley: *The Food of France*, Papermac, 1958.

Rose, Evelyn: *The New Jewish Cuisine*, Papermac, 1985; *The First Time Cookbook* (with Judi Rose), Penguin, 1984.

Ross, Janet, and Waterfield, Michael: *Leaves From Our Tuscan Kitchen*, Penguin, 1973.

Rosso, Julie, and Lukins, Sheila: *The Silver Palate Cookbook*, Ebury Press, 1979; *The New Basics Cookbook*, Workman, 1989.

Round, Jeremy: *The Independent Cook*, Barrie & Jenkins, 1988.

Roux, Albert and Michel: *The New Classic Cuisine*, Macdonald, 1983; *French Country Cooking*, Sidgwick & Jackson, 1989; *The Roux Brothers Cooking for Two*, Sidgwick & Jackson, 1991.

Sahni, Julie: *Classic Indian Cooking*, Dorling Kindersley, 1986.

Santa Maria, Jack: *Indian Meat and Fish Cookery*, Rider, 1977.

Scott, David, with Winata, Surya: *Indonesian Cookery*, Rider, 1984.

Segal, Stephanie: *The Winter Vegetarian*, Papermac, 1989; *The Summer Vegetarian*, Papermac, 1991.

Sekules, Veronica: *Friends of the Earth Cook Book*, Penguin, 1980.

Shulman, M. R.: *Chez Martha Rose*, Papermac, 1988.

Simon, André L.: *A Concise Encyclopedia of Gastronomy*, Penguin, 1952.

Simon, Nezih: *Eats Without Meats*, Tredolphin Press, 1983.

Simpson, Jane, and Maclennan, Gill: *The Apple Book*, Bodley Head, 1984.

Smart, Elizabeth, and Ryan, Agnes: *Cooking the French Way*, Spring Books, 1958.

Smith, Delia: *Complete Illustrated Cookery*, BBC Publications, 1989.

Smith, Michael: *Cooking with Michael Smith*, Papermac, 1981.

Spencer, Colin: *The New Vegetarian*, Elm Tree Books, 1986; *Cordon Vert*, Thorsons, 1985.

So, Yan Kit: *Wok Cookbook*, Piatkus, 1985.

Spieler, David and Marlena: *Naturally Good*, Faber, 1973.

Spunt, Georges: *The Step-By-Step Chinese Cookbook*, Penguin, 1980.

Stafford, Julie: *Taste of Life*, Sphere, 1983.

Stein, Richard: *English Seafood Cookery*, Penguin, 1988.

Strang, Jeanne: *Goose Fat and Garlic*, Kyle Cathie, 1991.

Stubbs, Joyce M.: *The Home Book of Greek Cookery*, Faber, 1963.

Style, Sue: *A Taste of Alsace*, Pavilion, 1990.

Tada, Tatsuji: *Japanese Recipes*, Tuttle, 1967.

Tanja, Meera: *Indian Regional Cookery*, Mills & Boon, 1980.

Thomas, Helen: *Biscuits*, Jill Norman, 1984.

Time-Life Books: *The Cooking of the British Isles*, 1970.

Torday, Jane: *A Little Book of Old-Fashioned Nursery Recipes*, Parsley Publications, undated.

Troisgros, Jean and Pierre, and Conran, Caroline (ed. and trans.): *The Nouvelle Cuisine of Jean and Pierre Troisgros*, Macmillan, 1980.

Trum Hunter, Beatrice: *The Natural Foods*, Faber, 1963.

Vernon, Tom: *Fat Man in the Kitchen*, BBC Publications, 1986.

Visser, Margaret: *Much Depends on Dinner*, Penguin, 1989.

Vongerichten, Jean-Georges: *Simple Cuisine*, Prentice Hall Press, 1990.

Walker, Clare, and Coleman, Gill: *The Home Gardener's Cookbook*, Penguin, 1980.

Wells, Patricia: *Bistro Cooking*, Kyle Cathie Ltd, 1989.

White, Marco Pierre: *White Heat*, Thames TV, 1990.

Willan, Anne: *La France Gastronomique*, Pavilion, 1991.

Wilson, C. Anne: *Food and Drink in Britain*, Penguin, 1973.

Wilson, Marie M.: *Siamese Cookery*, Tuttle, 1965.

Wood, Denis, and Crosby, Kate: *Grow and Cook It*, Faber, 1975.

Woolfert, Paula: *Good Food from Morocco*, John Murray, 1973; *The Cooking of South West France*, Papermac, 1983.

Worrall-Thompson, Antony: *The Small and Beautiful Cookbook*, Weidenfeld & Nicolson, 1984.

Yudkin, John: *The Penguin Encyclopaedia of Nutrition*, Penguin, 1985.

Index

ૢ